Commercial Contracts:
A Practical Guide to Standard Terms

Fifth Edition

Commercial Contracts: A Practical Guide to Standard Terms

Fifth Edition

Dr Saleem Sheikh LLB (Hons), LLM (Lond), PhD (Lond)

Susan Singleton LLB, Solicitor, Singletons, www.singlelaw.com

Bloomsbury Professional

LONDON • DUBLIN • EDINBURGH • NEW YORK • NEW DELHI • SYDNEY

BLOOMSBURY PROFESSIONAL
Bloomsbury Publishing Plc
41–43 Boltro Road, Haywards Heath, RH16 1BJ, UK

BLOOMSBURY and the Diana logo are trademarks of Bloomsbury Publishing Plc

British Library Cataloguing-in-Publication Data

A catalogue record for this book is available from the British Library.

ISBN:	PB:	978-1-52650-833-1
	ePDF:	978-1-52650-835-5
	ePub:	978-1-52650-834-8

Typeset by Evolution Design & Digital Ltd (Kent)
Printed and bound by CPI Group (UK) Ltd, Croydon, CRO 4YY

To find out more about our authors and books visit www.bloomsburyprofessional.com.
Here you will find extracts, author information, details of forthcoming events and the option
to sign up for our newsletters

Downloadable precedents

In previous editions of *Commercial Contracts: A Practical Guide to Standard Terms*, the precedents have been available separately on a CD-ROM.

For the new 5th edition, the precedents are available to download electronically from https://bloomsburyprofessionallaw.com/commercialcontracts.

They are password-protected and the password is YBU7DM.

They can be downloaded individually or in totality.

If you have any problems downloading the precedents or have any questions, please contact Bloomsbury Professional customer services on 01444 416119 or by email at customerservices@bloomsburyprofessional.com.

For a Licence agreement relating to the use of this Data, please see overleaf at p vi.

Licence agreement

Preface

Since the first edition of this book was published in 2002 much has changed. The fifth edition of this book is now fully updated incorporating the changes that have taken place since the fourth edition was published in 2014.

Commercial Contracts: A Practical Guide to Standard Terms aims to provide useful background and detailed advice on the law surrounding a wide range of commercial agreements and commercial concepts. This edition reflects the latest developments and modernisation of UK commercial law since the previous edition and aims to cover all significant legal developments relevant to its subject matter. Standard terms and commercial contracts raise complex issues and the book aims to provide useful practical guidance for those involved with such standard terms so they understand the background to the various legal issues which arise.

Commercial Contracts: A Practical Guide to Standard Terms has the following objectives:

(i)   to provide a detailed analysis of the key common clauses typically encountered in commercial agreements and when to use standard terms;

(ii)   to set out precedent commercial agreements relevant to those topics covered in this book, as well as commentary on the scope and context of the clauses with reference to case law, where applicable;

(iii)   to highlight the significant case law and legislation that has influenced and shaped the development of UK commercial law in relation to the standard terms given, including the legal and practical implications involved;

(iv)   to provide some practical tips arising from case law and legislation and their potential impact on commercial agreements; and

(v)   to provide a summary and checklists on the various topics covered in this book focussing on the main issues addressed in the chapters.

Dr Saleem Sheikh has written and edited Sections A, B1 and B2 and C of the book. Section A addresses the following:

Forming and Concluding Contracts

This covers the developing and recent case law on the essential requirements for the formation of contracts and its impact on commercial agreements. Some of the significant English law Supreme Court and Court of Appeal cases are considered and how these may affect some of the provisions in commercial agreements.

Common and Specific Clauses

This addresses the statutory implied terms and conditions relevant to commercial agreements. It also covers unfair terms and how this applies to exclusion of liability clauses and their treatment under the latest case law, as well as the modern law on penalties.

Export Contracts – Special Issues

This highlights the key legislative framework governing export control. It also covers provisions governing export of controlled goods; arms embargoes and trade control restrictions; obtaining an export licence; FOB and CIF contracts and Incoterms.

Software Contracts – Special Issues

This section covers the concept of software as 'goods'; consumer contracts and software; intellectual property in software; warranties and limitation of liability; and use and licensing of software.

Sections B1 and B2 cover Business-to-Business Contracts in the following areas:

Terms and Conditions for the Sale and Supply of Goods

This addresses principal legislation governing the sale and supply of goods with key cases; implied terms and conditions and exceptions; misrepresentation; and includes standard sale of goods terms and conditions.

Terms and Conditions of Purchase

Aspects covered in this chapter include a checklist of the essential issues to consider when purchasing goods from a buyer's perspective. A specimen precedent has also been drafted on the terms and conditions of purchase by the buyer. This includes commentary on each clause drafted including reference to applicable case law.

Section C of this book is concerned with Business-to-Consumer Contracts and addresses the following main topics:

Consumer Contracts – Distance Selling

This section covers the preliminary issues of incorporation. It sets out in detail a specimen precedent on a distance selling contract with commentary. It also includes rights to cancellation by the buyer.

Hire Purchase Contracts

This section highlights the key distinction between hire purchase and conditional sale agreements. It also addresses regulated hire purchase agreements and creditworthiness. A specimen precedent is provided for a hire purchase contract with detailed commentary and significant case law is described which has an impact on certain provisions in the agreement.

Online Terms and Conditions of Sale

This section covers applicable regulations relating to online contracts; the law on distance selling including statutory cancellation rights; contracts concluded by electronic means; implications of the *Data Protection Act 2018* and GDPR. A standard internet contract is provided with commentary.

Online Terms and Conditions for the Supply of Software

The final section addresses key issues including the distinction between offers and invitation to treat in an online context. It also covers key applicable regulations; and implications of the *Consumer Rights Act 2015*. This section also contains a precedent for a standard internet contract for software.

Sections B3–B7 have been written and updated by Susan Singleton and contain the following:

Licence of Computer Software

This section is drafted from the standpoint of the buyer/licensee covering licensed rights, intellectual property and other relevant issues.

Professional Services Agreements

This section comes in two forms: one drafted from the standpoint of a supplier of such services; and the other the buyer. It includes clauses required by the Provision of Services Regulations 2009 and this section has been fully updated for the fifth edition to cover recent legal changes relevant to consultancy agreements.

Export Terms and Conditions and Import Terms and Conditions

These apply to those exporting and importing products. Issues such as export control legislation, Incoterms such as FOB, retention of title, intellectual property, liability and standards are included. The commentary has been updated to cover the implications for these contracts of the UK leaving the EU and relevant competition law in relation to exports and imports.

This book also covers the latest significant cases and where they have affected the standard terms in the book, the terms have been accordingly updated. Key judgments are mentioned where relevant to particular topics and the practical application of these as they affect contract terms is given.

The standard terms reflect the laws of England and Wales and where relevant EU law.

The law is stated as at 31 December 2019.

Dr Saleem Sheikh, LLB, LLM, PhD
Susan Singleton, LLB, Solicitor, Singletons
London
December 2019

Preface to the First Edition

In the everyday life of a business, with the overriding need to secure contracts of sale or purchase, attention to the contract itself can often be overlooked. This can have disastrous consequences; an imprecise or non existent written contract can often leave the rights and obligations of the parties uncertain. As a consequence, businesses can be held up from running their usual operations, and – in many cases – expensive and protracted litigation results.

It is, of course, sometimes the case that entirely informal contracts are embarked on and work themselves out of the complete satisfaction of the parties. All too often, however, this does not occur.

It can be time-consuming and costly, particularly if the business has no immediate access to legal advice, for contracts to be drafted in the required form. This book, therefore, sets out model contracts for use in the type of agreements in which businesses will generally become involved. Whilst the specimen contracts will no doubt often need amending to suit the facts of the individual contract, we have prepared models which can serve as the basis, sometimes without any change at all, for a properly set out contract.

We have also been mindful of the type of contracts most often made by modern businesses. The sale and purchase of goods will remain the most common, but new technology has become of increasing important, and hence we have included specimen contracts dealing with software and with on-line agreements.

This book purports to be a handy tool for businesses, further than a legal text book. It was, however, necessary to explain the background to the contracts which we have prepared, and so the relevant legal principles lying behind them have also been set out.

Dr Richard Lawson, LLM PhD,
Partner, Lawmark
Susan Singleton, LLB, Solicitor
Singletons, Solicitors
www.singlelaw.com
2002

Acknowledgements

We owe profound gratitude and appreciation to the many people, companies, entities and organisations who assisted in our editing and research of *Commercial Contracts: A Practical Guide to Standard Terms*, including, in particular, The Institute of Advanced Legal Studies and the London School of Economics and Political Science for allowing the use of their library resources and general administrative support.

Dr Saleem Sheikh

My family has been, and will always be, the greatest inspiration in my life. To them I owe my sincere appreciation and I thank them for their kindness, patience, understanding and immense sense of humour in giving me the time, isolation, commitment and resolute determination to write and edit the various chapters for which I was responsible in this book. I pay particular tribute to my wife Shabena, my daughter Iram in successfully completing her MPharm at Nottingham University and pursuing her career in pharmacy, and my two sons, Kamil who is aspiring to achieve success in his business management course, and to Sohail who wants to be a lawyer; and to my son Hamza for diligently pursuing his higher academic studies towards a prosperous future career.

I have also been blessed with my remarkable parents, Fahmida and Tahir Jamil Sheikh. I pay tribute to my late mother and father for their relentless efforts in encouraging me in life, for loving me, for giving me determination, hope and confidence in life and for sharing the happiness, pain, suffering and sorrows together, for giving me the opportunity to look after them in their old age and care for their needs, and for allowing me to be with them when they needed me most. I salute them for inculcating their core values and beliefs in me which taught me to respect people of all walks of life and to give back to the community. They have made me strong, courageous and determined, and I owe my success to their laborious efforts and struggles. I only hope that I can replicate their hard work one day. I also thank my aunt, Saeeda Khan, for being there for me when I most needed her. To Raheem and Afifa who will soon be joining the family.

Susan Singleton

I would like to acknowledge the support of my family in the writing of this fifth edition and indeed the first to fourth editions of the book. I acknowledge the tolerance of my five children (and two grandchildren Rose and Frederick) whilst updating this book for the latest edition at weekends when client work is less likely to intrude into the working week: Rachel, a banking solicitor at

Acknowledgements

Macfarlanes, Rebecca, solicitor and Head of Legal at M&C Saatchi, Benjamin who works for Ocado and my twin sons Samuel and Joseph who graduate in 2020. My knowledge of the practical use of standard terms would be much less were it not for my clients over the years, both from when I worked for Slaughter and May and also Bristows and since I have been running Singletons, Solicitors. Every day my clients throw up new practical problems from which I learn.

This book is also dedicated to the memory of Dr Richard Lawson who was the co-author for the first to fourth editions, who sadly passed away in 2018.

These acknowledgements would not be complete without reference to our publishers, Bloomsbury Professional particularly to Ellie Mackenzie for all her assistance, patience, support and encouragement in the editing of the chapters. We are very fortunate to have worked with a team who displayed the highest professional standards in bringing their experience and skills to bear on this book.

The editing of this book has involved interesting research into new case law and legislation. We hope that the contracts in the book will be useful to the reader and that the commentary will provide the reader with a broader knowledge of commercial law and practice and how the topics covered fit within the wider European and international context.

Contents

Contents

Table of Statutes

Table of Statutory Instruments

Table of Cases

All references are to paragraph numbers

Table of Cases

Z

Section A: Commentary

A1:
Forming and Concluding
a Contract

At a glance A1.1

- Ideally, though not essentially, a contractual arrangement should be expressed in a formal document (that is to say in writing and signed by both parties).

- An agreement which is not formally expressed will still be binding but since the parties may have a different recollection of what exactly was agreed, there should always be a document setting out, if only in the form of bullet points, the heads of agreement.

- A binding agreement will normally be reached between parties if they have agreed on the essential points of the contract. Items such as the precise subject matter of the agreement and the price to be paid should usually be definitely agreed.

- Include all the key terms in a written agreement signed by all the parties before any obligations are performed by them.

- Contracts may sometimes be entered into unintentionally and care should be taken to ensure that nothing is mentioned in negotiations or correspondence that could be construed as binding the parties contractually.

- Ensure that the terms agreed are certain and contain sufficient detail to ensure enforceability. If the terms are vague or uncertain, the courts may determine the terms void.

- Recent judicial authorities have demonstrated that the courts will try and ensure that a contract is workable. Therefore, uncertain clauses should not be accepted on the basis that they may not be enforceable by the courts.

- The courts will objectively assess whether the parties by their words and conduct intended to create a legally binding relationship and that they had agree all the terms that the law requires as essential for that purpose.

- The relevant contract terms must be adequately brought to the attention of the other side. The terms themselves do not have to be

3

presented to the other side; it is enough if reference is made to them, eg by stating in a letter that copies of the contract terms are available on request.

- If the parties have formed contracts between themselves in the past, terms can be incorporated as a result of this normal course of dealing. It will be a matter of fact dependent on the circumstances of each case as to how many previous contracts need to have been made between the parties.

- Contract terms are categorised as 'conditions', 'warranties' or 'intermediate terms'. The remedies for breach depend on which category of term has been broken. Following enactment of the *Consumer Rights Act 2015*, however, this is no longer so in contracts made with consumers, but remains the case in business-to-business contracts.

- When parties send their own terms and conditions to each other, this is often called the 'battle of the forms'. In broad terms, the victor is the person who presents his terms last of all.

- For most contracts a signature is not required to make it binding although contracts relating to the sale of land are something of an exception to this rule. Provision has been made by statute for the treatment of electronic signatures.

- Any description applied to the goods in the contract must be very closely complied with. The courts generally assume that businessmen want goods exactly as described in the contract.

- Where the contract for sale is made by reference to a sample, similar provisions to those described above apply in relation to description, fitness and quality.

- One of the most important issues in a contract of sale is whether the risk of damage to the goods has passed to the buyer. Statute sets out basic rules, but these can be displaced by the specific terms of the contract.

- The passing of property is no less important than issues of risk. Again, statute sets out certain rules, but the parties in this case can displace them with the express terms of the contract.

- Sellers often seek security for payment by retaining title to the goods. This requires great care in the drafting of the specific terms.

- Parties are well advised to use exclusion or limitation clauses to ensure that they do not face open-ended liability in the event of a breach. At the same time, statute significantly restricts the effect of such clauses, making it difficult to use them in business-to-business contracts, and particularly difficult to exclude or limit liability in the case of a consumer contract.

- Damages for breach of contract are, by long-established principles, assessed on the basis of what the guilty party contemplated as the probable result of the breach. Principles have also been developed by the courts concerning the reimbursement of expenditure incurred by the innocent party.

- The basic rule laid down by statute is that no action for breach of contract can be brought after six years, though there are many exceptions to this rule. This can be addressed by the parties in the contract.

- A party may enter into a contract on the basis of a mistake or because of a misrepresentation which the other party might have made in the course of negotiation. A considerable body of law has developed as to the remedies available in such circumstances.

- There are strictly limited circumstances where a contract becomes void due to supervening circumstances.

- The so-called doctrine of privity of contract means that only the actual parties to the contract acquire rights and duties under it. This rule remains intact but has been considerably affected by legislation.

- Parties will often wish to protect their intellectual property. This can happen where the buyer is heavily involved in the development of the contract goods. Likewise, there will be matters which neither party may wish to be disclosed. These issues should be catered for in the contract when appropriate.

- To ensure correct delivery of documents, the contract should provide for the service of notices on each other.

- If the contract is made with a party overseas, care should be taken for the contract to have a term specifying which legal system applies.

- When drafting a contract, the parties should always bear in mind that certain aspects of the agreement, such as pricing, can fall foul of UK competition law.

- If a party wishes to ensure that no binding agreement is reached until a formal document has been signed, this must be stated in very clear words, such as a clear statement that all negotiations are 'subject to contract'.

Whether agreement has been reached   A1.2

Negotiations between the parties can often be a long, drawn out process, before being concluded by one side or the other. In such a case, there will often be a dispute as to whether a contract had been concluded, or whether the parties had simply been engaged in negotiations which had, in the end, achieved no result. For example, the parties may reach agreement on essential points of principle, but still leave some important points unsettled and whether the courts would enforce the contract despite the absence of certain terms from the parties' contractual relationship.

This arose in the leading Supreme Court case of *Wells v Devani* [2019] UKSC 4. This case concerned Mr Wells, a property developer and Mr Devani, an estate agent. Various correspondence and telephone exchanges took place between the parties for the sale of Mr Wells' remaining unsold properties. Subsequently, Mr Devani found a purchaser for the properties and claimed 2% plus VAT as his commission. The parties had not defined at what stage a commission would be payable to Mr Devani.

One of the issues raised on appeal concerned the agreement between the parties and whether it was complete and enforceable despite there being no express identification of the event which would trigger the obligation to pay the commission. The Supreme Court unanimously ruled in favour of Mr Devani. On the issue as to whether there was a binding contract, Lord Kitchin (with whom Lords Wilson, Sumption and Carnwath agreed) stated that the question was whether objectively assessed, the parties by their words and their conduct intended to create a legally binding relationship, and that they had agreed all the terms that the law requires as essential for that purpose: see *RTS Flexible Systems Ltd v Molkerei Alois Muller GmbH* [2010] 1 WLR 753. It may be the case that the words and conduct relied on are so vague that the court is unable to identify the terms on which the parties have reached agreement. However, the courts are reluctant to find an agreement is too vague or uncertain to be enforced where it is found that the parties had the intention of being contractually bound and have acted on their agreement: see *Scammel v Ouston* [1941] AC 251.

In this case, the Supreme Court was of the view that the parties had intended to create legal relations leading to a binding contract. On the issue of the commission, the Supreme Court stated that it would naturally be understood that payment of the commission would become due on completion of the purchase of the flats and the commission would be made from the proceeds of sale. Mr Devani and Mr Wells had agreed that if Mr Devani found a purchaser for the flats, he would be paid his commission. Therefore, it was not necessary to imply a term into the contractual relationship. The Supreme Court stated that if it had been necessary, it would imply such a term. According to Lord Kitchin: '…if, as here…the bargain is, in substance, 'find me a purchaser' and the agent introduces a prospective purchaser to whom the property is sold, then a reasonable person would understand that the parties intended the commission to be payable on completion and from the proceeds of sale'. This was the 'only sensible interpretation' from the parties' telephone conversation and surrounding circumstances. The Supreme Court applied *Marks & Spencer plc v BNP Paribas* [2015] UKSC 72 that such a term would be necessary to give the contract business efficacy and would not go beyond what was necessary for that purpose. On the issue of implying terms into a contractual relationship, Lord Kitchin stated that it was possible to imply something that was so obvious that it goes without saying, including something the law regards as no more than an offer. He stated that if the offer is accepted, the contract is made on the terms of the words used and what those words imply. Moreover, where it was apparent that the parties intended to be bound and to create legal relations, it may be permissible to imply a term to give the contract such business efficacy as the parties must have intended. For example, an agreement may be enforceable despite calling for some further agreement between the parties, say as to price, for it may be appropriate to imply a term that, in default of agreement, a reasonable price must be paid. On implying terms into a contractual relationship, see A1.9.

Lord Briggs agreed with Lord Kitchin and added that there are occasions, where the context in which the words are used to inform a person as much, or even more, about the essential terms of the bargain than the words themselves. This was the situation with Mr Wells and Mr Devani. Accordingly, a sufficiently certain and complete contract had been agreed between them. The Supreme Court's decision highlights the court's reluctance to find that an agreement is too vague or uncertain to be enforced where the parties intended to be bound and had acted on their agreement. The decision also highlights the importance of the parties ensuring that all key terms are expressly agreement between the parties and stated in the contract.

In *AMP Advisory & Management Partners AG v Force India Formula One Team Limited* [2019] EWHC 2426, Moulder J rejected the company's claim for commission for introducing a sports sponsorship opportunity. The judge was of the view that there was no binding oral or written contract between the parties for the commission to be payable particularly when the mandate agreement in question which would have triggered off the commission payment had not been signed by the parties. The High Court stated that viewed objectively, the verbal exchange between the parties was not intended to create legal relations or binding on the parties, having regard to the social nature of the meeting between the parties, and that one of the parties had no prior experience of acting as a sponsorship agent. On the issue of an unjust enrichment claim by the claimant, the evidence showed that a third party and not the claimant had introduced the sponsorship deal. Nevertheless, the Court recognised a limited contribution made by the claimant for its services in facilitating the sponsorship deal and awarded the sum of £150,000 as a result of the services provided on the basis that these services were an enrichment of the defendant at the expense of the claimant even where the contract did not materialise: *MSM Consulting Ltd v United Republic of Tanzania* [2009] EWHC 121. This decision emphasises the importance of ensuring that the principal terms of an agreement are clearly documented and signed by the parties to ensure their enforceability and to create legally binding relations, and opens up the possibility of a claim for unjust enrichment as an alternative in the absence of a binding contract.

Enforceability of incomplete contractual terms   A1.3

Recent judicial authorities demonstrate that the courts are inclined to give effect to a contractual term whose overall effect is explicit but whose detailed terms are incomplete. The courts will be slow to find contract terms void for uncertainty. In *Openwork Ltd v Forte* [2018] EWCA Civ 783, Forte was a financial adviser who entered into a franchise agreement with Openwork Limited for the sale of investment products. The franchise agreement provided for a clawback clause the effect of which was that Openwork was entitled to claim back a percentage of the commission which it had paid Forte, where an investment was withdrawn within three years. The clawback term did not however set out the percentage or formula for the calculation except that the commission would be calculated by reference to the amount invested, length of time invested and the amount withdrawn. Openwork sought to enforce the clawback provision. Forte contended that the clause was void for uncertainty.

The issue before the Court of Appeal was the extent to which the court could give effect to a contractual term whose overall effect was explicit, but whose detailed terms were incomplete. The Court of Appeal held that the clawback term was enforceable. According to Simon LJ, the court should strive to give some meaning to contractual clauses agreed by the parties if at all possible: see *WN Hillas v Arcos Ltd* (1932) 147 LJ 503. On the facts, the parties intended the words of the clawback provision to have some effect – otherwise the intent of the clause would be defeated. Although the clause did not set out a calculation formula, it did set out the necessary detail to identify the amount Forte would have to pay as part of the clawback. The effect of the Court of Appeal decision is that the court will attempt to give effect and meaning to a contract term if at all possible. Accordingly, the parties should not accept the inclusion of vague or uncertain terms on the basis that they will not be capable of enforcement. Where the terms are not clear, the court may try and determine their meaning, as it would be understood by a reasonable third party.

Effect of subsequent communications between parties and contractual enforceability   A1.4

From time to time the courts have recognised that there may be in existence certain factors that are inconsistent with the formation of a contractual relationship between the parties. Subsequent communications can be relevant to determining whether a contract has been concluded. The Court of Appeal considered this position in *Global Asset Capital, Inc v Aabar Block S.A.R.L* [2017] EWCA Civ 37, where the claimants claimed that on 6 May 2015, the defendants entered into a contract to sell them some rights and other debt interest for €250 million. The claimants contended that there was a valid contract between the parties and sought specific performance. As part of the background to the case, the parties agreed on the following facts.

- On 23 April 2015, the claimants sent an offer letter to the defendants headed 'Without Prejudice – Subject to Contract'.

- On 6 May 2015, there was a telephone conversation between the parties. One of the defendant's representatives stated that they accepted the offer subject to the claimants resending the offer letter in open and binding form; and also providing satisfactory evidence of their ability to fund the transaction.

- On 7 May 2015, the claimants emailed the defendants stating that they would provide the binding terms and funding commitment later in the day or following day.

- On 9 May 2015, the claimants sent the defendants a further offer letter setting out the main commercial terms of the previous offer which also included additional terms different from the original offer letter. The email from the claimants stated that the claimants looked forward to receiving confirmation of acceptance of the offer.

- On 10 May 2015, the defendants replied that the offer was not accepted.

A major matter in dispute between the parties was whether the court could consider events after the telephone conversation in deciding whether, during the conversation, a contract had been made. The Court of Appeal held that the parties' communications following 6 May 2015 telephone call should have been taken into account in determining whether a contract had been formed. In determining whether a contract had been made during the course of those negotiations, the court would consider the whole course of those negotiations, regardless of whether those negotiations were conducted in writing, orally or by conduct. By focusing on part of the communications in isolation, this could give a misleading impression that the parties had reached an agreement when they had not. Although the court will not consider subsequent events when interpreting the words of a contract, the issue in this case was not concerned with the interpretation of a contract but whether a contract had been entered into between the parties. The Court of Appeal decided that a contract had not been concluded during a telephone conversation following a 'subject to contract' offer letter, as this was inconsistent with the parties' subsequent communications.

According to the Court of Appeal, in spite of the parties' subsequent communications, the claimants had no real prospect of showing that there had been a binding offer and acceptance during the telephone conversation. There were certain factors which were inconsistent with the formation of a contract which included the fact that the claimants had marked the offer letter as 'subject to contract'. Further, the offer letter sent on 9 May referred to the purchase as the 'proposed transaction'; and that some of the terms of the contract provided the clause 'upon your agreement that you are willing to proceed…' which words indicated that a contract had not been formed. From a practical viewpoint when entering into negotiations, all correspondence should be marked 'subject to contract' to avoid entering into a contract prematurely, as in some circumstances, the courts may find that the 'subject to contract' status has been waived by a party. Further, the parties should ensure that they agree on all the terms of a contract between them set out in a written contract and signed by the parties.

An 'agreement to agree' provision   A1.5

Some provisions in a contract have the effect of 'an agreement to agree' at a future stage which are not binding on the parties to a contract. This aspect was considered in *Morris v Swanton Care & Community Limited* [2018] EWCA Civ 2763. In 2006, Morris sold his shares in a company to Swanton Care for an initial consideration subject to certain adjustments, through an earn-out provision. The terms of the agreement were set out in a Share Purchase Agreement. The earn-out provision stated that Morris 'shall have the option' to provide consultancy services for four years after completion and 'following such period as shall reasonably be agreed between [the parties]'. Although Morris had provided the consultancy services for four years, Swanton Care rejected his 'reasonable extension' to the earn-out period. Morris contended that he had a contractual right to a further earn-out period which would have earned him additional remuneration.

The Court of Appeal held that Morris did not have an enforceable right to provide the consultancy services during any earn out period other than the initial period agreed for four years. The further earn-out period was in essence an agreement to agree and was unenforceable for uncertainty of terms. Further, the parties intended to leave the issue of any extension to the period to be agreed. This necessarily meant that either of them would be free to agree or disagree about the matter and they would need to reach agreement between them. Accordingly, there was no bargain which the courts could enforce. There was no obligation on the parties to negotiate in good faith about the matter which remained to be agreed between them. See too *Walford v Miles* [1992] 2 AC 128. A practical point to note which arises from the Court of Appeal decision is that if the parties wish to create an enforceable agreement which takes into account an objective framework which can fill in any gaps later provided these are not uncertain in nature and scope, then the parties should consider setting out in detail how the objective framework should operate including the factors and circumstances that should be taken into account.

Effect of waiver on mode of acceptance   A1.6

One of the essential elements in the formation of a contract is the mode of acceptance of the offer made by the offeror. In some circumstances, the offeror may stipulate the particular mode of acceptance that is to be followed by the offeree. An issue arises as to the position where there is a waiver of specific mode of acceptance by subsequent conduct of the parties and whether this constitutes formal acceptance of the offer. This issue was considered in *Reveille Independent LLC v Anotech International (UK) Ltd [2016] EWCA Civ 433*, where the Court of Appeal posed the following question: 'In what circumstances will a contract result when a written offer document states that it is not binding until signed by the offeree and the offeree does not sign but performs in a manner contemplated by its terms?'

Reveille, a US television company issued proceedings against Anotech, a UK cookware distributor for breach of contract. Reveille alleged that there was an agreement whereby it had agreed to integrate and promote Anotech's products in episodes of the US MasterChef television series and license Anotech the right to use the MasterChef brand on its products. Although long form agreements negotiated between the parties were never completed, the parties began to negotiate a short written agreement ('Deal Memo'). The Deal Memo provided that it would not be binding on Reveille until executed by both Anotech and Reveille. Subsequently Anotech amended and signed the Deal Memo (which became a counter offer) but Reveille did not sign it.

The Court of Appeal held that the Deal Memo was binding on the parties as Reveille had accepted the contract by its conduct notwithstanding the prescribed mode of acceptance in that Reveille had not signed it. On the facts, Reveille had waived the requirement that there would be no binding contract in the absence of its signature on the Deal Memo by its subsequent conduct. There was no prejudice to Anotech. Reveille's actions such as integrating Anotech's products into episodes of MasterChef and approving Anotech's request to use the MasterChef brand at a show demonstrated that by its conduct it had waived the requirement for a signature. Further, both parties through subsequent conduct had confirmed the existence of a contract by performance of their respective obligations.

Cranston J summarised the following contractual principles required for contract formation.

- Consent to a contract is found in the acceptance of an offer. Acceptance can be by conduct as long as that conduct is objectively intended to constitute acceptance: *Brogden v Metropolitan Railway Co (1877)* 2 App Cas 666.

- An offer which is set out in a draft agreement can be accepted even though it is never signed by the parties: *Brogden v Metropolitan Railway Co.*

- If a party has a right to sign a contract before being bound, it is open to it by clear and unequivocal words or conduct to waive the requirement and conclude the contract without insisting on its signature: *Oceonografia SA de CV v DSND Subsea AS (Botnica)* [2006] EWHC 1360.

- Where signature is the prescribed mode of acceptance, the offeror will be bound by the contract if it waives that requirement and acquiesces in a different mode of acceptance as long as that has not prejudiced the offeror: *MSM Consulting Ltd v United Republic of Tanzania* [2009] EWHC 121.

- A draft contract can still have contractual force, although the parties did not comply with a requirement that to be binding it must be signed, if essentially all the terms have been agreed and their subsequent conduct indicates this: *RTS Flexible Systems v Molkeroi Alois Muller GmbH* [2010] 1 WLR 753.

- The subsequent conduct of the parties is admissible to prove the existence of a contract and its terms.

11

According to Cranston J, these contractual rules take effect against a background of legal policies recognised in case law. One such policy is the need for certainty in commercial contracts, commercial negotiations and the question of whether a contract has come into existence: *Cobbe v Yeoman's Row Management Ltd* [2008] 1 WLR 1752.

A second policy is that in commercial dealings, the reasonable expectations of honest, sensible business persons must be protected: see *RTS Flexible Systems Ltd*; and *G. Percy Trentham Ltd v Archital Luxfer Ltd* [1993] 1 Lloyd's Rep 25.

A practical point to note is that the parties to a contract should in advance sign an agreement before commencement of their obligations to ensure certainty in a contract. Further, this case demonstrates that a formal prescribed mode of acceptance can be waived by subsequent conduct.

The position where an agreement is subject to consent being obtained   A1.7

Some cases have demonstrated that a contract cannot be formed and there cannot be a legally valid binding contract where an agreement is expressed and is subject to board approval and therefore not binding until approval is given. This arose in *Goodwood Investments Holding Inc v ThyssenKrupp Industrial Solutions AG* [2018] EWHC 1056, where the court was required to consider whether an arbitration claim was settled in without prejudice correspondence between the parties' respective solicitors. The court held that a binding settlement had not been reached as the offer was made subject to the conclusion of a formal settlement agreement as well as subject to board approval which had not yet been obtained.

According to Males J, words such as 'subject to contract' indicated that the parties do not intend to be bound until a formal contract is entered into between them: *Generator Developments Ltd v Lidl UK GmbH* [2018] EWCA Civ 396. The same principles applied to an agreement which was stated to be subject to board approval of one or both parties. The effect of this is that the person concluding the agreement does not have the authority or is not prepared to commit the company unless the approval is forthcoming: see *RTS Flexible Systems Ltd v Molkerei Alois Muller GmbH & Co KG* [2010] 1 WLR 753; and *Pagan SpA v Feed Products Ltd* [1987] 2 Lloyd's Rep 601. In determining whether an agreement has become legally binding, the whole course of the parties' negotiations must be considered: *Global Asset Capital Inc v Aabar Block Sarl* [2017] EWCA Civ 37. Since the directors are required to exercise an independent judgment whether the transaction is in the best interests of the company, it was difficult to see how there could in such circumstances be any implied promise binding the company to the effect that approval will be forthcoming or that it is a mere formality or a 'rubber stamping' exercise.

Proper parties to the contract   A1.8

A contract which is entered into must ensure that appropriate parties are included in the contract to ensure enforceability against the party concerned. The decision in *Erith Holdings v Murphy* [2017] EWHC 1364 serves to highlight the importance of knowing who are the exact parties to the contract. In this case, a group of waste removal companies which provided services to a company that subsequently went into liquidation was not entitled to recover outstanding amounts from the company's owner. The court found that the agreement for works had been entered into with the company itself and the company's owner had not given any guarantee or indemnity in his personal capacity. Even where a guarantee had been given by the owner, it was merely oral and therefore unenforceable. A practical point to note is the importance of knowing who a party is contracting with to ensure enforceability. This case emphasises that terms should be formally set out in writing rather than relying on oral discussions. Where a guarantee is to be provided by the owner in an individual capacity, that party should be added to the agreement or that any such guarantee is properly documented.

Implied terms   A1.9

In certain circumstances, the courts may imply some terms into the contractual relationship between the parties. The law recognises two types of contractual implied terms:

1.   A term may be implied into a particular contract, in the light of the express terms, commercial common sense, and the facts known to both parties at the time the contract was made. This section is concerned with the first type of implied term.

2.   The second type of implied term arises because unless such a term is expressly excluded, the law (sometimes by statute or through the common law) imposes certain terms into certain classes of relationship (for example the *Supply of Goods and Services Act 1982*): see *Geys v Societe Generale* [2013] 1 AC 523, at para 55.

Over the years, there have been various classic judicial interpretations as to the requirements that have to be satisfied before a term can be implied into a commercial contract. Three principal tests have been highlighted: (i) business efficacy; (ii) necessity; and (iii) officious bystander.

The requirement for business efficacy test was set out in *The Moorcock (1889)* 14 PD 64. Bowen LJ stated that in all the cases where a term had been implied, 'it will be found that ...the law is raising an implication from the presumed intention of the parties with the object of giving the transaction such efficacy as both parties must have intended that at all events it should have.'

The business efficacy test was further developed in *Reigate v Union Manufacturing Co (Ramsbottom) Ltd* [1918] 1 KB 605. Scrutton LJ stated that a term can only be implied if it is necessary in the business sense to give efficacy to the contract. A term would only be implied 'if it is such a term that it can confidently be said that if at the time the contract was being negotiated, the parties had been asked what would happen in a certain event, they would both have replied 'of course. So and so will happen; we did not trouble to say that; it is too clear."

Shirlaw v Southern Foundries (1926) Ltd [1939] 2 KB 206 introduced the 'officious bystander' test. MacKinnon LJ stated that 'prima facie that which in any contract is left to be implied and need not be expressed is so obvious that it goes without saying.' Further, that a term would only be implied 'if, while the parties are making their bargain, an officious bystander were to suggest some express provision for it in their agreement, they would testily suppress him with a common 'Of, of course!" See too *Powell v Lowe* [2010] EWCA Civ 1419; and *Trollope & Colls Ltd v North West Metropolitan Regional Hospital Board* [1973] 1 WLR 601; and *Liverpool City Council v Irwin* [1977] AC 239.

Modern Test on Implied Terms **A1.10**

Given the nature of the diverse tests for implying a term into a contractual relationship, the leading test on implied terms has been set out by the Supreme Court in *Marks and Spencer plc v BNP Paribas Securities Services Trust Co (Jersey) Ltd* [2015] UKSC 72. Lord Neuberger stated that the classic tests for implied terms (considered above) represented a clear, consistent and principled approach, and that it would be dangerous to reformulate the principles. He favoured the approach to implied terms set out in the Privy Council decision by Lord Simon in *BP Refinery (Westernport) Pty Ltd v President Councillors and Ratepayers of the Shire of Hastings* (1977) 52 ALJR 20:

> '[F]or a term to be implied, the following conditions (which may overlap) must be satisfied: (1) it must be reasonable and equitable; (2) it must be necessary to give business efficacy to the contract, so that no term will be implied if the contract is effective without it; (3) it must be so obvious that 'it goes without saying'; (4) it must be capable of expression (5) it must not contradict any express term of the contract.'

Lord Neuberger added the following six observations to the above implied term principles enunciated by Lord Simon.

- There is no need to show an actual intention of the parties when negotiating the contract. The court is instead concerned with the notional intention of reasonable people in the position of the parties at the time at which they were contracting.

- A term should not be implied into a detailed commercial contract merely because it appears fair or merely because one considers that the parties would have agreed to it if it had been suggested to them. Those are necessary but not sufficient grounds for including a term.

- It is questionable whether (Lord Simon's first requirement) reasonableness and equitableness, will usually, if ever, add anything. If a term satisfies the other requirements, it is hard to think that it would not be reasonable and equitable.

- Business necessity and obviousness can be alternatives in the sense that only one of them needs to be satisfied.

- If one approaches the issue by reference to the officious bystander, it is 'vital to formulate the question to be posed by [him] with the utmost care.'

- Necessity for business efficacy involves a value judgment. The test is not one of 'absolute necessity', not least because the necessity is judged by reference to business efficacy. A term can only be implied if, without the term, the contract would lack commercial or practical coherence.

Lord Neuberger further stated that the exercise of implying a term into a contract was not the same as the exercise of interpreting a contract, particularly because the express terms of a contract must first be interpreted before considering any question of implication.

Practical Points **A1.11**

- The Supreme Court in *Marks and Spencer plc* has emphasised the strict nature of the legal test which must be met before a term can be implied into a contractual relationship.

- The process of construction of an express term will first be considered by the court and only thereafter will the issue of implication of a term will arise.

- When drafting a commercial agreement, set out expressly and specifically and clearly the objectives and intentions of the parties.

- The court will not rewrite provisions of a contract for the parties.

- The court will uphold the bargain struck by the parties as set out in the commercial agreement.

- A term cannot be implied into a commercial agreement if it contradicts an express term.

- The courts are now placing emphasis towards a more literal approach to contractual interpretation and in particular to the actual words set out in the commercial agreement.

- In *Kason Kek-Gardner Ltd v Process Components Ltd* [2017] EWCA Civ 2132, Lewison LJ applied the test for implying terms in commercial agreements: the term must be necessary to give the contract business efficacy, or it must be so obvious that it goes without saying. He also stated that that the necessity required by the test is necessity for the business efficacy of the contract itself and 'not some wider business purpose of the contracting party.'

- The *Marks and Spencer plc* case was applied by the Court of Appeal in JN *Hipwell & Son v Szurek* [2018] EWCA Civ 674, where Hildyard J (with whom Gross LJ agreed) stated:

  '….it is well established, and was not disputed before us, that a term may be implied where it is necessary to give business efficacy to the contract in question. In such a context, the touchstone is always necessity and not merely reasonableness, and the term is implied as a matter of fact in the particular case, rather than as a matter of law and as a legal incident of contracts of an identified type.'

- Since *Marks and Spencer plc* case, the courts have demonstrated that a strict approach will be taken when implying terms in a contractual relationship between the parties. Further, the courts will construe the express term first before considering whether or not to imply a term into the contract. In *Robert Bou-Simon v BGC Brokers LP* [2018] EWCA Civ 1525, BGC Brokers ('B') lent £336,000 to Simon ('S') under a loan agreement which assumed that S would become a partner in B. The agreement provided that the loan would be repaid from S's partnership distributions with interest. S resigned within four years and B claimed that the outstanding loan plus interest was due from S. B contended that the loan was due pursuant to a term which should be implied to that effect into the loan agreement. The Court of Appeal held that although the judge at first instance had identified the correct test for implied terms in *Marks and Spencer plc*, he had misapplied the test. The judge had implied a term in order to reflect the merits of the situation as they now appear. He did not approach the matter from the perspective of a reasonable reader of the loan agreement, knowing all its provisions and the surrounding circumstances at the time the agreement was made. It was not appropriate to apply hindsight and to seek to imply a term in a commercial contract merely because it appears to be fair or because one considers that the parties would have agreed to it if it had been suggested to them. Those are necessary but not sufficient grounds for the implication of a term. Further, the issue of implied terms should only be considered once the process of construing the express terms of the agreement had been completed.

- In *Takeda Pharmaceutical Company Limited v Fougera Sweden Holding AB* [2017] EWHC 1995, the High Court was required to consider whether a term for the parties to cooperate following completion was to be implied into a share purchase agreement ('SPA'). Arnold J relying on *Marks and Spencer plc*, held that an implied duty to cooperate could not be implied in the SPA. He noted that there was no dispute as to the principles to be applied in interpreting the SPA taking account of the decision in *Wood v Capital Insurance Services*. The Court's task was to ascertain the objective meaning of the language which the parties had chosen to express their agreement when read in the context of factual background known or reasonably available to the parties at the time of the agreement, excluding prior negotiations. The practical point to note is that if a party is seeking cooperation from the other party, it should be expressly drafted in the agreement as such a term will not be implied, particularly because on the facts Arnold J determined that the SPA had been professionally drafted on behalf of sophisticated and well-resourced parties, and was detailed and complex.

- In *Hayfin Opal Luxco 3 SARL v Windermere VII CMBS plc* [2018] 1 BCLC 118, Snowden J was of the view that where an analysis of the express term of a contract led to the clear conclusion that something was missing, the court could supply the missing words or terms by the process of correcting mistakes by construction or by the implication of terms. In either case, however, there was a strict test to justify such a result: the court would not supply additional words or imply terms simply because it was reasonable to do so in the circumstances which had arisen. The court would only add words to the express terms of the agreement if it was necessary to do so because the agreement was incomplete or commercially incoherent without them. Even then, the court had to be certain both that the absence of the missing words was inadvertent, and that if the omission had been drawn to the attention of the parties at the time of contracting they would have agreed what additional provisions should be made.

- In *Merthyr (South Wales) Ltd v Merthyr Tydfill County Borough Council* [2019] EWCA Civ 526, a dispute arose between the parties in connection with a planning permission granted by the Council to a mining company, which provided a requirement that the company fund restoration of the land after its mining operations concluded. The parties entered into an escrow agreement in 2015 establishing a fund to secure £15 million of the restoration costs. Clause 4.2(a) of the escrow agreement provided that 'subject to [subclauses (b) and (c)], on each Funding Date, the Company shall deposit an amount equal to £625,000 (as adjusted pursuant to [subclauses (c) and (d)]) into the Account.' The funding dates occurred quarterly and subclauses (b) and (c) set out that, subject to subclause (d), if a deposit or consecutive deposits were missed, the amount due on the next funding date would increase by the amount outstanding. Subclause (d) was a longstop provision, specifying that if the final deposit was missed, the company was to pay the outstanding balance of the £15 million by 30 June 2022. The company did not however make any deposits and the Council sought an order for specific performance. The company's defence was that the relevant provisions allowed the company to make quarterly deposits as long as the company paid £15 million by the longstop date. The High Court granted the specific performance and ordered the company to pay the deposits outstanding at that time into the escrow account. The Court of Appeal considered one of the issues regarding textual analysis and business common sense. According to the mining company, the escrow agreement should reasonably be understood to mean that, if a quarterly payment was missed, there was no enforceable obligation to make the payment until the longstop date. The company contended that this followed from the fact that the requirements to make the quarterly payments were expressed to be 'subject to' the provisions stating that missed payments would be rolled forward to the next funding date. The Court of Appeal rejected the company's purported interpretation of the escrow agreement based on the textual analysis and because it would be 'an extraordinary and improbable intention to attribute to contracting parties', which was contrary to business common sense. According to the Court of Appeal, the decision in *Arnold v Britton* cautioned against relying on considerations of commercial common sense where to do so would undervalue the importance of the commercial language used. Leggatt LJ stated that in this case no question arose of rejecting the natural meaning of the contractual language as there were no words in the agreement which had as their natural meaning that the amount to be deposited on each funding date ceased to be due if the company failed to pay it. Implying such a term would be inconsistent with the express terms of clause 4.2 which used terminology ('shall', 'fails to pay', 'payable', and 'outstanding') clearly indicating that payment of the amounts on the funding dates was a legal obligation rather than merely a statement of non-binding intention. Further, such a construction would undermine the commercial purpose of the escrow agreement which was to ensure that a fund of restoration money was established from the revenue generated from the mine. As a practical point, the decision in *Merthyr* demonstrates the importance of ensuring that all contractual provisions are drafted clearly. Where any assumptions or background information may be necessary to understand the purpose and intended operation of a particular provision, these should be set out in the contract by way of recitals or similar with clearly drafted provisions demonstrating the intentions of the parties. The Court of Appeal decision illustrates the strict operation of the common law rule against relying on evidence of pre-contractual negotiations to interpret contracts. The decision highlights that it is not only statements reflecting one party's subjective intentions or aspirations which are excluded for the purposes of interpreting a contract, but also communications that are capable of showing that the parties reached a consensus on a particular point or used words in an agreed sense in concluding the contract.

- *Triple Point Technology Inc v PTT Public Company Ltd* [2019] EWCA Civ 230 raised the issue of implying a term into a commercial contract to the effect that the independent contractor could suspend work and its services in the event of non-payment by the employer. The Court of Appeal rejected the implication of such a term on the basis that if the employer failed to make payments to the contractor on the due dates, the contractor would have all the usual remedies for non-payment rather than liquidated damages. These would include suing for the money due, applying for summary judgment, and treating the non-payment as a repudiation. Further, even if the contract were to favour one party strongly, there was no reason for the court to redress the balance by implying terms into the contract. Although there were express provisions dealing with suspension of work, these provisions did not specifically include non-payment. Therefore, a clause providing for liquidated damages for delay did not apply where the contractor failed to complete the contracted work.

Implied Duty of Good Faith in a Commercial Agreement and Relational Contracts   A1.12

The issue here is whether the courts would imply a duty of good faith where there is an oral commercial joint venture agreement or a long-term contract? Although there is no general principle of good faith in English contract law, there is a recognition that a duty of good faith may be implied in certain circumstances and to categories such as a fiduciary relationship or in contracts of employment.

In *Sheikh Tahnoon Bin Saeed Bin Shakhboot Al Nehayan v Ioannis Kent* [2018] EWHC 333, Leggatt LJ considered that 'there appears to be a growing recognition that such a duty may readily be implied in a relational contract.' A 'relational contract' is a contract that 'may require a high degree of communication and predictable performance based on mutual trust and confidence and involve expectations of loyalty which are not legislated for in the express terms of the contract but are implicit in the parties' understanding and necessary to give business efficacy to the arrangements': per Leggatt LJ in *Yam Seng Pte Ltd v International Trade Corp* [2013] EWHC 111. Relational contracts may include joint venture agreements, distribution agreements and franchise agreements. It includes a category of contract in which the parties are committed to collaborating with each other, typically on a long-term basis, which respect to the spirit and objectives of their venture, but which they have not tried to specify, and which may be impossible to specify, exhaustively in a written contract. Such 'relational' contracts involve trust and confidence but of a different kind from that involved in fiduciary relationships. The trust is not in the loyal subordination by one party of its own interests to those of another. It is the trust that the other party will act with integrity and in a spirit of cooperation. The legitimate expectations which the law should protect in relationships of this kind are embodied in the normative standard of good faith.

Leggatt LJ found the following features in the dealings between the parties to conclude that there was a relational contract:

- The nature of the parties' relationship was one in which they 'naturally and legitimately' expected of each other greater candour and cooperation and greater regard for each other's interests than ordinary commercial parties dealing with each other at arm's length.

- The two parties entered into a joint venture agreement which was intended to be a long-term collaboration, in which their interests were inter-linked and which they saw commercially albeit not in law, as a partnership. Their collaboration was formed and conducted on the basis of a personal friendship and involved much greater mutual trust than is inherent in an ordinary contractual bargain between shareholders in a company.

- Although the parties did not attempt to formalise the basis of their cooperation in any written contract, they were content to deal with each other entirely informally on the basis of their mutual trust and confidence that they would each pursue their common project in good faith.

On the facts, Leggatt LJ concluded that the joint venture agreement was a 'relational contract.' Therefore, the implication of duty of good faith in the contract was essential to give effect to the parties' reasonable expectations and satisfied the business necessity test as set out in the *Marks and Spencer plc* case.

The obligation to act in 'good faith' is an obligation to act honestly and with fidelity to the bargain. It is an obligation not to act dishonestly and not to act to undermine the bargain entered into or the substance of the contractual benefit bargained for. It is also an obligation to act reasonably and with fair dealing having regard to the interests of the parties (which will, inevitably, at times conflict) and to the provisions, aims and purposes of the contract, objectively ascertained.

The court identified two forms of 'furtive or opportunistic' conduct which would be incompatible with the obligation of good faith. First, it would be inconsistent with the duty of good faith for one party to agree or enter into negotiations to sell his interest or part of his interest in the companies which they jointly owned to a third party covertly and without informing the other beneficial owner. Second, it would be contrary to the obligation to act in good faith for either party to use his position as a shareholder of the companies to obtain a financial benefit for himself at the expense of the other.

In *Bates v Post Office Ltd (No 3)* [2019] EWHC 606, the High Court decided that certain contracts between the Post Office and sub-postmasters were 'relational contracts' and subject to an implied obligation on the parties to act in good faith. According to Fraser J, the obligation of good faith will not be implied in every commercial contract but in accordance with the decision in *Yam Seng Pte Ltd v International Trade Corp*, there was a recognition in English law that in relation to 'relational contracts' an obligation of good faith was implied into a commercial agreement. The nature of a relational contract depended on the circumstances of the relationship, defined by the terms of the agreement, set in its commercial context. Fraser J stated that it was not sufficient in the duty of good faith for the requirement that the parties only act honestly. Although the duty included honesty, it also required the parties to refrain from conduct which in the relevant context would be regarded as commercially unacceptable by reasonable and honest people.

The *Bates* case involved group litigation between 550 sub-postmasters and the Post Office pursuant to a sub-postmaster contract and subsequently the Network Transformation Contract between the respective parties. The terms of these contracts provided that the sub-postmasters and their personnel were solely responsible for any losses caused by negligence on their part, and they were required to make good any shortfalls to the Post Office. In the late 1990s, the Post Office introduced a computerised accounting system named Horizon which was to be used by all sub-postmasters in their branches. The Horizon system identified a number of shortfalls and discrepancies in the accounting systems in the various branches to which the sub-postmasters were required to contribute from their own personal resources despite their protestations that the Horizon system was defective with many becoming bankrupt and convicted of fraud and false accounting.

Having determined that there was a contractual relationship between the Post Office and the claimants, Fraser J focused on the characterisation of the contract as a 'relational contract' and whether there was an implied obligation of good faith in such a contract. Fraser J decided that the contract between the Post Office and the sub-postmasters was a relational contract:

> 'I consider that there is a specie of contracts, which are most usefully termed "relational contracts", in which there is an implied obligation of good faith (which is also termed "fair dealing" in some of the cases). This means that the parties must refrain from conduct which in the relevant context would be regarded as commercially unacceptable by reasonable and honest people.'

Fraser J decided that although there was no general duty of good faith implied into all commercial agreements, but 'such a duty could be implied into some contracts, where it was in accordance with the presumed intention of the parties.' In the course of his judgment, he set out the essential characteristics of a relational contract which carried the obligation of good faith:

- there is no specific express term in the contract that prevents a duty of good faith being implied;

- the contract is a long-term contract, with mutual intention of a long-term relationship;

- there is an intention to perform the parties' respective roles with integrity and fidelity to the bargain;

- there is a commitment to collaboration in the contract's performance;

- the 'spirits and objectives' of the parties' venture is incapable of exhaustive expression in a written contract;

21

- the parties reposing trust and confidence in each other (but of a kind different to that reposed in fiduciary relationships);
- there is a high degree of communication, cooperation and predictable performance based on mutual trust and confidence, and expectations of loyalty;
- there is a degree of significant investment by one or both parties;
- there is exclusivity of contractual relationship.

The above list of characteristics was not exhaustive of a relational contract and that no single factor was determinative with the exception of the first characteristic, so that if the express terms prevented the implication of a duty of good faith, such duty could not be implied in such contracts. Fraser J decided that each of the above characteristics was present in the contractual relations between the Post Office and the sub-postmasters, but with the following additional elements from the facts that lent support to a relational contract namely:

- the significant of the sub-postmaster's investment in buying or leasing premises for the branch;
- the Post Office's awareness of the size of the investment and the sub-postmaster's source of funds;
- the sub-post master's entitlement to certain benefits similar to those under an employment contract;
- the requirement on the Post Office to maintain branches widely, even in locations that would not normally be commercially viable;
- the importance of trust between the sub-postmaster and the public and the Post Office and the sub-postmasters.

The *Bates* case involved implying terms of good faith into the contractual relationship between the parties. However, the scope for implying further terms of good faith are very limited especially where there is an express duty to act in good faith. In *Teesside Gas v CATS North Sea* [2019] EWHC 1220 one of the clauses in the agreement between the parties stated that Teesside Gas had 'the right to dispute, in good faith, any amount specified in an invoice'. Butcher J held that 'The contract thereby defined, in my judgment exhaustively, the extent of any good faith obligations arising under it. It would be inconsistent with those terms to imply any wider duty of good faith'.

The issue and scope of the label 'relational contracts' and implied duty of good faith was considered in *UTB LLC v Sheffield United Ltd* [2019] EWHC 2322 including the circumstances in which a duty of good faith should be implied in an investment and shareholder agreement. According to Fancourt J:

> 'If by "relational contract" it is clear that one means a relational contract of the kind described by Leggatt LJ in *Sheikh Tahnoon*

and not all relational contracts in a broader sense, then there is no difficulty and the characteristics identified by Fraser J [in the *Bates* case] may assist to identify such a contract. But there is a danger in using the term "relational contract" that one is not clear about what exactly is meant by it. There is a great range of different types of contract that involve the parties in long-term relationships of varying types, with different terms and varying degrees of detail and use of language, and to characterise them all as "relational contracts" may be in one sense accurate and yet in other ways liable to mislead. It is self-evidently not all long-term contracts that involve an enduring but undefined, cooperative relationship between the parties that will, as a matter of law, involve an obligation of good faith: see *Globe Motors, Inc v TRW Lucas Varity Electric Steering Ltd* [2016] EWCA Civ 396.

Rather than seek to identify and weigh likely indicia of a "relational contract" in the narrower sense used by Leggatt LJ, it is, I consider, preferable to ask oneself first – as Leggatt LJ did in the *Sheikh Tahnoon* case – whether a reasonable reader of the contract would consider that an obligation of good faith was obviously meant or whether the obligation is necessary to the proper working of the contract. The overall character of the contract in issue will of course be highly material in answering that question but so will its particular terms, as recognised by the principle that (as restated in the *Marks and Spencer* case) no term may be implied into a contract if it would be inconsistent with an express term.

That approach is, in my respectful opinion, preferable also because the exact content of any implied obligation of fair dealing, or to act with integrity, or to act in good faith, will be highly sensitive to the particular context of the contract, as observed by Dove J in *D&G Cars Ltd v Essex Police Authority* [2015] EWHC 226 (QB) at [175]. The greater part of that context is the express terms of the contract. Thus, to imply a general obligation to act at all times in good faith towards the counterparty because the contract is a relational contract may fail to have regard to rights and obligations created by the express terms, to which any implied obligation must be tailored if it is not to be excluded as being inconsistent with them. In the instant case there is a real example of just such a question...'

On the facts, Fancourt J did not find that good faith should be implied in an investment and shareholder agreement.

Inconsistency between express and implied terms   **A1.13**

There may be some situations where the implied terms which are pleaded by a party are substantially inconsistent with the express terms of the contract between the parties because the express terms do not fully reflect the parties' intentions. The issue arises whether the courts will uphold the implied terms or the express terms. This aspect was considered by the Court of Appeal in *Irish Bank Resolution Corp Ltd (In Special Liquidation) v Camden Market Holdings Corp* [2017] EWCA Civ 7.

The bank, Irish Bank Resolution Corp Ltd ('IBRC') and the developer, Camden Market Group ('CMG') entered into a Facility Agreement in 2005 under which IBRC provided £195 million to CMG to purchase and develop properties at Camden Market with the extension of the loan in 2008 and 2012. Thereafter, IBRC was placed in special liquidation. The liquidators of IBRC were instructed to sell off IBRC's loan books including the loans made to CMG. The loan agreement between IBRC and CMG expressly allowed IBRC to assign any of its loans to another bank and to provide details of the loans to potential assignees who entered into a confidentiality undertaking. At the same time, CMG began to market the properties it had developed under the loan facilities to prospective buyers. IBRC's liquidators began to market CMG's loans as part of a package of loans containing distressed debt. It was contended by CMG that IBRC's marketing of CMG's facilities together with the distressed debt implied that CMG's facilities were also in default, which on the facts was not the case.

CMG issued proceedings against IBRC on the basis that IBRC's right to market the CMG's loans was qualified by an implied term that IBRC should not do anything to hinder CMG's ability to achieve the best price for CMG's properties. CMG alleged that it had suffered substantial losses owing to breach of the implied term. IBRC sought summary judgment and contended that the alleged implied term contradicted the express term in the loan agreements which allowed IBRC to assign the loans with CMG's parent company's consent, and to provide information to any prospective purchaser.

In the Court of Appeal, Beatson LJ affirmed the principles on implied terms set out by Lord Neuberger in *Marks and Spencer plc*, and that it was necessary first to consider the express terms in a contract before determining whether or not a term should be implied. If a term was to be implied, it would always be subject to the 'cardinal rule' that any implied term must not contradict any express term of the contract.

Beatson LJ distinguished between two types of inconsistencies: (a) direct linguistic inconsistency; and (b) substantive inconsistency. He decided that there was no linguistic inconsistency in IBRC's ability to market the loans under the express terms of the loan agreements. Beatson LJ held however that the implied term alleged by CMG would be substantively inconsistent with the express terms of the loan agreements. There would be a 'significant restriction' on IBRC's express power to disclose information to potential purchasers. The express terms and the implied term were therefore held to be substantively inconsistent.

The Irish Bank case signifies a stringent approach that the courts are taking when considering whether to imply terms in a commercial agreement between the parties. A term cannot be implied into a contract between the parties if it contradicts the express terms of the contract. The parties to the contract should therefore ensure that their rights are protected by express terms when entering into a contractual relationship and not to rely upon implied terms to supplement the express terms. The courts will uphold the bargain struck by the parties under the express terms of the contract. The court will only therefore apply the strict test set out in *Marks and Spencer plc* once it has addressed the express terms in the contract. Where an express term provides for an express power on a party to the contract, the express power cannot be qualified, limited or altered by an implied term: see too *Stevensdrake Ltd (Trading as Stevensdrake Solicitors) v Stephen Hunt (Liquidator of Sunblow Ltd)* [2017] EWCA Civ 1173 (terms of an earlier contract could not be implied into a subsequent agreement). See too *Merthyr (South Wales) Ltd v Marthyr Tydfill County Borough Council* [2019] EWCA Civ 526.

The incorporation of contract terms   A1.14

It is always open for the parties to agree expressly on a set of written terms. If this is the case, then those terms will be incorporated into the contract and form the basis of the agreement between them.

Many situations are not so clear-cut, and a number of issues can arise as in *Arcadis Consulting (UK) Ltd v AMEC (BCS) Ltd* [2018] EWCA Civ 2222. AMEC (BCS) Ltd, the claimant, was a contractor specialising in the design, manufacture and installation of pre-cast concrete for the civil engineering and construction industries. The claimant hired the defendant, Arcadis Consulting (UK) to carry out specific works for two large projects in the Wellcome Building and CastlePoint Car Park which was in anticipation of a wider agreement between the parties which did not subsequently materialise.

The claimant contended that the CastlePoint Car Park was defective and had suffered substantial losses as a consequence of the defect. The defendant denied liability and sought to rely on a contractual liability cap. A dispute arose between the parties as to the terms on which the defendant carried out the works as there was no formal written agreement between the parties when works commenced because it was still being negotiated and whether those terms had incorporated a cap on the defendant's liability. Various correspondence was exchanged between the parties during the negotiation period. At first instance, Coulson J found that there was a 'simple contract' between the parties evidenced partly in the exchange of correspondence between the parties and further by the defendant's conduct in undertaking the works. However, the judge found that terms and conditions had not been incorporated in the contract as no terms had been accepted which meant that the defendant's liability was uncapped. The Court of Appeal while finding that a contract had existed between the parties, also determined that the contract had incorporated the terms and conditions including the defendant's liability cap. The Court of Appeal found that the parties were working under an 'interim contract' pending final agreement between them and that from the exchange of correspondence, the terms and conditions had been incorporated into the interim contract. Accordingly, Arcadis's liability for defective design (if any) was limited to the reasonable costs of repair. The Court of Appeal's decision aligns with the position stated by Goff J in *British Steel Corp v Cleveland Bridge & Engineering Co Ltd* [1984] 1 All ER 504, in which Goff J stated that if parties are in a stage of negotiation and one party asks the other to begin work 'pending' the parties entering into a formal contract, it cannot be inferred from the other party acting on that request that he is assuming any responsibility for his performance, except such responsibility as will be assumed under the terms of the contract that both parties are confident will be shortly finalised.

A practical point to note is that the parties should agree at the outset as to the key terms including incorporation of any terms and conditions before works commence and pending resolution and agreement on the final contractual terms.

Notification of the relevant terms   A1.15

Generally, unless one party notifies the other of the particular terms before a contract is concluded between them, those terms will not apply. It is for a court, as a matter of law, to decide whether there is evidence for holding that the notice is reasonably sufficient.

Cases in which notice has been held to be insufficient have been those where the conditions were printed on the back of a document without any reference to them on the face, or where the conditions have been obliterated by a date stamp (*Sugar v London, Midland & Scottish Railway* [1941] 1 All ER 172; *White v Blackmore* [1972] 2 QB 651; *Richardson, Spence & Co v Rowntree* [1894] AC 217). It is important to understand, however, that it is not necessary for the contract terms themselves to be set out in the document which is tendered.

Whether there is sufficient notice   A1.16

> **Case Example:** *Lacey's Footwear v Bowler International* **[1997] 2 Lloyd's Rep 369**
>
> The defendant carriers had been soliciting work from the claimants by sending them mailshots and visiting them at their place of work. The first approach had been by telephone in May 1986, and this had been followed by a letter, the bottom of which bore a reference to the defendants' terms and conditions. These were on the reverse of the letter and in print 'so small and so faint as to be legible only to one of such tender years that he or she would be far too young to comprehend the meaning of them'. The reverse of the letter, in large print, indicated that a large print version was available. No contract was made at that stage.

Two years later, a letter was tendered to the claimants setting out terms and conditions on the reverse. Still no contract materialised, nor did an approach in 1991 result in a contract being formed. In October 1992, however, the claimants sought quotations from a number of carriers, including the defendants. The latter prepared a document which referred to the terms of trading, and they telephoned the claimants. In the proceedings which followed, the managing director of the claimants did not dispute that the letters from the defendants did have the terms and conditions on the back though as a matter of practice – he never read them. The court concluded that reasonable notice of the contract terms had not been given.

The opening move had been the call from the claimants, followed by the defendants' brief covering letter, which had small print at the foot of the page reading: 'Trading Conditions – See Reverse'. No other effort had been made to bring the defendants' conditions to the claimants' notice. The defendants' rate proposal specifically referred to the terms of trading in block capitals, but that reference specifically detailed 'from FOB Alicante to delivered London E2. Excluding customs clearance'. There was nothing in the proposal to refer back to the small print on the reverse of the covering letter. In reaching its decision, the Court said that it had borne in mind that this was an oral contract negotiated over the telephone, and made in a hurry. The rate proposals, which formed the basis of the contract, did not refer to the conditions of contract; it made no reference to the conditions set out on the reverse side of the accompanying letter.

Case Example: *SSL International plc v TTK Lig Ltd* **[2011] EWHC 1695**

The applicant English company (S) applied for a mandatory injunction requiring the first respondent Indian company to supply condoms pursuant to a supply agreement. S manufactured and marketed condoms. T also manufactured condoms and formed a joint venture with S, which was governed by Indian law. T was obliged to supply condoms to S. S generated a purchase order which purported to include S's standard terms and conditions which, among other things, included an exclusive jurisdiction clause. However, the purchase order was never seen by T; it only saw the purchase order number. Having gained effective control of the venture's board, T sought to implement a new arrangement that was not favourable to S. S accepted with a view to a later challenge. Under the terms of the joint venture T and S could each appoint four nominee directors to the board. Despite S's acceptance of T's proposal, T failed to resume supply of the condoms. Proceedings were commenced in India in which resumption of supply was ordered. T failed to comply, and enforcement proceedings were issued. S served one of the Indian nominee directors with a claim form when present in England at its offices. S submitted that: (1) the service of the claim form on the Indian nominee director was valid; (2) its standard terms and conditions had been incorporated in the contract.

The court held that in the circumstances, the applicable law was Indian law. The purchase order which referenced the terms and conditions on which S purported to contract was never seen by T. There was no way therefore that T could agree to or subscribe to those terms and, consequently, they were not incorporated into the contracts. Incorporation did not occur via dealings with the parties. The fact that one of S's nominated directors believed that the dealings with T were on the basis of the standard terms and conditions were irrelevant. There was no basis for attributing the belief of a nominee director on S's side of the joint venture to the joint venture company itself. One of the Indian directors might well have taken a different view.

Case Example: *Allen Fabrications Ltd v ASD Metal Services Ltd* **[2012] EWHC 2213**

The judge made this statement of principle: a party's standard terms could be incorporated into a contract in two principal ways other than where they are expressly agreed to for example by being signed:

'(1)   They may be on or referred to in a document which is 'contractual' that is to say provided to the other party prior to or at the time when the contract is made (leaving aside 'battle of the forms' cases); or

(2)   They may be on or referred to in a document not itself contractual but post contractual, like the advice notes and invoices here, but which are nonetheless held to have been incorporated because of a prior course of dealing between the parties using those documents from which it can be inferred, objectively, that the parties must have intended to contract on those terms.'

He went on to consider the case where such terms have not actually been read by the other party or where that party was not aware of their import or effect. In such a case, the basic principles governing their incorporation are:

(1)   If the person receiving the document did not know there was writing or printing on it, he is not bound.

(2)   If he knew that the writing or printing on it contained or referred to conditions, he is bound.

(3)   If the answer to (1) above is Yes but the answer to (2) is No, that party will be bound by the conditions if the tendering party did what was reasonably sufficient to give the other party notice of the conditions. He went on to say that, if this requirement is satisfied, it matters not that the party in question was (still) not subjectively aware of them. In the normal course, the judge said, the fact that the document contains the terms on its face or clearly refers to them as being on the reverse or being available elsewhere, is likely to be sufficient.

> **Case Example:** *FG Wilson Engineering Ltd v John Holt Ltd* **[2012] EWHC 2477**
>
> The position was put this way:
>
> > 'Where a party seeks to incorporate standard terms and conditions into a contract by reference, they will be incorporated if that party has taken such steps as are sufficient to give reasonable notice of the terms .... What is reasonable depends upon the circumstances of each case and the term or condition which is relied upon. Generally the more unusual or onerous the term, the greater the notice that must be given of it.'
>
> It is possible to incorporate contract terms by reference, ie by giving proper notice of them without setting them out in full. For examples, see *Parker v South Eastern Ry* (1877) 2 CPD 416; *Hood v Anchor Line (Henderson Bros) Ltd* [1918] AC 837. It is also the case, using this fact as a principle, that a written document can incorporate terms by referring to a website address where those terms are to be found, and vice versa.

The course of dealing   A1.17

There is an important qualification to the principle that advance notice must be given of the terms of a contract in that, where the parties have habitually and customarily dealt on the basis of certain terms in the past, they will be assumed to do so in the instant case, even though those terms were not specifically referred to. For this qualification to apply, a course of dealing must be established, and that depends on the circumstances of the particular case. The following cases are instructive.

Where there is a course of dealing   A1.18

> **Case Example:** *Henry Kendall & Sons v William Lillico & Sons* **[1969] 2 AC 31**
>
> The contract in dispute had been preceded by a verbal contract, followed the next day by a contract setting out the relevant terms and conditions. There had been more than 100 similar contract notes in the course of dealing stretching back over the previous three years. This was held to constitute a course of dealing, the result being that, in the instant case, the terms of the contract received the day after the contract was made were incorporated into it.

Case Example: *Petrotrade Inc v Texaco Ltd* **(23 May 2000, Court of Appeal)**

There was no dispute that, over the 13 months or so prior to the contract in question, there were five other contracts for the sale of similar, if not of the same, products on the same terms and effected in the same manner. That was held to be enough to establish a course of trading.

Case Example: *Allen Fabrication Ltd v ASA Metal Services* **(see A1.16)**

A course of dealing was held to be established when the parties had dealt with each other on over 250 occasions and the buyers had received the actual terms on advice notes and there had been a clear reference to the terms on invoices which would have been seen by them.

Where there is not a course of dealing   **A1.19**

Case Example: *McCutcheon v MacBrayne* **[1964] 1 WLR 125**

The claimant's agent had dealt with the defendants on a number of occasions, yet he had not always signed a note containing the contract terms. He had not signed the note on the relevant occasions to the case. It was held that no course of dealing had been established in this case which allowed the terms to be incorporated by course of dealing.

Case Example: *Hollier v Rambler Motors Ltd* **[1972] 2 QB 71**

There had been three or four contracts between the parties over a period of five years. On the last two of these occasions, but not when the contract in dispute was made, a note had been signed by the claimant. It was held that no course of dealing had been established.

Case Example: *Capes (Hatherden) Ltd v Western Arable Services Ltd* **[2009] EWHC 3065**

The judge in this case observed as follows:'In the present case, the course of dealing between the parties consists of four contracts in the same year, with an interval of five months between the last of them and the two contracts in question. Although a different crop was involved, the procedure by which the previous contracts were concluded was substantially the same. On each occasion the claimant received a contract note referring to Contract 1/04: but he was not required to respond positively to it (eg by signing and returning a copy). He did not in fact notice the reference to Contract 1/04 and it was never expressly discussed or drawn to his attention. In my judgment these facts fall right on the borderline. If there had been any persuasive evidence, either that the terms of Contract 1/04 were the usual terms on which grain merchants purchase grain from UK producers, or that Mr Capes knew that grain merchants commonly employed standard terms which provided for disputes to be settled by arbitration, I would have been likely to hold that Contract 1/04 was incorporated. In the absence of such evidence, I do not think that the previous contracts justify the conclusion that the AIC terms were incorporated. To put it another way, the limited course of dealing between the parties is not in my view such that an impartial observer would conclude that the parties had reached a common understanding that Contract 1/04 applied'.

Incorporation by conduct   A1.20

It may be that there is no history of previous dealings, but the parties might instead have incorporated the relevant terms by their conduct.

Case Example: *Picardi Architects v Cuniberti* **[2002] EWHC 2923**

The defendants in this case wanted the service of architects. They chose the claimants after contacting the Royal Institute of British Architects. The relevant work got under way but relations between the parties broke down, and an adjudication was made under the adjudication procedure established by the provisions of the terms and conditions tendered by the claimants. That adjudication went against the defendants. As a result, they declined to pay the amount awarded, hence the present action. As part of the defence, they argued that the architects' terms of contract had not been incorporated into the contract between them.

Following a meeting between the parties, some preliminary work was done on the redesign of the particular premises. An invoice was sent in relation to what were time-charged services. A further meeting between the parties followed, after which a letter from the claimants set out their fees for the next stage. Further work was done and invoices tendered for a specified number of chargeable hours. Soon after, the claimants wrote as follows to the defendants: 'Appointment. Please find enclosed the letter of appointment for your examination and signature. Should you have any query I will be happy to discuss it further.' An annexed document contained a covering letter which, under the heading Agreement, stated that: 'The client wishes to appoint the architect to the project, and the architect has agreed to accept such appointment upon and subject to the terms set out in this letter of appointment and the attached copy of the RIBA conditions of engagement for the appointment of an architect … as completed'. The architects signed and dated this draft agreement. It was never signed by the defendants. Paragraph 9.2 of the attached conditions of engagement stated: 'Where the law of England and Wales is the applicable law, any dispute or difference arising out of this agreement must be referred to adjudication by the client, or the architect, at any time. The adjudication procedure and the agreement for appointment of an adjudicator shall be as set out in the 'Model adjudication procedures' published by the Construction Industry Council … The adjudicator shall act impartially and shall be entitled to take the initiative in ascertaining the facts on the law relating to the dispute. The decision of the adjudicator shall be binding on both parties until the dispute is finally determined pursuant to clause 9.5 hereof.' There was something of a general offer to go through the contract. This particular clause set out the provisions for arbitration. There was also provision for the appointment of an adjudicator when no adjudicator was specified in the agreement. A further clause said that, without prejudice to the right of adjudication, any disputes could be referred to an arbitrator nominated by RIBA. RIBA had produced guidance notes on the terms of engagement which indicated that architects should explain specified clauses to a client, guidance which the present claimants did not follow.

There was a further meeting between the parties, followed by a letter which hoped that the earlier letter of appointment was clear but that, should there be any query, the architects should be contacted.

An important fact was that the defendants had had a bad experience previously with contracting on RIBA conditions, and that, following that experience, their solicitor had advised them never in the future to sign a contract incorporating RIBA conditions. Contrary to what the claimants had alleged, the judge found that the defendants had never said that there would be no problem about their signing the contract. At no stage, the judge found, had the claimants offered to explain the matters covered by the RIBA guidance notes.

The negotiations were continued with yet a further letter from the claimants which drew attention to the fact that the agreement had not been signed, asking the defendants to give the matter their attention. The judge found this letter inconsistent with the claim that the defendants had already signified their willingness to sign the agreement with the RIBA terms. While the defendants did not reply specifically to this letter, they did pay the accompanying invoice, a fact relied on heavily by the claimants. The invoice referred specifically to 'Agreement dated 9 March 2000 (to be signed by the client)'. The invoice was dated 10 April. A further invoice followed the same format. Further correspondence and work followed, and in the November the claimants were again seeking signature to the agreement. A further request for signature was made the following March, a year after the agreement had been first presented for signature. It was almost a year later that the claimants served the defendants with a notice of arbitration, referring to the provisions of the RIBA agreement.

The court noted that the various payments made by the defendants were always made under the reservation that the defendants, as the claimants acknowledged from time to time, were declining to sign the contract. The various payments were not, therefore, referable to any assent to the RIBA terms. The payments were instead referable to certain agreed percentage fees. The court said that the parties could have continued on this basis until the conclusion of the work, if the relationship between the parties had not deteriorated in the way it did. Its view was that the various payments made referred to a subsequent agreement that, pending conclusion of a more detailed agreement (if one could be agreed), the claimants would charge in accordance with the agreed percentages and in accordance with the stages in the RIBA contract, which were known to the defendants. In short, the terms set out in the RIBA contract were never agreed to by the defendants, nor were they incorporated by conduct.

Unusual or onerous terms   A1.21

Clauses should not be unusual or onerous and a court will strike out such clauses from a contract as if they had never been included in the contract unless the clause is highlighted or special prominence is given to it.

Clauses which are unusual or onerous   A1.22

Case Example: *Interfoto Picture Library Ltd v Stilleto Visual Programmes Ltd* **[1989] QB 433**

One of the provisions in a contract for the hire of transparencies provided for a holding fee of £5 a day to be charged if the transparencies were returned late. This was well above the industry norm, and was regarded by the court as an unreasonable and extortionate clause. Given that no effort had been made to bring the other side's attention to this clause, it was held not to be part of the contract, even though the relevant provision would, under the rules discussed above, have been incorporated into the contract. According to Dillon LJ, if a condition in a contract is particularly onerous or unusual, the party seeking to enforce it must show that the particular condition was fairly brought to the attention of the other party. Bingham LJ considered that the test was 'whether it would in all the circumstances be fair (or reasonable) to hold a party bound by any conditions or by a particular condition of an unusual and stringent nature.' Therefore, the more onerous and unusual a clause, the greater notice must be given to the other party.

Case Example: *AEG (UK) Ltd v Logic Resources Ltd* **[1996] CLC 265**

In this case a clause stated that: 'The purchaser shall return the defective parts at his own expense to the suppliers immediately on request of the latter'. This was a sub-clause in what was called a 'warranty'. Other sub-clauses contained a guarantee that the goods were free from defects caused by faulty materials and bad workmanship, adding that if the supplier were not the manufacturer, the warranty would extend only to the extent of any warranty provided by the manufacturer. The buyer was also required to notify the supplier of any defect within seven days of discovery and to tender proof of purchase and guarantee. Once goods had been returned, the buyer was to allow the supplier 'the time and opportunity requested as estimated' by the supplier. The buyer was also required to pay the costs of any tests on the goods should the supplier deny liability. This whole clause was held to be extremely onerous and, since no special effort had been made to draw the attention of the buyer to its content, it did not form part of the contract.

It will be a matter of evidence and of all the surrounding circumstances as to whether a term is onerous. In the *AEG* case, it was a majority decision that the clause in dispute was onerous, the dissenting judge ruling that it was 'in no way unusual for standard conditions to qualify obligations for sellers under a contract of sale. The clauses deal with a topic one would expect to be dealt with in the Conditions of Sale and they cover the type of points which would be commonly dealt with'.

Case Example: *Picardi Architects v Cuniberti* (see A1.20)

The contract by which the architects were engaged sought to incorporate the standard terms of the Royal Institute of British Architects. One of these terms related to adjudication on disputes arising between the parties. It was the case that the adjudication clause was incorporated by virtue of *s 108* of the *Housing Grants, Construction and Development Act 1996*, but that *s 106* of that Act provides that such provision was not to apply to private residents, such as the defendant in this case. The court concluded that the adjudication clause in this case was so unusual that it should have been brought to the attention of the defendant and individually negotiated. It was felt to be significant that RIBA's own guidance notes indicated that the adjudication clause should be brought specifically to the attention of the other contracting party.

For further information see *Thornton v Shoe Lane Parking Ltd* [1971] 2 QB 163 and *Bankway Properties v Dunsford* [2001] 1 WLR 1369.

In *Bates v Post Office Ltd (No 3)* [2019] EWHC 606, Fraser J held that certain contractual terms between the sub-postmasters and the Post Office were unusual and onerous. In the course of his judgment Fraser J stated that the effect of clauses which were unusual or onerous (or extraordinary, or harsh or outlandish) was that this led to the clause not being incorporated into the contract if the written contractual term is of an unusual and stringent or particularly onerous nature, unless it has fairly been brought to that person's attention. The degree of notice depends upon the nature of the clause; the more severe its effect, the greater the notice required. Such a clause must have the potential to act very severely to the detriment of the party in question. In such circumstances, it is also necessary to have full regard to the context and the respective bargaining positions of the parties. On the facts, the Post Office was in an extremely strong bargaining position and the incoming sub-postmaster could not bargain at all. Further any amendments to the contractual terms were not permitted. In the *Bates'* case, Fraser J highlighted that the provisions of the contract between the sub-postmasters and the Post Office were standard terms of business of the Post Office and were therefore subject to the requirement of reasonableness imposed by UCTA 1977, and the burden was on the Post Office to demonstrate that they were reasonable. Having regard to some of the provisions in the contract which were the subject of litigation, the Post Office had failed to satisfy this test in relation to terms concerning liability for losses; remuneration for the sub-postmasters in terms of suspension; and also reinstatement following suspension; termination provisions; no compensation for loss of office; and new terms which the Post Office sought to introduce governing the appointment of sub-postmasters. Accordingly, the Post Office could not rely on these clauses.

In *Goodlife Foods Ltd v Hall Fire Protection Ltd* [2018] EWCA Civ 1371, Coulson LJ stated that it was a well-established principle of common law that, even if A knows that there are standard conditions provided as part of B's tender, a condition which is 'particularly onerous or unusual' will not be incorporated into the contract, unless it has been fairly and reasonably brought to A's attention. On the facts, the exclusion clause was neither onerous nor unusual and had been fairly brought to the attention of the other party, but see *Thornton v Shoe Lane Parking Ltd* [1971] 2 QB 163. The authorities do not always agree on what amounts to an 'onerous' clause. In *Interfoto*, Bingham LJ called the clause in question 'unreasonable and extortionate.' Dillon LJ referred to 'particularly onerous' clauses. In *Circle Freight International Ltd (T/A Mogul Air) v Medeast Gulf Exports Ltd (T/A Gulf Exports)* [1988] 2 Lloyd's Rep 427, the clause in question which limited the carrier's liability to a very small sum, were found to be neither unusual nor 'Draconian.' According to Waksman J in *Allen Fabrications Ltd v ASD Ltd* [2012] EWHC 2213:

> 'So the mere fact that the clause is a limitation or exclusion clause does not seem to me to render it onerous without more. Much will depend on the context. It might be said that if in very common use it is less likely properly to be regarded as onerous especially between two commercial parties since that is the business in which they knowingly operate. Furthermore, where the terms, if incorporated, would be subject to scrutiny under UCTA it can be argued that a somewhat more flexible approach to what is truly "onerous" could be taken.'

For other cases on unusual or onerous clauses, see *Shepherd Homes Ltd v Encia Remediation Ltd* [2007] BLR 135; *Trebor Bassett Holdings Ltd v ADT Fire and Security plc* [2011 EWHC 1936; *Watford Electronics Ltd v Sanderson CFL Ltd* [2001] EWCA Civ 317; *Regus (UK) Ltd v Epcot Solutions Ltd* [2008] EWCA Civ 361; *Charlotte Thirty Ltd v Croker Ltd* (1990) 24 Con LR 46; and *Balmoral Group Ltd v Borealis (UK) Ltd* [2006] EWHC 1900.

Steps to be taken with possibly onerous clauses   **A1.23**

The precise steps to be taken by a party when seeking to incorporate an onerous or unusual clause depend on all the circumstances of the case. A useful point of reference is provided in *J Spurling Ltd v Bradshaw* [1956] 1 WLR 461, where it was stated there was a need for a clause to be in red ink, with a 'red' hand pointing to the particular clause.

Clauses which are not unusual or onerous   **A1.24**

Case Example: *Lease Management Services Ltd v Purnell Secretarial Services Ltd* **[1994] CCLR 127**

The following clause, in a contract for the lease of a photocopier was held not to be onerous:

'Our Exclusion and Limitation.

The equipment and the supplier have been selected by you relying entirely on your own judgement. If you require any warranties or guarantees in respect of the equipment, its maintenance or suitability for any purpose, you must obtain them from the supplier. We exclude all express or implied warranties, conditions or guarantees from this agreement, and in no event will our liability under this agreement exceed the aggregate of the rentals paid by you at the time the liability arises. In no event will we be liable to you in contract, tort, or otherwise including any liability for negligence:

- for any loss of revenue, business, anticipated savings or profits, or any loss of use or value; or

- for any indirect or consequential loss however arising. 'Anticipated savings' means any expense which you expect to avoid incurring or to incur in a lesser amount than would otherwise have been the case.'

A clause of such a nature was 'plainly to be expected ... in equipment leasing contracts with finance companies'.

Case Example: *Danka Rentals Ltd v Xi Software* **(1998) 17 Tr LR 74**

A contract for the lease of a photocopier to a business contained this clause:

'Our Exclusion and Limitation.

The equipment and the supplier have been selected by you relying entirely on your own judgement. If you require any warranties or guarantees in respect of the equipment, its maintenance or suitability for any purpose, you must obtain them from the supplier. We exclude all express or implied warranties, conditions or guarantees from this agreement, and in no event will our liability under this agreement exceed the aggregate of the rentals paid by you at the time the liability arises. In no event will we be liable to you in contract, tort or otherwise including any liability for negligence:

(a)   for any loss of revenue, business, anticipated savings or profits, or any loss or use or value; or

(b)   for any indirect or consequential loss howsoever arising. 'Anticipated savings' means any expense which you expect to avoid incurring or to incur in a lesser amount than would otherwise have been the case.'

The court held that, while this clause was widely drawn, 'it is plainly to be expected that clauses of that nature would be found in equipment leasing contracts with finance companies'. Furthermore, the facts disclosed that the lessee had looked at the terms and conditions and 'therefore, probably, understood the nature of what he was signing'.

Case Example: O'Brien v MGN Ltd Court of Appeal [2001] EWCA Civ 1279, CA

One of the terms in a scratchcard promotion provided that: 'Should more prizes be claimed than are available in any prize category for any reason, a simple draw will take place for the prize'. It was held that this was neither onerous nor unusual. Hale LJ (as she was then) stated that the words 'onerous or unusual' were not terms of art. They were simply one way of putting the general proposition that reasonable steps must be taken to draw that particular term in question to the notice of those who are to be bound by it and that more is required in relation to certain terms than to others depending upon their effect. On the facts, the defendants had just enough to bring the rules of the game to the claimant's attention as there was clear reference to the rules on the face of the card he used. Further, there was also a clear reference to the rules in the paper containing the offer of a telephone prize. There was nothing 'outlandish' about the rules of the game which made them onerous or unusual.

Case Example: *Sumukan Ltd v Commonwealth Secretariat* [2007] EWCA Civ 1148

The contract between the parties provided for disputes to be referred to the Commonwealth Secretariat Arbitral Tribunal for settlement by arbitration in accordance with its statute which formed part of the contract and was available on request. The statute provided that the judgment of the tribunal was to be final and binding on the parties and not subject to appeal. The court held that the exclusion agreement was not some form of unusual or onerous clause to which attention had to be drawn specifically before it could be relied on. It pointed out that the policy of the *Arbitration Act 1996* was to encourage the notion that persons should arbitrate and keep the resolution of their disputes out of the courts. Waller LJ stated: 'This was a commercial contract. True, Sumukan had no choice as to the terms of the contract so far as arbitration was concerned but that is a common feature of and the reality of many commercial contracts. Sumukan are not a consumer with the protection of consumer legislation and are bound by the terms of the contract they made.'

Case Example: *Otto Chan v Barts & The London NHS Trust* **[2007] EWHC 2914**

The claimant employee sought various declarations against the defendant following his summary dismissal for gross misconduct. Paragraph 190 of the Terms and Conditions for Hospital and Medical and Dental Staff, which had been incorporated into his contract of employment when he joined the Trust, provided for an appeal to the Secretary of State for Health against an unfair termination of employment by sending a notice of appeal during the period of notice of termination of the appointment. He was informed by the Trust in 2003 that it would be adopting a new standard consultant contract which was to be adopted nationally. The new contract removed the para190 procedures. It was held that the loss of the right of appeal was not such a fundamental change and was not so onerous or unusual as to require explicit and clear notification to the claimant.

Case Example: *Do-Buy 925 Ltd v National Westminster Bank plc* **[2010] EWHC 2862**

A contract between a jeweller, in relation to his acceptance of credit card payments, and a bank as merchant acquirer, contained this clause: 'You agree that as between You and Us it is Your responsibility to prove to Our Satisfaction that the debit of a cardholder's account was authorised by the genuine cardholder'. The court said that that the clause was neither a particularly unusual nor onerous term in allocating the risk of identity fraud to the merchant: 'In any event the Bank did more than was sufficient fairly to draw the attention of Do-Buy to this allocation of risk. It is expressly identified in the Merchant Operating Instructions. It is part and parcel of the system of chargebacks, which are also clearly identified in the contractual literature.'

The general trend of the cases is to find that a clause is not onerous or unusual. In the *Allen* case (see A1.7), the court thought that if a clause was in very common use, then it was less likely properly to be regarded as onerous 'especially between two commercial parties since that is the business in which they knowingly operate'. The court also made the point that if the dispute term was subject to the provisions of the *Unfair Contract Terms Act 1977*, it was arguable that a more flexible approach to what is truly 'onerous' could be taken.

In *Woodeston v Credit Suisse (UK) Ltd* [2018] EWCA Civ 1103, where some of the clauses were held not to be unusual or onerous, Longmore LJ stated that there was evidence that the anti-set off clauses in the contract between the parties were by no means unusual in mortgage transactions, even if not universal, even though they may operate harshly on a consumer. The first step that has to be taken is to consider each term which is said to be onerous or unusual and decide if it is correctly so characterised. Only if any one of them do, does one need to move to the second step of the process, and consider adequacy of notice. See too *Carewatch Care Services Ltd v Focus Caring Services Ltd* [2014] EWHC 2313; and *Goodlife Foods Ltd v Hall Fire Protection Ltd* [2018] EWCA Civ 1371.

The effect of express variation clauses   A1.25

Most commercial agreements usually provide for an express written variation only clause signed by the parties as a means of creating legal certainty rather than oral variations – known as 'NOM' clauses ('No Oral Modification'). The issue of NOM clauses was considered by the Supreme Court in *Rock Advertising Ltd v MWB Business Exchange Centers Ltd* [2018] UKSC 24.

Rock (R) entered into a Licence Agreement with MWB to occupy office space for a fixed term of 12 months. According to clause 7.6 of the Agreement:

> 'This Licence sets out all the terms as agreed between MWB and [Rock]. No other representations or terms shall apply or form part of this Licence. All variations to this Licence must be agreed, set out in writing and signed on behalf of both parties before they take effect.'

Subsequently R was in licence fee arrears. R's director proposed a revised schedule of payments to a Ms Evans, a credit controlled employed by MWB. Under this proposal, certain payments would be deferred and accumulated arrears would be spread over the remainder of the Licence term. The revised schedule was worth less to MWB than the original terms owing to the interest cost of deferral. A dispute arose as to whether Ms Evans had accepted R's director's proposal orally. R also sought damages for wrongful exclusion from the premises.

One issue on appeal to the Supreme Court was whether a contractual term precluding amendment of an agreement other than in writing ('NOM' clause) was legally effective. The Supreme Court ruled in favour of MWB. Lord

Sumption stated that the oral variation was unenforceable '…the law should and does give effect to a contractual provision requiring specified formalities to be observed for a variation.' He further stated that 'Party autonomy operates up to the point when the contract is made, but thereafter only to the extent that the contract allows. Nearly all contracts bind the parties to some course of action, and to that extent restrict their autonomy. The real offence against party autonomy is the suggestion that they cannot bind themselves as to the form of any variation, even if that is what they have agreed.'

According to Lord Sumption, NOM clauses are common for three reasons:

(1)   they prevent attempts, including abusive attempts, to undermine written agreements by informal means;

(2)   they avoid disputes not just about whether a variation was intended, but also about its exact terms;

(3)   they make it easier for corporations to police their own internal rules restricting the authority to agree variations.

Contract law does not normally obstruct the legitimate intentions of the parties except for overriding reasons of public policy. NOM clauses do not frustrate or contravene any policy of the law. According to Lord Sumption, parties who agree an oral variation in spite of a NOM clause do not necessarily intend to dispense with that clause. What the parties agreed was that oral variations will be invalid, not that they are forbidden. The natural inference from a failure to observe a NOM clause is not that the parties intended to dispense with it, but that they overlooked it. On the other hand, if they had it in mind, then they were courting invalidity with their eyes open.

The enforcement of NOM clauses involve the risk that a party may act on the varied contract but then find itself unable to enforce it. The safeguard against injustice lies in the various doctrines of estoppel. Reliance on an estoppel would require: (i) some words or conduct unequivocally representing that the variation was valid notwithstanding its informality; (ii) for this purpose, something more than the informal promise itself.

Accordingly, the oral variation in the present case was invalid for want of writing and signatures required by clause 7.6 of the Agreement. See too: *HSM Offshore SV v Aker Offshore Partner Ltd* [2017] EWHC 2979.

Some practical points to note are:

• A contract may be varied orally or by conduct. It is therefore essential to include a clause in the Agreement requiring all variations to be in writing, signed by the parties, and who has authority to agree amendments on behalf of each party.

• The parties to an Agreement should ensure that any variations should comply with the requirements that of the variation clause in the original contract. Any subsequent correspondence should state that a variation will not take effect until agreed in accordance with the variation clause.

The effect of signature A1.26

Although it has never been formally decided, it seems that the principles of the *Interfoto* case will not apply where the relevant document has been signed. In *Jonathan Wren & Co Ltd v Microdec plc* (1999) 65 Con LR 157, it was said that 'it is unlikely that the approach adopted in the *Interfoto* case would be applied to a written contract actually signed by the parties'. Again, in *Bankway Properties v Dunsford* [2001] 1 WLR 1369, Arden LJ thought it not clear that the *Interfoto* doctrine applies to a contract which a party signs. In *Ata v American Express Ltd*, Times, 26 June 1998, CA, Rix J was quite specific that the *Interfoto* principle did not apply to documents which had been signed.

The 'battle of the forms' A1.27

This is a shorthand expression which is often used to describe the occurrence when one party notifies the other that their terms apply to the contract they are negotiating, but the other responds by saying their terms will apply. 'Battle of the forms' issues tend to arise in cases involving retention of title and exclusion clauses. Neither clause is likely to feature in the buyer's terms. A court may be called on to decide whether the retention or exclusion clause has been incorporated into the contract prior to ruling on the validity of the particular clause.

The basic rule is that the person who refers to his terms and conditions last of all is the one whose terms and conditions prevail.

> **Case Example:** *Butler Machine Tools Ltd v Ex–Cell–O Corporation (England) Ltd* **[1979] 1 WLR 401**
>
> The sellers offered to supply goods subject to their terms and conditions, whereupon the buyers placed an order, but making it subject to their terms and conditions. This order contained a tear-off slip, to be signed and returned by the sellers, stating that the sellers accepted the order 'on the terms and conditions stated therein'. The sellers signed and returned the slip with a letter saying that they were 'entering the order' in accordance with the offer.
>
> It was held that the buyer's terms prevailed since the sellers, in the reference to the offer, were only identifying the goods and the letter was not made for the purpose of reiterating the seller's terms. It should be noted that a clause in the seller's terms and conditions providing that these terms and conditions would prevail over any others was ineffective in light of the circumstances.

Case Example: *BRS v Arthur v Crutchley Ltd* **[1968] 1 All ER 811**

The claimants delivered a consignment of whisky to the defendants for storage. Their driver handed the defendants a delivery note purporting to incorporate the claimants' 'conditions of carriage'. The defendants stamped the note: 'Received under [our] conditions'. It was held that this amounted to a counter-offer which the claimants had accepted by handing over the goods, thus incorporating the defendants' own terms and conditions.

Cases for Further Information

A Davies & Co (Shopfitters) v William Old (1969) 113 SJ 262; *OTM Ltd v Hydranautics* [1981] 2 Lloyd's Rep 211; *Muirhead v Industrial Tank Specialities Ltd* [1986] QB 507; *Souter Association v Goodman Mechanical Services* (1984) 34 Build LR 81; *Durabella Ltd v J Jarvis & Sons Ltd* (2001) 83 Con LR 145.

It is, however possible that the 'battle of the forms' will result in neither party's terms being incorporated.

Case Example: *GHSP Inc v AB Electronic Ltd* **[2010] EWHC 1828**

The court was required to determine a preliminary issue as to the terms on which the parties had contracted. The claimant was a designer and manufacturer of electro-mechanical controls systems for motor vehicles. It placed orders with the defendant supplier for the manufacture of pedal sensors to be incorporated into one of the claimant's products; an electronic throttle pedal, for on-sale to the Ford Motor Company. A defective batch of sensors was used which could lead to intermittent engine stumbling or uncontrolled deceleration and loss of power. The resultant losses were said to be very substantial including costs claimed by Ford in respect of the inspection of vehicles and replacement of parts. The preliminary issue was whether the parties had concluded a contract in relation to the supply of sensors by the defendant on the terms of the claimant's purchase orders, including the terms in the latter's supplier's manual, or on the defendant's terms and conditions of sale or on neither set of terms. The claimant argued that its purchase orders were accepted by the defendant's subsequent conduct; that contract was on the basis of its conditions, which had been disclosed to and discussed with the defendant and which the defendant knew were a pre-requisite for any contract between the parties. The defendant argued that it never accepted the claimant's purchase orders until it sent an acknowledgment of order which expressly incorporated and referred to its own conditions; therefore the claimant entered into a contract on the terms of the defendant's conditions by impliedly accepting the counter-offer contained in the acknowledgment of order.

It was held that the defendant did not during the course of negotiations agree to accept the claimant's conditions which purported to impose unlimited liability on the seller in respect of relevant breaches. On the other hand, there was never any discussion of the content, nor any suggestion as to the applicability, of the defendant's conditions at any meeting or in any email. Both parties were hoping that the other would come up with some kind of acceptable cap on liability, as opposed to the unlimited liability provided for by the claimant's conditions and defendant's conditions which almost entirely excluded liability. There was, in fact, deadlock. There was no possibility of the claimant accepting the defendant's conditions, but there had been discussion as to whether there could be some amelioration of the claimant's conditions, which the defendant would not accept without a cap on liability. In the circumstances, whenever precisely the contract was made, it did not incorporate either party's conditions: there was no express acceptance of the conditions or of an offer containing the conditions expressly or impliedly; there was no conduct by the defendant by which it accepted the claimant's terms contained in the purchase orders; there was no relevant conduct by the claimant after the acknowledgment of order.

The court further held that the contract had been concluded by acceptance by the defendant, when it accepted the claimant's production schedule. That contract was not accepted by the defendant on the terms of the claimant's conditions and certainly not on the terms of the defendant's conditions. If that was wrong, then the contract was accepted by, or as a result of, the defendant's acknowledgment of order, but not on the defendant's conditions. The acknowledgment amounted to an acceptance of the claimant's purchase order but not on the basis of the latter's conditions, because of the clear lack of consensus in that regard. The defendant's acknowledgment of order did not amount to a counter-offer. But even if it did, if it was accepted, it was accepted without incorporation of the defendant's conditions, because of the lack of consensus between the parties. The result was that the parties did not contract on either side's terms and the terms of the contract were those implied by the *Sale of Goods Act 1979 (SGA 1979)*.

The relative importance of the contract terms   A1.28

The rights and remedies available to the victim of a breach of contract will depend on the importance of a contract term. It has become traditional to classify the terms or conditions of a contract as 'conditions' in the strict sense, or as 'warranties'.

Essentially, a term is a 'condition' if it is a major term of the contract, whereas a term is a 'warranty' if it is of minor importance (*Wallis, Son & Wells v Pratt & Haynes* [1910] 2 KB 1003). The fact that a contract term might be described in the contract as a 'condition' does not mean that, on analysis, it is properly classified as a warranty (*Schuler v Wickman Machine Tool Sales Ltd*

[1974] AC 235). The effect of a breach of condition is to entitle the innocent party to terminate the contract and claim damages for loss of bargain.

In some cases, it is provided by statute into which category a term falls. The *SGA 1979* provides that terms relating to description, quality and fitness for purpose are conditions. Terms as to title are also conditions, while terms as to quiet possession and freedom from encumbrances are warranties. Corresponding provisions are contained in the *Supply of Goods (Implied Terms) Act 1973 (SG(IT) A 1973)* and the *Supply of Goods and Services Act 1982 (SGSA 1982)*. Following enactment of the *Consumer Rights Act 2015*, these enactments apply only in the case of business-to-business contracts. The terms of a consumer contract no longer refer to conditions or warranties, but only to 'terms'.

In the absence of any statutory provision as above, or where the parties have not themselves clearly identified terms as falling into one category or the other, it will be for the courts to decide on the facts of the particular case as to whether or not a provision is a condition or some other term. This issue arose in *Grand China Logistics Holding (Group) Co v Spar Shipping AS* [2016] EWCA Civ 982. The principal issue was whether the charterers' failure to pay an instalment of hire punctually under a time charterparty was a breach of a condition? Grand China Shipping Company was in substantial arrears under a charterparty. Spar therefore issued proceedings with a view to obtaining the balance of the hire due, and damages for loss of bargain for the remaining term of the charter. Subsequently, Grand China went into liquidation and Spar issued proceedings against the guarantor, Grand China Logistics.

In the event that prompt payment was considered to be a condition, this would entitle Spar to terminate the contract and claim for loss of bargain for the remainder of the charterparty. It should be noted that the agreement between the parties did not provide any sufficient clarity as to the remedy available apart from entitlement to damages. The Court of Appeal held that the term in question was not a condition but an innominate term. According to Gross LJ: 'Where...breaches of a term may have consequences ranging from the trivial to the serious, this is a strong indication that it is to be treated as an innominate term.' The contract between the parties had not clearly stipulated that the provision was a condition. A right to terminate under the contract was not sufficient to make that obligation a condition in respect of the remedies available following the breach. The court would also take account of business common sense and late payments must be considered according to contractual terms as well as significance of breach of the term in question. The emphasis, therefore, is to expressly stipulate in the commercial agreement that the term is a condition otherwise it will be construed as an innominate term.

Case Examples: Mercantile Contracts

In mercantile contracts, stipulations as to time are of the essence – for example:

- as to the time in which a ship must be ready to load (*Mihailis Angelos, The* [1971] 1 QB 164*)*;

- as to when goods must be delivered under a contract of sale (*Hartley v Hymans* [1920] 3 KB 475);

- as to the time in which certain oil company approvals should be obtained (60 days was stipulated) (*BS&N (BVI) v Micado Shipping Ltd (Malta)* [2000] 2 All ER (Comm) 169); and

- as to the time frames within which any force majeure (ie events outside the parties' control) should be notified, extensions of the shipping period could be claimed, and the option to cancel the contract (*Bremer Handelgesellschaft v Vanden Avenne-Izegem* [1978] 2 Lloyd's Rep 109).

Cases for Further Information

Glaholm v Hays (1841) 2 M&G 257; *Bentsen v Taylor, Sons & Co* [1893] 2 QB 274; *Re Comptoir Commercial Anversois and Power, Son & Co* [1920] 1 KB 868; *Astley Industrial Trust v Grimley* [1963] 1 WLR 584; *Bunge Cpn New York v Tradax Export SA Panama* [1981] 1 WLR 711; *State Corp of India Ltd v M Golodetz Ltd* [1989] 2 Lloyd's Rep 277; *Compagnie Commerciale Sucres et Denrees v Czarnikow Ltd* [1990] 1 WLR 1337; *Torvald Klaveness A/S v Arni Maritime Corp* [1993] 2 Lloyd's Rep 335.

Intermediate terms   A1.29

In recent years, the courts have moved away from a rigid classification of contract terms into conditions and warranties, and have recognised instead the category of 'intermediate' or 'innominate' terms.

Where a term falls into this category, the courts will instead look to the gravity or seriousness of the breach which is considered at the time of the termination taking into account what has happened and is likely to happen, and apply the appropriate remedies accordingly: *The Hansa Nord* [1976] QB 44. A term is most likely to be classified as intermediate if it is capable of being broken either in a manner which is trivial and capable of remedy by an award of damages, or in a way which is so fundamental as to undermine the whole contract. For instance, a shipowner's obligation in a charterparty to:

- provide a seaworthy vessel (*Hongkong Fir Shipping Co Ltd v Kawasaki Kisen Kaisha* [1962] 2 QB 26);

- load containers without any stability problem (*Compagnie Generale Maritime v Diakan Spirit SA* [1982] 2 Lloyd's Rep 574); or

- commence and carry out the voyage agreed on with reasonable despatch (*Freeman v Taylor* (1831) 8 Bing 124),

have all been classified as intermediate terms, the breach of which does not allow for discharge of the contract unless the consequences of breach are such as to deprive the charterer of substantially the whole benefit of the contract or to frustrate the object of the charterer in chartering the ship.

The uncertainty which can arise as to the classification of a contract term is to be avoided. If the matter is not specifically decided by statute, the contract itself should clearly state that a term is to be regarded as of the essence, and hence a condition; or should set out the consequences of a breach.

For the duty of a court to consider whether a term is a condition or warranty, see *RG Grain Trade LLP (UK) v Feed Factors International Ltd* [2011] EWHC 1889. The court said that in the absence of any clear agreement or prior decision this was to be a condition, it should lean in favour of construing this provision as to impurities as an intermediate term, only a serious and substantial breach of which entitled rejection.

Contractual interpretation   A1.30

The UK courts often resort to contractual interpretation to ascertain the meaning of a word or a phrase in the context of a commercial agreement. However, over the years, there have been some judicial inconsistencies as to the correct test to be applied in the context of contractual interpretation.

The Supreme Court's approach to Contractual Interpretation   A1.31

In *Rainy Sky SA v Kookmin Bank* [2011] 1 WLR 2900, Lord Clarke stated that the ultimate aim of interpreting a provision in a contract, especially a commercial contract, is to determine what the parties meant by the language used which involves ascertaining what a reasonable person would have understood the parties to have meant (see *Investors Compensation Scheme Ltd v West Bromwich Building Society* [1998] 1 WLR 896; *Pink Floyd v EMI* [2010] EWCA Civ 1429; *Chartbrook Ltd v Persimmon Homes Ltd* [2009] 1 AC 1101; *Wickman Machine Tools Sales Ltd v Schuler AG* [1974] AC 235; and *The Antaios* [1984] AC 91).

The issue on appeal in *Rainy* was the role to be played by considerations of business common sense in determining what the parties meant. According to Lord Clarke, the exercise of construction is essentially one unitary exercise in which the court must consider the language used and ascertain what a reasonable person, that is, a person who has all the background knowledge which would reasonably have been available to the parties in the situation in which they were at the time of the contract, would have understood the parties to have meant. In doing so, the court must have regard to all the relevant surrounding circumstances. If there are two possible constructions, the court is entitled to prefer the construction which is consistent with *business common sense* and reject the other.

Where the parties have used unambiguous language, the court must apply it. It is not necessary to conclude that a particular construction would produce an absurd or irrational result before proceeding to have regard to the commercial purpose of the agreement (see *Chalabi v Agha-Jaffar* [2011] EWHC 203). The courts will therefore take a commercial approach towards interpreting ambiguities in commercial contracts.

The leading authority on contractual interpretation is the Supreme Court decision in *Arnold v Britton* [2015] UKSC 36. Oxwich Leisure Park contained 91 chalets, each of which was let for a period of 99 years from 25 December 1974. The Appellants were the current tenants under 25 of the leases. Clause 3(2) of each lease contained a covenant to pay a service charge. Each lease also contained covenants by the lessor including an obligation to promote services to the Park such as maintaining roads, paths, fences, a recreation ground and drains, mowing lawns and removing refuse.

The respondent who was the current landlord, contended that the service charge provision in clause 3(2) required from the lessee an initial service charge of £90 which increased at a compound rate of 10% for the first 70 chalets to be let every three years, but for the last 21 chalets to be let, every year.

A typical service charge provision in every lease provided:

> 'To pay to the Lessor without any deduction in addition to the said rent a proportionate part of the expenses and outgoings incurred by the Lessor in the repair maintenance renewal and provision of services hereinafter set out the yearly sum of Ninety Pounds and value added tax (if any) for [the first three years or the first year] of the term hereby granted increasing thereafter to Ten Pounds per Hundred for every subsequent [three year period or year] or part thereof.'

The issue on appeal before the Supreme Court was whether the respondent's interpretation of Clause 3(2) in the 25 leases, where the increase was to be every year, was correct. The Supreme Court decided by a majority of 4-1 for the respondent. In the course of his judgment Lord Neuberger considered the issue of contractual interpretation of commercial agreements, taking account of the House of Lords and Supreme Court decisions in *Prenn v Simmonds* [1971] 1 WLR 1381; and *Rainy Sky SA v Kookmin Bank*. According to Lord Neuberger, when interpreting a written contract, the court must identify the intention of the parties by reference to 'what a reasonable person having all the background knowledge which would have been available to the parties would have understood them to be using the language in the contract to mean.' (see *Chartbrook Ltd v Persimmon Homes Ltd* [2009] 1 AC 1101). This involves focussing on the meaning of the relevant words in their documentary, factual and commercial context. That meaning had to be assessed in the light of:

- the natural and ordinary meaning of the clause.

- any other relevant provisions of the contract.

- the overall purpose of the clause and the contract.

- the facts and circumstances known or assumed by the parties at the time that the document was executed.

- commercial common sense.

However, subjective evidence of any party's intentions must be disregarded.

Lord Neuberger emphasised the following factors in contractual interpretation.

- The reliance placed in some cases on commercial common sense and surrounding circumstances should not be invoked to undervalue the importance of the language of the provision which is to be construed.

- The exercise of interpreting a provision involves identifying what the parties meant through the eyes of a reasonable reader, which meaning will be obtained from the language of the provision. Unlike commercial common sense and the surrounding circumstances, the parties have control over the language they use in a contract. Accordingly, the parties must have been specifically focussing on the issue covered by the provision when agreeing the wording of that provision.

- When it comes to considering the centrally relevant words to be interpreted, the less clear the words, the more ready the court can properly be to depart from their natural meaning. The clearer the natural meaning, the more difficult it is to justify departing from it. It does not justify the court embarking on an exercise of searching for or constructing, drafting infelicities in order to facilitate a departure from their natural meaning. If there is a specific error in the drafting, it may often have no relevance to the issue of interpretation which the court has to resolve.

- Commercial common sense should not be invoked retrospectively. The mere fact that a contractual arrangement, if interpreted according to its natural language, has worked out badly, or even disastrously, for one of the parties, should not be a reason for departing from the natural language. Commercial common sense is only relevant to the extent of how matters would or could have been perceived by the parties, or by reasonable people in the position of the parties, as at the date that the contract was made.

- Although commercial common sense is a very important factor to take into account when interpreting a contract, the court should not reject the natural meaning of a provision as correct simply because it appears to be a very imprudent term for one of the parties to have agreed, even ignoring the benefit of wisdom of hindsight. The purpose of interpretation is to identify what the parties have agreed, not what the court thinks they should have agreed. It is not the function of the court when interpreting an agreement to relieve a party from the consequences of his imprudence or poor advice. When interpreting a contract, the court should avoid re-writing it in an attempt to assist an unwise party or to penalise an astute party.

- When interpreting a contractual provision, one can only take into account facts or circumstances which existed at the time that the contract was made, and which were known or reasonably available to both parties. Given that a contract is a bilateral arrangement involving both parties, it cannot be right, when interpreting a contractual provision, to take into account a fact or circumstance known only to one of the parties.

- In some cases, an event subsequently occurs which was plainly not intended or contemplated by the parties, judging from the language of their contract. In such circumstances, if it is clear what the parties would have intended, the court will give effect to that intention: see *Aberdeen City Council v Stewart Milne Group Ltd* [2011] UKSC 56.

Practical Points

- In *Arnold v Britton*, the Supreme Court emphasised its approach towards literal interpretation of contracts rather than a purposive or commercial approach considered in *Rainy Sky v Kookmin Bank*. The Supreme Court in *Arnold* gives prime importance to the language of the provision which is to be construed. The courts will consider the language and provisions chosen by the parties to the contract. On the application of the literal approach, see *Exsus Travel Ltd v Baker Tilly* [2016] EWHC 2818; and *Metlife Seguros De Retiro v J P Morgan Chase Bank* [2016] EWCA Civ 1248.

- In *Wood v Capital Insurance Services Ltd* [2017] UKSC 24, the Supreme Court reaffirmed the principles of contractual interpretation as set out in *Arnold v Britton* as being the correct approach. Lord Hodge stated that the court's task was to ascertain the objective meaning of the language which the parties had chosen to express their agreement. In doing so, the court must also consider the contract as a whole and, depending on the nature, formality and quality of the drafting of the contract, giving more or less weight to elements of the wider context in reaching its view as to that objective meaning. Where appropriate, the court would also have regard to the factual background known to the parties at or before the date of the contract. Textualisation and contextualism were not conflicting paradigms in contractual interpretation. The court, when interpreting any contract, can use them as tools to ascertain the objective meaning of the language which the parties have chosen to express their agreement. The extent to which each tool will assist the court in its task will vary according to the circumstances of the particular agreement. Some agreements may be successfully interpreted principally by textual analysis because of their sophistication and complexity. The correct interpretation of other contracts may be achieved by a greater emphasis on the factual matrix because of their informality or brevity. Lord Hodge confirmed that on the approach to contractual interpretation, *Rainy Sky* and *Arnold* could be reconciled with one another. See too *Triple Point Technology Inc v PTT Public Company Ltd* [2019] EWCA Civ 230.

- In *Kason Kek-Gardner Ltd v Process Components Ltd* [2017] EWCA Civ 2132, the Court of Appeal emphasised that subsequent conduct of the parties to an agreement could not affect the true interpretation of the agreement, much less the subsequent conduct of those not party to the agreement. Lewinson LJ made reference to *Arnold v Britton* and stated that admissible background was limited to the facts that were known or reasonably available to both parties. It was not right to take into account facts that were only known to one of them. According to Lewinson LJ, reliance on commercial common sense and background should not be used to devalue the importance of the language of the provisions to be interpreted.

- In *MT Højgaard A/S v E.On Climate & Renewables UK Robin Rigg East Limited* [2017] UKSC 59, the Supreme Court was required to interpret provisions in a construction contract which imposed design obligations and performance obligations on the contractor. Lord Neuberger sought to give effect to the terms in the contract by applying a literal interpretation which had the effect that the contractor was liable for the remedial works in breach of its performance obligations which imposed higher standards. The court therefore seeks to give effect to, and not interfere in the freedom of parties to reach their own commercial agreements and recognise that they bear the burden involved in understanding and fulfilling the agreements that they make. The *Højgaard* decision reinforces the approach in *Arnold v Britton* of an approach towards the literal meaning of contractual provisions. The Supreme Court in Højgaard stated that the reconciliation of various terms in a contract, and the determination of their combined effect must be decided by reference to ordinary principles of contractual interpretation. While each case must turn on its own facts, the courts are generally inclined to give full effect to the requirement that the item as produced complies with the prescribed criteria, even if the customer or employer has specified or approved the design. Generally speaking, the contractor is expected to take the risk if he agreed to work to a design which would render the item incapable of meeting the criteria to which he has agreed.

- The Court of Appeal decision in *Classic Maritime Inc v Limbungan Makmur SDN BHD* [2019] EWCA Civ 1102 further highlights the modern judicial approach towards contractual interpretation. The Court of Appeal emphasised that the issue of contractual interpretation was not how the clause should be labelled (whether as an exceptions clause or a force majeure clause) but rather how it should be interpreted, based on its language and having regard to its context and purpose. According to Males LJ: 'As with most things, what matters is not the label but the content of the tin.' As a practical point, it is therefore essential to ensure that the parties' intentions are made absolutely clear in the language of the clause when drafting or entering into contracts.

- In *Merthyr (South Wales) Ltd v Merthyr Tydfill County Borough Council* [2019] EWCA Civ 526, the issue concerned the interpretation of a contract to establish an escrow account. The Court of Appeal highlighted the strict operation of the common law rule against relying on evidence of pre-contractual negotiations to interpret agreements. The Court of Appeal's decision emphasises that while it is permissible for a court to take account of pre-contractual material for the limited purpose of understanding the genesis and commercial aim of the transaction as a whole, this does not extend to admitting material in order to elucidate further on the genesis and aim of a particular contractual provision. Leggatt LJ summarised the law as follows:

'(1) Previous documents may be looked at to show the surrounding circumstances and, by that means, to explain the commercial or business object of a contract;

(2) The approach is, by considering the circumstances which led to the execution of the contract, to identify the purpose of the transaction and to construe the language used in the light of that purpose;

(3) Evidence of negotiations, or of the parties' intentions, ought not to be received;

(4) What is not permissible, is to seek to rely on evidence of what was said during the course of pre-contractual negotiations for the purpose of drawing inferences about what the contract should be understood to mean;

(5) It is also clear that it is not only statements reflecting one party's intentions or aspirations which are excluded for this purpose, but also communications which are capable of showing that the parties reached a consensus on a particular point or used words in an agreed sense;

(6) In other words, there is a line between referring to previous communications to identify the 'genesis and aim of the transaction' and seeking to rely on such evidence to show what the parties intended a particular provision in a contract to mean, may be hard to draw.'

- In *Stobart Group Ltd v Stobart* [2019] EWCA Civ 1376, the sellers agreed to sell all the issued share capital of Stobart Rail Ltd ('SRL') to the buyers, Stobart Group Ltd. Under the share purchase agreement (SPA) entered into by the parties, there were various tax warranties and covenants addressing the sellers' liability for tax incurred prior to the sale of the business including the ability of the buyers to claim against the sellers under the warranties and covenants. According to paragraph 6.3 of the SPA, the sellers were not liable in respect of a tax claim unless the buyers gave written notice of it within seven years of the sale completion. Also, the SPA provided the possibility of a claim, demand or notice being received from HMRC in respect of tax for which the sellers might be liable. In this respect, paragraph 7.1 required the buyers, if they became aware of any such claim, to notify the sellers within 10 business days. Therefore, two different and separate regimes operated for the service of the applicable notices under either paragraph 6.3 or paragraph 7.1.

In 2008, the buyers sent a letter to the sellers notifying them that under paragraph 7.1 of the SPA, HMRC had issued a claim against SRL for unpaid insurance contributions. Subsequently, in March 2015, the buyers sent a letter to the sellers which gave notice pursuant to the SPA of a 'potential liability to Taxation under the Tax Covenant'. The letter set out details as to the likely amount of the claim and asked the sellers whether pursuant to paragraph 7, the sellers wished to have continued conduct of discussions with HMRC in relation to the claim. The letter did not refer to any claim under paragraph 6.3 of the SPA. The buyers contended that the letter in 2015 was notification of a tax claim under paragraph 6.3, whereas the sellers contended that the letter only served to confirm a further paragraph 7.1 notice and not one under paragraph 6.3 so that as no tax claim was notified within the seven year period, the buyers were statute-barred from bringing any claim against the sellers. The Court of Appeal held that the letter sent by the buyers did not constitute a notice of a claim under the tax covenants in the SPA. The claim was not therefore properly notified within the contractual time limit and therefore time-barred. The Court of Appeal concluded that a person receiving the 2015 letter with knowledge of the terms of the SPA would have understood it to be a notice under paragraph 7.1 and not paragraph 6.3.

The Court of Appeal considered its approach towards construction of the notice provisions in the SPA following the ruling in *Wood v Capita Insurance Services Ltd* and the strict approach taken in respect of contractual notices. The Court of Appeal in *Stobart* considered the letter written by the buyers in March 2015 to the sellers and stated that the court's task when construing a unilateral contractual notice was similar to when construing agreed contractual terms. Its task was to ascertain the objective meaning of the language used. The question to be answered was what a reasonable recipient of the notice would have understood it to mean. In *Wood*, the Supreme Court stated that the court could be assisted in ascertaining the objective meaning by considering both the ordinary meaning of the language use and the relevant context or factual matrix known to the parties. It did not matter whether the language or the factual matrix is analysed first, provided the court balances the indications given by each. In *Stobart*, the Court of Appeal stated that the courts would not take account of the subjective understandings of the parties as to what was intended by a document. A subjective understanding could not displace the objective criteria for interpreting contractual notices. A recipient's subjective understanding may, however, be applicable in an estoppel context.

Signing a contract   **A1.32**

There is no general requirement in the law of contract that contracts have to be in some special form or signed. If the parties do stipulate that a contract will have no effect until signed, then, of course, there will be no contract until signature has been applied unless the parties have, by their conduct, indicated that they have dispensed with the need for signature (*Picardi Architects v Cuniberti* (see A1.20) and *Pretty Pictures v Quixote Films Ltd*. If a contract is signed, then the party signing will be bound by the contract whether or not he has read the terms or even understood them (*L'Estrange v Graucob* [1934] 2 KB 394).

Electronic signatures   **A1.33**

The *Electronic Communications Act 2000 (ECA 2000)* provides that an electronic signature incorporated, or logically associated, with a particular electronic communication or data, and the certification by any person of such signature, shall be admissible in evidence in relation to any question as to the authenticity of the communication or its integrity: section 7. There is, though, no presumption as to the validity of such signature. This will allow contractual documents and negotiations to be exchanged by email, and for any electronic signature to be used to confirm the authenticity of the transmission. For these purposes, an electronic signature is so much of anything in electronic form as:

(a)   is incorporated into or otherwise logically associated with any electronic communication or electronic data; and

(b)   purports to be used by the individual creating it to sign (see *The Electronic Notification and Trust Services for Electronic Transactions Regulations 2016, SI 2016/696*).

The term 'electronic communication' means a communication transmitted (whether from one person to another, from one device to another or from a person to a device or vice versa) (a) by means of an electronic communications network; or (b) by other means but while in an electronic form: section 15(2), *ECA 2000*.

ECA 2000 also provides for any legislation requiring documents to be in writing to be amended to allow for electronic communication. This power has been exercised in the *Unsolicited Goods and Services Act 1971 (Electronic Communications) Order 2001 (SI 2001/2778)* and the *Unsolicited Goods and Services Act 1971 (Electronic Commerce) (Amendment) Regulations 2005 (SI 2005/148)* (paragraph 2). This allows for the electronic communication of entries for directories, as previously such entries had to be requested in writing.

Checklist   A1.34

- Have you agreed on the key provisions of the proposed contract, such as:

    - the subject matter;

    - the price and terms of payment; and

    - the duration of the contract, if appropriate, including start date and end date?

- Have you ensured that your terms and conditions have been adequately brought to the attention of the other party?

- Have you made sure that you are the 'winner' in the 'battle of the forms'?

- Does the contract clearly spell out which terms are considered fundamental and which are considered to be of a more minor nature?

- Have you taken care to ensure that proper attention has been brought to any unusual or onerous terms?

- Have you considered the necessity for signature and made proper provision for securing it?

- Have you made sure that copies of the agreement are safely stored away?

A2:

Common and Specific Clauses and Terms

At a glance A2.1

- When the contract describes the goods, the description then becomes a major term of the contract. This description, once established, must be closely complied with by the seller. This applies even in the case of non-business sales.

- Statute requires all goods supplied under a contract to be of satisfactory quality and reasonably fit for their purpose. These apply only when the seller or supplier is acting in the course of business.

- There is scope, subject to restrictions, on the use of exclusion and limitation clauses. Careful note should be taken of possible criminal offences arising from the use of exclusion clauses in consumer contracts. Modern judicial authorities suggest that the courts will not necessarily give a narrow interpretation of exclusion clauses.

- It is not just the contract goods which are covered by the above obligations, but also all goods supplied under the contract, such as a free gift which might be supplied with the main item.

- Obligations as to fitness and quality also apply to contracts made by reference to a sample.

- A central feature of the contract is the passing of risk. There are statutory presumptions as to when risk passes but parties can provide in the contract for when risk is to pass.

- Equally important is the passing of property. Again, there are statutory presumptions which can be displaced by the terms of the contract.

- Suppliers should always consider retention of title clauses to secure their position in the event of a buyer's non-payment or other default.

- Following enactment of the *Consumer Rights Act 2015*, the *Unfair Contract Terms 1977* applies only to business to business contracts. *The Consumer Rights Act 2015* applies only to contracts made with consumers.

- An alternative to an exclusion or limitation clause is the liquidated damages clause and the enforceability of such clauses following modern judicial authorities.

- The modern test on penalty clauses is whether the impugned provision is a secondary obligation which imposes a detriment on the contract-breaker out of all proportion to any legitimate interest of the innocent party in the enforcement of the primary obligation. The courts will consider whether any (and if so) what legitimate business interest is served and protected by the penalty clause, and, whether, assuming such an interest to exist, the provision made for the legitimate interest is nevertheless in the circumstances extravagant, exorbitant or unconscionable.

- Damages for breaches of contract are assessed on the basis of what the wrongdoer contemplated would be the probable result of any breach. Recovery for loss of profits generally requires advance disclosure to the other side of the relevant facts relating to the purpose of the contract, eg that goods purchased are intended for resale.

- The victim of a breach of contract must do all that is reasonable to limit the loss which arises from the breach. This is the so-called 'duty to mitigate'.

- Actions for breach of contract must generally be brought within six years, but there are exceptions to the rule. The parties can provide for their own limitation periods.

- If a contract has been concluded on the basis of a mistake or a misrepresentation, much depends on the nature of the mistake or misrepresentation. A contract may be automatically void, or voidable, or it may be unaffected.

- Clauses excluding or limiting liability for misrepresentation are subject to statutory control.

- In strictly defined and limited circumstances, a contract affected by supervening events will be void for frustration. Special rules deal with the perishing of goods.

- There may be scope for contracting out of the rules relating to frustration and perishing.

- The consequences of frustration are spelled out by both common law and statute. Scope exists for the contract itself to deal with potential frustrating events.

- It is a fundamental rule of law that those who are not contracting parties have no rights under the contract. This principle has, however, been modified by statute.

- The parties are free to use contract terms protecting their intellectual property rights and securing that all necessary confidences are maintained.

- Provision can be made for the serving of notices on each party to the contract.

- Quite often, signature is not a pre-requisite to a binding contract. The provision of a signature does, however, commit the party to the full terms of the contract.

- Parties making overseas contracts can provide for which jurisdiction is to govern the contract. Certain restrictions are imposed on the parties' choice.

- Both domestic and European law impose restrictions on anti-competitive behaviour. Fines can be imposed.

Describing the goods or services   A2.2

Section 13 of the *Sale of Goods Act 1979 (SGA 1979)* provides that any description applied to the goods is a condition of the contract. Comparable provisions are to be found in the *Supply of Goods (Implied Terms) Act 1973 (SG(IT)A 1973)* and the *Supply of Goods and Services Act 1982 (SGSA 1982)*. Under the *Consumer Rights Act 2015*, terms as to description are implied into consumer contracts but they are not known as 'conditions'. Section 11 CRA 2015 states that every contract to supply goods by description is to be treated as including a term that the goods will match the description. If the supply is by sample as well as by description, it is not sufficient that the bulk of the goods matches the sample if the goods do not also match the description. A supply of goods is not prevented from being a supply by description just because the goods are exposed for supply; and they are selected by the consumer.

Key to description   A2.3

The key to description is identification. Statements in the contract as to the quality of the goods do not normally identify a product and hence are not part of its description. In the case of *Ashington Piggeries Ltd v Christopher Hill Ltd* [1972] AC 441 it was explained that:

> '… ultimately the test is whether the buyer could fairly and reasonably refuse to accept the physical goods proffered to him on the ground that their failure to correspond with that part of what was said about them in the contract makes them goods of a different kind from those he had agreed to buy'.

Terms held to be part of description   A2.4

Case Example: *Varley v Whipp* **[1900] 1 QB 513**

Statements as to the location, age and use of goods were all part of the description.

> **Case Example:** *Arcos Ltd v EA Ronaasen and Son* **[1933] AC 470**
>
> Stipulations as to the dimensions of wooden staves were held to be part of the contract description.

> **Case Example:** *MacPherson Train & Co Ltd v Howard Ross & Co Ltd* **[1955] 1 WLR 640**
>
> A statement that goods sold were 'afloat per SS Morton Bay due London approximately 8 June' was also held to be part of the description since it enabled the goods to be identified.

Terms held not to be part of description   **A2.5**

> **Case Example:** *T&J Harrison v Knowles and Foster* **[1918] 1 KB 608**
>
> Two ships were sold, each of which was stated in particulars supplied to the buyers to have a deadweight capacity of 460 tons. The capacity of each was, in fact, 360 tons. It was held that these statements were not part of the description.

> **Case Example:** *Harlingdon & Leinster Enterprises Ltd v Christopher Hull Fine Arts Ltd* **[1991] 1 QB 564**
>
> The statement that a painting was the work of a certain artist was held not to be part of the description. This was because the description was not, on the facts, an essential part of the sale. It was said that for all practical purposes 'there cannot be a contract for the sale of goods by description where it is not within the reasonable contemplation of the parties that the buyer is relying on that description'. In this case, the claimants were specialists in the particular work of art, while the defendants were not.

Compliance with description   **A2.6**

Once it is established that a statement is part of the description, strict compliance with that description is required.

> **Case Example:** *Arcos Ltd v EA Ronaasen & Son* **[1933] AC 470**
>
> The contract required wooden staves to be half an inch thick. Only 5% of the total delivered matched this description. A large proportion were over half an inch, but not more than 9/10 of an inch, in thickness; some were larger but less than 5/8 of an inch in thickness, and a very small

proportion larger than that. It was found as a fact that all the goods could be used for their intended purpose. It was also found that they did not correspond to their description. See too *Hazlewood Grocery Ltd v Lion Foods Ltd* [2007] EWHC 1887.

Case Example: *Re Moore & Co Ltd and Landauer & Co Ltd* **[1921] 2 KB 519**

The contract was for 3000 tins of fruit packed in cases of 30 tins. When the goods were delivered, it was found that about half the cases contained 24 tins, though the correct quantity was delivered. It was found that the goods did not conform to their description.

The effect of these rulings has been mitigated in business-to-business contracts by *s 15A* of the *SGA 1979*, which restricts a buyer's right to reject goods where the breach of the term as to description is so slight that rejection would be unreasonable.

Since *SGA 1979* does imply a term as to description, there is no particular need for a contract of purchase to contain any specific clause as to description. A contract of sale could state: 'The description of the goods has been given by way of identification only and the use of such description shall not constitute a sale by description'. It should be said, however, that such a clause might well be unsuccessful in its aim of avoiding the impact of the implied term, but, in certain circumstances, it might be enough to tip an argument in favour of the seller.

Case Example: *Farrans (Construction) Ltd v RMC Readymix Concrete (Scotland) Ltd* **[2004] ScotCS 51**

The contract had called for the delivery of C7 concrete. Because of the dispute which subsequently arose as to the quality of concrete actually supplied, it became necessary for the court to determine just what was meant by C7 concrete. After listening to a considerable amount of expert evidence, the judge concluded that when a civil engineer orders 'C7 foamed concrete' from a concrete supplier, it would be understood by reasonable men in the position of both parties as indicating two things. First, the concrete would be of relatively low strength and low density. Secondly, the strength of the concrete would be such that it could be broken easily, and thus put to the uses that are characteristic of C7 foamed concrete. If, therefore, concrete was supplied with typical compressive strengths in excess of 35 N/mm^2, that, the court said, would not conform to the description 'C7 foamed concrete'. The court further concluded that the concrete as delivered to the pursuers was in conformity with the description applied to it, namely C7 concrete. Any problems which were subsequently discovered with the concrete could be attributed to the faulty way it had been pumped into the relevant shaft by third parties.

Accordingly, there had been no breach of the express term of the contract that the concrete to be delivered would be C7 concrete; nor any breach of the condition implied by *s 13* of the *Sale of Goods Act 1979* that goods supplied under a contract must conform to their contract description.

Quality and fitness for purpose A2.7

Just as with matters of description, *SGA 1979* implies into contracts of sale conditions that the goods supplied under the contract will be of satisfactory quality and reasonably fit for their purpose. There are corresponding provisions in *SG(IT)A 1973* and *SGSA 1982*. It should always be borne in mind that, in business-to-business contracts, *s 15A* of the *SGA 1979* prevents a buyer from rejecting for a breach of these conditions where breach is so slight that rejection would be unreasonable. Under the *Consumer Rights Act 2015 (CRA 2015)*, terms as to quality and fitness for purpose are implied into consumer contracts but they are not known as 'conditions'. Section 9(1) CRA 2015 provides that every contract to supply goods is to be treated as including a term that the quality of the goods is satisfactory.

Satisfactory quality A2.8

When it comes to deciding if goods are of satisfactory quality, *SGA 1979* states that this is a matter of what a reasonable person would regard as satisfactory, taking into account any description applied to the goods, the price (if relevant) and all other relevant circumstances. The following are stated in *SGA 1979* to be aspects of quality in appropriate cases:

- fitness for all the purposes for which goods of the kind in question are commonly supplied;
- appearance and finish;
- freedom from minor defects;
- safety; and
- durability.

The *Consumer Rights Act 2015* provides that the quality of the goods will be considered as satisfactory if they meet the standard that a reasonable person would consider satisfactory, taking account of:

- any description of the goods;
- the price or other consideration for the goods (if relevant); and
- all the other relevant circumstances (see *s 9(5), CRA 2015: s 9(2), CRA 2015.*

The quality of the goods includes their state and condition, and the following aspects (among others) are in appropriate cases aspects of the quality of goods:

- fitness for all the purposes for which goods of the kind in question are usually supplied;

- appearance and finish;

- freedom from minor defects;

- safety;

- durability.

In the case of a sale of goods to a consumer, the following relevant circumstances will also be taken into account when deciding if goods were of satisfactory quality: any public statements on the specific characteristics of the goods made about them by the trader, the producer or any representative of the trader or the producer, particularly in advertising or on labelling: *ss 9(5)* and *(6) CRA 2015*. Such statement cannot, however, be considered if the trader shows that:

(a) at the time the contract was made, he was not, and could not reasonably have been, aware of the statement;

(b) before the contract was made, the statement had been withdrawn in public or, to the extent that it contained anything which was incorrect or misleading, it had been corrected in public; or

(c) the consumer's decision to buy the goods could not have been influenced by the statement: *s 9(7), CRA 2015*.

Where goods are of satisfactory quality A2.9

Case Example: *Thain v Anniesland Trade Centre* 1997 SLT (Sh Ct) 102

The buyer purchased a six-year old car for £2,995, which had 80,000 miles on the clock. A fortnight later, the buyer noticed a droning noise, and after six weeks, the car could no longer be driven. It was found that the cause of the trouble was the failure of a bearing in the automatic gearbox, which could have failed at any time. The court held that the car was of satisfactory quality and, because of the car's age, the buyer had no rights as to durability.

Case Example: *Jewson Ltd v Boyhan* [2003] EWCA Civ 1030

The purchaser had been supplied with boilers to be installed in certain flats. When they were subject to SAP (the Standard Assessment Procedure, designed to give a home energy rating to a particular residential dwelling), this came out lower than hoped for. This could have the effect of delaying or even ending a possible purchase. The High Court had held that a reasonable man would regard the boilers as of unsatisfactory quality if their installation in the flats led to SAP ratings which were so low that a proposed purchaser might delay purchasing the flats or pulling out of a purchase. The Court of Appeal did not agree, stressing that it was the function of the provision as to satisfactory quality to establish a general standard of quality which goods are required to reach. It was not designed to ensure that goods were fit for a particular purpose made known to the seller: 'There may be exceptions, but in general a particular purpose which is not one of the ordinary uses for which goods of the relevant type are generally supplied seems to me to be irrelevant. The question in most cases will be whether the goods are intrinsically satisfactory and fit for all purposes for which goods of the kind in question are supplied ... these boilers satisfied that criterion. They were satisfactory as boilers.'

Case Example: *Bramhill v Edwards* **[2004] EWCA Civ 403**

The appellant (B) appealed against a decision to dismiss his claim for breach of the implied term in respect of the purchase from E of a second-hand motor-home. The motor-home in question, a Dolphin, had been manufactured in and imported into this country from the USA. The vehicle was 102 inches wide, exceeding the maximum permitted by the *Road Vehicles (Construction and Use) Regulations 1986 (SI 1986/1078), reg 8*, which provided that the overall width of such a vehicle must not exceed the equivalent of 100 inches. According to B, E had made representations as to the width of the Dolphin, namely that its maximum width was 100 inches. B claimed that, when he was looking at the vehicle, he noticed a spacious feel to the interior and that E had stated that it was 100 inches and perfectly legal, adding that he would not import motor-homes of a width of 102 inches because they were illegal. B had ample opportunity to examine the vehicle and had purchased the vehicle, knowing at that time of the maximum permitted width. The High Court held that a reasonable person could reasonably have taken the view that on these facts the Dolphin was not of satisfactory quality but could have equally reasonably have felt that it was. The High Court thus concluded that it was not. The Court of Appeal, however, said that this conclusion was wrong since the burden is on the buyer to prove his case. The decision had therefore to be that the goods were of satisfactory quality.

Case Example: *Hi–Lite Electrical Ltd v Wolseley UK Ltd* **[2011] EWHC 2153**

The claimant contractor (H) sought a declaration that the defendant supplier (W) was liable for a fire started in premises operated by a hair salon (O) and that W should indemnify H for any sums it was liable to pay O. W denied liability and sought to pass on any claim to the third party (X).

H had been engaged by O to carry out maintenance work in the salon and had purchased a pump from W, which it installed in the salon nine weeks before the fire. O alleged that the fire was caused by the pump, and H was found liable in contract. H made the instant claim against W on the basis that the pump was not of satisfactory quality, contrary to the *Sale of Goods Act 1979 s.14(2)*. W began third party proceedings against the manufacturer of the pump (X), which accepted that if W was liable to H, then it would be liable to W. At the instant hearing, it was agreed that the fire started in a cable attached to the pump, but the cause of the fire was disputed.

H submitted that damage had been caused to the cable during manufacturing. W and X argued that the cable had been damaged in the installation or service of the pump; alternatively that if the damage had been caused by a defect for which they were responsible, H should have fitted a residual current device (RCD), which would have prevented the fire from developing. They further contended that damages arising were too remote, as damage by fire had not been contemplated by the parties as a likely result of the cable being defective. W and X also argued that if they were liable there should be apportionment of liability due to H's failure to install an RCD.

The High Court held that on the expert evidence, the fire had been caused by a fatigue failure of the cable caused by damage to the cable which, on the balance of probabilities, had been caused by O cutting it whilst cleaning the sump and cable. It was unlikely that any damage had been caused when the pump was installed. H had therefore not proved on the balance of probabilities that the cause of the fire was a manufacturing defect and there was no other likely cause which gave rise to W being liable under s.14

Where goods are not of satisfactory quality   A2.10

Case Example: *Bernstein v Pamson Motors (Golders Green) Ltd* **[1987] 2 All ER 220**

A new car was purchased for £8,000, but it broke down within three weeks having travelled a mere 140 miles. The fault was a minor defect in a piece of sealant, but this led to the engine seizing up, which meant that the car was unsafe. The court held that the car was 'unmerchantable', which was the test before the criterion of 'satisfactory quality' replaced it. The ruling would be the same under the new test.

Case Example: *Clegg v Olle Andersson* **[2003] EWCA Civ 320**

A yacht had been delivered with an overweight keel. This had unacceptable safety consequences. It had been argued that this was overcome by the margin of safety which had been built into the rig. Reliance was also placed on the fact that the cost of remedial work was low in relation to the cost of the yacht itself. Expert evidence, however, indicated that the margin of safety did not overcome the problem and the Court of Appeal said that the cost of remedial work was not of relevance. The yacht, therefore, was not of satisfactory quality.

Case Example: *KG Bominflot Bunkergesellschaft fur Mineralole MBH & Co KG v Petroplus Marketing AG sub nom The Mercini Lady* **[2009] EWHC 1088**

The court ruled that there was to be implied into an FOB contract to deliver goods, a term under the *SGA 1979, s 14(2)* that the goods would be of satisfactory quality, not only when the goods were delivered onto the vessel, but also for a reasonable time thereafter; such a term was also to be implied at common law with the additional dimension that the goods should remain in accordance with any contractual specification for a reasonable period. The court said that such a conclusion was fortified by the fact that the *SGA 1979, s 14(2B)* made durability an aspect of satisfactory quality.

Case Example: *Hazlewood Grocery Ltd v Lion Foods Ltd* **[2007] EWHC 1887**

Chilli powder provided under a contract of sale contained a minute quantity of an industrial dye that was not a permitted additive in food. The court said that the powder contaminated with measurable quantities of dye was not reasonably fit for its purpose or of satisfactory quality because products manufactured from it were liable to be posted on the Food Standards Agency website and to be subject to recall as a result of advice or instruction from the FSA. The decision of the FSA to advise a recall of products was predictable, in line with the decisions of other European countries and could not be said to have been unreasonable.

Case Example: *Cheeld v Alliott* **[2013] EWCA Civ 508**

By an oral contract, X had engaged C to construct and install a metal porch at the front of their property at a cost of £6,500. X paid a deposit of £2,000. After the porch was installed, X sought to reject it. They did not pay C and he issued proceedings in the small claims court seeking to recover £4,250, a slight reduction on the contract price as the porch's installation was not completed. C counterclaimed seeking the return of their deposit. The deputy district judge found accepted X's evidence that they were unhappy with the porch after its installation and had said to C that it might look better if it was painted. That painting work was carried out by a third party, but X remained dissatisfied with it. The DDJ found that there was a lack of symmetry in the frame of the porch and lack of finish and that C was in breach of contract since X had expected and were entitled to expect goods of the highest quality in an ornamental feature at the front of their home. However, she concluded that the defective workmanship amounted to a breach of warranty rather than a breach of condition entitling X to reject it.

The Court of Appeal ruled that the DDJ and the circuit judge had erred by failing to treat the defects found as a breach of condition. Not every defect in goods would amount to a breach of condition: it was a question of degree. Minor matters would amount to a breach of warranty, with a remedy in damages. Nothing turned on whether the contract fell under the 1979 or the 1982 Act: whichever Act applied, the nature of the defects, the cost of rectification, the practicalities of rectification and X's contractual expectation of work of the highest quality led to the clear conclusion that there had been a breach of the condition as to satisfactory quality.

Case Example: *Ward v MGM Marine Ltd* **[2012] EWHC 4093**

A vendor of a luxury motor yacht that caught fire and exploded 15 minutes after delivery was found liable for a breach of an implied term of satisfactory quality under the *Sale of Goods Act 1979* as there was no evidence that the fire occurred otherwise than as a result of engine defects present when the yacht was sold.

Case Example; *Dalmare SPA v Union Maritime Ltd and another* **[2012] EWHC 3537**

The vessel was a 1994 built motor tanker. The sale contract was on the Norwegian Saleform 1993. The first sentence of *cl 11* provided that the vessel was to be delivered and taken over 'as she was' at the time of inspection, fair wear and tear excepted. A month after delivery of the vessel the main engine broke down because of a defective crankpin. The arbitrators held that the engine had been likely to fail within a short period of normal operation after delivery, that there was a breach of the implied term as to satisfactory quality implied into the sale contract by the *Sale of Goods Act 1979, s 14(2)* as amended and that B was entitled to damages accordingly.

D submitted that the *s 14(2)* term was excluded, by virtue of *s 55(2)*, because it was inconsistent with *cl 11*, which provided that the vessel was sold 'as she was'.

The High Court held that the correct starting point was that the *s 14* implied terms would apply to the sale contract as to any other English law contract, unless the parties had contracted out of *s 14*. Second-hand ships were "goods" within the Act like any other piece of machinery or equipment. If commercial parties did not want to be subject to the statutory implied terms, they could contract out of them, as provided for by *s 55(1)*. The words "as she was' in the first sentence of *cl 11* were a necessary part of a sentence which recorded the obligation to deliver the vessel in the same condition as she was when inspected. They were part of a temporal obligation which arose because there would usually be a period of time of weeks or even months between inspection and delivery. However, those words did not say anything about what D's obligations were, either on inspection or delivery, as regards the quality of the vessel. Hence they did not exclude the implied term as to satisfactory quality under *s 14(2)*. The words 'as she was', in context, were incapable of bearing the same meaning as the free-standing words 'as is, where is' in a sale contract, assuming that those words did exclude the statutory implied terms. Even if a possible meaning of the words 'as she was' was to exclude the implied terms, that was not their only meaning in context, and the fact that they had more than one meaning was fatal to D's case, since it could not be said that they were inconsistent with the implied term, as *s 55(2)* required. The obligations in the second sentence of *cl 11* relating to class complemented or supplemented the obligation to deliver the vessel in a satisfactory condition rather than being inconsistent with it. The first sentence of *cl 11* did not exclude the implied term as to satisfactory quality. It was not necessary to decide whether the words 'as is' were apt to exclude the statutory implied terms, but it was difficult to see how, in the absence of some customary meaning, the words 'as is' could be said to be sufficiently clear and unequivocal to exclude them.

This interpretation was later said to be 'generous to the buyer', and unlikely to be 'an interpretation that would occur to anyone other than an ingenious lawyer': *Hirtenstein v Hill Dickinson LLP* [2014] EWHC 2711

Cases for Further Information

Sumner Permain and Company v Webb and Company [1922] 1 KB 55; *Niblett Ltd v Confectioners' Materials Co Ltd* [1921] 3 KB 387; *Mash & Murrell Ltd v Joseph I Emanuel Ltd* [1961] 1 WLR 862; *Lee v York Coach and Marine* [1977] RTR 35; *Rogers v Parish (Scarborough) Ltd* [1987] QB 933.

Avoiding the obligation as to satisfactory quality   **A2.11**

A distinction is to be drawn between contracts between businesses and contracts made with a consumer. In the former case, a seller can always try to exclude liability for any breach, but the test of reasonableness imposed by *UCTA 1977*, and the onus of proof being on the seller to show that it is a reasonable exclusion, makes it difficult, though not impossible, for the seller to succeed. In the case of a consumer contract, any such clause is rendered void by the *Consumer Rights Act 2015*. The *Consumer Protection from Unfair Trading Regulations 2008 (SI 2008/1277)* protects consumers from unfair or misleading trading practices. It also prohibits misleading omissions and aggressive sales tactics with the imposition of criminal offences. See *OFT v Ashbourne Management Services Ltd* [2011] EWHC 1237. See too the *Consumer Protection (Amendment) Regulations 2014 (SI 2014/870)*, which creates civil offences against the trader where a trader has created misleading actions or aggressive practices under the 2008 Regulations.

Since the term regarding satisfactory quality applies automatically, it does not need to be spelled out in a contract.

Business and consumer contracts **A2.12**

Since an exclusion clause can be simply invalid and void when used in a business contract, but a criminal offence can arguably result when present in a consumer contract, care must be taken when such clauses are used in contracts supplied to businesses and consumers alike. Where this is so, the contract should contain the clause:

> 'Terms in this contract excluding or limiting liability in relation to breach of the terms implied by the Consumer Rights Act 2015 do not apply when this contract is made with a consumer'.

Circumstances disapplying the implied obligation **A2.13**

SGA 1979 (and the other appropriate enactments) and the *CRA 2015* do, however, identify certain circumstances where, irrespective of the presence of any exclusion clauses, there will be no implied term as to satisfactory quality. This will be when:

- the defect is specifically drawn to the buyer's attention before the contract is made;

- the buyer examines the goods beforehand and that examination should reveal the defect; or

- where the sale was by sample, a reasonable examination of the sample would have revealed the defect.

Case Example: *Bramhill v Edwards* **(A2.9)**

As noted above, the problem with the Dolphin was that its external width exceeded that permitted by law. Before the sale had gone through, the sellers had pointed to the interior width of the Dolphin, and the Court of Appeal said that that should have alerted the buyers to the excessive exterior width. It ruled that this meant that there was no implied term as to satisfactory quality because of the first two points referred to above.

Reasonable fitness for purpose   A2.14

SGA 1979 provides, as do the other relevant enactments, and, in relation to consumer contracts, the *CRA 2015* that where a buyer, expressly or by implication, makes known any particular purpose for which the goods are wanted, there is a condition or term that the goods must be reasonably fit for that purpose. In *MT Højgaard A/S v E. On Climate & Renewables UK Robin Rigg East Limited* [2017] UKSC 59, one of the key contractual provisions in the construction contract provided:

> Clause 8.1(x) of the contract terms:
>
> '[Højgaard] must design, manufacture, test, deliver and install and complete the Works… so that each item of Plant and the Works as a whole shall be free from defective workmanship and materials and *fit for its purpose* as determined in accordance with the Specification using Good Industry Practice.'

Fitness for purpose was defined by reference to the Employer's Requirements. These included the 'Technical Requirements' which laid out minimum design requirements including the requirement that the design of the foundations will 'ensure a lifetime of 20 years in every aspect without planned replacement.' The Supreme Court decided, inter alia, that the contract contained a fitness for purpose obligation and required the turbine bases to have a service life of 20 years. Højgaard was in breach of that obligation (because the turbine bases clearly did not have a service life of 20 years) and so Højgaard was liable for the remedial costs involved. Although these obligation provisions were contained in the Technical Requirements attached as a schedule to the main contract, the Supreme Court held that these Technical Requirements were incorporated into the main contract by reference and were therefore enforceable obligations. The contractor was required to comply with the fitness for purpose obligation under the contract even though these obligations were contained in the technical schedules and to exercise reasonable skill and care and comply with an international standard. Where there is a contractual conflict requiring adherence to a certain specification and an obligation requiring adherence on certain performance criteria, the performance criteria obligation will generally prevail as this is a higher standard. The Supreme Court also held that the fitness for purpose obligation was to be given its natural effect and it was not inconsistent with other terms of the contract. The courts are therefore generally inclined to give effect to a requirement that a product complies with its contractual criteria.

Meaning of 'purpose'   **A2.15**

If the goods have only one normal purpose or purposes, there is no need for the seller to spell these out, since the seller will be automatically taken to know what the purpose is.

Case Example: *Priest v Last* **[1903] 2 KB 148**

The seller was assumed to know what a hot-water bottle was bought for even though this had not been mentioned by the buyer. This case demonstrated that the seller will not be liable, however, even if the goods are not fit for the purpose if there was something special, or unique, about the purpose for which the buyer wanted the goods and he had not disclosed this to the seller. The seller is not responsible if the reason for the unfitness lies in some undisclosed idiosyncrasy of the buyer.

Case Example: *Slater v Finning Ltd* **[1996] 3 All ER 398**

The House of Lords ruled against the buyer where camshafts were supplied for an engine which suffered an abnormality which created excessive torsion resonance in the shafts. The suppliers had not been made aware of the engine abnormality.

Case Example: *Griffith v Peter Conway Ltd* **[1939] 1 All ER 685**

The seller of a fur coat was not liable when the buyer contracted dermatitis since this was due to an abnormal skin condition not disclosed to the seller.

Note too that durability can be taken into account when assessing the fitness for purpose of particular goods. See the *Petro plus* (A2.10)

The burden of proof lies on the buyer to show on the evidence that the goods are not fit for their purpose: *Leicester Circuits Ltd v Coates Brothers plc* [2003] EWCA Civ 290.

Securing the benefit of this provision   **A2.16**

To overcome the problems associated with the burden of proof, the buyer should always take care to disclose all the relevant facts to the seller prior to contract and to make sure that these are provided in written form. It is, of course, always possible that the buyer himself is unaware of the relevant special factor. To avoid this further problem, the buyer should write into the contract a provision to this effect:

'The seller will provide goods which are in all respects fit for the buyer's intended use, whether or not such use, and any factors relevant to that use, have been disclosed, expressly or by implication, to the seller'.

Avoiding the obligation as to fitness for purpose   A2.17

A seller in a business to business contract can always try to exclude liability for any breach, but the test of reasonableness imposed by *UCTA 1977*, and the onus of proof being on him to show that it is a reasonable exclusion, makes it difficult, though not impossible, for the seller to succeed. See A2.11 as to any possible illegality when an exclusion clause is used in a consumer contract.

Circumstances disapplying the implied obligation   A2.18

SGA 1979 (and *SG(IT)A 1973, SGSA 1982* and, in relation to consumer contracts the *CRA 2015*) do, however, provide for the obligation as to reasonable fitness not to apply when:

- the buyer did not rely on the seller's skill and judgement;
- it was unreasonable for the buyer to rely on the seller's skill and judgement.

Where there has been no relevant reliance   A2.19

Case Example: *Wren v Holt* [1903] 1 KB 610

The claimant bought beer in a public house which he knew was a tied house. It was held that this meant there was no evidence as to the buyer having relied on the seller's skill and judgement.

Case Example: *Phoenix Distributors Ltd v LB Clarke Ltd* [1967] 1 Lloyd's Rep 518

The sellers sold potatoes for export from Northern Ireland to Poland. It was shown that a clearance certificate was required from the Northern Ireland Ministry of Agriculture. It was held that the buyers relied on the certificate rather than on the sellers in respect of matters covered by the certificate.

Case Example: *Knight v Mason* (1912) 15 GLR 300

The defendant was an ordinary small farmer, while the claimant was an experienced dealer in seeds. The latter asked for and received from the defendant a quotation for seed potatoes. He was shown a heap of mixed potatoes which he bought. The defendant had told the claimant that the potatoes were not blind, when, in fact, a large proportion were and hence were not reasonably fit for their purpose. The court stressed that the defendant was 'an ordinary farmer', while the claimant was a 'skilled dealer'. The claimant had completed the purchase after a 'very slight conversation'. In these circumstances, there was no evidence 'that the [claimant] relied on the judgement of the defendant'.

Case Example: *Jewson Ltd v Boyhan* (see A2.9)

The buyers had made it clear to the suppliers, and also to the manufacturers of the boilers, that the boilers were for installation in flats. They had provided no information as to the nature of the buildings being converted into flats. This meant that the suppliers were not given enough information on the basis of which they could form a view as to the possible effect of a low SAP (Standard Assessment Procedure) rating. The court agreed that the question of suitability in all the circumstances had been a question for the buyers and their advisers. There had, therefore, been no reasonable reliance.

Case Example: *Farrans (Construction) Ltd v RMC Readymix Concrete (Scotland) Ltd* (see above)

The contract was for the supply of C7 foamed concrete. When the contract was being negotiated, the evidence showed that the buyers had not relied on the skill and judgement of the suppliers in the selection of the concrete as a mix suitable for any particular purpose. In fact, the buyers had conceded this in cross-examination. More than that, the buyers had accepted that the decision to use the C7 had been made by the buyers in consultation with third parties. It also appeared from the evidence that the suppliers had not been told of the depth of the shaft into which the C7 was to be placed. Nor had the parties discussed how the pumping was to be carried out by the pumping contractor. As the court saw it, such circumstances supported the buyers' concession that no reliance had been placed on the suppliers' skill and judgement.

In any case, the court also said that, had there been such reliance, it would not have been reasonable. The buyers had employed a third party as a specialist drilling subcontractor. It was also the case that the buyers were experienced civil engineering contractors. The evidence was that the decision to use C7 had been made by the buyers and the third parties. In addition, the buyers had not told the suppliers how the pumping operation was to be carried out by the contractor, nor informed the suppliers of the proposed method of working on site, nor of the depth of the shaft.

Case Example: *BSS Group plc v Makers (UK) Ltd* **[2011] EWCA Civ 809**

B had supplied M with materials, including piping, adaptors and valves, for the installation of a new plumbing system in a public house. A particular make of part, 'Uponor', was used for the project. M requested further materials from B, specifically identifying that they were to be used in the same project. B supplied a different type of valve which was incompatible with the adaptor. A connection became insecure under pressure, resulting in substantial flooding of the public house. B were held to be liable. The judge found that M had expressly and, if not, by implication made it known to B that the valves were to be used with Uponor piping and had relied on B's skill and judgment as to the compatibility of the parts. He found that the valves were not compatible with the adaptors they were likely to be used with and were not therefore fit for purpose.

B contended that the judge had: (1) misdirected himself regarding the test for determining whether M had made known the purpose for which it would be using the valves; (2) wrongly concluded that M had communicated a sufficiently particular purpose to B; (3) wrongly concluded that the valves were not fit for purpose; (4) dealt inadequately with the issue of M's reliance on B's skill and judgment.

The Court of Appeal held that relevant questions for assessing a claim for breach of the implied term were: (a) whether the buyer, expressly or by implication, had made known to the seller the purpose for which the goods were being bought; (b) if so, whether they were reasonably fit for that purpose; (c) if they were not reasonably fit for that purpose, whether the seller had shown that the buyer had not relied upon its skill and judgment or, if it had, that it had been unreasonable to do so.

In this case, B had known that M was using a Uponor system and had previously supplied Uponor components for the same project. It was an irresistible inference from M's inquiry regarding further parts that it was making known to B its intention to use the valves as a device intended to regulate or control the flow of water in pipes used in the project. It was also an obvious inference that it was making known to B that it intended to use such valves in conjunction with the Uponor plastic piping that B was aware it was using. At the very least, it had to have been apparent to B that M was likely to so use the valves and M had therefore made known a particular purpose for which the valves were intended to be used.

The valves were not fit for the requisite purpose, as they were incompatible with the Uponor adaptors and would be likely to fail when used in conjunction with them

Where a buyer had made known its purpose, there was prima facie an implied condition of fitness which the seller could defeat only by proving that the buyer had not relied on, or that it had been unreasonable to rely on, the skill and judgment of the seller. The issue was whether B had discharged that burden. B's argument that M was content to buy any valve and was relying on B to do the tests necessary to ensure that it worked was unrealistic. B was a specialist dealer and M was relying on B to sell it a compatible valve. Although the judge had not expressly dealt with the issue of whether it had been reasonable for M to rely on B's skill and judgment, he could not have overlooked that issue as he had quoted the provisions of the Act before focusing on the issues to be decided. The inference to be drawn was that he was satisfied that there was no question of any reliance by M as having been unreasonable and that conclusion could not be criticised.

Cases for Further Information

Manchester Liners Ltd v Rea [1922] 2 AC 74; *Ashford Shire Council v Dependable Motors Pty Ltd* [1961] AC 336; *Young & Marten Ltd v McManus Childs Ltd* [1968] 2 All ER 1169; *Gloucestershire County Council v Richardson* [1968] 2 All ER 1181; *Hardwick v SAPPA* [1969] AC 31; *Corbett Construction Ltd v Simplot Chemical Co Ltd* [1971] 2 WWR 332; *Aswan Engineering Establishment Co v Lupdine Ltd* [1987] 1 WLR 1; *Hazlewood Grocery Ltd v Lion Foods Ltd* [2007] EWHC 1887.

When not reasonably fit   A2.20

Case Example: *Lowe v Machell Joinery Ltd* [2011] EWCA Civ 794

L were converting a barn for residential use and ordered a staircase from W. They paid for the goods but when delivered took the view that the staircase did not comply with W's obligations under the contract. L rejected the goods and issued proceedings to recover the price of the staircase. Shortly before trial, L took a new point, namely, that if the goods had been installed there would have been a breach of the building regulations which was another breach justifying their rejection of the goods. The judge held that W was in breach of contract as the building regulations had not been complied with but that did not justify rejection of the goods as the design could be easily modified by L when installed so as to avoid any breach.

The Court of Appeal held that, under the *Sale of Goods Act 1979*, the staircase had to be fit for the purpose of being installed in a building to be used as a residence and for use as such. The statutory provisions had to be implied into the contract unless it was a case in which L did not rely on the skill and judgment of W as a seller. The fact that the judge held that W should at the very least have warned L of the need to ensure that the building control officer would accept the particular design clearly supported the proposition that L did rely on, and were reasonable in relying on, W. As the goods supplied in exact conformity with the contract could not lawfully be used for their intended purpose, which was known to W, they were not reasonably fit for purpose and a reasonable buyer would not find them satisfactory. The judge was right to conclude that W was in breach of contract because the staircase, as designed and supplied, would not have complied with the building regulations when installed but wrong to hold that that did not entitle L to reject the goods. As such L were entitled to be repaid the price paid.

Note the goods supplied to a bespoke design, but which turn out not to be reasonably fit for the purpose, can still avoid being supplied in breach of the *Sale of Goods Act 1979* or the *Consumer Rights Act 2015*.

Case Example: *Trebor Bassett Holdings Ltd v Cadbury UK Partnership* **[2012] EWCA Civ 1158**

M manufactured popcorn and other confectionery. In the popcorn production area of the factory, corn was popped in pans of oil before being transported via an elevator to a hopper for packaging. The parties had contracted for the design and installation of an automatic 'CO2 suppression' system in the elevator and hopper. The system was supposed to discharge CO2 into the hopper upon fire being detected, thereby extinguishing the fire. A fire broke out in the hopper, but no CO2 was discharged. M's operatives ejected a burning ball of popcorn, together with the hopper's entire load, and tried to stamp out the fire. The fire consequently spread and destroyed the whole factory. The judge had found that although D was liable to M for design and installation faults, M shared responsibility for the damage because it had been negligent in failing to segregate the production area from the rest of the building, failing to install sprinklers, and encouraging the spread of the fire by taking inappropriate action upon its discovery. The judge made a 75% reduction in damages to reflect M's contribution. M's case on appeal was that the obligation on D to supply a system which met the desired specification and was fit for purpose was absolute, and the court therefore had no power under the Law Reform (Contributory Negligence) Act 1945 to reduce the ensuing damages because D's contractual duty extended beyond the tortious duty that it also owed. D's case was that even if M could establish that D had effectively guaranteed the efficacy of the system so as to provide absolute liability, it could not rely upon D's breach as causative of its losses because a similar fire one year earlier had broken the chain of causation. It also alleged that the panicked reaction of M's operatives to the fire had caused it to spread and had broken the chain of causation.

The Court of Appeal held that M had characterised its contract with D inappropriately. D could not be regarded as having supplied a system which could be equated with 'goods', thereby attracting the express requirement that it be of good quality and reasonably fit for purpose. It had not supplied an off-the-shelf product, but had offered to undertake the design and supply of a bespoke, tailor-made, system. It was not possible to say, in the abstract, that the system was not of good quality, because it did not have any inherent characteristics which could be independently assessed, and because there were no purposes for which it was commonly supplied. The shortcomings in the system were matters of design, not matters concerning the inherent quality of the goods.

Goods supplied under the contract A2.21

In relation both to the requirement as to satisfactory quality and fitness for purpose, the obligations laid down by the *SGA 1979, SG(IT)A 1973, SGSA 1982* and the *Consumer Rights Act 2015* apply to the goods supplied under the contract. The implied conditions therefore apply, not just to the goods directly the subject matter of the contract, but also to the goods supplied with them.

Where goods are supplied under the contract A2.22

Case Example: *Wilson v Rickett Cockerell & Co Ltd* **[1954] 1 QB 598**

A product called Coalite was supplied which, unknown to the parties, contained an explosive. It was held that *SGA 1979* applied to all products supplied under the contract, and not merely to the Coalite alone.

Case Example: Geddling v Marsh [1920] 1 KB 668

It was held that *SGA 1979* applied to the bottle in which a drink was supplied, even though the bottle remained the property of the seller.

Other pre-contract information treated as included in the contract A2.23

These particular provisions apply solely to consumer contracts as provided for under the *Consumer Rights Act 2015, s 12*. Certain information must be supplied to consumers when making on-trade contracts or off-trade premises by the *Consumer Contracts (Information, Cancellation and Additional Charges) Regulations 2013 (SI 2013/3134)*.

In the case of *on-trade premises contracts*, the following information must be provided pre-contract, if not already apparent from the context of the contract, and is to be regarded as incorporated into the contract as a term of the contract: *s 12(2), CRA 2015* and Sch 1 of the 2013 Regulations:

(a) the main characteristics of the goods or services, to the extent appropriate to the medium of communication and to the goods or services.

(b) the identity of the trader, such as his trading name, the geographical address at which he is established and his telephone number;

(c) the total price of the goods or services inclusive of taxes, or where the nature of the goods or services is such that the price cannot reasonably be calculated in advance, the manner in which the price is to be calculated, as well as, where applicable, all additional freight, delivery or postal charges or, where those charges cannot reasonably be calculated in advance, the fact that such additional charges may be payable;

(d) where applicable, the arrangements for payment, delivery, performance, the time by which the trader undertakes to deliver the goods or to perform the service, and the trader's complaint handling policy;

(e) in addition to a reminder of the existence of a legal guarantee of conformity for goods, the existence and the conditions of after-sales services and commercial guarantees,

where applicable;

(f) the duration of the contract, where applicable, or, if the contract is of indeterminate duration or is to be extended automatically, the conditions for terminating the contract;

(g) where applicable, the functionality, including applicable technical protection measures, of digital content;

(h) where applicable, any relevant interoperability of digital content with hardware and software that the trader is aware of or can reasonably be expected to have been aware of.

In the case of *off-trade premises contracts*, the following pre-contract information must be provided and is to be regarded as incorporated into the contract as a term of the contract: *s 12(2), CRA 2015* and Sch 2 of the 2013 Regulations:

(a) the main characteristics of the goods or services, to the extent appropriate to the medium of communication and to the goods or services;

(b) the identity of the trader, such as his trading name;

(c) the geographical address at which the trader is established and the trader's telephone number, fax number and e-mail address, where available, to enable the consumer to contact the trader quickly and communicate with him efficiently and, where applicable, the geographical address and identity of the trader on whose behalf he is acting;

(d)   if different from the address provided in accordance with point (b), the geographical address of the place of business of the trader, and, where applicable, that of the trader on whose behalf he is acting, where the consumer can address any complaints;

(e)   the total price of the goods or services inclusive of taxes, or where the nature of the goods or services is such that the price cannot reasonably be calculated in advance, the manner in which the price is to be calculated, as well as, where applicable, all additional freight, delivery or postal charges and any other costs or, where those charges cannot reasonably be calculated in advance, the fact that such additional charges may be payable. In the case of a contract of indeterminate duration or a contract containing a subscription, the total price shall include the total costs per billing period. Where such contracts are charged at a fixed rate, the total price shall also mean the total monthly costs. Where the total costs cannot be reasonably calculated in advance, the manner in which the price is to be calculated shall be provided;

(f)   the cost of using the means of distance communication for the conclusion of the contract where that cost is calculated other than at the basic rate;

(g)   the arrangements for payment, delivery, performance, the time by which the trader undertakes to deliver the goods or to perform the services and, where applicable, the trader's complaint handling policy;

(h)   where a right of withdrawal exists, the conditions, time limit and procedures for exercising that right as well as the model withdrawal form set out in the *2013 Regulations*

(i)   where applicable, that the consumer will have to bear the cost of returning the goods in case of withdrawal and, for distance contracts, if the goods, by their nature, cannot normally be returned by post, the cost of returning the goods;

(j)   that, if the consumer exercises the right of withdrawal after having made a request the consumer shall be liable to pay the trader reasonable costs;

(k)   where a right of withdrawal is not provided for, the information that the consumer will not benefit from a right of withdrawal or, where applicable, the circumstances under which the consumer loses the right to withdraw;

(l)   a reminder of the existence of a legal guarantee of conformity for goods;

(m)   where applicable, the existence and the conditions of after sale customer assistance, after-sales services and commercial guarantees;

(n)   the existence of relevant codes of conduct and how copies of them can be obtained, where applicable;

(o)   the duration of the contract, where applicable, or, if the contract is of indeterminate duration or is to be extended automatically, the conditions for terminating the contract;

(p)   where applicable, the minimum duration of the consumer's obligations under the contract;

(q)   where applicable, the existence and the conditions of deposits or other financial guarantees to be paid or provided by the consumer at the request of the trader;

(r)   where applicable, the functionality, including applicable technical protection measures, of digital content;

(s)   where applicable, any relevant interoperability of digital content with hardware and software that the trader is aware of or can reasonably be expected to have been aware of;

(t)   where applicable, the possibility of having recourse to an out-of-court complaint and redress mechanism, to which the trader is subject, and the methods for having access to it.

Where model seen or examined before contract   A2.24

The *Consumer Rights Act 2015, s 14*, provides that where a contract for the supply of goods is made by reference to a model of the goods that is seen or examined by the consumer before the contract is made, then the contract will include a term that the goods will match the model. There is an exception where to the extent that any differences between the model and the goods are brought to the consumer's attention before the contract is made.

There is no such statutory implication in the case of contracts with a business but it is right to say that such a term would be implied in such circumstances as being incorporated by virtue of the particular circumstances.

Digital content   A2.25

Under the *Consumer Rights Act 2015*, and hence only in relations to consumer contracts, certain terms are implied in the case of contracts for digital content: *Part 1, Ch 3, CRA 2015*. This a reference to data supplied and produced in digital form.

In relation to such contracts, there are implied like terms to those implied in relation to goods, ie correspondence with description, satisfactory quality and fitness for purpose, and title: see *ss 34-36 CRA 2015*.

It is likely that such provisions would be implied into business contracts by common law.

The *2015 Act* also incorporates into the contracts the pre-contract information required by the *2013 Regulations* (see A.2.23) other than information about (main characteristics, functionality and compatibility is to be treated as included as a term of the contract: *s 37, CRA 2015.*

Sales by sample   A2.26

Section 15 of *SGA 1979* implies into contracts for sale by sample a condition that the bulk corresponds with the sample in quality, and that the goods will be free from any defect, rendering the quality unsatisfactory, not apparent on a reasonable examination of the sample. There are like provisions in *SG(IT) A 1973* and *SGSA 1982. Section 13, CRA 2015* applies to a contract to supply goods by reference to a sample of the goods that is seen or examined by the consumer before the contract is made. In such circumstances there is an implied term that the goods will match the sample except to the extent that any differences between the sample and the goods are brought to the consumer's attention before the contract is made; and the goods will be free from any defect that makes their quality unsatisfactory and that would not be apparent on a reasonable examination of the sample.

When a contract is a sale by sample   A2.27

SGA 1979 and *SGSA 1982* (but not *SG(IT)A 1973*, though it can be assumed that the common law is to like effect) and the *CRA 2015* provide that a contract is a contract for sale by sample when there is an express or implied term to that effect. There seems no reason why a seller cannot avoid this implication by the use of the following:

> 'Notwithstanding that a sample of the goods has been exhibited to and inspected by the buyer, it is hereby declared that such sample was so exhibited and inspected solely to enable the buyer to judge for himself the quality of the bulk, and not so as to constitute a sale by sample'.

Such a provision would, though, not affect the general duties as to the supply of goods of satisfactory quality and of reasonable fitness. At the same time, such a clause could well be within the jurisdiction of *UCTA 1977* and hence valid only if reasonable. In the case of a consumer contract, and if held to be an exclusion clause, any such clause would be arguably illegal: See A2.11 above. In the case of a consumer contract, such a clause could also be unfair under the *Consumer Rights Act 2015.*

Effect of slight breaches   A2.28

Whenever, in the case of a contract with a business, any breach of the provisions as to description or quality of fitness is so slight that it would be unreasonable for a buyer to reject the goods, then he cannot reject them, but must keep them and sue instead for damages. This applies in relation to *SGA 1979*, *SG(IT)A 1973* and *SGSA 1982*.

Passing of risk   A2.29

The time at which risk in the goods passes to the buyer is crucial. If the risk of loss or damage is with the buyer, then he will still have to pay for them, however useless the goods might be. If the risk was on the seller at the time when the goods were damaged or destroyed, he cannot sue for the price.

Differing approaches of parties as to who bears risk   A2.30

The position as to who bears the risk when the contract is with a business buyer is set out in *s 20(1) SGA 1979* which provides that risk passes with property unless the parties agree otherwise. There is no equivalent provision in *SG(IT)A 1973* and *SGSA 1982*, but it can be assumed that the common law applicable to the relevant contracts is the same as the law set out in *SGA 1979*. The parties obviously have divergent views on this, and the buyer should always ensure that the contract provides for risk to pass only on delivery of goods in conformity with the contract; while the seller should, of course, seek to provide that risk passes as soon as possible when goods are transferred to the buyer. In the context of contracts made with a business buyer, but not where the buyer is a consumer, the law imposes no restraints in this context on what the contract may say. Thus, the conditions of purchase need simply say:

> 'The goods will be at the seller's risk until such time as goods in conformity with the contract are actually and physically delivered to and received by the buyer or his authorised agent'.

Such a clause could also say that any receipt must be evidenced in writing.

The conditions of sale would say:

> 'The risk in the goods will pass to the buyer at the time the goods are allocated to the contract and will remain at the buyer's risk thereafter'.

Where the buyer is a consumer, the *2015 Act* provides that risk does not pass until the goods are in the physical possession of the consumer or someone identified by the consumer to take possession: *s 29, CRA 2015*. This will not apply if the carrier was appointed by the consumer except where the carrier was named as an option provided by the seller. The *CRA 2015* states that the provisions in the Act as to the passing of risk cannot be excluded.

Passing of property   **A2.31**

There are two reasons why it is important to know when property (which can perhaps be better understood as ownership) passes to the buyer. As we saw in A2.29, it can, unless the contract states otherwise, determine where risk lies. Importantly, it is only when the buyer obtains property that he effectively becomes owner and can assert the normal rights of ownership. *Section 17 SGA 1979* provides that in a contract where the buyer is a business, the parties can state in the contract when property is to pass. If the contract says nothing on this point, then *s 18 SGA 1979* sets out a number of rules as to when property (and potentially risk) passes to the buyer. There are no equivalent provisions in *SG(IT)A 1973* and *SGSA 1982*, but it may be assumed that the applicable common law provisions are to like effect.

The *Consumer Rights Act 2015* has no provisions as to the passing of property. This would appear to mean, perhaps oddly, that the common law rules set down *SGA 1979* apply in those cases where the buyer is a consumer.

The five rules

Rule 1   **A2.32**

If the contract is for the sale of specific goods in a deliverable state, and the contract is unconditional, then property passes when the contract is made, regardless of payment time or delivery time. Unconditional in this context means that there are no pre-conditions to the passing of property, such as payment, while deliverable means, according to *s 61(5) SGA 1979,* goods which are in such a condition that the buyer would be bound to take delivery of them.

> **Case Example:** *Underwood Ltd v Burgh Castle Brick and Cement Syndicate* **[1922] 1 KB 343**
>
> Machinery was not in a deliverable state when still attached to the factory floor, and it had to be dismantled prior to delivery. See too the *Kulkarni* case below.

Rule 2   **A2.33**

This concerns specific goods not yet in a deliverable state. Where it is the seller's duty to do something to the goods in order to put the goods into a deliverable state, property passes when he has made the goods deliverable and informed the buyer.

Rule 3   **A2.34**

This concerns specific goods in a deliverable state, but where the seller has to do something to the goods, such as weigh or measure them, in order to work out the price. Property passes to the buyer when whatever is required has been done, and the buyer has been notified.

Rule 4   **A2.35**

This deals with the situation where goods are delivered to the buyer on approval, or on sale or return or similar terms. Property will pass when the buyer indicates acceptance or performs any act adopting the transaction. If he does neither, and fails to indicate rejection, then property will pass after the lapse of a reasonable time, or the expiry of a date set for the return of the goods.

> **Case Example:** *Kirkham v Attenborough* **[1897] 1 QB 201;** *London Jewellers Ltd v Attenborough* **[1934] 2 KB 206**
>
> These illustrate the point that if a buyer pledges or sells the goods, this will constitute approval or acceptance and property will pass under Rule 4.

> **Case Example:** *Elphick v Barnes* **(1880) 5 CPD 321;** *Re Ferrier* **[1944] Ch 295**
>
> These cases demonstrate that if the buyer is unable to return the goods through no fault of his own, as for example in the case of theft or seizure by a third party, this is not acceptance and Rule 4 will not apply.

> **Case Example:** *Atari Corporation (UK) Ltd v Electronics Boutique Stores (UK) Ltd* **[1998] QB 539**
>
> Unless the parties specify otherwise, a buyer can reject the goods by any indication to the seller which clearly shows that he does not wish to exercise the option to purchase. In this case, the Court of Appeal held that, in the absence of contrary indications, the notice rejecting the goods did not need to be in writing, nor did it need to identify with certainty the goods to which it related (as long as the generic description enabled them to be identified with certainty), and nor did the goods have to be physically capable of collection when the notice was issued (so long as they were available within a reasonable period).

Rule 5   **A2.36**

This is the one rule that relates to unascertained goods; that is to say goods which have not been agreed on and identified at the time of sale. It also applies to future goods. *Section 61(1)* of the *SGA 1979* defines these as 'goods to be manufactured or acquired by the seller after the making of the contract of sale'.

Case Example: *Healy v Howlett & Sons* **[1917] 1 KB 337**

Where Rule 5 applies, *s 17 SGA 1979* provides that property cannot pass until the contract goods are first ascertained. In this case, the buyer instructed the seller to send him 20 boxes of mackerel. The seller consigned 190 boxes to a railway company, instructing it to deliver 20 to the buyer, and the remaining boxes to other consignees. The train was delayed and the fish perished before reaching the train's destination. The court held that the goods had not been ascertained vis-à-vis the buyer since no specific boxes had been earmarked for him.

Once ascertained, Rule 5(1) provides for property to pass when the goods are unconditionally appropriated to the contract, by either party with the assent of the other, and such assent can be express or implied.

Case Example: *Aldridge v Johnson* **(1857) 7 E&B 885**

The claimant buyer agreed to buy 100 quarters of barley out of 200 which he had seen in bulk and approved. It was arranged that he would send 200 sacks for the barley, which the seller would fill and send to the buyer by rail. The seller filled 155 sacks, leaving 45 unfilled. On the eve of his bankruptcy, the seller emptied the barley from the sacks back into the bulk. It was held that the property in the 155 sacks had passed the instant they were filled.

Case Example: *Rohit Kulkarni v Manor Credit (Davenham) Ltd* **[2010] EWCA Civ 69**

Kulkarni had ordered a car from a company (G), knowing that G had no such car but intended to source one. G bought the car from Manor Credit under a hire purchase agreement signed on 14 March 2008 and delivered it to Kulkarni that day. However, three days earlier, on 11 March, it had given Kulkarni the car's registration number so he could insure it. Manor Credit discovered G's fraud and repossessed the car. Kulkarni claimed against Manor Credit in conversion, relying on a title derived under *s 27* of the *Hire Purchase Act 1964*. The issue was whether there had been a disposition of the car at a time when G was a hirer of it. The judge found that there had not. Applying the *SGA 1979, s 18, r 5(1)*, he found that the parties had intended property in the car to pass to Kulkarni when he had been given the registration number and that his insurance of the car amounted to an assent to G's appropriation of it within the meaning of the *SGA 1979, s 18, r 5(1)* in relation to goods which have been 'unconditionally appropriated to the contract' and *s 18, r 5(1)* insofar as it relates to the assent of the buyer. Kulkarni submitted that there had been no transfer of the property in the car until delivery because either the car had not been in a deliverable state until its registration plates had been attached on delivery; there could have been no assent to appropriation when G did not have property in the car; or that, in any event, *s 18, r 5(1)* was only a prima facie rule.

It was held that there was no evidence that the registration plates had been attached prior to delivery. Kulkarni would not have been bound to take delivery of the car without them and therefore it had not been shown to have been in a deliverable state before delivery. On that basis Kulkarni could establish that he had become a purchaser under a disposition which first took place upon delivery so that the exception in the *Hire Purchase Act 1964, s 27* applied. That was enough to entitle him to succeed.

The court said that, if that if that conclusion was wrong, the next question was whether there had been an unconditional appropriation of the car with Kulkarni's assent. Although the judge considered that there had been, authority suggested that the rule was not so easily fulfilled. If Kulkarni's insurance of the car was to be taken as an assent to G's appropriation, it might be said to have been given on the basis of G's implied representation that it had the necessary property in the car. Such assent would be no assent. There was force in Kulkarni's submission that in the case of the sale of a car to a consumer, property was not intended to pass until delivery. It was upon delivery that the buyer could inspect the car and receive its log book. Before solving the issue on the basis of the *SGA 1979, s 18, r 5(1)* the court would have needed good evidence that the parties had intended property in the car to pass before delivery. The judge thought that he had that in Kulkarni's insurance of the car but had made no finding as to the time the cover began. If, as had to be inferred in the absence of evidence, Kulkarni only insured it from the time of its expected delivery, then that pointed against a solution in terms of *SGA 1979, s 18, r 5(1)*. Moreover, G had never had property in the car and had no intention of fulfilling its contract to transfer property in it. It knew that any assent by Kulkarni to its appropriation was by reason of its own dishonest pretence. A seller who knew that he lacked the property in goods which he appropriated to a contract could not reasonably think that his buyer would assent to such an appropriation. In such a situation, *SGA 1979, s 18, r 5(1)* was unlikely to provide a solution. The rule assumed that the seller had property in the goods. If, therefore, he lacked property in the goods, his appropriation of them to the contract was unlikely to be reliable as an indication of the parties' intentions. The agreement to sell would only mature into a sale upon delivery. That would reflect the presumption in *SGA 1979, s 18*, r 5(2). In summary, in the instant case, delivery was looked to as the decisive act transferring possession and property; there was nothing in the parties' communications indicating an intention otherwise; there was no actual or constructive delivery; the car was not at Kulkarni's risk before delivery; and in the circumstances of G's fraud the parties should not be taken to have intended anything prior to actual delivery of the car to turn their agreement into a sale. In the circumstances, G's appropriation of the car was not to be regarded, under a merely presumptive rule, as intended to transfer the property to Kulkarni.

Rule 5(2) provides that there can be unconditional appropriation where, acting under the contract, the seller delivers the goods to the buyer, or hands them over to a third party for transmission to the buyer.

If the facts show, however, that the carrier is the seller's agent, or his employee, then this rule will not apply (*Badische Anilin und Soda Fabrik v Basle Chemical Works* [1898] AC 200).

Goods in bulk   A2.37

Rule 5(3) deals with goods which form part of an identified bulk. Where the bulk is reduced to the same (or a smaller) quantity ordered by the buyer, and he is the only buyer left with goods in the bulk, then the remaining quantity is taken as appropriated to the contract, and the property passes to the buyer. Rule 5(4) applies the foregoing rule to cases where, again, the amount left in the bulk is the same as or smaller than the agreed quantity, but are due to a single buyer under separate contracts.

Undivided shares in bulk   A2.38

Section 20A SGA 1979 was added to cater for the fact that property in goods forming part of an identified bulk cannot pass until the goods have been separated from the bulk, including by consolidation or exhaustion as demonstrated by Rules 5(3) and 5(4) above.

Where the buyer has paid for some or all of the goods, the buyer acquires ownership in common with others of a proportionate share of the bulk. This share is determined according to the ratio that the quantity of goods already paid for but not received bears to the entire bulk existing at that time.

Section 20B SGA 1979 makes it clear that each co-owner can deal with goods within his share without needing the consent of the other co-owners. It is also made clear that these provisions:

- do not impose any obligation on a buyer who takes delivery out of a bulk to compensate others who receive short delivery as a result;

- do not affect any contractual arrangement between the buyers for adjustments among themselves; or

- alter or diminish any contractual rights of the buyer against the seller.

The above will apply to contracts for the same of goods only.

Differing approaches of parties as to passing of property   A2.39

It should again be remembered that all the foregoing rules as to when property is to pass apply only if the parties have made no separate arrangement as to this. It will always be in the seller's interest to delay passing of property until the last minute (usually until he has been paid) and for the buyer to stipulate that property is to pass the moment the contract is made. Bearing in mind the presumption that risk passes with property unless the parties agree otherwise, the buyer should draft the relevant term as follows:

> 'Property, but not risk, in the contract goods shall pass to the buyer on the making of this contract'.

The corresponding seller's term is discussed in A2.40 below.

Retention of title   A2.40

It is, of course, always in the seller's best interests to postpone the passing of title for as long as possible. While property remains vested in the seller, the goods remain as a security against default by the buyer, and can thus always be repossessed. The importance of using a retention clause was indicated by Templeman LJ in *Borden (UK) Ltd v Scottish Timber Products Ltd* [1981] Ch 25, who stated: 'Unsecured creditors rank after preferential creditors, mortgagees and holders of floating charges, and they receive a raw deal'.

This right to reserve or retain title is expressly preserved in *s 19 SGA 1979* which allows the seller to retain title to the goods until certain conditions are fulfilled as stipulated by the seller. There are no equivalent provisions in *SG(IT)A 1973* and *SGSA 1982*, but it may be assumed that the applicable common law provisions are to like effect.

Case Example: *Aluminium Industries Vassen BV v Romalpa Aluminium Ltd* **[1976] 1 WLR 676**

The clause before the court was an English translation of the original Dutch:

> 'The ownership of the material to be delivered by AIV will only be transferred to the purchaser when he has met all that is owing to AIV, no matter on what grounds. Until the date of payment, purchaser, if AIV so desires, is required to store the material in such a way that it is clearly the property of AIV.
>
> AIV and purchaser agree that, if purchaser should make (a) new object(s) from the material, mixes this material with (an)other object(s) or if this material in any way whatsoever becomes a constituent of (an)other object(s), AIV will be given the

ownership of this (these) new object(s) as surety of the full payment of what purchaser owes AIV.

To this end AIV and purchaser now agree that the ownership of the article(s) in question, whether finished or not, are to be transferred to AIV, and that this transfer of ownership will be considered to have taken place through and at the moment of the single operation or event by which the material is converted into (a) new object(s), or is mixed with or becomes a constituent of (an)other object(s). Until the moment of full payment of what purchaser owes AIV, the purchaser shall keep the object(s) in question for AIV in his capacity of fiduciary owner and, if required, shall store this (these) object(s) in such a way that it (they) can be recognised as such.

Nevertheless, purchaser will be entitled to sell these objects to a third party within the framework of their normal carrying on of his business and to deliver them on condition that if AIV so requires purchaser, as long as he has not fully discharged his debt to AIV, shall hand over to AIV the claims he has against his buyer emanating from this transaction'.

The subject matter of this contract was aluminium foil. The seller, on the buyer going into receivership, successfully claimed to be entitled, as against the receiver, to foil worth £50,000 and to £35,000 held in a separate account which represented the proceeds of sub-sales of the unused foil. The court held that the unused foil was held by the buyer as bailee, and in a fiduciary capacity, and that, as a result, the seller was entitled to trade and claim the proceeds of any sub-sales in priority to both the bank appointing the receiver and the buyer's general creditors.

Case Example: *Borden (UK) Ltd v Scottish Timber Products Ltd* **[1981] Ch 25**

The relevant clause was as follows:

'Risk and property.

Goods supplied by the Company shall be at the purchaser's risk immediately on delivery to the purchaser or into custody on the purchaser's behalf (whichever is the sooner) and the purchaser should therefore be insured accordingly. Property in the goods supplied hereunder will pass to the customer when (a) the goods the subject of the contract; (b) all other goods the subject of any other contract between the company and the customer which at the time of payment of the full price of the goods sold under the contract, have been delivered to the customer but not paid for in full, have been paid for in full'.

The contract was for the supply of resin. This was supplied but a receiver was appointed to the buyer's affairs. When required for use, the resin was transferred to a separate tank where it was mixed with wax emulsion and hardeners to form a glue mix. It was then blended with desiccated timber and pressed to form chipboard. Of the final chipboard, the timber components comprised 24% by value and the resin 17%. The court held that once the buyers had used the resin in the manufacture of chipboard, the resin ceased to exist and there was nothing which the seller could trace.

The effect of the reservation of title clause was merely to reserve to the sellers the property in the resin so long as it remained unused. When the resin ceased to exist when incorporated into the chipboard the seller's title also ceased to exist. Furthermore, there was no express agreement and no ground to imply an agreement in the contract that the buyers were to provide substantial security for the resin used in the chipboard. The court questioned whether a tracing remedy could ever be applied where goods have been mixed and also queried how, if tracing were available, the proportion of the value of the manufactured product which the tracer could claim as property was attributable to his ingredient.

Case Example: *Re Bond Worth* **[1980] Ch 228**

The relevant terms were:

'(a) The risk in the goods passes to the buyer upon delivery, but equitable and beneficial ownership shall remain with us until full payment has been received (each order being considered as a whole), or until prior resale, in which case our beneficial entitlement shall attach to the proceeds of resale or to the claim for such proceeds.

(b) Should the goods become constituents of or be converted into other products while subject to our equitable and beneficial ownership, we shall have the equitable and beneficial ownership in such other products as if they were solely and simply the goods and accordingly sub-clause (a) shall as appropriate apply to such other products.'

The court interpreted this as creating a security interest rather than an ownership interest. The seller had not reserved equitable ownership at all, and the buyer had created a charge rather than a trust.

Cases for Further Information

Hendy Lennox Industrial Engineers Ltd v Grahame Puttick Ltd [1984] 1 WLR 485; *Re Peachdart Ltd* [1984] Ch 131; *Clough Mill Ltd v Martin*

[1985] 1 WLR 111; *Stroud Architectural Systems Ltd v John Laing Construction Ltd* [1994] BCLC 276; *Bulbinder Singh Sandhu (t/a Isher Fashions UK) v (1) Jet Star Retail Ltd (t/a Mark One) (In Administration) and others* [2010] EWHC 1936; *Fadallah v Pollak* [2013] EWHC 3159

Such clauses are most useful when dealing with easily identifiable goods. In such a case, a simple clause such as the following will suffice:

> 'Property in the goods will remain with the seller and shall not pass until payment in full for the goods has been received by the seller'.

The clause should also specify that risk has passed even though property has not; it should also give the seller the right to enter the buyer's premises to repossess and should stipulate that the buyer must have full insurance cover for the goods. The seller must always take care to reserve the whole title in the goods. A major problem with the use of such clauses arises from the fact that under *SGA 1979*, and the *Factors Act 1889*, and also under established principles of agency and estoppel, the buyer of goods – notwithstanding the presence of a retention clause – is still able to pass a valid title to a third party who acts in good faith and without notice of the clause. Problems will also arise where the buyer mixes or uses the goods in the normal course of business. In such cases, the seller will want to be able to trace the proceeds of sale or the goods in their new form.

Varieties of retention clause A2.41

To help deal with these and other problems, more elaborate retention clauses have been devised. These need expert drafting and will usually need to consider factors such as whether the buyer:

- will hold the goods as the seller's bailee and fiduciary agent;

- will store the goods separately so that they can be clearly identified as the seller's property;

- may resell the goods to a third party (although the buyer shall act as the seller's agent when sub-selling);

- is to be accountable for the entire proceeds of sale, not merely the sums owing to the seller, and will keep the proceeds in a separate, identified fund.

Examples of retention clauses A2.42

Sellers could consider the use of one or more of the clauses below as might fit their own circumstances. Expert guidance should always be taken.

- The intending purchaser acknowledges that before entering into an agreement for the purchase of goods from the company, he has expressly warranted and represented that he is not insolvent and has not committed any act of bankruptcy, or being a company with limited or unlimited liability, knows of no circumstances which would entitle any debenture holder or secured creditor to appoint a receiver, to petition for the winding up of the company or exercise any other rights over or against the company's assets.

- Goods the subject of any agreement by the company to sell shall be at the risk of the intending purchaser as soon as they are delivered by the company to his vehicles or his premises or otherwise to his order.

- Such goods shall remain the sole and absolute property of the company as legal and equitable owner until such time as the intending purchaser shall have paid to the company the agreed price (together with the full price of any other goods the subject of any other contract with the company).

- The intending purchaser acknowledges that he is in possession of goods solely as bailee for the company until such time as the full price thereof is paid to the company (together with the full price of any other goods the subject of any other contract with the company).

- Until such a time as the intending purchaser becomes the owner of the goods, he will store them on his premises separately from his own goods or those of any other person and in a manner which makes them readily identifiable as the goods of the company.

- The intending purchaser's right to possession of the goods shall cease if he, not being a company, commits an available act of bankruptcy or if he, being a company, does anything or fails to do anything which would entitle a receiver to take possession of any assets or which would entitle any person to present a petition for winding up. The company may for the purpose of recovery of its goods enter upon any premises where they are stored or where they are reasonably thought to be stored and may repossess the same.

- In the case of any purchaser who is not a company, the purchase price shall be payable in two instalments, namely 10% on receipt of the goods and the balance at the end of such time as may be separately agreed or in default of agreement 30 days after the delivery of the goods.

- Subject to the terms hereof, the intending purchaser is licensed by the company to process the said goods in such fashion as he may wish and/or incorporate them in or with any other product(s) subject to the express condition that the new product(s) or any other chattel whatsoever containing any part of the said goods shall be separately stored and marked so as to be identifiable as being made from or with the goods the property of the company; or

- Subject to the terms hereof the intending purchaser is licensed by the company to agree to sell on the company's goods, subject to the express condition that such an agreement to sell shall take place as agents, (save that the intending buyer shall not hold himself out as such), and bailees for the company, whether the intending buyer sells on his own account or not and that the entire proceeds thereof are held in trust for the company and are not mingled with other monies or paid into any overdrawn account and shall be at all times identifiable as the company's monies.

- If goods the property of the company are admixed with goods the property of the intending purchaser or are processed with or incorporated therein, the product thereof shall become and/or shall be deemed to be the sole and exclusive property of the company. If goods the property of the company are admixed with goods the property of any person other than the intending purchaser or are processed with or incorporated therein, the product thereof shall become or shall be deemed to be owned in common with that other person.

- The intending purchaser shall be at liberty to agree to sell on any product produced from or with the company's goods on the express condition that such an agreement to sell shall take place as agents and bailees for the company whether the intending buyer sells on his own account or not and that the entire proceeds therefore are held in trust for the company and are not mingled with any other monies and shall at all times be identifiable as the company's monies.

- If the intending purchaser has not received the proceeds of any such sale he will, if called upon to do so by the company, within seven days thereof assign to the company all rights against the person(s) to whom he has supplied any product or chattel made from or with the company's goods; or

- If the intending purchaser has not received the proceeds of any such sale, he will, if called on to do so by the company, within seven days thereof assign to the company all rights against the person(s) to whom he has supplied any product or chattel made from or with the company's goods.

The registration of retention clauses **A2.43**

A clause which only retains a beneficial or equitable interest creates an equitable charge. In order for this to be valid it must be registered under *Part 25 Companies Act 2006* (*CA 2006*) (*Re Bond Worth* [1980] Ch 228 and *Stroud Architectural Systems Ltd v John Laing Construction plc* [1994] 2 BCLC 276). *CA 1985* provides that a charge created by a company registered in England and Wales, if of the type described in the Act – so far as any security on the company's property or undertaking is conferred by the charge – is void as against the liquidator, administrator and any creditor of the company unless the charge is properly registered. The most important categories of registrable charges for present purposes are floating charges, charges on book debts and charges which, if executed by an individual, would require registration as a bill of sale (see further below).

Where the buyer is not a company, *CA 2006* will not apply. The consequences in respect of purported retention clauses over products and proceeds are similar, however, because of the operation of the *Bills of Sale Act 1878* and the *Bills of Sale Act 1882*, and of *IA 1986*. The provisions of these Acts effectively render void, as against the buyer's creditors, any unregistered attempt by the buyer to assign by way of security any interest in either the buyer's goods or his book debts.

Exclusion clauses and unfair terms   A2.44

The supplier of goods or services will typically wish to exclude altogether any liability, or at any rate restrict the level of any potential liability.

> **Case Example:** *Fujitsu Services Ltd v IBM United Kingdom Ltd* **[2014] EWHC 752**
>
> The exclusion clause read thus:
>
> > '20.7 Neither Party shall be liable to the other under this Sub-Contract for loss of profits, revenue, business, goodwill, indirect or consequential loss or damage, although it is agreed that:
> >
> > (a)   this Clause 20.7 shall not apply to exclude costs to PwC and other Participants of remedying failures and re-running activities, the cost of re-tendering, costs of engaging other providers in the case of Fujitsu failure, and cost of termination which would otherwise be recoverable from Fujitsu because they arose as a result of an event of default by Fujitsu (including its Sub-Contractors and Affiliates and their respective employees, servants and agents);
> >
> > (b)   actual agreed revenue share may be recoverable to the extent expressly agreed between the parties;
> >
> > (c)   loss of profits shall be recoverable only as specified in Schedule 13 (Finance) or as a basis which may be used for calculating damages payable for infringement of Intellectual Property Rights or breach of confidentiality claims; and
> >
> > (d)   third party claims, including where a party has agreed to indemnify the other, shall be recoverable to the extent that the underlying third party claim results directly from a failure of the indemnifying Party, provided that this Clause 20.7(d) shall not be interpreted to make loss of profits recoverable in circumstances where under Clause 20.7(c), loss of profit would not be recoverable.'

The court ruled that the words of the basic exclusion under review had to be read in the context of the whole exclusion clause, the contract as a whole, the material background and the circumstances at the time the sub-contract was entered into. On that approach, any liability for damages on the workshare, change control and money value claims fell within the basic exclusion as claims for loss of profits. In any event, the language of cl 20.7 was clear and unambiguous; there was nothing in the context of that clause that pointed to any different construction than a simple application of the words to the facts of the case. The words used rebutted any presumption that the parties did not intend to abandon their remedies for loss of profit for breach by the other.

Case for further information: *Kudos Catering (UK) Ltd v Manchester Central Convention Complex Ltd* **2013] EWCA Civ 38**

In recent years, the validity of such clauses has been considerably affected by the controls imposed by the *Unfair Contract Terms Act 1977* which applies only to business to business contracts. In respect of consumer contracts, unfair terms are governed by the *CRA 2015*.

The following clause may be regarded as typical of this category of clause:

- No liability whatsoever shall be incurred by the seller in respect of any representation made by the seller or his agents before the contract was made where such representation related or referred in any way to (a) the correspondence of the goods to any description; or (b) the fitness of the goods for any purpose whatsoever.

- No liability whatsoever shall be incurred by the seller to the buyer in respect of any express term of the contract whether a condition, warranty or intermediate stipulation (including any liability arising from the breach of such term) where the said term relates or refers in any way to (a) the correspondence of the goods to any description; or (b) the quality of the goods; or (c) the fitness of the goods for any purpose whatsoever.

- All implied terms, conditions or warranties – statutory, common law or otherwise – as to (a) the correspondence of the goods to any description; or (b) the satisfactory quality of the goods; or (c) the fitness of the goods for any purpose whatsoever (whether made known to the seller or not) are hereby excluded from the contract.

As indicated above, an alternative approach is for the seller to accept some responsibility rather than to exclude it altogether. For example, liability may be limited to the contract price, to a percentage of that price, or simply to a specific figure. It has been said that a person who limits his liability takes a 'very ordinary business precaution' (*Cellulose Acetate Silk Co v Widnes Foundry (1925) Ltd* [1933] AC 20).

Drafting commercial agreements represents the bargain that is struck between the parties. It reinforces the principle of freedom of contract in which the parties are engaged and dealings between each other. At times, commercial parties enter into restrictions, limitations and exclusion clauses, and the issue for the courts is whether widely drafted exclusion clauses will be upheld by the courts as part of accepting the commercial risk between the parties. This situation was considered in *Persimmon Homes Ltd v Ove Arup & Partners Ltd* [2017] EWCA Civ 373. The developers as claimants issued proceedings against the defendant engineers alleging that the engineers had negligently failed to identify and report on asbestos on their development site. The defendant sought to rely on the exclusion clauses in the development contract between the parties and warranties in the contract under the heading 'Professional Indemnity Insurance' which stated that the defendant would maintain professional indemnity insurance of not less than £5 million per event and that the defendant's liability for pollution and contamination would be limited to £5 million in the aggregate and that 'Liability for any claim in relation to asbestos is excluded.' The Court of Appeal (per Jackson LJ) rejected the claimant's argument that the exclusion clauses should be interpreted as covering only liability for *causing* pollution or contamination, or the spread of asbestos, rather than a failure to identify it. The Court of Appeal applied a natural meaning to the words and the application of business common sense. The Court stated that it would be nonsensical for the parties to have agreed that the defendant was not liable if asbestos was moved from one part of the site to another, but liable if it was left in place. The Court further noted that the particular clauses were clearly intended to limit the defendant's liability to the extent of the insurance cover. Therefore, it would be absurd to read the exemption clauses as confined to moving contamination from one place to another. The Court of Appeal decided that the exclusion clause was effective to exclude any liability on the part of the defendant for identifying and reporting on asbestos on a development site. The Court stated that the traditional principles or canons of construction relating to exclusion clauses had no part to play here. The courts will not necessarily apply a narrow interpretation of exclusion clauses as according to Jackson LJ: 'In major construction contracts the parties commonly agree how they will allocate the risks between themselves and who will insure against what. Exemption clauses are part of the contractual apparatus for distributing risk. There is no need to approach such clauses with horror or with a mindset to cut them down.'

In *Interactive E-Solutions JLT v 03B Africa Ltd* [2018] EWHC 186, the parties entered into a commercial services agreement where 03B provided satellite services in Pakistan and Interactive provided satellite-based infrastructure. Interactive refused to pay a service fee to 03B which fees were due when the relevant satellite system had been 'successfully placed into commercial operation' which was subject to approval from the Pakistan Telecommunication Authority ('PTA').

03B subsequently decided to terminate the agreement. Interactive claimed specific performance of the agreement and counterclaimed damages of US$55 million for breach of contract. The commercial agreement provided for a wide exclusion clause excluding 03B's liability for all events except fraud by either party: 'Nothing…limits the liability of either party arising from fraud.' Interactive contended that their claim was within the fraud exception to the exclusion clause, owing to a series of misstatements made by 03B's subcontractor of which 03B was likely to be aware, and that its claim for payment from Interactive was made fraudulently.

The Court of Appeal decided that the provision 'Nothing…limits the liability of either party arising from fraud' meant 'liability in relation to which fraud is a necessary averment, other the "liability" would not arise from fraud. It would arise from something else.' The term 'fraud' meant a cause of action in which dishonesty was a necessary element. Interactive had not been able to prove fraud on the part of O3B. Lewison LJ stated that the traditional approach of the courts towards exclusion clauses previously had been one of hostility. A strict and narrow approach to their interpretation held sway. This began to change with the passing of the *Unfair Contract Terms Act 1977*. Since then the courts have become more accepting of such clauses recognising (at least in commercial contracts made between parties of equal bargaining power) that exclusion clauses are an integral part of pricing and risk allocation: *Persimmon Homes Ltd v Ove Arup & Partners Ltd* [2017] EWCA Civ 373. In analysing exclusion clauses, commercial parties were entitled to allocate between them the risks of something going wrong in their contractual relationship in any way they choose. However, the court must still use its tools of linguistics, contextual, purposive and common sense analysis to discern what the clause really means: *Nobahar-Cookson v Hut Group Ltd* [2016] EWCA Civ 128.

In *Transocean Drilling UK Ltd v Providence Resources plc* [2016] EWCA Civ 3721, Providence which was an oil exploration company hired a rig from Transocean to drill a well. While drilling, a fault developed in the rig which resulted in a four-week suspension of operations. The hire purchase agreement entered into between the parties provided for liability to be apportioned between the parties through indemnities and a series of exclusion clauses. One exclusion clause sought to prevent the recovery of 'consequential loss' for both parties.

The Court of Appeal decided that although the clause was a mutual exclusion clause that the two parties of equal bargaining power had negotiated, the court was obliged to give effect to the contractual language used by the parties taking account of the principles in *Arnold v Britton*. Such exclusion clauses could be seen as an integral part of a broader scheme for allocating losses between the parties. The clause in question was not a simple exclusion clause of a kind at which the courts were willing to construe restrictively in order to avoid commercial oppression. The courts have recognised that artificial approaches to the construction of commercial contracts are to be avoided in favour of giving the words used by the parties their ordinary and natural meaning. The court should give the language used by the parties the meaning which it would be given by a reasonable person in their position furnished with the knowledge of the background of the transaction common to them both. Particular importance must be given to the language chosen by the parties to express their intentions.

The Court of Appeal stated that even where the parties have entered into onerous obligations in a commercial agreement, the court prefers the interpretation that reflects what the parties actually agreed. The court will uphold the principle of freedom of contract which requires the court to respect and give effect to the parties' agreement. Accordingly, as the parties have agreed to exclude any liability for damages for any breaches, the court would give effect to their agreement.

In *Classic Maritime Inc v Limbungan Makmur SDN BHD* [2019] EWCA Civ 1102, the shipowner (claimant) and the charterer (defendant) entered into a long-term contract for the shipment of iron ore pellets from Brazil to Malaysia. This case was concerned with the charterer's failure to provide a cargo for seven shipments during the period July 2015 to June 2016. The charterer defaulted in performing the first two shipments. Before the next five shipments were due to take place, a dam burst which stopped production at the relevant mine. The charterer relied on the 'Exceptions Clause' under clause 32 of the contract, which provided, inter alia:

> 'EXCEPTIONS
>
> Neither the… Charterers, Shippers or Receivers shall be Responsible for loss or damage to, or failure to supply, load, discharge or deliver the cargo resulting From: Act of God, act of war, act of public enemies, pirates or assailing thieves;… accidents at the mine…; or any other causes beyond the Owners', Charterers', Shippers' or Receivers' Control; always provided that any such events directly affect the performance of either party under This Charter Party…'

The parties agreed that the dam burst was an 'accident at the mine' for the purposes of clause 32.

The Court of Appeal decided in favour of the shipowner. It noted that although clause 32 was referred to as an 'Exceptions' clause, it shared some of the features of a typical force majeure clause. It listed a number of events or causes beyond the parties' control; it defined the effect on a party's performance of the contract which such events must have if the clause is to apply; and it specified the consequences on the parties' contractual responsibility when that occurred. Males LJ stated that the question was one of construction of clause 32 and this would be determined by the language of the clause which the parties had chosen, having regard to the context and the purpose of the clause. The purpose of clause 32 was, however, to be gathered from its terms. The labels attached to the contract were not conclusive as to construction. Applying *Wood v Capita Insurance Services Ltd* [2017] UKSC 24, the court was required to check its provisional conclusions against the terms of the contract as a whole, and the commercial consequences of the proposed construction. On the facts and construction of clause 32, the Court of Appeal held that the charterer could not rely upon the 'Exceptions' clause because the charterer could not prove that but for the dam bursting, it could and would have performed the contract, and that it could not be said that its failure to perform had 'resulted from' the dam burst, or that the dam burst had 'directly affected' its performance, as required by the clause. Males LJ referred to a number of features of clause 32 in the context of contractual interpretation and stated that any clause in a contract must be construed as a whole: first, clause 32 was a general exceptions clause of mutual application. It was not a force majeure clause and could not be construed as such because the clause was headed 'Exceptions' clause and this heading was part of the parties' contract. Second, the words 'loss or damage to cargo' referred to a particular cargo which was in fact lost or damaged as a result of one or more of the events listed in the clause. There was no scope for these words to apply unless, but for the event in question, the cargo would not have been lost or damaged. Third, the clause covered a wide range of miscellaneous events and in the construction context, the clause must be construed consistently. Fourth, the words 'resulting from' together with the requirement that the events in question 'directly affect the performance of either party' import a causation requirement. These are not merely events which happen to have occurred but 'causes' which impact on performance. Fifth, the 'time lost' provision in the concluding sentence of the clause was significant. Time cannot be lost due to an event or cause listed in the clause unless, but for the event, loading would have taken place during the time in question: see *Burnett Steamship Co Ltd v Danube & Black Sea Shipping Agencies* [1933] 2 KB 438.

Circumstances when an exclusion clause is incorporated in a contract   A2.45

There are some situations in which a party disputes whether an exclusion clause has been properly incorporated into a contract, and if so, whether the clause is valid under *s 2, UCTA 1977*. *Section 2, UCTA 1977* provides that any restriction of liability for negligence must satisfy the requirement of reasonableness set out in *s 11, UCTA 1977*.

In *Goodlife Foods Ltd v Hall Fire Protection Ltd* [2018] EWCA Civ 1371, HFP established an automatic fire sprinkler system at G's frozen foods factory in Warrington for the sum of £7,490. The contract did not include any maintenance obligations on HFP. The terms and conditions were attached to the quotation received by G. HFP had expressly excluded 'all liability, loss, damages or expenses consequential or otherwise… directly or indirectly resulting from [HFP's] negligence.' The quotation expressly stated that the terms and conditions 'did not provide for the imposition of any form of damages whatsoever.'

At least ten years after purchasing the sprinkler system, G had a fire at its factory. G issued proceedings against HFP for £6.6 million alleging that the system was defective. G contended that the clause excluding liability had not been properly incorporated into the contract. Further, it was unusual and onerous and had not been properly brought to G's attention. Further, G contended that if the exclusion clause was found to be properly incorporated, the clause was ineffective as it was unreasonable under *UCTA 1977*.

The Court of Appeal ruled in favour of HFP. The exclusion clause had been incorporated into the contract between the parties. The quotation had expressly referred to the terms and conditions that were attached. Further, although the exclusion clause was wide, it was not unusual or onerous and had been properly brought to G's attention: 'A buyer who started reading these conditions would have seen by the very first words used that, at the very least, at, at the very least, the conditions contained terms which were emphatically not in the buyer's interests. Obviously, the buyer should then have read on' per Coulson LJ.

With regard to the application of *UCTA 1977* to the exclusion clause, the Court of Appeal held that the clause satisfied the reasonableness test under *UCTA 1977*, taking account of the nature and value of the contract.

In the course of his judgment, Coulson LJ considered whether the exclusion clause was onerous or unusual and stated that this matter should be addressed by looking at the contract as a whole. Having regard to the fact that this was a one-off supply contract carried out for a modest sum and that HFP had no maintenance obligations or any other connection with G's premises, the exclusion clause was neither unusual nor onerous for HFP to protect themselves against the possibility of unlimited liability arising from future events.

Practical points on exclusion clauses

- The draftsman should ensure that all terms and conditions are properly incorporated into the contract.

- Ensure that any unusual or onerous clauses are fully brought to the attention of the other party to the contract.

- Always consider the application of *UCTA 1977* for business-to-business contracts taking into account that some liabilities cannot be limited, while others are subject to the reasonableness test.

- Exclusion clauses or limitation of liability clauses are construed taking account of the agreement as a whole.

- At all times, clear, unambiguous and specific wording should be used in exclusion clauses or limitation of liability clauses rather than relying on general wording.

The Unfair Contract Terms Act 1977   A2.46

The *Unfair Contract Terms Act 1977* (*UCTA 1977*) applies solely to contracts made business to business.

Negligence liability   **A2.47**

UCTA 1977 makes it impossible for any contract term or notice to avoid or exclude liability for death or personal injury resulting from negligence. Where any other form of loss, such as damage to property, is caused by negligence, liability can be excluded or restricted if the clause is reasonable. It is common to see contract terms which state:

> 'The supplier hereby altogether excludes liability for any loss or damage, howsoever arising, from any act of negligence on his part, except where such negligence results in death or personal injury'.

General exclusion clauses   **A2.48**

Where the contract is on written standard terms then the following categories of contract term or notice are valid only if shown to be reasonable:

- clauses seeking to exclude or restrict liability; and

- clauses seeking to allow a substantially different performance from that which was reasonably expected, or clauses seeking to allow no performance at all.

Meaning of 'written standard terms'   **A2.49**

The expression 'written standard terms' is referred to under s.3 UCTA 1977 but no definition is given of 'the term, but it has been considered on occasions by the courts.

> **Case Example:** *St Alban's City and District Council v International Computers Ltd* **[1995] FSR 686**
>
> It was accepted that a contract can be subject to some negotiation between the parties and yet be on written standard terms (see too *McCrone v Boots Farm Sales Ltd* 1981 SLT 103).

> **Case Example:** *British Fermentation Products Ltd v Compair Reavell Ltd* **[1999] BLR 351**
>
> It was said that a contract made on the terms and conditions of a trade association is not on one party's written standard terms except, perhaps, where these are adopted either by practice or by express statement as a party's own standard terms. See too *Langstane Housing Association Ltd v Riverside Construction (Aberdeen) Ltd* [2009] CSOH 52.

Case Example: *The Salvage Association v CAP Financial Services Ltd* **[1995] FSR 654**

It was said that the following matters should be taken into account when deciding if a contract is on written standard terms:

(1)   The degree to which the 'standard terms' are considered by the other party as part of the process of agreeing the terms of the contract.

(2)   The degree to which the 'standard terms' are imposed on the other party by the party putting them forward.

(3)   The relative bargaining power of the parties.

(4)   The degree to which the party putting forward the 'standard terms' is prepared to entertain negotiations with regard to the terms of the contract generally and the 'standard terms' in particular.

(5)   The extent and nature of any agreed alterations to the 'standard terms' made as a result of the negotiations between the parties.

(6)   The extent and duration of the negotiations.

See too *Yuanda (UK) Co Ltd v WW Gear Construction Ltd* [2010] EWHC 720 and *Softlanding Systems Inc v KDP Software Ltd* [2010] EWHC 326. It was said in the former case that it was (5) above which was the main consideration.

In *African Export-Import Bank v Shebah Exploration and Production Co Ltd* [2018] 2 All ER 144, the claimant was a syndicate bank which entered into a facility agreement with the defendant based on an industry standard form contract syndicated facility agreement (the Loan Market Association (LMA) model terms). The contract was executed after a process of negotiation and amendment by the parties' lawyers to the facility agreement. The defendant defaulted on its repayment obligations under the facility agreement and the claimant accelerated repayment of the entire debt. The defendant contended that it was dealing on the claimant's written standard terms of business within the meaning of *s 3, UCTA 1977*, so that the claimant could not rely on a set-off exclusion clause contained in the facility agreement as this clause was unenforceable except in so far as that provision satisfied the requirement of reasonableness. The trial judge granted the claimant summary judgment. On appeal, the Court of Appeal held that the complexity of standard business terms was of no relevance to the granting of a summary judgment. It stated that where a party alleges that an agreement has been made on the standard terms of business of the other party, the party making the allegation must produce some evidence of this. On the facts, there was evidence of detailed and substantial negotiations by the parties over the terms of the facility agreement based on various amendments that were made to the agreement before it was finalised. It was therefore 'impossible to say that either the LMA model form was, or the terms ultimately agreed were, the claimants' standard terms of business'. The Court of Appeal decided that in determining whether the parties are contracting on standard terms of business, it was not sufficient that the terms derive from the use of a model form. The essential questions are: (a) whether the relevant party habitually uses those terms; and (b) whether there have been more than insubstantial variations to the terms. However, each case will depend on its facts. From a practical viewpoint, the Court of Appeal decision highlights that where a party habitually uses a standard form document but its terms are negotiated, it is unlikely to be seen as contracting on standard terms for the purposes of *s 3, UCTA 1977* particularly where the negotiations result in 'more than insubstantial variations' to that standard form. The Court of Appeal stated that for *s 3, UCTA 1977* to apply, the party relying on UCTA must prove that: (a) the term is written; (b) the term is a term of business; (c) the term is part of the other party's standard terms of business; and (d) the other party is dealing on those written standard terms of business. It concluded that in determining whether a term is part of the other party's standard terms of business: '…it has to be shown that that other party habitually uses those terms of business. It is not enough that he sometimes does and sometimes does not. Nor is it enough to show that a model form has, on the particular occasion, been used; the party relying on the Act has to show that such model form is habitually used by the other party'.

Accordingly, the Court of Appeal upheld an order for summary judgment for sums due under the facility agreement. See too: *Hadley Design Associates v Westminster City Council* [2003] EWHC 1617; and *Yuanda (UK) Co Ltd v WW Gear Construction Ltd* [2011] Bus LR 360.

Meaning of a performance which is 'substantially different' or 'no performance' A2.50

Case Example: *Timeload Ltd v British Telecommunications plc* **[1995] EMLR 459**

BT made certain phone numbers available in a contract containing the following clause:

'Termination of service by notice. At any time after service has been provided this contract or the provision of any service under it can be ended:

(1) by one month's notice by us; or

(2) by seven days' notice by you'.

No final decision was reached on whether this clause was one allowing a contractual performance which was substantially different from that which was reasonably expected, but the court said that: 'If a customer reasonably expects a service to continue until BT has substantial reasons to terminate it, it seems … at least arguable that a clause purporting to authorise BT to terminate without reason purports to permit partial or different performance from that which the customer expected'. Reference should also be made to *Zockoll Group Ltd v Mercury Communications* [1999] EMLR 385.

Case Example: *Brigden v American Express Bank Ltd* [2000] IRLR 94

In this case a clause in an employment contract allowing for dismissal during the first two years of employment without recourse to the disciplinary procedure was held not to be a term allowing the employer to render a performance substantially different from that which was reasonably expected.

It was also stated that the clause under consideration was not one allowing the employer not to perform the contract at all.

See too *Harrison v Shepherd Homes Ltd* [2011] EWHC 1811.

Case Example: *Paragon Finance plc v Staunton* [2001] 2 All ER (Comm) 1025

The question in this case was which party's performance was relevant to the application of the Act. The case concerned the following clause in a consumer credit contract: 'Interest shall be charged at such rate as the Company shall from time to time apply to the category of business to which the Company shall consider the Mortgage belongs and may accordingly be increased or decreased by the Company at any time and with effect from such date or dates as the Company shall determine...' It was submitted on behalf of the borrowers that they were reasonably entitled to expect that, in performing their side of the bargain, the lender would not apply rates which were substantially out of line with rates applied by comparable lenders to borrowers in comparable situations to the borrowers. It was contended that the setting of interest rates was a 'contractual performance' within the meaning of *s 3(2)(b)* of *UCTA 1977*.

The Court of Appeal rejected this argument. It said that, in the present case, there was no relevant obligation on the lender, and therefore nothing that could qualify as 'contractual performance' for the purposes of *s 3(2)(b)(i)*: 'Even if that were wrong, by fixing the rate of interest at a particular level the [lender] is not altering the performance of any obligation assumed by it under the contract. Rather, it is altering the performance required of the appellants'.

In practice, the parties to a contract of sale will often reserve the right not to perform upon the happening of certain events. For example, the seller may refuse to deliver until payment has been received, or the buyer may refuse to pay until the seller has delivered. Such a clause is one that seeks to allow no performance at all and hence would be subject to the reasonableness test.

Excluding implied terms   **A2.51**

UCTA 1977 provides that no contract term can exclude or restrict the term as to title implied into contracts for the sale or supply of goods by *SGA 1979*, *SG(IT)A 1973* or *SGSA 1982*.

In the case of the implied terms as to fitness for purpose and satisfactory quality, such terms can be excluded or limited subject to the reasonableness test.

In the case of consumer contracts, identical terms are implied by the 2015 Act which provides that any term seeking to exclude or limit any such term is automatically void. Such a term is arguably also illegal: see the *Ashbourne* case (A2.11).

Misrepresentation   **A2.52**

The *Misrepresentation Act 1967 s 3*, as amended by *UCTA 1977*, provides that any clause seeking to exclude or restrict liability for misrepresentation, or to exclude or restrict any right or remedy available on a misrepresentation, is valid only if it satisfies the requirement of reasonableness under *s 11(1)*, *UCTA 1977*: see *Cleaver v Schyde Investments Ltd* [2011] EWCA Civ 929

Anti-avoidance measures   **A2.53**

Normally, the disputed clause will be set out directly in the contract between the parties. *UCTA 1977*, however, also covers those cases where a contracting party seeks to rely on a clause contained in another contract. If that clause would be caught by the Act had it been contained in the contract between the parties, then it will be caught even though contained in the other contract: *s 10, UCTA 1977*.

Limiting liability to a specific sum   **A2.54**

If liability is limited to a specific sum, a court must also consider:

- the resources which the relevant party could expect to be available for the purposes of meeting the liability should it arise; and
- how far it was open to that party to obtain insurance cover.

Case Example: *Overseas Medical Supplies Ltd v Orient Transport Services Ltd* [1999] 1 All ER (Comm) 981

A contract of carriage limited liability for loss or damage to approximately £600. The contract also stated that, by special agreement in writing, the carrier would accept a greater degree of liability 'upon the customer agreeing to pay the company's additional charges for accepting such increased liability. Details of the company's additional charges will be provided on request'. There was also a clause which provided for insurance cover to be effected if written instructions were given, and that, when effecting such insurance, the carrier would act as agent for the customer using its best endeavours to arrange such insurance. Instructions were given to take out insurance, but these were ignored.

The Court of Appeal held that the clause was unreasonable. The court pointed in particular to the fact that there was no equality of bargaining power; the contract failed to make it clear that the £600 limit would apply if the other party failed to take out insurance, so that there was 'no 'reality of consent' to the effect of the clause'; and that limit was in any event 'derisory'.

Case Example: *The Salvage Association v CAP Financial Services Ltd* **[1995] FSR 654**

The contract contained a limitation clause putting an upper limit of liability at £25,000. The facts disclosed that the respective parties were of equal bargaining power, that the contracts were freely negotiable and that there were other software houses to whom the relevant party could have gone and that the terms of one of the contracts were subject to considerable negotiation. It was also the case in regard to this particular contract, that advice had been sought from solicitors, accountants and insurance brokers. If these were all the relevant facts, the official referee acknowledged that he would have upheld the limitation clauses, noting the position of a party 'well able to look after itself [which] enters into a commercial contract, [and which] willingly accepts the terms of the contract which provide for apportionment of the financial risks ...'

There were, however, other circumstances which led to an opposite conclusion. The figure of £25,000 was entirely arbitrary and bore no relationship to company turnover, the level of insurance cover available, the value of the contract or the financial risk to which the other side was exposed and for which it could not obtain insurance cover. It had also been accepted that the upper limit of £25,000 should be increased to £1 million, and no reason was ever given as to why this had not been applied to these particular contracts.

These factors alone were held enough to justify a finding that the limitation clauses could not be shown to be reasonable. The official referee, however, thought that other factors could be taken into account as supporting this decision. To begin with, there had never been any suggestion by the party seeking to rely on the limitation clauses that they would fail to perform their contractual task. This task was not exceptionally demanding and it was well within the relevant party's range of skills. It was generally believed that the software system would be satisfactorily completed within a very short period of time. It was also the case that the party receiving the services under the contract was unable to obtain insurance against non-performance by the other side at anything like a reasonable cost, if at all. The official referee did add, however, that given the relatively straightforward nature of the task, there was no reason for any particular concern to be felt over the lack of insurance cover. In addition, the party providing the service had the resources to meet its possible liability. It also had insurance cover of £5 million with an excess of £500,000. These several factors reaffirmed the official referee's view that the limitation clauses in question did not satisfy the requirement of reasonableness.

Case Example: *Regus (UK) Ltd v Epcot Solutions Ltd* **[2008] EWCA Civ 361**

A series of exclusion clauses was followed by this clause: 'We will be liable: without limit for personal injury or death; up to a maximum of £1 million (for any one event or series of connected events) for damage to your personal property; up to a maximum equal to 125% of the total fees paid under your agreement up to the date on which the claim in question arises or £50,000 (whichever is the higher), in respect of all other losses, damages, expenses or claims'. The court upheld this term, finding the relevant maxima 'generous'.

The reasonableness test   **A2.55**

Central to the application of *UCTA 1977* is the reasonableness test. A clause challenged under the Act must be shown to be reasonable. The burden of proof, therefore, is on the person seeking to uphold the clause. A number of precedents are set out below, but it must always be remembered that each case must be judged on its individual facts and 'has to be considered in the light of the particular circumstances of the parties in question at the time the contract was made' (*British Fermentation Products Ltd v Compair Reavell Ltd* [1999] 2 All ER (Comm) 389). It is always possible that a clause found reasonable in one case will, because of the different contractual context, be found unreasonable in another.

In applying the reasonableness test, the courts are required by *UCTA 1977* to consider the following guidelines when the exclusion clause relates to any of the terms implied by the *SGA 1979* and the related Acts and is made in a contract with a business – See Schedule 2 ('Guidelines for the Application of Reasonableness Test'):

- the strength of the bargaining position of the parties relative to each other, taking into account (among other things) alternative means by which the customer's requirements could have been met;

- whether the customer received an inducement to agree to the term, or in accepting it had an opportunity of entering into a similar contract with other persons, but without having to accept similar terms;

- whether the customer knew or ought reasonably to have known of the existence and extent of the term (having regard, among other things, to any custom of the trade and any previous course of dealing between the parties);

- where the term excludes or restricts any relevant liability if some condition is not complied with, whether it was reasonable at the time to expect that compliance with the condition would be practicable; and

- whether the goods were manufactured, processed or adapted to the special order of the customer.

Although these guidelines are stated as applicable only to cases involving the implied terms, the courts have stated on many occasions that they consist of the matters which would be taken into account generally when considering whether or not a contract term is reasonable.

The reasonableness test – clause reasonable   **A2.56**

In assessing the reasonableness test in business contracts, the starting point must be the observations in *Photo Production Ltd v Securicor Transport Ltd* [1980] 1 All ER 556 that 'in commercial matters generally, when the parties are not of unequal bargaining power, and when risks are normally borne by insurance, not only is the case for judicial intervention undemonstrated, but there is everything to be said … for leaving the parties free to apportion the risk as they think fit and for respecting their decisions'.

> **Case Example:** *W Photoprint Ltd v Forward Trust Group Ltd* [1993] **12 Tr LR 146**
>
> A clause in a hire purchase contract contained a term to the effect that the customer had examined the goods and accepted that 'they are in every respect satisfactory and suitable for the purpose for which they are required and that he has relied on his own skill and judgement in choosing the goods'. The agreement also stated that, subject to the requirement of reasonableness, the defendants did 'not let the goods subject to any undertaking express or implied whether statutory or otherwise save the condition as to title.' These clauses were considered to be reasonable in all the circumstances of the case.

> **Case Example:** *British Fermentation Products Ltd v Compair Reavell Ltd* **[1999] 2 All ER (Comm) 389**
>
> The contract contained these terms:

- If within twelve months after delivery there shall appear in the goods any defect which shall arise under proper use from faulty materials, workmanship, or design (other than a design made, furnished, or specified by the purchaser for which the vendor had disclaimed responsibility), and the purchaser shall give notice thereof in writing to the vendor, the vendor shall, provided that the defective goods or defective parts thereof have been returned to the vendor if he shall have so required, make good the defects either by repair or, at the option of the vendor, by the supply of a replacement. The vendor shall refund the cost of carriage on the return of the defective goods or parts and shall deliver any repaired or replacement goods or parts as if [the contract terms as to delivery] applied.

- The vendor's liability under this Condition or under Condition 5 (Rejection and Replacement) shall be accepted by the purchaser in lieu of any warranty or condition implied by law as to the quality or fitness for any particular purpose of the goods and save as provided in this Condition the vendor shall not be under any liability to the purchaser (whether in contract, tort or otherwise) for any defects in the goods or for any damage, loss, death or injury (other than death or personal injury caused by the negligence of the vendor as defined in *section 1* of the *Unfair Contract Terms Act 1977*) resulting from such defects or from any work done in connection therewith.'

The court upheld these clauses, referring to their 'good business sense'.

Case Example: *BTE Auto Repairs v H&H Finance Factors Ltd* **(unreported, 26 January 1990)**

This involved a contract for the lease of machinery. The relevant clause was as follows:

'The lessee has satisfied himself as to the condition of the goods and acknowledges that no condition or warranty whatsoever has been or is given by the lessor as to their fitness for any purpose and all conditions or warranties express or implied and whether by statute or otherwise are expressly excluded and delivery of the goods to the lessor shall be conclusive evidence that the lessee has examined them and found them to be completely in accordance with the description overleaf, in good order and condition, fit for any purpose for which they may be required and in every way satisfactory. The lessee shall not be entitled to any remission of rental in respect of any period during which the goods or any of them are unserviceable and the lessor shall not be liable to provide the lessee with any replacement goods during any such period or at all. The lessor shall use all reasonable efforts to obtain for the lessee the benefit of the manufacturers guarantees and warranties (if any) given to the lessor'.

The Court of Appeal upheld the clauses.

Case Example: *Frans Maas (UK) Ltd v Samsung Electronics (UK) Ltd* **[2004] EWHC 1502**

The defendant counterclaimed to recover over £2 million arising from the theft of 25,738 Samsung mobile phones belonging to it from the warehouse of the claimant. Clause 27(A) of the terms of the British International Freight Association, which applied to the bailment between the parties and permitted the claimant to limit its 'liability howsoever arising', covered a loss by theft caused by the wilful default of the claimant's employees. It was held that this clause satisfied the requirement of reasonableness under *UCTA 1977*. There had been no inequality of bargaining power, terms such as this one were routinely used in the freight industry, and it was open to the defendant to agree with the claimant to a higher limit upon payment of additional charges, pursuant to clause 27(D) of the BIFA terms.

Case Example: *Axa Sun Life Services plc v (Campbell Martin Ltd) and others* **[2011] EWCA Civ 133**

The appellant company had appointed the respondents to act as its authorised representatives in providing insurance products to customers. The terms of appointment were set out in a standard form agreement. Under the agreement, the appellant could claw back commission paid to the respondent if customers cancelled their products and, upon termination of the agreement, the respondent was required to repay business benefit allowances provided by the appellants. Under clause 1.6 of Sch 4 any statement signed by the appellant about the monies the respondent owed would, save for manifest error, be binding. In determining whether these clauses were reasonable, the Court of Appeal said that the starting point was that the agreements were made between commercial organisations and in a commercial context. The respondent would have been expected to have read the agreement. Furthermore, the contractual provisions in issue were not unusual in the insurance industry; they were standard terms. Accordingly, the respondent 'knew or ought reasonably to have known of the existence and extent of the terms in question'. In relation to the Entire Agreement Clauses, these gave both sides certainty as to the terms of their contract; it was therefore a reasonable provision to have been included in the agreement, clause 1.6 of Sch 4 was also a reasonable provision. Appointed representatives could be expected to keep track of commission earnings and claw backs, and therefore would be able to demonstrate that any statement signed by the appellant for the purposes of clause1.6, if incorrect, was subject to a manifest error.

Case Example: *FG Wilson Engineering Ltd v John Holt & Co (Liverpool) Ltd* **[2012] EWHC 2477**

The applicant manufactured and sold generator sets and spare parts worldwide. It had supplied generators and spare parts to Holt for export to Nigeria. Holt had ordered the generators and parts from using the applicant's online ordering system. The sales were subject to the applicant's terms and conditions. The trading terms agreed between the parties allowed Holt extended credit. Invoices were not paid and a repayment plan was discussed. Holt contended that the discussions resulted in a binding repayment agreement. Holt was unable to meet the repayment terms and the applicant brought proceedings claiming US$12.6 million, the majority of which was for generators and spare parts supplied. The goods had been sold on by Holt to its Nigerian subsidiary. Holt claimed that the applicant had supplied generators to others within Nigeria over a number of years, in breach of exclusivity obligations owed to Holt. The applicant said that the no set-off clause in its terms and conditions meant that Holt could not set off claims for breach of the distributor agreement and/or for breach of the alleged repayment agreement against the applicant's claim under the contracts of sale.

Holt submitted that the no set-off clause did not satisfy the test of reasonableness.

The court said that the applicant had given reasonable notice of its terms and conditions. No set-off clauses were not unusual in standard terms and conditions. The no set-off clause was not particularly unusual or onerous and satisfied the test of reasonableness. The fact that it was wide enough to cover admitted credits was not of itself a bar to a finding of reasonableness. It was not unfair or unreasonable to require Holt to pay the price for products in full without any deduction for what was a mere claim, however arguable, even if for fraud or intentional wrongdoing. The parties' bargaining power was equal. The no set-off clause satisfied the test of reasonableness.

Case Example; *Allen Fabrications Ltd v ASD Ltd and others* **[2012] EWHC 2213**

A boat repair and maintenance company (B) had subcontracted another company (P) to supply and construct a rigid steel platform. P subcontracted the supply of the constituent elements of the platform to F, who in turn subcontracted the supply of grating and clips to S. In 2006 a part of the grating on the platform gave way and one of B's employees suffered extremely serious head injuries. B did not file a defence to a claim, and damages of around £7 million were agreed. B in turn brought negligence proceedings against various parties, including P and F, and sought contribution from them. F in turn alleged that the defendant (S) had breached tortious and contractual obligations owed to F. S denied it owed F any contractual or tortious duties, and sought to rely on various limitation or exclusion clauses under cl.8 of its standard terms and conditions, which it claimed had been variously incorporated into an agreement between it and F. The preliminary issues were: (i) whether S's standard terms and conditions had been incorporated; (ii) the effect of the limitation and exclusion clauses, cl.8.6 and cl.8.8, on F's claim; (iii) whether those clauses were reasonable under the *Unfair Contract Terms Act 1977*.

It was held that, although there was no explicit evidence that F, in applying for a credit facility with S, had signed a written application form which contained an acknowledgement and acceptance of S's terms of trading as the only ones governing sales contracts, the clear likelihood was that F did sign such a form. It followed that F had expressly agreed to be bound by those terms; it had not been suggested that a later version of the terms had been materially different. Accordingly, the terms had been expressly incorporated into the agreement. If wrong on that point, the terms had been incorporated via a course of dealing between the parties where F had dealt with S on over 250 occasions, had received the actual terms on advice notes and there had been a clear reference to the terms on invoices which would have been seen by F. Furthermore, it could not be said that the terms limiting and excluding liability were unusual in the industry: F knew that suppliers like S had to protect themselves by insurance and had used such terms themselves. On that footing, the terms were not onerous or unusual ones that abrogated statutory rights so as to require that their existence be specifically brought to F's attention. S only had to satisfy the normal 'notice' test for incorporation and course of dealing, which it was conceded it did. Accordingly, whether by express acceptance under the credit facility application, or through a course of dealing, the terms were incorporated. Unless the relevant clauses were invalid as unreasonable under the Unfair Contract Terms Act, their effect was to limit F's claim to the price of the goods. Clauses 8.6 and 8.8 were reasonable. Both parties were substantial commercial entities; the fact that both had insurance in place to protect themselves against such claims as those made by B and/or P meant that insurance was one of the ways in which a party in F's position protected itself against the recognised risk of buying goods from suppliers like S who had such clauses. Other factors which went to the reasonableness of the clauses were: the industry prevalence of such terms; their commonplace nature, which meant that F was aware there would be such terms, coupled with the fact that F had even more restrictive terms; F's conscious acceptance of the risks inherent in buying on such terms in order to get the best price amounted to F's real consent to those clauses. The clauses did not amount to a 'blanket exclusion' and were therefore not unreasonable on that basis. F could not show that there was industry non-reliance on such clauses and that they were therefore unreasonable

See too *Rohlig (UK) Ltd v Rock Unique Ltd* [2011] EWCA Civ 18.

Trade association terms   A2.57

It has been said that when a clause is in common use, and is well known in the trade following comprehensive discussions between reputable and representative bodies 'mindful of the considerations involved, the likelihood is that a clause will be held to be reasonable', because the clause 'reflects a general view as to what is reasonable in the trade concerned' (*Overland Shoes Ltd v Schenker Ltd* [1998] 1 Lloyd's Rep 498).

The reasonableness test-clause not reasonable   A2.58

It should always be remembered that the observation made in the *Photo Production Ltd* case (see A2.55 above) does no more than raise a presumption, at most, that a clause in a business–to–business contract will be upheld. Every case must be judged on its own facts.

> **Case Example:** *Edmund Murray Ltd v BSP International Foundations Ltd* **33 Con LR 1, CA**
>
> A contract for the supply of a rig was subject to a term providing that, while the supplier would make available to the buyer any rights afforded by his own supplier, this was to be in place of 'any other conditions, guarantees, liabilities or warranties expressed or implied statutory or otherwise and in no event shall the seller be liable for any loss, injury or damage however caused...' The Court of Appeal held this was not reasonable.
>
> A further clause in the contract excluded liability for loss of profit or for any other category of loss however caused, and also provided that the suppliers were not to be liable for damage arising from any 'stoppage or breakdown of the goods or in any other way from the performance of the goods in operation or any damage to the plant'. This too was held to be unreasonable.
>
> The provision in the contract whereby the suppliers agreed to repair or replace the goods was made subject to certain conditions, such as notification to the suppliers and to the return of the 'defective goods or part or parts thereof... satisfactorily packed, at the risk of the buyers, carriage paid, to the sellers' works, or to such other place as the sellers may direct'. This too was unreasonable.

> **Case Example:** *The Salvage Association v CAP Financial Services Ltd* **[1995] FSR 654**
>
> A limitation clause put a limit on liability, in a contract relating to the supply of computer software, at £25,000. This limit was arbitrary and there had been suggestions of raising it to £1m (these suggestions were not

acted on). It was also the case that the service to be provided was relatively straightforward. The recipient of the service could not obtain insurance cover, while the supplier could. The clause was held to be unreasonable.

Case Example: *Lease Management Services Ltd v Purnell Secretarial Services Ltd* **[1994] CCLR 127**

A contract for the lease of a photocopier contained a clause which offered to obtain for the lessee the benefits of any manufacturer's guarantee, but which excluded all liability:

> '…in respect of any conditions, warranties or representations relating to the condition of the equipment or to its merchantability or suitability or fitness for the particular purpose for which it may be required whether such conditions, warranties or representations are express or implied and whether arising under the agreement or under any prior agreement or in oral or written statements made by or on behalf of the lessor or its agents in the course of negotiations in which the lessee or its representatives may have been concerned prior to the agreement'.

Finding the clause unreasonable, the court said:

> 'We would like to think that the days of such blanket clauses, daunting to anyone and incomprehensible to an ordinary customer, are passed. One would hope that finance companies and suppliers of expensive equipment no longer use pre-printed standard conditions as a means to avoid liabilities otherwise attaching to them for breach of pre-sale representations or breach of implied warranties'.

Case Example: *Motours Ltd v Euroball (West Kent) Ltd* **[2003] EWHC 614**

A clause excluded liability for indirect loss even if caused by negligence, recklessness or breach of contractual duty to take reasonable care. The circumstances which were or ought reasonably to have been known or in the contemplation of the parties when they entered that agreement included the crucial importance of the telephone system being installed to M's business, that M needed six lines and would probably suffer loss of business and hence loss of profit if W did not provide those and that M was entirely dependent on W to provide the service for which it had contracted. The parties also knew or ought to have known that it was a very competitive market and that there would be some limitation on W's liability in order to protect its commercial interests. However, it would not have been in M's contemplation or knowledge that W would exclude all liability for all consequential loss, particularly if caused by W's negligence. The fact that M had little choice and that these were common clauses did not mean that they were fair and reasonable. W did not expect or encourage the customer to discuss or negotiate the terms on the back of the order form which were very difficult to read. W was a very large provider of telephone services and had substantial financial resources and capital. In approaching M with a financial incentive W had the financial strength and superior bargaining position. In the circumstances W had failed to establish that the exclusion clause was fair and reasonable.

Case Example: *Axa Sun Life Services plc v (Campbell Martin Ltd) and others* **[2011] EWCA Civ 133**

In that case, discussed above in relation to reasonable clauses, a further clause precluded the respondent from asserting any credit, set-off or counterclaim against the appellant. The Court of Appeal said that the clause, which prevented an appointed representative who was owed commission from being able to set-off what it was owed against its liability was, in the absence of any explanation of the appellant's requirement for that clause, unreasonable.

Case Example: *Hirtenstein v Hill Dickinson LLP* **[2014] EWHC 2711**

'Hill Dickinson LLP's liability for any one claim or series of connected claims shall not exceed £3 million.' Purchase had to be made at great speed with no chance of switching solicitors. The court also took note of Paragraph 2.07 of the Solicitor's Code of Conduct 2007, which was applicable at the time, and which permitted a firm of solicitors to limit its liability, provided that such limitation: (a) was not below the minimum level of insurance cover required (which was £3 million); (b) was brought to the client's attention; and (c) was in writing. The second of these conditions was not complied with by Hill Dickinson and reliance on clause 15 of their standard terms to limit their liability was therefore a breach of the solicitors' professional code. The court said that that did not automatically make the purported limitation of liability unreasonable for the purpose of the Unfair Contract Terms Act, but it was 'a powerful indication'.

Cases for Further Information

Green (RW) Ltd v Cade Bros Farms [1978] 1 Lloyd's Rep 602; *Walker v Boyle* [1982] 1 WLR 495; *Josef Marton v Southwestern General Property* (unreported, 6 May 1982); *George Mitchell (Chesterhall) Ltd v Finney Lock Seeds Ltd* [1983] 2 AC 803; *Fillite (Runcorn) Ltd v APV Pasilac Ltd* (The Buyer, July 1995); *Flamar Interocean v Denmac Ltd* [1990] 1 Lloyd's Rep 434; *AEG (UK) Ltd v Logic Resources* [1996] CLC 265; *McCullagh v Lane Fox & Partners Ltd* [1996] PNLR 205; *Danka Rentals Ltd v Xi Software* (1998) 17 TrLR 74;

South West Water Services Ltd v International Computers Ltd (1999) BLR 420; Horace Holman Group Ltd v Sherwood International (unreported, 12 April 2000); Nippon Yusen Kaisha Ltd v Scandia Steam Navigation Ltd [2000] 1 All ER (Comm) 700; Moore v Yakeley (2001) BLR 322; Messer UK Ltd v Britvic Soft Drinks Ltd [2002] EWCA Civ 548; SAM Business Systems v Hedley [2002] EWHC 2733; Expo Fabricks (UK) Ltd v Naughty Clothing Co Ltd (21 July 2003); Granville Oil & Chemicals Ltd v Davies Turner & Co Ltd [2003] 1 All ER (Comm);819 Hi-Flyers Ltd v Linde Gas UK Ltd [2004] EWHC 105; Deutsche Bank AG v Sebastian Holdings Inc [2013] EWHC 3463; Lloyd and Lloyd v Browning and Browning [2013] EWCA Civ1637; West v Ian Finlay and Associates [2014] EWCA Civ 316.

The Consumer Rights Act 2015   A2.59

The Act repeals and replaces the *Unfair Terms in Consumer Contracts Regulations 1999 (SI 1999/2083)*. The Act, like the Regulations goes beyond simply controlling exclusion clauses. Instead, the Act (which applies only where the seller or supplier is a business and the other party a consumer) applies to consumer contracts and condemns as unfair – and hence unenforceable – any term which 'contrary to the requirements of good faith.... causes a significant imbalance in the parties' rights and obligations arising under the contract, to the detriment of the consumer': s.62 CRA 2015. It has been established that as well as contracts for the sale and supply of goods and services, the Regulations and hence the Act also apply to contracts relating to land: *Khatun v London Borough of Newham* [2004] EWCA Civ 55. An unfair term of a consumer contract is not binding on the consumer: *s 62(1), CRA 2015*.

Meaning of 'good faith'   A2.60

In *Director General of Fair Trading v First National Bank* [2002] 1 All ER 97, the House of Lords interpreted 'good faith' to mean a duty to deal fairly and openly. Openness required that the terms should be expressed fully, clearly and legibly, containing no concealed pitfalls or traps. Appropriate prominence should be given to terms which might operate disadvantageously to the customer. Fair dealing required that a supplier should not, whether deliberately or unconsciously, take advantage of the consumer's necessity, indigence, lack of experience, unfamiliarity with the subject matter of the contract, weak bargaining position or any other factors listed in or analogous to those listed in *Schedule 2* to the Act (see A2.60 below).

The indicative list   A2.61

Schedule 2 of Part 1 to *CRA 2015* contains an indicative and non-exhaustive list of terms which may be regarded as unfair: *s 63, CRA 2015*. The list is headed by examples of exclusion clauses as follows:

1.   A term which has the object or effect of excluding or limiting the trader's liability in the event of the death of or personal injury to the consumer resulting from an act or omission of the trader.

2.   A term which has the object or effect of inappropriately excluding or limiting the legal rights of the consumer in relation to the trader or another party in the event of total or partial non-performance or inadequate performance by the trader of any of the contractual obligations, including the option of offsetting a debt owed to the trader against any claim which the consumer may have against the trader.

3.   A term which has the object or effect of making an agreement binding on the consumer in a case where the provision of services by the trader is subject to a condition whose realisation depends on the trader's will alone.

4.   A term which has the object or effect of permitting the trader to retain sums paid by the consumer where the consumer decides not to conclude or perform the contract, without providing for the consumer to receive compensation of an equivalent amount from the trader where the trader is the party cancelling the contract.

5.   A term which has the object or effect of requiring that, where the consumer decides not to conclude or perform the contract, the consumer must pay the trader a disproportionately high sum in compensation or for services which have not been supplied.

6.   A term which has the object or effect of requiring a consumer who fails to fulfil his obligations under the contract to pay a disproportionately high sum in compensation.

7.   A term which has the object or effect of authorising the trader to dissolve the contract on a discretionary basis where the same facility is not granted to the consumer, or permitting the trader to retain the sums paid for services not yet supplied by the trader where it is the trader who dissolves the contract.

8.   A term which has the object or effect of enabling the trader to terminate a contract of indeterminate duration without reasonable notice except where there are serious grounds for doing so.

9.   A term which has the object or effect of automatically extending a contract of fixed duration where the consumer does not indicate otherwise, when the deadline fixed for the consumer to express a desire not to extend the contract is unreasonably early.

10. A term which has the object or effect of irrevocably binding the consumer to terms with which the consumer has had

no real opportunity of becoming acquainted before the conclusion of the contract.

11. A term which has the object or effect of enabling the trader to alter the terms of the contract unilaterally without a valid reason which is specified in the contract.

12. A term which has the object or effect of permitting the trader to determine the characteristics of the subject matter of the contract after the consumer has become bound by it.

13. A term which has the object or effect of enabling the trader to alter unilaterally without a valid reason any characteristics of the goods, digital content or services to be provided.

14. A term which has the object or effect of giving the trader the discretion to decide the price payable under the contract after the consumer has become bound by it, where no price or method of determining the price is agreed when the consumer becomes bound.

15. A term which has the object or effect of permitting a trader to increase the price of goods, digital content or services without giving the consumer the right to cancel the contract if the final price is too high in relation to the price agreed when the contract was concluded.

16. A term which has the object or effect of giving the trader the right to determine whether the goods, digital content or services supplied are in conformity with the contract, or giving the trader the exclusive right to interpret any term of the contract.

17. A term which has the object or effect of limiting the trader's obligation to respect commitments undertaken by the trader's agents or making the trader's commitments subject to compliance with a particular formality.

18. A term which has the object or effect of obliging the consumer to fulfil all of the consumer's obligations where the trader does not perform the trader's obligations.

19. A term which has the object or effect of allowing the trader to transfer the trader's rights and obligations under the contract, where this may reduce the guarantees for the consumer, without the consumer's agreement.

20. A term which has the object or effect of excluding or hindering the consumer's right to take legal action or exercise any other legal remedy, in particular by:-

    (a) requiring the consumer to take disputes exclusively to arbitration not covered by legal provisions,

    (b) unduly restricting the evidence available to the consumer, or

(c)   imposing on the consumer a burden of proof which, according to the applicable law, should lie with another party to the contract.

Fairness   **A2.62**

In applying the test of fairness, *CRA 2015* requires the court to take into account the nature of the subject matter of the contract, In addition the court must take into account all the circumstances existing when the particular term was agreed and all the other terms of the contract or of any other contract on which it depends. Note; the cases cited below were decided under the Regulations but remain valid under the 2015 Act.

> **Case Example:** *Director General of Fair Trading v First National Bank* **[2002] 1 All ER 97**
>
> A credit agreement provided that the lender was entitled, on default of an instalment, to demand payment of the balance and interest outstanding. It further provided that interest on the amount that became payable would be charged at the contract rate until payment, after as well as before judgment, and that such obligation was to be independent of and not to merge with the judgment. In the absence of such a provision, a lender seeking to enforce an agreement in the county court would have been unable to recover post-judgment interest.
>
> The House of Lords, reversing the Court of Appeal, held that this term was not unfair. The essential bargain was that the bank would make funds available to the borrower which the latter would repay, with interest, over time. Neither party could suppose that the bank would willingly forgo any part of the principal money or interest. If the bank thought that this was the likely outcome, it would not lend. The House of Lords also said that the borrower's obligation to repay the principal money in full with interest was very clearly and unambiguously expressed in the conditions of the contract.

> **Case Example:** *Bairstow Eves London Central Ltd v Smith* **[2004] EWHC 263**
>
> An estate agency contract contained a term providing for 1.5% commission if paid within ten days of completion, failing which commission was charged at 3%.
>
> The county court judge had ruled the provision as to the payment of 3% commission unfair: 'The clause is a trap for consumers. It can operate where there is simply a misunderstanding between them and their solicitors, perhaps not even their fault, as indeed it was not their fault here. It can operate where, as here, the option was exercised effectively

when just £387 [out of a commission of £2925.75] was outstanding ... this is not a good standard of commercial morality or practice ... it falls comfortably within the Regulations, and it follows that the provisions of the marketing agreement which require a 3% commission to be paid are not binding on the consumer'. There was no appeal against this finding.

Case Example: *UK Housing Alliance (North West) Ltd v Francis* **[2010] EWCA Civ 117**

The appellant appealed against a decision that the respondent was not required to pay him the sum of £37,500. The appellant had sold his house for £125,000 to the respondent, whose business it was to buy residential properties and then lease them back to their former owners. The sum of £87,500 was payable on completion, while the balance of £37,500 (the final payment) was due on the expiry of ten years and the giving up of possession by the appellant. If the appellant terminated his tenancy at any time during the first six years, the final payment would not become payable. If he terminated it thereafter, he would receive a percentage of the final payment on a sliding scale depending on the date of termination. If, however, the respondent terminated the tenancy pursuant to any right to do so under the tenancy agreement, the sale contract provided that the appellant would cease to have any right to receive the final payment. The respondent terminated the tenancy for non-payment of rent. The clause was upheld.

Case Example: *Chesterton Global Ltd v Finney* **(Lambeth County Court, 30 April 2010)**

The claimant, a provider of property management services, sought payment of renewal commission under the terms of a contract it had made with the defendant landlord. The latter counterclaimed for payment of renewal commission that it had previously paid the claimant. He stated that he had bought the property to lease it, with the hope that he would profit on the capital and that the rent would pay the mortgage interest. Under the contract, the claimant was to find a tenant.

The contract stated that 10% of the total rent payable was due 'at the commencement of each tenancy and/or renewal'. A provision concerning renewed tenancies stated that commission was payable at 10% of the total rent. The claimant found a tenant and charged 10% of the rent payable for the initial term of the tenancy. The defendant agreed that the claimant had been entitled to do so.

The tenant, by signing a renewal contract, later exercised an option to renew the tenancy and pay increased rent. The claimant invoiced the defendant for renewal commission of 10% of the increased rent. The latter stated that he had queried that invoice but stated that the claimant had informed him that the fee was provided for in the contract and there was nothing that the defendant could do about it. Accordingly, he had paid that commission. The tenancy was later renewed again and the claimant invoiced for the commission but the defendant refused to pay it.

The clause was judged unfair.

Case Example; *West v Ian Finlay and Associates* **[2013] EWHC 868, [2014] EWCA Civ 316**

W had engaged F to change the layout of the house's ground and lower floors and agreed a specification of work on the basis that they would arrange the procurement of certain discrete parts of the work themselves, including a new kitchen. The contract included a net contribution clause providing that F's liability for loss or damage would be limited to the amount it would be reasonable to pay in relation to the contractual responsibilities of other contractors appointed by W. F introduced them to the contractors (X) subsequently engaged to install the kitchen. When W moved into the house after six weeks, by which time all the work was supposed to have been completed, they found extensive damp in the lower floor. Experts were called in and concluded that X had not carried out any proper waterproofing. An independent check of the mechanical services and electrical installations (M&E) revealed serious problems and led to a decision that the newly installed M&E services would have to be removed and replaced. In the course of remedial works, it was discovered that floor slabs installed by X in the lower ground floor were defective, requiring removal and replacement. X became insolvent, and W sought to recover from the costs of dealing with the problems and various consequential losses from F.

F contended that even if it had discovered the defective workmanship, it would never have been rectified and completed by X because of its poor financial position, and that the net contribution clause operated to limit its liability. W denied that the clause had that effect and questioned whether it was fair and reasonable.

It was held that in a contractual claim for negligence against a construction professional, a claimant had first to establish what would have happened if the professional had in fact exercised proper care and skill; if the claimant established that, had proper care and skill been used, he would have proceeded with the project in accordance with the professional's design, then the measure of damages would be the cost of remedying the defects, less any credit for higher costs which would have been payable for a proper design in the first place, In adopting the design it had for the waterproofing of the new slabs, F fell below the standard of a reasonably competent architect. The cost to W of carrying out the proper dampproofing work that should have been recommended was a loss flowing directly from F's negligence. W had been entitled to seek expert advice and adopt reasonable measures to deal with it. From correspondence with X, F should have been put on notice that the pipework in the kitchen was not being installed in accordance with the contract and taken steps to resolve the problem (para 164). The M&E installation had not been fitted in accordance with the specification and F had fallen below the standard to be expected of a reasonably competent architect in failing to notice that poor quality or take any steps to remedy it at an early stage, without additional delay or expense. Those were therefore defects for which F was liable to W. The remedial work was necessary as a direct result of F's breaches of duty. W were also entitled to recover the cost of a new kitchen. Given its breaches of duty, the onus was on F to show that even if it had acted with reasonable care the damage would probably still have occurred. On the evidence, F failed to establish that X would not have completed the works; its conduct was not that of a contractor who did not intend to complete them, and its financial position at the relevant time was not such that it never could have completed the contract. In the context of the contract's factual background, the net contribution clause did not apply so as to limit F's liability to W in a situation where X was the other party liable. In order to satisfy the test for unfairness under, a term had to be contrary to the requirements of good faith and cause a significant imbalance in the party's rights and obligations arising under the contact to the detriment of the consumer: it could not be said that F was guilty of any lack of good faith. W were entitled to recover damages in respect of the remedial work and various defects in the property, with interest awarded on actual expenditure at 7% over base rate/ It was appropriate to award W general damages for inconvenience, distress and discomfort, excluding damages for the stress and vexation of litigation. They were awarded a total of £14,000 general damages.

The High Court had held that F had breached its professional duties. It found that the losses were caused to some extent by X's breach of contract, but held that the net contribution clause did not limit F's liability to W where the other party liable was the main contractor.

The Court of Appeal reversed the High Court. The judge had erred in his construction of the NCC. He held that the parties' knowledge that W would instruct a number of specialist contractors directly meant that they should be taken to have intended the words referring to the persons to be 'appointed by [W]' to refer only to those persons appointed directly by W, and not to the main contractor appointed through F's agency. That placed too much reliance on that aspect of the contextual background. The first consideration in any construction exercise was to consider the normal meaning of the words. In the instant case, the normal meaning of the words was clear. There was no limitation on the words 'other consultants, contractors and specialists appointed by [W]', and they had to be taken to mean any such persons, including any main contractor ultimately appointed, excepting F. The NCC was not therefore ambiguous. It had a clear meaning and the relevant factual matrix did not lead to the conclusion that the parties should be taken to have used the wrong language to express their agreement. The NCC did grant F a beneficial limitation of liability and impose a corresponding disadvantage on W. It also imposed a disadvantageous risk on W, namely the risk of the insolvency of the contractors. It also forced W to bring proceedings against any defaulting contractor who might be jointly and severally liable with F, and to await the outcome of any contribution proceedings before obtaining full satisfaction. Contrary to F's submissions, it was the NCC which created the imbalance in the parties' rights under the contract, to W's detriment, as it reduced F's liability in the event of it being jointly and severally liable with a contractor. F's failure to draw W's attention to the NCC and its effect, and the particular formulation of the clause, were factors that weighed in the balance against a finding that its inclusion satisfied the requirements of good faith. However, the openness of the presentation of the clause, F's fair dealing in relation to it and the reasonable equality of bargaining power weighed in favour of a finding that its inclusion satisfied the requirement of good faith. Weighing those factors, the imbalance caused by the NCC was not significant and the NCC was not properly to be regarded as so weighted as to tilt the parties' rights and obligations under the contract significantly in F's favour, or as contrary to the requirement of good faith. The contention that the NCC was not binding on W was rejected. Were in an equal bargaining position with F and, although they received no inducement to agree to the NCC, they could have re-negotiated it, gone to another architect or even protected themselves from the risk posed by the NCC by some other commercial route. They should reasonably have known that the NCC existed, as it was prominently placed on the third page of the agreement. The NCC satisfied the requirement of reasonableness within the meaning of the 1977 Act and was, therefore, an effective limitation on F's liability. The NCC was a valid and binding clause and should have been given effect.

Cases for Further Information

Falco Finance Ltd v Michael Gough [1999] CCLR 16; *Murphy v Kindlance* (Consumer Law Today, November 1996); *Gosling v Burrard-Lucas* (4 November 1998); *Broadwater Manor School v Davis* (8 January 1999); *Lowell Products v Legg and Carver* [2003] BLR 452; *Westminster Building Co Ltd v Beckingham* [2004] EWHC 138; *Governor and Company of Bank of Scotland v Singh* (17 June 2005); *Ofir Scheps v Fine Art Logistic Ltd* [2007] EWHC 541; *Governors of the Peabody Trust Ltd v Reeve* [2008] EG 116 (CS); *UK Housing Alliance (North West) Ltd v Francis* [2010] EWCA Civ 117; *Deutsche Bank (Suisse) SA v Khan* [2013] EWHC 482; *AJ Building and Plastering Ltd v Turner and others* [2013] EWHC 484.

Core terms   **A2.63**

The *CRA 2015* provides that a term is not subject to an assessment of its fairness if it specifies the main subject matter of the contract; or if the assessment relates the appropriateness of the price payable under the contract by comparison with any goods, services or digital content: *s 64(1), CRA 2015*.

As well as satisfying these requirements, term must be 'transparent and prominent': *s 64(2), CRA 2015* and *s 68, CRA 2015*. In turn, in order to meet this requirement, the term must be in 'plain and intelligible language' and, if written, legible: *s 64(3), CRA 2015*. A term is prominent if brought to the consumer's attention in such a way that the average consumer would be aware of it: *s 64(4), CRA 2015*.

The Regulations referred only to 'plain and intelligible language'. The further refinements added by the *CRA 2015* reflect how the Regulations had been interpreted rather than bringing about any change in the law. Accordingly, the cases below remain valid precedents.

> **Case Example:** *Director General of Fair Trading v First National Bank* **[2002] 1 All ER 97**
>
> It was held that the terms referred to above were not a core provision. It did not concern the adequacy of the interest earned by the bank as its remuneration, but was designed instead to ensure that its entitlement to interest did not come to an end on the entry of judgment. It was an ancillary provision, not one concerned with the adequacy of the bank's remuneration for the services supplied.

> **Case Example:** *Bairstow Eves London Central Ltd v Smith* **[2004] EWHC 263**
>
> As noted above, the court had ruled on the fairness of the term. The court had further said that, before it could give any such ruling, it had first to be determined whether the fairness test applied at all, and this raised the question whether the relevant terms were a core provision. The court said that this issue turned on the question:
>
> (1)   Did the agreement provide for a 3% rate with the sellers having the option, but no obligation, to pay 1.5%; or
>
> (2)   Did the agreement place the sellers under an obligation to pay a price of 1.5% with a default provision, exercisable at the option of the agency, to insist on a payment of 3%?
>
> If it were the former, then the term would be a core provision; if the latter, then it would fall to be judged on its fairness.

The court held that it was clear on the evidence that the parties contemplated that the second alternative was the case, and that was for the following reasons:

(a)   The branch manager had recognised that, in the then state of the market, it would not have obtained business had 3% been the commission rate.

(b)   It was not disputed that the negotiations had focused exclusively on the 1.5%.

(c)   The parties had proceeded on the basis that the commission would be paid within ten days. They had no reason to suppose otherwise. The completion monies would of necessity be available from day one of the period.

Furthermore, the fact that the 3% was stated to be payable only at the agency's option militated against the 3% being the contract price. In addition, the provision as to interest being payable assumed an obligation to pay the 1.5% commission in full within the ten-day period.

The existence of the interest provision was not appropriate to the idea that payment of the 1.5% commission was only an option on the part of the sellers. The provision charging 3% was not therefore a core provision and its fairness had to be judged.

Case Example: *Office of Fair Trading v Abbey National & others* [2009] UKSC 6

The charges imposed by the banks, and which were at the heart of the case, comprised unpaid item charges, paid item charges, overdraft excess charges and guaranteed paid item charges (the relevant charges). These were held to be core provisions. The Supreme Court said that there could be 'no justification for excluding from the application of [the rules as to core provisions] any term as to price or remuneration on the ground that it was an 'ancillary or incidental price or remuneration' if it is possible to identify such price or remuneration as being paid in exchange for services, even if the services are fringe or optional extras'. See too the *Ashbourne* case: A2.11.

Case Example: *Árpád Kásler and Hajnalka Káslerné Rábai v OTP Jelzálogbank Zrt* (European Court of Justice; 30 April 2014)

Mr Kásler and Ms Káslerné Rábai concluded a contract for a mortgage denominated in a foreign currency with a Hungarian bank. The bank granted the borrowers a loan of 14 400 000 Hungarian Forints (HUF) (approximately €46 867).

The contract stipulated that the fixing in Swiss francs of the amount of the loan was to be made on the basis of the buying rate of exchange of that currency applied by the bank on the day the funds were advanced. In accordance with that term, the amount of the loan was fixed at CHF 94 240.84. However, under the contract, the amount in Hungarian forints of each monthly instalment to be paid was to be determined, on the day before the due-date, on the basis of the rate of exchange applied by the bank to the sale of Swiss francs.

Mr and Mrs Kásler brought an action before the Hungarian court challenging the term, which authorises the bank to calculate the monthly instalments due on the basis of the selling rate of exchange of the Swiss franc. They rely on the unfairness of that term, in so far as it provides, for the purpose of repayment of the loan, for the application of a rate different from that used when the loan was made available.

The Court stated that a term defining the main subject matter of the contract was exempt from an assessment of its unfairness only if it was in plain, intelligible language. In that connection, the Court said that that requirement was not limited to clarity and intelligibility from a purely structural and grammatical point of view. The point was that the loan contract must set out in a transparent fashion the reason for and the particularities of the mechanism for converting the foreign currency. That meant it was for the national court to determine whether the average consumer, who was reasonably well informed and reasonably observant and circumspect, on the basis of the promotional material and information provided by the lender in the course of negotiating the loan contract, would not only be aware of the existence of the difference between the selling rate of exchange and the buying rate of exchange of a foreign currency, but also be able to assess the consequences arising from the application of the selling rate of exchange for the calculation of the repayments and for the total cost of the sum borrowed.

Case Example: *Foster-Burnell v Lloyds Bank*: **Taunton CC; 21 June 2014**

Oliver Foster-Burnell sued Lloyds TSB for the return of bank charges levied against his current account. Deputy District Judge Stockdale held that despite the Supreme Court judgment, the unarranged overdraft charges levied on Mr Foster-Burnell were contrary to the requirement of good faith under the 1999 Regulations. The bank was ordered to reimburse the claimant £743 in charges plus interest. The court also awarded the claimant non-pecuniary damages of £1000 for a related incorrect default to his credit file.

Plain, intelligible language   **A2.64**

The Regulations provided that if a term was not expressed in plain, intelligible language, any doubt as to the meaning of the term will be interpreted in favour of the consumer.

Case Example: *Bankers Insurance Co Ltd v South* **[2003] EWHC 380**

The following clause in an insurance policy was held plain and intelligible. It required the 'reporting in writing to us as soon as possible, full details of any incidents which may result in a claim under the policy', and also 'forwarding to us immediately upon receipt, every writ, summons, legal process or other communication in connection with the claim'.

Case Example: *Office of Fair Trading v Foxtons Ltd* **[2009] EWHC 1681**

These clauses fell for consideration: '2.14.3 Renewal commission will become due in respect of renewals, extensions and hold-overs or new agreements where the original tenant remains in occupation. It will also become due where the incoming tenant is a person, company or other entity associated or connected with the original tenant, either personally, or by involvement or connection with any company or other entity with whom the original tenant is or was involved or connected. Where there is more than one tenant, renewal commission will be payable in full where any or all of them remain in occupation. Commission is due whether or not the renewal is negotiated by Foxtons. 2.14.4 Renewal commission is charged in advance, either as a percentage of the rental value of the new agreed term or where the tenant extends and/or holds over indefinitely, commission will be payable for the same period as the initial agreement subject to clause 1.5 above. The scale of commission fees charged is as set out on page 1.' The first of these was held not to be plain and intelligible; the other was.

Enforcement   **A2.65**

It is the duty of the Competition and Markets Authority to consider any complaint made to it that a contract term drawn up for general use is unfair, other than those complaints it considers frivolous or vexatious: *s 70, CRA 2015* and *Sch 3*. The CMA can then seek a court injunction against any person appearing to be using or recommending an unfair term drawn up for general use in consumer contracts. Alternatively, an undertaking may be sought. The CMA has authority to publish details of the injunction or the undertaking. For the CMA approach to unfair terms, see. https://www.gov.uk/government/collections/cma-consumer-enforcement-guidance.

Qualifying bodies   A2.66

Schedule 3 to the *CRA 2015* Act lists a number of 'qualifying bodies' who may apply for injunctions against the use of unfair terms. These bodies are:

(a)   The Competition and Markets Authority,

(b)   the Department of Enterprise, Trade and Investment in Northern Ireland,

(c)   a local weights and measures authority in Great Britain,

(d)   the Financial Conduct Authority,

(e)   the Office of Communications,

(f)   the Information Commissioner,

(g)   the Gas and Electricity Markets Authority,

(h)   the Water Services Regulation Authority

(i)   the Office of Rail Regulation,

(j)   the Northern Ireland Authority for Utility Regulation; or

(k)   the Consumers' Association.

Provision of Services under the CRA 2015   A2.67

Part 1, Chapter 4 to the *CRA 2015* applies to a contract for a trader to supply a service to a consumer (otherwise known as 'a contract to supply a service'): *s 48(1), CRA 2015*. It does not include a contract of employment or apprenticeship: *s 48(2), CRA 2015*.

Every contract to supply a service is to be treated as including a term that the trader must perform the service with reasonable care and skill: *s 49(1), CRA 2015*.

The *CRA 2015* further provides that every contract to supply a service is to be treated as including a term of the contract anything that is said or written to the consumer, by or on behalf of the trader, about the trader or service, if:

(a)   It is taken into account by the consumer when deciding to enter into the contract; or

(b)   It is taken into account by the consumer when making any decision about the service after entering into the contract: *s 50(1), CRA 2015*.

Anything taken into account by the consumer as mentioned in subsection (1) (a) or (b) is subject to:

(a)   anything that qualified it and was said or written to the consumer by the trader on the same occasion; and

(b)   any change to it that has been expressly agreed between the consumer and the trader (before entering into the contract or later): *s 50(2), CRA 2015*.

Any information provided by the trader in accordance with regs 9, 10 or 13 of the *Consumer Contracts (Information, Cancellation and Additional Charges) Regulations 2013 (SI 2013/3134)* is to be treated as included as a term of the contract: *s 50(3). CRA 2015*.

A change to any of the information mentioned in *s 50(3), CRA 2015*, made before entering into the contract or later, is not effective unless expressly agreed between the consumer and the trader: *s 50(4), CRA 2015*.

Section 51, CRA 2015 addresses the position where a reasonable price is to be paid for a service. It applies to a contract to supply a service if:

(a)   the consumer has not paid a price or other consideration for the service,

(b)   the contract does not expressly fix a price or other consideration, and does not say how it is to be fixed; and

(c)   anything that is to be treated under *s 50, CRA 2015* as included in the contract does not fix a price or other consideration either: *s 51(1), CRA 2015*.

In that case, the contract is to be treated as including a term that the consumer must pay a reasonable price for the service, and no more: *s 51(2), CRA 2015*. What is a reasonable price is a question of fact: *s 51(3), CRA 2015*.

The *CRA 2015* also identifies the duration period when a service must be performed. *Section 52, CRA 2015* applies to a contract to supply a service, if:

(a)   the contract does not expressly fix the time for the service to be performed, and does not say how it is to be fixed; and

(b)   information that is to be treated under s 50, CRA 2015 as included in the contract does not fix the time either: s 52(1), CRA 2015.

In that case the contract is to be treated as including a term that the trader must perform the service within a reasonable time: s 52(2), CRA 2015. What is a reasonable time is a question of fact: s 52(3), CRA 2015.

The *CRA 2015* provides the consumer with specific rights to enforce terms about services: *s 54, CRA 2015*. If the service does not conform to the contract, the consumer's rights are: (a) the right to require repeat performance; and (b) the right to a price reduction: *s 54(3), CRA 2015*.

If the trader is in breach of a term that *s 50, CRA 2015* requires to be treated as included in the contract but that does not relate to the service, the consumer has the right to a price reduction (see *s 56, CRA 2015* for provisions about that right and when it is available): *s 54(4), CRA 2015*.

If the trader is in breach of what the contract requires under *s 52, CRA 2015* (performance within a reasonable time), the consumer has the right to a price reduction (see *s 56, CRA 2015* for provisions about that right and when it is available): *s 54(5), CRA 2015*.

The consumer is not prevented from seeking other remedies for a breach of a term to which any of *ss 54(3)-(5)* applies, instead of or in addition to a remedy referred to there (but not so as to recover twice for the same loss): *s 54(6), CRA 2015*. Those other remedies include any of the following that is open to the consumer in the circumstances:

(a)   claiming damages;

(b)   seeking to recover money paid where the consideration for payment of the money has failed;

(c)   seeking specific performance;

(d)   seeking an order for specific implement;

(e)   relying on the breach against a claim by the trader under the contract;

(f)   exercising a right to treat the contract as at an end: *s 54(7), CRA 2015*.

Penalty clauses   A2.68

English contract law has long been based on the notion of freedom of contract: the parties essentially deciding the contractual provisions entered into between them. This contractual freedom entailed the ability to negotiate freely on the contractual terms as well as setting the parameters for the level of compensation to which a party may be entitled to claim under the contract following a breach of contract. Judicial attitudes were favourable towards the awards of compensation that a party could claim under the contract, but this did not prevent the courts from intervening in disputes between the parties on compensation provisions in the contract, particularly in relation to liquidated damages and penalty clauses.

Over the years, the courts have considered clauses addressing liquidated damages and penalties. In respect of liquidated damages, the parties would typically set out a genuine pre-estimate of losses that may be incurred owing to a breach of contract. Therefore, where amounts under the contract were a genuine pre-estimate of loss, the courts would usually uphold such claims as liquidated damages. In other contracts, the amounts claimed are not based upon a genuine pre-estimate of losses incurred but are usually far greater than the maximum possible losses that parties may incur following a breach of contract. Such claims are considered as 'penalties' and are punitive in nature and serve as a warning to a party not to breach a particular provision otherwise that party may incur excessive penalties. Where a clause was considered as a penalty, the courts would not award any compensation in such circumstances and preferring instead to award compensation for the actual losses incurred by a party following the contractual breach. In this regard, the tasks of the courts has been to distinguish between a liquidated damages clause and a penalty clause – this has been a matter of construction and interpretation by the courts based on the language used by the parties in the contract. This section addresses the penalty rule and liquidated damages and modern judicial attitudes towards these concepts,

The penalty rule in England has been described as 'an ancient, haphazardly constructed edifice which has not weathered well…' per Lords Neuberger and Sumption in the conjoined appeals in *Cavendish Square Holding B.V. v Talal El Makdessi*; and *Parking Eye Ltd v Beavis* [2015] UKSC 67 (the former case concerning a commercial contract and the latter a consumer contract). The penalty rule has been considered as an interference with the freedom of contract and undermining the certainty which the parties are entitled to expect.

Over the years, there have been judicial inconsistencies over the application of the penalty rule and as to what constituted a 'penalty'. In *Legione v Hateley* (1983) 152 CLR, Mason and Deane JJ defined a penalty as follows: 'A penalty, as its name suggests, is in the nature of a punishment for non-observance of a contractual stipulation; it consists of the imposition or an additional or different liability upon breach of the contractual stipulation…'

Overview of the Penalty Rule   **A2.69**

The penalty rule has its origins in equity and common law. At common law, the courts prevented the parties to the contract from agreeing terms which had the effect of punishing a contract-breaker by extending liability for a specific breach of contract beyond a genuine pre-estimate of the financial losses that an innocent party to the contract might suffer owing to the breach of contract. The courts refused to enforce such terms on the basis that such penalty clauses were contrary to public policy.

The common law courts introduced a distinction between a provision for the management of a sum representing a genuine pre-estimate of damages and a penalty clause in which the sum was out of all proportion to any damages liable to be suffered. English law appeared to accept clauses which prescribed the amount of damages payable following a contractual breach, where the parties had specified that the amount represented a genuine attempt by them to predict in advance the losses that might be suffered owing to the breach. This became known as the 'liquidated damages' clause. The distinction between a clause providing for a genuine pre-estimate of damages and a penalty clause has remained fundamental to the modern law. The issue as to whether a damages clause is a penalty clause was a matter of interpretation of the contractual provision, at the time that it was agreed. This is because it depended on the character of the provision and not on the circumstances in which it fell to be imposed. The penalty rule was considered to be a species of agreement considered by the common law to be by its very nature, contrary to the policy of the law, thereby making such clauses unenforceable. The innocent party is therefore left to his remedy under the general law.

In English law, the courts have taken the view that a provision could not be a penalty unless it provided an exorbitant alternative to common law damages, and a provision operating upon a breach of contract. The main objective of the law relating to penalty clauses was to prevent the claimant recovering a sum of money in respect of a breach of contract committed by a defendant which bore little or no relationship to the loss actually suffered by the claimant as a result of the breach by the defendant. The penalty rule regulates only the remedies available for breach of a party's primary obligations and not the primary obligations themselves.

The view of the penalty rule was set out in *Dunlop Pneumatic Tyre Company Ltd v New Garage and Motor Company Ltd* [1915] AC 79. Dunlop contracted to supply tyres, covers and tubes to New Garage and that New Garage would not resell any of these goods to private customers at prices below those specified by Dunlop. According to clause 5 of the agreement, in the event that New Garage failed to comply with this prohibition, it would pay £5 to Dunlop for each of the goods sold in breach of the agreement, as and by way of liquidated damages and not as a penalty. The House of Lords held that this was a valid liquidated damages clause. Lord Dunedin formulated the following test in determining whether or not a particular clause was penal:

- Where the sum stipulated for is extravagant and unconscionable in amount in comparison with the greatest loss that could conceivably be proved to have followed from the breach.

- Where the breach consisted only in the non-payment of money and it provided for the payment of a larger sum.

- There was a presumption that it would be penal if it was payable in a number of events of varying gravity.

- It would not be treated as penal by reason only of the impossibility of precisely pre-estimating the true loss.

Lord Dunedin applied the four tests and determined that clause 5 was enforceable as a liquidated damages clause, because the exact amount of Dunlop's loss would have been difficult to identify and it was 'quite reasonable for parties to contract that they should estimate that damage at a certain figure…'.

Lord Dunedin's four tests appeared to have achieved the status of a quasi-statutory code subsequently followed by the courts. However, these were only tests that could be applied to a particular case and were not necessarily of universal application.

Following *Dunlop*, some courts advanced the possibility of a broader test of 'commercial justification' for clauses which might otherwise be regarded as penal: see *Scandinavian Trading Tanker Co AB v Flota Petrolera Ecuatoriana (The 'Scaptrade')* [1983] 2 AC 694; and *Lordsvale Finance plc v Bank of Zambia* [1996] QB 752.

However, the Supreme Court in *Makdessi* pointed out that the law relating to penalties had become the prisoner of artificial categorisation, itself the result of unsatisfactory distinctions between a penalty and genuine pre-estimate of loss, and between a genuine pre-estimate of loss and a deterrent. These distinctions originated from an over-literal reading of Lord Dunedin's four tests and a tendency to treat them as rules of general application. The real question when a contractual provision is challenged is whether it is penal, not whether it is a pre-estimate of loss. The fact that the clause is not a pre-estimate of loss does not necessarily mean it is penal.

Modern Penalty Test   A2.70

The law on penalties is now governed by the Supreme Court judgment in the joined cases of *Cavendish v El Makdessi* and *Parking Eye v Beavis* [2015] UKSC 67.

The Supreme Court in *Makdessi* and *Parking Eye* advanced the following modern test for penalty clauses:

> 'The true test is whether the impugned provision is a secondary obligation which imposes a detriment on the contract-breaker out of all proportion to any legitimate interest of the innocent party in the enforcement of the primary obligation'.

The innocent party can have no proper interest in simply punishing the defaulter. His interest is in the performance or in some appropriate alternative to performance. In the case of a straightforward damages clause, that interest will rarely extent beyond compensation for the breach and in such cases, Lord Dunedin's four tests in *Dunlop* apply to determine its validity.

In applying the *Makdessi* test, the circumstances in which the contract was made are not entirely irrelevant. In a negotiated contract between properly advised parties of comparable bargaining power, the strong initial presumption must be that the parties themselves are the best judges of what is legitimate in a provision dealing with the consequences of breach.

Abrogation of the Penalty Rule?   A2.71

The Supreme Court decided against the abrogation of the penalty rule. This is because it was a long-standing principle of English law and was common to most systems of law internationally. Further, although statutory regulation had made further inroads into the penalty law (eg *UCTA 1977*), it would still be inappropriate to abrogate the penalty rule as it continues to be a developing area where the common law principles would still apply. The penalty rule is consistent with other well-established principles developed by judges and which involve the court declining to give full force to contractual provisions, such as relief from forfeiture, equity of redemption and refusal to grant specific performance in certain circumstances. The Supreme Court also decided against extending the scope of the penalty rule.

In *Cavendish v El Makdessi*, by an agreement, Mr El Makdessi agreed to sell to Cavendish a controlling stake in the holding company of the largest advertising and marketing communications group in the Middle East. The agreement stated in clause 5.1 that if Mr El Makdessi was in breach of certain restrictive covenants against competing activities, he would not be entitled to receive the final two instalments of the price paid by Cavendish. Further under clause 5.6, Mr El Makdessi could be required to sell his remaining shares to Cavendish, at a price excluding the value of the goodwill of the business. Subsequently, Mr El Makdessi breached these covenants. He contended that clauses 5.1 and 5.6 were unenforceable penalty clauses.

The Supreme Court held that clauses 5.1 and 5.6 were valid and did not contravene the penalty rule. The Court was of the view that clause 5.1 was a price adjustment clause. It was not a secondary provision but a primary obligation. The sellers earn consideration for their shares by observing the restrictive covenants. The Court stated that there was 'no reason in principle why a contract should not provide for a party to earn his remuneration, or part of it, by performing his obligations'. Further, clause 5.1 was 'plainly not a liquidated damages clause' and was 'not a contractual alternative to damages at law'.

Whilst clause 5.1 had no relationship with the measure of loss attributable to the breach, Cavendish also had a legitimate interest in the observance of the restrictive covenants, in order to protect the goodwill of the Cavendish Group generally. The goodwill of the business was critical to Cavendish and Mr El Makdessi's loyalty was critical to the goodwill. The Court could not assess the precise value of that obligation or determine how much less Cavendish would have paid for the business without the benefit of the restrictive covenants. Accordingly, the parties were the best judges of how it should be reflected in their agreement.

The Court applied the same analysis to clause 5.6 of the agreement. The aim of clause 5.6 was to sever the connection between the parties in the event of a breach of the restrictive covenants. This clause was also a primary obligation and it could not be treated as invalid without rewriting the agreement. Clause 5.6 was said to be penal because the formula excluded goodwill from the calculation of the payment price. It did not represent the estimated loss attributable to the breach. However, it reflected the reduced consideration which Cavendish would have been prepared to pay for the acquisition of the business on the hypothesis that they could not count on the loyalty of Mr El Makdessi.

In *Parking Eye v Beavis*, Parking Eye Ltd agreed with the owners of the Riverside Retail Park to manage the car park at the site. Parking Eye displayed a number of notices throughout the car park, stating that failure to comply with the two-hour time limit would 'result in a parking charge of £85'. The car park notice also provided:

> '2 hour max stay…Failure to comply…will result in a parking charge of £85…A reduction of the Parking Charge is available for a period as detailed in the Parking Charge Notice. The reduced amount payable will not exceed £75, and the overall amount will not exceed £150 prior to any court action, after which additional costs will be incurred.'

On 15 April 2003, Mr Beavis parked in the car park, but overstayed the two-hour limit by almost an hour. Parking Eye demanded payment of the £85 charge. Mr Beavis contended that the charge of £85 was unenforceable at common law as a penalty. Further, he argued that it was unfair and unenforceable by virtue of the *Unfair Terms in Consumer Contract Regulations 1999* (see now *Part 2 of the CRA 2015*).

The Supreme Court dismissed Beavis' appeal by 6-1. It held that the £85 charge did not contravene the penalty rule nor the 1999 Regulations. According to the Supreme Court, Mr Beavis had a contractual licence to park in the car park on the terms of the notice posted at the entrance of the car park, including the two-hour limit. The charge had two main objectives: (1) the management of the efficient use of parking space in the interests of the retail outlets and their users by deterring long-stay or commuter traffic; and (2) the generation of income in order to operate the scheme. According to the Supreme Court, these 'two objectives appear to us to be perfectly reasonable in themselves. Subject to the penalty rule and the Regulations, the imposition of a charge to deter overstayers is a reasonable mode of achieving them. Indeed, once it is resolved to allow up to two hours free parking, it is difficult to see how else those objectives could be achieved.'

Unlike in *Makdessi*, the penalty rule was engaged. The parking charge fell within the rule against penalties. This was because principally, there was a contractual agreement which concerned the provision by Parking Eye to Beavis of a licence to park on private land which was subject to Beavis' agreement to comply with the conditions for parking. It was only when Beavis failed to comply with the terms of the contractual licence that an obligation to pay the parking charge arose. The payment obligation was therefore a secondary obligation arising on the breach which was subject to the penalty rule. However, in applying the new test, the Supreme Court determined that the £85 charge was not a penalty. Both Parking Eye and the landowners had a legitimate interest in charging overstaying motorists, which extended beyond the recovery of any loss. The interests of the landowners was the provision and efficient management of customer parking for the retail outlets. The interest of Parking Eye was in income from the charge, which met the running costs of a legitimate scheme plus a profit margin. Further, the charge was neither extravagant nor unconscionable having regard to the practice in the UK, and taking into account the use of this particular car park and the clear wording of the notices.

The same principles applied to the 1999 Regulations. Although the charge may fall under the description of potentially unfair terms under paragraph 1(e) of Schedule 2, it did not come with the basis test for unfairness in Regulations 5 and 6(1) (see now *CRA 2015*).

Any imbalance in the particular rights did not arise 'contrary to the requirements of good faith', because Parking Eye and the owners had a legitimate interest in inducing Mr Beavis not to overstay in order to efficiently manage the car park for the benefit of the generality of the users of the retail outlets. The charge was no higher than was necessary to achieve that objective. Objectively, the reasonable motorist would have, and often did, agree to the charge.

The Supreme Court further relied on the following to uphold the validity of the clause:

- The £85 charge amount was less than the maximum charge stated by the British Parking Association in its Code of Practice.

- Local authorities would charge a slightly lower amount, but may not offer 2 hours of free parking.

- Similar parking charge schemes were applied across the United Kingdom.

In *Makdessi*, Lord Mance stated:

> 'In my opinion the development of the law indicated by the authorities discussed in paragraphs 145 to 151 above is a sound one. It is most easily explained on the basis that the dichotomy between the compensatory and the penal is not exclusive. There may be interest beyond the compensatory which justify the imposition on a party in breach of an additional financial burden. The maintenance of a system of trade which only functions if all trading partners adhere to it (the Dunlop case) may itself be viewed in this light. So can terms of settlement which provide on default for payment of costs which a party was prepared to forego if the settlement was honoured (the *Cine Bes* case), likewise also the revision of financial terms to match circumstances disclosed or brought about by a breach: *Lordsvale* and other cases. What is necessary in each case is to consider first whether any (and if so) what legitimate business interest is served and protected by the clause, and, second, whether, assuming such an interest to exist, the provision made for the interest is nevertheless in the circumstances

extravagant, exorbitant or unconscionable. In judging what is extravagant, exorbitant or unconscionable, I consider (despite contrary expressions of view) that the extent to which the parties were negotiating at arm's length on the basis of legal advice and had every opportunity to appreciate what they were agreeing must at least be a relevant factor.'

Lord Hodge stated as follows:

'I therefore conclude that the correct test for a penalty is whether the sum or remedy stipulated as a consequence of a breach of contract is exorbitant or unconscionable when regard is had to the innocent parties' interest in the performance of the contract. Where the test is to be applied to a clause fixing the level of damages to be paid on breach an extravagant disproportion between the stipulated sum and the highest level of damages that could possibly arise from the breach would amount to a penalty and thus be unenforceable. In other circumstances a contractual provision that applies on breach is measured against the interest of the innocent party which is protected by the contract and the court asks whether the remedy is exorbitant or unconscionable.'

Whilst Lord Toulson stated as follows:

'On the essential nature of penalty clause I would highlight and endorse Lord Hodge JSC's succinct statement at para 255 that:

"the correct test for a penalty is whether the sum or remedy stipulated as a consequence of a breach of contract is exorbitant or unconscionable when regard is had to the innocent party's interest in the performance of the contract".'

The Position Post Makdessi and Parking Eye   **A2.72**

In *Holyoake v Candy* [2017] EWHC 3397, Holyoake (H) desired to purchase a property in Belgravia, London and raised funds for the purchase including an amount from the CPC Group Ltd (CPC). CPC contended that H was in default of loan payments and subsequently CPC rescheduled the loan with H paying extension fees. H thereafter sold the property and paid off the loan and the extension fees. He issued proceedings against CPC on the basis that certain clauses in the loan agreements and extension agreements were in effect penalties. With regards to the early repayment clause, it provided that H had the option to repay the loan earlier but all interest which would have accrued over the term of the loan would also have to be repaid.

Nugee J held that this was not a penalty clause. The clause was not stated to operate on breach of the agreements. It set out only the sums that were due upon early repayment. Following *Makdessi* and *Parking Eye*, the effect of the early repayment clause was to ensure that CPC received the interest accrued over the loan, whether or not the loan was repaid earlier. The clause imposed a primary obligation on H and was not a penalty.

With regard to the loan extension, Nugee J decided that these agreements did not fall with the penalty rule. The extension fees were 'expressly made payable in return for the extension of time.' Further, where sums were payable under the contract, the parties are free to decide what these sums are payable for. The judge held that the extension payments were payments in return for consideration and not payments due owing to breach of an obligation.

The final aspects concerned double interest charges. Although one clause was upheld as not a penalty clause, there was another interest clause which provided that interest would not be charged had H adhered to the payment schedule. According to Nugee J, the failure to keep to the repayment schedule was the key trigger for the interest and that this was in breach of the extension agreements, and therefore a penalty clause. However, Nugee J decided that the clause protected a legitimate business interest and it was not extravagant or exorbitant or unconscionable. He stated that clauses providing for the whole balance of the debt to become due on default were standard provisions in such agreements. Further, charging further interest in addition to this amount was also standard practice. Additionally, such clauses were also commercially justified because once the debtor is in default, the creditor is not only being kept out of his money but also running an enhanced risk.

See too *Edgeworth Capital (Luxembourg) SARL v Ramblas Investments BV* [2016] EWCA Civ 412, where the Court of Appeal held that a cross-default clause did not breach the penalty rule, as the fee payable had nothing to do with damages for breach of contract: the fee was payable on the happening of a specified event.

In *Vivienne Westwood v Conduit Street* [2017] EWHC 350 (Ch), Fancourt J stated as:

> 'The *Cavendish* case shows clearly that, in considering whether a contractual stipulation is or is not a penalty, one must address first the threshold issue – is a stipulation in substance a secondary obligation engaged upon breach of a primary contractual obligation; then identify the extent and nature of the legitimate interest of the promisee in having the primary obligation performed, and then determine whether or not, having regard to that legitimate interest, the secondary obligation is exorbitant or unconscionable in amount or in its effect.'

See too: *Cargill International Trading Pte Ltd v Uttam Galva Steels Ltd* [2019] EWHC 476.

In relation to liquidated damages clauses, the Court of Appeal in *Triple Point Technology Inc v PTT Public Company Ltd* [2019] EWCA Civ 230 held that a clause providing for liquidated damages for delay did not apply where the contractor failed to complete the contracted work which concerned the installation of a new software system. Accordingly, under the contract the employer was entitled to recover damages for breach of contract based on ordinary contractual principles rather than claiming liquidated damages.

The dispute concerned a contract entered into between the claimant, Triple Point, and defendant, PTT, for the supply of a software system.

Under the contract, Triple Point were to provide the new software system in two phases, with each phase having multiple stages of work. Phase 1 of the project was to be delivered by a certain time and the contract provided that if Triple Point failed to deliver the work by that time then it was:

> 'liable to pay the penalty at the rate of 0.1% (zero point one percent) of undelivered work per day of delay from the due date for delivery up to the date PTT accepts such work...' (Article 5.3).

Article 12.3 of the contract provided that Triple Point's total liability to PTT was limited to the contract price received by Triple Point.

According to the Court of Appeal, the issue of whether such a clause applied in these circumstances would depend on the wording of the clause itself. In respect of the specific clause before the court, the clause was focussed specifically on delay between the contractual completion date and when the work was actually completed by the contractor and accepted by the employer. If that never occurred, the clause on liquidated damages did not apply. The Court of Appeal rejected the appellant's argument that the liquidated damages clause should be struck out as a penalty clause as it imposed a detriment 'out of all proportion to any interest of the innocent party' under the test set out in *Makdessi*. However, the Court of Appeal noted that although the contractual formula was not perfect, the total sums as calculated under the clause were modest when compared to the financial consequences of delays in installing the software and concluded that it was a genuine pre-estimate of loss likely to flow from the delay.

Practical Points to Note

- The penalty rule has not been abrogated or abolished by the Supreme Court in *Makdessi* and still retains its place in English law.

- However, the penalty rule has been significantly reduced in its scope and effect coupled with the Supreme Court's difficulty in providing any justification or underlying policy reasons for its operation.

- The Supreme Court did not fully resolve the distinction to be made between primary and secondary obligations. According to the Supreme Court, only secondary obligations, that is, obligations that are triggered on breach of primary obligations, are capable of being penalties. The Court in *Makdessi* was split as to whether the obligation to sell shares was a primary or a secondary obligation. While a clause could be drafted to transform a secondary obligation into a primary one, there is still a risk that the court may determine that the clause is a secondary obligation and potentially a penalty.

- A 'legitimate interest' is an important element to the *Makdessi* test. However, there is no guidance by the Court as to what constitutes a legitimate interest that requires protection, but it is part of the test and the parties may well use this expression in the enforceability of clauses and setting out the circumstances giving rise to the legitimate interests.

- There is also no guidance on when a clause is 'out of all proportion' to the legitimate interests being protected.

- It is likely that the courts will still have regard to the four tests enunciated by Lord Dunedin in *Dunlop* together with the 'legitimate interest test' as set out in *Makdessi*.

- In identifying whether an amount is 'exorbitant or unconscionable' consideration will be given to the innocent party's legitimate interests in the performance of the contract on a wider basis. This will not be limited to the level of damages that the innocent party could have expected to flow directly and measurably from the breach.

- The effect of the *Makdessi* and *Parking Eye* decisions is that it will be more difficult for a party to successfully contend that a clause is an unenforceable penalty.

- The courts are likely to have regard to the commercial interests of the parties rather than only the financial implications of the breach.

- When drafting, consider the commercial justifications for the inclusion of secondary obligations in the agreement. This could set out the nature of the legitimate interests and the commercial considerations that led to the penalty amount being negotiated by the parties. This would then provide a factual background that should assist in the construction of the provision and the rationale for its inclusion.

Liquidated damages clauses   A2.73

A contract will frequently contain a clause which spells out the amount payable by the other party in the event of a breach where specific target dates or milestones have not been met. This has the practical value that such a clause could avoid litigation over the precise amount due in the event of a breach. Care must be taken in the drafting of such a clause, however, since the courts will only uphold a clause which is properly regarded as a 'liquidated damages' clause and which is not in fact a 'penalty clause' particularly following the Supreme court decision in *Makdessi*.

Determining whether a clause is a penalty clause or a liquidated damages clause – the position before Makdessi **A2.74**

Case Example: *Dunlop Pneumatic Tyre Co v New Garage & Motor Co Ltd* **[1915] AC 79**

The House of Lords stressed that the description given to the clause by the parties was not relevant to the test, so a clause described in the contract as a penalty clause could well, on analysis, prove to be a liquidated damages clause (and vice versa).

In this case, the company had supplied tyres subject to a price maintenance agreement which was then lawful. If there was any breach of the agreement, £5 was payable in respect of every tyre sold in breach of the agreement. This was held to be a valid liquidated damages clause because, while the sum itself might seem excessive, news of any undercutting would spread and the damage to Dunlop's selling organisation would be impossible to estimate.

Case Example: *Ford Motor Co v Armstrong* **(1915) 31 TLR 267**

The defendant retailer agreed not to sell supplies obtained from Ford below the list price, not to sell Ford cars to other dealers, nor to exhibit any Ford car without permission. He agreed to pay £250, for 'the agreed damage which the manufacturer will sustain'. This was held to be an unenforceable penalty; it was made payable for various breaches differing in kind, and its very size prevented it from being a reasonable pre-estimate of the probable damage.

The test for determining the category into which a clause fell was this: 'The essence of a penalty is a payment of money stipulated' in such a way as effectively to coerce a party to perform the contract, while a liquidated damages clause is one which is a 'genuine covenanted pre-estimate of damage'.

See also *Lombard North Central plc v Butterworth* [1987] QB 527.

It was stated in the *Dunlop* case that there will be a presumption that a clause is a penalty when 'a single lump sum is payable by way of compensation, on the occurrence of one or more or all of several events, some of which may occasion serious and others but trifling damage'. This rule has caught out a number of contract draftsmen and clauses have been held to be penal because they failed to distinguish between serious and trifling breaches of the agreement.

The fact that, in many cases, precise pre-estimation is almost impossible will not be a bar to a clause still being a valid liquidated damages clause. This was stated by the House of Lords in the *Dunlop* case. This is likely to be of more significance where the obligation of the party in breach is to perform a particular obligation other than payment. In such a case, it may be very difficult to calculate the financial consequences of breach, and the courts take the view that the parties are in a better position to assess the consequences of breach than the courts themselves. The courts are unwilling to second-guess the parties in such cases, as explained in *Clydebank Engineering and Shipbuilding Co v Don Jose Ramos* [1905] AC 6. The same case also shows that the courts have generally insisted for there to be a large disproportion before the clause is classified as a penalty clause.

Interpreting a liquidated damages clause   A2.75

Case Example: *Cenargo Ltd v Empresa Nacional Bazan de Construcciones Navales Militares SA* **[2002] EWCA Civ 524**

A clause in a contract for the building of a line of ferries provided that:

> 'if the actual trailer-carrying capacity of the Vessel is less than 146 Units of 13 metres each the Builder shall pay to the Buyer as liquidated damages one hundred and fifty thousand United States Dollars ($150,000) for each trailer unit by which the Vessel is deficient but excluding the first one (1) in respect of which deficiency no liquidated damages shall be payable. If the deficiency in trailer carrying capacity is ten (10) or more the Buyer as an alternative to receiving the aforementioned liquidated damages may rescind the contract'.

The particular deficiencies in the vessels as delivered were minor in that they could have been rectified in a matter of hours at little cost. The Court of Appeal held that where a substantial sum was payable in respect of deficiencies, a court should 'lean naturally to the conclusion that the clause was intended to apply only to major breaches'. Presumably, a clause drafted to cover minor breaches, but providing for payment of the same sum as for major breaches, would in any event be construed as penal and hence unenforceable (see A2.70 below).

Case Example: *McAlpine v Tilebox* **[2005] EWHC 181**

The applicant applied for a declaration that a liquidated damages clause contained in a contract between themselves and the respondent was in fact a penalty clause and unenforceable. The respondents had acquired the leasehold of a property with the view to developing it for commercial office use. They entered into a development funding agreement (DFA) with a third party whereby the third party agreed to finance the development in return for a long lease on the property. Under that agreement, the respondents were entitled to a fee for managing the development and a development completion payment (DCP) which reduced if completion was delayed. The respondents engaged the applicants as main contractor for the development on an amended JCT standard contract with contractor's design. That contract contained a liquidated and ascertained damages clause that provided for payment by the applicants to the respondents at a specified rate for any delay on the project. Work on the project was in fact severely delayed and the applicants sought a declaration that the damages clause was a penalty clause and unenforceable. The respondents submitted that the rate of damages provided for in the clause was a reasonable pre-estimate of damages at the time the contract was entered into and that the DFA imposed a continuing liability on it to the third party so that its foreseeable losses included that liability.

The court ruled that pre-estimated damages did not have to be right to be acceptable. There had to be an unacceptable difference between the pre-estimated damages and the likely damages before the pre-estimated damages could be said to be unreasonable. The test for whether a clause was a penalty clause did not turn on the honesty or genuine nature of a party as the test was primarily an objective one. The court said that, because the penalty clause rule was an anomaly, it was predisposed to uphold the terms of an agreement and in particular where the agreement was made in a commercial context between two parties of an equal bargaining power. In the instant case on a proper construction the DFA imposed a continuing liability on the respondents to the third party. In the circumstances, even without taking into account the diminution of the DCP to the respondents, the payment by the applicants to them at the rate specified in the liquidated damages clause was reasonable. The fact that the DCP had, over the period of delay incurred, eroded to nothing, did not mean the inclusion of an allowance for erosion to the DCP in the calculation of the rate specified in the liquidated damages clause rendered it a penalty clause as when the clause was agreed neither party had anticipated the length of delay incurred.

Case Example: *Murray v Leisureplay plc* **[2005] EWCA Civ 963**

The appellant appealed against a High Court ruling that a clause in his service agreement with the respondent company providing for the payment of a year's gross salary in the event of the termination of his employment without one year's notice was a penalty clause and hence unenforceable. The appellant had been given only seven and a half weeks' notice of termination rather than the 12 months' notice to which he was entitled under the agreement. His case was that the termination of his employment constituted wrongful termination for the purposes of the agreement so that he was entitled to payment of liquidated damages under the relevant clause. The terms of his service agreement had been approved by the board and the respondents had been advised by solicitors.

The court said that, when deciding in a case such as the instant case whether a clause was a penalty clause, the court should consider what breaches of contract the clause applied to, what amount was payable on breach, what amount would be payable if a claim for damages for breach of contract had been brought at common law, what were the parties' reasons for agreeing the relevant clause and whether the amount payable under the clause was imposed as a deterrent or whether it constituted a genuine pre-estimate of loss. The disputed clause in this case had to be construed as meaning that if less than one year's notice was given the payment of gross salary, pension contributions and other benefits in kind was reduced to the extent that those payments had been duly made in the notice period. In the events which happened, the respondents became liable under the clause (if enforceable) to pay 44 and a half weeks' gross salary, pension contributions and other benefits to the appellant. This meant, therefore, that the sum payable under the clause was likely greatly to exceed the damages which the appellant could have obtained at common law since he would have had to mitigate his damages by giving credit for remuneration he could reasonably have earned in the period of one year. That issue had to be judged as at the date of the agreement. That comparison was no more than a guide to the assessment of a provision as a deterrent rather than compensatory. The court could not go behind the High Court's finding that the appellant had been able to determine the terms of the service agreement within broad limits. There was no question of the respondents showing that the clause was imposed as a deterrent. Since the context in which it had been agreed was commercial, the question whether it was a penalty or not had to be assessed by reference to commercial considerations. The restrictions which the appellant undertook to observe on termination were important and significant. There were other potential advantages to the respondents and disadvantages to the appellant on a termination. The respondents had been content to take the right to elect to make a payment of one year's salary in lieu of notice without any discount for mitigation. In all the circumstances, the respondents had not discharged the burden of showing that the clause was not a genuine pre-estimate of damage or that it was not otherwise justifiable.

Case Example: *Azimut-Benetti SpA v Healey* [2010] EWHC 2234

The defendant had commissioned a yacht from the claimant. He had given a personal guarantee for the cost. A clause in the yacht construction contract entitled the claimant to suspend construction of the yacht if the defendant failed to pay any monies due. The clause further entitled the claimant in such circumstances to charge 20% of the full contract price in liquidated damages for its estimated losses arising from non-completion of the contract and required the claimant to promptly return any balance over and above that amount to the defendant. Another clause specified that the defendant, as guarantor, was not to be released from liability even if the contract was found to be invalid in some way. As negotiations between the parties proceeded, the defendant's solicitors and yacht brokers were independently retained for the purchase of another yacht from the claimant (the second yacht purchase) and in those negotiations there was considerable discussion about whether the latter's entitlement to liquidated damages should be reduced to 10%. He refused, explaining his commercial reasoning and offering an alternative model of calculation. Negotiations for the second yacht purchase continued, with various drafts of the contract passing between the parties. The contract however, had to be concluded within a shorter timescale. It was agreed that the same basic draft contract would be used for both transactions. The defendant signed his contract while discussions continued between the legal teams regarding the second yacht purchase. There was no specific discussion in the defendant's case of the 20% liquidated damages clause, which remained in the contract at the time the defendant signed it. The defendant failed to pay the first instalment of the purchase price so the claimant terminated the contract and demanded an amount equal to 20% of the contract price. The defendant refused to pay on the basis that the liquidated damages percentage was not a genuine pre-estimate of the loss that the claimant would suffer, but was a penalty and that there was no liability on which the guarantee could fasten. The claimant submitted that the negotiations for the two yachts had proceeded 'in tandem', with amendments agreed in relation to the second purchase being transposed into the defendant's contract. It maintained that its justification in the second yacht negotiations of a 20% liquidated damages charge could be attributed to the defendant and that the defendant had chosen the liquidated damages clause over the alternative clause. The claimant relied on the express provision in the contract that the guarantor's liability would not be discharged even if the contract was found to be invalid. The defendant argued that the matter should proceed to a full trial so that the court could properly quantify the claimant's loss by reference to disclosure and evidence.

The High Court ruled that the mere assertion by the claimant that the liquidated damages clause was a genuine pre-estimate of damage did not advance matters. The negotiations regarding the second yacht purchase were admissible as 'inherent circumstances' surrounding the making of the contract, but matters negotiated in one transaction could not simply be transposed into the other merely because the agents concerned happened to be the same. The liquidated damages clause, read as a whole, was commercially justifiable. It placed obligations on both parties and, on the evidence, was not even arguably a penalty. The terms of the contract, including the liquidated damages clause, had been freely entered into and both parties had had the benefit of expert representation. In a commercial contract of the instant type, the court should normally uphold what the parties had agreed.

Determining whether a clause is a penalty clause or a liquidated damages clause – the position after *Makdessi*   **A2.76**

Liquidated damages clauses are typically found in construction contracts. They represent a secondary obligation to pay an agreed sum of money arising upon breach of a primary obligation of the contract which will usually be a delay event such as failure to complete the works by a specified date. In *Makdessi*, the Supreme Court considered that the true test on penalties was whether the impugned provision is a secondary obligation which imposes a detriment on the contract-breaker out of all proportion to the legitimate interest of the innocent party in the enforcement of the primary obligation. The court will also consider whether the sum or remedy stipulated as a consequence of a breach of contract is exorbitant or unconscionable when regard is had to the innocent party's legitimate interest in the performance of the contract. The Supreme Court reformulated the rule on penalties from the longstanding 'genuine pre-estimate of loss' test established in *Dunlop* into the 'legitimate interest' test. The reliance on a clause being a penalty clause is often pleaded by a party owing to a dispute arising in, for example, a construction contract to defeat a claim for liquidated damages for delay.

In relation to liquidated damages clauses following termination of a contract, previous cases have held that an employer will usually be entitled to claim liquidated damages for delay up to the point of termination, but must bring a claim for general damages for any delays which accrue after that date. The Court of Appeal in *Triple Point Technology Inc v PTT Public Company Ltd* [2019] EWCA Civ 230 held that a clause providing for liquidated damages for delay did not apply where the contractor failed to complete the contracted work which concerned the installation of a new software system. Accordingly, under the contract the employer was only entitled to recover damages for breach of contract based on ordinary contractual principles rather than claiming liquidated damages.

The dispute concerned a contract entered into between the claimant, Triple Point, and defendant, PTT, for the supply of a software system.

Under the contract, Triple Point were to provide the new software system in two phases, with each phase having multiple stages of work. Phase 1 of the project was to be delivered by a certain time and the contract provided that if Triple Point failed to deliver the work by that time then it was:

> 'liable to pay the penalty at the rate of 0.1% (zero point one percent) of undelivered work per day of delay from the due date for delivery up to the date PTT accepts such work...' (Article 5.3).

Article 12.3 of the contract provided that Triple Point's total liability to PTT was limited to the contract price received by Triple Point.

According to the Court of Appeal, the issue of whether such a clause applied in these circumstances would depend on the wording of the clause itself. In respect of the specific clause before the court, the clause was focussed specifically on delay between the contractual completion date and when the work was actually completed by the contractor and accepted by the employer. If that never occurred, the clause on liquidated damages did not apply. The Court of Appeal rejected the appellant's argument that the liquidated damages clause should be struck out as a penalty clause as it imposed a detriment 'out of all proportion to any interest of the innocent party' under the test set out in *Makdessi*. However, the Court of Appeal noted that although the contractual formula was not perfect, the total sums as calculated under the clause were modest when compared to the financial consequences of delays in installing the software and concluded that it was a genuine pre-estimate of loss likely to flow from the delay.

The issue of liquidated damages and whether they were penalties was considered in *GPP Big Field LLP v Solar EPC Solutions SL* [2018] EWHC 2866. GPP appointed Prosolia to construct five solar power plants in the UK under five separate EPC contracts. Four of the EPC contracts included guarantees by Solar EPC Solutions SL which was Prosolia's Spanish parent company. Prosolia subsequently failed to complete the projects by the completion dates and later became insolvent. Accordingly, GPP claimed against Solar under its guarantees. Solar contended that the liquidated damages clauses were in effect penalties and therefore unenforceable because they were expressly set out as and described as a 'penalty' under clause 21.5 which stated that 'In the event of the delay of more than fifteen (15) calendar days of commissioning the Contractor shall pay to the [Employer] a penalty…The maximum amount of the penalty for the delays to the Works shall be two hundred and fifty thousand pounds sterling per MWp ($£250,000$/MWp)'. Further, the five EPC contracts provided the same 'penalty' of $£500$ per day per MWp, despite the fact that each of the solar energy plants would generate different amounts of energy. Solar contended that the pre-determined amount could not be based on a genuine pre-estimate of GPP's losses. Solar also contended that as one of its EPC contracts had been terminated, the liquidated damages clause did not survive termination of the contract.

The High Court decided that the liquidated damages clauses were not penalties and were enforceable. The court stated that clauses dealing with liquidated damages for delay were common in construction contracts and that GPP and Prosolia were experienced commercial parties of equal bargaining power to assess the commercial implications of such clauses. Further, the court stated that it was in the nature of liquidated damages clauses that they were often used when precise prediction of the likely loss was difficult. The fact that the loss resulting from the breach may vary in amount depending on the actual circumstances at the time did not of itself give rise to any inference that the sum agreed was a penalty, provided it was not extravagant and unconscionable in comparison with the greatest loss that might have been expected, at the time when the contract was made, to follow from the relevant breach. The court also stated that ultimately, the sum specified did not exceed a genuine attempt to estimate in advance the loss which GPP would be likely to suffer from the relevant breach. It was not in any way extravagant or unconscionable in comparison to GPP's legitimate interest in ensuring that the project was ready on time. The references to 'penalty' in the clause were only 'equivocal indications': it was the substance of the matter that was relevant. Further, the court also held that the liquidated damages provisions survived the termination of the contract as a 'matter of principle' because otherwise this would reward the defendant for their own default: *Hall v Van Der Heiden (No 2)* [2010] EWHC 586. A practical point to note following *Makdessi* is that the court will still have regard to the liquidated damages test as to whether the liquidated damages were a genuine pre-estimate of loss flowing from the breach of contract. However, the court will ultimately apply the test in *Makdessi* namely whether the amount stipulated is exorbitant or unconscionable having regard to the innocent party's interest in the performance of the contract. The court had regard to the 'genuine pre-estimate of loss' test set out in *Dunlop* which still therefore remains a relevant consideration in determining whether or not a clause is a penalty clause. The court had regard to the following aspects in upholding the liquidated damages clauses in the EPC contracts:

- The liquidated damages clauses as set out in the EPC contracts were commonly found in construction contracts.

- Both the parties were experienced and sophisticated commercial parties of equal bargaining power capable of assessing the commercial implications of the liquidated damages provisions. There was no requirement for any detailed negotiations between the parties on the liquidated damages.

- The court found that the amount of liquidated damages under each EPC contract was stated to be a round sum paid irrespective of the effect of the delay. However, it was in the nature of liquidated damages clauses that they were often used in cases where precise prediction of the likely loss was difficult and therefore often expressed in round figures.

- The amount provided for in each of the liquidated damages clause was payable only on a single type of breach. The fact that the loss resulting from the breach may vary in amount depending on the actual circumstances at the time did not of itself give rise to any inference that the sum agreed to be paid is a penalty, provided that it is not extravagant and unconscionable in amount in comparison with the greatest loss that might have been expected when the contract was made to be likely to flow from the breach.

- The legitimacy of a liquidated damages clause is not just about compensation but it was also concerned with whether the clause can be commercially justified.

With regards to the position of whether liquidated damages were payable for delay after termination, the judge in *GPP Big Field* held that they were payable on the basis that if liquidated damages were not payable for delay after termination, the contractor would effectively be rewarded for his own default. Accordingly, the judge decided that the employer was entitled to claim liquidated damages for the entire period of delay, including delays which exceeded beyond the date of termination. The court arrived at this decision based on the actual wording of the contract. The *GPP Big Field* decision is inconsistent with the Court of Appeal ruling in *Triple Point Technology* which in the latter case the Court of Appeal emphasised that the outcome as to whether liquidated damages are awarded following termination of the contract will depend upon the wording of the contract and that there was no blanket rule that applied by default.

Prepayments and forfeitures A2.77

A seller will be in a much stronger position if he requires the buyer to make a payment to him in advance. Should the buyer default, the seller's right to recover depends on the nature of the prepayment. Where the sum has been paid as part of the purchase price, the buyer can recover what he has paid. Where the sum, however, has been paid as a deposit, it is generally irrecoverable unless the deposit is an unreasonable one, or unless the court thinks that it has jurisdiction to grant relief against forfeiture (that is to say, relief against the buyer having to forfeit or lose his deposit) (*Stockloser v Johnson* [1954] 1 QB 476).

Limitation periods A2.78

Section 5 of the *Limitation Act 1980 (LA 1980)* provides that no action on a simple contract 'can be brought once six years have passed from the date when the cause of action accrued'. A 'simple contract' is, essentially, one not made by deed. A contract made by deed is a 'specialty contract', for which s 8 of *LA 1980* prescribes a limitation period of twelve years. In the case of any action for breach of contract where the damages claimed consist of or include damages for personal injuries, *ss 11* and *14* of *LA 1980* specify that the limitation period is three years from:

- the date on which the cause of action accrued, or
- the date of the claimant's knowledge (if later) of certain facts relevant to his right of action.

The general rule in contract is that the cause of action accrues when the breach takes place. As a result, time begins to run from the moment the contract is broken, and not from the time when any damage is actually sustained. For example, in an action for breach of warranty or condition against a seller, the cause of action accrues when the goods are delivered, and not when the damage is discovered.

Under *s 14, LA 1980*, the references to a person's date of knowledge in *s 11, LA 1980* are references to the date on which he first had knowledge of the following facts:

(a)   that the injury in question was significant, and

(b)   that the injury was attributable in whole or in part to the act or omission which is alleged to constitute negligence, nuisance or breach of duty, and

(c)   the identity of the defendant, and

(d)   if it is alleged that the act or omission was that of a person other than the defendant, the identity of that person and the additional facts supporting the bringing of an action against the defendant;

and knowledge that any acts or omissions did or did not, as a matter of law, involve negligence, nuisance or breach of duty is irrelevant.

LA 1980 also contains a number of provisions which extend the limitation period.

Fraud, concealment, mistake   **A2.79**

Section 32 of *LA 1980* applies:

- if the action is based on the fraud of the defendant;

- any fact relevant to the claimant's right of action has been deliberately concealed from him by the defendant;

- or if the action is for relief from the consequence of a mistake.

The limitation period in these cases does not run until the claimant discovers the fraud, concealment or mistake (as the case may be) or could with reasonable diligence have discovered it.

Case Example: *Cave v Robinson Jarvis & Rolf* **[2002] 2 All ER 641**

The House of Lords laid down the following principles for the application of *LA 1980, s 32*. It deprived a party of a limitation defence:

- where that party took active steps to conceal his own breach of duty after he had become aware of it, and

- where he was guilty of deliberate wrongdoing and concealed or failed to disclose it in circumstances where it was unlikely to be discovered for some time.

Case Example: *Allison and another v Horner* **[2014] EWCA Civ 117**

In January 2003, T had made a number of fraudulent representations to H, and H had been induced by those representations to invest in a tax relief scheme that she was operating. The lower court found T liable to H in deceit, subject to limitation. Ordinarily, the limitation period for deceit would have expired in January 2009, but H had not commenced proceedings until 19 July 2010. However, the judge held that the *Limitation Act 1980 s 32(1)* applied. He found that H could not, with reasonable diligence, have discovered the fraud until August 2004, and that consequently, limitation did not expire until August 2010. Although the Revenue had announced in January 2004 that it would be making inquiries into H's claim for tax relief under the scheme, it had not begun its investigations until later that year. It was not until August 2004 that it concluded that the scheme was a sham, and required H to repay the monies he had obtained through it by way of tax relief. At trial, T argued that H had been aware of the fraud by May 2004 and that his claim had been brought out of time.

The Court of Appeal held that, in reaching a decision on the applicability of *s 32(1)*, the first question for the judge was whether, on or before July 19, 2004, H had discovered the precise fraud that he subsequently pleaded. The question was not whether the fraud was obvious, but whether H had discovered it. Moreover, he had to have discovered the precise fraud pleaded; knowledge of fraud in a more general sense was not sufficient to start the limitation period running under *s 32(1)*. If H had not discovered the fraud, the question was then whether he had proved that he could not have discovered it with the exercise of reasonable diligence. In that respect, he bore the burden of showing that he could not have discovered the fraud without taking exceptional measures which it was not reasonable to expect him to take. The court said it was important to bear in mind that the issue of whether T's statements were false would only arise for H if and when he suffered a relevant loss, namely the repayment of any tax rebate he had managed to obtain through the scheme. On the assumption that it was not self-evident that T's statements were false, it would only have been reasonable for H to have investigated them if he needed to do so. Whether he knew that T had made fraudulent misstatements depended on whether he knew the true state of affairs, and there was no evidence that he did. It was only in August 2004 that the Revenue stated definitively that the scheme was a sham and that the tax relief that H had obtained would have to be repaid. Moreover, T had run the scheme with an associate who, the judge found, had believed it to be legitimate. In those circumstances, H could not have been expected to have investigated the legitimacy of the scheme himself before August 2004. The real question was what was required of him by way of reasonable diligence. The judge did not consider any date for possible knowledge of the fraud before 30 April 2004. Even if H had engaged a forensic accounting expert on that date, it was unlikely that results would have been produced before 19 July 2004 which would have enabled him to conclude that T's representations were false. In any event, engaging a forensic accounting expert would have been well beyond the requirements of reasonable diligence. Thus, H had proved that he could not, with the exercise of reasonable diligence, have discovered the fraud on or before 19 July 2004, and the judge had not erred in his application of *s 32(1)*.

Latent damage   **A2.80**

Section 14A of *LA 1980* provides for a limitation period running from:

- six years from the date on which the cause of action first started to accrue, or

- three years from the earliest date on which the claimant first had both the knowledge required for bringing an action and a right to bring the action (if that three year period expires later than the six year period). This provision only applies, however, to actions in negligence, and even then does not cover actions involving personal injuries (see A2.72 above). It does not apply to contract actions, and will be of use only to contracting parties who have a concurrent or independent cause of action in negligence.

Acknowledgement and part payment   **A2.81**

Section 29 of *LA 1980* lays down a uniform rule applicable to both simple and specialty contracts by providing that where a person acknowledges the claim, or makes any payment in respect of it, the right is to be treated as accruing on the date of acknowledgement or payment.

Section 30 says that an acknowledgement must be in writing and signed by the person making it.

What counts as writing   **A2.82**

Case Examples

- *Re River Steamer Co* (1871) LR 6 Ch App 822 (correspondence (unless written 'without prejudice')).

- *Hony v Hony* (1824) 1 Sim & S 568 (an account rendered).

- *Howcutt v Bonsor* (1849) 3 Exch 491 (a recital in a deed).

- *Re Gee & Co (Woolwich) Ltd* [1975] Ch 52 (a company's balance sheet).

- *Goode v Job* (1858) 1 E&E 6 (a pleading).

Acknowledgement is a question of construction, to be decided on the facts of the instant case, and it has been said that the decided cases are of little value as precedents (*Spencer v Hemmerde* [1922] 2 AC 507). Under the present law, all that is needed from the debtor is an admission that there is a debt or other liquidated pecuniary claim outstanding, and of his legal liability to pay it.

Guidelines for determining acknowledgement **A2.83**

> **Case Example:** *Jones v Bellgrove Properties Ltd* **[1949] 2 KB 700**
>
> This case explained that it is not necessary for the acknowledgement to specify the amount of the debt if it can be ascertained by other means.

> **Case Example:** *Howcutt v Bonsor; Re Gee & Co (Woolwich) Ltd* **[1975] Ch 52**
>
> The acknowledgement must, though, acknowledge a claim, and not merely that there might be a claim, and it must further acknowledge that the claim exists at the date of acknowledgement or that it existed on a date which falls within the appropriate period of limitation next before action is brought.

> **Case Example:** *Consolidated Agencies Ltd v Bertram Ltd* **[1965] AC 470**
>
> This case showed that acknowledgement of past liability, however, is ineffective.

Shortening the limitation period **A2.84**

The parties to a contract can always agree on a shorter period than allowed for by *LA 1980*. Such provisions are not uncommon in commercial agreements and their effect may be, depending on the exact wording, to bar or extinguish a right of action, or deprive a party of their right of recourse to particular proceedings after the expiry of the agreed time limit. It should be realised though that such clauses, if contained in a contract made on written standard terms, will be valid only if they can be shown to be reasonable.

Remedy itself barred not the right **A2.85**

If time has lapsed under *LA 1980*, this means that the remedy of court action has gone, but not the particular right. If, for example, a buyer pays a debt which is time-barred, he cannot subsequently recover that payment on the ground that it was no longer due.

Excluding liability for misrepresentation **A2.86**

The *Misrepresentation Act 1967 (MA 1967)*, *s 3*, provides that any contract term excluding or restricting any liability for misrepresentation, or excluding or restricting a remedy otherwise available because of misrepresentation, is valid only if it satisfies the test of reasonableness laid down in the *Unfair Contract Terms Act 1977* . The Act applies only in the case of business to business contracts. In the case of consumer contracts, such clauses are subject to the fairness test laid down in the *Consumer Rights Act 2015.*

When a clause has not been reasonable A2.87

Case Example: *Howard Marine and Dredging Co Ltd v A Ogden & Sons (Excavations) Ltd* **[1978] QB 574**

A term provided that:

> '…charterer's acceptance of handing over the vessel shall be conclusive that [she is] … in all respects fit for the intended and contemplated use by charterers and in every other way satisfactory to them'.

The Divisional Court found that it was not fair and reasonable to rely on this clause, a view which the majority of the Court of Appeal were not prepared to disturb though no specific view was expressed. Lord Denning, however, pointing out that the parties were commercial concerns of equal bargaining strength, and that the term was not foisted by one party on another, but contained in a contract the drafts of which had been passed between the parties, and also noting that the dispute which had arisen was just what such a clause sought to avoid, ruled that it was fair and reasonable to rely on this clause.

Case Example: *Walker v Boyle* **[1982] 1 WLR 495**

A clause in the then edition of the National Conditions of Sale provided that there was no right of rescission for errors, misstatements or omissions in the preliminary answers, or in the sale plan or special conditions, 'nor (save where the error, misstatement or omission is in a written answer and relates to a matter materially affecting the description or value of the property) shall any damages be payable or compensation allowed by either party in respect thereof'.

Without specifying his reasons, the judge ruled that this clause had not been shown to be reasonable. He appears to have been influenced by the fact that the condition excluded compensation for any oral misstatement, however grave, even to the extent of being fraudulent.

Case Example: *Cleaver v Schyde Investments Ltd* **[2011] EWCA Civ 929**

The appellant sellers (C) appealed against a decision that a contract for the sale of land to the respondent (S) should be rescinded on the ground of innocent misrepresentation. The property was used for a garage business. C had orally agreed to sell the property to S with a view to residential development. A local doctor (W) was interested in purchasing the property for development as a medical centre. C had replied to the commercial property standard enquiries from S's solicitors to the effect that there was no planning application, letter or notice outstanding in relation to the property. C then received notice from W that he had made a planning application for the erection of a health centre and four flats on the property. C informed their solicitor but the latter failed to correct the answers to the enquiries. Contracts were exchanged incorporating the *Standard Conditions of Sale* (4th edition). W pursued his planning application notwithstanding that the property had been sold and that came to the attention of S. S thought that W's application, if successful, would create real difficulties in the way of any application for purely residential development. S therefore gave notice to rescind. It was accepted that C's replies to the standard enquiries had contained innocent misrepresentations which would have entitled S to rescind but for standard condition 7.1.3 which excluded error or omission except in the case of fraud or recklessness or where the property differed substantially in quantity, quality or tenure from what the purchaser had been led to expect. The judge held that standard condition 7.1.3 was not fair and reasonable in the circumstances and was therefore of no effect by virtue of the *Misrepresentation Act 1967, s 3* and the *Unfair Contract Terms Act 1977, s 11*. Therefore S was entitled to rescind. C submitted that the judge had not given sufficient weight to the facts that the parties were represented by solicitors, the standard conditions had been varied by a number of special conditions, the standard conditions were endorsed by the Law Society and standard condition 7 had a long history.

It was held that there was nothing self-evidently offensive, in terms of reasonableness and fairness, in a contractual term which restricted a purchaser's right to rescind in the event of the vendor's misrepresentation to cases of fraud or recklessness or where the property differed substantially in quantity, quality or tenure from what the purchaser had been led to expect, and to confine the purchaser to damages in all other cases. The argument in favour of upholding such a provision was particularly strong where, as in the instant case, the term had a long history, it was a well-established feature of property transactions, it was endorsed by the Law Society, both sides were represented by solicitors and the parties had negotiated variations of other standard provisions. The issue, however, on the appeal was whether the judge had erred in principle or was obviously wrong, It would require some exceptional feature or combination of features to enable a court to conclude that standard condition 7.1.3 failed to satisfy the test of reasonableness. The judge was entitled to find that W's planning application had a significant negative impact on S such that had it known of the application it would not have exchanged contracts for the purchase. At the date of the contract C knew of the planning application and that it would be material to S's intentions. C had that knowledge and failed to disclose the fact that the application had been made at the very time that they were entering into a contract which would remove the right that S would otherwise have to rescind for misrepresentation. Moreover, they were doing so notwithstanding their express promise in the standard enquiries to notify S on becoming aware of anything which might cause any reply they had given to be incorrect and notwithstanding the fact that the replies to pre-contract enquiries were excluded by agreement from the entire agreement clause in special condition 12. The judge was entitled to regard that combination of circumstances as taking the case out of the general run and to hold that C failed to show that standard condition 7.1.3 was fair and reasonable in the instant case

Case Example: *Josef Marton v Southwestern General Property* **(unreported, 6 May 1982)**

Land had been bought at auction in reliance upon a misrepresentation. The relevant clause stated:

> 'The property is believed to be and shall be taken to be correctly described and any incorrect statement, error or omission found in the particulars or conditions of sale shall not annul the sale or entitle the purchaser to be discharged from his purchase.'

The purchaser was also denied the right to take any point under town and country planning legislation, requiring him to 'take the properties as they are under the said Acts, rules and regulations'.

A further clause, 'quite obviously designed to avoid the effects' of *MA 1967* provided:

> 'All statements contained in the foregoing particulars are made without responsibility on the part of the auctioneers or the vendor and are statements of opinion and are not to be taken as or implying a statement or representation of fact and any intending purchaser must satisfy himself by inspection or otherwise as to the correctness of each statement contained in the particulars. The vendor does not give or make any representation or warranty in relation to the property nor has the auctioneer or any person in the employment of the auctioneer any authority to do so on his behalf.'

The vendors argued that the circumstances of auction sales necessitated such clauses, while the purchaser said that the misrepresentation was derived from matters solely within the knowledge of the vendors. The vendors further argued that the particulars did stress the need for purchasers to make their own enquiries, and that they were catering not just for private buyers, such as the present party, but also for other categories including speculators.

The judge, however, ruled that parties might well come to an auction, as did this particular buyer, when time no longer allowed for enquiries to be made. He stressed that he was to judge this particular contract and the particular circumstances of the case, also noting that the facts on which the misrepresentation was based were central to the purchase and peculiarly within the vendors' knowledge.

He held that they had not shown that the exclusion was reasonable; if it were otherwise, the vendors could have avoided liability 'for a failure to tell more than only a part of the facts which were among the most material to the whole contract of sale'.

Where a clause has been reasonable   **A2.88**

Case Example: *McCullagh v Lane Fox and Partners Ltd* **[1996] PNLR 205**

This case involved the purchase of property which had a smaller acreage than stated in the particulars. An exclusion clause was upheld, not least because the purchaser 'had ample opportunity to regulate his conduct having regard to the disclaimer. He could have obtained, had he so chosen, an independent check on the acreage. Indeed, he appears to have accepted in evidence that, even within the tight timetable which he was following, he did have the opportunity had he wished to avail himself of it.'

Case Example: *EA Grimstead & Son Ltd v McGarrigan* **[1998–99] Info TLR 384**

An agreement for the purchase of shares contained clauses by which the purchaser confirmed that he had not relied on any warranty or representation not expressly contained in the agreement.

The evidence showed that the draft accounts had been available and the purchaser had had the chance to make a full investigation of the books and records. When the agreement was made, both sides had the benefit of advice from solicitors and accountants. It was also the case that the party making the allegedly false statements was only prepared to enter the contract on the basis that the purchasers relied on his own investigations and judgement. The court said that:

'In such a case, it seems ... wholly fair and reasonable that the purchaser should seek his remedies ... within the four corners of the agreement and should not be permitted to rely on pre-contractual representations which are, deliberately, not reflected in contractual warranties.'

Case Example: *Morgan v Pooley* **[2010] EWHC 2447**

An action for misrepresentation was excluded by the following non-reliance clause: '6. The Buyer acknowledges that this Contract has not been entered into by the Buyer in reliance upon any representations made by or on behalf of the Seller except those made in writing by the Seller's conveyancers prior to the date hereof as being representations upon which reliance is placed and such as were not capable of independent verification by the Buyer.' The clause was said to be reasonable.

Case Example: *Lloyd and Lloyd v Browning and Browning* **[2013] EWCA Civ 1637**

L had retained a planning consultant and an architect before exchanging contracts to purchase farmland from B. Planning permission had been granted for conversion of a barn on the land. Although B had initially obtained plans which included an extension of the barn, those plans were amended when the local authority indicated that such an extension would be contrary to its policies. However, relying on an alleged oral statement by B, L believed that the permission included the extension. L's discussions with their architects were based on the original, unamended plans. When L's planning consultant inspected the planning file there was no planning permission filed. Owing to an error, the amended plans had never been placed on the local authority's files available for public inspection. The planning consultant reported that there was nothing to indicate that there was permission for an extension, but that she did not consider that to be a cause for concern because the extension was mentioned in the estate agent's letter and shown on the plans. The contract for the sale contained a clause, which had been in common usage by a regional law society, stating that the buyer had entered into the agreement solely on the basis of an inspection that he had undertaken, and that he had not been induced by any statement made by the seller, except for written responses by the seller's conveyancers to written pre-contractual enquiries by the buyer's conveyancers. Following completion, L became aware that there was no permission for an extension and brought a claim against B for misrepresentation. The judge held that, although L had been induced by a misrepresentation that there was planning permission for an extension, and although the land was worth approximately £55,000 less without that permission, the exclusion clause had removed B's liability. The issue was whether the exclusion clause was fair and reasonable.

L submitted that the judge should have found that the exclusion clause breached the requirement of reasonableness in the *Unfair Contract Terms Act 1977, s 11* and had erred in placing too much reliance on the fact that the parties had been legally represented, adopting an overly formulaic approach.

The Court of Appeal held that the general purpose behind such clauses was to achieve certainty and to forestall disputes that could lead to trials on contested issues of fact. That was a reasonable position for each party to be presumed to wish to take and a reasonable aim for them to wish to achieve. The features relevant to the assessment of reasonableness of a condition such as the instant one and was to be endorsed. Each side had had legal advisers and L had instructed architects and planning consultants. The contract was one for a sale of land, which had a status of formality as the law required all agreed terms to be in one contractual document to be signed by both parties. The clause was not an example of the 'take it or leave it' condition of the type sometimes imposed in small print in consumer agreements. It was a special condition that had been agreed by both parties' lawyers, with equal negotiating positions. That the term was used by the regional law society meant that it was in common use, which indicated reasonableness. It was particularly striking that, had L wished to rely on an oral statement, they could have made a written pre-contractual enquiry and relied upon the written response. B could not have been expected to know that the local authority had not placed the amended plans on the public file, or that L's planning consultant and architect would not have been able to identify the true position before exchange. The planning consultant's report had indicated potential problems and L could have made enquiries to establish the planning position. The condition was fair and reasonable.

Unfair terms A2.89

In the context of a consumer contract, a term excluding or restricting liability for misrepresentation would be subject to the fairness test laid down in the *Consumer Rights Act 2015*.

Entire agreement and non-reliance clauses A2.90

It has been said that an 'entire agreement' clause is designed to prevent the parties to a contract from 'threshing through the undergrowth and finding in the course of negotiations some (chance) remark or statement ... on which to found a claim ... such as ... to the existence of a collateral warranty': *Inntrepreneur Pub Company (GL) v East Crown Ltd* [2000] 2 Lloyd's Rep 611. In that case, the relevant clause provided: 'Any variations of this Agreement which are agreed in correspondence shall be incorporated in this Agreement where that correspondence makes express reference to this Clause and the parties acknowledge that this Agreement (with the incorporation of any such variations) constitutes the entire Agreement between the parties'. In the judge's view, an entire agreement clause constituted a binding agreement between the parties that the full contractual terms were to be found in the contractual document and not elsewhere.

Case Example: *Deepak v ICI* **[1999] 1 Lloyd's Rep 387**

The clause read:

'This contract comprises the entire agreement between the parties ... and there are not any agreements, understandings, promises or conditions, oral or written, express or implied, concerning the subject matter which are not merged into this contract and superseded thereby...'

This was held to be wide enough to exclude all liability for collateral warranties, but not misrepresentations.

Case Example: *Alman & Benson v Associated Newspapers Group Ltd* **(unreported, 20 June 1980)**

It was provided that a contract 'constituted the entire agreement and understanding between the parties with respect to all matters therein referred to'.

The court held that the language was apt to exclude all liability for a collateral warranty.

An alternative approach, designed to achieve the same end, is to reduce the clause to an acknowledgment by the parties that the agreement constitutes the entire agreement between them. In the *Inntrepreneur* case, the court considered that this form of clause was also sufficient to constitute an agreement that 'the full contractual terms to which the parties agreed to bind themselves are to be found in the agreement and nowhere else'. The relevant clause ran: 'Any variations to this Agreement which are agreed to in correspondence shall be incorporated in this Agreement where that correspondence makes express reference to this Clause and the parties acknowledge that this Agreement (with the incorporation of any such variations) constitutes the entire Agreement between the parties'. It was also held that an entire agreement clause did not itself preclude a claim in misrepresentation. The denial of contractual force to a particular statement could not affect the status of that statement as a representation.

See too the observation that 'the suggestion....that in some way that provision [a non-reliance provision] should be struck down as unreasonable under *sections 3 and 11 of the Unfair Contract Terms Act 1977* is hopeless', per Flaux J in *Barclays Bank plc v Svizera Holdings BV and another* [2014] EWHC 1020.

In *Al-Hasawi v Nottingham Forest Football Club* [2018] EWHC 2884, concerned a share purchase agreement (SPA) entered into between H and the Club. The buyer alleged that the seller had misrepresented the target company's liabilities. The seller contended that the entire agreement clause in the SPA prevented the buyer from claiming for misrepresentation. The clause comprised only of an entire agreement statement but there was no clause on non-reliance or any exclusion of liability. The clause provided:

> 'This agreement…constitutes the entire agreement between the parties and supersedes and extinguishes all previous discussions, correspondence, negotiations, drafts, agreements, promises, warranties, representations and understandings between them…relating to its subject matter.'

The SPA also set out a contractual indemnity clause for any losses incurred by the buyer by reason of any misstatement or misrepresentation of the target company's liabilities.

HHJ David Cooke emphasised the position that clear words are needed to exclude liability for misrepresentation. He stated that although it might have made commercial sense to exclude a claim in misrepresentation for the indemnified loss, the parties had not set this out in the agreement, and the court could not therefore intervene. The High Court therefore allowed the buyer's appeal and stated that a contractual mechanism to allow a remedy did not carry with it the implication that other remedies (such as misrepresentations) were excluded or defeated. If the parties wish to exclude the right to claim for misrepresentation, clear language to that effect is required.

In *First Tower Trustees Ltd v CDS (Superstores International) Ltd* [2019] 1 WLR 637, the landlord, First Tower Trustees, leased property to CDS. Unknown to the tenant CDS but known to the landlord, the property was contaminated with asbestos and dangerous to enter. The Landlord had misrepresented the position in response to CDS's formal enquiries that the landlord had not been notified of any environmental problems. The solicitors representing the landlord did not pass the information on asbestos to CDS despite a requirement in the enquiry form. Subsequently, CDS terminated the lease and claimed misrepresentation. The landlord relied on the non-reliance clause in the lease which provided:

> 'The tenant acknowledges that this lease has not been entered into in reliance wholly or partly on any statement or representation made by or on behalf of the landlord.'

The Court of Appeal held that the landlord's representations in the reply to the enquiries were false and the non-reliance clause was an attempt to exclude liability for misrepresentation under *s 3, MA 1967*.

According to the Court of Appeal, the non-reliance clause was not simply describing the parties' primary obligations, but was an attempt to exclude liability for misrepresentation. It was therefore subject to *s 3, MA 1967* and *s 11, UCTA 1977* on the reasonableness test. In any event, the non-reliance clause did not satisfy the reasonableness test under *UCTA 1977*.

Frustration   A2.91

A contract is frustrated when 'a contractual obligation has become incapable of being performed because the circumstances in which performance is called for would render a thing radically different from that which was undertaken by the contract' (*Davis Contractors Ltd v Fareham Urban District Council* [1956] AC 696, 729). The effect of frustration is to discharge the parties from any further obligation under the contract. The application of the doctrine of frustration depends on the actual terms of the contract:

- to define the nature and basis of the performance, so that it can be determined whether the circumstances that have occurred have made performance radically different, and

- secondly, to determine whether the parties provided in the contract for the very event which occurred.

Other limits are that the impossibility of contemplated performance must not have been foreseen by the parties, and must not be brought about by the fault or the choice of either party.

Case Example: *Dany Lions Ltd v Bristol Cars Ltd* [2013] EWHC 2997

D owned a very rare vintage car. It had participated in email communications with B about the possibility of B carrying out radical restoration works on the car. One email from B laid out the various works it proposed to do, including fitting an automatic gearbox, and said that it would deduct £15,000 from the quoted figure of £168,000 to leave a total of £153,000. The terms and conditions in the email provided that D would make a first payment of £50,000, a second of £40,000, and a final one of the 'balance of the invoice price'. In the event, B did not perform the works and D commenced proceedings for alleged breach of contract. In the instant hearing, D brought two applications for summary judgment in relation to various issues: first, it sought an order that, on a proper construction of the email exchange, it was a term of the contract between the parties that the price of the works would not exceed £153,000; second, it sought an order to the effect that B could not avoid its contractual obligations on the basis of common mistake, and that the contract had not been frustrated.

B argued that: (1) whilst its email was in the nature of an offer, it included no fixed price and the reference to 'balance of the invoice price' meant that the total price due from D had not been finalised; (2) the contract was void because it was based on the parties' fundamental mistaken view that it would be possible to convert D's car to automatic transmission without affecting its full functionality, or alternatively, that the contract had been frustrated when the parties realised the impossibility of carrying out the proposed works.

The court held that the only possible interpretation of the email exchange was that B had offered to carry out the works for no more than £153,000.

It was entirely plain that B's case that there had been no agreed maximum price was wholly unsustainable. Accordingly, it was a term of the parties' contract that the price of the works would not exceed £153,000, and it was appropriate to award D summary judgment on that issue. It was also held that B had agreed to adapt the engine; it did not agree to see if it could do so. Therefore, the starting point for considering B's arguments based on common mistake and frustration was that B had assumed a positive liability to achieve a result. B's case was not that that result could not be achieved, but that that result would have affected the car's functionality. Whilst that might have been the case, it did not relieve B of its obligation to satisfy its contractual liability. On a proper construction of B's email, which amounted to the offer to do the works, it had warranted that it would be possible to fit an automatic gearbox. The supply of the gearbox was important but not so fundamental to the contract as a whole as to render impossible all of B's contractual obligations. As a result, B had no real prospect of showing that the contract was void for common mistake or that it was frustrated by the realisation that the works could not be completed.

Frustration under the Sale of Goods Act 1979   **A2.92**

Section 7 of the *Sale of Goods Act 1979* (*SGA 1979*), which still applies to consumer contracts, provides that where there is an agreement to sell specific goods, and the goods without any fault on the part of the seller or buyer perish before risk has passed to the buyer, the agreement is at an end.

Meaning of 'perish'   **A2.93**

Case Example: *Horn v Minister of Food* [1948] 2 All ER 1036

The contract was for the sale of potatoes, which rotted and became useless. The court held that they could still be described as potatoes, for all that they had rotted, so *SGA 1979* did not apply.

When a contract is rendered void by the above provisions, the buyer can recover the price if already paid. There can be no adjustment for benefits conferred or expenses incurred before the time when the goods perished.

Case Example: *Turnbull v Rendell* (1908) 27 NZLR 1067

The contract was for the sale of 'table potatoes' from a specific crop. At the time of the contract, some of the potatoes were so badly affected with secondary growth that they could no longer be described as 'table potatoes'. It was held that the potatoes had perished.

It would appear that goods can be said to have perished if they have been stolen (*Barrow, Lane & Ballard Ltd v Phillip Phillips & Co Ltd* [1929] 1 KB 574); or destroyed by fire (*Oldfield Asphalts v Grovedale Coolstores 1994 Ltd* [1998] 3 NZLR 479).

Contracting out of Section 7   **A2.94**

Unlike many other provisions of *SGA 1979*, such as those relating to property and risk, the Act says nothing about the parties making their own provision as to the effect of perishing. It is arguably within the spirit of the Act to allow parties to allocate risk as they wish, so the following clause could be considered by a supplier:

> 'In those cases where the goods have perished before delivery to the buyer, the contract will be at an end, but the buyer will be liable for any costs and expenses incurred by the supplier in preparing for performance of the contract, and the buyer will be further liable to pay a reasonable sum for any benefits received. In no circumstances, however, will the buyer be liable for more than the contract price'.

Cases for Further Information

Duthie v Hilton (1868) LR 4 CP 138; *Asfar v Blundell* [1895] 1 QB 126.

Frustration outside the Sale of Goods Act 1979   **A2.95**

Where *s* 7 of the *SGA 1979* does not apply, a contract can be frustrated by any reason which makes performance radically different from that which was undertaken in the contract.

Instances of frustrating events   **A2.96**

Case Examples

- Illegality due to the outbreak of war (*Re Badische Co Ltd* [1921] 2 Ch 331).

- Requisitioning of goods (*Shipton Anderson & Co v Harrison Brothers & Co* [1915] 3 KB 676).

- Government restrictions on the purchase of contractual goods (*Societe Co-operative Suisse des Cereales et Matieres Fourrageres v La Plata Cereal Company SA* (1947) 80 LL.R 530).

- Inability to obtain export licences (*AV Pound & Co Ltd v MW Hardy & Co Inc* [1956] AC 588).

- Where goods were to be loaded on a particular vessel which was so damaged that it could not be loaded within the contractual period (*Nickoll & Knight v Ashton, Eldridge & Co* [1901] 2 KB 126).

Contracting out of the rules on frustration   **A2.97**

It will be difficult to draft a clause which excludes the possibility of frustration altogether. This is because it will be for the court to decide if it covers the events which have happened and even the widest of clauses might still not cover a very unusual or catastrophic event.

> **Case Example:** *Metropolitan Water Board v Dick Kerr & Co* [1918] **AC 119**
>
> A contract for the construction of a reservoir provided for an extension of time in the event of delay 'whatsoever and howsoever occasioned'. This was held not to cover cessation of work due to government order, since the delay was such that it 'vitally and fundamentally changes the condition of the contract, and could not possibly have been in the contemplation of the parties when it was made'.

Consequences of frustration outside the Sale of Goods Act 1979   **A2.98**

The position in such cases is regulated by the *Law Reform (Frustrated Contracts) Act 1943* (*LR(FC)A 1943*). Any sums paid or payable can be recovered or will cease to be payable: *s 1(2)*. The other side can, however, retain or recover payment in whole or in part to cover their costs, if the court considers it just to do so having regard to all the circumstances of the case. This would mean that, in a contract for the sale of goods where *SGA 1979, s 7* did not apply, any expenses involved in manufacturing the goods, or in customising manufacturing equipment, or in packing or transporting the goods is potentially recoverable.

LR(FC)A 1943 also provides that if before the frustrating event one party has conferred a valuable benefit on the other, the court may order the payment to the first party of such sum as it considers just, taking into account the valuable benefit: *s 1(3)*.

LR(FC)A 1943 specifically allows the parties to make their own provisions in the contract for the effect of frustration, and thus to avoid the foregoing provisions.

Third party rights

Privity of contract A2.99

Under the 'privity of contract' doctrine, parties who are not actually parties to the contract cannot enforce it, even if the contract was specifically entered into for their benefit.

Case Example: *Tweddle v Atkinson* **(1861) 1 B & S 393**

The groom's father, John Tweddle, agreed with the bride's father, William Guy, to pay the groom, William Tweddle, £200. William Guy died, and the estate would not pay. So William Tweddle sued. The courts ruled that the promisee could not bring an action unless the consideration for the promise moved from him. Consideration must move from party entitled to sue upon the contract. Third parties to a contract do not derive any rights from that agreement nor are they subject to any burdens imposed by it.

Case Example: *Beswick v Beswick* **[1968] AC 58**

A widow was refused enforcement in her own right of a contract made between her late husband and her nephew which required the latter to pay her £5 a week in return for the transfer to him of her husband's business.

Cases for Further Information

Gandy v Gandy (1885) 30 Ch D 57; *The Pioneer Container* [1994] 2 AC 324; *Darlington BC v Wiltshier Northern Ltd* [1995] 1 WLR 68; *White v Jones* [1995] 2 AC 207.

Contracts (Rights of Third Parties) Act 1999 A2.100

The position stated above remains the basic position, but significant inroads have been made into it by the *Contracts (Rights of Third Parties) Act 1999* (*C(RTP) A 1999*). *Section 1* of the Act provides that a person who is not actually a party to a contract may still enforce a term of the contract, if:

- the contract expressly provides that he may; or
- the term purports to confer a benefit on that party.

This, however, will not apply if, on a proper construction of the contract, it appears that the actual parties to the contract did not intend the term to be enforceable by the non-party: *s 1(2)*.

The third party must be expressly identified in the contract by name, as a member of a class or as answering a particular description but need not be in existence when the contract is entered into: *s 1(3)*. This would allow references in the contract to companies which have yet to be formed.

In *Chudley v Clydesdale Bank plc* [2019] EWCA Civ 344, the Court of Appeal held that a letter of instruction ('LOI') between a bank and its customer conferred a benefit on third party investors. The third party investors who were not customers of the bank, were held to be part of a sufficiently identified class in the LOI for the purpose of *s 1(3)* of the 1999 Act. The Court of Appeal was required to ascertain the level of identification required in order for a third party to establish that a contract conferred a benefit on them which was enforceable under *s 1(3)* of the Act. The Court of Appeal held that it was not necessary for the LOI to specify a third party investor by name. It determined that the reference to 'a client account' in the LOI together with the name of the investment scheme was express identification of the class who were clients of the bank's customer who were investing in the scheme that was the subject of the LOI.

Sample Clause

Draftsmen of commercial contracts would be well advised to consider, as a standard part of the drafting process, whether each provision which benefits a third party, who is also expressly designated in the contract, is capable of being directly enforced by that third party. If so, the draftsman will avoid all uncertainty if a right of enforceability is expressly conferred on the third party. If not, a provision should be included expressly excluding the third party rights of enforcement. For example, the draftsman might wish to provide that:

> 'except as otherwise expressly provided by this agreement, none of the terms and conditions of this agreement shall be enforceable by any person who is not a party to it',

so as to avoid any accidental conferring of enforceable rights on a third party.

Exclusion clauses and third parties   A2.101

C(RTP)A 1999 states that, where the exclusion clause is one seeking to exclude or restrict liability for negligence (other than relating to death or personal injury), the controls on such clauses imposed by the *Unfair Contract Terms Act 1977* shall not apply where the breach was in relation to the third party. In such cases, common law rules as to interpretation will apply. The absence of any reference to other provisions of *UCTA 1977*, or to the *Unfair Terms in Consumer Contracts Regulations 1999 (SI 1999/2083)*, will mean that they will apply in relation to third party actions on the contract.

> **Case for further information:** *Fortress Value Recovery Fund ll and another v Blue Skye Opportunities Fund LP* [2013] EWCA Civ 367

Arbitration clauses A2.102

C(RTP)A 1999 states that where a third party right of enforcement is given subject to a term of the contract which requires the submission of disputes to arbitration, the third party should be required to submit to arbitration to enforce his rights, and should be treated as a party to the arbitration agreement for that purpose: *s 8, C(RTP)A 1999.* See too the case cited immediately above.

Intellectual property rights A2.103

There will be many contracts, such as licensing or technology agreements, or when the supplier of goods first develops and manufactures them with guidance from the buyer, where it will be necessary for intellectual property rights to be settled in the contract itself.

Sample Clauses

The contract term should first define just what is meant by 'intellectual property rights'. Thus:

> "Intellectual Property' means all rights in patents, registered and unregistered designs, copyright, trade marks, know-how and all other forms of intellectual property wherever in the world enforceable'.

It then becomes necessary to establish where ownership of such intellectual property is to lie, as follows:

> 'All intellectual property rights used in or produced from or arising as a result of the performance of this contract shall, so far as not already so vested, become the absolute property of ourselves, and you will do all that is reasonably necessary to ensure that such rights vest in us (as, (without prejudice to the generality of the foregoing) by the execution of appropriate instruments or the making of agreements with third parties).'

If it is considered appropriate, the clause could go on to grant the other side a licence to use the intellectual property, as follows:

> 'At our discretion, we shall grant you a licence to use such intellectual property on such terms as to time, extent and royalty, and other appropriate matters, as we think appropriate.'

Confidentiality, non-disclosure and trade secrets   A2.104

As with intellectual property, it is first necessary to define what is meant by 'confidential information'. Confidential information is protected through case law in the UK. It has generally been accepted that in order to demonstrate that there has been a breach of confidence, it is necessary to show three elements were present:

(1)   The information has the necessary quality of confidence in that it is not generally known by the general public or persons who specialise in that subject.

(2)   The information was shared in circumstances imparting an obligation of confidence (that is, that a reasonable person would have realised that the information was being given in confidence).

(3)   There has been an unauthorised use of that information to the detriment of the party communicating it in that it has been used by the recipient beyond the owner's consent or disclosed to third parties without the owner's consent: see per Megarry J in *Coco v Clark* [1969] RPC 41.

In *Vestergaard Frandsen SIA v Bestnet Europe Ltd* [2013] UKSC 31, the Supreme Court further refined the law on confidential information by holding that an action for breach of confidence was based ultimately on conscience. In order for the conscience of the recipient to be affected, he must have information which he has agreed, or knows, is confidential, or he must be party to some action which he knows involves the misuse of confidential information. More broadly, the law had to maintain a realistic and fair balance between (i) effectively protecting trade secrets and other intellectual property rights, and (ii) not unreasonably inhibiting competition in the market place. The protection of intellectual property, including trade secrets, was a vital contribution of the law to research and development. However, the law should not discourage former employees from benefitting society and advancing themselves by imposing unfair potential difficulties on their honest attempts to compete with their former employers.

Trade secrets constitute valuable business assets. They can be used by businesses alongside formal intellectual property rights (patents, designs, trade marks and copyright), or as an alternative to them, to provide competitive advantage in the marketplace. They come in various forms and consist of a wide range of confidential information such as commercial data, technological information and product information. Trade secrets are protected by contract and/or the common law of confidence.

At the European level, the *EU* Trade Secrets *Directive* SI 2016/943 on the protection of undisclosed know-how and business information (trade secrets) against their unlawful acquisition, use and disclosure was approved by the European Parliament and Council in 2016. Its main objective was to achieve the smooth-functioning internal market by establishing a sufficient and comparable level of redress for trade secret holders in the event of the unlawful acquisition, use or disclosure of their trade secrets. The Directive provided a minimum level of protection across the EU Member States available for litigants where there has been misappropriation or misuse of a trade secret. The Directive has sought to improve the environment for innovation and knowledge transfer within the EU by enhancing the effectiveness of the legal protection available for trade secrets.

At the national level, the UK has enacted the *Trade Secrets (Enforcement, etc) Regulations 2018, SI 2018/597* which came into force in June 2018. A number of the provisions of the Directive have already been implemented in the UK by the principles of common law and equity relating to breach of confidence in confidential information, statute and court rules. The 2018 Regulations address those areas where gaps occur or where the implementation of the provisions of the Directive will ensure legal certainty, making the law more transparent and coherent across all of the UK's jurisdictions with respect to proceedings concerning the unlawful acquisition, use or disclosure of a trade secret. It is likely that actions could be brought both under the 2018 Regulations and the common law in the alternative as the definition of a trade secret under the common law is perceived to be wider than under the 2018 Regulations.

The Regulations define a 'trade secret' as information which:

(a)   is secret in the sense that it is not, as a body or in the precise configuration and assembly of its components, generally known among, or readily accessible to, persons within the circles that normally deal with the kind of information in question;

(b)   has commercial value because it is secret, and

(c)   has been subject to reasonable steps under the circumstances, by the person lawfully in control of the information, to keep it secret': Regulation 1 to the 2018 Regulations.

(see also Article 2(1) of the EU Directive and Article 39(2) of the World Trade Organisation Agreement on Trade-Related Aspects of Intellectual Property (TRIPS)).

Regulation 2 to the 2018 Regulations defines related terms:

'infringer' means a person who has unlawfully acquired, used or disclosed a trade secret;

'infringing goods' means goods, the design, functioning, production process, marketing or a characteristic of which significantly benefits from a trade secret unlawfully acquired, used or disclosed;

'trade secret holder' means any person lawfully controlling a trade secret.

The 2018 Regulations are intended to operate alongside existing UK law on trade secrets. This is achieved by Regulation 3 which provides for a wider protection by stating that:

(1) The acquisition, use or disclosure of a trade secret is unlawful where the acquisition, use or disclosure constitutes a breach of confidence in confidential information.

(2) A trade secret holder may apply for and a court may grant measures, procedures, and remedies available in an action for breach of confidence where the measures, procedures and remedies:

   (a) provide wider protection to the trade secret holder than that provided under these Regulations in respect of the unlawful acquisition, use or disclosure of a trade secret, and

   (b) comply with the safeguards referred to in Article 1 of *Directive (EU) 2016/943* of the European Parliament and of the Council of 8 June 2016 on the protection of undisclosed know-how and business information (trade secrets) against their unlawful acquisition, use and disclosure.

(3) A trade secret holder may apply for and a court may grant the measures, procedures and remedies referred to in paragraph (2) in addition, or as an alternative, to the measures procedures and remedies provided for in these Regulations in respect of the unlawful acquisition, use or disclosure of a trade secret.

Therefore, under Regulation 3, claims under existing breach of confidence law are likely to be brought alongside the 2018 Regulations. The Regulations do not replace the existing law.

The limitation period for bringing a claim under the 2018 Regulations is six years in England and Wales. This period begins with the later of (a) the date on which the unlawful acquisition, use or disclosure that is the subject of the claim ceases; and (b) the day of knowledge of the trade secret holder: Regulations 4-9.

Under Regulation 10(4), a court may order any of the measures set out in Regulation 10(5) as may be necessary to preserve the confidentiality of any trade secret or alleged trade secret used or referred to in the course of the proceedings. In this regard, the court may:

(a) restrict access to any document containing a trade secret or alleged trade secret submitted by the parties or third parties, in whole or in part, to a limited number of persons;

(b) restrict access to hearings, when trade secrets or alleged trade secrets may be disclosed, and to the record or transcript of those hearings to a limited number of persons, and

(c)   make available to a person, who is not one of the limited number of persons referred to in sub-paragraph (a) or (b), a non-confidential version of any judicial decision, in which the passages containing trade secrets have been removed or redacted.

In deciding whether or not to grant these measures, and in assessing their proportionality, the court must take into account:

(a)   the need to ensure the right to an effective remedy and to a fair trial;

(b)   the legitimate interests of the parties, and

(c)   any potential harm for the parties: Regulation 10(7). The term 'parties' includes, where appropriate, third parties: Regulation 10(8).

Various measures are provided under Regulations 11–15 which includes the power of the court to make various interim and final measures, including the prohibition of the unlawful activity and the seizure or delivery up of infringing goods.

A court may order compensation in lieu of an injunction or corrective measures under Regulation 14: Regulation 16. Under Regulation 17(1), on the application of an injured party, a court must order an infringer, who knew or ought to have known that unlawful acquisition, use or disclosure of a trade secret was being engaged in, to pay the trade secret holder damages appropriate to the actual prejudice suffered as a result of the unlawful acquisition, use or disclosure of the trade secret.

A court may award damages under Regulation 17(1) on the basis of either Regulations 17(3) or (4).

Under Regulation 17(3), when awarding damages, a court must take into account all appropriate factors, including in particular:

(i)   the negative economic consequences, including any lost profits, which the trade secret holder has suffered, and any unfair profits made by the infringer, and

(ii)   elements other than economic factors, including the moral prejudice caused to the trade secret holder by the unlawful acquisition, use or disclosure of the trade secret.

Under Regulation 17(4), when awarding damages under Regulation 17(1), a court may, where appropriate, award damages on the basis of the royalties or fees which would have been due had the infringer obtained a licence to use the trade secret in question.

In proceedings for the unlawful acquisition, use or disclosure of a trade secret, a court may order, on the application of the trade secret holder and at the expense of the infringer, appropriate measures for the dissemination of information concerning the judgment, including its publication in whole or in part: Regulation 18(1). In deciding whether to order a measure under Regulation 18(1) and when assessing whether such measure is proportionate, the court must take into account where appropriate:

(a)   the value of the trade secret;

(b)   the conduct of the infringer in acquiring, using or disclosing the trade secret;

(c)   the impact of the unlawful use or disclosure of the trade secret;

(d)   the likelihood of further unlawful use, or disclosure of the trade secret by the infringer, and

(e)   whether the information on the infringer would be such as to allow an individual to be identified and, if so, whether publication of that information would be justified, in particular in the light of the possible harm that such measure may cause to the privacy and reputation of the infringer.

Sample Clauses

The definition of confidential information can be dealt with using the following clause:

> "Confidential Information' shall mean all information disclosed by us to you in any form or manner, provided that each such item of information would appear to a reasonable person to be confidential or is specifically stated by us to be confidential.'

This would then be followed by the following further clause:

> 'You will take all proper steps to keep confidential all confidential information disclosed to, or obtained by, you under or as a result of this agreement, and will not divulge such information to any third party. Without prejudice to the foregoing, such information may be divulged where this is necessary for the proper performance of this agreement and providing you ensure that the recipient of such information is under a like obligation to that spelled out in this clause. In addition, no liability will attach in relation to confidential information which, through no fault on your part, enters the public domain. It is further agreed that, on termination of this agreement, for whatever reason, you will promptly return to us all equipment, articles, items, products and data, in whatever form recorded, and without retaining any copies, provided for the purposes of this agreement. Notwithstanding the termination of this contract, for whatever reason, the obligations and restrictions imposed by this clause shall be valid for a period of [x] years from the date of such termination.'

Notices A2.105

Proper provision for the service of notices is a necessary part of most agreements. Any such clause has to provide for the place or places at which notice is to be served, the method of service, and when any such notice will be deemed to have been delivered. Although oral notice is possible and permissible, the need for evidence of delivery effectively precludes such form of notice.

Sample Clause

'All notices and communications given under this agreement shall be in writing or other durable form and shall be deemed to have been given:

- when delivered, if delivered personally or by messenger during normal business hours (or on the commencement of the first working day thereafter);

- when sent, if transmitted by telex, facsimile or electronic mail including thereby SMS text service during normal business hours or on the commencement of the first working day thereafter), or

- on the second business day following mailing by recorded or registered mail.

In all the above cases, the communication will be deemed to have been sent or delivered to the correct address or number if sent to the last address or number of which we have been advised by you.'

Major issues can arise where a party does not adhere to the notice provisions in the agreement. Some cases demonstrate that the courts take a strict approach towards the notice provisions in order to ensure compliance with the contractual agreement. In *Teoco UK Ltd v Aircom Jersey 4 Ltd* [2018] EWCA Civ 23, the parties entered into a share purchase agreement (SPA). Teoco claimed damages for breach of various warranties contained in the SPA. The SPA stated that any liability of Aircom under the warranties were subject to Teoco giving Aircom notice of such claims 'setting out reasonable details of the claim (including the grounds on which it is based and [Teoco's] good faith estimate of the amount of the claim…'.

The notices sent by Teoco to Aircom in respect of two of the claims only alleged breach of the 'Tax Warranties and the General Warranties'. The notices did not identify any specific warranties. Aircom therefore applied to strike out the claims on the basis that Teoco had not complied with the notification requirements in the SPA.

The Court of Appeal recognised that every notification clause turns on its own individual wording (see *Forrest v Glasser* [2006] EWCA Civ 1086). The Court of Appeal held that Teoco had not properly notified Aircom of the warranty claims which required Teoco to set out the grounds of the claim with explicit reference to particular warranties rather than a general reference. This could be achieved without referencing a specific warranty where the facts unequivocally pointed towards a particular warranty. The 'omnibus reference' to 'Warranty Claims' or 'Tax Claims' was not sufficient as they did not serve to identify the 'grounds' of the claims, and further, the references were not clear nor certain. The Court of Appeal also stated that the notices were broadly framed by Teoco so as to keep its options open. By failing to identify the warranties or other provisions, Teoco had not complied with the notice provisions.

The Court of Appeal in *Teoco* also noted the following cases which provide assistance on notification claims:

- *Senate Electrical Wholesalers Ltd v Alcatel Submarine Networks Ltd* [1999] 2 Lloyd's Rep 423, concerned a provision requiring a purchaser of a business to give notice in writing of a claim to the vendor 'setting out such particulars of the grounds on which the claim is based and are known to the Purchaser promptly.' This required the notice to be sufficiently clear and unambiguous as to leave no room for argument about the particulars of the complaint. Notice in writing is required in order to constitute the record which dispels the need for further argument and creates the certainty. Stuart-Smith LJ further stated that 'certainty is only achieved when the vendor is left in no reasonable doubt not only that a claim may be brought, but of the particulars of the grounds upon which the claim is to be based.'

- In *RWE Nukem Ltd v AEA Technology plc* [2005] EWHC 78, in which the clause stipulated that the vendor of a business would be under no liability in respect of a claim 'unless written particulars of such Claim giving details of the specific matters as are available to the Purchaser in respect of such Claim is made', had been given to the vendor within a specified period. This largely depended upon the nature of the Claim, the facts known to the vendor at the date of the notice, and whether it was realistic to put any monetary quantification on the amount claimed. The court could not lay down too rigid a formula for ascertaining what precise particulars or details have to be provided – it all depends upon the circumstances of each case. At the very least, the compliance notice would identify the particular warranty that was alleged to have been breached with some particularisation of the facts upon which such allegation was based, and to indicate what loss had been suffered as a result of the breach of warranty.

In *Stobart Group Ltd v Stobart* [2019] EWCA Civ 1376, the Court of Appeal decided that a letter sent by a party to a share purchase agreement did not constitute a notice of a claim under tax covenants in the agreement. This resulted in a defective notice being served in that the claim was not properly notified within the contractual time limit and was time-barred.

Signature   A2.106

A signature is only required in those cases where a contract must be in writing, such as contracts relating to real property, insurance and certain agreements relating to consumer credit. If, of course, a document is signed, that makes it that much easier to show that the contents were acknowledged and that a binding contract has resulted.

Binding nature of signature   A2.107

Case Example: *L'Estrange v Graucob* [1934] 2 KB 394

The buyer of a cigarette vending machine was bound by a clause which appeared in 'regrettably small print' in the seller's order form, and which the buyer signed.

Although probably not a major issue in commercial dealings, it should be noted that a person will only be allowed to deny the validity of his signature if he can show that the document signed was of an altogether different nature from what he thought he was signing (*Foster v McKinnon* (1869) LR 4 CP 704; *Saunders v Anglia Building Society* [1971] AC 1004). Under the provisions of the *Electronic Communications Act 2000*, provision is made for the use of electronic signatures. See for example, Article 4 of the *Consumer Credit Act 1974 (Electronic Communications) Order 2004 (SI 2004/3236).* This enables agreements to be concluded electronically and to enable the creditor or owner to include in the signature box contained in the agreement information about the process or means of providing, communicating or verifying the signature made by the debtor or hirer. See too the *Unsolicited Goods and Services Act 1971 (Electronic Communications) Order 2001 (SI 2001/2778)* and the *Unsolicited Goods and Services Act 1971 (Electronic Commerce) Regulations 2005 (SI 2005/148)* which allow for the electronic communication of an order for an entry in a directory.

It has been held that a consumer credit agreement can be entered into electronically and that clicking the 'Accept' button amounts to the provision of a signature: *Bassano v Toft and others* [2014] EWHC 377

Either party can stipulate that a contract will take effect only when signed by or on behalf of both parties.

Proper law clauses   A2.108

If goods are supplied to a party outside the jurisdiction, it is always advisable to include what is called a 'proper law' clause specifying whose law is to apply.

Sample Clause

A typical clause would run: 'This agreement shall be governed by and construed in accordance with English law'. This is often bracketed with further wording giving English courts the exclusive right to determine any issues which may arise: 'Each party also agrees to submit to the exclusive jurisdiction of the English courts'.

Avoiding restrictions on exclusion clauses   A2.109

Although the parties have considerable flexibility in choosing the proper law, there are some restraints. Under the *Unfair Contract Terms Act 1977*, the Act will still apply if the parties choose a proper law outside the United Kingdom, if this was done to evade the operation of the Act; or if one of the parties was a consumer who was habitually resident in the United Kingdom, and the 'essential steps necessary' for making the contract were taken in the United Kingdom. Conversely, the Act also provides that where United Kingdom law applies only by virtue of a proper law clause, the provisions of the Act will not apply. As the 1977 Act no longer applies to consumer contracts, comparable provisions are found in the *Consumer Rights Act 2015*.

Competition issues   A2.110

Article 101 of the Treaty on the Functioning of the European Union prohibits all agreements between undertakings, decisions by associations of undertakings and concerted practices which may affect trade between EU member states and which have as their object or effect the prevention, restriction or distortion of competition within the common market. The Treaty prohibits restrictions which:

- directly or indirectly fix purchase or selling prices or any other trading conditions;

- limit or control production, markets, technical development or investment;

- share markets or sources of supply;

- apply dissimilar conditions to equivalent transactions with other trading parties, thereby placing them at a competitive disadvantage; and

- make the conclusion of contracts subject to acceptance by the other parties of supplementary obligations which, by their nature or according to commercial usage, have no connection with the subject of such contracts. Such restrictions should therefore be left out when a contract is being drafted. The European Commission can impose fines of up to 10% of turnover.

Under the Treaty, an agreement which is anti-competitive can also be beneficial, and, if this is felt to be the case, an application can be made to the European Commission for an individual exemption.

There are specific European enactments detailing the application of at 101 as follows:

- Vertical agreements (Vertical agreements in general and motor vehicles);
- Horizontal agreements;
- Licensing agreements for the transfer of technology
- Specific sector legislation:
- Agriculture
- Insurance
- Postal services
- Professional services
- Transport
- Telecommunications

Equivalent domestic provisions A2.111

The Treaty broadly applies to agreements affecting trade within the European Union. Much the same provisions are, however, applied to transactions having only a domestic effect by the *Competition Act 1998 (CA 1998)*. The so-called Chapter I prohibition applies to agreements, decisions and concerted practices between undertakings or associations of undertakings which are implemented in the United Kingdom, and the purpose or effect of which is the prevention, restriction or distortion of competition in the UK. Exemptions can be granted by the Competition and Markets Authority. The Secretary of State may issue block exemptions. The CMA may impose fines of up to 10% of turnover.

Case Example

Penalties were imposed on two bus companies, Arriva and FirstGroup. Staff from the companies had met and agreed that Arriva would withdraw from two routes, leaving FirstGroup with no competition on these routes. In turn, FirstGroup would withdraw from routes which Arriva would take on. Arriva was fined £318,175 and FirstGroup £529,852. These penalties were then reduced under the OFT's leniency programme under which businesses that inform the OFT about cartel activity and co-operate fully can be granted leniency. FirstGroup asked for leniency at an early stage and was granted 100% leniency, thus eliminating the fine. Arriva asked for leniency second and co-operated, and its fine was reduced to £203,632.

Case Example

The OFT found that Hasbro, Argos and Littlewoods had entered into an overall agreement and/or concerted practice to fix the price of certain Hasbro toys and games infringing the Chapter I prohibition contained in *s 2* of the *Competition Act 1998*. Financial penalties totalling £22.65 million were imposed in respect of the infringements. The Competition Appeals Tribunal upheld the decision on the companies' liability.

Case Example

The OFT found that a number of sportswear retailers (including but not limited to Allsports Ltd and JJB Sports plc), Manchester United plc, the Football Association Ltd and Umbro Holdings Ltd had entered into price fixing agreements in relation to replica football kit infringing the Chapter I prohibition contained in *s 2* of the *Competition Act 1998*. Financial penalties totalling £18.6 million were imposed in respect of the infringements. The first two companies mentioned above lost an appeal to the Tribunal.

Abuse of dominant position   **A2.112**

Article 102 of the Treaty, in provisions which are also matched in the *CA 1998*, prohibits the abuse of a dominant position.

Equivalent domestic provisions   **A2.113**

The so-called Chapter II prohibition contained in *CA 1998* is in comparable terms to that of the Treaty on the Functioning of the European Union. Any conduct by an undertaking which amounts to an abuse of a dominant position will offend the prohibition. The Office of Fair Trading may impose fines of up to 10% of turnover.

Case Example

NAPP Pharmaceutical was fined £2.2 million for supplying drugs used by cancer patients at excessively high prices to patients in the community while supplying hospitals at discount levels which blocked competition. Community prices were typically more than ten times Napp's hospital prices and up to six times higher than export prices. At least one competitor withdrew from the market.

Checklist   A2.114

- Have the goods to be supplied been clearly and closely defined?

- Are you, as a supplier, fully aware of your duties as to the supply of goods which are reasonably fit for their purpose and are of satisfactory quality?

- Have you, as a buyer, made known to the supplier just why you want the goods and what intentions, such as resale, you have in relation to the goods?

- Have you, as a supplier, made best use of the ways to avoid liability for the quality of the product?

- Do you think that any exclusion or limitation clauses you have drafted could be unreasonable or unfair?

- Are you sure that no exclusion or limitation clause you have used is going to give rise to a criminal offence?

- What provisions have been made as to the passing of property and the passing of risk?

- If the contract was meant to be by reference to a sample, has this been made clear?

- Do you understand the implications of the fact that duties can be imposed not just in relation to the actual contract goods, but also to all goods supplied under the contract?

- What measures have you, as supplier, taken to ensure that you have a proper retention of title clause in your contract? Have you considered the possibility that your goods might be used in the manufacture or construction of others?

- If you have drafted such a clause, have you considered that it might need registering to ensure that it is valid?

- What measures have you taken to exclude or limit your possible liability? Have you taken fully on board that there are statutory controls over the use of such clauses?

- When drafting such clauses, have you considered the possibility of making the clause a two stage one, so that there will be a limitation of liability as an alternative to a total exclusion of liability?

- Have you considered the modern test for penalty clauses and drafting liquidated damages clauses?

- If the contract you have made is with a consumer, have you ensured that the terms and any guarantee are drafted in plain and intelligible language?

- Have you considered making special provision in the contract for frustration, or for the impact on the contract of some supervening event?

- Have you considered the use of an entire agreement and non-reliance clauses?

- Have you considered if a non-party is to acquire benefits under your contract, and have you taken the appropriate steps to ensure that such person can enforce those rights?

- Have you ensured that you have secured all your intellectual property rights and also made provision for the non-disclosure of confidential information and considered the modern definition of 'trade secrets' in confidentiality clauses?

- What provision has been made to ensure that notices are served on the right people at the right address and that the notice provisions are strictly adhered to?

- Have you ensured that all necessary signatures have been provided?

- If the contract is made with a party outside the jurisdiction, have you checked the contract to make sure that express provision is made for the governing law?

- Are you certain that nothing in the agreement, or in your conduct, infringes competition law?

- And, bearing in mind enactment of the *Consumer Rights Act 2015*, has your drafting been updated to recognise that the *Unfair Contract Terms Act 1977*, the *Sale of Goods Act 1979* and the *Unfair Terms in Consumer Contracts Regulations 1999* no longer apply to consumer contracts or, in this last case, have been repealed?

A3:
Export Contracts –
Special Issues

At a glance   A3.1

- There are various statutory provisions that impact upon controlling export sales.

- Proper export documentation must be obtained.

- There are various categories of invoice to be supplied.

- Sale of goods rules will apply when the export contract is subject to English law.

- There are a number of well-established categories of contract used in export sales, of which FOB (free on board) and CIF (cost, insurance, freight) contracts are the best known.

- The seller under a CIF contract takes on more obligations than under an FOB contract.

- A model set of terms and conditions for the sale of goods internationally has been prepared by the International Chamber of Commerce. This is called 'Incoterms' which are amended from time to time – usually every ten years. Incoterms 2020 have replaced Incoterms 2010 and which will take effect from 1 January 2020.

- Incoterms are, however, generally restricted to matters relating to delivery of goods.

- There are rules operating among EEA countries (the European Economic Area, which consists of the 28 EU states plus Norway, Iceland and Liechtenstein) for determining which country's law shall apply. Special provision is made as to the applicability of UK law on exclusion clauses and unfair terms.

- A person dealing as 'consumer' is given special protection as to which country's law will apply.

- There are also provisions determining the separate issue of which country's courts within the EEA have jurisdiction. A distinction is drawn between consumer and business contracts.

- There are restrictions on opting out of the rules on jurisdiction.
- Whether Internet advertising is directed at a particular country will depend on the circumstances of the case.
- Provision is made for the mutual recognition and enforcement of judgments within the EEA.
- Provision is also made for bringing actions against parties outside the EEA.

Legislative framework   A3.2

Under the *Export Control Act 2002*, the government has the power to:

(a)   impose controls on exports from the UK in relation to goods of any description – the term 'export controls' in relation to any goods means the prohibition or regulation of their exportation from the United Kingdom or their shipment as stores;

(b)   impose controls on the transfer of technology of any description from the UK and by UK persons anywhere by any means (other than by the export of goods);

(c)   impose controls on the provision of technical assistance of any description overseas – the term 'technical assistance' means services that are provided or used, or which are capable of being used, in connection with the development, production or use of any goods or technology;

(d)   impose controls on the acquisition, disposal or movement of goods or on activities which facilitate such acquisition, disposal or movement (this is often referred to as trafficking and brokering) – a person 'acquires' goods if he buys, hires or borrows them or accepts them as a gift. A person 'disposes' of goods if he sells, lets on hire, lends or gives them;

(e)   apply measures in order to give effect to EU legislation on controls on dual-use items (ie items with a civil and potential military application);

(f)   prescribe licensing procedures in respect of any of the controls imposed;

(g)   require the Secretary of State to report annually to Parliament on the controls imposed on both strategic and cultural exports under the Act;

(h)   require the Secretary of State to issue guidance about the general principles to be followed when exercising licensing powers;

(i)   enable penalties for export control offences to be imposed, increased or varied to reflect the seriousness of the offences.

Current strategic export control legislation   **A3.3**

Overview of legislation on exporting controlled goods

The *Export Control Order 2008 (SI 2008/3231)* as amended by *The Export Control (Amendment) Order 2017 (SI 2017/85)* and *The Export Control (Amendment) Order 2018 (SI 2018/165)* are the main pieces of legislation that controls the exports of military and dual-use goods. It consolidates and updates previous legislation in one legal document and provides details of how the legislation will be applied. The 2017 Order and 2018 Order makes a small number of changes to Schedule 2 to the 2008 Order, which lists the military goods, software and technology subject to export controls.

The Export Control Joint Unit (ECJU) is responsible for maintaining, updating and implementing export control legislation and licensing for military and dual-use items which potentially affects any exporter of specified controlled goods. The ECJU is part of the Department for International Trade ('DIT'). It brings together operational and policy expertise from the DIT, Foreign and Commonwealth Office ('FCO') and the Ministry of Defence ('MOD'). The DIT has overall responsibility for the statutory and regulatory framework of export controls, and for decisions to grant or refuse an export licence.

What the Export Control Order covers

The *Export Control Order* controls the:

- export of strategic goods;
- transfer of technology and the provision of technical assistance;
- trade of military equipment between overseas countries where any part of the activity takes place in the UK;
- trade controls with destinations where an arms embargo has been imposed by the UK following EU or Organisation for Security and Co-operation in Europe regulations or declarations.

It also details any exemptions if applicable and the practicalities of record-keeping requirements.

The Order includes a number of attached schedules. These currently include:

- *Schedule 1, Part 1* – category A goods;
- *Schedule 1, Part 2* – category B goods;
- *Schedule 2* – the UK Military List;
- *Schedule 3* – UK Controlled Dual-Use Goods, Software and Technology;
- *Schedule 4* – Countries and Destinations subject to stricter export and trade controls.

Category A and B goods are military items which are subject to stricter export and trade controls. The UK Military List and the UK Controlled Dual-Use Goods, Software and Technology List both comprise parts of the Control Lists.

Arms embargoes and trade control restrictions A3.4

Sanctions are restrictions on exports implemented for political reasons by countries and international organisations to maintain international peace and security. Sanctions measures include arms embargoes and other trade control restrictions.

An arms embargo is a prohibition or sanction against the export of weaponry and dual-use items. An arms embargo might be imposed through various routes such as by the UN or the EU and where the UK has imposed regulations as a result.

There are embargoes and stricter trade controls in relation to the following countries: Armenia; Azerbaijan; Belarus; Burma; Democratic Republic of Congo; Democratic People's Republic of Korea (North Korea); Eritrea; Iran; Lebanon; Libya, Republic of Guinea; Syria; South Sudan; Sudan; Venezuela; Zimbabwe.

UN embargoes A3.5

There are UN embargoes and transit controls for military goods in the following countries: Iraq; Somalia.

Partial EU embargoes A3.6

China is subject to a partial EU embargo and also to transit controls for military goods.

Other countries listed in the Export Control Order A3.7

Schedule 4, Part 3 to the 2008 Order states that the following countries are subject to transit controls for military goods: Afghanistan; Argentina; Burundi; Macao Special Administrative Region; Rwanda; Tanzania; Uganda.

Transit control for category B goods A3.8

The *Export Control Order 2008* includes a wider list of countries that are subject to transit controls for Category B goods. Category B of the trade controls comprises small arms and light weapons, unmanned aerial vehicles, long-range missiles and man portable air-defence systems. This list can be found in *Schedule 4, Part 4* to the *Export Control Order.*

Military end-use controls   A3.9

Some goods which are not on the UK Military List may need an export licence under the military-end-use control. The following countries are subject to military end-use controls: Armenia; Azerbaijan; Belarus; Burma; Democratic Republic of Congo; Democratic People's Republic of Korea (North Korea); Eritrea; Iran; Iraq; Ivory Coast; Lebanon; Liberia; Libya Republic of Guinea; Sierra Leone; Somalia; South Sudan; Sudan; Syria; Zimbabwe.

Other restrictions   A3.10

There is a wider list of countries that are subject to other types of restrictions. In particular, the ECJU is concerned with the restrictions listed below.

(i) Restrictions for the maintenance of regional peace and stability

The Economic Community of West African States (ECOWAS) adopted a Convention on Small Arms and Light Weapons, their ammunition and other related materials and a moratorium on Import, Export and Manufacture of Light Weapons in June 2006. For the latest information, consult www.gov.uk/arms-embargo-on-west-african-states.

(ii) Restrictions on non-conventional and dual-use items

In June 2018, the Minister of State for Foreign and Commonwealth Affairs announced a revised policy on exports to, and trade (trafficking and brokering) in controlled goods and technology for the Argentina military. The UK's position is that it will continue to refuse licences for export and trade of goods judged to enhance Argentine military capability.

However, where like-for-like equipment is no longer available, the UK may grant licences where it is judged they are not detrimental to UK's defence and security interests.

Licence applications for equipment and defence technology which meet the above criteria will still be assessed on a case by case basis against the consolidated EU and national arms export licensing criteria.

Argentina is subject to transit control for military goods.

As of 10 November 2008, the UK reviewed its policy towards nuclear-related exports to India. Restrictions on nuclear exports to Pakistan remain in force.

(iii) *Countries whose sustainable development might be damaged by arms exports*

There is a list of countries eligible for loans from the World Bank's International Development Association (IDA). The IDA's remit is to help the world's poorest countries by providing interest-free credits and grants for development programmes. This list includes countries where:

- there are already specific sanctions and embargoes in place;

- arms exports might seriously hamper its economic or sustainable development. Consult www.worldbank.org/ida/borrowing-countries.htm.

(iv) *Other non-arms-related restrictions*

There are various non-arms-related restrictions relating to UK exports in force, such as visa and financial sanctions. The Foreign and Commonwealth Office is responsible for overall UK policy on international sanctions. HM Treasury is responsible for the implementation and administration of international financial sanctions in the UK. The following countries are currently subject to financial sanctions: Afghanistan; Belarus; Democratic Republic of Congo; Egypt; Eritrea; Federal Republic of Yugoslavia and Serbia; Iran (Human Rights); Iran (Nuclear Proliferation); Iraq; Ivory Coast; Lebanon; Liberia; Libya; North Korea (Democratic People's Republic of Korea); Republic of Guinea; Republic of Guinea-Bissau; Somalia; Sudan; Syria; Tunisia; Zimbabwe.

(v) *Counter financing of terrorism*

The following counter financing of terrorism designations currently apply:

- ISIL (Da'esh) and Al-Qaida organisations;
- terrorism and terrorist financing.

The UN Security Council has imposed measures against terrorist organisations in relation to financial and visa sanctions, and arms embargos.

All UN member states are obliged to:

- freeze without delay the funds and other financial assets or economic resources, including funds derived from property owned or controlled directly or indirectly;

- prevent entry into, or the transit through, their territories;

- prevent the direct or indirect supply, sale, or transfer of arms and related material, including military and paramilitary equipment, technical advice, assistance or military training.

In conjunction with these measures the EU has implemented restrictive measures on the Taliban and Al-Qaida network as specified by *Council Regulation (EC) SI 881/2002* (as amended by *Council Regulation (EU) SI 754/2011* ('the Al-Qaida Regulation') and *Council Regulation (EU) SI 753/2011*('the Taliban Regulation').

These regulations include prohibitions on the technical advice, assistance or training related to military activities to any person, body or entity listed in Annex I to the Al-Qaida Regulation. They also prohibit technical assistance related to goods and technology listed in the Common Military List of the European Union to any person, group, undertaking or entity listed in Annex I of the Taliban Regulation. The Common Military List is published in the UK as the UK Military List, which forms part of the UK Strategic Export Control Lists.

Both of these EU Council Regulations came into force on 2 August 2011 and are directly applicable in all EU member states (including the UK).

The UK has subsequently introduced a new legislative order – the Export Control (Al-Qaida and Taliban Sanctions) Regulations 2011 – which came into force on 30 November 2011.

This regulation creates new offences and penalties in respect of the EU restrictive measures directed at certain persons, groups and entities associated with the Al-Qaida network and with the Taliban in view of the situation in Afghanistan.

(vi) EU sanctions

The European Commission website has an up-to-date list of EU Sanctions in force. This list includes details of financial and other restrictions, as well as arms embargoes and sanctions.

Consult http://eeas.europa.eu/cfsp/sanctions/index_en.htm.

(vii) EU code of conduct on arms exports

The EU Code of Conduct on Arms Exports is a set of standards drawn up by the Council of the EU for the transfer of conventional arms by all EU member states. Consult www.consilium.europa.eu/uedocs/cmsUpload/08675r2en8.pdf.

(viii) Consolidated EU and national arms export licensing criteria

All licence applications to export arms and other controlled goods are considered on a case-by-case basis.

The UK also prohibits the export of specific goods to any country, including:

- portable devices – components for devices designed or modified, for riot control purposes or self-protection, to administer an electric shock;

- anti-personnel landmines and their component parts;

- binding laser weapons;

- significant new nuclear supplies or materials to countries other than recognised nuclear weapon states, where there are unsafeguarded nuclear installations;

- Man-Portable Air Defence Systems (MANPADs) to non-state end users.

Exporters need to be aware of the following EU legislation, which is directly applicable in the UK:

- the *EU Dual-Use Regulation, Council Regulation (EC) No 428/2009)*;

- the *EU Regulation on Torture, Council Regulation (EC) No 1236/2005*;

- the guide on controls on torture goods.

Exporters should also be aware of the following specific UK legislation:

- the *Export Control Act (2002)*;

- the *Export Control Order 2008 (SI 2008/3231)* as amended and the *Export of Radioactive Sources (Control) Order 2006 (SI 2008/1846)*.

(ix) The UK Strategic Export Control Lists

These are important documents which comprise an essential part of the legislation. They are a list of controlled items, which indicate if a product needs an export licence (listed under a 'control entry heading' or 'rating'). The Control Lists comprise several different parts, including:

- the UK Military List;

- the EU Dual-Use List. Consult www.gov.uk/uk-strategic-export-control-lists-the-consolidated-list-of-strategic-military-and-dual-use-items.

(x) End-use items

Even if an item is not listed on the Control Lists, an export licence may still be required as a result of End-Use controls. These are so-called 'catch-all' controls where there are concerns about the end user. End-Use controls fall into two categories: Military End-Use Control; and Weapons of Mass Destruction (WMD) End-Use Control. Consult www.gov.uk/military-end-use-control-guidance-notes; and also consult www.gov.uk/weapons-of-mass-destruction-wmd-end-use-control. If an exporter is unsure whether their goods are listed on the UK Strategic Control Lists, then view the guidance about strategic exports: when to request an export licence. Consult www.ecochecker.bis.gov.uk/.

(xi) Russia sanctions

The Russia (sanctions) (EU Exit) Regulations 2019 (SI 2019/855) apply if the UK leaves the EU without a deal. For further details see www.gov.uk/government/publications/russia-sanctions-guidance/russia-sanctions-guidance.

Getting an export licence **A3.11**

The main categories of licences are:

Open General Export Licences (OGELs)

These are licence-controlled goods that are of a less restricted nature, or being exported to less sensitive destinations. Using an OGEL can potentially save time and money. Exporters are therefore advised to register for an appropriate licence if they are able to fulfil all the stated terms and conditions. If exports are unable to fulfil these terms and conditions they can apply for a Standard Individual Export Licence.

Standard Individual Export Licences (SIELs)

If the goods are controlled and an OGEL is not suitable for export, exporters will need to apply for the standard licence type, known as a SIEL. An SIEL allows the export of a quantity of specified goods to a specified importer as set out in the licence. The goods must be addressed to a stated person or company, and it may be necessary to identify the end user. The goods must be of the same quantity and value as described on the licence.

A SIEL is a form of export licence for controlled goods specific to one exporter and one consignee. Controlled goods are items of strategic importance, including:

- dual-se goods (military and civilian);
- torture goods (including drugs used in execution by lethal injection);
- radioactive sources;
- military goods;
- electronic technology.

189

SIELS are normally valid for two years and allows the export of:

- specific items as listed on the licence;
- specific quantities and values of each item;
- specific consignees and end users of the products.

Open Individual Export Licence (OIELs)

This is a 'concessionary' licence for exporters with either a track record in export licensing or with a business case. It is designed to cover long-term contracts, projects or repeat business. This licence is specific to an individual exporter and allows multiple shipments of specified goods to specified destinations.

Other specific licences issued by the ECJU for particular trading activities (such as 'trafficking and brokering' or transhipment) are:

- trade control licences for brokering;
- transhipment licences;
- Global Project Licences (GPL).

Those seeking export licences should consult www.spire.bis.gov.uk/spire/fox/espire/LOGIN/login.

Case Example:

Mr Philip Bisgrove of Morecombe, Lancashire, was the owner of NDT Mart, a company that exports non-destructive testing equipment. He was questioned by HMRC investigators about his export activities, particularly those involving sales of dosimeters to an Iranian company called Sakht Afzar Farayand Eng Co (SAFCO).

Dosimeters are items that measure either an individual or an object's exposure to the environment.

Between May 2007 and June 2008, Mr Bisgrove made ten supplies of dosimeters and doserate meters to Iran without the required authorisation. These goods require a licence, for which Mr Bisgrove did not apply. Between November 2007 and July 2008 he also made three supplies of MY–2 Electromagnets to Iran, also without an export licence. Finally, in September 2008, Mr Bisgrove shipped a consignment of radiation detection equipment to Iran via Taiwan. The total value of the exported goods was over £14,500.

As part of the investigation into Mr Bisgrove's export activities, HMRC investigative officers searched his home. The officers took emails, invoices and other documents as evidence that he had known all along that the deals were illegal. For instance, emails from Mr Bisgrove's contact at SAFCO, Peyman Rostami, had discussed shipping goods via Dubai, Malaysia and China in order to avoid export licence controls. To try to cover his tracks, Bisgrove also paid a separate company, RSM Motorsport, to ship and receive goods on behalf of NDT Mart.

When interviewed by HMRC, Bisgrove tried to mislead, avoid and confuse issues regarding his deals with the Iranian firm, claiming he did not know a licence was required to export the dosimeters. However, when faced with the evidence – particularly his own emails – he admitted he knew all along he needed a licence for the exports to be legal.

Mr Bisgrove was sentenced at Southwark Crown Court on 15 October 2010. He pleaded guilty to five counts of being knowingly concerned in the export of prohibited or restricted goods. Confiscation proceedings were also instituted.

Case Example: *R v Ramin* **[2013] EWCA Crim 158**

In September 2009, P had exported electronic switchgear to Iran. Electrical switchgear were dual-use items under *SI 2009/428, art 2*. In October 2009, the Department for Business Innovation and Skills Export Control Organisation (BIS) wrote to P, informing him that authorisation was required under art 4(1) and an export licence was required because there were grounds for believing that the goods listed in the invoice would be used in connection with activities relating to the proliferation of weapons of mass destruction. It then informed him that an export licence had been refused. The refusal schedule listed the generic part numbers of the items in the invoice. P was not prosecuted because he had not been 'informed' beforehand of what was required for the purposes of art 3. P then attempted to export further goods listed in another invoice. On 3 December he received a letter from BIS, informing him that he needed an export licence. On 21 December the goods were seized. P maintained that the 3 December letter was his first notification that an export licence was required for the particular goods listed in the second invoice, because every export was dealt with separately. The judge ruled that to be a matter for the jury. During the trial, a juror wrote to the judge, indicating that he had relevant professional experience supervising similar transactions. He acknowledged his duty to judge the case based on the information provided, but indicated that he would find it difficult to forget about specific details which were definite red signals in his professional environment. The judge allowed the juror to continue. He directed the jury that one juror had professional knowledge of freight forwarding, that there was no impediment in sitting on a case in which a juror might have some professional understanding, and that it might be of some benefit. He stated that the case was to be tried on the evidence given and no other evidence.

P submitted that the conviction was unsafe because of (1) the judge's refusal to rule, as a matter of law, that the October letters were incapable of amounting to a relevant notification; (2) inappropriate and prejudicial comments in the prosecution's final speech; (3) the judge's refusal to discharge the jury after receiving the juror's note.

The court ruled that the word 'informed' and the expression 'items in question' in *SI 2009/428, art 4.1* were straightforward words which could be given their ordinary meaning. There was nothing which required any interpretation as to its meaning or effect. The words 'items in question' were not to be interpreted as consistent with a case-by-case consideration only of specific items and not those of some generic description. Annex 1 contained long lists of items which were all particularised in generic form. In the overall context of what was being described, the terminology was in favour of general, and not specific, particularisation of the 'items in question'. The judge had been correct to rule that the letters were capable of amounting to the requisite notification and whether they did was a matter for the jury.

The court also held that the prosecution's closing speech had not contained factually incorrect, unjustified or improper comments. In any event, no complaint had been made at the time, such that the judge could have addressed it in his summing up.

In a final ruling, the court said that the juror's actions and the contents of his note showed that he took his duties very responsibly and was committed to returning a true verdict according to the evidence. As such, he was not biased against P. However, that did not resolve the question of whether a fair-minded and informed observer would have concluded that there was a real possibility of unconscious bias. It was relevant that although the juror had asked for the rest of the jury to be made aware of his knowledge and experience, the judge's direction did not alert the jury to the caution they should exercise in relation to the views expressed by that juror. If anything, it did the reverse. The direction that the case was to be tried on the evidence given in the courtroom and not on other evidence was correct, but insufficient in the context of a full understanding of the contents of the note and the underlying possible risk of unconscious bias inherent within it. The juror's special knowledge and experience were directly related to the issue in the trial, namely whether P's actions had been prohibited. That issue was not addressed in either the decision to permit the juror to remain on the jury, or the subsequent direction to the whole jury. A fair-minded and informed observer would have concluded that there was a real possibility of unconscious jury bias such that a fair trial was not possible.

In 2019, a UK exporter was punished for brokering goods without a licence. In this regard, Her Majesty's Revenue & Customs issued a compound penalty of £10,234.26 to the UK exporter/trader. The penalty was in relation to unlicensed trading of body armour. The goods were not exported from the UK, but the transaction involved a UK national contrary to the Export Control Order 2008 (as amended): see Notice to Exporters 2019/06.

Cases for Further Information

Sufflet Negoce SA v Bunge SA [2010] EWCA Civ 1102; *Rohlig (UK) Ltd v Rock Unique Ltd* [2011] EWCA Civ 18.

FOB contracts   A3.12

The duties of a seller under an FOB, or 'free on board' contract, ultimately depend on the terms of the contract. While it is always open to the seller to assume additional duties, the seller's general duty is to place the goods free on board a ship to be named by the buyer during the contractual shipment period. If the goods are damaged on board the vessel, this will be the responsibility of the buyer. The seller's obligations extend to all charges incurred before shipment, including loading charges, but not freight or insurance. It is the duty of the buyer to select both the port and date of shipment, as well as to make arrangements for shipment. Adequate notice must be given to the seller of the ship nominated. Compliance with the obligation to ship at the nominated port is a condition of the contract, meaning that breach entitles the buyer to claim damages and rescind the contract (*Petrograde Inc v Stinnes Handel GmbH Times*, 27 July 1994).

Under a free on board contract for the sale of goods to be imported by the seller that allowed for delivery at a range of places in the country of destination, the right and duty to nominate the place of delivery lay with the seller (*Zenziper Grains & Feed Stuffs v Bulk Trading Corporation Ltd*, 6 December 2000 unreported).

Failure of seller to load   A3.13

A seller who fails to deliver the goods on board the vessel or fails to load the goods is not necessarily in breach of contract. It will usually be the buyer who is in breach for failure to nominate an effective ship or provide effective shipping instructions.

Where the buyer under FOB contracts for the sale of rice had nominated a vessel but given short notice of the vessel's estimated time of arrival for the purpose of loading, the notices were not invalid and of no effect and the seller had in the circumstances repudiated the contracts by indicating that it had no cargo available for loading (*Thai Maparn Trading Co Ltd v Dreyfus Commodities Asia Pte* Ltd [2011] EWHC 2494).

Seller only obliged to deliver on board   **A3.14**

While the seller is bound to put the goods on board the vessel in accordance with the terms of the contract, he is not generally obliged to deliver the goods in any other way (*Maine Spinning Co v Sutcliffe & Co* (1917) LJKB 288).

Delivery at port of shipment   **A3.15**

The fact that a supplier chose not to make goods available for shipment, thus rendering performance by the seller impossible, was not of itself sufficient in the circumstances to frustrate an FOB contract (*CTI Group Inc v Transclear SA* [2008] EWCA Civ 856).

Indicating port of shipment   **A3.16**

The terms of the contract should indicate the port of shipment, though this can be left to the option of either party. Where there is an option as to the port of shipment, the choice will be that of the buyer unless the circumstances show that the choice was to be that of the seller.

Cases for Further Information

David T Boyd & Co Ltd v Louis Louca [1973] 1 Lloyd's Rep 209; *Gill & Duffus v Soc pour L'Exportation des Sucres* [1985] 1 Lloyd's Rep 621.

Stipulations as to time   **A3.17**

Not least because of the costs involved in shipping, time is an important factor in the performance of FOB contracts. The contract will generally create a timetable for performance and it is essential for the timetable to be met in order to keep costs down. *Section 10, Sale of Goods Act 1979* says that whether a stipulation as to time is of the essence is a question of the circumstances of the case. In FOB contracts, it is normally the case that time is of the essence.

Case Example: *Bunge Corporation New York v Tradax Export SA Panama* [1981] 1 WLR 711

The contract provided that the 'buyers shall give at least 15 consecutive days' notice of probable readiness of vessel(s)'. The last day of the delivery period for the June shipment was 30 June, so the last day for notice was 12 June, though notice was not given until 17 June.

The House of Lords ruled that this was a major term, and hence a condition, of the contract. It rejected the argument that a condition must be such that breach must deprive the victim of the substantial benefit of the contract. It was also the case that the law had generally treated stipulations as to time in commercial contracts as of the essence. Certainty was important in commercial contracts and that favoured classification of the term as a condition.

Account also had to be taken of the buyer's duty to notify the seller, and of the latter's duty to nominate the port of shipment. The court further stressed that the experience of businessmen was thought to support the conclusion that time stipulations were conditions. It was also the case that damages for breach of the term would be difficult to assess, and this pointed to the clause being a condition, breach of which allowed termination.

Completion of loading   A3.18

The seller must ship the goods at the latest by the end of the shipment period specified in the contract. The obligation so to do is a condition of the contract, so that any failure gives the buyer the right to terminate the contract (*Yelo v SM Machado & Co Ltd* [1952] 1 Lloyd's Rep 183).

Arrival at destination   A3.19

In an FOB contract, the seller is not generally under any obligation in relation to the arrival of the goods. The seller's obligation is to place the goods on board the vessel. It is, therefore, the time of shipment which matters, not the time at which the buyer takes delivery.

Case Example: *Frebold and Sturznicke (Trading as Panda OHG) v Circle Products Ltd* **[1970] 1 Lloyd's Rep 499**

It was a term of the contract for the sale of toys that 'delivery of the consignment would be effected in good time for [the defendants] to catch the Christmas trade'. The goods were put on board on 2 November and reached their destination on 13 November. The buyers were not notified of the arrival and, on 27 December, cancelled the order. The seller's claim for damages succeeded. The vital factor was that the contract between the parties was FOB so that delivery was complete when the goods were put on board on 2 November. This being the case, the sellers were not responsible for what happened subsequently.

Cost of putting goods on board   A3.20

While the seller in an FOB contract is to bear the cost of putting the goods on board, he is not required to bear any subsequent carriage costs unless the terms of the contract so require. The parties can always agree that the seller will bear the cost of stowing the goods on board the vessel and other incidental costs incurred after the goods have been placed on board, hence the use of the terms 'FOB stowed' and 'FOB stored and trimmed'.

Seller's duty as to contract of carriage   **A3.21**

In what is sometimes called the 'classic' FOB contract, the contract for the carriage of the goods is between the seller and the shipowner. This means that the seller must, unless the contract is to the contrary, comply with *s 32(2)* of the *SGA 1979* and 'make such contract with the carrier on behalf of the buyer as may be reasonable having regard to the nature of the goods and the other circumstances of the case and if the seller omits to do so, and the goods are lost or damaged in the course of transit, the buyer may decline to treat the delivery to the carrier as delivery to himself, or may hold the seller responsible in damages'.

> **Case Example:** *Thomas Young & Sons Ltd v Hobson & Partners* **(1949) 65 TLR 365**
>
> Goods were damaged in transit because they were insecurely fixed. Had the sellers made a reasonable contract with the carriers (ie had they sent the goods at the company's risk as per the usual practice for goods of that kind instead of at owner's risk) the loss would not have occurred. The Court of Appeal held the buyers were entitled to reject the goods.

Insurance   **A3.22**

While the terms of the contract may require the seller to insure the goods while they are in transit, the general rule is that an FOB seller is not responsible for insuring the goods while they are in transit (*Wimble Sons & Co v Rosenberg* [1913] 3 KB 743).

Incoterms guidelines   **A3.23**

Incoterms 2010 A3 (which will later be replaced by Incoterms 2020) expressly state that the seller is under no obligation in relation to the contract of insurance. The FOB seller is, however, required by *s 32(3)* of the *SGA 1979* to give notice to the buyer to enable him to insure the goods during sea transit. Incoterms 2010 A3 further states that:' the seller must provide the buyer, at the buyer's request, risk and expense (if any) with information that the buyer needs for obtaining insurance'.

Accordingly, Incoterms place the onus on the buyer to request such information.

Passing of risk and property **A3.24**

The almost universal rule is that risk passes as soon as the goods are over the ship's rail. This is because the duty of the seller is to deliver the goods free on board. Once they are on board, the seller has delivered them to the buyer, thus making it natural that they should thereafter be at the buyer's risk (see *Frebold and Sturznicke (Trading as Panda OHG) v Circle Products Ltd* [1970] 1 Lloyd's Rep 499 at A3.19 above).

The loading of the goods is probably an unconditional appropriation of the goods, which passes the property in the goods to the buyer under *s 18, r 5* of the *SGA 1979*. In modern times, any general presumption that property passes with risk on shipment in an FOB contract has probably largely disappeared. Although this may sometimes be the case if the contract contains no contrary provision, the practice of treating the shipping documents as security for payment is now so well established in international sales that contractual terms requiring payment in exchange for the shipping documents is the norm in FOB contracts. Where payment is to be made only against the documents, the seller will normally have himself named as the consignee in the bill of lading (ie the goods will be deliverable to or to the order of the seller), so the provisions of *s 19* of *SGA 1979* become relevant. A bill of lading is a document acknowledging the shipment of a consignor's goods for carriage by sea, often used when the ship is carrying goods belonging to a number of consignors.

Section 19(1) provides that a seller may reserve the right of disposal of the goods until certain conditions are fulfilled, with the result that, notwithstanding delivery of the goods to the buyer, carrier or other bailee for transmission to the buyer, property does not pass until the particular conditions are fulfilled. *Section 19(2)* provides that, where goods are shipped, and the bill of lading states that the goods are deliverable to the order of the seller, the seller is prima facie to be taken as having reserved the right of disposal. The result is that shipment is treated as amounting only to a conditional appropriation, the condition being that the seller must be paid before property passes.

Obtaining a licence **A3.25**

For details as to the licences which are required in export contracts, see A3.11 above.

The obligation of the seller is simply to pay the cost of putting the goods on board the vessel at the port of shipment unless he assumed some further obligation under the terms of the contract. It follows that he is, therefore, not responsible for the cost of obtaining the licence which might be required for export.

Incoterms guidelines A3.26

Incoterms 2010 (which will later be replaced by Incoterms 2020) draw a clear line between import and export licences. The obligation of a seller is, where applicable, to 'obtain at its own risk and expense any export licence or other official authorisation and carry out, where applicable, all customs formalities necessary for the export of the goods'. The buyer is stated to be obliged, where applicable, to 'obtain at his own risk and expense any import licence or other official authorisation and carry out all customs formalities for the import of the goods and for their transit through any country'.

In the absence of any express term in the contract governing the matter, there will be occasions where there will be an implied duty on the buyer to obtain the export licence.

Case Example: *HO Brandt & Co v HN Morris & Co Ltd* **[1917] 2 KB 784**

The parties entered into a contract for the sale of aniline oil FOB Manchester. The contract was for monthly deliveries over a period of five months but, after the contract was made, the export of this product was banned by government order and the prohibition ran for the greater part of the five months, although licences were granted in certain cases. The buyers sued for non-delivery. It was held that it was the duty of the buyers to obtain the necessary export licences, therefore, they could not maintain an action for damages when the failure of the seller to deliver was due to their own failure to obtain the requisite licences. The Court of Appeal indicated that it was generally the duty of the buyer under an FOB contract to obtain the necessary export licences.

Case Example: *AV Pound & Co Ltd v MW Hardy & Co Inc* **[1956] AC 588**

This ruling somewhat limited the scope of the above case. The House of Lords said that the earlier case was authority 'only for the proposition that where a British buyer has bought goods for export from Britain, and a British prohibition on export except with a licence supervenes, then there is a duty on such buyer to apply for a licence, because not only is he entitled to apply to the relevant British authority but he alone knows the full facts regarding the destination of the goods'.

In the *Pound* case itself, a US company agreed to buy from an English company Portuguese gum spirits of turpentine FAS (free alongside ship). The sellers knew at the time when they made the contract that the goods were for East Germany. Under Portuguese law, the goods could not be exported without a licence and that licence could be obtained only by the seller's suppliers, the name of whom had not been disclosed to the buyers. The sellers then bought the goods from their Portuguese suppliers on terms expressly subject to the grant of a licence. A licence was refused. The buyers' vessel arrived in Lisbon and was ready to load the goods on board, but loading did not take place because the buyers declined to provide another destination for the goods and a licence for export to East Germany had been refused. The sellers failed in their action against the buyers because it was their duty to obtain a licence. The factors which persuaded the House of Lords to decide that it was the sellers' duty to obtain the licence were that the sellers knew that the buyers wished to export the goods to East Germany and that only their suppliers, whose identity had been deliberately withheld, could apply for the necessary licence.

It would seem to follow from this ruling that, where the parties are in different countries, the duty to obtain the export licence will be that of the seller, since he is in the better position to do so.

Whoever bears the duty of obtaining a licence, the further question remains whether that duty is absolute, or whether the relevant party is required only to use his best endeavours. If this is not covered by the contract itself, the prima facie approach of the courts is to require only that the relevant party uses his best endeavours or reasonable diligence (*Re Anglo-Russian Merchant Traders and John Batt & Co (London) Ltd* [1917] 2 KB 679).

Documentary obligations   A3.27

It is essentially a question of the terms to determine if the seller has any documentary obligations. The terms of any letter of credit may be particularly relevant in this context. The terms of the contract may impose other documentary obligations on the seller, such as a duty to supply a certificate of quality in relation to the goods.

Force majeure or prohibition of export clauses   A3.28

The implication referred to in A3.26 above that the duty to obtain a licence is a duty to use best endeavours is not inevitable, since the courts have on occasions found that a more onerous obligation has been assumed. An important factor in determining this issue can be the presence in the contract of a force majeure or prohibition of export clause. Force majeure is the term generally used to indicate some supervening event, outside the control of the parties, which makes performance of the contract impossible or impractical.

Case Example: *C Czarnikow Ltd v Centrala Handlu Zagranicznego 'Rolimpex'* [1979] AC 351

Where there is such a clause, and the clause states that the failure to obtain a licence is not a force majeure event, the court may be prepared to accept that the parties intended that the obligation to obtain a licence was stricter than an obligation merely to use best endeavours.

Case Example: *Colonie Import–Export v Loumidis Sons* **[1978] 2 Lloyd's Rep 560**

Conversely, where the force majeure clause makes no reference to the failure of one party to obtain a licence, the court may be more willing to infer that the duty is only to use best endeavours.

Case Example: *Great Elephant Corp v Trafigura Beheer BV* **[2013] EWCA Civ 905**

T was a purchaser at the top of the chain. The sale contract was pursuant to the General Conditions of the Nigerian National Petroleum Corporation for the sale of Nigerian Crude Oil (NNPC Terms). The oil had originated from a terminal operator in Nigeria, who sold it to C, who sold it to V, who sold it to T. T chartered a vessel from G to load the oil at the Nigerian terminal. Loading began in breach of local regulations in the mistaken belief by the terminal operator that such loading had been authorised. As a result, the necessary documentation was not completed and the ship was detained for about six weeks. It was only released upon payment of a 'fine' imposed by the Minister of Petroleum Resources. G claimed against T for demurrage. The court held that G was entitled to full demurrage for the first week because the delay during that period was attributable to the lack of paperwork. It held the remaining delay attributable to a new cause, namely an abuse of power by the Minister in imposing the 'fine', and ordered demurrage at half the full rate for the remaining period. T sought to pass its liability to V, V to C and so on down the chain. It was held that liability could not be passed down the chain because of a force majeure clause in the sale contract. The issues were: (i) whether the court had been right to hold that the delay had been caused by an unforeseeable force majeure event; (ii) if not, whether the delay was beyond the reasonable control of V and C; (iii) whether the judge had been right to find that the Minister's unlawful act broke the chain of causation so that any liability of V or C was to be confined to the delay occurring in the first week.

It was held that in considering whether the delay attributable to the lack of paperwork had been within the control of the terminal operator, the court had not taken sufficient account of the fact that the channel of communication had been between the operator and the Nigerian authorities. Although the operator's representative might have acted entirely reasonably, and could not be considered 'culpable', culpability was not the fundamental issue. The real question was whether the operator, as a complete entity, had acted reasonably, and why it had not sought official clearance until the vessel began to load. The court had assumed that as the loading of the vessel was T's responsibility under the charter, and as the loading could only be performed by the operator, the latter was the former's agent for the purposes of the force majeure clause. The delay had not been beyond the operator's control or 'reasonable' control. It had chosen not to follow official channels for seeking loading clearance. That had been a choice which carried a risk; exercising such a choice was doing something within one's control.

The question then arose whether T could say that even if the cause of the demurrage had been within the terminal operator's control, it had not been within the control of T or 'their servants and agents' within the meaning of the force majeure clause. Strictly speaking, T had delegated its loading responsibility to V, who were its agents, and likewise V to C. The intention of the charterparty was that if anything went wrong with the loading operation, T was to bear the liability and look down the line of contracts for indemnity. It would be inconsistent with that concept if charterers were able to excuse themselves or their immediate contracting party on the basis that the event causing the damage was outside of their control. Therefore, T was contractually liable to G, V to T, and C to V. The force majeure clause excused a seller for delay in the performance of its obligations if performance was hindered by an 'unforeseeable' act. If an act was within a party's control, it was very likely that it was also 'foreseeable'. In the instant case it had certainly been foreseeable that if official channels were bypassed, the vessel would not be allowed to leave until questions were answered. T had undertaken the responsibility of loading the vessel and, in their respective FOB contracts, V and C had undertaken the same. They could not rely on the force majeure clause unless they could show that the relevant events had been beyond the control of the terminal operator, that being the entity which discharged the responsibility. The chain of causation had not been broken by the Minister's abuse of power. The imposition of the 'fine' did not displace the original breaches of contract by V and/or C.

Other issues A3.29

The terms of the contract may impose other obligations on the seller than those set out above.

> **Case Example:** *KG Bominflot Bunkergesellschaft fur Mineraloele MBH & Co KG v Petroplus Marketing AG* **[2010] EWCA Civ 1145**
>
> Gasoil was sold FOB Antwerp. The properties of the gasoil were set out in clause 4 of the contract. By clause 12, quality and quantity were to be determined by independent inspection at loading which was to be final and binding for both parties, save for fraud or manifest error. By clause 15, risk and title were to pass on loading. Clause 18, headed 'Other Conditions',

contained, among other terms, an exclusion clause which provided that there were no guarantees, warranties or representations, express or implied, of merchantability, fitness or suitability of the oil for any particular purpose or otherwise which extended beyond the description of the oil set forth in the agreement. The gasoil was inspected at Antwerp and the loading determination found the cargo to be within specification. After a four-day voyage to the first discharge port in Spain the cargo was tested and found to be off specification as to sediment. The goods were accordingly rejected by the receivers and B claimed against P. P accepted that the implied statutory condition of satisfactory quality under the *Sale of Goods Act 1979, s 14(2)* would ordinarily require the capability of the gasoil delivered at Antwerp to withstand a normal voyage of reasonable duration such as that to Spain with its satisfactory quality intact, but relied on the exclusion in clause 18. B argued, and the judge deciding preliminary issues held, that the contract contained a further implied common law term that the goods would remain on specification for a reasonable time after delivery. He further held that clause 18 did not preclude the implication of the *s 14(2)* term or the additional common law term.

P submitted that the additional implied term was inconsistent with the express terms of the contract, in particular clauses 4 and/or 12 and 15, and unnecessary in the light of the basic statutory implied condition. In relation to clause 18, B submitted that there was long-standing and high authority to the effect that the Act implied that conditions could not be excluded without express reference to the exclusion of 'conditions'.

It was held that there was nothing to suggest, let alone require the alleged implication, which was novel. On the contrary, the contract made it clear that the specification had to be met at the time of delivery, that the intention was that the gasoil should be inspected by an independent inspector prior to loading, and that the inspector's determination should be conclusive. The intention of the contract was that specification should be determined conclusively at loading. Therefore it mattered not that things might change thereafter, or even, once a conclusive determination had been made, that things might not change but that a new test might show a different result which was outside specification limits. After delivery the buyer assumed all risks pertaining to the product under clause 15. That included the risk of transport and the risk of cargo instability. A clause for conclusive inspection and determination on loading replaced or redefined the implied terms as to quality pro tanto. A fortiori it prevented any further implication that it was legitimate to take account of changes in the cargo's specification after delivery.

The court held that it would be superfluous to discuss whether or not the additional implied term was necessary or not in the light of the acceptance of the *s 14(2)* term. The additional implied term was simply not part of the intention of the parties to the contract and would not have been understood by reasonable merchants to have been part of its meaning. If it were otherwise, the whole point of a final and binding determination by an independent inspector on loading would be rendered pointless, and the certainty in international sale of goods, which such inspection clauses were designed to provide, would be lost.

As a final point, the court said that a principle had been established, on the highest authority, that *Sale of Goods Act* implied conditions could not be excluded by reference to guarantees or warranties and required clearer language extending to 'conditions' themselves. It was not open to the court to depart from that long-established consensus.

Incoterms guidelines   **A3.30**

Incoterms 2010 A10 (which will later be replaced by Incoterms 2020) states that:

'The seller must where applicable, in a timely manner, provide to or render assistance in obtaining for the buyer, at the buyer's request, risk and expense, any documents and information, including security-related information, that the buyer needs for the import of the goods and/or for their transport to the final destination.

The seller must reimburse the buyer for all costs and charges incurred by the buyer in providing or rendering assistance in obtaining documents and information as envisaged in B10.'

B10 provides:

'The buyer must, in a timely manner, advise the seller of any security information requirements so that the seller may comply with A10. The buyer must reimburse the seller for all costs and charges incurred by the seller in providing or rendering assistance in obtaining documents and information as envisaged in A10. The buyer must, where applicable, in a timely manner, provide to or render assistance in obtaining for the seller, at the seller's request, risk and expense, any documents and information including security-related information, that the seller needs for the transport and export of the goods and for their transport through any country.'

Sample Clause

'We undertake to furnish you with a 10% guarantee that we will deliver the goods to your forwarding agents in Antwerp as soon as we receive confirmation from your bankers that the necessary letter of credit, valid not less than six weeks, will be established in our favour in free transferable US dollars.'

(*Heisler v Anglo-Dal Ltd* [1954] 1 WLR 1273.)

The contract might contain special terms precluding any deduction from the invoice.

Sample Clause

'Payment shall be made without discount, deduction, withholding, set-off or counterclaim in United States Dollars ... on or before the due date ... against presentation to Buyer of hard copy or telex invoice together with original bills of lading or letter of indemnity ...'

It was held that, on a proper construction of the contract, the special terms prevented any deduction from a presented invoice. In making a lesser payment based on short shipment, the relevant party had made a deduction that was not permitted.

(*Totsa Total Oil Trading SA v Bharat Petroleum Corp Ltd* [2005] EWHC 1641.)

CIF contracts   A3.31

A seller under a CIF contract (cost, insurance, freight) assumes more obligations than the seller under an FOB contract. Under an FOB contract, the seller is merely responsible for delivery of the goods to the port of origin; they will then be transported. The seller under a CIF contract agrees to sell the goods at an inclusive price which covers the cost of the goods, and also their insurance and freight. Here, the seller insures the goods transported up until they arrive at the port whereupon the risk and insurance becomes the responsibility of the buyer. The seller pays for the delivery of the goods and their export including insurance.

Case Example: *Omv Supply & Trading ag v Kazmunaygaz Trading AG* [2014] EWCA Civ 75

A price clause in a CIF contract for the sale of diesel, which provided that 'customs duties and penalties incurred by non-EU origin' would be deducted from the invoice, entitled the buyer to recover from the seller anti-dumping duties incurred on import to the EU, but where the duties exceeded the price paid, the buyer could not recover the balance from the seller.

Shipment   A3.32

Unless the terms of the contract stipulate to the contrary, the CIF seller is not obliged physically to load the goods on board a particular vessel. Instead, he can purchase goods already on board and allocate them to the particular contract. The terms of the contract will dictate the obligations of the seller in this regard.

The terms of the contract dealing with time and place of shipment are generally regarded as conditions, breach of which entitles the buyer to rescind the contract and to claim damages.

> **Case Example:** *Bowes v Shand* **(1877) 2 App Cas 455**
>
> Shipment was to be 'during the months of March and/or April 1874'. In fact, the vast majority of the goods were shipped in February and, of four bills of lading, three were issued in late February. It was held that shipment could be rejected.

> **Case Example:** *Suek AG v Glencore International AG* **[2011] EWHC 1361**
>
> Where a CIF contract permitted notice of readiness to be given by the seller at the usual waiting place if the berth was occupied, notice of readiness was validly given at the usual waiting place where the vessel was unable to reach the berth because it was occupied and because of the tidal conditions.

Time of notification of appropriation **A3.33**

When the seller is required by the contract to give the buyer notice of appropriation, the time limits specified for giving notice must be complied with, so that a failure to comply will generally entitle the buyer to reject the documents and the goods (*Societe Italo-Belge pour le Commerce et l'Industries SA v Palm and Vegetable Oils (Malaysian) Sdn Bhd (The Post Chaser)* [1982] 1 All ER 19).

The terms of the contract may specify in some detail the form and content of the notice and the seller must comply with those requirements; a failure to do so will allow the buyer to rescind the contract and claim damages.

The entitlement of the seller to withdraw a notice once given may be regulated by the terms of the contract. It is not uncommon for a contract to contain a provision to the effect that 'a valid notice of appropriation when once given shall not be withdrawn' (*Ross T Smyth & Co Ltd v TD Bailey, Son & Co* [1940] 3 All ER 60).

Such a clause applies only to attempts by the seller to withdraw a notice, not to correct or amend it. The right of a seller to amend or correct a notice may be limited by the terms of the contract. In particular, where the contract contains a term which entitles the seller to amend or correct a notice of appropriation within certain narrow limits, this contractual entitlement to correct or amend may be held to be the sum total of the seller's right to do so, with the result that a seller who fails to comply with the term of the contract entitling him to correct will have no further power to do so.

Sample Clause

An instance of a term entitling the seller to amend or correct a notice of appropriation is:

> 'Every such notice of appropriation shall be open to correction of any errors occurring in transmission, provided that the sender is not responsible for such errors and for any previous error in transmission which has been repeated in good faith.'

(*Kleinjan and Holst NV Rotterdam v Bremer Handelgesselschaft mbH Hamburg* [1972] 2 Lloyd's Rep 11.)

Route of shipment – deviation provisions   **A3.34**

The contract of sale may provide for a particular route of shipment. Where this is the case, the seller must tender a bill of lading for shipment via the route specified in the contract. So-called deviation clauses are now a common feature of bills of lading, however, and it may be that such a clause may no longer entitle the buyer to reject such a bill. A buyer who wishes to ensure that the goods are carried straight to the agreed destination should ensure that the contract contains a clause which states that the ship shall sail direct from the port of loading to the destination for unloading of cargo.

Insurance   **A3.35**

The seller must tender to the buyer insurance documentation which covers the goods for the duration of their sea transit. The documents must relate to an enforceable contract. The main cause of uncertainty in this area is not the existence of the seller's obligation to tender insurance documents, but the nature of the documentary obligation which has been assumed by the seller or, possibly, imposed on him. The question which arises is whether the seller is to tender the insurance policy itself, or whether it is enough for the seller to tender a certificate of insurance entitling the buyer to call for the policy itself.

Incoterms guidelines   **A3.36**

There is no clear authority on this point at the moment, so this is a matter which must be covered in the contract. As a result, Incoterms 2010 A3 (which will later be replaced by Incoterms 2020) state that:

'The seller must obtain at its own expense cargo insurance complying at least with the minimum cover provided by Clause (C) of the Institute Cargo Clauses (LMA/IUA) or any similar clauses. The insurance shall be contracted with underwriters or an insurance company of good repute and entitle the buyer, or any other person having an insurable interest in the goods, to claim directly from the insurer.'

The reference to Institute Cargo Clauses is to the ICC 2009 version of those clauses. The remainder of A3 deals with issues such as additional cover, the minimum coverage, the period of cover, provision of the policy itself and further information required in relation to additional insurance.

Clause B3 states that: 'The buyer has no obligation to the seller to make a contract of insurance. However, the buyer must provide the seller, upon request, with any information necessary for the seller to procure any additional insurance requested by the buyer' as envisaged in A3 above.

In the absence of such a provision as Incoterms A3, it would be necessary to look at the common law, although the relevant cases are somewhat old and do not reflect modern commercial practice.

Invoice   **A3.37**

The seller must tender to the buyer an invoice for the goods. The form and content of the invoice may be regulated by the terms of the contract itself. Buyers who wish to obtain an invoice in a particular form, or with a particular content, should stipulate for this in the contract of sale.

Other documents   **A3.38**

The seller may be required by the terms of the contract to tender other documents to the buyer. For instance, the seller may be required to tender a certificate of origin, quality or inspection.

Incoterms guidelines   **A3.39**

It will generally be the responsibility of the seller to obtain an export licence for the goods (Incoterms 2010 A2 and *Congimex Compahania Geral SARL v Tradax Export SA* [1983] 1 Lloyd's Rep 250). Import licences are more likely to be a matter for the buyer (Incoterms 2010 B2 and *Mitchell Cotts & Co v Hairco Ltd* [1943] 2 All ER 552).

Tender of shipping documents   **A3.40**

The contract will generally make provision for the time at which the documents are to be tendered to the buyer. Where the contract requires the buyer to pay against the documents, a provision which fixes the date on which the buyer is to make payment may also fix the date on which the seller must tender the documents (*Alfred C Toepfer v Lenersan-Poortman NV* [1980] 1 Lloyd's Rep 143).

As for the place of tender, there is no clear authority. In practice, therefore, this is an issue usually dealt with in the terms and conditions. For example, if the contract provides for payment to be made by letter of credit, the place of tender is likely to be the offices of the collecting bank.

The time at which the goods arrive at the port of destination is normally of no concern to the seller. That said, it may be particularly important for the buyer to know when that delivery will take place. In such a case, the buyer must insert into the contract an express term imposing on the seller an obligation to ensure that delivery takes place within a particular period of time, or an obligation to give the buyer appropriate notice of the arrival of the vessel. The clause should be drafted in such a way as to impose on the seller an obligation to ensure that the goods actually arrive at the port of destination within the stipulated period of time and not in such a way as to impose nothing more than an obligation to load the goods at such a time as will enable the ship to arrive at the port at the relevant time.

Incoterms   **A3.41**

When quoting and pricing for export it must be quite clear to buyer and seller which party is responsible for the various costs, tasks and responsibilities in the export supply chain. To facilitate this, the International Chamber of Commerce publishes a set of terms which, when used to qualify a price, establishes:

- which costs are included in the price, for example:
    - documentation;
    - export packing;
    - inland freight;
    - terminal charges at port/airport of export;
    - overseas freight;
    - cargo insurance;
    - terminal charges at port/airport of arrival;
    - import customs clearance;
    - payment of import duties and taxes; and
    - inland freight to buyer's premises;

- the point at which risk passes from seller to buyer;
- the delivery and transport responsibilities of the parties;
- the division of functions between seller and buyer; and
- the overall division of responsibilities.

Incorporating Incoterms A3.42

Incoterms 2010 (which will later be replaced by Incoterms 2020 with effect from 1 January 2020) should be included in all international trade contracts and, additionally, all export invoices should include the clause 'Subject to Incoterms 2020 (or such later version if Incoterms has been replaced or amended)'.

Incoterms designation – the codes A3.43

Each Incoterm under Incoterms 2010 is designated by a three letter code. The code must precede a named place, for example: 'EXW Liverpool'.

The individual codes and their meanings are set out below.

- EXW: ex works.
- FCA: free carrier.
- FAS: free alongside ship.
- FOB: free on board.
- CFR: cost and freight.
- CIF: cost, insurance, and freight.
- CPT: carriage paid to.
- CIP: carriage and insurance paid to.
- DAP: delivered at place.
- DAT: delivered at terminal.
- DDP: delivered duty paid.

NOTE

Incoterms 2010 have been replaced by Incoterms 2020 which will come into effect on 1 January 2020. At the time of publication of this book, full details of Incoterms 2020 have not been published. Some of the above-listed Incoterms are likely to be repealed and replaced by new codes and terms. Consideration should therefore be given to the new Incoterms 2020 when they are published. According to ICC's website, the following changes in Incoterms 2020 include:

- *Incoterms 2020* provides for demonstrated market need in relation to bills of lading (BL) with an on-board notation and the Free Carrier (FCA) Incoterms rule.

- *Incoterms 2020* aligns different levels of insurance coverage in Cost Insurance and Freight (CIF) and Carriage and Insurance Paid To (CIP).

- *Incoterms 2020* includes arrangements for carriage with own means of transport in FCA, Delivery at Place (DAP), Delivery at Place Unloaded (DPU), and Delivered Duty Paid (DDP).

- There is a change in the three-letter name for Delivered at Terminal (DAT) to DPU.

- Incoterms 2020 includes security-related requirements within carriage obligations and costs.

Case Example: *Stora-Enso Oyj v Port of Dundee* [2006] CSOH 40

In their contract, the parties agreed that the contract would be on a CIP basis. In fact, the agreement as to costs did not match precisely what Incoterms meant, but CIP had been used as it most closely described what the parties had intended. Reference was made by the court to the words of Roskill LJ in *The Albazero* [1977] AC 774: 'It is a trite observation that what is sometimes called a true f.o.b. or a true c.i.f. contract is a comparative commercial rarity. Contracts vary infinitely according to the wishes of the parties to them. Though a contract includes the words f.o.b. or c.i.f. amongst its terms, it may well be that other terms of the contract clearly show that the use of those letters is intended to do no more than show where the incidence of liability for freight or insurance will lie as between buyer and seller but it is not to denote the mode of performance of the seller's obligations to the buyer or of the buyer's obligations to the seller. In other cases, though the letters c.i.f. are used, other terms of the contract may show that the property is intended to pass on shipment and not upon tender of and payment against the documents so tendered or though the letters f.o.b. are used, other terms may show that the property was not intended to pass on shipment but upon tender and payment, the seller by the form in which he took the bill of lading intending to reserve his right of disposal of the property until he was paid against the shipping documents'. The court in the present case held that the evidence showed that neither party had intended to incorporate Incoterms. They had used CIP simply as a convenient form of shorthand to record that part of the agreement relating to what was covered in the price. The fact that Incoterms were referred to in the invoice was irrelevant since, by then, the terms of the contract had already been agreed. In fact, the terms on which they had agreed were often referred to as FOM (Free on Motor), but that was not an Incoterm.

Matters not covered by Incoterms   **A3.44**

Incoterms say nothing about the price of goods or the method of payment. Nor do they deal with the transfer of ownership or the consequences of breach.

In areas outside the scope of Incoterms, the contracting parties should be careful to set out the relevant contract terms as to sale and purchase.

Jurisdiction and choice of law   **A3.45**

The presence in any contract of what might be called a 'foreign element' necessitates a discussion of issues as to which country's law will apply; and which country has jurisdiction to hear disputes arising under the contract.

Applicable law   **A3.46**

The *Rome Convention* applies to litigation within the EEA between sellers and buyers wherever situated. The EEA consists of the 28 EU states, Norway, Iceland and Liechtenstein. It is given effect in the United Kingdom by the *Contracts (Applicable Law) Act 1990*.

The choice of the parties   **A3.47**

The general rule is that a contract is in the first place to be governed by the law chosen by the parties.

In the absence of such a choice, the contract will be governed by the law of the country with which it is most closely connected. It is presumed that the contract is most closely connected with the country where the party who is to effect the performance which characterises the contract has – at the time of the contract – his habitual residence (or, in the case of a body corporate or unincorporate, its central administration).

> **Case Example:** *Lawlor v Sandvik Mining & Construction Mobile Crushers & Screens Ltd* **[2012] EWHC 1188**
>
> Since approximately 1994, L had been a sales agent for a company (E) whose business had been bought by S in 2007. E had been an Irish company, but had operations in England. L was E>s agent in Spain, selling mobile screens and crushing equipment. Arrangements were informal and there was never a written agreement recording the terms or applicable law of the agency. S terminated the agency in 2009 and it was agreed that L was entitled to compensation. The question of whether the agency agreement was governed by Spanish or English law affected the amount

of compensation which would be payable. There was a dispute about how much time L spent in Spain and to what extent his responsibilities extended to other countries. L claimed that he spent less than six months a year in Spain and spent a lot of time in Andorra as a tourist as well as visiting E›s English factory regularly.

L submitted that (1) although there had been no express choice of law, a choice of English law was implied; (2) even if no choice of law was implied, the fact that he had regularly been required to travel to the English factory meant that his agency required him to effect performance in both Spain and the United Kingdom and it was therefore impossible to determine the country of the characteristic performance of his agency for the purposes of the *Rome Convention 1980, art 4(2), (3)* under *art 4(5)* of the Convention, the contract was more closely connected with England than Spain.

The court held that, if the parties had made a choice of law, it would have been English law, but that did not point to a choice having been made. Given the casual and informal circumstances in which the agency took effect it was very unlikely that choice of law was considered, let alone discussed. Since the parties had no clear intention of making a choice, the situation was governed by *art 4*, in accordance with guidance contained in Guiliano and Lagarde, 'Report on the Rome Convention', Official Journal of the Communities, 31 October 1980

Whatever the importance of the visits to the English factory, the agency agreement required L to effect performance primarily in Spain at the relevant time, which was the time of the conclusion of the contract under *art 4(2)*. The instant case involved a straightforward application of facts to *art 4(2)*. The correct characteristic performance of the agency by L was undoubtedly in Spain.

Under *art 4(5)*, the presumption in *art 4(2)* did not apply if, among other things, it appeared from the circumstances as a whole that the contract was more closely connected with another country than it was with a country indicated by the presumption. L had been S's agent in Spain throughout the agency and spent much less time in England than in Spain. He also spent more time in Spain, as opposed to Andorra, than he admitted. In time, he came to work in other territories, but only to a limited extent. The connections with England included the factory which he visited, the express choice of English law for contracts for the sale of machinery; payment of commission in sterling in the early years; and the likelihood that if the parties had applied their minds to the matter, L's agency contract would have been seen to be governed by English law. Considering the circumstances as a whole, the Spanish connection remained much deeper and more extensive than that of England. An examination of the broader circumstances under *art 4(5)* produced the same result as the application of *art 4(2)*. Spain remained the country with which the contract was most connected.

For a further examples see *Halle v Fr Lurssen Werft gmbh & Co KG* [2010] EWCA Civ 587; *British Arab Commercial Bank plc v Bank of Communications* [2011] EWHC 281.

The parties are at any time entitled to agree to subject the contract to a law other than that which previously governed the contract.

Case Example: *Mauritius Commercial Bank Ltd v Hesta Holdings Ltd* [2013] EWHC 1328

The court held that there was no rationale or policy reason why parties to a contract should not be permitted to amend the governing law of that contract.

Unfair terms   A3.48

In certain circumstances, a party may wish to rely on the *Unfair Contract Terms Act 1977 (UCTA 1977)*, even though the contract is not to be governed by English law. The position is that, under *s 27(2)* of *UCTA 1977*, the provisions of the Act will apply regardless of any contract term which seeks to apply the law of a country outside the United Kingdom where that term was imposed wholly or mainly to enable the relevant party to evade the Act.

Similarly, *s 74* of the *Consumer Rights Act 2015* has a mandatory effect, in that the Act will apply notwithstanding any term seeking to apply the law of a country outside the EEA if the contract has a close connection with the territory of a Member State. The Act states that if no choice is made or the choice is the law of an EEA state, then the law of that EEA state will apply, or, where there is no choice, the law of the state with which the seller has the closest connection.

Uniform law on international sales   A3.49

The *Uniform Law on International Sale of Goods 1964* was implemented in the United Kingdom by the *Uniform Laws on International Sales Act 1967*. Under the Act, the Convention applies only if chosen by the parties. The Convention deals with the obligations of the parties, the availability of remedies and the passing of risk, but not the passing of property. The Convention is very rarely used.

Jurisdiction   A3.50

Separate from the question of whose law is to apply is the further question of which courts have the jurisdiction to apply the relevant law. Between the Member States of the EEA, this is governed by *Council Regulation (EC)*

No 44/2001 of 22 December 2000 on jurisdiction and the recognition and enforcement of judgments in civil and commercial matters whatever the nature of the court or tribunal. The jurisdiction does not extend to revenue, customs or administrative matters. The Regulation was implemented in the UK by the *Civil Jurisdiction and Judgments Order 2001 (SI 2001/3929)*, which came into force on 1 March 2002.

Any contractual choice as to jurisdiction must be properly incorporated into the contract: *SSL International plc v TTK LIg Ltd* [2011] EWHC 1695.

For further examples, see *Smeg UK Ltd v NAA Appliances Ltd* [2013] EWHC 1300; *Mar-Train Heavy Haulage Ltd v Shipping.DK Chartering a/s (t/a Frank & Tobiesen A/S)* [2014] EWHC 355.

Business contracts – the rules   A3.51

- In the case of persons (which will include both natural and legal persons) domiciled in a Member State, whatever their nationality, they are to be sued in the courts of that Member State.

- Persons who are not nationals of the Member State in which they are domiciled shall be governed by the rules of jurisdiction applicable to nationals of that state.

- Persons domiciled in a Member State may be sued in the courts of another Member State only by virtue of the rules set out in the Regulation.

- If the defendant is not domiciled in a Member State, the jurisdiction of the courts of each Member State shall be determined by the law of that Member State.

- As against such a defendant, any person domiciled in a Member State may, whatever his nationality, avail himself in that state of the rules of jurisdiction there in force.

- A person domiciled in a Member State may, in another Member State, be sued in matters relating to a contract, in the courts for the place of performance of the obligation in question. For the purpose of this provision and unless otherwise agreed, the place of performance of the obligation in question shall be:
  - in the case of the sale of goods, the place in a Member State where, under the contract, the goods were delivered or should have been delivered;
  - in the case of the provision of services, the place in a Member State where, under the contract, the services were provided or should have been provided; or
  - as regards a dispute arising out of the operations of a branch, agency or other establishment, in the courts for the place in which the branch, agency or other establishment is situated.

- A person domiciled in a Member State may also be sued:

  - where he is one of a number of defendants, in the courts for the place where any one of them is domiciled, provided the claims are so closely connected that it is expedient to hear and determine them together to avoid the risk of irreconcilable judgments resulting from separate proceedings;

  - as a third party in an action on a warranty or guarantee or in any other third-party proceedings, in the court seised of the original proceedings, unless these were instituted solely with the object of removing him from the jurisdiction of the court which would be competent in his case; or

  - on a counter-claim arising from the same contract or facts on which the original claim was based, in the court in which the original claim is pending.

Place of domicile   A3.52

A company or other legal person or association of natural or legal persons is domiciled at the place where it has its:

- registered office or, where there is no such office anywhere, the place of incorporation or, where there is no such place anywhere, the place under the law of the country where the formation of the contract took place;

- central administration; or

- principal place of business.

Contracting out of the Regulation   A3.53

If the parties, one or more of whom is domiciled in a Member State, have agreed that a court or the courts of a Member State are to have jurisdiction to settle any disputes which have arisen or which may arise in connection with a particular legal relationship, that court or those courts shall have jurisdiction. Such jurisdiction shall be exclusive unless the parties have agreed otherwise.

Agreements conferring jurisdiction – the rules   A3.54

Such agreements must be:

- in writing or evidenced in writing;

- in a form which accords with practices which the parties have established between themselves; or

- in international trade or commerce, in a form which accords with a usage of which the parties are or ought to have been aware and which in such trade or commerce is widely known to, and regularly observed by, parties to contracts of the type involved in the particular trade or commerce concerned.

Any communication by electronic means which provides a durable record of the agreement shall be equivalent to 'writing'.

Where such an agreement is concluded by parties, none of whom is domiciled in a Member State, the courts of other Member States shall have no jurisdiction over their disputes unless the court or courts chosen have declined jurisdiction.

Consumer contracts – the rules   **A3.55**

Articles 15–17 of the Regulation confer additional jurisdiction over a contractual dispute between a consumer and a business on the courts of the consumer's country of domicile when certain tests are met. *Article 15* states:

- In matters relating to a contract concluded by a person, the consumer, for a purpose which can be regarded as being outside his trade or profession, jurisdiction shall be determined as below if:

  (a)   it is a contract for the sale of goods on instalment credit terms; or

  (b)   it is a contract for a loan repayable by instalments, or for any other form of credit, made to finance the sale of goods; or

  (c)   in all other cases, the contract has been concluded with a person who pursues commercial or professional activities in the Member State of the consumer's domicile or, by any means, directs such activities to that Member State or to several States including that Member State, and the contract falls within the scope of such activities.

- Where a consumer enters into a contract with a party who is not domiciled in the Member State but has a branch, agency or other establishment in one of the Member States, that party shall, in disputes arising out of the operations of the branch, agency or establishment, be deemed to be domiciled in that State.

- This provision shall not apply to a contract of transport other than a contract which, for an inclusive price, provides for a combination of travel and accommodation.

- There are separate provisions on insurance contracts in *arts 8–14*.

Article 17 of the Regulation prevents the parties to a consumer contract from agreeing to depart from the above provisions before a dispute has arisen.

For example, a business could not enforce a contractual term in which the consumer waived the right to sue in his own country's courts in the event of a dispute.

A consumer may sue at home if the trader 'pursues commercial ... activities in the Member State of the consumer's domicile or, by any means, directs such activities to that Member State ...'

Internet websites   **A3.56**

Article 15.1(c) raises a question about when an internet website would be said to be directed to one or more Member States. There are no detailed rules and no case law. The Department for Business, Energy & Industrial Strategy has provided the following general guidance:

- it would be necessary to look at the nature of any given website;

- websites giving information in different Community languages and currencies and offering to deliver to EU countries might well be covered by *art 15*;

- some websites (eg a site in English with prices in pounds and confining orders to UK customers) might be hard to describe as directed anywhere but the UK. See further the case considered below.

Case Example: *Peter Pammer v Reederei Karl Schlüter GmbH & Co KG and Hotel Alpenhof GesmbH v Oliver Heller* **(European Court of Justice; 10 December 2010)**

In its judgment, the ECJ listed the various elements allowing a court to decide whether a website is 'directed to' consumers in another Member State:

- international nature of the activity, such as travel or hotel booking services;

- description of itineraries from one Member State to the place where the service is provided;

- mention of telephone numbers with the international dialling code;

- use of a top-level domain name such as '.com' or '.eu', instead of a national one such as '.be' or '.fr';

- mention of an international clientele;

- the fact that a website allows a language or currency other than that used in the trader's Member State.

One of the above cases concerned a travel agency in Germany which sold an Austrian resident travel on a freighter from Italy to the Far East.

The Austrian resident refused to embark on the freighter arguing that the conditions of the boat did not correspond to the descriptions given by the travel agency and he claimed his money back. The travel agency only reimbursed part of the paid amount; therefore the Austrian resident brought proceedings before Austrian courts. The agency argued that they lacked jurisdiction and that it did not pursue any commercial activity in Austria.

In the other case, a German resident reserved rooms in a Hotel in Austria, by email with the hotel. The German resident was unhappy with the quality of the hotel services and refused to pay his bill. The hotel brought an action before Austrian courts for payment of the bill. The German resident argued a lack of jurisdiction saying that he could only be sued in German courts. The precise answer to the issue was to be determined by the national courts in the light of the judgment of the ECJ.

Contracts entered into by consumers when they are outside their country of domicile   A3.57

It is not necessary that the consumer must have taken the steps to conclude the contract while in his country of domicile. For example, a UK consumer who buys goods while on holiday in France would be able to sue in the UK court if the trader (who would not necessarily be French) had pursued or by any means directed his activities to the UK.

Recognition and enforcement   A3.58

The Regulation provides that a judgment given in a Member State shall be recognised in the other Member States without any special procedure being required.

Non-recognition of a judgment – the rules   A3.59

In certain circumstances a judgment will not be recognised where:

- such recognition is manifestly contrary to public policy in the Member State in which recognition is sought; or where it was given in default of appearance, if the defendant was not served with the document which instituted the proceedings or with an equivalent document in sufficient time and in such a way as to enable him to arrange for his defence, unless the defendant failed to commence proceedings to challenge the judgment when it was possible for him to do so;

- if it is irreconcilable with a judgment given in a dispute between the same parties in the Member State in which recognition is sought; or

- if it is irreconcilable with an earlier judgment given in another Member State or in a third state involving the same cause of action and between the same parties, provided that the earlier judgment fulfils the conditions necessary for its recognition in the Member State addressed.

A judgment given in a Member State and enforceable in that state shall be enforced in another Member State when, on the application of any interested party, it has been declared enforceable there.

In the United Kingdom, such a judgment shall be enforced in England and Wales, in Scotland, or in Northern Ireland when, on the application of any interested party, it has been registered for enforcement in that part of the United Kingdom. The application shall be submitted to the court or competent authority indicated in the Regulation (which, for England and Wales, is the High Court). The declaration of enforceability shall be served on the party against whom enforcement is sought, accompanied by the judgment, if not already served on that party.

Seller outside the EEA   A3.60

For an English buyer to sue a seller outside the EEA, leave to serve the claim outside the jurisdiction must be obtained under the Civil Procedure Rules.

Bringing claims outside the EEA – the rules   A3.61

Broadly, claims in contract may be brought with leave of the court if the contract:

- was made within the jurisdiction;
- was made by or through an agent trading or residing within the jurisdiction on behalf of a principal trading or residing out of the jurisdiction;
- is by its terms, or implication, governed by English law; or
- contains a term to the effect that the High Court shall have jurisdiction to hear and determine any claim in respect of the contract.

Case Example: *Brinkibon v Stalig Stahl under Stahlwarenhandelgessellschaft MBH* **[1983] 2 AC 34**

The issue was whether the contract had been made within the jurisdiction. An English company sought leave to appeal to serve an Austrian company for breach of contract (Austria not at that time being an EU member). The contract had been made by telex with the buyer in London accepting a counter-offer made by the seller situated in Vienna. It was held that the contract had been made in Vienna where the acceptance had been received.

Case Example: *Scottish and Newcastle International Ltd v Othon Ghalanos Ltd* **[2008] UKHL 11**

O had agreed to buy cider from S. The parties' contract of sale was governed by English law. The cider had been shipped from Liverpool to Limassol where O had taken delivery, but had never paid. S had sued O for the price of the goods. The issue for determination was whether the English court had jurisdiction to entertain the action. It was common ground that in terms of *SI 2001/44, art 5(1)(b)*, the English courts did not have jurisdiction unless, according to English law, the cider was 'delivered' on shipment at Liverpool. The sale contract had provided for S to send the goods to O and to pay the freight, but O had designated the carrier to be used. The contract was expressed to be 'delivery cost and freight Limassol' and the invoices referred to the place of delivery as Limassol. The Court of Appeal had found that the delivery terms 'delivery cost and freight Limassol' meant that possession would be transferred to O on shipment on terms that S would procure for O a contract of carriage to carry the goods to Limassol and that risk, title and possession were all intended to pass on shipment. It had found that the reference in the invoices to 'place of delivery Limassol' did not turn the contract into an ex ship contract and that there was therefore no express term that delivery was to be effected at Limassol. O submitted that the instant contract was a typical CIF contract and that the *Sale of Goods Act 1979, s 32(1)* was of limited scope and did not apply where the carrier was the servant or agent of the seller. The section provides that: 'Where, in pursuance of a contract of sale, the seller is authorised or required to send the goods to the buyer, delivery of the goods to a carrier (whether named by the buyer or not) for the purpose of transmission to the buyer is prima facie deemed to be a delivery of the goods to the buyer'.

The House of Lords held that the contract was in all essential respects an FOB contract. By shipping the containers on board the vessels at Liverpool with the intention that O should be in a position to take delivery of them immediately on their arrival in Limassol, S was deemed, under *s 32(1)* of the Act, to have delivered the cider to O at Liverpool. Therefore, in terms of *art 5(1)(b)* of the Regulation, the English court had jurisdiction to hear the case. Although delivery of goods to a carrier did not automatically mean that delivery had been effected to the buyer, *s 32(1)* gave a prima facie rule, which would have to yield if the terms of the contract between the parties indicated that the seller was to keep, rather than to transfer, possession. In the instant case, the carriers were properly to be regarded as O's agents for the purposes of *s 32(1)* and S had no continuing interest in the cider once it had been shipped.

It was also stated by one Law Lord that, although it was unnecessary to consider what the position might have been after the passing of property and risk on shipment if S had not only made a special contract with the carriers, but had also retained possession of the goods, it was clear, bearing in mind the general aim of *art 5(1)(b)* and the general nature of FOB contracts, that the place of shipment was also the place of delivery in all types of FOB contracts, including those which provided for the seller to retain the bills of lading.

Checklist   A3.62

- Have you made sure that all necessary export licences have been obtained?

- Are you sure that your documentation, particularly with regard to invoices, is in order?

- Have you decided on what kind of contract you are going to use: in particular, has consideration been given to whether the contract will be FOB or CIF?

- Has proper attention been given to the terms of the particular contract, not least with regard to such matters as delivery, loading and payment?

- Does the contract make special provision for the passing of property and risk and for obtaining necessary export licences?

- Has thought been given to using trade association terms or those drafted by the ICC?

- Has the contract made provision as to which country's law is to apply?

- If the contract is with a consumer, has note been taken of the restrictions imposed on determining the applicable law?

- Have you given thought to using the Uniform Law on International Sales?

- Are you fully aware of the provisions as to jurisdiction and enforcement?

- Have you determined the precise place of domicile of the other party?

- To what extent have you contracted out of the rules on jurisdiction and to what extent, when so doing, have you distinguished between business and consumer contracts?

- Are you aware of what must be done to sue a seller based outside the EEA?

A4:
Software Contracts – Special Issues

At a glance

- A software contract can involve both goods (the disk) and services (the actual software).

- Issues as to whether the contract is for goods and/or services can be settled by an appropriate contract term.

- There is automatic copyright protection in a computer program, but this can be reinforced by a specific contract term.

- Failure to provide clear instructions for use of the software can produce a breach of contract.

- Licensees should take care to ensure that the functional specifications of the software are drafted to meet their special needs. These specifications should be accompanied by appropriate systems specifications.

- The licence should clearly indicate what rights there are as to user manuals.

- Warranties are often linked to exclusion or limitation clauses. The latter are subject to statutory control and their use can arguably give rise to a criminal offence.

- The buyer receives automatic statutory protection to the effect that his use of the software will not of itself violate the intellectual property rights of a third party. As above, these rights can be excluded or limited subject to strict statutory control.

- Software writing contracts can make provision for who will own copyright.

- The terms and conditions contained within a shrink-wrap purchase, insofar as they relate to the manufacturer and not the actual supplier, probably have no legal validity in contracts between businesses because of the absence of consideration.

- When goods are bought from a retailer, the general rule is that a manufacturer's guarantee is unenforceable. It is otherwise, however, where the buyer is a consumer.

- Customer registration cards often found in shrink-wrap purchases could, if returned to the manufacturer, provide consideration to make the terms and conditions binding.

- A licence clause will set out the rights of the purchaser in relation to his use of the software.

- The contract can provide for acceptance tests to be imposed as a pre-condition to the licensee accepting the software.

- The licence can set out specific restrictions on the use of the software.

- The contract should contain specific provisions as to confidentiality and disclosure, if only to affirm provisions implied by law.

- Provision can and should be made for the source code to be lodged with a third party.

- The contract should set out details of any training provided in the use of the software.

- An indemnity can be offered against the use of the software by the licensee infringing the rights of a third party.

- There are a number of points which should be considered in the case of a contract for bespoke software.

Whether software is 'goods'   A4.2

It is clear from the observations in *St Albans City and District Council v International Computers Ltd* [1996] 4 All ER 481, that a computer disk falls within the definition of 'goods'. Accordingly, the terms implied by the *Sale of Goods Act 1979* and the *Consumer Rights Act 2015* as to description, quality and fitness for purpose will apply to the goods. Similarly, the sale of an entire computer system, including hardware and software, will be a sale of 'goods'. Under *s 61, Sale of Goods Act 1979* the term 'goods' is defined as all personal chattels other than things in action or money.

This, however, is clear only in respect of the disk itself. What is less clear is the status of the software contained within the disk.

> **Case Example:** *Advent Systems Ltd v Unisys Corporation* (1991) 925F.2d 670
>
> In this American case, it was indicated that software does 'constitute' goods for the purposes of sale of goods legislation.

Case Example: *St Albans City and District Council v International Computers Ltd* (above)

In this case, in contrast, it was stated that the computer program itself is not goods, but the sale of the disk 'onto which a program designed and intended to instruct or enable a computer to achieve particular functions has been encoded' can constitute a sale of goods.

Case Example: *Beta Computers (Europe) Ltd v Adobe Systems (Europe) Ltd* 1996 SLT 604

A Scottish court said that an order for a standard package to upgrade an existing system was a discrete category of agreement which contained elements of a contract of sale and a contract of licence. It was said to be an essential feature of such a contract that the supplier undertook both to supply the medium on which the program was recorded, and the right to access and use the software.

Case Example: *Toby Construction Products Pty Ltd v Computer Bar Sales Pty Ltd* (1983) 50 ALR 684

In this Australian case, the claimant purchased a computer system from the defendants under a contract which apportioned the total price between 'software' and 'hardware' referring to it collectively as 'the equipment' and claimed against the defendant for losses alleged to have been caused by defects in the system. As to whether the contract was for 'the sale of goods' under the New South Wales Sale of Goods Act 1923, it was held that the substance of the contract was for the sale of a computer system and although the software was intangible and the product of research which might not on its own be within the statutory description of 'goods' the sale of the software and the hardware collectively was within the description.

Ultimately, the point may be more academic than practical. If the agreement is one for the supply of goods, then the implied terms referred to above will apply. If the contract falls within the remit of the *Supply of Goods and Services Act 1982*, then identical provisions apply. If, for whatever reason, no particular Act applies, then the common law will certainly apply much the same terms in any event.

Case Example: *Horace Holman Group Ltd v Sherwood International Group Ltd* (12 April 2000)

The court felt it 'probable' that a contract for the supply of software was not a contract for the supply of goods, in which case a term as to reasonable fitness (and one may assume satisfactory quality) would be implied at common law.

225

Case Example: *Southwark LBC v IBM UK Ltd* **[2011] EWHC 549**

The claimant local authority claimed damages for breach of contract against the defendant company. The local authority had contracted with IBM for the provision of third-party software and associated consultancy services for the implementation of a 'master data management' system to rationalise information recorded on a number of the authority's computer systems. The software was to be provided under licence from the manufacturer). The latter warranted that the software would be virus free and would perform to specification. Any additional implied conditions or warranties of fitness for purpose by IBM were excluded. The standard conditions provided that IBM warranted that the goods were of satisfactory quality. The project was ultimately abandoned by the local authority. It claimed that the software had been unfit for purpose because it did not properly deal with its requirements for data matching and security provisions. The issues for determination were: (i) what express or implied suitability obligations IBM had with regard to the software; and (ii) whether the *Sale of Goods Act 1979* applied.

It was held that the parties had contracted on the basis that warranties and indemnities relating to the software were the manufacturer's responsibility. Other than that, IBM gave no warranties. Any implied conditions or warranties as to quality or fitness for purpose were agreed to be excluded. There was a contractual provision that the software would be satisfactory, and this fell to be determined by reference to the contractual appendices which stipulated, among other things, that it should be virus free and should provide extensive data searching facilities. If parties to such a contract spelt out what software had to do, it would be satisfactory if it achieved what the contract dictated it should achieve. There was no room in the contract for some interpretation which suggested that IBM was warranting that the software would, in some abstract way, be suitable for the authority's purpose.

It was also held that there was no 'transfer' of property in goods for the purpose of the *1979 Act*. The contract specifically stipulated that 'title, copyright and all other proprietary rights in the software' remained vested in the manufacturer. Indeed, the termination provision required the authority to return to the manufacturer or destroy all copies, forms and parts of the software covered by the licence, intimating that property remained vested in the manufacturer. The court said, without making a specific finding to such effect, that software could be 'goods' within the meaning of the *1979 Act*. Compact discs impressed with software were physical objects and there was no reason why they should not be considered as goods.

A purchaser would be well advised to avoid any problems as to whether the *Sale of Goods Act 1979* applies by specifically incorporating into the contract appropriate terms.

> **Case Example: Fern Computer Consultancy Ltd v Intergraph Cardworx and Analysis Solutions Inc [2014] EWHC 2908**
>
> X owned software products. The software was generally provided on a CD, accompanied by a dongle.
>
> It was said that where software was supplied on CDs, there was a real prospect of success in arguing that that was a supply of goods.

Sample Clause

'It is agreed that the subject matter of this contract, including both hardware and software, in whatever form, in all respects corresponds with any description made, and is, in all respects, of satisfactory quality and reasonably fit for the purpose for which it is supplied. These undertakings are in addition to, and not in derogation from, any other applicable provisions implied by law'.

Consumer contracts   A4.3

The discussion above as to whether software can be categorised by goods no longer applies in the case of contracts made with a consumer. Chapter 3 of the *Consumer Rights Act 2015* deals specifically with contracts having 'digital content', which it defines as 'data which are produced and supplied in digital form'. The Act then provides for the provisions of terms as to description, quality and fitness for purpose in terms identical to those which would apply were the contract for the sale of goods. These provisions also apply where software is downloaded. The Act also provides consumers with a remedy if the digital content causes damage to a device or other digital content and if such damage could have been avoided by the exercise of reasonable care and skill.

Intellectual property   A4.4

A computer program as well as preparatory design material for a computer program or a database is stated to be a literary work under the provisions of *s 3(1)* of the *Copyright, Designs and Patents Act 1988* (*CDPA 1988*). This applies if the program is 'written'. *Section 178* states that 'writing' includes (so the definition is illustrative rather than exhaustive) 'any form of notation or code, whether by hand or otherwise and regardless of the method by which, or medium in or on which, it is recorded'. It is difficult to envisage any form of software which would not be in writing.

Given that a computer program does have copyright protection, this means that it cannot be copied in whole or in substantial part without the consent

227

of the copyright owner. The copyright in computer-generated works lasts for 50 years from the end of the year in which the work was made (*s 12(7)* of the *CDPA 1988*). Whether or not a software program is computer-generated will depend on an analysis of the facts leading to its creation. It is thought likely that the individual skill of the program-writer will mean that in many, perhaps most, cases the software will not be computer-generated. In such a case, copyright protection will last for 70 years from the end of the year in which the program-writer died; or 70 years from the year in which the program was first made available if the author is unknown (*s 12(1)* of the *CDPA 1988*). This particular period of protection will, however, not apply if the country of origin of the work is outside the European Economic Area and the author is not an EEA national, in which case the duration of copyright is that of the country of origin so long as that does not exceed the 70-year period (*s 12(6)* of the *CDPA 1988*). The EEA consists of the Member States of the European Union, Norway, Liechtenstein and Iceland.

Although it is strictly unnecessary for the supplier to spell out his copyright protection, it may be useful to do so, perhaps with a limited permission to make copies.

Sample Clause

'No part of any software may be copied or stored in any medium without the supplier's prior written consent, except that no more than [X] copies may be made for back-up or archive purposes.'

Instructions for use   A4.5

It is an unfortunate fact that many of the instructions accompanying computer material are sometimes misleading, and more often than not confusing, and thus making the subject matter of the contract difficult or even impossible to use (see further A4.11 below).

Case Example: *Wormell v RHM Agriculture (East) Ltd* **[1987] 1 WLR 1091**

It was accepted that misleading instructions would mean that the goods would not be reasonably fit for their purpose, and, one would imagine, not of satisfactory quality.

Where goods are ordered from a non-English speaking country by a party in the United Kingdom, the buyer presumably takes the risk that the instructions might not be in English (see further A4.11 below).

Documentation   A4.6

The nature and quality of the documentation provided with the software will be of particular importance. The most important documentation will be as set out in A4.7 to A4.9 below.

Functional specification   A4.7

This will set out, in ordinary language and in some detail, the functions to be performed by the software. In the case of packaged software, this may be the supplier's document stating what the software does, rather than stating the customer's requirements. From the licensee's point of view, it is far better that the specifications should have been drawn up by the licensee, setting out his requirements for the software. In this case, the supplier will be concerned to ensure either that he can meet the specifications, or that he states the respects in which he will not.

The commercial purchaser of a standard, as opposed to a bespoke, computer software package is under an implied duty to cooperate with the supplier of the software in order to achieve as good a 'fit' as is reasonably possible, and had, if necessary, to modify its systems and/or expectations to that end.

> **Case Example:** *Anglo Group plc v Winther Brown & Co Ltd* **(1 March 2000)**
>
> WB, a distributor of goods for the DIY market, entered into a written agreement on BML's standard terms that BML would supply computer hardware and a standard software package called Charisma (collectively referred to as 'the equipment') to WB. WB alleged that BML made a number of representations to WB in order to induce it to enter into a standard form leasing agreement with Anglo in respect of the equipment. WB alleged that the equipment, principally the software, suffered from numerous defects, such that Anglo, by reason of the representations made by its agent BML, was in breach of a condition or warranty as to the fitness or quality of the equipment, which was to be implied into the leasing agreement under the *Supply of Goods and Services Act 1982*. In reliance upon that breach, WB purported to terminate the leasing agreement.
>
> It was held that it was clear that WB was only ever interested in, and willing to pay for, a standard computer system rather than a bespoke system. The court said that it was almost inevitable that Charisma would not be a perfect 'fit', and hence it was also inevitable that WB would have to adapt to Charisma. In such circumstances, there was an implied duty on both WB and BML to cooperate in achieving reasonable solutions to problems as and when they emerged. The specific aspects of that duty were the equivalent of BML's written terms of business which required WB to accept responsibility for the selection of the computer system.

System specification   **A4.8**

This will consist of the detailed, technical specification of the software, setting out how the functional requirements will be realised.

User manual   **A4.9**

This will describe how the software is to be used.

The right of the user to obtain copies of the above documents, the number to which he is entitled, when they are to be delivered, his right to copy, and the ownership in them, should all be clearly addressed in the licence.

Warranties and limitation of liability   **A4.10**

It is not uncommon to find in a contract a provision which both offers a limited warranty on the product, but which also takes away from the buyer such other rights as he might have at law.

Sample Clause

> 'We make no warranties or conditions with respect to the items supplied under this contract other than to guarantee the original items against faulty materials or workmanship for 90 days from the date the items were supplied.'

This may then be followed by such a clause as:

> 'The foregoing warranty is in lieu of all other conditions or warranties, express or implied, including, but not limited to, the implied conditions or warranties as to description, quality and fitness for purpose. In no event will we be liable for consequential damages even if we have been advised in advance of the possibility of such damages.'

The 90-day warranty is lawful, but there may be a problem with the exclusion of liability if this occurs in a contract made between businesses. On the safe assumption that the clause is part of a contract on written standard terms, then, under the provisions of the *Unfair Contract Terms Act 1977 (UCTA 1977)*, it will be valid only if the party seeking to rely on it can show that it is reasonable.

Case Example: *Southwark LBC v IBM UK Ltd* **[2011] EWHC 549**

In this case, the contract included this term:

'Except as expressly stated in this Contract, all warranties and conditions, whether express or implied by statute, common law or otherwise (including fitness for purpose) are hereby excluded to the extent permitted by law.'

This was held to be reasonable. The court said that this was a case in which the parties were of broadly equal bargaining strength. The local authority had the opportunity to contract with the manufacturer and also chose the benefit of standard framework agreement terms. The court said that there could be no suggestion that the authority did not or could reasonably not have known of the terms which excluded the implied terms; it had gone through a protracted process negotiating the terms and had lawyers involved. Finally, it appeared that there was some enhancement of the software by the manufacturers to reflect what the authority said it wanted. The reality was, the court said, that the contract was not, objectively looked at, an unfair or unreasonable one. Under the provisions of the contract, the authority was to get exactly what its staff wanted and was or would have been in the position by virtue of the contract to have all breaches remedied, to recover damages, albeit somewhat but not overly limited, and indeed to terminate if there were material defaults which were not remedied within specified times.

If the purchaser of the system was a private consumer, then the position is more stringent. The *Consumer Rights Act 2015* provides that the exclusion clause is automatically void. Furthermore, under the provisions of the *Consumer Protection from Unfair Trading Regulations 2008 (SI 2008/1977)*, it may be the case that the use of the exclusion clause will constitute a criminal offence (this does not apply if the clause is used in a business-to-business contract).

The legal status of guarantees A4.11

When goods are bought other than from a manufacturer, as when they are bought from a shop or other source of supply, there is no contract with the actual manufacturer of the goods and therefore any guarantee provided by the manufacturer is, in principle, not legally binding. In the case of a consumer contract, the *Consumer Rights Act 2015* specifically makes manufacturers' guarantees enforceable even in the absence of a direct contract with the manufacturer. Furthermore, the Act states that the guarantor shall ensure that the guarantee sets out in plain, intelligible language the contents of the guarantee and the essential particulars necessary for making claims under the guarantee, notably the duration and territorial scope of the guarantee as well as the name and address of the guarantor. Furthermore, they also state that, if the goods are marketed in the United Kingdom, the guarantee must be in English.

Purchaser's safeguard against intellectual property infringements **A4.12**

It will be implicit in any contract between businesses involving the supply of software that the buyer can lawfully use that software; that is to say, that his doing so will not infringe the intellectual property rights, such as copyright or patent rights, of a third party. This is made explicit in the case of consumer contracts by the *Consumer Rights Act 2015*. Insofar as any clause seeks by implication (or it might expressly spell it out) to exclude or limit such a duty, then it will fall to be governed in the case of business-to-business contracts by *UCTA 1977*. In the case of consumer contracts, the *Consumer Rights Act 2015* provides that, such a clause cannot be excluded.

UCTA 1977 does not apply to contracts so far as the contract relates to the creation or transfer of any right or interest in intellectual property, but a contract for the supply of items, even though they may be subject to copyrights or patents, is not such a contract. The *Consumer Rights Act 2015* contains no exclusion of terms relating to intellectual property rights.

The scope of the exclusion from *UCTA 1977* of terms relating to the creation of transfer of intellectual property rights has been subject to a restrictive interpretation.

> **Case Example:** *The Salvage Association v CAP Financial Services Ltd* **[1995] FSR 654**
>
> The contract in dispute related to the installation of computer software. It was argued that, since all the issues in the case related to the creation or transfer of interests in intellectual property, then the matter fell within the exclusion. This argument was rejected. The court ruled that the exclusion applied only to those provisions of a contract actually dealing with the creation or transfer of a right or interest in the relevant intellectual property:
>
> > 'It does not extend generally to all the terms of a contract simply because the contract is concerned overall with the provision of a service, performance of which will result in a product to which the law affords the protection of one or more of the specified intellectual property rights.'
>
> The court agreed that the exclusion from *UCTA 1977* would apply to any term concerned with the creation or transfer of a right or interest in intellectual property; but if a term was one concerned with other aspects of the contract, then the exclusion would not apply. Where a term does fall within the exclusion from *UCTA 1977*, then it will be judged on common law principles, which effectively means that the court will construe it to determine its precise scope and applicability.

Use and licence of software A4.13

A contract for the supply of a specially written computer program can provide for the writer to retain copyright or for copyright to pass to the client, though the former is more usual.

Shrink-wrap licences A4.14

Many software packages sold in shops are wrapped in cellophane, or some other wrapper, on which there appears a notice indicating that, by opening the package, the buyer agrees to be bound by various terms supplied alongside the notice or inside the package. Typically, the 'shrink-wrap' terms will include an undertaking by the purchaser not to claim against the manufacturer for consequential loss arising out of defective software, as well as restrictions on the use of the software itself. In return, the manufacturer might agree to replace defective disks.

It has yet to be decided in the courts if the purchaser is bound by the licence, but it is unlikely that he would be. His contract would only be with the supplier of the goods, and not with the manufacturer. Even if the purchaser expects to be aware that there will be terms and conditions contained in the package (perhaps from previous purchases), he has supplied no consideration to the manufacturer and hence still cannot be bound by them. For the position as to manufacturers' guarantees in the case of consumer contracts, see A4.11.

Customer registration A4.15

It is frequently the case that a shrink-wrap licence will contain a term asking the purchaser to complete a registration card and return it to the manufacturer. This could entitle him to updates and the use of a telephone helpline and other assistance. It is arguable that, by returning the card, the purchaser is accepting the terms and conditions contained in the licence and providing the consideration to support a contract containing those terms, though this point still remains to be settled.

Licence clause A4.16

The main purpose of a licence is to grant a permission to do something which the licensee would otherwise have no right to do. For instance, unless the licence expressly gives the right to make back-up or archive copies, there is no right to do so. The licence would also have to consider an 'internal purposes' clause. The reason for such wording would be to prevent the software being used for the provision of a bureau service to businesses or persons who would otherwise themselves have to obtain a licence from the supplier. It will also have the effect of restricting use to the purposes of the particular company which obtained the licence. Where the company is a member of a group, and it is envisaged that other members of the group may wish to use the software, the licence should specifically cover such use.

Acceptance tests   A4.17

The idea of acceptance tests is important in relation to software. The purpose of such tests is to determine whether the software performs required functions, so that the licensee can decide whether to accept the software and proceed with the contract, or terminate the contract, return the software and obtain a return of any money paid.

The nature of the acceptance tests can vary widely. At one extreme will be a detailed set of tests, comprehensively stated in a document negotiated as part of the contract. At the other extreme, acceptance may be a simple provision by which the licensee will be taken to have accepted the software if he uses it for a fixed period without rejection. The key to such provisions is that they should be clear and definitive; they should not involve an agreement to agree unless there is a procedure established for the determination of issues in the event of a disagreement.

Restrictions on use   A4.18

The basic restrictions on the use of the software will be contained in the licence clause (see A4.16 above) since, by saying what can be done, this will preclude any other use. Software licences do, however, often lay down further restrictions, the most common of which are set out below.

No modifications   A4.19

The licensee will, in practice, be unable to create any modifications without the software source code. Legally, however, in the absence of an express prohibition, there would seem to be no reason why he should not modify the software except to the extent that by doing so he does something impermissible such as infringe the copyright in the software.

Use with other hardware or software   A4.20

The terms of the licence will often limit the hardware with which the software can be used. In addition, the licensee may be restricted from using the software with other software. For example, the licensee may decide to write some software of his own to perform additional functions, or alter the way in which the licensed software operates. A restriction as to the hardware to be used with the software will normally be reasonable provided that it permits use with replacement or standby hardware. The licensee should resist limits on the source of such hardware; the test should be compatibility with the software, not the source.

Use by skilled operator in accordance with manual   A4.21

The supplier may impose some such restriction because of a concern for problems which may reflect unfairly on him. Such a restriction is, though, difficult to police.

Confidentiality   A4.22

Software is generally protected by the law of copyright and the law of confidence. The latter does not require the existence of any specific provision in the contract, but enforcement becomes more straightforward if the licensee explicitly agrees to maintain confidentiality. Accordingly, in most software licences, the supplier will impose an obligation on the licensee to keep the software, and all associated documentation, confidential including data protection.

Such a clause is reasonable so long as the items to be protected are confined to those belonging to the licensor. If they are, for example, extended to include data or specifications belonging to the licensee, this will impinge on the latter's business. The licensee should also ensure that the clause permits him to disclose the software to his employees, or at least those who need to know, and others with a legitimate right to know (such as auditors, consultants, lawyers or other advisers), and that the obligation of confidence ceases when the information falls into the public domain. The clause should also not impinge on the scope of the licensee to use the software. If, for example, subsidiaries of the licensee are permitted to use the software, disclosure to them should not be a breach of the undertaking as to confidentiality.

Sample clause on data protection:

> 'You [the licensee] shall comply with all relevant data protection legislation including without limitation the Data Protection Act 2018 and UK GDPR policies in force from time to time in the performance of the Contract.'

Source code escrow   A4.23

The default or disappearance of the licensor will almost certainly have serious consequences for the licensee. For example, the licensee may no longer be able to have errors corrected or modifications carried out. The licensee will generally have only the object code version of the software and, without the source code, will be unable to do any of these things for himself.

The solution to this is the 'source code escrow agreement'. A tripartite agreement is entered into between the licensor, the licensee and the escrow agent. The licensor agrees to deposit a copy of the software source code with the agent, and to update it as and when new releases of the software are supplied to the licensee. The licensor will agree with the licensee that, on the happening of a number of defined events (such as the insolvency of the licensor, or his failure to provide maintenance), the source code will be released to the licensee. The escrow agent agrees that he will release the source code when such events are notified to him.

Training   A4.24

Training may constitute an important part of the arrangements for both parties. Full details of any courses offered, their location, the payment of travel and accommodation expenses, the number of persons who can attend each course, and the like, should be included in the licence.

Patent/copyright indemnity   A4.25

Generally, licensors will be prepared to give a limited indemnity in relation to the infringement by the software of any intellectual property rights owned by a third party. This would constitute a breach by the licensor of the provisions of *SGA 1979* and *SGSA 1982*, as to quiet possession and freedom from encumbrances (*Niblett v Confectioners' Materials Co Ltd* [1921] 3 KB 387; *Microbeads AG v Vinhurst Road Markings Ltd* [1975] 1 WLR 218). In the case of a consumer contract, the *Consumer Rights Act 2015* has no such provisions, saying only that the supplier of any digital content must have the right to supply such content.

Indemnities often contain a limitation to the effect that they will not apply if the infringement arises from the combination of the licensor's goods with those not so supplied. Patents can be granted for new combinations of old inventions, and, as a result, infringements can occur when two non-infringing items are combined. Insofar as any such limitation clause relates to the obligations as to quiet possession and freedom from encumbrances, which in any event apply only in relation to business contracts, then they will be subject to the reasonableness and test imposed by *UCTA 1977*.

Drafting tips

Practical drafting points to bear in mind are that the person providing the indemnity will:

- wish to have control, or the right to take control, of any action brought or negotiations for its settlement;

- require the other party to notify him immediately of any claim; and

- require him not to make any admission of liability.

Provision is often made to the effect that, in the event of a claim, the indemnifying party may modify the equipment so that it ceases to infringe, or obtain a licence from the third party who brought the claim, or terminate the agreement.

Bespoke software   A4.26

While a contract for the provision of bespoke software will have many similarities to what might be called off-the-shelf software, there will be differences arising from the fact that such software has been expressly written for the purposes of the particular contract.

> **Case Example:** *Saphena Computing Ltd v Allied Collection Agencies Ltd* **[1995] FSR 616**
>
> The Court of Appeal said that it should be kept in mind that software may have to be tested and modified as necessary: 'it would not be a breach of contract at all to deliver software in the first instance with a defect in it'. Reference was made to an expert witness who had said: 'Just as no software developer can reasonably expect a buyer to tell him what is required without a process of feedback and reassessment, so no buyer should expect a supplier to get the programs right first time. He too needs feedback on whether he has been successful'. The Court of Appeal said that the supplier should be allowed a reasonable time, which will be determined according to the circumstances of the individual case.

Functional specification   A4.27

The question arises as to how to define the user's requirements. The answer will lie in the functional (or requirements) specification which will describe, in detail, the functions to be performed by the software. The preparation of the functional specification should be undertaken with great care, since it will become the benchmark for the project and will determine whether or not the supplier fulfils or breaches its obligations, is entitled to be paid, and whether or not the software meets the user's requirements. The functional specification is best prepared by the user alone, possibly with the help of independent consultants, or by a combination of the user and the supplier, with the user maintaining the ultimate control over content. It should not be prepared by the supplier alone since the essence of the specification is that it sets out what the user wants, not what the supplier is willing or able to supply.

It is important that the copyright and other rights in the specification should vest in the user. If the intention is that the rights to the software itself should vest in the user, then any different agreement as to the specification could lead to legal difficulties. Furthermore, the user should be able to take the functional specification to any software supplier and have the software written by them; if the rights in the functional specification are vested in a third party, such as the software house concerned in the preparation, this would be prevented.

A system specification and user manual should also be produced as part of the contract (see A4.8 and A4.9 above).

Defining responsibilities A4.28

The primary obligation will be on the supplier to write and deliver software complying with the user's requirements. At the same time, the supplier will be dependent on the user providing him with information about the latter's business, accepting the functional specification as complete, supplying trial data, providing employees of the required standard for training and so forth. The contract should spell these matters out, so that the division of responsibilities is clear. This should be done in the implementation plan, a document which sets out the detailed timing of the project. It will set dates for the exchange of information, the production of specifications, the availability of the site, the achievement of various planned stages, acceptance testing and the delivery of documentation.

Dealing with changes A4.29

The contract should set out a procedure for specifying and agreeing on changes to the contract work. The procedure should allow the user to specify a change, with a period allowing the supplier to respond with a statement as to the cost of implementing the change, the consequences for delivery and other dates, and any other consequences. It should be made clear who is to pay for the cost of such response.

It would also be sensible for the contract to provide for any changes which might be suggested by the supplier.

Price and payment A4.30

The price for bespoke software can either be a fixed price agreed in advance, or on a time and materials basis. The former suits the user, the latter, the supplier. Just which payment method is adopted will depend on the negotiations between the parties, and, in particular, their relative bargaining strengths. As a general rule, it would be unusual for bespoke software to be written entirely on a time and materials basis.

Performance stages   A4.31

The contract should specify details as to the:

- delivery of functional specifications;
- delivery of system specifications; and
- acceptance of software.

Many other stages may be identified as suitable for consideration in the contract. Where the software consists of a number of discrete modules, the stages might be linked to the achievement of particular stages in relation to each module, with overall system acceptance being the final stage.

Acceptance testing   A4.32

Acceptance testing will generally test each separate phase of the development as it is completed, and then the total installation. The acceptance tests should be specified in a contractual document and agreed at the outset. If the tests cannot be agreed on at the outset, a procedure should be laid down for determining the tests in the event of a failure to agree, such as determination by an independent third party.

Intellectual property   A4.33

A major area of possible dispute concerns the ownership of the intellectual property in bespoke software, not least because there is no general presumption in English law that the person who commissions, and pays for, a piece of work owns the copyright in it. If the parties expressly agree on the matter, that will resolve any disputes. If not, the courts will have to decide what has been implied as to ownership. To do this, it will look at all the circumstances of the case, such as the amount paid, the extent to which the software was specifically written for the user, the extent to which it embodied the supplier's standard software, and whether it was intended to confer a commercial advantage on the user.

An indication in the agreement that will be of major significance will be a licensing clause. If the user is licensed to use the software, this will be almost conclusive evidence that the intellectual property belongs to the supplier. The absence of a licence may indicate that intellectual property vests in the user.

Case Example: *Saphena Computing Ltd v Allied Collection Agencies Ltd* **(22 July 1988)**

The Recorder rejected a customer's submission that the commissioning of a computer program of itself vested the copyright in that program in the customer. He also declined to find any basis on which to imply a term that the beneficial interest should pass to the customer.

This issue was not raised before the Court of Appeal (see A4.26)).

The matter should normally be explicitly addressed in a bespoke contract, and will often constitute a major area of negotiation.

It is important for companies to remember that the *Copyright, Designs and Patents Act 1988* contains certain general exceptions to copyright infringement which a company that has commissioned work to a software developer can make use of, no matter what terms a court may or may not imply where there is no agreement regulating the question of copyright. Firstly, by *s 50A* a company paying for a computer program is entitled to make a backup copy so long as this will be used for lawful purposes. It may also copy or adapt a computer program if this is necessary for its lawful use: *s 50C*. Under *s 296A* another exception will be made to copyright infringement where a company observes, studies or tests the performance of a computer program in order to become familiar with the ideas and principles which lie behind the program. Finally, under limited circumstances a company wishing to develop new software that will be compatible with the existing commissioned software is entitled to decompile the software in order to ascertain how this is possible: *s 50B*. Certain conditions must be met before decompilation is permissible.

Matters to consider

- Ownership may be clearly allocated to one side or the other, but a range of intermediate solutions is possible taking into account such matters as the distinction between trade secrets and general skill and experience.

- The supplier can legitimately be expected not to claim ownership of anything which is a trade secret of the user, but could expect to make use of the general knowledge and experience acquired while performing the contract.

Distinction between specially written and standard codes **A4.34**

The bespoke software may be written entirely for the user, or may consist of modifications to a standard package. It may be agreed that the whole of such specially written software should belong to the user. Even within the specially written software, however, there might be segments of code which are standard and owned by the supplier. It might, therefore, be agreed that the supplier should retain ownership of the standard code, so that only the copyright in the codes written specifically for the user should belong to him.

Joint ownership **A4.35**

This is something which can arise in two ways. Firstly, the software may be created by programmers employed by both parties. In the absence of any specific agreement, such software will belong jointly to both parties.

Secondly, the parties may themselves agree on joint ownership. The respective rights of joint owners of copyright at law are unclear, but it would seem that each party would have the right to use the software and reproduce it for his own use, but could not sub-licence its use without the consent of the other.

Marketing rights **A4.36**

Rather than ownership of the rights, the user's main concern may be to prevent the competition from obtaining the advantage of similar software too quickly or too early. The supplier, in contrast, will be concerned that if it relinquishes ownership of the software, it will be hampered in future work by concern that it is infringing the rights of the user. The solution could lie in an agreement as to the marketing of the software similar to that written for the first user. For example, the rights might vest in the supplier, but it might be prevented from marketing any similar systems for a defined period, or to defined types of customer. It may also agree on the payment of a royalty on sales to other customers as a quid pro quo for its ownership of the rights. The arrangement need not necessarily involve the supplier owning the rights; they could vest in the user, with an exclusive licence being granted to the supplier allowing it to market the software.

Sub-contractors **A4.37**

It may well be that the supplier needs the assistance of third parties to fulfil the contract with the user. If there is nothing personal about the reason the user contracted with the particular supplier, the latter will be able to sub-contract all or part of the task. If, therefore, the user is particularly concerned that only employees of the supplier should work on the contract, this should be spelled out in the contract.

Matters to consider

- Prohibitions on disclosure of information should cover sub-contractors.

- The sub-contractor should agree that, as between himself and the supplier, the copyright and other rights in the software will vest in the supplier. If the user is actually to own these rights, this will happen automatically under the main contract.

- The user should consider taking direct undertakings from the sub-contractor as to such matters as quality, performance and non-disclosure. Since there is no direct contract with the sub-contractor, these undertakings should be made under seal, or supported by a nominal consideration.

Non-competition clauses A4.38

The user may require the supplier to enter into an agreement not to market similar software to any competitor within a defined period. Any such clause, however, is subject to both the Treaty on the Functioning of the European Union and the *Competition Act 1998*, to the effect that an agreement is void if it has the object or effect of preventing, restricting or distorting trade or is an abuse of a dominant position. A fine of up to 10% of turnover can also be imposed.

Solicitation of employees A4.39

Since there may well be close cooperation between one party and the employees of the other, even to the extent of employees working on the other's premises, it can be worthwhile stating in the agreement that neither party can entice, solicit or even employ another's employee for a period of, say, 12 months from the termination of the contract. Any such clause would have to be reasonable to avoid being an unfair restraint on trade, and possibly also anti-competitive as referred to immediately above.

Other terms A4.40

Reference should be made to the terms considered above in relation to software contracts generally.

Checklist A4.41

- Has the issue of whether software can cover the supply of goods and also the supply of services been properly addressed in the contract, particularly if it is a business-to-business contract?

- Has thought been given to the protection of your intellectual property rights?

- Has care been taken to ensure that the instructions for use have been given in clear, intelligible language?

- Has thought also been given, particularly in the case of a consumer contract, to how the guarantee is worded and whether it too, is in English, and in plain, intelligible language?

- Has proper thought been given to all the contents of the documentation?

- Has full use been made of exclusion and limitation clauses? Has care been taken to avoid the use of any such clauses which might be illegal?

- Are you sure that the use by the buyer/licensee of the software will not infringe third-party intellectual property rights?

- As the manufacturer of software, are you aware that the terms and conditions you seek to impose might not be binding against a party who buys from a retail supplier?

- Has use been made of a registration card as a possible way of a buyer providing consideration?

- Have the rights of the licensee been clearly spelled out? In particular, have all the relevant restrictions on use been clearly identified?

- As a purchaser, have you set out the acceptance tests which must be run before you are prepared to accept the software?

- What provision has been made in relation to confidentiality and non-disclosure?

- Has consideration been given to compliance with the *Data Protection Act 2018* and the UK GDPR?

- Does this agreement contain provision for the deposit of the source code with a third party?

- What provision has been made for training in the use of the software?

- Has an indemnity been offered against any possible infringement of a third party's intellectual property rights?

- Bespoke software raises special problems. Have all the relevant issues been considered in the contract?

- Does the grant of the licence cover all the licensee's anticipated usage?

- Has consideration being given for the licensee's rights to extend to affiliates, subsidiaries and other third parties?

- Where will the software be located?

- Are there any territorial restrictions on the use of the software?

- Is there a process for expanding the licensee's rights to include other users if required?

- Is the licence perpetual or for a fixed period? Will it be renewed?

- Is there a definition of 'software'? What does it cover? Does the definition include everything licensee is ordering or the licensor is delivering?

- What specific restrictions are placed on the licensee in the use of the software? Can the licensee fully comply with those restrictions?

- What performance and conformance warranties are being provided in the license agreement and are they limited in duration? Are there any disclaimers?

- Are there any restrictions on the assignment of the license agreement on the licensee?

- What support and maintenance services will the licensor be providing to the licensee for the duration of the agreement?

Section B:
Business-to-Business Contracts

B1:
Terms and Conditions for the Sale and Supply of Goods

At a glance B1.1

- A contract for the sale of goods means a contract where property in those goods passes or transfers from one party to another for a consideration.

- Generally speaking, no formalities are required for a contract of sale of goods.

- Statute implies obligations as to title into contracts for the sale of goods.

- Statute also implies a requirement that goods must conform to their contract description.

- Statute further requires that goods supplied must be of a particular quality and capacity and fit for their purpose.

- The obligations as to description and quality are strict, meaning that blame or intention is irrelevant to the question of a breach.

- There are obligations incurred by the seller when the sale is a sale by sample.

- Exclusions are permitted from the obligations as to quality and capacity in certain well-defined circumstances.

- Apart from the above, statute places severe control on the use of exclusion or limitation clauses and addresses the fairness of such clauses.

- Exclusion clauses can be subject to a reasonableness test.

- There are statutory provisions as to when property and risk is to pass.

- These statutory provisions are, however, subject to the terms of the contract.

- It is a general rule that a person who has no title cannot himself pass a valid title, but there are exceptions to this rule.

- Prompt payment is not generally of the essence of the contract, although this is subject to the terms of the contract.

- Late payment can incur statutory interest.

- Duties are imposed on a seller as to delivery, and as to delivery of the right quantity of goods.

- A buyer has rights as to the examination of the goods, but these are subject to the terms of the contract.

- Acceptance of the contract goods carries with it the loss of the right to reject by the buyer.

- Acceptance is defined by law.

- An unpaid seller of goods has certain rights, such as a right to a lien and a right to stop the goods in transit.

- Such a seller also has rights of resale and to damages.

- Provision is also made for the seller to sue for the actual price.

- Statute also provides for the rights of the buyer, notably with regard to specific performance and damages.

General   B1.2

Many aspects of contract of sale and of purchase of goods are determined by the *Sale of Goods Act 1979* (*SGA 1979*). Contracts of supply other than sale are dealt with in like terms to the *Sale of Goods Act* by the *Supply of Goods (Implied Terms) Act 1973* – which deals with hire-purchase – and the *Supply of Goods and Services Act 1982* – all other contracts of supply and contracts for the provision of services. These enactments are limited to business-to-business contracts. In the case of consumer contracts, corresponding provisions are contained in the *Consumer Rights Act 2015*. In many ways, the distinction between a contract of sale and other contracts is academic in that legislation such as the *Supply of Goods (Implied Terms) Act 1973* and the *Supply of Goods and Services Act 1982* and the *Consumer Rights Act 2015*, imply terms into the contract identical in most respects to those implied by the *SGA 1979*.

Case Example: *Cheeld v Alliott* [2013] EWCA Civ 508

By an oral contract, X had engaged C to construct and install a metal porch at the front of their property at a cost of £6,500. X paid a deposit of £2,000. After the porch was installed, X sought to reject it. They did not pay C and he issued proceedings in the small claims court seeking to recover £4,250, a slight reduction on the contract price as the porch's installation had not been completed. X counterclaimed, seeking the return of their deposit. The deputy district judge accepted X's evidence that they were unhappy with the porch after its installation and had said to C that it might look better if it was painted. That painting work was carried out by a third party, but X remained dissatisfied with it. The deputy district judge found that there was a lack of symmetry in the frame of the porch and lack of finish and that C was in breach of contract since X had expected and was entitled to expect goods of the highest quality in an ornamental feature at the front of their home. However, she concluded that the defective workmanship amounted to a breach of warranty rather than a breach of condition entitling X to reject it. The deputy district judge ordered X to pay C £2,000, a reduction on the £4,250 claimed to take account of the cost of remedying the defective workmanship. X appealed on the basis that the deputy district judge had wrongly held there was no breach of condition, and that the reduction of £2,250 was an arbitrary figure. The circuit judge allowed the appeal to the extent that he found no proper basis for assessing the cost of remedying the defects as £2,250, and he ordered the parties to file evidence in that respect. He rejected X's contention that C had breached a condition of the contract.

X contended that a further hearing in the small claims court was unnecessary and disproportionate and that the circuit judge should have held that there was a breach of condition, or left that issue open. They submitted that the monetary value of the defects arrived at by the deputy district judge as one-third of the contract's value indicated a breach of condition rather than a breach of warranty, and that by the *Sale of Goods Act 1979 s 14(2)* and *(6)*, 'satisfactory quality' was a condition entitling them to reject the defective porch and succeed on their counterclaim. C contended that the contract was not one for the sale of goods but a supply of skill and labour under the *Supply of Goods and Services Act 1982*. He asserted that since the finding of a breach of warranty was not perverse, the instant court should not interfere with it, and that X had, in any event, lost their right to reject by having the porch painted and affirming the contract.

The Court of Appeal held that the circuit judge should not have requested further evidence on the defective workmanship issue. The matter was to have been determined informally by the small claims procedure without expert evidence. The deputy district judge and the circuit judge had erred by failing to treat the defects found as a breach of condition. Not every defect in goods would amount to a breach of condition: it was a question of degree. Minor matters would amount to a breach of warranty, with a remedy in damages. Nothing turned on whether the contract fell under the 1979 or the 1982 Act: whichever Act applied, the nature of the defects, the cost of rectification, the practicalities of rectification and X's contractual expectation of work of the highest quality led to the clear conclusion that there had been a breach of a condition under *s 14(6)* of the 1979 Act or *s 4(2)* of the 1982 Act.

Definition of 'sale'   B1.3

Section 2(1) of the *SGA 1979* defines a 'sale' as a contract by which the seller 'transfers or agrees to transfer the property in goods to the buyer for a money consideration ...' This definition excludes contracts of hire purchase, contracts of hire, contracts for the supply of goods and services, and barter or exchange which are, respectively, covered by the 1973 and 1982 Acts.

Case Example: *Southwark London Borough Council v IBM UK Ltd* [2011] EWHC 549

The Borough had contracted with IBM for the provision of third-party software and associated consultancy services for the implementation of a 'master data management' system to rationalise information recorded on a number of the Borough's computer systems. The software was to be provided under licence from the manufacturer. A question arose as to whether this constituted a contract of sale. The court held that it did not. The contract specifically stipulated that 'title, copyright and all other proprietary rights in the software' remained vested in the manufacturer. Further, the termination provision required the Borough to return to the manufacturer or destroy all copies, forms and parts of the software covered by the licence, intimating that property remained vested in the manufacturer.

Formalities   B1.4

There are no formalities attached to a contract of sale, nor requirements as to copies. A contract can be made in any form (entirely oral, entirely written, or a combination). In commercial contracts, of course, a written agreement is, for practical purposes, essential and necessary to ascertain what the parties have agreed and to ensure that all key terms have been agreed before entering into a contractual relationship.

Implied terms as to title   B1.5

The following sections set out implied terms as to title in a business-to-business contract.

Conditions   B1.6

In a contract of sale, *section 12, SGA 1979* states that there is an implied condition that the seller has the right to sell the goods. A 'condition' is a major term of the contract which means that, on breach, the buyer can rescind the contract and claim damages (*Wallis, Son and Wells v Pratt and Haynes* [1910] 2 KB 1003). There are corresponding provisions in the 1973 and 1982 Acts.

Warranties   **B1.7**

The *Sale of Goods Act 1979* and the 1973 and 1982 Acts also imply warranties as to title. A 'warranty' can be regarded as a minor term of the contract, breach of which entitles the buyer to claim damages, but the contract remains valid and cannot be rescinded. The implied warranties are that:

- the goods are free from any charge or encumbrance not disclosed or known to the buyer when the contract is made; and

- the buyer will enjoy quiet possession of the goods except so far as it may be disturbed by the owner or other person entitled to the benefit of any charge or encumbrance so disclosed or known.

In many cases, the implied warranties will overlap with the implied condition.

Case Example: *Azzurri Communications Ltd v International Telecommunications Equipment Ltd* **[2013] EWPCC 17**

In 2010, C had entered into a major contract to supply a motoring association with large numbers of telephone handsets for its call centres. The contract was for specified handsets in respect of which the manufacturer (V) had registered trade marks. C acquired some of the handsets from the defendant supplier (S). C installed the handsets, but it emerged that those supplied by S were faulty. C approached V, which began to investigate the problem. However, V discovered a mismatch of the serial numbers and realised that the handsets were either refurbished or counterfeit. It emailed C, indicating that it refused to support the products in any way. C then approached S, which offered to carry out a warranty repair and asked for sample telephones for testing. Instead, C replaced all the handsets supplied by S with replacement handsets from an authorised distributor. V's solicitors wrote a letter before action to C, alleging that it had infringed V's trade marks. C settled any claim which V had against it and complied with V's request that it should deliver up the offending handsets to V. S admitted that it had infringed V's trade marks by selling the handsets to C.

It was held that the principal loss to C, caused by the breach of the implied terms in *s 12(1)* and *s 12(2)* of the Act, that the seller had a right to sell and that the buyer would enjoy quiet possession of the goods, was the cost of buying replacement telephones. Because C had delivered up the stock of handsets to V, that was the full cost and not just the difference between the total sum paid for the replacement handsets and the price paid to S. C was entitled to the sum paid for replacement telephones as damages for breach of either or both of the *s 12(1)* and *s 12(2)* terms.

Case Example: *Mason v Burningham* **[1949] 2 KB 545**

The purchaser of a stolen typewriter was entitled to recover the cost of repairs for breach of the warranty as to quiet possession, when he could equally have succeeded in an action for breach of the implied condition.

At the same time, it is possible for there to be breaches of the warranties in circumstances when there would be no breach of condition.

Case Example: *Microbeads AG v Vinhurst Road Markings Ltd* **[1975] 1 All ER 529**

This involved the sale of a product over which a third party had a patent and who could, therefore, seek delivery of the patented product.

Case Example: *Rubicon Computer Systems Ltd v United Paints Ltd* **(2000) 2 TCLR 453**

A computer was installed with a time-lock device, which rendered the computer unusable, this being held to infringe the warranty of quiet possession.

It can be seen from the above cases that there can be a breach of the implied warranties without there being a breach of the implied condition as to the right to sell.

Limited title **B1.8**

In those circumstances where it is to be inferred that the seller is transferring only such title as he or a third person may have, none of the foregoing implied conditions or warranties apply. Instead, there is an implied warranty that all charges and encumbrances known to the seller were disclosed to the buyer prior to the making of the contract, and an implied warranty that none of the following will disturb the buyer's quiet possession:

- the seller;
- the third party (in those cases where the seller is to transfer only such title as a third party might have); and
- anyone claiming through or under the seller or third party, except in relation to a charge of encumbrance disclosed or known to the buyer before the contract was made.

Implied terms as to description   **B1.9**

Section 13, SGA 1979 implies a condition into contracts of sale by description that the goods will correspond with the description given. Corresponding provisions are found in the 1973 and 1982 Acts.

A contract is a sale by description when 'even though the buyer is buying something displayed before him on the counter; a thing is sold by description, though it is specific, so long as it is sold not merely as a specific thing but as a thing corresponding to a description' (*Grant v Australian Knitting Mills* [1936] AC 85 at 100).

A sale will, therefore, not be by description if the buyer makes it clear that he is buying a particular thing because of its own unique qualities and that no other will do. Nor will a sale be by description if it was not within the contemplation of the parties that the buyer will be relying on the description (*Harlingdon & Leinster Enterprises Ltd v Christopher Hull Fine Arts Ltd* [1991] 1 QB 564).

Close conformity to description required   **B1.10**

Any variation from the agreed description will cause an infringement.

Case Example: *Arcos Ltd v Ronaasen and Son* **[1933] AC 470**

A contract was for the supply of a quantity of staves for use in making cement barrels, and it stated that the staves were to be half an inch thick. A breach of the implied term arose when only 5% conformed to the description, even though all the staves remained fit for their intended use.

See too *Wilensko Slaski Towarzstwo Drewno v Fenwick & Co Ltd* [1938] 3 All ER 429.

Case Example: *Hazlewood Grocery Ltd v Lion Foods Ltd* **[2007] EWHC 1887**

The written contract between the parties provided that the food was to be free from foreign and extraneous matter. The chilli powder provided was contaminated by an industrial dye. Citing the *Arcos* case, the court said that the words 'free from' meant what they said: absolutely free from.

Microscopic variations will, however, be disregarded on the *de minimis* principle. This requires the courts to disregard anything which can be fairly regarded as too small or insignificant to be worthy of notice.

Case Example: *Shipton Anderson & Co Ltd v Weil Bros & Co Ltd* **[1912] 1 KB 574**

The sellers contracted to sell 4,500 tons of wheat, plus or minus 10%. In fact, the sellers delivered 4,950 tons 55lbs, but the sellers did not seek payment for the 55lbs. It was held that the excess was so slight that the *de minimis* rule applied.

Case Example: *Moralice (London) Ltd v E, D & F Man* **[1954] 2 Lloyd's Rep 526**

It was said that, where the price is payable by means of a documentary credit against shipping documents, the *de minimis* principle had no application as between seller and bank. The shipping documents were to comply strictly with the requirements of the letter of credit.

It should be noted that *s 15A* of *SGA 1979* provides that, where a breach is so slight that it would be unreasonable to allow rejection, then only damages can be claimed because the breach is not treated as a breach of condition but as a breach of warranty. This is subject to the terms of the contract or unless a contrary intention appears in or to be implied from the contract, and it is for the seller to show that *s 15A* applies to the case in hand.

Breadth of 'description'   **B1.11**

The description can include the way in which goods are packed.

Case Example: *Re Moore & Co and Landauer & Co's Arbitration* **[1921] 2 KB 519**

It was held that packing tins in cases of 24, when the contract specified 30, infringed the implied condition even though the correct number of tins had been packed.

Case Example: *Albright & Wilson UK Ltd v Biachem* **[2001] 2 All ER (Comm) 537**

It was held that, where a buyer contracted with different sellers for the supply of different chemicals, but delivery was to be by the same firm, there was a breach of the implied term as to description where one supply of chemicals was accompanied by a delivery note referring to the other supply.

Strict liability B1.12

There is a breach of *s 13, SGA 1979*, regardless of any element of blame and therefore one of strict liability. An infringement arises if the goods do not conform to the contract description, whether or not the breach was innocent or inadvertent.

Satisfactory quality B1.13

Section 14(2), SGA 1979 implies a condition that the goods supplied under the contract must be of satisfactory quality. The same applies under the 1973 and 1982 Acts.

Meaning of 'satisfactory' B1.14

Section 14(2A), SGA 1979 provides that goods will meet this standard if a reasonable person would regard them as satisfactory, taking account of any description of the goods, the price (if relevant) and all the other relevant circumstances.

The 'quality' of the goods is said by *SGA 1979, s 14(2B)*, and again there are comparable provisions in the 1973 and 1982 Acts, to include their state and condition and the following (among others) are examples laid down by the Act of the matters to be taken into account as to aspects of the quality of the goods:

- fitness for all the purposes for which goods of the kind in question are commonly supplied;

- appearance and finish;

- freedom from minor defects;

- safety; and

- durability.

> **Case Example:** *Jewsons v Kelly* **[2003] EWCA 1030**
>
> In 1997 K acquired a former school building with planning permission for conversion into flats. K bought 12 electric boilers from Jewsons along with other materials. K did not pay for the goods and Jewsons issued proceedings in which K claimed to set off damages for breach of the contract to supply the boilers. K's case was that the boilers were neither of satisfactory quality nor reasonably fit for their purpose (see B1.15 below) because they reduced the Standard Assessment Procedure ('SAP') energy ratings of the flats, in that their dependence on peak rate electricity made them expensive to run, producing ratings which made the flats difficult to market. As a result K could not keep up repayments on the loan he had taken out to

finance the purchase of the building and the lender repossessed it. The deputy judge trying the preliminary issues held that although the boilers intrinsically worked satisfactorily, they were not of satisfactory quality and were not reasonably fit for the purposes for which the boilers were being bought, because of their adverse impact on the SAP ratings for the flats.

The Court of Appeal held that, under the statutory scheme set out in *s 14* of the *SGA 1979*, it was the function of *s 14(3)* (which deals with fitness for purpose), not *s 14(2)* (which deals with satisfactory quality), to impose an obligation tailored to the particular circumstances of the case. In the circumstances of this case the Court of Appeal said that it would be 'startling' if Jewsons was liable for breach of the implied terms in *s 14(2)* and not of the implied terms in *s 14(3)*.

For the purposes of *s 14(3)*, K made it clear to Jewsons that he was buying the boilers for installation in flats which were being converted for resale. The boilers were not reasonably fit for that purpose because of their effect on the SAP ratings. K did not, however, rely on the skill and judgement of Jewsons, save as to the intrinsic qualities of the boilers. The question whether they were suitable, having regard to their effect on the flats' SAP ratings, was a matter for K and his advisers. In all the circumstances, it was not reasonable for K to rely on the skill and judgement of Jewsons in relation to the effect on the SAP ratings. In the respect in which K could reasonably have relied on the skill and judgement of Jewsons as sellers of the boilers, they were reasonably fit for their purpose. As a result, Jewsons was not in breach of the term implied by *s 14(3)* of the *SGA 1979*. There was equally no breach of *s 14(2)*. There was nothing wrong with the quality of the boilers and a reasonable man would so conclude. They were of satisfactory quality for use in flats and whether they were fit for a particular purpose made known to the seller was the function of *s 14(3)*. Once it was held that it was not reasonable of K to rely on the skill and judgement of Jewsons with regard to the potential impact of the boilers on the flats' SAP ratings, it was clear that a reasonable man would not conclude that the boilers were not of satisfactory quality.

Case Example: *Bramhill v Edwards* **[2004] EWCA Civ 403**

The appellant appealed against a decision to dismiss his claim against the defendant for rescission or damages for misrepresentation and/or for breach of the implied warranty of satisfactory quality under *SGA 1979*, *s 14* in respect of the purchase from E of a second-hand motor-home. The motor-home in question had been manufactured in and imported into this country from the United States of America. The vehicle was 102 inches wide, exceeding the maximum permitted by the *Road Vehicles (Construction and Use) Regulations 1986 (SI 1986/1078)*, *reg 8*, which provided that the overall width of such a vehicle must not exceed the equivalent of 100 inches. According to B, E had made representations as to the width of the Dolphin, namely that its maximum width was 100 inches. B claimed that, when he was looking at the vehicle, he noticed a spacious feel to the interior and that E had stated that it was 100 inches and perfectly legal, adding that he would not import motor-homes of a width of 102 inches because they were illegal. B had ample opportunity to examine the vehicle and had purchased the vehicle, knowing at that time of the maximum permitted width. The judge concluded that E had made a representation about the width of the vehicle but only as to its interior width and unaccompanied by any reference to the maximum permitted width. Accordingly, he found that there had been no misrepresentation. The judge held that there would have been a breach of the statutory implied term, not because of uninsurability of the vehicle but because of the perception of risk of prosecution for non-compliance with the regulations, but that by virtue of *s 14(2C)(b)*, B was not entitled to rely on that term because his examination of the vehicle before the purchase should have revealed the defect (see below *Exceptions to obligation as to quality*). The judge held that, had any liability been established, he would have found that B had not proved any damage. B contended that the judge's finding of no misrepresentation was perverse; that the judge should have held that the statutory implied term was breached on the ground of uninsurability as well as of perception of risk of prosecution and challenged the disapplication of the statutory implied term under *s 14(2C) (b)*; the vehicle had no saleable value in the United Kingdom at the time of sale or at any material time thereafter and that the judge's finding had been predicated on the failure of the claim on liability.

The Court of Appeal ruled that the judge's decision on misrepresentation was not perverse. The relative credibility of B and E was essentially a matter for the judge. None of the other evidence was sufficient to undermine the judge's finding, still less to render it perverse. Nor was there any basis upon which the court could substitute its own and a different conclusion on the critical issue as to what was said before contract about the width of the vehicle. The fact that the judge's finding was not that for which either side had contended was no bar to its acceptability, if, on the whole of the evidence before him, a picture emerged which produced a more probable version than that of either side. It followed from the judge's reasoning that the vehicle was of unsatisfactory quality within the statutory test. The Court of Appeal said, however, that his reasoning was equally capable of leading to it being of satisfactory quality within the test, since he had found that a reasonable man could take either view. His reasoning was not apt in this context where a court was required to decide whether a reasonable person in the position of the buyer and with his knowledge of the background acts 'would' not regard the goods as unsatisfactory. The judge's error lay in overlooking the requirement that, where a decision on the facts of and/or on the inference to be drawn from them is evenly balanced, it was for the party making the assertion to prove it. Accordingly, the judge's conclusion on this issue should be set aside.

See also *Lowe and Lowe v Machell Joinery Ltd* [2011] EWCA Civ 794.

Case Example: *Venables v Wardle* **[2002] EWHC 2073**

The claimants began to build the property over a period of time beginning spring 1993. The claimants engaged Wardle to install pipework as well as to undertake other work at the property. The claimant said that he carried out work between 1993 and 1997. He said that he installed pipework in 1993 and 1994. The court made no findings on those matters. It did appear, however, that in 1995, he filled the hot and cold systems with water, checked for leaks, flushed the systems and left them for the claimants to use. The claimants did not move into the house until February 1997. Between 1995 and February 1997 other workmen drew water from taps in the house for use in construction.

The first leak occurred in May 1996. Further leaks occurred in 1998, and again in April, July and September 1999. Leaks occurred in relation to both 22mm and 28mm copper pipe. The pipes leaked because they had corroded. They corroded because periods of low and/or intermittent use of the pipes resulted in poor or partial formation of a protective layer of cuprous oxide on the inside of the pipes.

There was no allegation that Wardle failed to exercise skill or care. The claimant's case was that the 22mm and the 28mm copper pipe was defective, in that it was not of satisfactory quality nor fit for the purpose, because it corroded within a short time after having been installed. It was not of satisfactory quality nor fit for the purpose in that it was not suitable for use in a property with low and/or intermittent water use.

The evidence was that this was an extremely unusual problem. The pipes failed because of corrosion caused by intermittent water use and stagnancy, not because of defects in the pipes. To avoid corrosion of the sort experienced here, there needed to be a continuous flow of water to build up a protective film. The crucial features were the intermittent flow and the fact that pipes were left partially full at times. Corrosion could not have occurred until the water use began, then became intermittent. If the water supply after the plumbing system was fitted in 1995 had been constant but nevertheless at low volume, the crucial factors would probably not have occurred. The evidence was that the first few months of service of copper pipework systems were critical. This was when the normal protective adhering copper oxide layer was formed in a regular flow of fresh water. The development of such a layer was straightforward, but, if this does not happen and another layer or film of material forms or deposits instead of the protective copper oxide, then the pipe surface will be vulnerable to corrosion. In this case, the claimants' use of the water systems during the extended period from 1995, when they were filled, until February 1997 when the claimants moved into the property was low and intermittent. There was probably insufficient flow for the protective layer of cuprous oxide to have been deposited. As a result, the risk of corrosion was exacerbated by the practice of shutting off the mains water when the claimants left the house. This use was 'abnormal or idiosyncratic'.

The court said that, in this case, there was misuse, in the sense that there was insufficient water flow through the pipes to permit a build up of the protective cuprous oxide layer. The pipes were fit for any dwellinghouse including those with intermittent usage. The claimants' practice of shutting off the mains when leaving the property amounted to misuse of pipes which had not acquired sufficient protection. The court said that there was no good reason why copper pipes should not now be used at the property. The only difference which would arise would be in respect of usage: water flow through the pipes should be maintained and water should not be allowed to stagnate in the pipes.

The conclusion was that the pipes were of merchantable quality (the facts of this case straddled the period of time when the test in *SGA 1979* moved from merchantable to satisfactory quality).

Case Example: *Clegg v Olle Andersson* **[2003] EWCA Civ 320**

By a written agreement in December 1998, C had agreed to buy a new yacht with a shoal draught keel 'in accordance with the manufacturer's standard specification' from the respondent for £236,000. The yacht had been delivered by the manufacturers to Andersson on 25 July 2000 and by him to C on 12 August 2000. Andersson had realised and informed C when he had delivered the yacht that its keel was substantially heavier than the manufacturer's specification. Negotiations had ensued and on 6 March 2001, C's solicitors had written to Andersson asserting C's entitlement to reject the yacht and had thereby done so. Andersson had disagreed. C sued, seeking the return of the purchase price and damages for breach of contract. The High Court had concluded that: (i) there had been no breach of condition under either *s 13(1)* (as to description (see B1.9) or *s 14(2)* of the *Sale of Goods Act 1979*; and (ii) if there had been such a breach C had lost the right to reject the yacht before 6 March 2001 (see B1.41). The judge had dismissed the claim.

The Court of Appeal said that it had been established beyond doubt by the evidence before the judge that the effect of the overweight keel on the safety of the rig was both adverse and unacceptable to the manufacturers of the rig. The yacht as delivered had required some remedial treatment. The judge had underestimated the effect, as agreed by both expert witnesses, of the overweight keel on the safety of the rig to a significant extent. On the basis of all the evidence, a reasonable person would have considered that the yacht as delivered had not been of satisfactory quality because of the overweight keel, the adverse effect it would have had on rig safety and the need for more than minimal remedial work on it. C had established a breach of the requirement as to satisfactory quality.

Case Example: *Ward v MGM Marine Ltd* **[2012] EWHC 4093**

The first claimant (W), a keen yachtsman, had purchased a luxury motor yacht from one of the defendant boat dealers; the exact identity of the vendor was in dispute, as was the purchase price. W contended that the purchase price was £269,000, which had been funded through a mortgage loan of £188,000. In order to fund the purchase W had also entered into an arrangement with one of the defendants, whereunder an existing mortgage over W›s old boat would be paid off, and they would delay seeking repayment. Very shortly after taking delivery of the vessel, W and a passenger heard an unusual noise and saw that blue smoke was being emitted from the port exhaust. W shut down the engine, but realised that there was a serious problem and called for help. Both passengers prepared to abandon ship, and although they managed to escape on a lifecraft, both suffered serious burns. The vessel, along with equipment belonging to C, was destroyed. Although W and his passenger were both smokers, they denied having smoked on board the vessel. C relied on three expert evidence reports which concluded that the yacht may have had an inadequate fire design; the expert was unaware of any of C›s actions that may have caused the fire; the fire was caused by a deficiency or fault that was present when the yacht was handed over, and that the fire started in the port main engine.

C submitted that a boat that burst into flames within 15 minutes of delivery was neither fit for purpose of going to sea, nor for carrying passengers or crew, and that it lacked the necessary safety and durability required by *s 14(2)* of the *Sale of Goods Act 1979*. D submitted that C had failed to discharge the relevant burden of proof.

It was held that, although C's expert did not identify the source of the fire with precision, the cause of the fire had, no doubt, resulted from a deficiency in the yacht; it was noteworthy that the defendants did lead expert evidence of their own to test the veracity of W's expert evidence. Under *s 14(2)*, there was an implied term that goods supplied under a contract were of a satisfactory quality and that they were fit for all the purposes for which they had been supplied, including their safety and durability. In the instant case, there was no obstacle to C's claim. Although it was right to say that it was for C to prove that there had been a breach of *s 14(2)*, there was no evidence that the fire on the yacht occurred otherwise than a result of engine defects. There was no reason to believe that C had been smoking on the vessel; the court had no difficulty in concluding that C's version of events was correct.

Case Example: *Bominflot Bunkergesellschaft fur mineralole MBH v Petroplus Marketing AG* **[2012] EWHC 3009**

Gasoil had been tested before loading onto a vessel chartered for the purpose and found to be on specification. When the gasoil arrived at its destination port four days later, it was off-specification as to sediment. B alleged that the sediment had increased so quickly because the gasoil had been unstable on delivery; unstable gasoil, even before sediment formation, could not be used for any of the relevant grade of gasoil's usual purposes, and therefore the gasoil had been, on delivery, not of satisfactory quality. B could not sell it on to its intended buyer. It therefore found an alternative buyer (M), which also sold B replacement gasoil for delivery to the original intended buyer. B claimed damages for loss in the gasoil's value, calculated as the difference between the price it paid P and the price obtained from M for the unsound gasoil, plus the difference between what it paid M for the replacement gasoil and what it had paid P.

It was held that, on the evidence, the sediment increases had not been due to contamination on board the vessel. The only alternative conclusion was that the gasoil had been unstable on delivery. An unstable gasoil was not of satisfactory quality; accordingly, the instant gasoil had not been of satisfactory quality for the purposes of *s 14(2)*. The instability had been a latent vice which the specification tests had left undiscovered. Instability had not been a characteristic of the cargo covered by the specifications. Once it was accepted that *s 14(2)* was otherwise to be implied, it was hard to see why the buyer should be held to take the risk of an inherent vice which was not tested at the loadport and would therefore not be revealed there, but which meant that the cargo could not be used for any of its usual purposes and was therefore not of satisfactory quality. As the gasoil had not been of satisfactory quality for the purposes of the *s 14(2)* term, P had breached that term; the fact that the result of the instability was the later formation of sediment did not alter that.

Case Example: *Dalmare SPA v Union Maritime Ltd* **[2012] EWHC 3537**

The appellant seller (D) appealed against an arbitrators' decision that the respondent buyer (B) was entitled to damages for breach by D of a contract for the sale of a vessel.

The vessel was a motor tanker built in 1994. The sale contract was on the Norwegian Saleform 1993. The first sentence of clause 11 provided that the vessel was to be delivered and taken over 'as she was' at the time of inspection, fair wear and tear excepted. A month after delivery of the vessel, the main engine broke down because of a defective crankpin. The arbitrators held that the engine had been likely to fail within a short period of normal operation after delivery, so there was a breach of the implied term as to satisfactory quality implied into the sale contract by *s 14(2)* of the *Sale of Goods Act 1979*. Accordingly, B was entitled to damages.

D submitted that the *s 14(2)* term was excluded, by virtue of *s 55(2)*, because it was inconsistent with clause 11, which provided that the vessel was sold 'as she was'.

The court held that the correct starting point was that the *s 14* implied terms would apply to the sale contract, as to any other English law contract, unless the parties had contracted out. Second-hand ships were 'goods' within the Act like any other piece of machinery or equipment. If commercial parties did not want to be subject to the statutory implied terms, they could contract out of them, as provided for by *s 55(1)*.

The court said that the words 'as she was' in the first sentence of clause 11 were a necessary part of a sentence which recorded the obligation to deliver the vessel in the same condition as she was when inspected. They were part of a temporal obligation which arose because there would usually be a period of time of weeks, or even months, between inspection and delivery. However, those words did not say anything about what D's obligations were, either on inspection or delivery, as regards the quality of the vessel. Hence they did not exclude the implied term as to satisfactory quality under *s 14(2)*. The words 'as she was', in context, were incapable of bearing the same meaning as the free-standing words 'as is, where is' in a sale contract, assuming that those words did exclude the statutory implied terms. Even if a possible meaning of the words 'as she was' were to exclude the implied terms, that was not their only meaning in context; the fact that they had more than one meaning was fatal to D's case, since it could not be said that they were inconsistent with the implied term, as *s 55(2)* required. The obligations in the second sentence of clause 11 relating to class complemented or supplemented the obligation to deliver the vessel in a satisfactory condition rather than being inconsistent with it. The first sentence of clause 11 did not exclude the implied term as to satisfactory quality.

The court also said that it was necessary to decide whether the words 'as is' were apt to exclude the statutory implied terms, but it said that it was difficult to see how, in the absence of some customary meaning, the words 'as is' could be said to be sufficiently clear and unequivocal to exclude them.

Case Example: *Hi-Lite Electrical Ltd v Wolseley UK Ltd* [2011] EWHC 2153

The claimant contractor (H) sought a declaration that the defendant supplier (W) was liable for a fire started in premises operated by a hair salon (O) and that W should indemnify H for any sums it was liable to pay O. W denied liability and sought to pass on any claim to the third party (X).

H had been engaged by O to carry out maintenance work in the salon and had purchased a pump from W, which it installed in the salon nine weeks before the fire. O alleged that the fire was caused by the pump and H was found liable in contract. H made the instant claim against W on the basis that the pump was not of satisfactory quality, contrary to *s 14(2)* of the *Sale of Goods Act 1979*. W began third-party proceedings against the manufacturer of the pump (X), which accepted that if W was liable to H, then it would be liable to W. At the instant hearing, it was agreed that the fire started in a cable attached to the pump, but the cause of the fire was disputed.

H submitted that damage had been caused to the cable during manufacturing. W and X argued that the cable had been damaged in the installation or service of the pump; alternatively, that if the damage had been caused by a defect for which they were responsible, H should have fitted a residual current device (RCD), which would have prevented the fire from developing. They further contended that damages arising were too remote, as damage by fire had not been contemplated by the parties as a likely result of the cable being defective. W and X also argued that if they were liable there should be apportionment of liability due to H's failure to install an RCD.

It was held that, on the expert evidence, the fire had been caused by a fatigue failure of the cable caused by damage to the cable which, on the balance of probabilities, had been caused by O cutting it whilst cleaning the sump and cable. It was unlikely that any damage had been caused when the pump was installed. H had therefore not proved on the balance of probabilities that the cause of the fire was a manufacturing defect and there was no other likely cause which gave rise to W being liable under *s 14*. In any event, H had failed to carry out the installation properly because it had failed to fit an RCD which, on the balance of probabilities, would have tripped before the fire started.

Whilst the existence of the RCD would have prevented the fire, if W had been liable, the failure to fit the RCD could not be said to deprive any breach by W of its potency, so that it would remain an effective cause, and W would not have escaped liability. The fact that there were two causes did not deprive one cause of its causative effect.

The correct question in respect of remoteness was whether, at the time of the contracts, a fire was not unlikely to result from a manufacturing defect in the cable or there was a serious possibility of loss by fire arising from that defect. The important point was what would be expected, at that time, on the basis of a breach of contract in the form of a manufacturing defect in an electrical cable. An electrical fire was not unlikely to result from that defect. Therefore, the fire or the damages which H had to pay O would not have been too remote. The provisions of *s 14(2)* were those of strict liability and a party liable under them could not reduce their liability by an apportionment to take account of the negligence of the other party. See *Hall Hotel Ltd v Red Sky IT (Hounslow) Ltd* [2010] EWHC 965; *Choil Trading SA v Sahara Energy Resources Ltd* [2010] EWHC 374.

Exceptions to obligation as to quality   **B1.15**

Section 14(2C), SGA*1979* (and the corresponding provisions of the 1973 and 1982 Acts) provides that the implied term as to satisfactory quality is inapplicable where:

- the defects were specifically drawn to the buyer's attention before the contract was made; or

- where the buyer examines the goods beforehand, in relation to defects which that examination ought to have revealed.

Case Example: *Bramhill v Edwards* **[2004] EWCA 403**

The facts of this case are given above.

The High Court had concluded that the defence had made out the second of the exceptions referred to above. It stated that the evidence was that, before the sale of the Dolphin had been concluded, the Bramhills had parked the motor-home they were giving in part-exchange alongside the Edwards' premises, and had moved into the Dolphin. The evidence was that they had lived in the Dolphin for a few days prior to its purchase. That had led the High Court to conclude that Mr Bramhill had had adequate opportunity to examine the purchase. His evidence was that, when the question as to width had been raised in January 2000, he had measured the Dolphin and had found it to be 102 inches wide. His evidence was that, in June 1999, he had known that the vehicle exceeded the permitted width. This had led the High Court to conclude that an examination of the vehicle on that date ought to have revealed the width, and that the width had not been revealed because Mr Bramhill had not then measured it. The Court of Appeal, however, while upholding the decision to allow reliance on the exclusion from the implied term, did so in relation to the first exception referred to above. The Edwards sought to uphold the High Court's ruling on the ground that the evidence showed that the defects had in fact been pointed out to the Bramhills. The Court of Appeal accepted that Mr Edwards had made a representation as to interior width and that should have alerted the Edwards to the fact that the width exceeded the legal limit. At the same time, the Court of Appeal accepted that the High Court had also been right to accept the argument based on the second of the above exceptions.

Note that, under *s 15A* of the *Sale of Goods Act 1979*, in non-consumer cases, rejection is not allowed if the breach is so slight that rejection would be unreasonable. The right to damages remains intact.

Reasonable fitness for purpose

Section 14(3), *SGA 1979* (with like provisions found in the 1973 and 1982 Acts) provides that where the buyer in the course of a business expressly or by implication makes known any particular purpose for which the goods are being bought, there is an implied condition that the goods should be reasonably fit for that purpose whether or not that is a purpose for which such goods are commonly supplied. The requirement to make known any particular purpose is automatically fulfilled when the goods have only one ordinary purpose. If the goods have more than one purpose, the duty is on the seller to provide goods fit for such of the purposes as the seller indicated: see the *Australian Knitting Mills* case at B1.9 above. The seller will not, however, be in breach if the unsuitability of the goods arises from a special feature relating to the buyer not disclosed to the seller.

Case Example: *BSS Group plc v Makers (UK) Ltd* **[2011] EWCA Civ 809**

The appellant company (B) appealed against a decision that it had breached the implied term as to fitness of purpose under the *SGA 1979, s 14(3)* when supplying materials to the respondent plumbing contractors (M). B had supplied M with materials, including piping, adaptors and valves, for the installation of a new plumbing system in a public house. A particular make of part, 'Uponor', was used for the project. M requested further materials from B, specifically identifying that they were to be used in the same project. B supplied a different type of valve which was incompatible with the adaptor. A connection became insecure under pressure, resulting in substantial flooding of the public house. B were held to be liable. The judge found that M had expressly and, if not, by implication made it known to B that the valves were to be used with Uponor piping and had relied on B's skill and judgement as to the compatibility of the parts. He found that the valves were not compatible with the adaptors they were likely to be used with and were not therefore fit for purpose. B contended that the judge had: (1) misdirected himself regarding the test for determining whether M had made known the purpose for which it would be using the valves; (2) wrongly concluded that M had communicated a sufficiently particular purpose to B; (3) wrongly concluded that the valves were not fit for purpose; (4) dealt inadequately with the issue of M's reliance on B's skill and judgement.

It was held:

(1)   The relevant questions for assessing a claim for breach of the implied term imposed by *s 14(3)* were identified by Clarke LJ in *Jewson Ltd v Boyhan* (see above): (a) whether the buyer, expressly or by implication, had made known to the seller the purpose for which the goods were being bought; (b) if so, whether they were reasonably fit for that purpose; (c) if they were not reasonably fit for that purpose, whether the seller had shown that the buyer had not relied upon its skill and judgement or, if it had, that it had been unreasonable to do so.

(2)   B had known that M was using a Uponor system and had previously supplied Uponor components for the same project. It was an irresistible inference from M's inquiry regarding further parts that it was making known to B its intention to use the valves as a device

intended to regulate or control the flow of water in pipes used in the project. It was also an obvious inference that it was making known to B that it intended to use such valves in conjunction with the Uponor plastic piping that B was aware it was using. At the very least, it had to have been apparent to B that M was likely to so use the valves and M had therefore made known a particular purpose for which the valves were intended to be used.

(3)   The valves were not fit for the requisite purpose, as they were incompatible with the Uponor adaptors and would be likely to fail when used in conjunction with them.

(4)   Where a buyer had made known its purpose, there was prima facie an implied condition of fitness which the seller could defeat only by proving that the buyer had not relied on, or that it had been unreasonable to rely on, the skill and judgement of the seller. The issue was whether B had discharged that burden. B's argument that M was content to buy any valve and was relying on B to do the tests necessary to ensure that it worked was unrealistic. B was a specialist dealer and M was relying on B to sell it a compatible valve. Although the judge had not expressly dealt with the issue of whether it had been reasonable for M to rely on B's skill and judgement, he could not have overlooked that issue as he had quoted *s 14(3)* before focusing on the issues to be decided. The inference to be drawn was that he was satisfied that there was no question of any reliance by M as having been unreasonable and that conclusion could not be criticised. The judge was entitled to reach the conclusions he had.

Case Example: *Slater v Finnings Ltd* **[1996] 3 All ER 398**

A new camshaft fitted to a fishing vessel failed, as did two further replacement camshafts. This failure was not due to the camshafts themselves, but to the fact that the vessel had an abnormal tendency to produce excessive torsional resonance when fitted with the new type of camshaft which, in turn, caused excessive wear on the camshaft. The House of Lords held that there was no breach of the implied term where the failure of the goods to meet their intended purpose arose from an abnormal feature or idiosyncrasy, not made known to the seller, in the buyer or in the circumstances of the use of the goods by the buyer, regardless of whether or not the buyer himself was aware of such abnormality.

For a further example, see *Griffith v Peter Conway Ltd* [1939] 1 All ER 685.

Exceptions to obligation as to fitness for purpose   B1.16

The implied term is stated by *SGA 1979, s 14(3)* as inapplicable where the circumstances show that the buyer does not rely on the seller's skill or judgement, or that any reliance was unreasonable. It was said in the *Australian Knitting Mills* case (see B1.9 above) that this provision is generally interpreted in favour of the buyer.

Case Example: *Henry Kendall & Sons v William Lillico & Sons Ltd* **[1969] 2 AC 31**

It was said that the fact that the buyer proposed to analyse or test the goods on delivery does not mean an absence of reliance.

Case Example: *Wren v Holt* **[1903] 1 KB 610**

Where the buyer was aware that the seller could supply only one particular brand, there was evidence of an absence of reliance.

Case Example: *Phoenix Distributors Ltd v L B Clarke (London) Ltd* **[1967] 1 Lloyd's Rep 518**

It was said that a buyer who is given a certificate as to the goods supplied by an independent third party can be said not to be relying on the seller in respect of matters covered by the certificate.

Case Example: *Cammell Laird & Co v Manganese Bronze and Brass Co Ltd* **[1934] AC 402**

Partial reliance suffices if the breach is in the area of such reliance.

Case Example: *Farrans (Construction) Ltd v RMC Ready Mixed Concrete (Scotland) Ltd* **[2004] Scot CS 51**

The contract had called for the delivery of C7 concrete. Because of the dispute which subsequently arose as to the quality of concrete actually supplied, it became necessary for the court to determine just what was meant by C7 concrete. The court concluded that when a civil engineer orders 'C7 foamed concrete' from a concrete supplier that would be understood by reasonable men in the position of both parties as indicating two things. First, the concrete would be of relatively low strength and low density. Secondly, the strength of the concrete would be such that it could be broken easily, and thus put to the uses that are characteristic of C7 foamed concrete. If, therefore, concrete was supplied with typical compressive strengths in excess of 35 N/mm^2, that, the court said, would not conform to the description 'C7 foamed concrete'. The court further concluded that the concrete as delivered to the pursuers was in conformity with the description applied to it, namely C7 concrete. Any problems which were subsequently discovered with the concrete could be attributed to the faulty way it had been pumped into the relevant shaft by third parties. Accordingly, there had been no breach of the express term of the contract that the concrete to be delivered would be C7 concrete; nor any breach of the condition implied by *s 13* of the *Sale of Goods Act 1979* that goods supplied under a contract must conform to their contract description (see B1.9).

It was further argued that the defenders knew that the concrete was to be supplied to the particular shaft by pump, and that it was not fit for this particular purpose.

This argument was rejected. When the contract was being negotiated, the evidence showed that the pursuers had not relied on the skill and judgement of the defenders in relation to the selection of C7 concrete as a mix suitable for any particular purpose. Such a point had in fact been conceded by the pursuers in cross-examination. More than that, the pursuers had accepted that the decision to use C7 foamed concrete had been made by the pursuers in consultation with third parties. Furthermore, it appeared from the evidence that the defenders had not been told anything about the pursuers' method of working on site, and had not been informed of the depth of the shaft into which the concrete was to be placed. Nor had the parties discussed how the pumping operation was to be carried out by the pumping contractor. These circumstances, as the court noted, strongly supported the concession that no reliance was placed on the defenders' judgement in the selection of C7 concrete as a mix suitable for any particular purpose.

The court also said that the argument failed because, if they had relied on the defender's skill and judgement, then they had been unreasonable so to do. The pursuers had employed a third party as a specialist drilling sub-contractor. It was also the case that the pursuers themselves were clearly very experienced civil engineering contractors. In evidence, they had stated that the decision to use C7 foamed concrete had been made by the pursuers and the third party. In addition, the pursuers had not told the defenders how the pumping operation was to be carried out by the pumping contractor, nor informed them of the pursuers' proposed method of working on site, nor told them the depth of the shaft into which the concrete was to be poured. In these circumstances, the court felt that it could not have been reasonable for the pursuers to rely on the skill and judgement of the defenders in the selection of C7 concrete as suitable for being placed by pump. See too the *Jewsons* case discussed above.

Case Example: *Lowe v Machell Joinery Ltd* **[2011] EWCA Civ 79**

The appellants (L) appealed against a decision that whilst the respondent (W) was in breach of contract, L was not entitled to reject the goods and were not entitled to any relief as a result of the breach of contract.

L were converting a barn for residential use and ordered a staircase from W. They paid for the goods but on delivery, took the view that the staircase did not comply with W's obligations under the contract. L rejected the goods and issued proceedings to recover the price of the staircase. Shortly before trial, L took a new point, namely, that if the goods had been installed there would have been a breach of the building regulations, which was another breach justifying their rejection of the goods. The judge held that W was in breach of contract as the building regulations had not been complied with, but that did not justify rejection of the goods as the design could be easily modified by L when installed so as to avoid any breach.

L contended that having found that W had breached the contract, as the staircase did not comply with building regulations, he was wrong to find that L was not entitled to reject the goods.

The court held that, under the *Sale of Goods Act 1979,* the staircase had to be fit for the purpose of being installed in a building to be used as a residence and for use as such. It also had to be of satisfactory quality. *Section 14(3)* had to be implied into the contract unless it was a case in which L did not rely on the skill and judgment of W as a seller. The fact that the judge held that W should, at the very least, have warned L of the need to ensure that the building control officer would accept the particular design, clearly supported the proposition that L did rely on, and were reasonable in relying on, W. As the goods supplied in exact conformity with the contract could not lawfully be used for their intended purpose, which was known to W, they were not reasonably fit for purpose and a reasonable buyer would not find them satisfactory. The judge was right to conclude that W was in breach of contract because the staircase, as designed and supplied, would not have complied with the building regulations when installed but was wrong to hold that that this did not entitle L to reject the goods. As such L were entitled to be repaid the price paid.

Note that, under *s 15A* of the *SGA 1979,* in non-consumer cases, rejection is not allowed if the breach is so slight that rejection would be unreasonable. The right to damages remains intact.

Liability does not depend on any blame on the part of the seller.

Case Example: *Frost v Aylesbury Dairy Co Ltd* **[1905] 1 KB 608**

Milk was sold which was infected by typhoid. At the time, there was no test which could have disclosed this. The seller was still held liable for failing to supply goods which were reasonably fit for their purpose.

Sales by sample   B1.17

Section 15, SGA 1979 provides that a contract is a sale by sample when there
is an express or implied term to that effect. To satisfy this test, the parties
must contract by reference to a sample on the understanding that the sample
provides a description of the quality of the goods and that the bulk must
conform to the sample (*Drummond v Van Ingen* (1887) 12 App Cas 284).

Section 15 further provides that, when a contract is a sale by sample, then
certain conditions are implied. These are:

- that the bulk will correspond with the sample in quality; and

- that the goods are free from any defect, making their quality unsatisfactory.

If the sale is by description then there is an implied term that the goods must
also correspond with the description.

Excluding the implied terms   B1.18

The *Unfair Contract Terms Act 1977* severely limits the effectiveness of clauses
by which a seller seeks to exclude or limit his liability for breach of any
of the above implied terms in business-to-business contracts. Except for
the case of the implied terms as to title (which cannot be excluded or
limited in a business-to-business contract) any such clause will be valid only
if shown to be reasonable. If the contract is made with a consumer, that is
to say someone not buying in the course of a business, then, in the case of
the implied terms as to description, quality, fitness for purpose, and those
implied when the contract is a sale by sample, an exclusion or limitation
clause will be of no effect by virtue of the *Consumer Rights Act 2015*. In fact,
its inclusion in the contract might possibly be a criminal offence under the
Consumer Protection from Unfair Trading Regulations 2008 (SI 2008/1277)). If,
in a business-to-business contract, liability other than in relation the above
implied terms (the seller might exclude liability for late delivery; or the
buyer liability for non-acceptance), *UCTA 1977* also applies if the contract
is on written standard terms and any such clause will be valid only if it can
be shown to be reasonable.

What is meant by 'written standard terms'   B1.19

No definition is given of 'written standard terms' under *UCTA 1977*, but it
seems that a contract is still made on written standard terms even if some of
the terms have been individually negotiated (*McCrone v Boots Farm Sales Ltd*
1981 SLT 103; *Salvage Association v CAP Financial Services Ltd* [1995] FSR 654
at 671–672; *St Albans City and District Council v International Computers Ltd*
[1996] 4 All ER 481 at 491); *Yuanda (UK) Co Ltd v WW Gear Construction Ltd*
[2010] EWHC 720.

Non-breach cases   **B1.20**

Where the clause is in a contract made on written standard terms as above, a clause is subject to the reasonableness test if it:

- seeks to exclude or restrict liability for breach;

- seeks to allow the provision of a contractual performance which is a substantially different performance from that which was reasonably expected; or

- seeks to allow no performance at all: *s 3, UCTA 1977.*

Case Example: *Zockoll Group Ltd v Mercury Communications* **[1998] FSR 354**

The case was concerned with the free call number 0500 FLIGHTS. When tapped out on an alphanumeric keypad, this would give the number 0500 354 448, the addition of the final S being irrelevant since the final number 7 would not affect the dialling of what in fact was a six-digit number. Zockoll acquired 53 numbers from Mercury, including the FLIGHTS number. These numbers had all been acquired by Zockoll under an agreement made with Mercury on 15 December 1993. That agreement contained a number of clauses, clause 8.1 reading:

> 'It is hereby acknowledged that the telephone number(s) allocated by Mercury to the Customer as part of the Agreement do not belong to the Customer and Mercury shall be entitled at its sole discretion at any time to withdraw or change any telephone number used by the Customer on giving the Customer reasonable notice in writing. The Customer accepts that it shall acquire no rights whatsoever in any telephone number allocated by Mercury and the Customer shall make no attempt to apply for registration of the same as a trade or service mark, whether on its own or in conjunction with some other words or trading style.'

Mercury invoked this clause when they decided that the number was better allocated to a firm called Manchester Flights. In response, Zockoll maintained that the clause was subject to the above provisions, in that it purported to entitle Mercury to provide a performance of the contract which was substantially different from what was reasonably expected. Blackburne J said that a broad view of the Act had to be taken: 'So regarded, it seems to me that the contractual performance reasonably expected of Mercury was to provide 53 numbers (of which 50 were apparently random) for use as free call numbers'. If that approach were adopted, the judge said, it would then become impossible to contend that a withdrawal, in reliance on clause 8.1, coupled with the offer of a substitute, was 'to render a contractual performance substantially different

---

from that which was reasonably expected'. The point was, he said, that the other 49 random numbers remained with Zockoll, as well as what the judge called 'three golden numbers'. The fact that the number which was withdrawn could be converted to FLIGHTS was 'irrelevant'. This was because, when the agreement was made, Mercury simply did not know of the attributes of the apparently random numbers which it was providing: 'A condition of what was reasonably expected of [Mercury] by way of contractual performance, cannot … be coloured by Mercury's subsequent knowledge of the attributes of the disputed number'. He added that, even if the contractual performance reasonably expected of Mercury was that no number would be withdrawn without good reason, Zockoll were no more able to show that Mercury was claiming, by its reliance on clause 8.1, to be entitled to render a contractual performance which was 'substantially different' from that expectation.

See too *Timeload Ltd v British Telecommunications plc* [1995] EMLR 459; *Harrison v Shepherd Homes Ltd* [2011] EWHC 1811.

Case Example: *Brigden v American Express Bank Ltd* **[2000] IRLR 94**

The disputed clause, contained in an employment contract, provided that 'an employee may be dismissed by notice and/or payment in lieu of notice during the first two years of employment, without implementation of the disciplinary procedure'. The court held that this clause, while expressed in negative terms, was neither a term which provided for no performance at all nor one which entitled the defendants to render a contractual performance substantially different from what was reasonably expected.

It was later said that the Act did not apply to such contracts, but this does not affect the validity of the above observations of the court; *Commerzbank AG v Keen* [2006] EWCA Civ 1536.

Case Example: *Do-Buy 925 Ltd v National Westminster Bank plc* **[2010] EWHC 2862**

Do-Buy claimed the sum of £359,000 from the defendant bank acting in its role as a merchant acquirer. Do-Buy was a jewellery trader and had entered into an agreement with the bank whereby the bank would provide services enabling Do-Buy's customers to pay for goods with debit or credit cards via a portable electronic terminal. The bank's agreement contained this term: ('You agree that as between You and Us it is Your responsibility to prove to Our satisfaction that the debit of a cardholder's account was authorised by the genuine cardholder'). The argument was that this clause would allow the Bank to render a performance substantially different from that which was reasonably to be expected of it or to render no performance at all in respect of all or part of its contractual obligation. The court rejected this argument, saying that the bank's contractual obligation, and the performance which could reasonably be expected of it, was to pay for authorised transactions. The court said that this conclusion was supported by the General Terms and Conditions Clause 4.1 (which emphasises that the card must be offered by the card holder), Clause 6.2 (which emphasises that the only transactions within the scope of the Agreement were between the merchant and the cardholder), Clause 9.3.4 (which entitled the Bank to reimbursement for all payments if it processed 'invalid card transactions') and Clause 16.1 (which dealt with chargeback rights).

It may be supposed, however, that a force majeure clause is an example of the type of clause which falls into the 'no performance' provisions. Typically, a force majeure clause will specify that, in certain circumstances (such as fire, lock-outs, flooding or outbreak of war), the relevant party will not be liable for any failure to perform his obligations under the contract. A clause which went further, and gave that party an unfettered right not to perform at all, with no reference to any qualifying circumstances, would almost certainly be of itself ineffective since it would reduce the contract to the level of a mere declaration of intent, something that the courts would seek to deny. It would in any case certainly fail the reasonableness test.

Excluding liability for negligence   **B1.21**

In relation to business-to-business contracts, *UCTA 1977* provides that no contract, whether on written standard terms or not, can exclude or limit liability for negligence resulting in death or personal injury. Subject to the test of reasonableness, however, a clause can exclude or limit liability for negligence having other consequences, such as damage to property, or which causes economic loss.

The reasonableness test   **B1.22**

Where *UCTA 1977* applies the reasonableness test, each case must be judged on its own merits. This, in effect, means that a decision in one case cannot be a binding precedent for another case with an identical clause, since the circumstances of each case will differ. See *Fillite (Runcorn) Ltd v Pasilac Ltd* (unreported, 26 January 1995).

Cases where the reasonableness test has been applied

Flamar Interocean Ltd v Denmac Ltd [1990] 1 Lloyd's Rep 434; *The Salvage Association v CAP Financial Services Ltd* [1995] FSR 654; *St Albans City and District Council v International Computers Ltd* [1996] 4 All ER 481; *Overland*

Shoes Ltd v Schenkers Ltd [1998] 1 Lloyd's Rep 498; *British Fermentation Products v Compare Reavell Ltd* [1999] 2 All ER (Comm) 389; *Overseas Medical Supplies Ltd v Orient Transport Services Ltd* [1999] 2 Lloyd's Rep 273; *Watford Electronics Ltd v Sanderson FL Ltd* [2001] EWCA Civ 317; *Britvic Soft Drinks Ltd v Messer UK Ltd* [2002] EWCA Civ 548; *Granville Oil and Chemicals Ltd v Davis Turner & Co Ltd* [2003] 1 All ER (Comm) 819; *Frank Maas (UK) Ltd v Samsung Electronics Ltd* [2004] EWHC 1502; *Kingsway Hall Hotel Ltd v Red Sky IT (Hounslow) Ltd* [2010] EWHC 965; *Do-Buy 925 Ltd v National Westminster Bank plc* [2010] EWHC 2862; *Robinson v P E Jones (Contractors) Ltd* [2011] EWCA Civ 9; *Axa Sun Life Services plc v Campbell and others* [2011] EWCA Civ 18; *Rohlig (UK) Ltd v Rock Unique Ltd* [2011] EWCA Civ 133; *Harrison v Shepherd Homes Ltd* [2011] EWHC 1811; *Cleaver v Schyde Investments Ltd* [2011] EWCA Civ 929; *Allen Fabrications Ltd v ASD Ltd* [2012] EWHC 2213; *FG Wilson (Engineering) Ltd v John Holt & Co (Liverpool) Ltd* [2012] EWHC 2477; *Deutsche Bank AG v Sebastian Holdings Inc* [2013] EWHC 3463; *West v Ian Finlay & Associates* [2014] EWCA Civ 316.

Excluding liability for misrepresentation   **B1.23**

In the case of any contract, a term seeking to exclude or limit liability for misrepresentation is only valid, under the terms of the *Misrepresentation Act 1967,* if it can be shown to be reasonable.

A misrepresentation cannot be relied on if the contract contains a non–reliance clause: *Morgan v Pooley* [2010] EWHC 2447. See, too, *Barclays Bank plc v Svizera Holdings BV* [2014] EWHC 1020.

Cases where the reasonableness test has been applied

Josef Marton v Southwestern General Property (unreported, 6 May 1982); *Walker v Boyle* [1982] 1 WLR 495; *McCullagh v Lane Fox & Partners* [1995] EGCS 195; *Cleaver v Schyde Investments Ltd* [2011] EWCA Civ 929; *Lloyd and Lloyd v Browning and Browning* [2013] EWCA Civ 1637.

As to whether decisions as to reasonableness can give rise to a binding precedent, see B1.26).

Passing of property and risk   **B1.24**

The parties are always free to make their own provision as to when the property (which may be equated with ownership) of the goods passes. The seller will want it to pass at the latest possible moment, usually on full payment; while the buyer will want it to pass no later than delivery.

If the contract says nothing on this point, then certain Rules laid down by *s 18* of the *SGA 1979* will apply. Note that, in relation to consumer contracts, the position set out in *SGA* still applies. It is also to be noted that the 1973 and 1982 Acts say nothing about the passing of property. Since *SGA* represents the common law, the rules it lays down can be given a general application.

Specific and identified goods **B1.25**

In the case of specific goods (those agreed on and identified when the contract is made), property passes when the contract is made so long as the goods are in a deliverable state (*Rule 1*).

Where something remains to be done to put the goods in a deliverable state, property passes when this has been done and the buyer has been informed (*Rule 2*).

Where the goods are in a deliverable state, but the price has yet to be ascertained, property passes when this is done and the buyer informed (*Rule 3*).

Where the goods are delivered to the buyer on approval, or subject to sale or return or similar terms, property passes when the buyer does any act adopting the transaction, for example:

* by signifying acceptance or approval;
* if the goods are retained without notice of rejection after the time fixed for their return; or
* if the goods are retained after the lapse of a reasonable time if no specific time was fixed (*Rule 4*).

Non-specific goods **B1.26**

If the goods are not specific, that is to say, they had not been specifically agreed on and identified at the time of the contract, property passes when goods of the relevant description are unconditionally appropriated to the contract by either party with the assent of the other, express or implied. Assent can be given before or after appropriation (*Rule 5*).

> **Case Example:** *Kulkarni v Manor Credit (Davenham) Ltd* **[2010] EWCA Civ 69**
>
> The court said that a seller who knows that he lacks the property in goods which he appropriated to a contract could not reasonably think that his buyer would assent to such an appropriation. In such a situation, *r 5(1)* was unlikely to provide a solution. The Rule assumed that the seller had property in the goods. If, therefore, he lacked property in the goods, his

appropriation of them to the contract was unlikely to be reliable as an indication of the parties' intentions. The agreement to sell would only mature into a sale upon delivery. That would reflect the presumption in *r 5(2)*.

There are also specific rules as to the passing of property of goods contained within a bulk.

Passing of risk   B1.27

Just as with the passing of property, the parties are left free by *SGA 1979* to provide for when risk is to pass. In this instance, the seller will want risk to pass as soon as possible, while the buyer will only want risk to pass when he has safely received the goods in good condition. If, however, nothing is said in the contract as to the passing of risk, the Act provides that it passes with property: *s 20, SGA 1979*. Nothing is said in the 1973 and 1982 Acts as to passing of risks, but the *Sale of Goods Act* represents the common law which will govern contracts within those two Acts.

In the case of consumer contracts, the *Consumer Rights Act 2015* provides that, risk cannot pass until the goods are in the physical possession of the buyer or someone nominated by the buyer. This does not apply if the goods are delivered to a carrier commissioned by the buyer and who was not named by the seller: *s 29, CRA 2015.*

The provisions as to risk in a consumer contract cannot be excluded.

Transfer of title by non-owner   B1.28

Although property might not have passed to the buyer, it is always possible that he will seek to sell the goods on, innocently or fraudulently.

Section 21(1), SGA 1979, which continues to apply to consumer sales, contains the basic rule that any such disposition cannot pass title even to an innocent third party, but numerous exceptions to this rule are laid down, both in the Act and elsewhere. There is nothing in the 1973 and 1982 Acts as to this issue so, again, it can be assumed that the *Sale of Goods Act*, representing as it does the common law, probably applies also to contracts within these Acts.

The exceptions   B1.29

The seller can be estopped by his conduct. This means that he can act in such a way that he gives the impression that a third party, not himself, is the owner of the goods, or that a third party has the authority to sell or dispose of the goods. The common law principles of principal and agent can also apply. If one person is the agent of another, the agent might appear to be authorised to sell the principal's goods, even if this is not the case.

In addition, *ss 24* and *25, SGA 1979* apply exceptions in the case of the seller and buyer in possession. Thus, under *s 24*, a seller who remains in possession of goods after a sale can make a further sale of the same goods to a third party and pass a valid title to him.

Section 25 further provides that a person who has bought or agreed to buy goods, and who obtains possession of them with the seller's consent, can pass a good title to a third party. When the buyer is paying for the goods in instalments, and where title only passes on payment of the final instalment, he does not count as someone who has agreed to buy goods if the amount of credit advanced to him is not more than £25,000. This limit can be changed and a check should always be made on the current limit.

> **Case Example:** *Angara Maritime Ltd v Ocean Connect UK Ltd and others* **[2010] EWHC 619**
>
> The claimant ship owner (C) claimed a declaration that it was not liable for bunkers supplied by the defendants (O), an English company and its US parent engaged in the sale and supply of bunkers for shipping, to a third-party company (B), who had chartered vessels from C. B had found itself in financial difficulties and made early redelivery to C of a number of vessels. One of those vessels had bunkers on board that had been supplied by O to B but which B had failed to pay for. Under O's standard terms it retained title in the bunkers until they were paid for. On redelivery of the vessel, C gave B credit, pursuant to the charterparty between the parties, against B's outstanding hire charges for the bunkers that were on board the vessel. C contended that it had converted the bunkers after the redelivery of the vessel but that it had purchased the bunkers from B, which had said that it was 'buyer in possession' in good faith and without notice of O's rights so that under *s 25(1)* of the *Sale of Goods Act 1979*, it had acquired good title to the bunkers. O contended that *s 25* was inapplicable as there had been no contractual redelivery of the vessel by B to C so that there was no delivery of the bunkers to C. O submitted that C had failed to show that it had acted in good faith and without any notice of O's rights.
>
> The court said that the sequence of steps to be adopted in the instant case was, accordingly: (a) whether the person who bought or agreed to buy the goods, namely B, obtained possession of the goods with the consent of O; (b) whether there was delivery, within the meaning of *s 25*, of the bunkers by B to C; (c) whether C received the bunkers in good faith and without notice of any lien or other right of O in respect of the goods; (d) whether, if the preceding steps were satisfied by C, it was apparent, from *s 25(1)*, that if there was a delivery by B to C pursuant to a sale, B was acting in the ordinary course of its business as charterer and was doing

something, namely delivering goods pursuant to a sale, which constituted acting in the ordinary course of business if it was a mercantile agent. It was apparent that step one was met. Step two was also met as the issue was whether as a matter of fact there was a voluntary act by B amounting to delivery and, on the evidence, there clearly was. It was a question of fact not contractual analysis. Even if that analysis was required it was clear that B and C had agreed to redelivery otherwise than under the charterparty and thus had varied the terms of the deal between them. Step three was met as C had acted in good faith and without notice of O's rights because there was, on the evidence, nothing to put them on notice that B had not paid for the bunkers or of O's rights. The fourth step was also satisfied and as C purchased bunkers from B upon redelivery in good faith and without notice of any adverse right, what would otherwise have been a good claim in conversion by O had to fail.

The *Sale of Goods Act 1979* specifically preserves the operation of the *Factors Act 1889*, in relation to mercantile agency. A mercantile agent is one who, in the normal course of his business, has the authority to sell goods, consign goods for the purposes of sale, to buy goods or to raise money on the security of goods. Any sale by a mercantile agent to a bona fide third party passes the latter a good title.

The *Hire Purchase Act 1964* must also be considered. This provides that the disposition by any party of a motor vehicle to a bona fide third party who is not a dealer passes good title to that party. This also applies to conditional sale agreements within the financial limit referred to above.

Case Example: *G E Capital Bank Ltd v Rushton & Jenking* **[2005] EWCA Civ 1556**

The appellant bank (G) appealed against the recorder's decision that the first respondent (R) had acquired good title to motor cars as a private purchaser in good faith and without notice under the *Hire Purchase Act 1964*. G had lent money to a motor dealer (T) under a master trading agreement to enable T to purchase motor vehicles for the purposes of its business. The agreement provided that title to a purchased vehicle remained vested in the bank until the whole sum advanced in relation to that vehicle had been repaid. T ran short of money and approached R for a loan. The loan had been provided by R's friend, the second respondent (J), through J's company, which took a debenture from T to secure the loan. Some weeks later J demanded repayment of that loan and in order to repay it T sold its remaining stock of vehicles to R. R, with the assistance of J, took possession of the cars and stored them pending disposal. T went into liquidation. The bank took proceedings against R and J seeking the return of the cars or their value, damages for conversion and interest. G submitted that R had not been a private purchaser and had not acted in good faith.

It was held that the Act drew a clear distinction between a private purchaser who obtained the protection of the Act and a trade purchaser who did not. The trade purchaser carried on a business that consisted of purchasing motor vehicles for sale and the private purchaser did not. The expression 'carries on a business' could in an appropriate context refer to a single transaction in the way of business. The purpose of the legislation was to provide protection to those who did not buy in the course of trade. In context, the reference in the *HPA 1964* to a person carrying on a business that consisted wholly or partly of purchasing motor vehicles for the purpose of offering or exposing them for sale was intended to direct attention not only to the business of the purchaser immediately before and at the time of the disposition but also to the purpose for which the vehicle was bought. This meant that a person was not necessarily to be regarded as a private purchaser simply because he had not previously bought motor vehicles with a view to selling them in the way of business. When R bought the vehicles from T he had not taken any steps to set himself up as a motor dealer but he clearly decided to purchase them as a business venture with a view to selling them at a profit. At the time he bought the vehicles, R was a trade purchaser and not a private purchaser within the meaning of the Act. As a result, R did not obtain a good title to the vehicles when he bought them from T.

It was also said that, in order to assess R's bona fides it was necessary to know what he thought the cars were worth when he purchased them, as to which the evidence was far from clear. R clearly believed that he was buying at a discount to the trade price. The discount appeared to be about 20% and that was not strong evidence of dishonesty. There were insufficient grounds for overturning the recorder's decision that R had acted in good faith.

See too the *Kulkarni* case above.

Duty as to payment   B1.30

Under *s 8, SGA 1979*, the price in a contract of sale may be fixed by the contract, or may be left to be fixed in a manner agreed by the contract, or may be determined by the course of dealing between the parties. Where the price is not determined, the buyer must pay a reasonable price. What is a reasonable price is a question of fact dependent on the circumstances of each particular case.

The *SGA 1979*, which continues to apply to consumer sales, provides that, once the price has been agreed, it is the duty of the buyer to pay that price. It also says that unless a different intention appears from the contract, the time for payment is not of the essence. This means that late payment does not allow the seller to terminate the contract and claim damages, but he can claim damages alone: see *Newland Shipping & Forwarding Ltd v Toba Trading*

FZC [2014] EWHC 661. The seller who wishes to protect his position, therefore, should always write into the contract a term specifically stating that time of payment is of the essence. This will allow termination of the contract in the event of non-payment. There is nothing in the 1973 and 1982 Acts as to this issue so, again, it can be assumed that *SGA*, representing as it does the common law, probably applies also to contracts within these Acts.

The seller's position in relation to late payment has also been much affected by the *Late Payment of Commercial Debts (Interest) Act 1998 (LPCD(I)A 1998)*. This provides – whether or not it is specified in the contract itself – interest of 8% above base rate on all overdue payments. Payment is late where a supplier has agreed, either orally or in writing, a credit period with the purchaser, and payment is made after the last date of the credit period. If no credit period has been agreed, *LPCD(I)A 1998* sets a period of 30 days after which interest can run. The 30-day period starts from whichever is the later of:

- the delivery of the goods or the performance of the service by the supplier; or

- the day on which the purchaser has notice of the amount of the debt.

Certain changes were introduced by the *Late Payment of Commercial Debts Regulations 2013 (SI 2013/395)*. If no payment terms are agreed in business-to-business contracts, the default period remains at 30 days. However, payment terms must not exceed 60 days unless both parties agree and the extension is not grossly unfair. The public sector must pay within 30 days. The Regulations further provide that, where required, a procedure or verification period of goods or services must not exceed 30 days unless agreed and not grossly unfair to the creditor.

Case Example: *Yuanda (UK) Co Ltd v WW Gear Construction Ltd* **[2010] EWHC 720**

It was a term of this contract that interest on late payment should be paid at 5% above base rate. The Act allows for a contract term to exclude this rate so long as the contract itself provides a 'substantial contractual remedy' for late payment. *Section 8(1) of LPCD(I)A 1998* provides that a term displacing the statutory rate will not be regarded as providing a substantial remedy for late payment if:

'(a)   the remedy is insufficient either for the purpose of compensating the supplier for late payment or for deterring late payment; and

(b)   it would not be fair or reasonable to allow the remedy to be relied on to oust or (as the case may be) to vary the right to statutory interest that would otherwise apply in relation to the debt.'

The Act goes on to say that regard shall be had to 'all the relevant circumstances at the time the terms in question are agreed'. The Act also says that regard must be had when deciding this issue to:

'(a)   the benefits of commercial certainty;

(b)   the strength of the bargaining positions of the parties relative to each other;

(c)   whether the term was imposed by one party to the detriment of the other (whether by the use of standard terms or otherwise); and

(d)   whether the supplier received an inducement to agree to the term.'

It was the view of the court that it was not the intention of the Act to treat a contractual rate of interest for late payment as not meeting the 'substantial remedy' test simply because it was materially lower than the statutory rate.

The court then applied the criteria referred to above. As to the benefits of 'commercial certainty', the court took this to mean that, where the rate is not obviously unreasonable and appears to have been the product of genuine consensual agreement, 'it should not be set aside lightly'. As for the relative strength of the bargaining positions of the parties, the court thought that there was not much to choose between the parties. It did say that as time went on, Yuanda's bargaining position would have improved since it would become increasingly difficult for Gear to find another curtain walling trade contractor within the required time frame. It was also noted that this was not a case where Yuanda received an inducement to agree to the term. The court pointed to the fact that, in the standard printed form of JCT Trade Contract, the rate was 5% over base, which might suggest that this was thought by those responsible for drafting the contract to be a fair rate of interest for late payment in the context of the construction industry. Given this, when taken together with the other considerations referred to above, the court said it could see no reason why 5% over base should not be regarded as a substantial remedy within the meaning of the Act, even though 3% less than the statutory rate. It went on to say that a case could be made for saying that 3–4% would provide a substantial remedy for late payment, particularly if the rate had been specifically discussed and agreed between the parties. In the present case, though, Yuanda's rate, was much lower at 0.5% over base. What appeared to have happened was that the rate was effectively imposed on Yuanda, although it did have the chance to protest about it had it noticed the provision and wished to do so. This was regarded by the court as being 'marginally' in favour of Yuanda's argument.

The court's verdict was that the rate of 0.5% could not be regarded as a substantial remedy within the meaning of the Act in the absence of special circumstances relating to the parties and the making of the contract. There were, the court said, no such circumstances here. Ultimately, there was no reason why it would be fair or reasonable to allow Gear to oust the statutory rate. It would not be 'fair or reasonable to allow Gear to take advantage of the fact that during the pre-contract negotiations Yuanda failed to spot the amendment in the rate of interest'. The result was that the statutory rate of interest at 8% above base rate was to be substituted for the contractual rate of 0.5%.

If a clause in a contract seeks to postpone the time at which interest would otherwise start to run, the *LPCD(I)A 1998* treats such a clause as subject to the reasonableness test under the *Unfair Contract Terms Act 1977*.

Under the *Late Payment of Commercial Debts Regulations 2002 (SI 2002/1674)* once a party becomes entitled to statutory interest, he can also claim a fixed sum up to the following maxima:

- for a debt less than £1,000, the sum of £40;

- for a debt of £1,000 or more, but less than £10,000, the sum of £70;

- for a debt of £10,000 or more, the sum of £100.

If the compensation fees do not cover the cost of your claim, it is now possible to claim 'reasonable' additional costs. For example, if you use the services of a debt recovery agency, you can now add that to your claim.

The Regulations also provide that a representative body may bring proceedings in the High Court on behalf of small and medium-sized enterprises where standard terms put forward by a purchaser into contracts to which the *LPCD(I)A 1998* applies include a term purporting to oust or vary the right to statutory interest in relation to debts created by those contracts. The court may grant an injunction restraining use of the term, where it finds that the term is void under the provisions of *ss 8* and *9* of the *LPCD(I)A 1998*, on such basis as it sees fit.

'Small and medium-sized enterprises' are defined in *Annex 1* to *Commission Regulation EC/70/2001* of 12 January 2001 on the applications of *Articles 107* and *108* of the *Treaty on the Functioning of the European Union* (TFEU) to state aid to small and medium-sized enterprises. In summary, they are enterprises which have fewer than 250 employees and have either an annual turnover not exceeding €40 million, or an annual balance sheet not exceeding €27 million, and conform to the criterion of independence which in general limits the ownership of such enterprises by other enterprises, falling outside the definition of small and medium-sized enterprises, to 25% of the capital or voting rights.

'Representative body' is defined as an organisation established to represent the collective interests of small and medium-sized enterprises in general or in a particular sector or geographical area.

Duty as to delivery   B1.31

Section 27, SGA 1979 states that it is the duty of the seller to deliver the goods, a duty which is stated to be concurrent with the buyer's duty to pay the price.

Meaning of 'delivery'   B1.32

Section 61, SGA 1979 defines 'delivery' to mean a 'voluntary transfer of possession'. *Section 29* says that whether it is for the buyer to take possession, or for the seller to send, depends on the express or implied terms of the contract. It is always better for the contract to be specific on this point, rather than leave it to what may be implied from the contract.

Delivery of the incorrect amount   B1.33

The *Sale of Goods Act 1979* provides for several situations where the wrong amount of goods is delivered.

Where less is delivered   B1.34

Where less than the agreed amount is delivered, the *SGA 1979* gives the buyer the right to reject what is delivered, or accept it, paying the contract rate.

Where too much is delivered   B1.35

Similarly, *SGA 1979* provides that if more is delivered, the buyer can reject the surplus, reject the whole consignment, or accept the whole consignment paying for it at the contract rate.

Minimal variations   B1.36

The Act also imposes a *de minimis* rule so that if the shortfall or excess is so small that rejection would be unreasonable, and the buyer is acting as a business, then rejection will not be allowed. It is for the seller to show that rejection would be unreasonable.

Delivery in instalments   B1.37

SGA 1979 provides that, unless otherwise agreed, the buyer is not obliged to accept delivery in instalments, nor demand such delivery.

Examination   **B1.38**

Subject to what the contract might say, *SGA 1979* gives the buyer the right on request to a reasonable opportunity to examine the goods before he accepts delivery and, in the case of a contract for sale by sample, to compare the bulk with the sample (see B1.17 above).

Acceptance   **B1.39**

Whether or not a buyer has accepted the goods is crucial, since *SGA 1979* provides that, on acceptance, the buyer loses his right of rejection for any breach, although not his right to damages.

When the buyer has accepted the goods   **B1.40**

Acceptance arises when the buyer intimates acceptance of the goods.

> **Case Example:** *Libau Wood Co v WH Smith & Sons Ltd* (1930) **37 Ll L Rep 296**
>
> The mere receipt of goods without more, however, is not an intimation of acceptance.
>
> Acceptance also arises where the goods have been delivered to the buyer and the buyer performs an act which is inconsistent with the ownership of the seller. An example might be making use of the goods, particularly if this has the effect of consuming them.

> **Case Example:** *Mitchell v BJ Marine Ltd* [2005] **NIQB 72**
>
> The subject matter of the contract was a yacht. It was argued by the seller that a trip by the buyer with his family on the yacht constituted just such an act inconsistent with the ownership of the seller. The court, however, saw the relevant form of acceptance as applying only when the goods in question could not be returned to the seller and the buyer's trip with his family did not fall into this category.

> **Case Example:** *Filobake Ltd v Rondo Ltd* [2005] **EWCA Civ 563**
>
> The contract concerned the supply of commercial bakery equipment. The Court held that the buyers had accepted the goods by making the final payment, by mortgaging the equipment and by using it over a two-year period.

Section 35(1), SGA *1979*, however, provides that although a buyer might have appeared to have accepted goods within either of the above examples, he will not have done so if the goods were delivered to him and he had not previously examined them, until such time as he has had a reasonable chance to examine the goods for the purpose of:

- ascertaining whether they are in compliance with the contract; or

- comparing the bulk with the sample, where the sale is by sample.

Acceptance also arises where the buyer retains the goods for more than a reasonable time.

What constitutes a 'reasonable time'   **B1.41**

The *Sale of Goods Act 1979* provides that a 'reasonable time' is a question of fact, to be determined in all the circumstances of the case; and that in considering if a reasonable time has elapsed a court is to consider whether the buyer had a reasonable opportunity to examine or compare the goods as above.

Case Example: *Mitchell v BJ Marine Ltd* **[2005] NIQB 72**

A yacht had been delivered in June 2004. It was rejected by the buyer on 21 July. The court accepted that some form of commissioning period might be allowed, since yachts were more complex than most consumer purchases. By 28 July, the experts had identified most of the defects, thus indicating that they would perhaps have been discovered weeks before. The court said, however, that *s 35* does not imply an examination by experts, and that rejection had in fact taken place within a reasonable time.

Case Example: *Jones v Gallagher* **[2004] EWCA Civ 10**

The contract concerned the sale and supply of kitchen equipment. The equipment was put in place on 28 April. On 9 May, the purchasers complained to the suppliers that some of the items supplied were not as they should be. In particular, it was said that 'furniture finished colour does not match dresser with runs and inconsistencies'. On 16 May, the suppliers indicated by letter how they would remedy this problem. Further correspondence followed over the next four months. On 3 August, the purchasers pointed again to the problems with colour and advised that the matter was to be resolved within seven days, or action would be taken. They obtained expert reports, and eventually dismantled the entire kitchen. It proved impossible to obtain satisfactory quotations from other suppliers to restore the kitchen. Proceedings were commenced in the October of the following year.

It was held that a reasonable time had elapsed. The High Court pointed out that: the goods had been used; items had been stored in the cupboards; ornaments had been put on the shelves; and the colour mis-match must have been clear at the time the contract was made. In addition, the goods had been delivered at the end of April, and there had been no mention of rejection until the September.

The main focus of the appeal was whether it was correct to find that a reasonable time had elapsed. The Court of Appeal referred to *s 35* of the *Sale of Goods Act 1979*, which states in part that: 'The buyer is also deemed to have accepted the goods when after the lapse of a reasonable time he retains them without intimating to the seller that he has rejected them'. The section also states that a buyer is not, by virtue of any of the provisions contained within it as to acceptance, deemed to have accepted the goods merely because 'he asks for, or agrees to, their repair'.

The appeal in the present case was dismissed, the Court of Appeal finding that there was ample evidence on the basis of which the judge could hold that a reasonable time had elapsed. The main complaint related to colour and that, it was held, was visible when the goods were delivered. No complaint was made until some two weeks later, and, allowing time for a request for a remedy, no further complaint was made for some three months. Even then, it was a further seven weeks before rejection was first intimated. It was also pointed out that none of the other defects were latent. The Court of Appeal agreed that asking for the defects to be remedied, and allowing time for this to be done, did not count against the purchasers but that, on the facts, a reasonable time had clearly elapsed. It did add, though, that mere use of the kitchen equipment would probably not have amounted to acceptance.

Case Example: *Feldarol Foundry plc v Hermes Leasing (London) Ltd* **[2004] EWCA Civ 747**

A motor vehicle, bought on hire purchase, had a number of defects, notably with the steering and brakes. It was argued that the car had been accepted because the hirer had initially agreed to continue with his payments while he negotiated for a replacement vehicle. Possession of the car had been taken on 6 July and returned on 24 July. Two days earlier, the hirer had written to the credit broker, who copied the letter to the finance company, explaining that the car did not really suit him, and that he was seeking to 'roll over' the original agreement and obtain a replacement. Such an arrangement never came about. On 9 August, the hirer wrote to the dealer saying that the car had been returned to it following his rejection. He added that arrangements had been made for a replacement car without prejudice to his rights and remedies. He copied this letter to the finance company on 12 August. It was not until 19 August that the hire purchaser actually told the credit broker that the car was defective, information which they immediately passed to the finance company. On 23 August, the hire purchaser's solicitors wrote to the finance company advising them that the car had been rejected.

It had been argued that the purchaser had lost his right to reject, since he had in fact affirmed that contract by seeking to substitute the car, roll over the original agreement, and paying the first instalment even though aware of the defects.

Upholding the judge's ruling that the contract had not been affirmed, the Court of Appeal said that it was a matter of judging objectively from what had been said or done as to whether there had been acceptance or rejection. In the present case, there was 'only one answer'. The finance company had been told in a very short time of the purchaser's dissatisfaction with the car, and had returned it within days to the dealer. The letter of 12 August was a clear rejection, and payment had been made only in anticipation of a substitute vehicle being provided. The fact that the reasons for rejecting the car only emerged later was 'not to the point'.

Case Example: *Fiat Auto Financial Services v Mr Laurence Connelly Snr* **(Sheriff's Court, 19 December 2006)**

It was held that the buyer of a defective car had not lost his right to reject when rejection took place seven months and 44,000 miles after purchase. Unsuccessful attempts had been made at repair, and the garage, as the court said, had been 'stringing the customer along'.

Actions not constituting acceptance **B1.42**

As noted above, *SGA 1979* further provides that a buyer is not taken to have accepted goods under any of the above provisions if he has done no more than ask for, or agreed to, the repair of the goods by or under an arrangement with the seller; or because the goods have been delivered to a third party under a sub-sale or other disposition.

Goods sold in units **B1.43**

Special provision is made in *SGA 1979* for the sale of goods making up one or more commercial units (division of which would materially impair the value of the goods or the character of the unit). Acceptance of any of the goods in such a unit is taken to be acceptance of them all. For example, the buyer who purchases a fleet of cars is deemed to have accepted them all if he accepts just one.

Rejection   **B1.44**

Where a buyer validly rejects goods, *SGA 1979* provides that unless there is an agreement to the contrary, the buyer is not obliged to return the goods. It is enough that he indicates to the seller that he has rejected them. On receipt of such notice, the seller is entitled to have the goods placed at his disposal so as to allow for his resumption of possession (*Kwei Tek Chao v British Traders & Shippers Ltd* [1954] 2 QB 459). Until the seller does resume possession, the buyer is a bailee of the goods and must take reasonable care of them (*Galbraith and Grant Ltd v Block* [1922] 2 KB 155).

Where the defects in goods delivered affects only part of them, *SGA 1979* permits the buyer to reject the affected goods and to retain the balance. The parties are, however, free to include a term in the contract which excludes this particular right.

Additional rights of consumer   **B1.45**

Where the buyer is a non-business buyer, and the goods do not conform to the contract, *SGA 1979* (as amended by the *Sale and Supply of Goods to Consumers Regulations 2002 (SI 2002/3045)*) provides the buyer with the right to require the seller to repair or replace the goods; or to require the seller to reduce the price by an appropriate amount or to rescind the contract.

If the buyer opts for repair or replacement, the seller is obliged to act within a reasonable time, without causing significant inconvenience, and without charge to the buyer. The buyer cannot, however, require repair or replacement if this would be disproportionate or impossible.

The right of a buyer to rescind the contract or require a reduction in the price applies only when he cannot, for the reasons given above, require repair or replacement; or if the seller has not acted within a reasonable time and without causing significant inconvenience.

The buyer's right to reject the goods and terminate the contract is suspended for a reasonable time if he has required repair or replacement.

If the buyer does allow the seller to repair the goods, he has to take them back when they are repaired unless there are special circumstances making it reasonable for the buyer to refuse to accept them back: *Ritchie Ltd v Lloyd Ltd* [2007] UKHL 9.

The above rights cannot be excluded or limited by any contract term.

It is also the case that if, in the case of a non-business buyer, the goods become defective within six months, then they will be assumed to be defective at the time of delivery.

> **Case Example:** *O'Farrell v Moroney* **(Edinburgh Small Claims, 17 October 2008)**
>
> The case involved the purchase of falcon which died soon after purchase. The evidence was that this was caused by the buyer placing too much stress on the bird and the court concluded that the bird had been in conformity at the time of delivery.

Rights of unpaid seller   B1.46

The unpaid seller has a number of rights against the goods, and as to damages, as follows. Under *SGA 1979*, a seller is unpaid if the whole of the price has not been paid or tendered; or if a negotiable instrument, such as a cheque, has been handed over and has been dishonoured.

Lien   B1.47

Even if property has passed, *SGA 1979* gives an unpaid seller a right to a lien for the price while he is in possession of the goods. The Act goes on to say that if property has not passed, the seller has the right to withhold delivery similar to and co-extensive with the right to a lien.

Although these rights exist only when the seller is in possession, a clause in the contract which gives the seller the right to resume possession in the event of default revives the lien once possession has been resumed (*Bines v Sankey* [1958] NZLR 886).

Stoppage in transit   B1.48

The *Sale of Goods Act 1979* provides that where the buyer has become insolvent, the unpaid seller who has parted with possession may resume possession of the goods if they are in transit and retain them until payment. The position is the same whether or not property has passed.

Meaning of 'insolvency'   B1.49

This is defined by *s 61(4)*, SGA *1979* thus:

> 'A person is deemed to be insolvent within the meaning of this Act if he has either ceased to pay his debts in the ordinary course of business, or he cannot pay his debts as they fall due, whether he has committed an act of bankruptcy or not ... '

The mere fact of insolvency is not by itself a repudiation of the contract. The trustee in bankruptcy can always tender the amount due to the seller.

Resale   B1.50

The *Sale of Goods Act 1979* provides that the exercise of the right to a lien or
to stop the goods in transit does not automatically end the contract. If such
a buyer re-sells, however, then the Act further provides that the new buyer
obtains a valid title.

Perishable goods   B1.51

The *Sale of Goods Act 1979* further provides that where the goods are perishable,
or the seller has given notice of his intention to resell, and the buyer still does
not pay within a reasonable time, the seller can then resell the goods and
recover any loss occasioned by the breach, such as having to sell for a lower
price. Where the seller invokes a contractual right of resale in the event of
default, the Act provides that the resale of the goods terminates the contract,
but without prejudice to the seller's claim for damages.

Damages   B1.52

The *Sale of Goods Act 1979* also gives the seller a right to claim damages where
the buyer wrongfully neglects or refuses to accept and pay for the goods. The
measure of damages is the estimated loss which directly and naturally results in
the ordinary course of events from the breach. See *Aercap Partners 1 Ltd v Avia
Asset Management* AB [2010] EWHC 2431.

The *Sale of Goods Act 1979* says that the prima facie measure of loss is the
difference between the contract price and the market price at the time when
the goods should have been accepted, or at the time of refusal to accept if no
time was fixed for acceptance.

Claiming special loss   B1.53

The *Sale of Goods Act 1979* makes it clear that this is only the prima facie
measure and that, in appropriate circumstances, the seller can claim loss
based, for example, on his loss of profit. To do so, he will have to show
that the buyer contemplated such loss, on the basis of facts known to him
when the contract was made, as a probable result of any breach (*Hadley v
Baxendale* (1854) 9 Ex 341). See too *Transfield Shipping Inc v Mercator Shipping
Inc* [2008] UKHL 48.

Action for price   B1.54

Where property has passed and the buyer fails to pay, the seller is entitled
by *SGA 1979* to sue for the price. There are no specific provisions as to the

position where property has passed and the buyer wrongfully refuses to accept the goods. In such a case, the seller presumably has the option to sue for the price or to claim damages.

If property has not passed **B1.55**

The seller cannot sue for the price if property has not passed, since he is still the owner of the goods, and this is so even if it was the buyer who prevented property from passing (*Colley v Overseas Exporters* [1921] 3 KB 302). The *Sale of Goods Act 1979* does provide that if the price is payable on a 'day certain', an action for the price can be brought, regardless of whether or not property has passed.

Rights of buyer **B1.56**

The buyer has a number of rights against the goods, and as to damages, as follows.

Specific performance **B1.57**

Where there is a breach of a contract for specific or ascertained goods (ie goods identified and agreed on at the time the contract is made), the buyer may seek under *SGA 1979* an order from the court specifically enforcing the contract without the seller being given the option of retaining the goods on payment of damages.

Discretionary nature of remedy **B1.58**

Specific performance, however, is a discretionary remedy, and not an order to which a buyer is automatically entitled. Generally, the courts will refuse an action if damages are an adequate remedy.

> **Case Example:** *Sky Petroleum Ltd v VIP Petroleum Ltd* [1974] 1 All ER 954
>
> The claimants obtained an interlocutory injunction to restrain the defendants from breaking a contract to supply the claimants with all their petroleum requirements for ten years. The court treated the injunction as in effect a decree of specific performance, saying that the general rule against the grant of such a decree was inapplicable where damages would clearly not be an adequate remedy. In this case, there was a real danger that the claimants would be forced out of business if the defendants broke their contract at a time of exceptional disturbance in the oil market.

Damages   **B1.59**

Where the seller wrongfully neglects or refuses to deliver the goods, *SGA 1979* provides the buyer with an action in damages for non-delivery.

Prima facie measure   **B1.60**

The prima facie measure of damages laid down is the difference between the contract price and the market price at the time when the goods ought to have been delivered, or the time of refusal to deliver if no time was fixed.

Where the breach relates to quality, the *SGA 1979* provides that the prima facie measure of damages is the amount by which the goods have been diminished in value.

Claiming special loss   **B1.61**

The buyer will be able to displace the prima facie measure of damages and claim special damages. This can be done if the buyer can show that the seller, on the basis of facts known to him at the time the contract was made, contemplated that the special loss would be a probable result of any breach by him (*Hadley v Baxendale* (1854) 9 Ex 341). See, too, *Transfield Shipping Inc v Mercator Shipping Inc* [2008] UKHL 48.

Case Example: *Re R&H Hall Ltd and WH Pim (Junior) & Co's Arbitration* **[1928] All ER Rep 763**

The sellers sold a specific cargo of corn in a specific ship to the buyers at 51 shillings and ninepence per quarter. The buyers resold at 56 shillings and ninepence but, when the vessel arrived, the market price had fallen to 53 shillings and ninepence. The sellers failed to deliver and the question was whether the measure of damages was the difference between the contract price and the resale price, or the contract price and the market price. It was held that the former was correct. The two critical factors were that the sale was of a specific cargo on a specific ship and it was this same specific cargo which had been resold, and secondly the contract of sale by its terms actually provided for resale by the buyer in the sense that various contractual provisions dealt with this eventuality.

See too, *Bence Graphic International Ltd v Fasson UK Ltd* [1997] 1 All ER 979; *Louis Dreyfus Trading Ltd v Reliance Trading Ltd* [2004] EWHC 525.

Checklist B1.62

- Are you sure that the contract is one for sale (ie one where property in the goods is to pass for a money consideration)?

- Have you considered if this is one of the rare cases where the contract does require certain formalities?

- Are you certain that, as a seller, you can comply with the obligations as to title which are imposed on you; or have you considered the possibility of providing only a limited title?

- Are you satisfied that you will have no problems in meeting the statutory implied duties as to description, quality and fitness for purpose?

- Have you considered if the buyer might lose his rights in relation to fitness and quality by, for example, prior examination of the goods, or absence of reliance on the seller?

- Have you considered the possible use and effectiveness of any exclusion or limitation clauses and, in particular, whether any such clause is reasonable or fair and whether they have been fairly brought to the attention of the other party?

- Have you considered whether you should make special provision as to the passing of property and risk, or are you content to rely on the statutory provisions?

- When considering a special term as to passing of risk, have you first asked if the buyer is not buying in the course of a business?

- Are you aware of the exceptions to the basic rule that a person who has no valid title cannot himself pass a valid title?

- What provision has been made in the contract as to prompt payment? Are you aware that statutory interest may become payable?

- Are you aware of the duties relating to delivery of the goods and the position arising on delivery of too much or too little?

- Is provision made in the contract for a specific right to examine the goods?

- Are you aware of what constitutes acceptance of goods and of the consequences, in terms of remedies, of acceptance?

- Are you aware of the rights and duties of the parties in the event of rejection?

- Have you considered including a clause preventing a buyer from exercising a right to reject only some of the goods?

- Are you fully aware of the rights and remedies available to either party in the event of breach?

- Have you taken care to secure your rights to special damages by acquainting the other side, before the contract was made, of all the relevant circumstances and of any special factors which might give rise to loss?

- Ensure that all terms and conditions have been incorporated in the agreement and that any unusual or onerous terms have been brought to the attention of the buyer.

Precedent – Terms and Conditions of Sale; Specimen Contract

B1.63

1. GENERAL

These terms and conditions apply in preference to and supersede any terms and conditions referred to, offered or relied on by the buyer whether in negotiation or at any stage in the dealings between the parties with reference to the goods with which this contract is concerned. Without prejudice to the generality of the foregoing, the seller will not be bound by any standard or printed terms tendered by the buyer, unless the buyer specifically states in writing, separately from such terms, that it wishes such terms to apply and this has been acknowledged by the seller in writing.

Comment

The aim of this clause is to ensure that the contract is solely on the seller's terms and conditions. It can, however, only operate if the seller ensures that the contract is made on his terms and conditions in the first place. To do this, he must ensure that he is the winner in the so-called 'battle of the forms' (see A1.27).

---

2. VARIATION

Neither the seller nor the buyer shall be bound by any variation, addition to, or amendment of, these terms unless such is agreed in writing by the parties and signed on their behalf by a duly authorised party.

Comment

Parties are always free to vary their agreements in whatever way they wish, and in whatever form. To avoid the problems which purely verbal variations may cause, this clause stipulates that changes must be in writing and signed. Even so, this clause cannot be regarded as fool proof, since a verbal agreement to override it is binding, if perhaps difficult to prove. As to the effect of express variation clauses and no oral modification clauses ('NOM'), see the Supreme Court decision in *Rock Advertising Ltd v MWB Business Exchange Centers Ltd* [2018] UKSC 24.

---

3. DESCRIPTION

Any description given or applied to these goods has been given by way of identification only and the use of such description shall not constitute a sale by description. For the avoidance of doubt, the buyer hereby affirms that he did not in any way rely on any description when entering into the contract.

Comment

The *Sale of Goods Act 1979* implies into contracts of sale a condition that the goods will conform to that description and, if there is a breach, the buyer can rescind the contract and claim damages (for further information see B1.6 above). The implied condition operates only if there is a sale by description and if the buyer relied on the description, hence the wording of this clause. It is, however, subject to the reasonableness test imposed by the *Unfair Contract Terms Act 1977* and hence the seller will have to show it is reasonable if the buyer challenges it. Its success cannot be guaranteed, but it should be used just in case the seller can succeed in showing that the clause is reasonable. Such a clause has no validity in a consumer contract under the *Consumer Rights Act 2015*.

---

4. SAMPLE

Notwithstanding that a sample of the goods might have been shown to and inspected by the buyer, the parties hereto accept that such sample was so shown and inspected for the sole purpose of enabling the buyer to judge for himself the quality of the bulk, and not so as to constitute a sale by sample.

Comment

The aim of this clause is to avoid the terms otherwise implied in the case of a sale by sample. Since the clause is judged under the terms of the *Unfair Contract Terms Act 1977*, the comments made in relation to clause 3 above apply. Again, such a clause would have no effect in a consumer contract under the *Consumer Rights Act 2015*.

---

5. LIABILITY

(a)   No liability of any nature shall be incurred or accepted by the seller in respect of any representation (whether express or oral) made by the seller, or on his behalf, to the buyer, or to any party acting on his behalf, prior to the making of this contract where such representations were made or given in relation to:

(i)   the correspondence of the goods with any description; or

(ii) the quality of the goods; or

(iii) the fitness of the goods for any purpose(s) whatsoever.

(b) No liability of any nature shall be accepted by the seller to the buyer in respect of any express term of this contract where such term relates in any way to:

(i)   the correspondence of the goods with any description; or

(ii) the quality of the goods; or

(iii) the fitness of the goods for any purpose(s) whatsoever.

(c) All implied terms, conditions or warranties, statutory or common law, as to:

(i)   the correspondence of the goods to any description; or

(ii) the satisfactory quality of the goods; or

(iii) the fitness of the goods for any purpose whatsoever (whether made known to the seller or not),

are hereby excluded from the contract.

(d) Each provision of this clause is to be construed as a separate limitation, applying and surviving even if for any reason one or other of the foregoing provisions is held inapplicable or unreasonable in any circumstances, and shall remain in force notwithstanding termination of this contract howsoever caused.

Comment

Clause 5(a) above seeks to exclude liability for a misrepresentation made prior to the contract. Such clauses are regulated by the *Misrepresentation Act 1967*. The position is that this clause will have no effect unless it can be shown to be reasonable.

Clause 5(b) is one of the two clauses which deal with the terms of a contract. It confines itself to express terms. The seller is attempting to exclude liability for any express terms incorporated into the contract. This clause too is subject to the reasonableness test set out in the *Unfair Contract Terms Act 1977*. It should also be borne in mind that doubt has been expressed whether it is ever possible to exclude express terms: *Lease Management Services Ltd v Purnell Secretarial Services Ltd* [1994] CCLR 127. This should not, however, stop the draftsman from including such a clause.

Clause 5(c) is intended to exclude liability for breach of those terms which otherwise would be implied into the contract by the *Sale of Goods Act 1979* but is again subject to the reasonableness test. Note again that the implied terms cannot be excluded in consumer contracts under the *Consumer Rights Act 2015.*

UCTA 1977 states that a clause is reasonable if it is 'a fair and reasonable one to be included' having regard to the circumstances known to the parties when the contract was made. The Act also provides a number of guidelines. Strictly, these apply only to cases concerning those contracts which contain a clause such as clause 5(c) above, but the courts have said on many occasions that the guidelines represent the factors to be taken into account whenever the issue of reasonableness is raised. There are three important guidelines which are set out below.

Bargaining strength

This was a factor emphasised by Lord Wilberforce in *Photo Production Ltd v Securicor Transport Ltd* [1980] 1 All ER 556, who stated: 'After the [1977] Act, when the parties are not of unequal bargaining power, and when the risks are normally borne by insurance ... there is everything to be said ... for leaving the parties free to apportion the risks as they think fit and for respecting their decision'. This is, of course, not a factor which can be dealt with in the conditions of sale as it depends on extrinsic circumstances.

Choice

A court is also to consider whether the buyer could have entered into a contract with a different party, but without the exclusion clause. This points to an alternative method of drafting, which is to offer the buyer a 'two-tier system'. This would be a choice of business terms, with the seller accepting full liability for a higher price, but offering the goods at a lower price on terms which exclude liability. If the buyer chooses the latter, to save money, the courts are likely, though not certain, to find the clause reasonable.

Knowledge

This guideline asks if the buyer 'knew or ought reasonably to have known of the existence and extent of the term'. This factor too can be taken into account in the drafting. For example, the seller's position is likely to be weaker if the wording of the clause is complex, or the print is small and hardly legible, or the exclusion clause is hidden away in later clauses which are unlikely to be read. Some degree of clarity and prominence is therefore required. The clause should be clearly conspicuous and drawn to the attention of the buyer.

Clause 5(d) has the aim of ensuring, should any of the clauses be held unreasonable, that the other clauses will remain in being. By also providing that the clause survives termination, clause 5(d) allows the exclusion clauses to be invoked in relation to claims accrued at the date of termination.

6. LIMITATION OF LIABILITY

Where any court or arbitrator determines that any part of clause 5 above is, for whatever reason, unenforceable the seller will accept liability for all direct loss or damage suffered by the buyer but in an amount not exceeding the contract price.

Comment

This takes note of the fact that the total exclusion imposed by the preceding clause could well fail the reasonableness test, and hence proposes an alternative approach. Even this, however, cannot be guaranteed success, since it too is subject to the reasonableness test. *UCTA 1977* says that the reasonableness of a limitation clause should be judged by reference to the resources which the relevant party could expect to be available for the purposes of meeting any liability, and how far it was open to that party to obtain insurance cover.

In *Overseas Medical Supplies Ltd v Orient Transport Services Ltd* [1999] 1 All ER (Comm) 981, a contract of carriage contained terms limiting liability to approximately £600. The contract also said that, by special agreement in writing, the carrier would accept a greater degree of liability 'upon the customer agreeing to pay the company's additional charges for accepting such increased liability. Details of the company's additional charges will be provided on request'. There was also a clause providing for insurance cover to be effected if written instructions were given by the customer, and, when taking out a policy, the carrier would act as the customer's agent using its best endeavours to arrange such insurance. Instructions were given, but these were ignored. The clause was held to be unenforceable. The limit of £600 was said to be 'derisory'. The court noted that the carriers were offering the service of carriage and insurance, yet were limiting liability in each case. While there might well be cases involving package deals where a broad brush approach to limitation of liability might be reasonable, it was 'unjust and inappropriate' in the present case.

Each case must be judged on its facts, and this case does not mean that a fixed limit is always unreasonable. On the other hand, it does indicate that a more flexible limitation should perhaps be considered. Sellers could, therefore, try limiting damages to 50% of all loss suffered. They should also ensure that they have insurance cover covering the actual loss that may occur.

---

7. SELLER'S WARRANTY

The seller undertakes that it will, at its option, either repair or replace defective goods where defects are found notwithstanding the proper use of the goods, within [...] months from the date of delivery, provided that:

(a) notice in writing of the claimed defects is given to the seller immediately on their appearance;

(b) such defects are found to the seller's satisfaction to have arisen solely from faulty design, workmanship or materials; and

(c) the goods claimed to be defective are promptly returned to the seller at the expense of the buyer if so requested by the seller.

Any repaired or replacement goods shall be redelivered by the seller free of charge to the original point of delivery, but otherwise in accordance with these conditions of sale.

As an alternative to the above, the seller shall be entitled in its absolute discretion to refund the price of the defective goods in the event that such price has already been paid.

The remedies contained in this clause are without prejudice to the other terms of this contract, including, but without limitation, clauses 5 and 6 above.

Comment

The aim of this clause is to give the seller a better chance of showing that clauses 5 and 6 are reasonable. Support for the efficacy of such clauses was given in *British Fermentation Products Ltd v Compair Reavell Ltd* [1999] 2 All ER (Comm) 389, where the clause, linked to an exclusion clause, was said to represent 'good business sense'. The clause itself provided:

> 'If within 12 months after delivery there shall appear in the goods any defect which shall arise under proper use from faulty materials, workmanship, or design (other than a design made, furnished or specified by the purchaser for which the vendor had disclaimed responsibility), and the purchaser shall give notice thereof in writing to the vendor, the vendor shall, provided that the defective goods have been returned to the vendor if he shall have so required, make good the defects either by repair or, at his option, by the supply of a replacement. The vendor shall refund the cost of carriage on the return of the defective goods or parts and shall deliver any repaired or replaced goods or parts as if [the contract terms as to delivery] applied.'

---

8. ACKNOWLEDGEMENT OF EXAMINATION

The buyer hereby acknowledges and accepts that he has satisfied himself as to the condition of the goods and acknowledges that no condition or warranty whatsoever has been given or is given by the seller as to their quality or fitness for any purpose and that all conditions or warranties whether express or implied and whether by statute or otherwise are expressly excluded, and delivery of the goods to the buyer shall be conclusive evidence that the buyer has examined them and found them to be in complete accordance with the contract description, in good order and condition, of satisfactory quality and fit for any purpose for which they may be required.

Comment

In *BTE Auto Repairs v H&H Factors Ltd* (unreported, 26 January 1990), the county court was 'not impressed' by this clause, particularly since the relevant defects were not apparent at the time, indicating, perhaps that the clause might pass the reasonableness test under the *Unfair Contract Terms Act 1977* only in relation to patent defects. The case went to the Court of Appeal but no definitive finding was made. In *EA Grimstead & Sons Ltd v McGarrigan* [1998] EWCA Civ 1523 an examination clause was upheld as being reasonable.

This last case is also illustrative of the uses of such a clause as giving rise to an estoppel; that is to say, the buyer, having entered a contract with such a clause, cannot later deny its effect. In the case, the clause ran:

> 'The purchaser confirms that it has not relied on any warranty or representation or undertaking of or on behalf of the vendors (or any of them) or of any other person in respect of the subject matter of this agreement save for any representation or warranty or undertaking expressly set out in the body of this agreement and for the avoidance of doubt no representation or warranty is given in respect of any of the matters contained in Schedule 2 save in respect of the facts and to the extent as expressly therein stated.'

This was coupled with a clause which stated that the agreement set out the entire agreement between the parties, and which also stated that the other party had not relied on any representations, warranties or undertakings not set out in the agreement.

The Court of Appeal stated that these clauses could act as an estoppel against the other party, but that this could be so only if three conditions were met, namely:

- the statements in the disputed clauses were clear and unequivocal;
- the purchaser had intended the other party to act on the statements in the clause; and

300

- the other party must have believed the statements to be true and to have acted on them.

The Court of Appeal held that the seller had failed in relation to this last requirement. In the absence of specific evidence, it would not be safe to conclude that the seller had entered into the agreement on the basis that the buyer was not relying on the relevant representations. If the representations had been made as alleged, then that could only have been to persuade the buyer to enter the contract. In such a case, it would be open to hold that the seller knew that the acknowledgement of non-reliance clauses did not reflect the true position. If that were the case, then the seller could not rely on the estoppel which might otherwise have arisen.

Although the above cases suggest that it will always be very difficult to make use of non-reliance or examination clauses, there still remains the outside chance of success and they should be used. The chance of success would be enhanced if latent defects were specifically excluded; and if prominence were given to the clause as, perhaps, by placing it in a box or underlining it. This would support the argument that the buyer had accepted the clause specifically and that the seller had relied on that acceptance.

If the contract goes further and, rather than saying that no representation has been relied on, states instead that no representation has been made, this will be effective to deny any argument that a representation has been made: and relied on. Even if it was not in fact the case that there had been no representations, the parties are free to agree that it was so and base their contractual relations on that state of affairs. See *Trident Turboprop (Dublin) Ltd v First Flight Couriers Ltd* [2008] EWHC 1686.

9. PRICE

(a) All quotations and estimates issued by the seller are, except where expressly stated otherwise, subject to variation on or after acceptance.

(b) Without prejudice to the generality of the foregoing, any change in the applicable rate of VAT or of any other Government tax or levy shall be to the buyer's account.

Comment

There are no statutory controls on such clauses. It does not seem sustainable to argue that either clause purports to provide a performance substantially different from that which was reasonably expected within the *Unfair Contract Terms Act 1977* since nothing in it affects the seller's performance.

---

10. PAYMENT

(a)   Payment for goods supplied is due 30 days after delivery.

(b)   If payment of the price or any part thereof is not made by the due date, the seller shall be entitled to:

> (i)   charge interest on the outstanding amount at the rate of 9% per annum above the Bank of England's base rate, accruing daily;
>
> (ii)   require payment in advance of delivery in relation to any goods not previously delivered;
>
> (iii)   refuse to make delivery of any undelivered goods whether ordered under the contract or not and without incurring any liability whatever to the buyer for non-delivery or any delay in delivery;
>
> (iv)   terminate the contract.

Comment

One aspect to this clause – (b)(iv) – is that it overcomes the presumption contained in s *10* of the *Sale of Goods Act 1979* that time of payment is not of the essence. If this presumption were not corrected, the seller could not terminate a contract for late payment.

At the same time, the clause extends credit to the buyer, when this is not required, since the basic position is that payment is due on conclusion of the contract.

The provision in (b)(ii) can readily be dispensed with, since the *Late Payment of Commercial Debts (Interest) Act 1998* provides for interest to be payable on overdue bills at 8% above base rate, but the contract can provide for its own rate of interest, certainly where this provides for a 'substantial remedy', as it is put in *s 8* of the *1998 Act*. It is even possible for an interest rate set just below the statutory rate of interest to be substantial. The one query which must remain is that if the contract sets an interest rate higher than the statutory rate, this could well constitute a penalty clause and therefore be unenforceable.

---

11. DELIVERY

The seller will deliver the goods carriage paid within the United Kingdom by such method of carriage as the seller may choose.

> **Comment**
>
> Under this provision, the price includes the cost of delivery. The seller is always free to provide that the price is 'ex works', such that carriage charges are paid by the buyer. *Section 29* of the *SGA 1979* says that it depends on the express or implied terms of the contract as to whether it is for the buyer to collect the goods or for the seller to send them.

12. RISK

The risk in the goods will pass to the buyer at the moment the goods are dispatched from the seller's premises. Where the buyer chooses to collect the goods himself, risk will pass when the goods are entrusted to him or set aside for his collection, whichever happens first.

> **Comment**
>
> This takes advantage of the provision in *SGA 1979* that the parties are free to determine for themselves when risk is to pass. Since the buyer will have an insurable risk in the goods, even if property has not passed (see the following clause) the clause could indicate that the seller will arrange insurance cover on written request and at the buyer's expense.
>
> Note that special rules as to passing of risk apply where the buyer is not acting in the course of a business.

13. PROPERTY

The property in the goods will not pass to the buyer until payment of the price has been made in full to the seller.

> **Comment**
>
> This is the simplest form of retention of title clause and takes advantage of the provisions of *SGA 1979* that the parties are free to make their own contract as to when property is to pass.
>
> The real value of such clauses is that they offer the seller protection in case of the buyer's insolvency, since the seller can recover the goods as he has priority over other creditors of the buyer.

When drafting such clauses, it is crucial to reserve the whole title (as the above clause does) since anything less will reserve only what is called an equitable interest while still passing legal title to the buyer. An equitable interest is valid only if registered under the *Companies Act 2006* (*Re Bond Worth* [1980] Ch 228).

The clause drafted above is useful when the contract relates to goods which are easily identifiable as the seller's property, such as unique capital goods and equipment, which often have identifying serial numbers.

There are certain useful ancillary provisions which could be added, such as those permitting the seller access to the buyer's premises to recover the goods.

Alternative Clauses to the Above

The following more elaborate clause could be considered to cover these various matters:

'Title in the goods will not pass to the buyer but shall be retained pending payment in full of the contract price. Until such time as title passes to the buyer, the seller shall have absolute authority to retake, sell or otherwise deal with or dispose of all or any part of the goods in which title remains vested in him.

For the purposes specified above, the seller or any of his agents or authorised representatives shall be entitled at any reasonable time during normal working hours to enter without notice onto any premises where the goods or any part of the goods are installed, stored or kept or are reasonably believed to be for the purposes of possession of the goods.

The seller shall also be entitled to seek an injunction to prevent the customer from selling, transferring or otherwise disposing of the goods.'

Comment

It should be noted that, where a receiver contests a retention clause, but offers an undertaking to return the goods or their proceeds, the court is unlikely to grant an injunction (*Lipe Ltd v Leyland DAF* [1994] 1 BCLC 84). There is, though, nothing to stop the seller attempting to enforce his rights by refusing to deal with the receiver, by way of supply of further goods, unless the receiver chooses to return the goods immediately or pay their price (*Leyland DAF Ltd v Automotive Products plc* [1994] 1 BCLC 245).

It should always be remembered that, notwithstanding the presence of a retention clause, a buyer can still pass a good title in some circumstances to a third party. To cater for this possibility, the seller could extend the retention clause so that it provides:

> 'Where the buyer sells or disposes of the goods prior to full payment being received by the seller, the buyer shall immediately pay the proceeds of such sale or disposition into a separate bank account clearly denoted as an account containing monies deposited for the benefit of the seller by the buyer acting in a fiduciary capacity.'

Such a clause would impose a trust in relation to the proceeds by virtue of the fiduciary relationship, with the result that the seller would be able to recover the proceeds which are easily identifiable as being held by him on trust in the separate account.

14. FORCE MAJEURE

If delivery is delayed by strikes, lock-outs, fire, accidents, defective materials, delays in receipt of raw materials or bought-in goods or components or any other cause beyond the reasonable control of the seller, a reasonable extension of time shall be granted and the buyer shall pay such reasonable extra charges as shall have been occasioned by the delay. If the delay persists for such time as the seller considers unreasonable, he may, without liability on his part, terminate the contract.

Comment

Such a clause is necessary, because English law generally only excuses breach of contract where the contract has become literally impossible to perform. The clause above extends this right and, since it seeks to excuse what would otherwise be a breach of contract, it will be valid only if reasonable under the provisions of *UCTA 1977*. While success cannot be guaranteed, its limitation to events beyond the reasonable control of the seller should go some way to ensuring its validity.

---

15. DELAYED DELIVERY

If a firm delivery date is specifically provided for, and the seller fails to deliver the goods by such time for reasons other than matters beyond its reasonable control, the buyer shall be entitled to claim a reduction in price by giving the seller notice in writing within a reasonable time, unless it can be reasonably concluded from the circumstances that no loss has been suffered. Such reduction shall in no circumstances exceed 5% of the price.

Comment

Since this clause limits liability, it will have to survive the reasonableness test laid down in the *UCTA 1977*. Bearing this in mind, the seller in an individual case, with full knowledge of the contract goods and their intended use, should adjust the limit so that it has a better chance of being proved reasonable.

---

16. RELATIONSHIP OF PARTIES

Nothing in this agreement shall be construed as establishing or implying any partnership or joint venture between the parties, and nothing in this agreement shall be deemed to constitute either of the parties as the agent of the other or authorise either party:

(a)   to incur any expense on behalf of the other party;

(b)   to enter into any engagement or make any representation or warranty on behalf of the other party;

(c)   to pledge the credit of, or otherwise bind or oblige the other party;

(d)   to commit the other party in any way whatsoever, without in each case obtaining the other party's prior written consent.

Comment

In the absence of any express provision such as this, many types of commercial agreement can set up unwanted relationships of agency or partnership between the parties. The general effect of any such relationship would be that one party could bind the other towards third parties, or one party could become liable to third parties in respect of acts or omissions of the other.

If an agency or partnership is not a real possibility in the circumstances of a particular contract, this provision can be omitted.

---

17. ASSIGNMENT AND SUB-CONTRACTING

This agreement shall not be assigned or transferred, nor the performance of any obligation sub-contracted, in either case by the buyer, without the prior written consent of the seller.

> **Comment**
>
> The case law on topics such as sub-contracting and assignment is complicated and not entirely certain. In addition, sub-contracting is often permitted under the general law since the original party to the contract remains liable for the performance of the sub-contractor. As a result, these are matters which should be expressly regulated under the contract, particularly if the identity of the party is important.

18. COSTS AND OTHER EXPENSES

Except as specifically agreed to the contrary, any costs in relation to this agreement and its subject matter which are incurred by either of the parties shall be borne in full by that party.

> **Comment**
>
> On general legal principles, the costs of performance remain with the party who incurred them. The general law also provides as to which party is liable to bear sales or transfer taxes, VAT and stamp duties payable in respect of a transaction. It is useful to have these matters set out expressly, if only to avoid subsequent disagreements.

19. SEVERABILITY

If any terms or provision in this agreement shall be held to be illegal or unenforceable, in whole or in part, under any enactment or rule of law, such term or provision or part shall to that extent be deemed not to form any part of this agreement, but the validity and enforceability of the remainder of this agreement shall not be affected.

> **Comment**
>
> This provision recognises that the provisions of the contract might turn out to be illegal (perhaps because of a subsequent change in the law) or unenforceable (perhaps because a clause is successfully challenged under *UCTA 1977*). It accordingly provides that, notwithstanding such matters, the agreement remains in force.

20. TIME TO BE OF THE ESSENCE

Time shall be of the essence of this agreement, both as regards the dates and periods mentioned and as regards any dates and periods which may be substituted for them in accordance with this agreement or by agreement in writing between the parties.

Comment

Where time is stated in a contract to be of the essence, failure to perform an obligation on time entitles the other party to terminate the contract immediately. Generally, time is not of the essence unless the contract actually says so, or by the subsequent service of a notice. Under English law, in a contract for the sale of goods, neither the time for payment nor of delivery are of the essence, unless expressly stated so in the contract. The above clause may be considered too severe in many cases, so it can always be drafted so as to apply only to particular clauses.

---

21. WAIVER

The waiver or forbearance or failure by or of a party to insist on due and proper performance of the contract, whether by design or inadvertence, shall not be construed in any circumstances as a waiver or abandonment of that party's rights to future performance of such provision and the other party's obligation in respect of such future performance shall continue in full force and effect.

Comment

Under general principles, the failure of a party to enforce rights under an agreement can, in some circumstances, be construed as a waiver of those rights not just on the particular occasion, but also for the future. Since parties often either deliberately or inadvertently fail to enforce their rights under an agreement, it is advisable to provide for this situation by an express provision.

---

22. PROPER LAW

This agreement shall be governed by and construed in accordance with English law and each party agrees to submit to the exclusive jurisdiction of the English courts as regards any claim or matter arising under this agreement.

> **Comment**
>
> Such a clause can be useful if the parties to the contract are in differing jurisdictions (and remember that Scotland is a different jurisdiction to England).

23. ARBITRATION

Any disputes which arise out of or in connection with this agreement of whatsoever nature shall, if practicable, be settled amicably by negotiation between the parties and, if required, escalated to senior management for resolution. If such disputes are not resolved within 21 working days of such negotiations commencing, then the matter shall be referred to arbitration, the ruling in such arbitration being binding on the parties. The parties shall agree on the identity of the arbitrator and, in the event of their failure to agree, the arbitrator shall be appointed by the President of the London Chamber of Commerce.

> **Comment**
>
> The fairly obvious point of this clause is to seek to have disputes resolved speedily and without recourse to expensive litigation. The parties can of course nominate such party as they choose as the arbitrator, and could nominate someone from a relevant trade association.

24. DISPUTE SETTLEMENT

If any dispute arises between the parties with respect to any matter within the expertise of a technical expert, then such dispute shall at the instance of either party be referred to a person agreed between the parties, and, in default of agreement within 21 working days of notice from either party to the other calling upon the other so to agree, to a person chosen on the application of either party by [insert appropriate body, such as British Computer Society]. Such person shall be appointed to act as an expert and not as an arbitrator and the decision of such person shall be final and binding. The costs of the expert shall be borne equally by the parties unless the expert decides that one party has acted unreasonably, in which case he shall have discretion as to the award of costs.

Comment

Where the parties try to resolve a problem of fact, such as compliance with a technical specification, whether a particular standard has been reached, or the value of an item, it is possible (indeed advisable) to use an expert and to provide for his decision to be binding.

---

25. SET-OFF

Whenever under this contract any sum of money is recoverable from or payable by any party, the same may be deducted from any sum then due or which at any time thereafter may become due to that party under this or any other contract between the parties. Any exercise of the rights granted by this contract shall be without prejudice to such other rights or remedies as may be available to the party exercising such right.

Comment

The inclusion of an express right of set-off makes the use of this remedy easier, since the general law might impose some restrictions. The clause above is a wide one, since set-off is permitted not just of sums owed under the particular contract, but also of sums owed under other contracts with the party concerned.

Although the inclusion of such clauses is common, equally common are clauses excluding those rights, such as the following:

> 'All amounts due under this agreement shall be paid in full, without any deduction or withholding other than such as may be required by law, and the party owing such amounts shall not be entitled to assert any credit, set-off or counterclaim against the other party in order to justify the withholding of payment of any such amount in whole or part'.

Such a term is, however, within the remit of the *UCTA 1977* and is valid only if it can be shown to be reasonable (*Stewart Gill Ltd v Horatio Myer & Co Ltd* [1992] QB 600 and *Esso Petroleum v Milton* [1997] 1 WLR 938), although the Court of Appeal has raised some doubt as to whether this is really the case: *Society of Lloyd's v Leighs* [1997] EWCA Civ 2283. It does, however, now seem accepted that the Act will apply: *Barclays Bank plc v Alfons Kufner* [2008] EWHC 2319.

---

26. PRESERVATION OF RIGHTS

The provisions of this agreement, and the rights and remedies of the parties under this agreement, are cumulative and without prejudice and in addition to any rights or remedies a party may have at law or in equity; no exercise by a party of any right or remedy under this agreement, or in law or in equity, shall (save to the extent, if any, provided expressly in this agreement or at law or in equity) operate so as to hinder or prevent the exercise by it of any other such right or remedy.

Comment

There is sometimes a presumption that the parties have written down the whole of the rules governing the relationship between them and, in so doing, have displaced any additional remedies that might otherwise be available. This clause preserves rights under the general law in addition to any rights specifically granted by the contract.

B2:
Terms and Conditions of Purchase: buyer

Checklist

- Are you sure that the contract is one for sale; that is to say is it one where property in the goods is to pass for money consideration?

- Have you considered if this is one of the rare cases where the contract does require certain formalities to be observed?

- Are you certain that, as buyer, you will benefit fully from the implied obligations as to title; or, as a buyer, have you considered the possibility that you might be getting only a limited title?

- Are you, as buyer, satisfied that you will have the benefit of the statutory duties imposed on the seller as to description, quality and fitness for purpose?

- Are you, as buyer, sure that you have not lost your rights in relation to fitness and quality by, for example, your prior examination of the goods, or your absence of reliance on the seller?

- Have you considered the possible use and effectiveness and reasonableness of any exclusion or limitation clauses?

- Have you considered whether you should make special provision as to the passing of property and risk, or are you content to rely on the statutory provisions?

- Are you aware of the exceptions to the basic rule that a person who has no valid title cannot himself pass a valid title?

- What provision has been made in the contract as to prompt payment for the goods? Are you aware that statutory interest may become payable?

- Are you aware of the duties relating to delivery of the goods and the position arising on delivery of too much or too little?

- Is provision made in the contract for a specific right to examine the goods?

- Are you aware of what constitutes acceptance of goods and of the consequences, in terms of remedies, of acceptance?

- Are you aware of the rights and duties of the parties in the event of rejection?

- Are you fully aware of the rights and remedies available to you in the event of breach of contract?

Precedent – Terms and Conditions of Purchase by buyer; Specimen Contract

B2.2

1. GENERAL

These terms and conditions apply in preference to and supersede any other terms and conditions referred to, offered or relied on by the supplier whether in negotiation, and howsoever presented, at any stage in the dealings prior to conclusion of this contract. Without prejudice to the generality of the foregoing, the buyer will not be bound by any standard or printed terms presented by the seller in any of its documents, unless the seller specifically states, in writing, separately from such terms that it intends such terms to apply and the buyer separately acknowledges such notification in writing.

Comment

The clear aim of this clause is to ensure that it is the buyer's terms and conditions which will prevail. To do this, the buyer will have to take care that he is the winner in any 'battle of the forms'. In essence, this means that he must ensure that he is the last person to state that his terms and conditions apply: *Butler Machine Tool Co v Ex-Cello Corpn* [1979] 1 All ER 965.

An alternative version could read as follows:

'This agreement hereby cancels all previous agreements (if any) between the parties relating to the subject matter of this agreement, and also cancels and nullifies all rights (if any) of either party arising against the other by virtue of all or any of the said prior agreements, or any of the provisions thereof, notwithstanding the existence of any provision in any such prior agreement that any such rights or provisions shall survive its termination.'

Comment

It is important to refer to the survival provisions of the previous agreement or the cancellation may be incomplete.

---

2. VARIATION

Neither party to this contract shall be bound by any variation, waiver of, or addition to these conditions except where such is agreed to in writing by both parties and signed on behalf of each.

Comment

There is always a level of concern that employees in the buyer's organisation may prejudice the position of the organisation by agreeing on some change to the contract. If the relevant employee is part of the purchasing department, he will often appear to have the relevant authority, and thus be able to commit the organisation. Although, in legal principle, such variations may well not be enforceable, since no consideration is supplied for the variation, incorporation of such a clause as the above should avoid such problems from the outset.

An alternative clause to the above is:

> 'The parties may expressly agree in writing on any variation in the terms of this contract, provided that, unless expressly so agreed, no such agreement shall constitute or be construed as a general waiver of any of the provisions of this contract by any of the parties and the rights and obligations of the parties shall remain in full force and effect notwithstanding any variation agreed between the parties on any particular occasion.'

---

3. QUALITY, ETC OF GOODS

The supplier warrants and guarantees that all goods supplied under this agreement will be free from any defects, patent or latent, in material and workmanship, conform to applicable specifications and drawings and, to the extent that detailed designs were not provided by the buyer, will be free from design defects and in every aspect suitable for the purposes intended by the buyer, as to which the supplier hereby acknowledges that he has had due notice. The approval by the buyer of any designs provided by the seller shall not relieve the seller of its obligations under any provision contained in this term.

Comment

The above clause restates the provisions which would be implied into the contract by virtue of the *Sale of Goods Act 1979* as to description, quality and fitness for purpose. It also removes any doubt as to the applicability of the term as to fitness for purpose by avoiding any argument from the supplier that there was no reliance on his skill or judgement, or that such reliance was unreasonable. It is always useful for the supplier's duties and responsibilities to be clearly spelled out in the contract, not least because businessmen cannot be assumed to know of the statutory provisions.

The above clause could usefully be supplemented with a statement of the buyer's remedies and the period of time for which they are applicable. The following also contains a 'revolving warranty' in that the relevant repaired or replaced item can itself be repaired or replaced until it lasts for the appropriate time. The suggested addition is:

> 'The seller's obligations under this clause shall extend to any defect or non-conformity arising or manifesting itself within [period] from delivery. The buyer, without thereby waiving any rights or remedies otherwise provided by law and/or elsewhere in this agreement, may require the supplier:
>
> (*a*)   to make good or replace such items at the seller's risk and expense; or
>
> (*b*)   to refund such portion of the price as is equitable under all the circumstances.
>
> Items repaired or replaced shall be subject to the provisions of this agreement in the same manner as those originally delivered under the agreement. If the supplier refuses or fails promptly to repair or replace items when requested under this provision, the buyer may itself, or through an agent or sub-contractor, or otherwise, repair or replace any item himself and the seller agrees to promptly reimburse the buyer for any costs or expenses incurred.'

4. GUARANTEE AS TO TITLE

The supplier:

(*a*)   holds full, clear and unencumbered title to all of the goods;

(*b*)   will on the date of delivery hold such title in and to all the goods; and

(*c*)   will on the date of delivery have the full and unrestricted right, power and authority to sell, transfer and deliver all of the goods to the buyer at which point the latter will acquire a valid and unencumbered title to the goods.

Comment

This clause restates the provisions of the *SGA 1979* as to title (implied terms as to title B1.5), and hence makes the supplier fully aware of his obligations at the outset. It should be remembered that, even if there is a breach of this provision, the buyer will in some circumstances be able to act as though he did have full title in the goods (transfer of title by non-owner B1.28).

---

5. PRICE

The prices stated in the contract are inclusive of all taxes and cannot be varied without the express prior consent of the buyer given in writing and signed by a duly authorised party.

Comment

Many buyers think that, unless the contract expressly states the price to be fixed, the supplier is entitled to increase the cost to cover any increase in overheads since the agreement was made. In fact, the true legal position is that the price is fixed unless the contract itself states to the contrary. The above clause clarifies the position.

---

6. PAYMENT OF THE PRICE

The buyer will pay for the goods at the end of the month following the month in which the goods are received or in which the invoice for such goods is received, whichever is the later. In the event of late payment by the buyer, he shall be liable to pay the seller interest at a rate which compensates him for such loss as has been directly caused by late payment so long as this does not exceed the rate of statutory interest provided for in the *Late Payment of Commercial Debts (Interest) Act 1998*. In no circumstances shall the time for payment be of the essence of the agreement.

Comment

Under the *SGA 1979*, any time stated for payment is not of the essence unless the contract states otherwise. The final sentence to this clause ensures that time for payment is not of the essence. In the event of late

---

payment, however, there will still be a breach, for which the seller is entitled to compensation. Under the *Late Payment of Commercial Debts (Interest) Act 1998 (LPCD(I)A 1998)*, statutory interest of 8% above base rate is automatically payable by the buyer. *Section 8* of the *LPCD(I)A 1998*, however, allows for contracting out so long as the contract provides for a 'substantial remedy'. A remedy is 'substantial', by virtue of *s 9* of the *LPCD(I)A 1998*, unless it is insufficient for the purpose of compensating the seller or deterring late payment; and if it would not be fair and reasonable to allow the remedy stated in the contract to stand.

The above clause seeks to avoid payment of statutory interest, but still to ensure that the seller is compensated for his loss. An alternative approach would be to specify that any interest payable by the buyer shall be no more than 2% above base rate. In most cases, this would be enough to meet the requirements for a substantial remedy. See *Yuanda (UK) Co Ltd v WW Gear Construction Ltd* [2010] EWHC 720.

7. DELIVERY

The goods are to be delivered, carriage paid, to such location as the buyer shall direct. Any time agreed between the parties for such delivery shall be of the essence of the contract.

Comment

The *SGA 1979* provides that it is a question of fact whether any stipulations as to time are of the essence. By making delivery time of the essence, the buyer thus secures his right to terminate the contract and to seek damages where the date for delivery is not met.

The *SGA 1979* also provides that it is up to the parties to specify whether the buyer is to collect the goods or have them sent; and that the goods are to be delivered to the buyer's place of business unless the contract says otherwise. The above clause clarifies the position in the buyer's favour.

8. DELIVERY IN INSTALMENTS

Unless agreed by the parties in writing, and in a document signed on the buyer's behalf, delivery is not to be made in instalments. Where there is such an agreement (or where the buyer agrees in any case to accept delivery in instalments), breach in relation to any instalment, of whatsoever nature, shall entitle the buyer, without prejudice to such other remedies as he might have, to terminate the contract and to claim damages.

Comment

The *SGA 1979* states that the buyer is not obliged to accept instalments unless the contract states otherwise. It also states that where a contract is for separate instalments, it depends on the terms of the contract and the circumstances of the case as to whether a breach in relation to any instalment results in a repudiation of the entire contract. Although the *SGA 1979* requires satisfaction of two conditions, it must inevitably be the case that a specific term of the contract as above would allow the buyer to repudiate the entire agreement in the event of a breach in relation to just one instalment.

---

9. PASSING OF PROPERTY

The property in the goods will pass to the buyer when the goods are unconditionally appropriated (by either party or by or with the consent of either party) to the contract, or on delivery to the buyer, whichever happens first.

Comment

The *SGA 1979* sets out a number of rules (Rules 1–5) as to when property is to pass. These, however, apply only if the contract is silent on this point. The above clause takes advantage of this and ensures that property, which can be regarded as full ownership of the goods, passes from the earliest possible moment.

---

10. PASSING OF RISK

The goods will be and shall remain at the seller's risk until such time as they are delivered to the buyer (or at his direction), and are found to be in accordance with the requirements of the contract. It shall be the duty of the seller at all times to maintain a contract of insurance over the goods and, on request from the buyer, to assign to the buyer the benefits of such insurance. Without prejudice to the generality of the foregoing, the seller accepts the risk of deterioration in the goods which is necessarily incident to the course of transit or storage at his premises or at any premises on his behalf.

Comment

The *SGA 1979* provides that risk passes with property unless otherwise agreed. The above clause takes advantage of this and, taken with the previous

319

clause, gives the buyer property from the earliest possible moment, while delaying the passing of risk until the last.

The final part of the clause derives from a further provision in the *SGA 1979* which states that where the seller agrees to deliver at his own risk the buyer must still – unless the contract provides to the contrary – take any risk of deterioration which is necessarily incident to the course of transit. In *Bull v Robison* (1854) 10 Ex 342, steel was despatched by the carrier and rusted in transit. This was held to be a normal incident of the journey. In *Mash & Murrell Ltd v Joseph I Emanuel Ltd* [1961] 1 WLR 862, potatoes deteriorated during transit from Cyprus to England. This was said not to be a normal incident of the journey but happened because of a defect in the goods when the journey got under way. The above clause also makes the seller liable for any deterioration arising during storage by him or on his behalf.

11. ACCEPTANCE

The buyer shall not be deemed to have accepted the goods until such time as, in writing signed by him, he has notified the seller that he has accepted the goods as being in complete compliance with the requirements of the contract. Notwithstanding any such acceptance as aforesaid, the buyer will remain entitled to reject the goods and to claim damages if, within [period] of any such written notice, the goods are found not to be in complete compliance as aforesaid.

Comment

Acceptance of goods eliminates the right of the buyer to reject the goods for breach of contract. Under the *SGA 1979*, acceptance can take place when acceptance is intimated; after the lapse of a reasonable time, or when the buyer does an act inconsistent with the seller's ownership. Although the provisions stated in the *SGA 1979* as to acceptance are not stated to apply unless the parties agree otherwise, it is assumed that they are nevertheless free to specify in the contract just when acceptance takes place.

An alternative formulation of this clause is:

'If any of the goods, or the packages containing the goods, do not comply with the order or with any term of this contract including, but not limited to, those relating to quantity, quality or description, the buyer shall be entitled to reject those goods or any part at any time after delivery, regardless of whether the buyer is to be regarded under the *Sale of Goods Act 1979* (or such other enactment as might replace that Act) or otherwise as having accepted them. Any acceptance of such goods by the buyer shall be without prejudice to any rights that the buyer might have against the supplier. The buyer shall be entitled to return any rejected goods, carriage paid by the supplier, at the risk of the supplier.'

12. NON-DELIVERY

If the supplier does not deliver the goods or any part within the time specified in the contract, the buyer will be entitled to terminate the contract, purchase other goods of the same or similar description, and to recover from the seller the amount by which the cost of so purchasing exceeds the price which would have been payable to the supplier in respect of the goods replaced by such purchase, and all without prejudice to any other remedy for breach of contract (see clause 13 below).

Comment

In one sense, this condition is superfluous, since it essentially restates the law as expressed in the *SGA 1979* and as it also exists at common law. Its presence is due to the fact that it alerts the supplier to his duties, and thus avoids any possible recourse to litigation. Linked with the provision in clause 7 above, making time of delivery of the essence, this clause allows the buyer to take action if the goods are only, say, one day late. It will always be an option for the buyer, of course, to accept delivery of the goods in such a case (see clause 20 below).

The general rules about damages, based on the ruling in *Hadley v Baxendale* (1854) 9 Ex 341, is found in *s 51* of the *SGA 1979* which provides that an action for damages for non-delivery is available 'where the seller wrongfully neglects or refuses to deliver the goods', going on to say that damages will normally be 'the difference between the contract price and the market or current price of the goods at the time or times when they ought to have been delivered'.

---

13. CONSEQUENTIAL LOSS

Without prejudice to clause 12 above, or to such other rights as the buyer might have under statute or at law, the supplier shall also be liable, in the event of any breach of contract, for all indirect or direct consequential loss following from the breach howsoever caused. The supplier also expressly acknowledges that he was aware at all times of such circumstances as might affect any loss suffered by the buyer as a result of any breach.

Comment

The aim of this clause is in some ways to side-step the difficulties caused by *Hadley v Baxendale* and the *SGA 1979* which state that the type of loss covered here is available only if the supplier had specific knowledge of all the relevant circumstances (such as that the buyer was buying for the purposes of a profitable resale) which might produce such loss in the event of a breach.

The presence of this clause will overcome the problems inherent in decisions such as *Victoria Laundry (Windsor) Ltd v Newman Industries Ltd* [1949] 2 KB 528. Here the defendants contracted to supply the claimants with a boiler. They knew that it was to be put to immediate use in the claimants' laundry business. The boiler was delivered several months late and the claimants sued for profits lost because of the delay. The Court of Appeal held that the defendants were liable for the loss of profit which naturally flowed from their breach, but that they were not liable for the loss of profit on some exceptionally lucrative government contracts. The defendants had not known of the existence of these contracts at the time the contract had been made. Had the contract contained such a clause as the above, the further losses could also have been recovered.

---

14. INDEMNITY

The supplier shall indemnify the buyer and keep the buyer indemnified and held harmless against all those claims, costs and expenses which the buyer may incur and which arise, directly or indirectly, howsoever caused, from the supplier's breach of any of its obligations under this contract.

Comment

While this clause states what would anyway be the position, it makes it plain to the supplier that should the buyer, for example, incur costs through defending an action in relation to the goods (they might be defective and cause damage to a third party, or infringe a third party's patent or trade mark), then the supplier will be liable for such costs as legal fees.

---

15. ASSIGNMENT AND SUB-CONTRACTING

The supplier shall not assign or transfer the whole or any part of this contract, or sub-contract the production or supply of any goods to be supplied under this contract, without the prior written consent of the buyer.

Comment

Since buyers pay much attention to the quality of the goods produced by prospective suppliers, they will generally not want the supplier to hand over the contract to a third party. This will be despite the fact that the original supplier will remain liable on the contract and hence be responsible for any failures on the part of the third party. The general rule is that a contract can be assigned or sub-contracted unless it is evident in all the circumstances that a supplier was chosen for his unique qualities. This clause changes the rules to prevent any assignment or sub-contracting without prior written consent.

There will, of course, be cases where the supplier of a product which is to be manufactured might wish to contract out certain aspects of manufacture to specialists. In such cases, this clause can be removed, since the buyer will obtain adequate protection by drafting the contract specifications in as clear and tight a way as possible. Alternatively, the clause could be retained but have the following wording added to the end:

'... provided that such consent shall not be necessary where any assignment or sub-contracting is reasonably necessary for the due performance of the contract by the supplier.'

16. FORCE MAJEURE

The buyer shall not be liable for any failure to fulfil its obligations under the contract where such failure is caused by circumstances beyond its reasonable control.

Comment

It can be the case that the events which prevent a buyer from carrying out the contract will cause the contract to be frustrated, so that no liability would arise anyway. On the other hand, frustration is narrowly defined as occurring 'whenever the law recognises that without default of either party a contractual obligation has become incapable of being performed because the circumstances in which performance is called for would render it a thing radically different from that which was undertaken by the contract' (*Davis Contractors Ltd v Fareham UDC* [1956] AC 696).

It is unlikely that, for example, industrial action, or the drying up of the sole source of supply of an essential ingredient, would count as frustration. In *The Super Servant Two* [1990] 1 Lloyd's Rep 1, the defendants agreed to carry the claimants' drilling rig in one of two barges owned by them. The

323

defendants scheduled barge A for use in other contracts, and barge B for use in this contract. The latter was destroyed in an accident. The Court of Appeal said that the contract was not frustrated since it had been the defendants' choice to use barge B in performance of the contract. It is arguable that the above clause would have relieved the defendants in this case.

The above clause can be varied in two main ways.

- As well as using the broad phrase 'circumstances beyond its reasonable control', specific causes can be identified as potentially disrupting the contract, for example, fire, flood, or industrial disputes. If such illustrations are added, they should be accompanied by the phrase 'without prejudice to the generality of this clause', so as to make it clear that these examples are illustrative only and that the clause is not limited to such examples.

- The clause might be drafted so as to provide for an extension of time. Since it can rarely be clear in advance how long a particular circumstance will prevail, the clause should do no more than provide for the suspension of the contract 'for a reasonable time, such to be in the sole discretion of the buyer'.

A further question is whether such clauses are valid under the provisions of *UCTA 1977*. Since the clause seeks to excuse what would otherwise be a breach of contract by the buyer, it will be valid only if shown to be reasonable. Given that it applies to circumstances beyond the buyer's reasonable control, the clause ought to be regarded favourably.

17. PROPER LAW

This contract shall be governed by and construed in accordance with English law. Each party agrees to submit to the non-exclusive jurisdiction of the English courts as regards any claim or matter arising under this contract.

Comment

The grant of exclusive jurisdiction to the English courts does not prevent the use of an arbitration clause (see the following clause).

---

18. ARBITRATION

All disputes and differences which arise out of or in connection with this contract or its construction, operation, termination or liquidation shall, if practicable, be settled by means of negotiation between the parties. If the parties cannot settle any such dispute or difference within 28 days after first conferring, then such dispute or difference shall be settled by arbitration. The place, date and the arbitrator shall be agreed between the parties or, where the parties cannot so agree within a further 28 days, by the London Chamber of Commerce.

Comment

The value of this clause is that it can enable disputes to be settled promptly and without undue expense. Provision should always be made for an independent third person to appoint an arbitrator if the parties cannot themselves agree on an appointment.

---

19. SUPERVENING ILLEGALITY

If any term of this contract is held by any court of law or in arbitration to be illegal or unenforceable, or is so rendered by any enactment, in whole or in part, such term or part shall to that extent be deemed not to be part of this contract.

Comment

It is always possible that a subsequent change in the law can render a contract term unenforceable or illegal, or that a clause is deemed unenforceable, if it is found to fail the reasonableness test imposed by the *Unfair Contract Terms Act 1977*. The above clause seeks to overcome any problems which this might cause. It may be, however, that the invalid clause was central to the contract, with the result that its disappearance could fundamentally alter the nature of the contract. To cover this, the following words can be added:

> 'Provided that, where the buyer is of the view that it would not have entered into the contract in the absence of the particular term, it may terminate the contract forthwith by notice in writing to the supplier and without liability on its part, but without prejudice to such rights on its part which had already accrued.'

---

20. WAIVER

Any waiver by the buyer of its rights under this contract shall not be construed as a waiver of its rights in any future case and the supplier's obligations in respect of future performance shall continue in full force and effect.

> **Comment**
>
> It is always possible for a court to rule that a party's failure to enforce its rights has amounted to a permanent waiver of those rights. This clause avoids this by providing that an instance of forbearance does not amount to a waiver of the same obligation in the future. Since a forbearance can actually happen by inadvertence, a clause such as this is essential.

21. COSTS AND OTHER EXPENSES

Except as specifically agreed to the contrary, any costs in relation to this agreement and its subject matter which are incurred by either of the parties shall be borne in full by that party.

> **Comment**
>
> On general legal principles, the costs of performance remain with the party who incurred them. The general law also provides as to which party is liable to bear sales or transfer taxes, VAT and stamp duties payable in respect of a transaction. It is useful to have these matters set out expressly, if only to avoid subsequent disagreements.

22. FURTHER ASSURANCES

The supplier agrees to use its best endeavours to do, or cause to be done, all those things which are necessary, proper, or advisable to execute this contract including, without limitation, the performance of such further acts or the execution and delivery of any additional instruments or documents as may be necessary, and to obtain any permits, approvals or licences which may be required for the proper performance of this contract. Without prejudice to the generality of the foregoing, the supplier also agrees to use its best endeavours to provide the buyer with the benefits of any third party warranty to the extent that such warranty enhances the degree of protection available to the buyer under this contract.

> **Comment**
>
> It is always possible that the performance of a contract requires other documents to be produced or obtained, such as formal assignments of a contract, the transfer of intellectual property rights, or approvals from regulatory authorities. Although an obligation to do these things is

probably implied by law, it is convenient for them to be spelled out in the contract. Since third parties, such as manufacturers, might offer warranties in relation to the goods or components (which could not be enforced by the buyer), this clause also gives the buyer the protection of such warranty.

23. NO PARTNERSHIP, ETC

This contract shall not operate so as to create a partnership or joint venture of any kind, or make either party the agent of the other.

Comment

In the absence of an express clause such as this, many types of commercial agreement could set up unwanted relationships between the parties. If, for example, an agency were constituted, one party could bind the other to third parties, or one party could become liable to third parties in respect of the acts or omissions of the other.

Other possible considerations

Packaging **B2.3**

If the buyer has detailed requirements as to packaging, these may be specified in a separate condition. Such requirements may arise because the goods have to be shipped by sea or air, handling facilities in the buyer's warehouse might need special containers or pallets, or detailed information is required on the outside of the package to ensure safe use by employees or purchasers.

Instruction manuals **B2.4**

With complex items such as computers, instruction manuals will be crucial to proper use. The supplier can be placed under a contractual obligation to provide these facilities, perhaps also extending to instruction courses and to ensure that the instruction manuals are updated on a regular basis and communicated to the buyer at the supplier's own cost and expense.

Spares and after sales service **B2.5**

Some machines and equipment can be serviced only by the manufacturer and, unless spares continue to be available, the goods can become unusable.

In *L Gent & Sons (a firm) v Eastman Machine Co Ltd* [1986] BTLC 17, it was held that where there is no trade custom to such effect, a buyer has no cause of action where the contract does not contain an express term to the effect that a supply of spare parts will be available. Furthermore, where there is no such custom, a failure by a supplier to have spare parts is not of itself grounds for alleging that the goods are not of satisfactory quality. Accordingly, the existence of spare parts should be a matter actively considered by buyers in appropriate cases.

Performance tests   **B2.6**

Where the seller is to design an item to meet certain standards and performance criteria, the buyer will generally require tests to be carried out to satisfy him that these standards and criteria have been reached. The contract will need to provide for the type of tests to be carried out, the time, place and allocation of costs of such tests, and for the effect of any failure and that the buyer must be satisfied as to the tests carried out.

Cancellation   **B2.7**

A somewhat stringent clause sometimes inserted by buyers gives them the right to cancel the contract regardless of any breach. Since such an arbitrary clause would almost certainly be unreasonable under the *UCTA 1977*, it should at the very least state that the buyer will pay for the agreed goods which have been wholly or partly manufactured prior to cancellation, as well as for the cost of materials bought in and which now cannot be used.

Confidentiality   **B2.8**

Where, in the course of design and manufacture, confidential information, drawings, specifications and other materials come into the hands of the seller, the buyer may wish to provide expressly that the seller will keep such matters confidential, and will promptly return all such drawings and documents on completion or termination of the contract.

Insolvency   **B2.9**

The insolvency of the seller will not bring an end to the contract unless this is expressly provided for in the contract. If the seller does have financial difficulties, the buyer, particularly if the contract is a long term one, may wish to terminate the contract and seek a more secure source of supply.

B3:
Licence of Computer Software
– Buyer/Licensee

At a glance   B3.1

- Drafted to favour the Licensee/Buyer.
- Covers licence of software and provision of computer support services.
- For software on Licensee's system (not 'cloud computing').
- Detailed contract.

Commentary   B3.2

- This standard contract should be used by companies wishing to take a licence of computer software from a software licensor for relatively major procurements where the Supplier's standard software licence is inadequate or too one-sided. Some users/licensees will instead buy a hosted service whereby they access the software on the system of the licensor, in which case a different contract would be needed. Such hosted software known as a service (SaaS) contracts are becoming increasingly common although installed traditional software licences are still used by many. Some users take a licence, instead, of commercial off-the-shelf (COTS) products or slightly more complex out of the box (OOTB) software products. The precedent in B3 however is a straight forward traditional software licence.

- The agreement also includes software support. If the Buyer will not be taking software support from the Supplier then this contract should not be used.

- These kinds of contract vary substantially in practice. Rarely will any example such as this be appropriate for every arrangement or Supplier/Buyer. Customisation, ideally after taking legal advice, is usually necessary.

- The contract lists the main 'variables' such as the parties' names on the front page. This could instead be on a schedule. It is simply a matter of personal preference.

- In clause 3.1(a) the contract allows for one named software package to be supplied or as an alternative for the contract to be set up for all future

329

purchases of software from time to time ordered and documented by the parties.

- Clause 3.1 sets out the various supplies which the Supplier/licensor may undertake including software support and also training. This will vary from contract to contract.

- Clause 4 sets out strong warranties which protect the Buyer. A licensor would not want such stringent requirements. Strong Buyers are often, however, able to negotiate such provisions.

- Clause 5 contains the software licence clause. The Buyer needs to consider carefully the full extent of any licence which is required. Issues to consider include where the software may be used and by what legal entities, whether an outsourcing or facilities management company acting on behalf of the Buyer may use the software or not and whether there may be any special considerations such as a proposed future sale of assets which should be anticipated in the licence clause. Clause 5.2 sets out the different kinds of licence which a user may require. Often a Supplier will charge very different fees depending on which of these kinds of licence are envisaged. The decision of the CJEU in *Usedsoft GbmH v Oracle International Corp* (Case C-128/11 2012) has the effect that if a licence is perpetual yet purports to restrict the licensee from assigning it, such restriction may well be void under EU/UK competition law. However, this needs to be capable of being proved. In 2015 Usedsoft (despite winning the CJEU case) agreed to cease use of Oracle software as it could not prove the licences it was 're-selling' were perpetual licences nor other requirements of the CJEU decision. Parties should take legal advice on how this applies to them as the law is complex. Buyers wanting a right to assign ('resell' the licence after they stop using the product) should ensure there is no express restriction in the contract. They should, perhaps, even include an express right requiring the licensor to assign the benefit and burden of the agreement, whether to group companies in due course or any third-party outsider. Many licensors will fight such provisions, however. If the licensee plans to export the software and use it in other countries it should take legal advice. Some licences are specific to one country. UK and EU competition law can affect which restrictions are permitted in that respect and in some cases the rights owner cannot assert their copyright against an importer once the rights are 'exhausted' by a first sale in the EU/EEA. *The Intellectual Property (Exhaustion of Rights) (EU Exit) Regulations 2019 (SI 2019/265)* provide that after the UK leaves the EU the UK will recognise the EU exhaustion of rights and not prevent imports of software in which rights are exhausted by an earlier first sale in the EU/EEA but not vice versa. This has the effect that rights owners in the EU/EEA after Brexit may well be able to assert their copyright to prevent the export of a software product out of the UK even if they had put on the market in the UK or which their licensee had put on the market in the UK.

- Clause 7 is a fairly stringent security clause. Buyers not so concerned about the conduct of Supplier personnel at their premises may not require the entirety of these provisions.

- Clause 8 provides that the secret source code part of the software which is needed to repair faults and which the Supplier rarely gives to the Buyer will be lodged to protect the Buyer with a third party 'escrow agent'. NCC (see www.nccgroup.trust/uk/our-services/software-escrow-and-verification/) is suggested as an agent, although other software escrow agents exist. The agent should be one familiar with software and ideally with the expertise to undertake verification of what is lodged. Whether Supplier or Buyer pays the fees, which fees can be expensive, is a matter of negotiation in each case. If instead the contract provided that the Supplier would hand the source code to the licensee if the Supplier went out of business or failed to support the software then there is a risk that may not happen. In a liquidation, the liquidator of the Supplier would have a right to set aside onerous contracts under insolvency legislation, hence the necessity for deposit with a third party. If a Buyer is able to negotiate possession of the source code of course, which is rare, that is even better.

- Clause 9 provides for payment and is drafted in the Buyer's favour.

- Clause 10 – Confidentiality and Data Protection assumes little personal data will be supplied between the parties but does make reference to data protection legislation and duties under the Data Protection Act 2018 and UK GDPR.

- Clause 11 is an intellectual property indemnity clause which all licensees of software will require. Software is protected by copyright and it is hard for a licensee to check ownership, as the right in the UK is unregistered, whether the licensor is the true owner of the rights; thus an indemnity which should protect the licensee in the event that the licensee is sued where the software infringes a third-party right, is common. Even Suppliers in their own standard software licence agreements will include such a provision.

- Clause 15.1 excludes both parties' liability for consequential loss to the other. A very tough Buyer might not include such a provision but many Suppliers, particularly where in a strong negotiating position, may require it, so it is better that it is in the standard contract of the Buyer. Some stronger software licensors will want the Buyer/licensee to have unlimited liability in three areas – infringement of copyright and other IP rights in the software, breach of confidentiality and breach of data protection legislation (where fines can be up to 4% of annual global turnover or €20 million, whichever is greater (2020 rates) and breach is a criminal offence). Similarly, there is no legal reason why a Buyer has to exclude the Supplier's liability for consequential loss, but this contract does so as that tends to be the norm.

- Appendix 1 is the maintenance schedule and is only relevant if software support is to be provided by the other party.

- Appendix 2 would set out a description of the software.

- Appendix 3 would contain any detail about training to be provided.

Precedent – Licence of Computer Software and Purchase of Support Services

B3.3

Contract Number: _____

Estimated Contract Value: _____

Contract relating to:

The supply of software and related services.

[date]

CONTRACT

Between

'Buyer': _____ Ltd
Registered Office: _____
Company Number: _____ ; and
'Supplier': _____ Ltd
Registered Office: _____
Company Number: _____

For the fees set out in this Agreement paid by the Buyer, the Supplier shall supply to the Buyer such software and services (as the case may be) as the Buyer may order from time to time within the Contract Period in accordance with this contract which comprises this front sheet and the following appended documents:

Number	Description
1	Conditions
2	Appendix 1 – Maintenance
3	Appendix 2 – Software, Licence Types and Pricing
4	Appendix 3 – Training

These, in the case of conflict, have precedence in the order listed above.

Signed for and on behalf of the Supplier (name, position):

_____   _____

Signed for and on behalf of the Buyer (name, position):

_____   _____

CONDITIONS

1. Definitions

In the Contract, the following expressions shall have the meanings, if any, ascribed to them:

- 'Acceptance' – deemed acceptance of the Supplies by the Buyer in accordance with the Condition headed 'Faulty Supplies'. 'Accept' and 'Accepted' in the context of 'Acceptance' shall be construed accordingly.

- 'Buyer' – _____ Ltd, its successors and assigns and, for the purposes of all obligations of the Supplier and of all rights and licences granted by the Supplier, all companies within the Buyer's group of companies.

- 'Buyer's Commercial Contact' – _____

- 'Commencement Date' – _____

- 'Contract' – this contract.

- 'Contract Price' – the total sum payable to the Supplier by the Buyer for Supplies.

- 'Contract Period' – _____ years from Commencement Date.

- 'Contract Personnel' – the Supplier's employees, sub-contractors and agents (and their employees, sub-contractors and agents) engaged in the performance of the Contract.

- 'Functional Specification' – the Supplier's functional specification for the Software as supplied to the Buyer or as published by the Supplier.

- 'Information' – information whether written or oral or any other form, including, but not limited to, documentation, specifications, reports, data, notes, drawings, models, patterns, samples, software, computer outputs, designs, circuit diagrams, inventions, whether patentable or not and know-how.

- 'Intellectual Property Right(s)' – any patent, unitary patent, petty patent/ utility model, registered design, copyright, database right, unregistered design right, semiconductor topography right, know-how or any similar right exercisable in any part of the world and shall include any applications for the registration of any patents or registered designs or similar registrable rights in any part of the world.

- 'Site' – premises specified by the Buyer, upon which the Supplier is to install and/or deliver Supplies.

- 'Software'– all the Supplier's proprietary computer programs that may be supplied to the Buyer under the Contract as currently listed in Appendix 2 (including all updates, enhancements, modifications, versions, and all replacement or amendment products from time to time offering the same or similar functionality) and all appropriate documentation necessary to enable their proper operation and functionality.

- 'Supplier's Commercial Contact' – _____

- 'Supplies' – all Software and related services to be supplied to the Buyer under the Contract.

- 'Support Period' – _____ years.

- 'Virus'– any code which is designed to disrupt, disable, harm, or otherwise impede in any manner, including aesthetic disruptions or distortions, the operation of the Software, or any other associated hardware, software, firmware, computer system or network, or would disable the Software or impair in any way its operation based on the elapsing of a period of time, exceeding an authorised number of copies, advancement to a particular date or other numeral, or that would permit the Supplier or any other person to access the Software to cause such disablement or impairment, or which contains any other similar harmful, malicious or hidden procedures, routines or mechanisms which would cause such programs to cease functioning or to damage or corrupt data, storage media, programs, equipment or communications, or otherwise interfere with operations. It includes, without limitation, computer programs commonly referred to as worms or Trojan horses.

2. Duration

The Contract shall last for the Contract Period unless ended sooner in accordance with its terms.

3. Supply

3.1   The Supplier shall:

   (a)   supply, deliver and install [the Software] [such Software as is ordered by the Buyer from time to time during the Contract Period] at the respective Sites specified by the Buyer;

   (b)   maintain the Software in accordance with Appendix 1 for a period of 12 months from its respective Acceptance at no additional charge to the Buyer;

(*c*) if so requested by the Buyer in writing, maintain the Software in accordance with Appendix 1 within the Support Period (or any part of it as required by the Buyer) at the price stated in the Contract, or, if no such price is stated, at a fair and reasonable price;

(*d*) provide training to the Buyer's personnel in accordance with Appendix 4; and

(*e*) provide the Buyer's Commercial Contact with quarterly reports detailing the Buyer's quarterly and cumulative expenditure under the Contract.

4. Quality of Supplies

4.1 The Supplier warrants:

(*a*) that notwithstanding anything to the contrary in the Contract, the Buyer may freely disclose all Information concerning such compatibility to third parties;

(*b*) that the Software is free from:

  (i) all Viruses that could have been detected by using the latest (at the date of despatch) commercially available virus detection software; and

  (ii) all forms of 'electronic repossession' and 'logic bombs' (which expressions shall have meanings as they are generally understood within the computing industry) and the Supplier indemnifies the Buyer against all actions, claims, proceedings, damages, costs and expenses arising from any breach of this warranty;

(*c*) that, after Acceptance by the Buyer, the Software will perform in accordance with the Functional Specification;

(*d*) that it has and shall use and adopt only good quality materials, techniques and standards in performing the Contract with the standards of care, skill and diligence required of good computing practice;

(*e*) that it shall comply with:

  (i) the requirements of any written requirement of the Buyer, all applicable legislation, regulations or by-laws of a Local or other Authority; and

  (ii) any Buyer site regulations that may be notified to the Supplier; and

(*f*) that it has obtained all necessary licences, authorities, consents and permits for the unrestricted export of the Software to the Buyer, and export or re-export to such countries as the Buyer shall have notified to the Supplier at any time before delivery to the Buyer and the Supplier indemnifies the Buyer against all costs, claims or demands resulting directly or indirectly from any breach of such warranty.

5. Licence

5.1 The Supplier grants to the Buyer an irrevocable, non-exclusive, non-transferable, perpetual licence from its respective date of delivery to the Buyer for the Buyer by itself or by third parties on its behalf to use, copy, install, maintain, modify, enhance and adapt the Software for all Buyer design and development purposes in accordance with the relevant Licence Type (as described in paragraph 2 of this Condition).

5.2 The relevant Licence Type shall be as stated in Appendix 2 or as may be ordered by the Buyer and shall be either:

(a) Processor Licence – limited to a specified processor(s) irrespective of the power of the processor, size or model group, whether physically or logically linked. No limitation on location or number of users;

(b) Site Licence – limited to a specified geographical location(s). No limitation on type or power of processors or number of users;

(c) Corporate Licence – no limitation on type or power of processor(s), location(s) or number of users;

(d) Enterprise Wide Licence – as Corporate Licence save that the expression 'Buyer' shall be deemed to include also any undertaking or entity in which the Buyer has a commercial interest from time to time anywhere in the world; or

(e) Other – having limitations as may be agreed from time to time by the parties in writing.

5.3 Notwithstanding any limitations imposed by a relevant Licence Type, the Buyer shall have the right, without charge, to:

(a) use any alternative processor for Software test and evaluation purposes or where Software cannot for any reason be used on any specified processor;

(b) copy, install and use Software on any processor for back-up, archive or disaster recovery purposes;

(c) transfer any Processor Licence to an alternative processor (whether or not at the same location); and

(d) require the Supplier to promptly deliver and install (and the Supplier shall so deliver and install), where the Buyer elects to change an operating system, a new version of the Software compatible with such new operating system.

5.4 Notwithstanding any other Condition, the Supplier grants to the Buyer non-exclusive, royalty free, worldwide rights, by or on behalf of the Buyer, to copy and use Information supplied under the Contract or derived by the Buyer from the Supplies as necessary for the purpose of interfacing with other equipment as may form part of the Buyer Network or any other telecommunications network. For such purpose, the Supplier shall promptly provide such additional Information as the Buyer may request. The Buyer shall pay the costs of the collation, reproduction and despatch of the Information. In this Condition 'Buyer Network' means all exchange equipment, transmission equipment, network terminating equipment, line plant, power plant and ancillary equipment, owned or operated by the Buyer.

5.5 In this paragraph, 'lawful user' is as defined in the *Copyright (Computer Programs) Regulations 1992 (SI 1992/3233)*.

Notwithstanding any other Condition, the Supplier grants to the Buyer non-exclusive, royalty free, worldwide rights to any Software supplied under the Contract to the effect that the Buyer has:

(*a*) all the rights of a lawful user of the Software; and

(*b*) the rights to copy, disclose and use for any purpose any Information which:

(i) has been derived by the Buyer from observing, studying or testing the functioning of the Software;

(ii) relates to the ideas and principles which underline any element of the Software; and

(iii) is not subject to the Supplier's (or its licensor's) copyrights in the United Kingdom.

5.6 For the avoidance of doubt, nothing in the Contract shall prevent the Buyer from selling or deploying products, systems and services that are developed by the Buyer using the Software.

6. Faulty Supplies

The Buyer may reject any Supplies that do not accord with the Contract within 45 days of their respective delivery. The Buyer shall not be liable for any fees or charges in relation to such Supplies. The Buyer shall be deemed to have accepted Supplies that are not so rejected.

7. Security

7.1 The Supplier shall ensure that Contract Personnel conform to all security including personal data security, safety and works regulations and such other local instructions, as may be notified by the Buyer whilst on any

Buyer site or customer premises. In addition the Supplier shall comply with the Buyer's UK General Data Protection Regulation (GDPR) data security and related UK GDPR policies in force from time to time.

7.2   The Buyer may remove from and refuse entry and re-admission to a Buyer site or customer premises any person who is, in the reasonable opinion of the Buyer, not conforming to these requirements or not a fit person to be allowed on Buyer premises.

7.3   The Buyer may, at its discretion, search any Contract Personnel or their vehicles, or equipment upon any Buyer site or upon entry to and departure from any Buyer site or customer premises. The Supplier shall use its best endeavours to ensure that Contract Personnel are aware of and comply with these requirements and that no Contract Personnel unwilling to comply will be employed on any Buyer site.

7.4   The Supplier shall (and shall ensure Contract Personnel shall) access only those parts of Buyer sites strictly necessary for the purposes of the Contract.

7.5   The Supplier shall ensure that no Buyer equipment, facilities or materials are used or removed from any Buyer site without the Buyer's written consent and shall immediately notify the Buyer of any known or suspected breach of security in relation to the Contract and give the Buyer full cooperation in any investigation.

7.6   The Supplier shall supply on request details (name, address, date of birth) of any Contract Personnel who might have access to a Buyer site or customer premises under the Contract.

7.7   The Buyer may examine any Information relating to the handling, processing, transportation and storage of information or property of or supplied by the Buyer and held by the Supplier under the Contract, which Information shall be kept by the Supplier for at least one year after the termination or expiry of the Contract.

7.8   The Buyer shall not be responsible for safeguarding any property or money of Contract Personnel.

8. Escrow

8.1   The Supplier warrants that on the first delivery of each item of Software, and on each anniversary of such delivery where there has been any new release of that item during the preceding 12-month period, it shall place with NCC (www.nccgroup.trust/uk/our-services/software-escrow-and-verification/) ('Escrow Agent') in the UK a copy of the relevant source code, listings, programmer's notes and other documentation sufficient to enable the Buyer to maintain or have maintained the Software ('the Escrow Documents').

8.2   If the Supplier fails, or is in the Buyer's reasonable opinion unable or unwilling to maintain the Software, the Supplier shall at the Buyer's request deliver the Escrow Documents to the Buyer and the Buyer shall be entitled to use them for the purpose of maintaining the Software or having it maintained by a third party.

9. Pricing and Payment

9.1 The Contract Price and all other prices payable by the Buyer shall be:

(*a*) as stated in Appendix 2; and

(*b*) inclusive, where relevant, of all non-returnable packing, delivery to Site, any licence fees, installation, testing and commissioning and all other charges associated with Supplies but shall exclude VAT.

9.2 The Buyer shall pay invoices submitted in accordance with this Condition within 45 days from receipt of a valid invoice. An invoice shall not be valid until the Supplies to which it relates have been Accepted.

9.3 When payment becomes due, the Supplier shall forward invoices to: _____.

9.4 Each invoice shall specify: its date; the Contract Number; any order reference (purchase order number and any other required reference number or code required by the Buyer); the full Buyer description of the Supplies to which the invoice relates (as defined in the Contract); the portion of Supplies for which payment is due; and, if appropriate, the cumulative amount invoiced to date.

10. Confidentiality and Data Protection

10.1 Subject to the Condition headed 'Licence', either party receiving Information ('the Recipient') from the other shall not without the other's prior written consent use such Information except for Contract purposes or disclose such Information to any person other than Buyer people or Contract Personnel who have a need to know. The Recipient shall return documentation containing such Information to the other party when no longer required for such purposes.

10.2 Paragraph 1 of this Condition shall not apply to Information that is:

(*a*) published except by a breach of the Contract;

(*b*) lawfully known to the Recipient at the time of disclosure and is not subject to any obligations of confidentiality;

(*c*) lawfully disclosed to the Recipient by a third party without any obligations of confidentiality; or

(*d*) replicated by development independently carried out by or for the Recipient by an employee or other person without access to or knowledge of the Information.

10.3 The Supplier shall ensure that any sub-contractor is bound by similar confidentiality terms to those in this Condition.

10.4 Without prejudice to any prior obligations of confidentiality it may have, the Supplier shall ensure that no publicity relating to the Contract shall take place without the prior written consent of the Buyer.

10.5 The Supplier undertakes fully to comply with all relevant UK and other data protection legislation in force from time to time including without limitation the *Data Protection Act 2018* and UK GDPR in performance of the Contract and if any authorised contractor is used by the Supplier the Supplier shall impose the same requirements on such contractor. The Supplier will notify the Buyer as soon as any data subject access request, data deletion/erasure request or data protection investigation by the UK Information Commissioner or any other regulator is made or takes place which may relate to this Contract or data handled under it in any way.

10.6 The Supplier shall not export any personal data supplied to it by the Buyer outside the UK without the Buyer's prior written consent.

10.7 The Supplier shall not supply to the Buyer any personal data for which it does not have a lawful basis to transfer the data to the Supplier.

10.8 The Supplier will comply with all Buyer's data protection policies and security requirements supplied to the Supplier from time to time.

11. Intellectual Property Indemnity

11.1 The Supplier indemnifies the Buyer against all actions, claims, proceedings, damages, costs, and expenses arising from any actual or alleged infringement of Intellectual Property Rights or breach of confidentiality by the Buyer's possession or use of any of the Supplies anywhere in the world provided such possession or use is in accordance with the rights and licences granted pursuant to the Contract.

11.2 The Buyer shall notify the Supplier in writing of any such allegation received by the Buyer and shall not make any admissions unless the Supplier gives prior written consent.

11.3 At the Supplier's request and expense, the Buyer shall permit the Supplier to conduct all negotiations and litigation relating to Intellectual Property Rights claims brought against Buyer. The Buyer shall give all reasonable assistance and the Supplier shall pay the Buyer's costs and expenses so incurred.

11.4 The Supplier may, at its expense, modify or replace the Supplies to avoid any alleged or actual infringement or breach. The modification or replacement must not affect the performance of the Supplies.

11.5 This indemnity shall not apply to infringements or breaches arising directly from the combination of the Supplies with other items not supplied under the Contract.

12. Force Majeure

12.1 Neither party shall be liable to the other party for any delay in the performance of the Contract directly caused by any event beyond its reasonable control ('the Force Majeure Period') provided such party shall have first given the other party written notice within seven days after becoming aware that such delay was likely to occur.

12.2 If the Supplier is so delayed and the Force Majeure Period exceeds 28 days, the Buyer shall have the option by written notice to the Supplier to terminate the Contract forthwith in whole or in part and have no liability for the whole or part so terminated.

12.3 For the avoidance of doubt, the provisions of this Condition shall not affect the Buyer's right to terminate the Contract under Paragraph 4 of the Condition headed 'Termination'.

13. Termination

13.1 If the Supplier commits a material breach or persistent breaches of the Contract (or any other contract with the Buyer related to the Supplies), and in the case of a breach which is capable of remedy, fails to remedy the breach within seven days (or such longer period as the Buyer may at its option agree in writing) of written notice from the Buyer to do so then the Buyer shall have the right:

(*a*) at any time to terminate the Contract forthwith as a whole or (at the Buyer's option) in respect of any part of the Contract to be performed; and

(*b*) to recover from the Supplier all directly resulting losses and expenses (including, without limitation, the additional cost of completing Supplies, or having Supplies completed by another Supplier, to a similar standard).

13.2 The Buyer shall have the right at any time to terminate the Contract forthwith and to recover from the Supplier all directly resulting losses and expenses (including, without limitation, the additional cost of completing the Supplies, or having the Supplies completed by another Supplier, to a similar standard) if the Supplier shall become insolvent or cease to trade or compound with its creditors; or a bankruptcy petition or order is presented or made against the Supplier; or where the Supplier is a partnership, against any one partner, or if a trustee in sequestration is appointed in respect of the assets of the Supplier or (where applicable) any one partner; or a receiver or an administrative receiver is appointed in respect of any of the Supplier's assets; or a petition for an administration order is presented or such an order is made in relation to the Supplier; or a resolution or petition or order to wind up the Supplier is passed or presented or made or a liquidator is appointed in respect of the Supplier (otherwise than for reconstruction or amalgamation).

13.3 The Buyer may at any time on written notice terminate the Contract forthwith if the ownership or control of the Supplier is materially changed to (in the Buyer's reasonable opinion) the Buyer's detriment.

13.4 The Buyer may at any time on written notice terminate the Contract forthwith. Where the Buyer terminates the Contract under this paragraph 4 and does not have any other right to terminate the Contract, the following shall apply:

   (a)   The Buyer shall, subject to sub-paragraph (b) below, pay the Supplier such amounts as may be necessary to cover its reasonable costs and outstanding and unavoidable commitments (and reasonable profit thereon) necessarily and solely incurred in properly performing the Contract in relation to Applicable Supplies (as defined below) prior to termination.

   (b)   The Buyer shall not pay for any such costs or commitments that the Supplier is able to mitigate and shall only pay costs and commitments that the Buyer has validated to its satisfaction. The Buyer shall not be liable to pay for any Applicable Supplies that, at the date of termination, the Buyer is entitled to reject (including any Supplies for which the Buyer may have issued a Certificate of Commercial Service) or has already rejected. The Buyer's total liability under sub-paragraph (a) above shall not in any circumstances exceed the price that would have been payable by the Buyer for Applicable Supplies if the Contract had not been terminated.

   (c)   In this paragraph 4, 'Applicable Supplies' means Supplies in respect of which the Contract has been terminated under this paragraph, which were ordered by the Buyer under the Contract before the date of termination, and for which payment has not at that date become due from the Buyer.

   (d)   Sub-paragraphs (a) and (b) above encompass the total liability of the Buyer for termination pursuant to this Paragraph 4 and the Buyer shall be liable for no other costs, claims, damages, or expenses consequent upon such termination.

13.5 Each right of the Buyer under this Condition is without prejudice to any other right of the Buyer under this Condition or otherwise.

14. Indemnity

Without prejudice to any other rights or remedies available to the Buyer, the Supplier shall indemnify the Buyer against all loss of or damage to any Buyer property to the extent arising as a result of the negligence or wilful acts or omissions of the Supplier or Contract Personnel in relation to the performance of the Contract; and all claims and proceedings, damages, costs and expenses arising or incurred in respect of:

342

(*a*) death or personal injury of any Contract Personnel in relation to the performance of the Contract, except to the extent caused by the Buyer's negligence;

(*b*) death or personal injury of any other person to the extent arising as a result of the negligence or wilful acts or omissions of the Supplier or Contract Personnel in relation to the performance of the Contract;

(*c*) loss of or damage to any property to the extent arising as a result of the negligence or wilful acts or omissions of the Supplier or Contract Personnel in relation to the performance of the Contract; or

(*d*) under *Part I* of the *Consumer Protection Act 1987* in relation to Supplies.

15. Limitation of Liability

15.1 Subject to Paragraph 3 of this Condition, neither party shall be liable to the other under the Contract for any indirect or consequential loss or damage.

15.2 Subject to Paragraph 3 of this Condition, the total liability of either party to the other under the Contract shall not exceed the greater of either:

(*a*) £_____; or

(*b*) 200% of the total of all sums paid or due to the Supplier for Supplies.

15.3 Paragraphs 1 and 2 of this Condition shall not apply to loss or damage arising out of or in connection with:

(*a*) death or personal injury caused by that party's negligence or for fraud; or

(*b*) the wilful failure of either party to perform its contractual obligations; or

(*c*) paragraph (*d*) of the Condition headed 'Indemnity'; or

(*d*) the Conditions headed 'Intellectual Property' and 'Confidentiality and Data Protection'; or

(*e*) the payment of liquidated damages; or

(*f*) the Buyer's obligation to pay the Contract Price.

16. Insurance

16.1 The Supplier shall at its own expense effect and maintain for the Contract Period such insurances as required by any applicable law and as appropriate in respect of its obligations under the Contract. Such insurances shall include third party liability insurance with an indemnity limit of not less than £_____ for each and every claim.

16.2 If the Supplier cannot provide evidence of such insurance to the Buyer on request, the Buyer may arrange such insurance and recover the cost from the Supplier.

16.3 The Supplier shall notify the Buyer as soon as it is aware of any event occurring in relation to the Contract which may give rise to an obligation to indemnify the Buyer under the Contract, or to a claim under any insurance required by the Contract.

16.4 This Condition shall not be deemed to limit in any way the Supplier's liability under the Contract.

17. Contract Change Procedure

The Contract may only be varied by written agreement between each party's Commercial Contact who shall each respond in writing within ten days of receipt of a proposal for a variation from the other.

18. Notices

Notices required under the Contract to be in writing shall be delivered by hand, post or facsimile transmission to the Commercial Contact of the recipient and shall be deemed to be given upon receipt (except notices sent by facsimile transmission, which shall be deemed to be given upon transmission).

19. Assignment and Sub-contracting

19.1 The Supplier shall not, without the Buyer's written consent, assign or sub-contract the whole or any part of the Contract. Any consent, if given, shall not affect the Supplier's obligations or liabilities under the Contract.

19.2 The Supplier shall allow the Buyer access to its sub-contractors for technical discussions provided that the proposed agenda for such discussions and the outcome shall be promptly notified to the Supplier. The Buyer will notify any changes or proposals identified during such discussions to the Supplier who will process them in accordance with the Contract.

20. General

20.1 The headings to the Contract provisions are for reference only and shall not affect their interpretation.

20.2 (*a*) No delay, neglect or forbearance by either party in enforcing any provision of the Contract shall be deemed to be a waiver or in any way prejudice any rights of that party.

(b)   No waiver by either party shall be effective unless made in writing or constitute a waiver of rights in relation to any subsequent breach of the Contract.

20.3 The Contract governs the relationship between the parties to the exclusion of any other terms and conditions on which any quotation or tender response has been given to the Buyer.

20.4 The Contract is governed by English law and subject to the non-exclusive jurisdiction of the English courts.

20.5 The Supplier shall not be, nor in any way represent itself as, an agent of the Buyer and shall have no authority to enter into any obligation on behalf of the Buyer or to bind the Buyer in any way.

20.6 Except as expressly set out in the Contract:

(a)   no assignment of or licence under any Intellectual Property Right or trade mark or service mark (whether registered or not) is granted by the Contract; and

(b)   no right is conferred on any third party.

20.7 The following provisions of the Contract shall survive its termination or expiry in addition to those provisions relating to intellectual property and those which by their content or nature will so survive:

- Licence;
- Confidentiality;
- Indemnity;
- Intellectual Property Indemnity; and
- Quality of Supplies.

Appendix 1

(PROVISION OF MAINTENANCE SERVICES)

[Editorial Note: It is important to be clear what the support requirements are before contracting. This condition is a suitable standard for many cases. However, where defined customer requirements exist, they should be used instead of the relevant parts of this condition.

The requirements of Condition 3.1 may be replaced by the following in less critical cases:

(a)   The mean time to restore shall not be greater than five hours.

(b)   The mean outstanding time for problems shall not be greater than 20 weeks.

(c)   The mean time to fix shall not be greater than ten weeks.

(d)   [X%] of the problems shall be answered in ten weeks.]

The Supplier shall supply maintenance services for the Software in accordance with the following requirements:

Installation

Maintenance services shall include the installation of the Software and of subsequent releases of the Software by the Supplier on [*Buyer's licensed processors*] at no charge to the Buyer for a period of [X] years from the date of Acceptance of the Software.

Help-Desk

During Monday to Friday 8 am to 6 pm excluding Bank Holidays (hereinafter referred to as 'normal working hours') the Supplier shall provide a Hot-line or Help-Desk service manned by competent staff able to provide technical support and advice for the Software. The Supplier shall provide support outside normal working hours should the Buyer so require on terms and conditions to be agreed.

Meetings/Boards

The Supplier shall provide representatives with appropriate qualifications and decision-making powers to attend regular technical and management review meetings/boards with the Buyer.

The Supplier shall be prepared to undertake the maintenance of the Software for a period of [X] years from the Acceptance date. However, the Buyer shall have the option to have the maintenance undertaken either by itself or by a third party.

The documentation provided with any updates of the Software shall be defined and subject to the Buyer's agreement. As a minimum such documentation shall identify:

- the reason for the update (ie all faults cleared, etc);
- all new features and functions provided along with the invocation instructions;
- any impact upon the reliability of the Software;
- installation instructions for the update; and
- the update's compatibility with previous releases of the hardware and the Software.

The Supplier shall ensure all faults in the Software shall be classified and handled as follows.

Failures shall be classified as to the severity of effect that they have on the working system. The severity classification shall be used to determine the response time for returning the system to its fully operational state. The severity classifications shall be:

Severity Class A

Emergency. Any hardware or Software problem resulting in serious loss or degradation of service or serious loss of functionality.

Severity Class B

Urgent. Any hardware or Software problem that reduces system security or data integrity, or which represents a serious threat to service.

Severity Class C

Non-urgent. Low level hardware, Software or procedural problem requiring resolution in defined time scales.

Severity Class D

Low. Other low level hardware, Software or procedural problem.

The following targets shall be adopted by the Supplier for returning the system to its fully operational state:

Severity Class A – within two hours of receipt of a report from the Buyer.

Severity Class B – within four hours of receipt of a report from the Buyer.

Severity Class C – within five days of receipt of a report from the Buyer.

Severity Class D – by the next Software release.

The Buyer shall determine the severity classification of failures as they arise.

Failures shall also be classified as to the priority that should be given to the permanent rectification of the underlying fault. The criteria for prioritisation shall be agreed with the Buyer and shall include at least:

- the frequency of occurrence of the failures;
- the severity of the failures; and
- the maintenance effort needed to deal with the failures.

The priority classifications shall be:

Priority Class 1 – Very High;

Priority Class 2 – High;

Priority Class 3 – Medium;

Priority Class 4 – Low; and

Priority Class 5 –Very Low.

The priority classification given to failures shall be reviewed from time to time as more information becomes available as to the frequency of occurrence of the failures.

The following targets shall be adopted by the Supplier for providing a tested correction for the fault:

Priority Class 1 – within five days of receipt of a report from the Buyer;

Priority Class 2 – within ten days of receipt of a report from the Buyer;

Priority Class 3 – within one month of receipt of a report from the Buyer;

Priority Class 4 – within two months of receipt of a report from the Buyer; and

Priority Class 5 – by the next Software release.

If the Supplier fails to meet any of the timescales for returning the system to its fully operational state, the buyer may invoke the Escalation Procedure, as set out below:

ESCALATION LEVEL	LEVEL OF SEVERITY		
	Severity A	*Severity B*	*Severity C*
The Supplier's Help Desk Supervisor or Account Representative	Within four hours of the Buyer reporting the problem	Within eight hours of the Buyer reporting the problem	Within ten days of the Buyer reporting the problem
The Supplier's Technical Support Manager	Within six hours of the Buyer reporting the problem	Within 24 hours of the Buyer reporting the problem	Within 21 days of the Buyer reporting the problem
The Supplier's Technical Director/Managing Director	Within eight hours of the Buyer reporting the problem	Within one week of the Buyer reporting the problem	

The Supplier shall use the failure data to calculate the Mean Time Between Failures of Software incidents by severity.

The Supplier shall determine the root cause of each defect in the Software. This is essential for all *Severity A* and *Priority 1* defects. Other defects can be analysed on a sample basis to be agreed with the Buyer.

The Supplier shall record where the Software defects were discovered and where they were introduced and shall use the Information to improve the performance of the Software. The sources of introduction shall at least include:

- specification;
- design;
- coding;
- testing; and
- maintenance.

The Supplier shall classify the type of Software defects reported by the Buyer or the Supplier.

The maintenance service described in this condition shall be provided at no cost to the Buyer by the Supplier for 12 months following Acceptance of the Software. Thereafter the service, if the Buyer should require it, shall be chargeable at £ _____ per annum for a minimum of _____ years.

Appendix 2

(SOFTWARE, LICENCE TYPES AND PRICING)

Appendix 3

(TRAINING)

B4:
Professional Services Agreement – Supplier

At a glance   B4.1

- Drafted by the supplier and favours the supplier – see Chapter B5 for the equivalent buyer contract.

- Used where a supplier provides services, but not goods, to a customer. For sale of goods see Chapter B1.

- Consultancy contracts are rarely 'standard' as the services differ widely – this is an example only.

Commentary   B4.2

- Clause 1 requires that the parties agree in writing in advance the work which will be done. Such document agreeing the work to be done is called a project document here but this title is for convenience only. If there is no project document, clause 1.2 provides that timesheets will be completed. Some projects will be charged on the basis of the time spent on the matter and others on a fixed fee basis.

- Clause 2 addresses payment. It allows the consultant to charge reasonable expenses in addition to the fee. Buyers' contracts such as those in Chapter B3 and Chapter B5 may provide that only limited expenses may be claimed. Clause 2.3 makes reference to the off payroll taxation rules which only apply (from April 2020) to suppliers who are not sole traders and thus to whom taxation rules known as IR35 apply and only where the client is a large- or medium-sized business or a public sector body. The rules require the Buyer to establish in such cases the Consultant's taxation status and to deduct tax at source under PAYE where the Consultant is to be treated as an employee for such purposes. Guidance on these rules is at www.gov.uk/guidance/april-2020-changes-to-off-payroll-working-for-intermediaries.

- Clause 3.3 provides for a liquidated damages payment if the customer terminates the contract early. Any such sum must be a genuine pre-estimate of the supplier's losses in such a case, otherwise the clause will be void under common law as comprising a 'penalty clause'. However, it is sensible to consider including liquidated damages because then the parties know reasonably certainly what sum will be claimed for an early termination.

- Clause 4.5 provides that the supplier will own all copyright and other intellectual property rights in the materials it generates under the contract. The *Copyright, Designs and Patents Act 1988* has the effect that unless there is agreement to the contrary, the author of copyright works such as computer software, web page designs, etc will own the rights (or their employer, if they are employed). Thus consultants retain copyright unless the agreement says so even if the buyer is paying for the work. The buyer simply receives a licence to use the rights. Buyers wanting ownership, therefore, need to reverse this position by a contract term. This chapter is drafted from the supplier's perspective, however, so the supplier retains copyright and it is preferable to state this expressly rather than relying on the default position under the copyright legislation. Where a registered or unregistered design right or database right may be generated then the position was the reverse until October 2014 – the party paying (the commissioner) would own the rights unless the agreement said otherwise. From October 2014, the *Intellectual Property Act 2014* harmonised copyright and designs law in this area. *Section 2* of the Act changed the initial ownership of unregistered designs which have been created on commission from a third party, by amending *s 215* of the *Copyright, Designs and Patents Act 1988*. This change means that, in the absence of a contract to the contrary, the designer (for designs since October 2014) is the initial owner of the design, not the person who commissioned it. This brought UK law into line with the EU regulations in this area. It removed the situation in which a UK right is automatically owned by whoever commissioned the design, and an EU right (which includes the UK in its scope) is instead automatically owned by the designer. It brought UK design law into line with UK copyright law and means that the initial ownership of closely related rights will no longer end up with different parties. In practice, it is best if the contract makes such ownership rights very clear. There will be contracts where no material protected by rights is generated, but it is sensible to have a clause such as this just in case.

- In clause 4.5, the reference to reverse engineering carefully follows the provisions of the *EU Software Directive 2009/24*. This provides that any clause restricting all reverse engineering and decompilation in the EU is void unless that all-important caveat 'except in so far as the law applies' or as in clause 4.5 of the precedent – "Except to the extent expressly permitted under applicable law" or other words to the same effect are included,. Therefore, for EU contracts, do not remove those qualifying words, otherwise the entire attempt to restrict other forms of decompilation will be invalid. The EU right is very limited; it simply allows the licensor to write interoperable programmes subject to certain other limitations.

- Clause 5 provides limited warranties such as that the services will be provided with due care and skill. This should be contrasted with the contract in Chapter B5 – the equivalent buyer's contract for procuring services where much more stringent warranties to the disadvantage of the supplier are proposed.

- This precedent is based on provision of computer consultancy services, hence references to computer software. Other agreements would not need such references nor require clauses relating to ownership of copyright in software, etc.

- Schedules set out the variables of the agreement such as the nature of the work to be done and the fees.

Precedent – Professional Services Agreement – Supplier
B4.3

_____ LIMITED

PROFESSIONAL SERVICES AGREEMENT

Agreement Reference ....
....

BACKGROUND

Supplier has agreed to provide consultancy services to the Customer under the terms and conditions of this Agreement.

1. Consultancy Services

1.1 All professional services provided by the Supplier to the Customer shall be governed by the terms of this Agreement. At the commencement of the services the Supplier may submit to the Customer a statement of work and/or other similar documents describing the services to be provided by the Supplier (such documents being collectively referred to as a 'Project Document') which shall specify the services to be performed and the fees payable. All Project Documents will reference this Agreement by number and be subject to the terms set out herein. The Customer shall notify the Supplier Project Manager immediately if the Customer does not agree with the contents of the Project Document. Upon the completion of the services described on the applicable Project Document, the Customer shall sign and return one copy of the Project Document to the Supplier.

The parties may, from time to time, mutually agree upon and execute new Project Documents. Any changes in the scope of services to be provided hereunder shall be set forth in the Project Document, which shall reflect the changed services, schedule and fees.

Alternatively, for projects not using Project Documents, the Supplier shall submit timesheets to the Customer from time to time. The Customer shall sign such timesheets to indicate its acceptance of the professional services described on such timesheet.

1.2   All daily rates are based on an eight hour day, inclusive of travel time. Any services requested that are in excess of an eight hour day shall be charged at the prorated hourly rate, as applicable. Scheduled service dates shall be mutually agreed upon and subject to availability of the Supplier's personnel or the Supplier's authorised representative. Except as may be otherwise agreed to in writing by the Supplier Project Manager, time shall not be of the essence in the performance of any professional services, but the Supplier shall use all reasonable endeavours to complete services within the estimated time frames.

2. Payment

2.1   The Customer shall pay to the Supplier the fees set forth in the applicable Project Document or as may be otherwise agreed between the parties. The Supplier will invoice the Customer monthly in arrears for services rendered in the previous month and for reasonable out-of-pocket expenses incurred in providing those services. Value Added Tax is due at the VAT rate prevailing at the time of invoice in addition on all fees quoted.

2.2   Invoiced amounts shall be due and payable within thirty (30) days of receipt of invoice. The Customer shall pay interest on overdue amounts at a rate equal to two per cent (2%) above the base lending rate of National Westminster Bank plc as may be set from time to time. In the event that the Customer's procedures require that an invoice be submitted against a purchase order to payment, the Customer shall be responsible for issuing such a purchase order before the services are rendered.

2.3   The Supplier is responsible for its own tax due on any payment hereunder. Where the off payroll taxation rules apply to the Customer and provided the Supplier is not a sole trader in which event such rules will not apply, the Customer shall notify the Supplier of the application of such rules to the Customer and fully co-operate with the Supplier in establishing the Supplier's taxation status in relation to the relevant services.

3. Customer's Obligations

3.1   To enable the Supplier to perform its obligations hereunder the Customer shall:

(*a*)   co-operate with the Supplier;

(*b*)   provide the Supplier promptly with all information and documentation reasonably required by the Supplier;

(*c*)   make computer time and resources available as necessary;

(*d*)   give at its own expense reasonable access to hardware and software;

(*e*)   make appropriate staff available who are familiar with the Customer's computer systems;

(*f*)   provide suitable working space and facilities; and

(*g*)   comply with such other requirements as may be set out in any Project Document or otherwise agreed between the parties.

3.2   The Customer shall be liable to compensate the Supplier for any additional expense incurred by the Supplier through the Customer's failure to follow the Supplier's reasonable instructions, or through the Customer's failure to comply with clause 3.1.

3.3   Notwithstanding the generality of the foregoing, in the event that the Customer unlawfully terminates/cancels the services which have been agreed, the Customer shall be required to pay to the Supplier as agreed damages and not as a penalty the full amount of any third party costs to which the Supplier has committed and in respect of cancellations of less than five working days' written notice the full amount of the services contracted for as set out in the applicable Project Document, without prejudice to the Supplier's other rights. The Customer agrees this is a genuine pre-estimate of the Supplier's losses in such a case. For the purposes of this clause, the Customer's failure to provide the Supplier with adequate manpower or comply with its other obligations under clause 3.1 to enable the Supplier to perform its obligations shall be deemed to be a cancellation of the services and subject to the payment of the damages set out in this clause.

3.4   In the event that the Customer or any other third party, not being a sub-contractor of the Supplier, shall omit or commit anything which prevents or delays the Supplier from undertaking or complying with any of its obligations under this Agreement or any Project Document ('Customer's Default'), then the Supplier shall notify the Customer as soon as possible and:

(*a*)   the Supplier shall have no liability in respect of any delay to the completion of any project resulting from the Customer's Default;

(*b*)   if applicable, the project timetable will be modified accordingly; and

(*c*)   the Supplier shall notify the Customer at the same time if it intends to make any claim for additional documented costs incurred as a result of the Customer's Default and the payment of such costs and expenses shall be subject only to receipt of an itemised statement of expenditure.

3.5   *Change control.* Should either party request any alteration to this Agreement or an agreed Project Document insofar as it relates to services, such requests and any subsequent alterations will be subject to the change control procedures set out in the *Supplier Request for Change* form. Until such time as any alteration is formally agreed between the parties in accordance with such change control procedures, the parties will, unless otherwise agreed, continue as if such alteration had not been requested. The Supplier shall be entitled to make a reasonable charge for investigating a proposed alteration requested by the Customer. An 'alteration' includes any proposed amendment to this Agreement or any Project Document whether in whole or in part. For each such alteration which is agreed by the Supplier and the Customer, this Agreement or any relevant Project Document, as the case may be, shall be amended to the extent necessary to give effect to that alteration.

4. Rights in Material

4.1   The Supplier will specify Materials, if any, to be delivered to the Customer. 'Materials' are defined as being literary works or other works of authorship (such as programs, program listings, programming tools, documentation, reports, drawings and similar works) that the Supplier may deliver to the Customer as part of the consultancy services the Supplier provides.

4.2   The Supplier will deliver one copy of the specified Materials to the Customer. The Supplier grants the Customer a non-exclusive, worldwide licence to use, execute, reproduce, display, perform and distribute, within its company only, a copy of the Materials. The Supplier will, unless otherwise specified on the Schedule, retain ownership of all copyright, patent and other intellectual property rights in the Materials. Such licence shall be on the terms of the Supplier's Software Licence Agreement save as varied by this Agreement and its schedule.

4.3   The Customer shall reproduce the copyright notice and any other legend of ownership on any copies made under the licences granted in this clause.

4.4   Except as may be otherwise agreed by the Supplier in writing, the Supplier shall have no obligation to provide support services for the Materials.

4.5   The Supplier retains all intellectual property rights in all pre-existing Supplier materials used in the Materials supplied to the Customer. The Supplier grants to the Customer a non-exclusive, non-transferable licence to use the same for the Customer's internal use only. The Customer may make one copy of such materials for archival or backup purposes only and shall include all existing copyright and other proprietary notices in such copy. No title to ownership of such materials or any of its parts, nor any applicable intellectual property rights therein such as patents, copyrights and trade secrets, are transferred to the Customer. Except to the extent expressly permitted under applicable law, the Customer shall not reverse engineer, reverse compile or reverse assemble the Materials or any pre-existing materials of the Supplier in whole or in part.

4.6 The Customer shall be responsible for promptly obtaining and providing to the Supplier all Required Consents necessary for the Supplier to access, use and/or modify software, hardware, firmware and other products used by the Customer for which the Supplier shall provide services hereunder. A Required Consent means any consents or approvals required to give the Supplier and its sub-contractors the right or licence to access, use and/or modify (including creating derivative works) the Customer's or a third party's software, hardware, firmware and other products used by the Customer without infringing the ownership or licence rights (including patent and copyright) of the providers or owners of such products.

4.7 The Customer agrees to indemnify, defend and hold the Supplier and its affiliates harmless from and against any and all claims, losses, liabilities and damages (including reasonable attorneys' fees and costs) arising from or in connection with any claims (including patent and copyright infringement) made against the Supplier, alleged to have occurred as a result of the Customer's failure to provide any Required Consents.

4.8 The Supplier shall be relieved of the performance of any obligations that may be affected by the Customer's failure promptly to provide any Required Consents to the Supplier.

4.9 Except as otherwise provided herein, no licence including any licence by implication, estoppel or otherwise, or any intellectual property right including but not limited to patents, copyrights, trade secrets and trademarks is transferred to the Customer.

5. Warranty; Disclaimer of Other Terms

5.1 The Supplier warrants that the services performed under this Agreement will be performed using reasonable skill and care, and of a quality conforming to generally accepted industry standards and practices.

5.2 *Warranties.* Except as expressly stated in this agreement and its schedules and without prejudice to clause 5.1 above, there are no warranties, express or implied, by operation of law or otherwise offered by the Supplier to the Customer in relation to the licensed software or user documentation or services to be provided. The express warranties contained in this agreement and its schedules shall not be expanded, diminished or affected by and no obligation or liability will arise or grow out of the Supplier's rendering of technical, programming or other advice or service in connection with any licensed software and user documentation provided hereunder.

5.3 *Indemnity.* The Supplier will indemnify the Customer against injury (including death) to any persons or loss or damage to any property, which may arise out of the default or negligence of the Supplier, its employees or agents in consequence of the Supplier's obligations under this Agreement and against all claims, demands, proceedings, damages, costs, charges and expenses whatsoever in respect thereof and in relation thereto.

5.4 *Limitation.* Except in respect of injury, including death to a person, due to negligence and fraud for which no limit applies, the Supplier's liability arising out of this Agreement, regardless of the form of the action, whether in contract or tort, will not exceed the fee paid by the Customer in relation to the services or software to which the cause of action relates.

5.5 *Referrals.* The Supplier may direct the Customer to third parties having products or services which may be of interest to the Customer for use in conjunction with the Services. Notwithstanding any Supplier recommendation, referral or introduction, the Customer will independently investigate and test third party products and services and will have sole responsibility for determining suitability for use of such products and services. The Supplier shall have no liability with respect to the Supplier relating to or arising from use of third party products and services.

5.6 *Exclusion of Consequential Loss.* Subject to clause 5.7 in no event shall the Supplier be liable for:

(a) any incidental, indirect, special or consequential damages, including but not limited to loss of use, revenues, profits or savings, even if the Supplier knew or should have known of the possibility of such damages and even if an exclusive remedy fails of its essential purpose;

(b) claims, demands or actions against the Customer by any person; or

(c) loss of or damage to customer's data from any cause.

5.7 *No Exclusion for Death or Personal Injury or Fraud.* Nothing in this Agreement or its schedules shall exclude or limit the Supplier's liability for death or personal injury caused by its negligence, nor for fraud.

6. Indemnification

The Customer shall indemnify and hold the Supplier harmless against any claim brought against the Supplier alleging that any Materials or other products or services provided by the Supplier in accordance with the Customer's specifications infringes a patent, copyright or trade secret or other similar right of a third party.

7. Protection of Proprietary Information

7.1 *Definition.* For purposes of this provision 'Proprietary Information' means any information and data of a confidential nature, including but not limited to proprietary, technical, developmental, marketing, sales, operating, performance, cost, know-how, business and process information, computer programming techniques and all record bearing media containing or disclosing such information and techniques, which is disclosed pursuant to this Agreement.

7.2 *Nondisclosure.* Each party ('Receiving Party') shall hold the other party's ('Originating Party') Proprietary Information in confidence and protect it from disclosure to third parties and shall restrict its use as provided in this Agreement. Each Receiving Party acknowledges that unauthorised disclosure of Proprietary Information may cause substantial economic loss to the Originating Party or its licensors. The Receiving Party shall inform its employees of their obligations under this provision and instruct them so as to ensure such obligations are met.

7.3 *Limitation.* The obligation of non-disclosure shall not apply to information that:

(a) was in the possession of or known by the Receiving Party prior to its receipt from the Originating Party;

(b) is or becomes public knowledge without fault of the Receiving Party;

(c) is provided to the Receiving Party without restriction on disclosure by a third party, who did not violate any confidentiality restriction by such disclosure;

(d) is made available on an unrestricted basis to the Receiving Party by the Originating Party or someone acting under the Originating Party's actual control;

(e) is independently developed by the Receiving Party without reference to the Proprietary Information and without violation of any confidentiality restriction; or

(f) is disclosed by the Receiving Party pursuant to statute, regulation or the order of a court of competent jurisdiction, provided the Receiving Party has previously notified the Originating Party in order to permit the taking of appropriate protective measures.

7.4 *Survival.* This clause 7 shall survive termination of this Agreement.

8. Termination

8.1 *Duration.* This Agreement shall continue unless and until terminated as provided below.

8.2 *Termination for Default.* Without prejudice to other remedies, either party may terminate this Agreement for material breach if, upon written notice, the other party, in the case of a remediable breach, fails to cure the matters set forth in said notice within thirty (30) calendar days from the date of said notice.

8.3 *Termination for Liquidation.* If either party shall convene a meeting of its creditors or if a proposal shall be made for a voluntary arrangement within *Part I* of the *Insolvency Act 1986* or a proposal for any other composition scheme or arrangement with (or assignment for the benefit of) its creditors or if the other party shall be unable to pay its debts within the meaning of *section 123* of the *Insolvency Act 1986* or if a trustee, receiver, administrative receiver or similar officer is appointed in respect of all or any part of the business or assets of the other or if a petition is presented or a meeting is convened for the purpose of considering a resolution or other steps are taken for the winding up of the other or for the making of an administration order (otherwise than for the purpose of an amalgamation or reconstruction) then the other party may terminate this Agreement immediately upon written notice to said party.

The Customer shall pay to the Supplier the fees set forth in the applicable Schedule A to the relevant agreement or as may be otherwise agreed between the parties.

9. General Provisions

9.1 *Publicity.* Neither party shall reveal the terms of this Agreement to any third party without the prior written consent of the other, except to its professional advisers. The Supplier may in publicity materials refer to the Customer as being a customer of the Supplier. This provision shall survive expiration, cancellation or termination of this Agreement.

9.2 *Export.* The Customer shall not, without the prior written consent of the Supplier, export, directly or indirectly, any computer software generated under this Agreement or otherwise licensed by the Supplier to the Customer whether under this or any other agreement between the parties, to any country outside of the United Kingdom. The Customer also shall obtain any and all necessary export licences for any such export or for any disclosure of such software or its documentation to a foreign national where the Supplier has approved such export.

9.3 *Notices.* Any notice required or permitted by this Agreement to either party shall be deemed to have been duly given if in writing and delivered personally or sent by first class post to the party's address first written above, by registered or certified mail, postage prepaid, to the party's address first written above or by facsimile transmission.

9.4 *Assignment.* The Customer shall not assign its rights or obligations or delegate its duties hereunder without the prior written consent of the Supplier. Any attempted assignment or delegation in contravention of this clause shall be void and of no effect.

9.5 *Non-waiver.* The waiver by either party hereto of any default or breach of this Agreement shall not constitute a waiver of any other or subsequent default or breach.

9.6 *Non-Solicitation.* During the term of this Agreement and for a period of twelve months thereafter neither party shall solicit or permit any subsidiary or associated undertaking to solicit the employment of any employee, agent or sub-contractor of the other who is directly involved in the performance of this Agreement. If either party breaches this clause with respect to an employee of the other, the breaching party shall pay to the other party by way of agreed damages and not as a penalty an amount equal to the wages or salary (together with all associated employer costs) paid by the other party in respect of such employee for twelve months preceding the date of the breach. For the solicitation of an agent or sub-contractor of the other, the breaching party shall pay all damages actually incurred by the non-breaching party.

9.7 *Use of Supplier Trademarks.* The Customer shall not use the name, trademark or trade name of the Supplier in any manner without the prior written approval of the Supplier.

9.8 *Independent Contractors.* The Supplier and the Customer are contractors independent of each other, and neither has the authority to bind the other to any third person or act in any way as the representative of the other, unless otherwise expressly agreed to in writing by both parties. The Supplier may, in addition to its own employees, engage sub-contractors to provide all or part of the services being provided to the Customer. The engagement of such sub-contractors by the Supplier shall not relieve the Supplier of its obligations under this Agreement or any applicable Schedule.

9.9 *Data Protection.* The Customer agrees that the Supplier or any Related Company may process personal data (for example contact details) provided by the Customer in connection with this Agreement ('Customer Data') for the purpose of this Agreement and/or for the purposes connected with the Customer's or any Related Company's business relationship with the Supplier. The Customer shall ensure it obtains all similar data protection consents needed from its employees and contractors and others whose personal data it supplies to the Supplier to give effect to this clause or otherwise passes such data to the Supplier on a lawful basis under relevant data protection law from time to time including with limitation the *Data Protection Act 1998* and UK GDPR and hold the Supplier harmless for any loss arising from breach by the Customer of this provision. Such processing may also included transferring Customer Data to other Related Companies worldwide and its storage in a centralised database. The Customer shall comply with all relevant data protection and privacy policies of the Supplier and shall notify the Consultant as soon as any subject access or data deletion request is obtained or Information Commissioner's investigation is begun relating to any data supplied hereunder. For the purposes of this clause, Related Company shall mean any holding company from time to time of the Supplier and/or any subsidiary from time to time of the Supplier or any such holding company (for which purposes the expressions 'holding company' and 'subsidiary' shall have the meanings given in *section 1159* of the *Companies Act 2006*) including for these purposes bodies incorporated outside the UK.

9.10 *Governing Law and Severability.* This Agreement shall be governed by and construed in accordance with the laws of England and the parties submit to the jurisdiction of the English courts. If any provision of this Agreement is held invalid or unenforceable under any applicable law or be so held by applicable court decision, the parties agree that such invalidity or unenforceability shall not affect the validity and enforceability of the remaining provisions of this Agreement and further agree to substitute for the invalid or unenforceable provision a valid or enforceable provision which most closely approximates the intent and economic effect of the invalid provision within the limits of applicable law or applicable court decisions.

9.11 *Force Majeure.* Neither party shall be liable for non-performance or delays from causes beyond its reasonable control including, but not limited to, strikes (of its own or other employees), fires, insurrection or riots, embargoes, container shortages, wrecks or delays in transportation, inability to obtain supplies and raw materials, or requirements or regulations of any civil or military authority. In the event of the occurrence of any of the foregoing, the date of performance shall be deferred for a period equal to the time lost by reason of the delay. The affected party shall notify the other in writing of such events or circumstances promptly upon their occurrence.

9.12 *Entire Agreement.* This Agreement and its schedules set forth the entire agreement and understanding between the parties as to the subject matter hereof and merges all prior discussions between them, save that a confidentiality or non-disclosure agreement between the parties shall continue. Neither of the parties shall be bound by any conditions, definitions, warranties, understandings or representations with respect to such subject matter other than as expressly provided herein or as duly set forth on or subsequent to the date of acceptance hereof in writing and signed by an authorised representative of the party to be bound thereby.

9.13 *No Third Party Rights.* Nothing in this Agreement is intended to, nor shall it, confer any right on a third party whether under the *Contracts (Rights of Third Parties) Act 1999* or otherwise.

Professional Services Agreement Reference

Schedule A

COMPANY NAME:

ADDRESS:

REGISTERED OFFICE ADDRESS:

DESCRIPTION OF SERVICES:

LOCATION WHERE SERVICES
ARE TO BE RENDERED: ....

CONSULTANCY RATES (EXCLUDING EXPENSES):

Title	Daily Rate	No of Days	Total Fee (excl VAT)

The above quoted prices remain valid provided the customer calls of the services by DD/MM/YYYY.

Signatures

We indicate by our signatures that we accept the terms and conditions of this agreement.

Signed by _____ Signed by _____

Name: _____ Name: _____

Title: _____ Title: _____

Date: _____ Date: _____

For and on behalf of _____ For and on behalf of Customer
Limited

B5:
Professional Services
Agreement – Buyer

At a glance   B5.1

- Drafted from the perspective of a buyer buying services from a service provider/consultant.

- For provision of services by supplier please refer to Chapter B4.

- Includes strong protection for the buyer.

- For purchase of goods use Chapter B2 and for licensing of software use Chapter B3.

Commentary   B5.2

- These conditions are to be used by buyers, not suppliers. They are drafted from the perspective of the buyer. For conditions for suppliers use Chapter B4.

- The agreement sets up a structure under which individual purchase orders can be placed for the ordering of services which in each case would reference this contract.

- Under clause 3.2(d) the agreement says the Deliverables will meet the Specification. It is important, therefore, that the buyer does ensure an adequate specification is drawn up which reflects its needs and requirements. It is not acceptable for this to be drawn up at a later date as then it becomes an 'agreement to agree' on which the parties may never reach agreement and thus an unacceptable uncertainty.

- Some buyers have problems with suppliers constantly changing the personnel assigned to undertake the services. Clause 4 is designed to provide protection in this respect.

- Clause 5 sets out provisions as regards the fees for the services. Under clause 5.6 the fees are fixed once the initial agreement has been reached under the relevant purchase order. However, the parties could agree to vary any of these provisions by agreement in writing and document the differences from the standard contract on the purchase order concerned. The clause also addresses situations where from April 2020 where the off payroll taxation rules apply. These rules apply to the private sector from April 2020 to suppliers who are not sole traders and thus to whom taxation rules known as IR35 apply and only where the client (the Buyer here) is a large- or medium-sized business or a public sector body. The rules require the Buyer to establish in such cases the Company's taxation status and to deduct tax at source under PAYE where the Company supplying the services is to be treated as an employee for such purposes. Guidance on these rules is at www.gov.uk/guidance/april-2020-changes-to-off-payroll-working-for-intermediaries.

- Clause 7 includes acceptance tests/criteria. There may be some services where this is not appropriate, such as provisions for training. However, if there are any deliverables such as computer software, website designs, drawings, etc then the buyer will want a chance to check the deliverables before they are accepted. Suppliers offering acceptance testing normally give themselves a right to submit the work for retesting if the tests are failed. Buyers will usually want, as in this precedent, a 'cut off point' after which the deliverables can be rejected and the contract terminated and monies refunded. Often payment of a final tranche of monies due is payable on final acceptance.

- Clause 10 provides that intellectual property rights in the materials/deliverables will be owned by the buyer when they are created. Some suppliers will want to retain such ownership and only give a licence. Others will only want ownership to pass on payment. In other services contracts no intellectual property protected items will result.

- Attachment 2 is a change control attachment. Procedures the parties use to ensure all alterations to the requirements of what is to be produced can be documented.

- Attachment 3 is an individual confidentiality undertaking. This can be useful to emphasise to individual users the very confidential nature of the information provided.

- Attachment 5 is an expenses policy which some buyers are able to impose on their suppliers, depending on the parties' respective negotiating position.

Precedent – Professional Services Agreement – Buyer

B5.3

THIS SERVICES AGREEMENT is made on _____
(the 'Commencement Date')

BETWEEN:

ABC LIMITED a company incorporated in England and Wales (registered no _____), and whose registered office is at _____ ('the Buyer'); and

[   ] a company incorporated in England and Wales (registered no _____) and whose registered office is at _____ ('the Company').

1. DEFINITIONS

In this Agreement the following words will have the following meanings:

- **'Acceptance Certificate'** means a document signed by an authorised representative of the Buyer confirming that the Acceptance Criteria have been met.

- **'Acceptance Criteria'** means the evaluation and/or tests defined in the Work Package that the Deliverables must pass in order for the Services to be deemed as completed.

- **'Agreement'** means these terms and conditions comprising preamble, attachments and clauses 0 to 20 together with the terms of any applicable Purchase Order.

- **'Business Day'** means a day other than a Saturday, Sunday or Bank Holiday in the United Kingdom.

- **'Company Material'** means documents, notes, information, software, know-how, or other like material owned or licensed by the Company prior to the commencement of this Agreement, or obtained (whether created, purchased or licensed) by the Company separately from and otherwise than in connection with the Services.

- **'Company Personnel'** means any employee or contractor supplied by the Company to provide the Services.

- **'Confidential Information'** means any information that is marked as or is manifestly confidential and is disclosed (whether before or after the date of this Agreement, in writing, verbally or otherwise and whether directly or indirectly) by or on behalf of the Disclosing Party to the Receiving Party in connection with the Services.

- **'Deliverables'** means the items described in a Work Package or as otherwise agreed by the parties in writing from time to time to be delivered by the Company as part of the Services.

- **'Disclosing Party'** means the party to this Agreement disclosing the Confidential Information.

- **'Expenses'** means costs and expense incurred in the provision of the Services, which have been agreed in advance by the Buyer and conform to the Expenses policy as detailed in Attachment 5.

- **'Fees'** means the charges, expenses and fees, as set out in a Work Package and agreed in a Purchase Order, payable by the Buyer for the performance of the Services.

- **'Force Majeure'** means any of the following events and the effects thereof if and only to the extent that such event is not caused by, and the effects are beyond the reasonable control of, the affected party including: war or civil war (whether declared or undeclared) or armed conflict, invasion and acts of foreign enemies, blockades and embargoes; acts of Government or local authority or regulatory body; civil unrest, commotion or rebellion; any act, or credible threat, of terrorism; lightning, earthquake or extraordinary storm or weather conditions; nuclear, chemical or biological contamination; explosion, fire or flooding; non-availability of power; general strikes or other industrial action of general application.

- **'Buyer Group Company'** means a subsidiary of the Buyer or a holding company of the Buyer, or another subsidiary of a holding company of the Buyer.

- **'Intellectual Property Rights'** means all patents, topography rights, design rights, trade marks, copyrights, rights in databases and computer data, generic rights and all other intellectual property rights of a similar nature in any part of the world and all applications and rights to apply for the protection of any of the foregoing.

- **'Key Personnel'** means the personnel supplied by the Company and listed in the Work Package who will contribute to the provision of the Services.

- **'Project Plan'** means a plan listing the specific Deliverables and acceptance tests and the dates when both parties have agreed they are due to start and for completion.

- **'Purchase Order'** means the standard Buyer document which refers to the Work Package and provides a unique reference number and maximum value payable by the Buyer to the Company, which will be concluded in accordance with clause 0.

- **'Receiving Party'** means the party to this Agreement to whom the Confidential Information is disclosed.

- **'Services'** means the services specified in any Work Package and confirmed in a Purchase Order including but not limited to Work and Deliverables.

- **'Specification'** means the detailed statements and documents setting out the functionality and requirements of each component of the Deliverables as detailed or referred to in a Work Package or Purchase Order.

- **'Term'** means the duration of this Agreement as specified in clause 2.

- **'Variation'** means any change or variation to this Agreement or any Work Package that is agreed pursuant to the change control procedure set out in Attachment 2.

- **'Work'** means any Deliverable, idea, method, invention, discovery, design, business process or method, communication, analysis, drawing, composition, database, writing, computer software, computer data or any other similar item (in any media) which is produced by the Company and/ or the Company Personnel in connection with performing the Services.

- **'Work Package'** means the standard form of work package set out in Attachment 1 agreed by the Company and the Buyer prior to the commencement of the Services being supplied to the Buyer. A Work Package shall not be valid unless referenced by Purchase Order and signed by an authorised representative of each party.

2. STRUCTURE AND TERM

2.1 This Agreement will govern the provision of Services by the Company pursuant to one or more Purchase Orders.

2.2 If the parties agree that the Company will provide specific Services, then such Services will be documented in the standard form of Work Package. The Work Package will, at a minimum, set out the following information:

(*a*) Buyer contact person.

(*b*) Services to be performed including, but not limited to, a description and Specification of the Deliverables and a Project Plan.

(*c*) The Company's Fees for the Services and method of calculation (eg hourly, daily or otherwise).

(*d*) Names of Key Personnel performing the Services.

2.3 The Work Package will be deemed to have been agreed by the Buyer only after a Purchase Order has been issued and the Work Package has been signed by the relevant authorised Buyer representatives.

2.4 Unless the parties expressly amend the terms of this Agreement in a Work Package in relation to the subject matter of the Work Package, to the extent there is any conflict between this Agreement and a Work Package, the terms of this Agreement shall prevail. The parties agree, however, that the terms of this Agreement and a Work Package shall always prevail over the terms of any Purchase Order except that no Fees identified in a Work Package shall be due to the Company unless a Purchase Order to the value of the Fees has been issued by the Buyer.

2.5 The term of this Agreement will commence on the Commencement Date and, unless terminated earlier pursuant to clause 6, shall continue in force for an initial term of 12 months and thereafter until terminated by notice pursuant to clause 6.

3. COMPANY WARRANTIES AND OBLIGATIONS

3.1 In consideration of the Fees, the Company agrees to carry out the Services and provide the Deliverables in accordance with the terms of this Agreement.

3.2 The Company warrants, represents and undertakes that:

(*a*) it will provide the Services promptly and with all due skill, care and diligence, in a good and workmanlike manner and otherwise in line with best practice within its industry ('Best Industry Practice');

(*b*) the Company Personnel will possess the qualifications, professional competence and experience to carry out such services in accordance with Best Industry Practice. For the avoidance of doubt, the Company shall be responsible for any training of the Company Personnel that may be required to enable the Company Personnel to perform the Services, and the Buyer shall not be liable for any charges, fees or expenses in relation to any such training;

(*c*) the Services will not in any manner or way infringe or violate any Intellectual Property Rights, trade secrets, or rights in proprietary information, nor any contractual, employment or property rights, duties of non–disclosure or other rights of any third parties;

(*d*) the Deliverables shall upon delivery conform in all material respects to the Specification, be fit for purpose and of satisfactory quality;

(*e*) upon termination of this Agreement, any Work Package or Purchase Order, the Company shall afford all reasonable assistance to any incoming supplier and where requested promptly provide them with all necessary documentation and assistance to ascertain the status of the Deliverables and the Work required to complete them in accordance with the Specification and the Project Plan; and

(*f*) it has full capacity and authority to enter into this Agreement and that it has or will obtain prior to the Commencement Date, any necessary licences, consents, and permits required of it for the performance of the Services.

3.3 The Buyer engages the Company to provide the Services and the Company agrees to provide the Services in accordance with this Agreement.

3.4 The Company will procure that where required, the Company Personnel will provide the Services at such places and between such hours as set out in the Work Package.

3.5 The Company will provide the Buyer with such progress reports, evidence or information concerning the Services as may be requested by the Buyer from time to time.

3.6 The Company will be responsible for maintaining such insurance policies in connection with the provision of the Services as may be appropriate or as the Buyer may require from time to time.

3.7 The Company will procure that the Company Personnel take all reasonable steps to safeguard their own safety and the safety of any other person who may be affected by their actions, and the Company agrees to indemnify and keep indemnified the Buyer from all and any liabilities, obligations, costs and expenses whatsoever arising from any loss, damage, or injury caused to the Buyer or any third party by the Company Personnel in this regard.

3.8 The Company will procure that the Company Personnel co-operate with the Buyer's employees, officers and agents and comply with the instructions of the Buyer in providing the Services, including without limitation, any applicable internal Buyer policies notified to the Company or the Company's Personnel.

3.9 The Company will be responsible for implementing any required disciplinary action with respect to any of the Company Personnel.

4. COMPANY PERSONNEL

4.1 Where required and documented in the Work Package, identified parts of the Services shall be performed by the Key Personnel.

4.2 The Company shall make no change to such Key Personnel without the prior approval of the Buyer which shall not be unreasonably withheld or delayed. If the Buyer approves of or requires a change to the Company Personnel in accordance with this Agreement, the Company shall submit to the Buyer the names and full *curricula vitae* of any proposed substitute and shall permit the Buyer to interview any proposed substitute. The Buyer may in its absolute discretion refuse to accept any proposed substitute, in which case the Company shall as soon as reasonably possible submit to the Buyer further names and full *curricula vitae* of proposed substitutes until a substitute is accepted.

4.3 The Buyer may, in its sole discretion, require termination of the involvement of any Company Personnel performing the Services ('Individual') by providing written notice to the Company with immediate effect. The Company will provide a suitable replacement for such an Individual without delay in accordance with the process set out in clause 4.2.

4.4 To the extent that the Work Package requires Company Personnel to be dedicated to the provision of the Services on a full-time basis, the Company will procure that such Company Personnel are fully dedicated to performing the Services and do not work for third parties other than the Buyer until the Work Package is complete.

4.5 Neither party shall, during the term of this Agreement and for a period of six (6) months after the termination howsoever caused, directly or indirectly solicit or entice away or endeavour to solicit or entice away from the other party any employee of the other party who has been engaged in the provision of Services for the performance of this

Agreement. Nothing in this Agreement is intended to prevent any person from seeking employment by responding from to a *bona fide* recruitment advertisement placed by (or on behalf of) the new employer.

4.6   Neither party will be liable to the other for any charges or fees, whether transfer fees or otherwise, where a person takes up any employment having responded to a *bona fide* recruitment advertisement.

4.7   If any Company Personnel are unable due to illness or other incapacity or for any other reason to supply the Services on any day on which the Company is required to provide the Services, the Company will notify or will procure that the relevant Company Personnel will notify the Buyer as soon as practicable.

4.8   The Buyer will be under no obligation to pay the Company in respect of any periods during which any Company Personnel are unable to carry out the Services due to illness or other incapacity in the event that the fees have been calculated on a time and materials basis.

4.9   If applicable, timesheets for hours or time worked by the Company Personnel will be submitted weekly to the person designated in the Purchase Order as the Buyer contact for approval. All such timesheets will be submitted by the Company with the relevant invoice.

4.10 The Company will procure that Company Personnel performing the Services will not provide any services that are the same as or similar to the Services to any direct or indirect competitor of the Buyer during the period beginning on the Commencement Date and ending on the date which is six (6) months after the latest expiration date of any Purchase Order or Work Package relating to Services with which such Company Personnel have been involved.

4.11 During the period beginning on the Commencement Date and ending on the date which is six (6) months after the latest expiration date of any Purchase Order or Work Package, the Company shall not attempt to discourage any person, firm or company or any supplier who is at the date of cessation or has at any time during the continuance of this Agreement been a client, customer or supplier of the Buyer from dealing with the Buyer.

4.12 The Company warrants that the Key Personnel have a right to work in the jurisdiction in which they will provide the Services, that no bribes or secret commissions have been paid in relation to this Agreement or by or involving such Key Personnel, that such Key Personnel have written contracts which provide at least as much protection as this agreement including without limitation in relation to confidentiality, non-competition, intellectual property, liability and data protection and that no Services nor any part of the relevant supply chain has involved nay breach of the UK's *Modern Slavery Act 2015* and that all Key Personnel are paid at least as much as the UK's National Minimum Wage.

5. FEES AND PAYMENT TERMS

5.1 The Fees and Expenses for the Services will be as specified in the Work Package provided that such Fees and Expenses are agreed and set out in the applicable Purchase Order. If such Fees are not set out in a Work Package then the Fees and Expenses set out in Attachment 4 and Attachment 5 will apply and the Buyer's then current expenses policy (as the same is notified to the Company from time to time) will apply.

5.2 VAT (where applicable) will be payable by the Buyer in addition to the Fees subject to presentation to the Buyer by the Company of a valid VAT invoice. The Buyer agrees to settle correctly presented, valid and undisputed VAT invoices at the end of the month following the month in which the invoice is received.

5.3 The Company will invoice the Buyer monthly in arrears or as otherwise specified in accordance with the Purchase Order, as per the Buyer's standard terms of payment.

5.4 The Buyer will not be responsible for any expenses, charges or fees other than the Fees and Expenses set out in the Purchase Order.

5.5 If the parties agree that the Company is to provide services or resources in addition to those specified in a Purchase Order, then such agreement will be reflected in a further Purchase Order, which on execution will be deemed incorporated into this Agreement.

5.6 Once a Work Package has been agreed by the Buyer the Fees for the Services will be fixed.

5.7 The Company is responsible for its own tax due on any payment hereunder. Where the off payroll taxation rules apply to the Buyer and provided the Company is not a sole trader in which event such rules will not apply, the Company shall provide all details required by the Buyer to prove its tax status under such rules and any other tax legislation which is relevant to this Agreement and the Company shall accept deduction of tax and national insurance contributions at source by the Buyer where such tax rules require it; in which event payment after deduction of such tax and national insurance shall be full payment hereunder..

6. TERMINATION

6.1 The Buyer may terminate this Agreement, a Purchase Order or any Work Package for any reason by providing at least 15 days prior written notice to the Company at any time.

6.2 The Buyer may terminate this Agreement, a Purchase Order or any Work Package with immediate effect by providing written notice to the Company if:

(a) the Company becomes insolvent, has a receiver or manager appointed, commits an act of bankruptcy or commences to be wound up (except for amalgamation or reconstruction);

(b) the Company or the Company Personnel commit any material or persistent breaches of this Agreement;

(c) the Company unreasonably fails or refuses after written warning to procure that the Company Personnel provide the Services properly required of them in accordance with this Agreement;

(d) the Company or the Company Personnel acts or omits to act in a manner calculated or likely to bring the Buyer or any Group Company into disrepute;

(e) the Company fails to meet any Acceptance Criteria on three consecutive occasions; or

(f) the Company or the Company Personnel fails to comply with any applicable internal Buyer policies.

6.3 Upon termination of this Agreement or any Purchase Order or Work Package for whatever reason, the Company will deliver, and procure that the Company deliver, to the Buyer's offices or such other location as the Buyer may direct:

(a) all Work whether complete or partially complete;

(b) all books, documents, papers, materials, equipment, customer lists, technical information and data, reports; and

(c) any other property (including copies, summaries and excerpts) in whatever form or medium relating to the business of the Buyer or any Group Company,

which are in the possession or control of the Company or the Company Personnel at the time of termination.

7. ACCEPTANCE

7.1 The Services will be deemed to have been accepted by the Buyer when the Acceptance Criteria specified in a Work Package have been met and an Acceptance Certificate has been issued. Where no Acceptance Criteria are specified in a Work Package, the Services will be deemed accepted 180 days after delivery of the Deliverables to the Buyer, provided the Buyer has raised no earlier objections, issues or concerns regarding the Services.

7.2 Subject to any alternative acceptance procedure agreed in a Work Package, where a Deliverable is rejected under clause 7.1, the Company shall have two opportunities to resubmit the non-performing Deliverable but should it continue to fail to perform to the Buyer's satisfaction, the Buyer shall have the right to reject that Deliverable and recover any Fees associated with the same that it has paid to the Company and no further Fees shall be due to the Company.

8. STATUS AND LIABILITIES

8.1 Neither the Company nor any Company Personnel will have authority to act as agent for the Buyer or to contract on the Buyer's behalf.

8.2 The Company Personnel will at no time be deemed to be employed, or otherwise engaged by the Buyer and the Company will comply with all the Buyer's requests in relation to establishment of tax status under off pay roll rules where applicable as provided under clause 5.7 above..

8.3 The Company will be responsible for paying the Company Personnel and for making any deductions required by law in respect of income tax and National Insurance contributions or similar contributions relating to the provision of the Services. The Company agrees to indemnify the Buyer and any Buyer Group Companies in respect of any claims that may be made by the relevant authorities against the Buyer or any Buyer Group Companies in respect of tax demands or National Insurance or similar contributions relating to the provision of the Services by the Company.

8.4 The Company will, and will procure that the Company Personnel will, comply with all applicable laws, statutes, rules, orders and regulations in providing the Services, including all immigration and employment requirements imposed by any applicable jurisdiction, and the Company will indemnify and hold harmless the Buyer or any Buyer Group Companies from damages arising out of any failure to do so.

9. CONFIDENTIALITY AND DATA PROTECTION

9.1 Each party undertakes to keep the other party's Confidential Information confidential and to use the other party's Confidential Information solely for purposes related to this Agreement.

9.2 The Receiving Party will not disclose, copy, reproduce or distribute the Disclosing Party's Confidential Information to any person, except:

(a) with the prior written consent of the Disclosing Party;

(b) to its employees, professional advisors, consultants and authorised representatives (including to such persons representing its group undertakings), but only to the extent that disclosure is necessary for the purposes related to this Agreement; or

(c) where disclosure is required by law, by a court of competent jurisdiction, by the rules of any stock exchange or by another appropriate regulatory body, provided that all reasonable steps to prevent such disclosure will be taken, the disclosure will be of the minimum amount required, and the Receiving Party consults the Disclosing Party first on the proposed form, timing, nature and purpose of the disclosure.

9.3   The obligations under clauses 9.1 and 9.2 will not apply to Confidential Information:

> (*a*)   to the extent it is or becomes generally available to the public other than through a breach of this Agreement;
>
> (*b*)   which the Receiving Party can show by its written or other records was in its lawful possession prior to receipt from the Disclosing Party and which had not previously been obtained from the Disclosing Party or another person under an obligation of confidence; or
>
> (*c*)   which subsequently comes into the possession of the Receiving Party from a third party who does not owe the Disclosing Party an obligation of confidence in relation to it.

9.4   The Company will procure that all Company Personnel execute the form deed of confidentiality undertaking attached hereto as Attachment 3 prior to commencing any Services.

9.5   The Company shall comply with all data protection policies supplied to it by the Buyer from time to time and shall notify the Buyer as soon as it receives a data protection subject access or data deletion request or notice of an investigation by the Information Commissioner in all cases where relevant to this Agreement. The Company shall comply with the Buyer's data retention policies notified to the Company from time to time and in any event shall retain all personal data and other data and information relevant to this Agreement for a period of at least six years after this Agreement ends. Where this Agreement will involve data processing by the Company for the Buyer the Company shall enter into all data processing contracts and documentation required by the Buyer. The Company shall comply with the *Data Protection Act 2018* and UK GDPR and other relevant data protection legislation relating to this Agreement at all times. Where any data security breach occurs at the Company it shall forthwith notify the Buyer. The Buyer shall have a right of audit of the security systems of the Company from time to time on notice to check compliance with this clause 9.5 and such referenced data policies. The Company shall not export or hold or send any personal data supplied to it by the Buyer outside the UK without the Buyer's prior consent. The Company shall not supply any personal data to the Buyer unless it has a lawful basis to supply it to the Buyer.

9.6   This clause 9 shall apply without limit as to time.

10. INTELLECTUAL PROPERTY

10.1 Subject to the exceptions in clauses 10.2 and 10.3 below, the Company agrees and will procure that the Company Personnel agree that Intellectual Property Rights in the Work will vest in the Buyer on its creation and the Company hereby assigns, and agrees to procure that the Company Personnel will assign, to the Buyer with full title guarantee (by way of present and future assignment) such rights throughout the world for as long as such rights shall last. The Company further agrees to procure that the Company Personnel will agree to do such acts and sign such documents as will be necessary to give effect to the matters contemplated by this clause 10.

10.2 Clause 10.1 will not apply if and to the extent:

(*a*) the Intellectual Property Rights belong to a third party other than the Company Personnel; or

(*b*) prior to this Agreement, such copyright formed part of any Company Material.

10.3 The Company retains all Intellectual Property Rights, whether owned or licensed, in Company Material, provided that where any Company Material is delivered as part of the Services the Company hereby grant to the Buyer or any Buyer Group Company a worldwide, non-exclusive, perpetual, irrevocable, royalty free licence to use or modify Company Material unless and to the extent that a licence in respect of some or all of the Company Material concerned is granted subject to a separate agreement between the parties.

10.4 The Company hereby waives and agrees to procure that the Company Personnel waive all moral rights the Company or the Company Personnel has or may have under the *Copyright, Designs and Patents Act 1988* or otherwise in all Works.

10.5 The Company undertakes to defend the Buyer and all Buyer Group Companies from and against any claim or action that the use or possession of any Deliverable infringes the Intellectual Property Rights of a third party ('IPR Claim') and shall fully indemnify and hold the Buyer and all Buyer Group Companies harmless from and against any losses, damages, costs (including legal fees) and expenses incurred by the Buyer and/ or any Buyer Group Company or awarded by a court of competent jurisdiction against the Buyer and/or any Buyer Group Company as a result of or in connection with such an IPR Claim. The Company shall be promptly informed by the Buyer or the relevant Buyer Group Company in writing and furnished with a copy of each communication, notice or other action relating to the alleged infringement, and the Buyer or the relevant Buyer Group Company shall provide the Company with all reasonable authority, information and reasonable assistance (at the Company's expense) necessary for the Company to defend or settle such an IPR Claim provided always that in doing so the Company shall not take any step which the Buyer or a Buyer Group Company reasonably believes to be detrimental to its commercial interests.

10.6 The foregoing indemnity shall remain in effect notwithstanding any termination of this Agreement.

10.7 If any IPR Claim is made, or in either party's reasonable opinion is likely to be made, against the Buyer or any Buyer Group Company, the Company shall, with minimal disruption to the Buyer and the Buyer Group Companies, at its option, promptly and at its own expense either:

(*a*) procure for the Buyer and the Buyer Group Companies the right to continue using and possessing the Work; or

(*b*) modify or replace the infringing part of the Work (without prejudice to the representations and warranties made as to such Work and without diminishing or curtailing any of the required Specification, functions, facilities or the performance of the Services) so as to avoid the infringement or alleged infringement.

10.8 In the event that the Buyer or any Buyer Group Companies are not reasonably satisfied with any modification or replacement Work provided by the Company pursuant to this clause 10, the Buyer may terminate this Agreement and, without prejudice to its other rights and remedies, receive a refund of all sums paid under the Agreement to the Company.

10.9 The Company's indemnity obligations hereunder shall not apply to the extent that the infringement arises out of any modification of the Work made by anyone other than the Company or the Company Personnel or the combination, operation or use of the Work with other computer software if such infringement was directly caused by such combination, operation or use of the Work with other computer software.

11. OTHER AGREEMENTS

This Agreement, together with any Work Package or Purchase Order(s) executed in accordance with clause 2, will supersede all other agreements or discussions whether written or oral between the Buyer and the Company and comprise the entire agreement between the parties with respect to the subject matters described herein.

12. VARIATIONS

No changes or variations to this Agreement or any Work Package shall be effective unless agreed in writing pursuant to the change control procedure set out in Attachment 2.

13. PUBLICITY

The Company shall not disclose in its publicity material or otherwise the existence of this Agreement or the terms of its relationship with the Buyer without the prior written consent of the Buyer.

14. ASSIGNMENT

The Company will not sub-contract or assign its obligations hereunder to any third party without the Buyer's prior written consent.

15. WAIVER

The failure of either party to enforce or to exercise any term of this Agreement does not constitute a waiver of such term and will in no way affect that party's right later to enforce or to exercise it.

16. THIRD PARTY RIGHTS

A person not party to this Agreement shall have no rights under the *Contracts (Rights of Third Parties) Act 1999* to enforce its terms.

17. FORCE MAJEURE

If either party is prevented or delayed in the performance of any of its obligations under this Agreement by Force Majeure that party shall forthwith serve notice in writing on the other party specifying the nature and extent of the circumstances giving rise to Force Majeure, and shall, subject to service of such notice, have no liability in respect of the performance of such of its obligations as are prevented by Force Majeure during the continuation of the events, and for such time after they cease as is necessary for that party, using all reasonable endeavours, to recommence its affected operations in order for it to perform its obligations.

18. SEVERABILITY

In the event that any provision of this Agreement or any part of any provision shall be determined to be partially void or unenforceable by any court or body of competent jurisdiction or by virtue of any legislation to which it is subject or by virtue of any other reason whatsoever, it shall be void or unenforceable to that extent only and no further, and the validity and enforceability of any of the other provisions or the remainder of any such provision shall not be affected thereby.

19. NOTICES

19.1 Any notice or other communication to be given under this Agreement shall be in writing and signed by or on behalf of the Party giving it and may be served by leaving it or sending it by fax, delivering it by hand or sending it by first class post to the address and for the attention of the relevant Party set out in clause 19.2 (or as otherwise notified from time to time under this Agreement). Any notice so served by hand, fax or post shall be deemed to have been received:

- in the case of delivery by hand, when delivered;
- in the case of fax twelve (12) hours after the time of confirmation of despatch;

- in the case of post, at the expiration of two (2) Business Days or (in the case of air mail) five (5) Business Days after the envelope containing the same was delivered into the custody of the postal authorities;

provided that where, in the case of delivery by hand or by fax, such delivery or transmission occurs after 6pm on a Business Day or on a day which is not a Business Day, service shall be deemed to occur at 9am on the next following Business Day.

19.2 The addressees of the parties for the purpose of Clause 19.1 are as follows:

Party: _____

Buyer: _____

Address: _____

_____

Fax No: _____

Attention Of: _____

Party: _____

Buyer: _____

Address: _____

_____

Fax No: _____

Attention Of: _____

20. APPLICABLE LAW

This Agreement will be construed in accordance with the laws of England and Wales and the parties agree to submit to the exclusive jurisdiction of the Courts of England and Wales.

EXCECUTED by the parties on the date first above written:

SIGNED by for and on behalf of   _____

[BUYER] Limited

Print Name: _____

Date: _____

SIGNED by for and on behalf of   _____

[SUPPLIER] Limited

Print Name: _____

Date: _____

Attachment 1
Standard Work Package

(SPECIMEN WORK PACKAGE)

PROJECT NUMBER/DESCRIPTION/PRIMAVERA ID:

This Work Package is issued in accordance with the Professional Services Agreement ('the Agreement') between [XXXXXX] Limited ('the Company') and [XXXXXX] Limited ('the Buyer') executed on [COMMENCEMENT DATE] and is subject to the terms and conditions contained therein.

PART 1. STATEMENT OF WORK

Description of Services: _____

_____

_____

_____

Deliverables:

The Deliverables under this
Work Package are: _____

_____

_____

The Deliverables will
be produced in the
following formats.

1. Documentation: _____

2. Project Reports: _____

3. Prototypes: _____

4. Project Definition: _____

Additional Buyer Requirements:

Overview and Aim of   _____
the Project:

Specific Project Objectives: _____

Start Date: _____

End Date: _____

Fee (Fixed Fee/Rates)

(if different from the   _____
agreement):

PART 2. PROJECT PLAN

Delivery Dates: _____

_____

_____

_____

Other Key Milestones: _____

_____

_____

_____

Company: Key Personnel:

_____

_____

Key Contact:

_____

Project Manager:

_____

Buyer's Personnel: Key Contact:

_____

Delivery Manager:

_____

Project Sponsor:

_____

PART 3. ADDITIONAL/SPECIAL TERMS (IF ANY)

Note: Intellectual Property (the parties should specify here if any or all intellectual property rights are to vest in the Company).

For the purposes of this Work Package, the following provisions shall take precedence over the provisions of the Agreement:

- Clause [ ] shall be amended as follows:

_____

_____

_____

_____

- Clause [ ] shall be amended as follows:

_____

_____

_____

_____

Payment Terms (if different from the Agreement)

_____

_____

_____

_____

Confidentiality Requirements (over and above those contained within the Agreement)

1. _____
2. _____
3. _____

Acceptance Testing (if applicable)

Name (and date) of party who is to prepare the schedule of acceptance criteria:

_____

Name (and date) of party who is to prepare the schedule of acceptance
test procedures:

_____

Period(s) allowed for agreeing/rejecting acceptance criteria and acceptance
test procedures:

_____

Name (and date) of party responsible for preparing acceptance test data:

_____

Period allowed for acceptance testing (using acceptance test data):

_____

Acceptance Criteria

_____

_____

Additional Resources (if applicable)

_____

_____

**Signed for and on behalf of
the Buyer:**

Signature: _____

Name: _____

Title: _____

Date: _____

**Signed for and on behalf of
the Company:**

Signature: _____

Name: _____

Title: _____

Date: _____

Acceptance Certificate

I hereby acknowledge the services described in this Work Package have been delivered to the Buyer and the Acceptance Criteria have been met.

_____   _____

Signature   Date

For and on behalf of the Buyer

Attachment 2
Change Control Procedure

1. INITIATION OF CHANGE CONTROL PROCEDURE

1.1 The Buyer and the Company shall discuss Variations proposed by either party and such discussion shall result in either a written request for a Variation by the Buyer; or a written recommendation for a Variation by the Company.

1.2 Where a written request for a Variation is received from the Buyer, the Company shall, unless otherwise agreed, submit a Change Control Note ('CCN') to the Buyer within five (5) Business Days.

1.3 A written recommendation for a change by the Company shall be submitted as a CCN direct to the Buyer at the time of such recommendation.

1.4 Each CCN shall conform to the pro-forma set out below.

PRO-FORMA CCN

Title of the Variation
Originator and the date of request or recommendation for the Variation:
Reason for the Variation:
Impact analysis indicating the impact of the Variation on the following:
(a)   the Services, Company Software, Buyer Environment and other aspects of the Work;
(b)   the Project Plan;
(c)   the Charges;
(d)   the contractual documentation; and
(e)   staff resources.

| Full details of the Variation including any Specifications and user facilities: |
| Price, if any, of the Variation: |
| Timetable for implementation together with any proposals for Acceptance of the Variation: |
| Schedule of the cost of the Variation: |
| Date of expiry of validity of the CCN (which shall not be less than [xx] working days): |
| Provision for signature by the Buyer and the Company: |

2. APPROVAL OR DISAPPROVAL OF CCN

For each CCN submitted the Buyer shall, within the period of validity of the CCN:

(*a*)   allocate a sequential number to the CCN;

(*b*)   evaluate the CCN and as appropriate either:

    (i)   request further information;

    (ii)   approve the CCN; or

    (iii)   notify the Company of the rejection of the CCN.

If approved, two copies of the approved CCN will be signed by or on behalf of the Buyer and the Company. The signing of the CCN will signify acceptance of the Variation by both the Buyer and the Company.

Attachment 3

Form Deed of Confidentiality Undertaking

Name of Address

_____

_____

_____

_____

RE: CONFIDENTIALITY UNDERTAKING – SERVICES AGREEMENT BETWEEN [XXXXXX] AND THE BUYER

Dear Sir or Madam:

1. In connection with the Services Agreement executed by _____ Limited ('the Buyer'), and [XXXXXX] ('the Company'), I acknowledge that the Buyer may make available certain of its confidential information, for the purpose of my performing the functions described in that agreement ('the Purpose'). This letter relates to information that the Buyer or any of its group undertakings (including each of their respective officers, employees, advisers, agents and representatives) may supply in connection with the Purpose ('the Information').

2. In consideration of the disclosure of the Information to me, I agree and undertake to:

    (a) use the Information solely to the extent necessary for the Purpose;

    (b) take all reasonable steps necessary to prevent unauthorised publication or disclosure of the Information; and

    (c) hold the Information in strict confidence and not disclose, copy, reproduce or distribute any Information to any person, other than as permitted by the Buyer, or to those of the Buyer's employees who need access strictly for the Purpose, and on the basis that they themselves will not disclose, copy, reproduce or distribute it to any person who is not so authorised (together, the 'Authorised Recipients').

3. The above undertakings will not apply to Information which:

    (a) at the time of supply is in the public domain;

    (b) subsequently comes into the public domain, except through breach of the undertakings set out in this letter;

    (c) is already in my lawful possession or that of an Authorised Recipient (as evidenced by written records);

    (d) subsequently comes lawfully into my possession or that of an Authorised Recipient from a third party who does not owe the Buyer an obligation of confidence in relation to it; or

    (e) is required to be disclosed by law, regulation, the rules of any stock exchange or any governmental or competent regulatory authority, as long as I consult with the Buyer first on the proposed form, timing, nature and purpose of the disclosure.

4. On request, I agree to destroy or return to the Buyer any documents or other materials (including any note, analysis, memorandum or other

material that I prepare) containing Information and any copy which may have been made, and take reasonable steps to expunge all Information from any computer, word processor or other device containing Information.

5.   I understand that no right or licence is granted to me in relation to the Information except as expressly set out in this letter, and the Buyer will retain all rights, title and interest to its Information.

6.   I acknowledge and agree that the undertakings set out in this letter will survive completion of the Purpose.

7.   I acknowledge and agree that if I breach this letter in any manner the Buyer will be entitled to terminate either my provision of the Services or the Services Agreement immediately, at the Buyer's sole discretion.

8.   If any provision of this letter is held to be invalid or unenforceable, that provision will (so far as it is invalid or unenforceable) be given no effect and will be deemed not to be included in this letter, but without invalidating any of the remaining provisions.

9.   I confirm that I am acting in this matter as principal and not as an agent or broker for any other person.

10.   I agree that this letter and the relationship between the parties will be governed by, and construed in accordance with, English law, and each party submits to the exclusive jurisdiction of the English courts.

This letter will take effect as a deed

Yours faithfully,

_____

Print Name: _____

Date _____

Agreed and accepted and signed and delivered as a deed

_____

_____ Limited

Print Name: _____

Date _____

Signed in the presence of Witness

Signature of witness _____

Full Name of witness _____

Occupation of witness _____

Attachment 4
(Non) Work Package Rates

XXXXXX Rate Chart for Buyer	
Rate	£

All Prices GBP exclusive of VAT

Attachment 5
Expenses

The aim of this document is to explain what expenses are allowed and how to claim.

The basic guidelines are simple:

- All Expenses must be 'wholly, exclusively and necessarily' incurred in the proper performance of the provision of the Services related to Buyer.

- All Expenses incurred must be reasonable, and substantiated with written receipts.

- All Expenses must be planned in a Forecast by the Company and submitted to the Buyer in advance with each Forecast for Consultancy, and the Company shall ensure such Forecast Expenses are approved by the Buyer Project Manager and are covered by a Purchase Order, otherwise the Buyer will not be obliged to reimburse the Company for such expenses.

ALLOWABLE EXPENSES:

Note: Basis

No handling charge – all expenses charged at cost. All receipts to be provided. In the isolated case of an unreceipted expense claim, full supporting detail must be provided as to the cause of the claim, or reimbursement may be delayed or withheld. Entertainment and time used whilst travelling are non–chargeable.

2.5 *B5: Professional Services Agreement – Buyer*

Exceptions to Basis

- Company car mileage shall be charged at ___ p per mile, for mileage incurred whilst engaged on execution of the Services (unreceipted expense).

- Overnight accommodation with breakfast: max £__ per night.

- Subsistence (refreshments/meals/out-of-pocket expenses): max £__ per day.

- Taxi/bus/air fares charged at cost; rail fares charged at cost for standard class travel.

- Venue costs (room hire, equipment hire, food, etc) in the implementation of the programmes – chargeable at cost.

B6:
Terms and Conditions for Sale of Goods by Export – Supplier

At a glance   B6.1

- Drafted from point of view of supplier.

- For terms and conditions of a purchaser who imports, please refer to Chapter B7.

- Ensures it is clear which of the Incoterms 2010 are used – FOB, Ex works, DDP, DDU, etc can all be used (see Chapter A3 for further information).

Commentary   B6.2

- These conditions are a short and simple set to apply where a supplier sells goods for export. Where the supplies will be to another UK customer then modifications need to be made (eg reference to Incoterms 2010 would not then be appropriate). In such a case, Chapter B1 could be used instead. These are terms for sale of goods. They are not a distribution agreement for formal appointment of a local distributor to buy and then resell goods for a stated territory and period. Usually such distribution agreements incorporate sale terms such as these by reference or attach them at the back of the contract so the supplier can regularly update its terms of sale without changing the underlying distribution agreement. Instead, these terms are for one-off sales rather than appointment of a dealer or distributor.

- Export control legislation needs to be considered, particularly if sensitive technology or goods which can be used in the arms industry are involved, or if the sale is to a territory where exports can cause problems, such as Yemen, North Korea, Vietnam, Cuba or Syria. If the export from the United Kingdom of particular goods or technology is subject to control, then those goods or technology may not legally be exported without a licence. The export of other types of goods and certain activities are subject to control as well as a result, for instance, of the imposition of European Community or United Nations trade sanctions or arms embargoes against particular countries or regions.

- Licences to export arms and other goods controlled for strategic reasons are issued by the Department for Business, Energy and Industrial Strategy (BEIS). The Export Control Joint Unit (ECJU) administers the UK's system of export controls and licensing for military and dual-use items. ECJU is part of the Department for International Trade. Licences are approved on the advice of the Foreign and Commonwealth Office, the Ministry of Defence and, where sustainable development issues are involved, the Department for International Development. See www. gov.uk/business-and-industry/export-controls. There are many UK, EU and US laws imposing Iranian and other sanctions, which were in part ameliorated in 2014. HM Treasury summarises these well at: www. gov.uk/government/collections/financial-sanctions-regime-specific-consolidated-lists-and-releases.

- Trade Controls were introduced by the *Export Control Act 2002* which made the trading (often called trafficking and brokering) of goods from one overseas destination to another a licensable activity. The Government licenses the transfer of military goods, which fall into this trafficking and brokering category, between one overseas destination to another. If there are more than two countries involved in any transaction, including the export of goods from the UK, exporters should note that a licence may still be needed to move goods between all the countries concerned. Exporters should also remember that just because they have been granted a UK Trade Licence this does not remove the requirement for them to obtain permission of the authorities of the appropriate countries to remove or receive goods from or to that territory as necessary. Many UK contracts are subject to US export controls as the goods originated there. For export control legislation after the UK leaves the EU see the UK Guidance at www.gov.uk/guidance/exporting-controlled-goods-after-eu-exit.

- Where the Customer intends to re-export the goods from the UK after purchase consideration should be given to the *Intellectual Property (Exhaustion of Rights) (EU Exit) Regulations 2019 (SI 2019/265)* after the UK's departure from the EU as such export may be prohibited by the EU/EEA states where the Goods are protected by intellectual property rights which previously would have been 'exhausted' (incapable of being asserted) but after such departure may not be so.

- Clause 2 provides that payment is by letter of credit. Often letters of credit are rejected by the bank because of an error on the documentation. This clause requires the customer to pay any such bank charges which then arise, which can be considerable.

- Under clause 4, time for delivery is not of the essence, because these conditions are drafted for the benefit of the supplier.

- Clause 5 deals with when ownership of the goods sold will pass, and risk. These issues may be implied by the Incoterm used so the clause states that the default provisions in the agreement apply unless otherwise required by the Incoterm under which the parties have agreed the goods will be supplied.

• The terms state that English law applies and that the parties submit to the non-exclusive jurisdiction of the English courts in connection with any dispute.

Precedent – Terms and Conditions for Sale of Goods by Export
B6.3

ABC LIMITED

[ADDRESS]

[TEL]

[E-MAIL]

TERMS AND CONDITIONS OF SALE

1. TERMS

These terms and conditions apply to all supplies of goods by the Supplier to Customers. They prevail over any terms supplied by the Customer. No prior statements or correspondence forms part of this Agreement and the Customer accepts it has not relied on any representations in entering into this Agreement.

In these terms:

(a) 'Supplier' means ABC Limited of [address].

(b) 'Bespoke Goods' means Goods or parts of Goods specifically made or customised for the Customer.

(c) 'Customer' means the customer buying the Goods who is named on the Order.

(d) 'Goods' means the products to be sold by the Supplier to the Customer named on the Order.

(e) 'Order' means the Customer's purchase order for the Goods or, if none, described in the confirmation of order of Supplier or otherwise agreed in writing by the parties.

(f) 'Price' means the charge to be paid by the Customer to the Supplier for the Goods.

2. SUPPLY AND PAYMENT

The Supplier sells the Goods to the Customer on the terms of this Agreement in consideration of the payment by the Customer of the Price. Payment for the Products shall be in UK pounds sterling and shall be made by confirmed, transferable, irrevocable without recourse letter of credit providing for payment at sight allowing partial deliveries and collections and issued by a reputable first class bank acceptable to the Supplier. The Customer shall also pay any handling and shipping or other incidental costs and expenses the Supplier has incurred or will incur in relation to the Goods. Prices are exclusive of VAT or other sales taxes which are payable in addition by the Customer and are to be paid in full without deduction of taxes, charges or duties imposed. The parties shall collaborate to take advantage of any double taxation treaties in force. Where there is an error on the letter or credit, or for whatever reason the Supplier's bank rejects the letter or credit, the Customer shall pay all the bank charges and other costs of the Supplier in relation to such error and ensure that a correct letter of credit is issued forthwith. The Supplier shall not offer any credit to the Customer. The Distributor shall not pledge the credit of the Supplier. The Customer shall open each letter of credit within seven (7) days after the Customer's receipt of the Supplier's acceptance of the Order and it shall remain open for at least 30 days or such longer period as may be agreed by the parties in relation to individual letters of credit. The terms of the letter of credit may be specified by the Supplier from time to time and payment for Goods shall be made in full without deduction, set off or counterclaim. For payment of the Price as to time and amount, time shall be of the essence.

The Price includes packaging charges. Delivery charges shall be paid where so specified in clause 3 below. The Price shall remain fixed for the Order unless otherwise agreed in writing by the parties. Where credit has been agreed in writing between the parties, all invoices shall be paid by the Customer within 30 days of the date of invoice. No right of set off shall arise. The Supplier may charge interest at 3% above base rate from time to time of National Westminster Bank plc on all late payments of invoices. Once an Order is placed the Customer may not cancel or alter such Order without the prior written consent of the Supplier.

3. DELIVERY CHARGES

Delivery charges shall, where supply is specified on the Order as on the basis that the Supplier shall deliver to the Customer, be stated on the Order and are payable by the Customer. Supply shall be on the Incoterm 2020 specified on the Order – DDP, CIF, Ex works, etc.

4. DELIVERY

The Supplier shall deliver the Goods to the address specified on the Order, unless otherwise agreed in writing. Time for delivery specified on the Order, if any, is an estimate only and time shall not be of the essence. Where a carrier delivers Goods which the Customer believes are not the quantity or kind ordered or which are damaged, the Customer must notify the Supplier by telephone immediately on receipt and confirm this in writing within seven (7) days of delivery otherwise the Supplier accepts no liability for this. Where on investigation the Supplier agrees the incorrect quantity was delivered or the Goods were damaged, the Supplier shall ensure the correct quantity is supplied and the Customer will return any over supply and/or the Supplier shall replace the damaged Goods with undamaged Goods and this shall be the Customer's only remedy in such a case. The Customer shall return any damaged Goods at its own expense to the Supplier. Where the Supplier, after inspection, agrees the Goods were damaged it shall refund to the Customer the carriage costs of such return, but not otherwise.

5. PASSING OF TITLE

Title to the Goods shall pass to the Customer unless otherwise required by the Incoterm under which the parties have agreed the Goods will be supplied, or, if no such agreement exists, when payment is made to the Supplier for those Goods. Until payment is made the Customer shall not resell the Goods or combine them with other Goods and shall ensure they are kept separately from other goods and are clearly marked as the Supplier's property. The Supplier may, until such time as payment is made, enter the Customer's premises to retrieve its Goods. Risk in the Goods shall pass on delivery unless otherwise required by the Incoterm under which the parties have agreed the Goods will be supplied.

6. INTELLECTUAL PROPERTY RIGHTS AND SERVICES

The Supplier owns all copyright, design and registered design rights, trade mark and other intellectual property rights in the Goods and in Bespoke Goods. The Customer shall not register any intellectual property right or claim any such right in the Goods or the Bespoke Goods and shall keep any rights notice of the Supplier's on the Goods or Bespoke Goods and notify the Supplier if it discovers any infringement of the Supplier's such rights by a third party. In particular, the Customer acknowledges that it has no right or licence by virtue of having purchased the Goods or Bespoke Goods or otherwise itself to manufacture the Goods or Bespoke Goods. It shall ensure its employees, agents, customers and contractors are aware of the Supplier's such intellectual property rights. Where the Customer requests specific modifications or additions the Customer shall ensure the Supplier is given all information it requires to make such modifications and the Customer shall fully indemnify the Supplier against any loss or liability arising from the Supplier following the Customer's instructions and/or performing such services or making Bespoke Goods. Any manufacturing data, product or other confidential or commercial information supplied by the Supplier to the Customer, whether marked as confidential or not, shall be held in strict confidence by the Customer and only used for the purposes for which it was supplied.

7. LIABILITY

The Supplier shall use all reasonable endeavours to ensure:

(i)   the Goods comply with their description on the Order; and

(ii)   are of satisfactory quality and/or fit for their purpose; and

(iii) are delivered to the Customer.

Where the Supplier fails to use such reasonable endeavours, the Customer shall notify the Supplier within seven (7) days of delivery in writing and the Supplier's sole obligation shall be to repair, replace or supply the Goods. Save as provided in this clause, the Supplier's liability to the Customer is otherwise excluded, including, without limitation, implied conditions to the fullest extent permitted by law. The Supplier limits its liability to the Price of the Goods in relation to any claim relating to Goods supplied and excludes all liability for consequential, indirect loss, loss of profit revenue and goodwill. The Supplier shall not be liable for any delay or failure caused by circumstances beyond its reasonable control, including, without limitation, liability arising from failures by sub-contractors, manufacturers, terrorist activity, Government action or Acts of God. However, nothing in these terms shall exclude the Supplier's liability for death and personal injury caused by its negligence. Where a Customer's modification to the Goods or combination of the Goods with other Goods or other Customer action, including without limitation, installation, results in a loss to, or liability of, the Supplier, the Customer shall fully indemnify and hold harmless the Supplier against all such loss and liability.

8. STANDARDS

It is the responsibility of the Customer to ensure that the Goods comply with any safety or other standard and for the product or market in which the Goods will be used or resold or used and that the Goods will not infringe the intellectual property rights of any person in the market in which the Customer intends to sell the Goods. Whilst the Supplier shall use its reasonable endeavours to assist Customers, where further information in this respect is required, the Supplier reserves the right to levy a charge, which will be estimated to the Customer in advance, for any significant research or investigations required to satisfy the Customer's detailed enquiries in relation to such matters, and does not accept liability for statements made in providing such assistance. The Customer shall fully indemnify and hold the Supplier harmless against all loss and liability, including legal fees on an indemnity basis, arising from claims by the Customer's customer arising from non-compliance of the Goods with any local law or intellectual property right. The Customer shall ensure it fully complies with all relevant data protection legislation and will only process any personal data supplier to it by the Supplier in accordance with such legislation and the data protection policies of the Supplier as supplied by the Supplier to the Customer from time to time.

9. GENERAL

This Agreement is subject to English law and the Supplier and the Customer agree to submit to the non-exclusive jurisdiction of the English courts in relation to any dispute. Notices shall be served on the Supplier at the address above and the Customer at the address on the Order. The failure to enforce a right under this Agreement shall not amount to a waiver of it by the Supplier. Where any provision of this Agreement is held to be void, the other provisions of this Agreement shall continue notwithstanding to apply.

B7:
Terms and Conditions for Purchase of Goods and Services by Import – Buyer

At a glance

- These terms are for use by a buyer, not a supplier.

- They are to be used where a UK buyer is buying goods or services from abroad by way of import.

- These terms are not suitable for suppliers to use when selling goods or services.

Commentary

- These terms and conditions are prepared from the standpoint of the buyer of the goods, not the supplier. They therefore include provisions favourable to buyers such as ensuring goods are of good quality and can be rejected if unsuitable. The terms can also be used where services are used. As with the last set, they are not a long-term distribution agreement which would be a different contract. They are the terms instead for a one-off sale or purchase of goods. It is vital they are seen by the other party before the contract is made and any other party's terms are rejected, otherwise they may well not apply as they are not signed by both parties. They should be sent to the other party as often as possible and included with and on the buyer's purchase order in addition to being sent when the parties start their discussions. Any acknowledgement of the order from the seller referring to seller terms instead should be rejected.

- The terms are designed where goods are imported from abroad and thus in particular address issues of foreign imports, intellectual property including trade mark issues, and other related areas of law. As Incoterms are referenced provisions relating to customs, duties are therefore incorporated by reference. However, if regulatory changes arising from the UK's departure from the EU affect the Goods or Services concerned, or may do, the Buyer may wish to include further detail on those issues. In addition, if the import is from the EU/EEA and could be affected by the EU exhaustion of rights rules, legal advice should be sought as to the impact of such rules following the UK's departure from the EU. Reference should be made to the *Intellectual Property (Exhaustion of Rights) (EU Exit) Regulations 2019 (SI 2019/ 265)* where the goods being imported are protected by intellectual property rights.

- They are not to be used where goods are sold, rather than purchased. Sellers will have terms which favour them which should be used instead.

- Clause 13 provides that the buyer will own the intellectual property rights in any customised work undertaken. If this is not provided then by default under English law most rights will remain with the supplier, even though the buyer is paying.

Precedent – Terms and Conditions for Purchase of Goods and Services (Import)

B7.3

_____ LIMITED

[ADDRESS]

[TEL]

[EMAIL]

Terms and Conditions of Purchase of Goods and Services – Import

1. CONDITIONS

These Conditions shall apply to all orders for the purchase of goods and services by us from our suppliers and sub-contractors from outside the UK. Any qualification of these Conditions by you or any other Conditions which you seek to impose will be inapplicable unless expressly accepted in writing, signed by us. We agree to buy the goods or services specified on the order from you on the terms set out below. Only written orders on our official purchase order form and signed by an authorised person are valid. Reference must be made to our purchase order number in all correspondence, invoices and delivery notes enclosed with the goods. Failure to include such a delivery note may result in our incurring additional costs, which you shall pay. If further documentation is required this will be stated on the order or on annexed delivery instructions.

2. ORDER NUMBER

Any delivery against this order must be accompanied by an advice and/or packing note quoting the order number. If your invoice does not quote our order number payment will be subject to delay.

3. DEFINITIONS

(a)   'Goods' means machinery, apparatus, materials, instruments, articles, parts and things of all kinds to be provided or work to be done under the order.

(b)   'Services' means the services you will perform for us described on our purchase order.

(c)   'We' means _____ Limited of _____,
Tel _____ Email _____.

(d)   'You' means the supplier of goods or services or our sub-contractor whose name and address appears on our purchase order.

4. IDENTIFICATION

All goods supplied against our drawings must be marked with our drawing number except where such a number cannot physically be incorporated. Packages containing goods supplied against our drawings, part numbers or catalogues must be marked with the appropriate reference.

5. PRICES

Prices shall remain firm as quoted by you for the whole of this order and shall not be subject to variation unless we agree in writing and unless we also have been given 28 days' notice of such proposed variation. If we do not accept the variation we shall be entitled to cancel the whole or any part of the order, at our discretion, without prejudice to our other rights and remedies. Any deposit or sum paid by us in advance shall immediately be repaid by you. Any VAT shall be deemed included in the price except where specified separately on the order. VAT shall be stated separately on the invoice.

6. INVOICES

Invoices which do not refer to our purchase order number will be rejected. All invoices must be received by the fourth of the month following the date of despatch of the Goods or performance of the Services, otherwise payment will be delayed. All statements of account shall be rendered by you to us by the ninth of each month. Unless otherwise agreed invoices are due for payment 60 days from the date of invoice where the terms of this agreement in relation to this invoice are met. We reserve the right to charge interest at 3% above National Westminster Bank plc base rate from time to time on all sums overdue hereunder.

The price shall be deemed to include all materials, expenses and costs except where expressly stated on the purchase order.

Payment shall be in UK pounds sterling unless otherwise stated on the purchase order and shall be made by the payment means specified on the purchase order, or, where not so specified, by letter of credit. Prices are exclusive of VAT or other sales taxes which are payable in addition by us. You agree to collaborate to take advantage of any double taxation treaties in force.

7. PACKING MATERIAL

Packing cases, skids, drums and other packaging are to be supplied free of charge by you to us. Empty packaging where relevant will be returned at your expense upon request to you by us, but we can accept no liability for their return in safe condition. Returnable containers must be stencilled with your name and address together with an addressed reversible label.

The type of packing material shall be such as will adequately protect the Goods in transit for storage at our premises or those of our customer. You will mark the goods in accordance with our instructions. Such instructions shall not obviate the need for you to mark the Goods according to their nature such as 'Fragile'.

8. DELIVERY

Unless otherwise specified on the purchase order, you shall deliver the Goods to us or provide Services to us at the address on the purchase order. Title to, and risk in the Goods shall pass on delivery. Where terms on the order such as FOB, Ex works, etc are used these shall be construed in accordance with Incoterms 2020. The Goods and/or Services must be delivered or provided not later than the delivery date on the purchase order or otherwise agreed in writing by us or where delivery is to be by instalments not later than the agreed date. Time shall be of the essence. Where additional goods or work are delivered or modifications are made you shall not be entitled to extra time for delivery except where agreed in writing with us in advance. You shall only be entitled to payment for the quantity of goods specified on the purchase order which comply with these terms and the purchase order.

We shall be under no obligation to accept delivery of Goods or provision of Services before the agreed date. Should we agree to accept early delivery we shall be entitled to withhold payment in respect of such deliveries until the agreed date. We shall be entitled to reject all the Goods or Services if any part is not delivered by the agreed date or any agreed extension of such date. The time for delivery shall be extended by a reasonable period if delay in delivery is caused by industrial dispute or by circumstances beyond your control, provided that you have notified us immediately on becoming aware of the likelihood of any such delay and we agree such extension and provided, where relevant, our own customer accepts an extension. The delays of your approved sub-contractors or suppliers shall not be treated as a cause beyond your reasonable control. Any failure by you to make delivery occasioned otherwise than by *force majeure*, entitles us to damages in addition to or by way of alternative to compensation. If due to industrial dispute or circumstances beyond our control we are unable to accept delivery on the agreed date you will arrange for storage and the reasonable cost of such storage shall be borne by us. No responsibility can be accepted by us for Goods received damaged. In such cases you will be notified and required at our option to credit or exchange the Goods.

9. INSPECTION

The Goods will be subject to inspection by us and/or our customer after delivery and any rejected Goods may be returned to you at your expense. We shall also examine Services provided. We will advise you of any rejects and you will be given reasonable opportunity to advise disposition. We reserve the right to inspect at your works any material or equipment the subject of the order at any stage in the process of manufacture.

10. DEFECTS AFTER DELIVERY AND WARRANTY

All Goods and Services supplied by you to us shall be of first class material and workmanship throughout and in accordance with the contract, the description on the purchase order, their specification, if any, and otherwise as represented to us by you. You will only use new parts, not second hand or reconditioned parts, unless agreed by us. You shall use materials in providing the Goods or Services, such as paint, which comply with our requirements set out on the purchase order, specification or other document. All Goods shall be of reasonable commercial quality and you shall be responsible for ensuring they are fit for their intended use where stated or where such use is clear. You shall comply with any contractual requirements of our customer set out on our purchase order and shall indemnify us for any loss suffered by us arising from any breach of these terms, including, without limitation, where such breach causes us to breach our contract with a customer. All Services shall be provided with reasonable skill and care by competent staff. You will make good by repair, or at our option by the supply of a replacement, defects which under proper use appear in the Goods and Services within a period of 36 months after supply and/or installation at the ultimate location where the Goods will be used or such alternative period as may be specified on the purchase order, without prejudice to our other rights and remedies. The repaired or new Goods or Services will be delivered by you free of charge as provided in Clause 8 above. You shall hold product liability insurance relevant to damages caused by default in the quality of the Goods or Services.

Work under this agreement may not be sub-contracted without our prior written consent. Where we agree to sub-contracting it shall be sub-contracted on the same terms as this agreement, in particular, but without limitation, in relation to ownership of intellectual property rights and quality and you shall ensure your sub-contractors contract on such terms.

Any international standards to which the goods must comply shall be stated on the purchase order and shall be the latest such standards.

11. REJECTIONS AND TESTING

We shall be entitled to reject any Goods or Services not in accordance with the contract within a reasonable time after they have been received. All such rejected Goods or Services must be replaced and the Goods or Services shall not be deemed to have been delivered until such rejected goods are replaced. No payment shall be made for any rejected Goods or Services. If you are unable to replace rejected Goods or Services within a reasonable time after being notified of their rejection we shall be entitled to cancel the order in respect of the rejected Goods or Services and obtain equivalent goods or services elsewhere and any extra expense to which we may be put shall be paid for by you, without prejudice to our other rights and remedies.

Where formal acceptance tests are to be undertaken by us or our customer or quality audits undertaken by such customer or us, these shall be specified on the purchase order. You shall provide us with test certificates indicating the character, scope and results of the tests performed. Where we or our customer require(s) a test to be carried out in our joint presence this shall be at a venue and on a date which is convenient to us or our customer at your expense. You shall provide all equipment and tools necessary for such tests. We shall be entitled to check all equipment used in such tests. In addition to tests specified in the order we are entitled to check the Goods otherwise comply with the contract. Where Goods fail a test they shall be retested only where we agree. We will not normally demand a retest for slight defects. The passing of an acceptance test does not remove any right for us to claim any breach of contract or warranty under this agreement.

Our signature of your delivery note shall, notwithstanding any notice on such note, not comprise acceptance of the Goods or Services nor an acknowledgement that they comply with the contract.

12. INTELLECTUAL PROPERTY RIGHTS INDEMNITY

You warrant that the Goods do not infringe any third party intellectual property right. You will indemnify us against any claim of infringement of patent, registered design, design right, trade mark, copyright, database right or any other intellectual property right by the use or sale of the Goods/any article or material supplied by you to us and against all costs and damages, including legal fees, which we may incur in any action or threatened action for such infringement or for which we may become liable in any such action, provided always that this indemnity shall not apply to any infringement which is due to your having followed a design or instruction furnished or given by us or to the use of such article or material in a manner or for a purpose or in a foreign country not specified by us or disclosed to you, or to any infringement which is due to the use of such article or material in association or combination with any other article or material not supplied or approved by you. We will give you immediate notice of any such claim and permit you to defend the same and to conduct any litigation that may ensue and all negotiations for a settlement of the claim.

13. OWNERSHIP OF INTELLECTUAL PROPERTY RIGHTS AND TOOLS, CONFIDENTIALITY AND DATA PROTECTION

We shall own all intellectual property rights in tools, gauges, dies, jigs, fixtures, patterns of drawings, computer software, plans, diagrams or other materials specially made by you for us ('Tools') for the purposes of this order automatically on their creation. You waive all moral rights therein. You shall not register any rights in such Tools and shall not use them except for the purposes of performance of your obligations under this agreement. Where you have incurred costs in purchase of physical materials or parts for such Tools and the purchase order does not specify that we obtain ownership of the physical property in the Tools as part of the price, we shall own such physical property where we pay you its written-down value as appearing in your accounts at the date we exercise such right. You will give us credit for any payment made for Tools towards the original cost of purchase or manufacture.

Where we supply Tools of the kind specified above, including without limitation, patterns, measuring devices and packaging, to you so you can perform the contract, they remain our property and should be returned to us immediately on request and only used for the purposes of the contract. We shall supply a list of such Tools to you. You shall store our Tools separately from your property and name them as our property. We shall have a right of entry to your premises to recover them. You shall maintain, insure and store them at your expense and to our required standards. You will not modify, move or alter them without our consent. You will inform us when they cease to produce acceptable products or when additional Tools, models, etc are required.

Where samples are to be produced you shall send them to us free of charge as soon as possible or by the date on the order, if any. We shall examine them and notify you of any alterations required and where another sample shall be sent. The acceptance of the sample shall not limit your guarantee obligations. We shall notify you within two (2) weeks of our receipt of the sample as to whether it is acceptable.

You shall not use our name in any publicity or claim any connection with us without our prior consent in writing. You shall put any patent numbers, names or other signs we or our customer requires on the Goods.

You shall keep confidential all information you obtain about us whether as to our customers, products, supplies or other commercially sensitive material without limit as to time and not disclose or use this save as expressly required for the purposes of this agreement.

You shall comply with all relevant data protection legislation and will only process any personal data we supply to you in accordance with such legislation and our data protection policies as supplied by us to you from time to time.

14. HEALTH AND SAFETY AND REGULATORY MATTERS

All goods shall have all necessary safety devices fitted. You are responsible for compliance with the *Health and Safety at Work etc. Act 1974* in relation to Goods and Services and will indemnify us against any liability, costs, losses or expenses we may sustain if you fail to do so.

When you are working at our premises or the premises of our customer in the performance of any Services or installation of the Goods you shall ensure your staff comply with our or our customer's reasonable requirements at the premises.

You shall ensure you give nor receive any bribe contrary to the *UK Bribery Act 2010* in relation to supplies under this Agreement nor breach any relevant competition laws nor the *Modern Slavery Act 2015* in relation to any of the supplies hereunder of Goods or Services.

15. GENERAL

Headings to the Clauses in these Conditions are for convenience only and shall not affect the construction thereof.

If any provision in these Conditions (or part thereof) shall be found to be invalid or unenforceable, the invalidity or unenforceability of such provision (or part thereof) shall not affect any other provision (or the other part of the provision).

Nothing in these Conditions shall give any right to any third party whether under the *Contracts (Rights of Third Parties) Act 1999* or otherwise.

Our failure to insist on strict performance of any of your obligations shall not be construed as a waiver and shall not affect our right to require strict performance of all your obligations.

These terms are personal to you and may not be assigned or transferred by you. We may assign and/or sub-contract our obligations under this agreement.

These Conditions shall be governed by and construed in accordance with the laws of England and you agree to submit to the non-exclusive jurisdiction of the English courts where disputes arise.

_____ Ltd – Conditions of Purchase (Import).

Section C:
Business-to-Consumer Contracts

C1:
Consumer Contracts – Distance Selling

At a glance

- Distance selling terms and conditions should be provided to the potential purchaser before conclusion of the contract in a clear and comprehensible manner.

- There is a distinction made between off-premises contracts and distance selling contracts.

- The Consumer Contracts (Information, Cancellation and Additional Charges) Regulations 2013 have particular application to distance selling contracts.

- Distance selling contracts allow for a cooling-off period and a mode of cancellation of the contract.

- The Data Protection Act 2018 and UK GDPR apply to the processing of personal data.

- Certain consumer contracts are outside the ambit of the 2013 Regulations such as gambling and financial services, to which different legal regimes apply.

- Particular details are required to be given by the supplier to its acknowledgement of order placed by the customer.

- Certain formalities apply in the use of telephone calls to conclude a distance contract.

Preliminary issues of incorporation and terminology
C1.2

It should be stressed at the outset that distance selling terms and conditions should be presented to a potential buyer prior to the conclusion of the contract, otherwise they will not be binding. If the initial contact is with the consumer through, for example, a direct mail shot or media advertising, then the terms and conditions should be contained in that initial contact, or, at the very least, reference to the terms and conditions should be made in that contact if the potential supplier is not inclined to spell them all out immediately. In particular, this may be the case where the initial contact is by radio or television, or over the telephone. If the supplier wishes to incorporate the terms and conditions by reference only, the initial contact, in whatever form it is made, should state something along the lines of:

> 'This contract is made subject to our terms and conditions. Copies are available on request from…'

The following distinction should be noted for 'off-premises' contracts and distance selling contracts:

- **Off-premises contracts.** There are four types of these contracts:

    (1)   A contract made where a consumer and trader are together and agree the contract in a place that is not the trader's business premises – for example, in a consumer's home or place of work.

    (2)   A contract made where a consumer and trader are together, and an offer is made by the consumer in a place that is not the trader's business premises – for example, where a consumer signs an order form during a visit to their home and the trader agrees the contract later.

    (3)   A contract that is agreed on a trader's business premises or through any means of distance communication immediately after a meeting with a consumer in a place that is not the trader's business premises. For example, a salesperson meets a consumer in the high street and convinces them of the benefits of buying a water filter; the consumer is then taken to the local office of the trader to sign the contract for the equipment. An example of this scenario using distance communication would be if the salesperson in the high street meets the consumer and immediately enters into a contract with them using a tablet computer.

    (4)   A contract made with the consumer during an excursion organised by the trader with the aim of selling or promoting goods or services to the consumer. The 2013 Regulations (see below) do not define an 'excursion'; however, it is possible that this will cover a situation where a trader meets a consumer on holiday and invites them to travel with the trader to a different venue to be sold goods or services.

- **Distance contracts.** A contract made between a trader and a consumer where they are not together, which is negotiated and agreed by one or more organised means of distance communication – for example, by phone, post or over the internet. There must be an organised distance scheme for selling goods and/or services, so the 2013 Regulations are unlikely to affect a business that sells a product at a distance as a one-off. For instance, a knitting wool shop that does not normally sell at a distance would not fall within the definition of a distance contract when a consumer rings to ask for a ball of wool to be posted to them because they are unable to call into the shop; this is unlikely to be classed as an 'organised' distance selling scheme.

Precedent – Specimen Distance Selling Contract

C1.3

1. This contract is for the supply and delivery of the items specified herein.

Comment

The particular items to be supplied will be specified here. *The Consumer Contracts (Information, Cancellation and Additional Charges) Regulations 2013 (SI 22013/3134)* ('Regulations') also require the contract to describe the main characteristics of the goods, such as 'inkjet business cards' or 'arum lily white'.

Provision may be made for the products listed to be identified by code and for the quantity of each particular product being ordered.

---

2. We will endeavour to deliver all products ordered within 28 days of receipt of order, but delivery time cannot be guaranteed.

Comment

The Regulations provide that the supplier is to perform the contract within 30 days from the day following the day the consumer sent the order. By stating that delivery time cannot be guaranteed, the supplier is taking advantage of the further provision in the Regulations that the 30 day period applies 'unless the parties agree otherwise'.

---

3. The products displayed here are illustrative only and the actual product delivered may differ in some respects.

Comment

Occasionally, particularly if the item to be supplied has not actually been manufactured, or if an enhanced version of an existing product is expected,

---

the supplier might wish to take advantage of some such clause as this. It should be noted though, that, while it is not infrequently used, its success cannot be guaranteed. While it might avoid any allegation that the goods supplied do not conform to their description, it is less clear that such a clause will avoid the provisions of the *Consumer Protection from Unfair Trading Regulations* 2008 *(SI 2088/1277)* which penalises misleading practices. The 2008 Regulations do, though, allow for the defence of due diligence.

Case Example: Norman v Bennett [1974] 1 WLR 1229

A supplier can always qualify any description, but the rule laid down in this case is that any such qualification must be as 'bold, precise and compelling' as the description itself. This would mean that any such statement as above must be in immediate proximity to the product or the product description, so that the customer sees them simultaneously. Though decided under provisions of the *Trade Descriptions Act* 1968 now repealed, this is still a useful precedent in relation to the 2008 Regulations.

---

4. Your payment must be enclosed with this order. Payment can be by personal cheque drawn on a UK bank and must be crossed 'A/C payee only' if not already so crossed. Payment may also be made by debit, credit or charge card by completing the following details...

Comment

It should be added that, under *s 75* of the *Consumer Credit Act 1974*, the credit card company is as liable as the supplier in the event of there being a misrepresentation or breach of contract by the supplier, where the cash price of the relevant item is at least £100 and not more than £30,000. Note, however, this applies only to credit cards, ie cards where the debt can be paid off in instalments. It does not apply to debit cards, but the banks operate a non-statutory scheme called Chargeback which works in much the same way.

Changes introduced by the Consumer Credit Act 2006 give further rights to the consumer against the card company when there is a claim against the supplier, but only when these conditions are met:

(a)   that the supplier cannot be traced;

(b)   that the debtor has contacted the supplier but the supplier has not responded;

(c)   that the supplier is insolvent, or

(d)   that the debtor has taken reasonable steps to pursue his claim against the supplier but has not obtained satisfaction for his claim.

Furthermore, these rights apply only if the cash price is less £30,000 or less and the credit extend does not exceed £60,260.

Alternatively, the supplier might provide for payment by instalments, in which case account should also be taken of the *CCA 1974*. When the Act applies, the supplier must be licensed by the Financial Conduct Authority. Various formalities must also be observed as to the form and content of the contract and the provision of copies. Breach of these requirements means that the agreement can be enforced only on a court order and, in some cases, not at all.

A supplier can avoid these provisions, however, if the agreement is exempt from control under the provisions of the *Consumer Credit (Exempt Agreements) Order 1989 (SI 1989/869)*. The relevant exemption refers to agreements where the credit is repayable in not more than four instalments over not longer than one year.

Section 75 covers transactions made when the consumer is abroad: *Office of Fair Trading v Lloyds TSB Bank plc* [2006] 2 All ER 821.

Where a consumer validly cancels a contract for the supply of goods, a credit agreement taken out in relation to the contract also comes to an end: *Durkin v DSG Retail* Ltd [2014] UKSC 21

5. Credit account applications are granted subject to status and to checks made through credit reference agencies. If you do not wish us to contact such agencies, please advise us accordingly.

Comment

The supplier will make use of such a clause if he offers a credit account against which customers can charge their purchases.

6. You have a right to cancel this agreement at any time up to fourteen days from the day after your receipt of the goods. In the event of cancellation by you, the goods must be returned to us at your expense or you can arrange for us to collect the goods at your expense.

Comment

The 2013 Regulations give a right to the 14-day cooling-off period and require that this is stated in the contract. The supplier does not have to say that the goods have to be returned if this is not the case, but must indicate if collection or return is required at the customer's expense. The supplier is always free to bear the costs himself.

The consumer can exercise a right to cancel by using the model cancellation form which the trader must supply or by making any other clear statement as to the decision to cancel. If the trader gives the consumer the option of filling in and submitting such a form or other statement on the trader's website:

(a)   the consumer need not use it, but

(b)   if the consumer does, the trader must communicate to the consumer an acknowledgement of receipt of the cancellation on a durable medium without delay.

The Regulations do not preclude a supplier from offering better terms, of which the following is an example:

> 'Any item ordered will be accepted for return for any reason within 30 days of receipt by the customer. If you are not completely satisfied with the product, we will provide a complete refund and provide you with a reply-paid label for the return of the product'.

7. We guarantee that this product will be free of any defects rendering it unfit for its purpose or not of satisfactory quality for 12 months from the date of purchase. In the event of a breach of this guarantee, we will repair or replace the product free of charge, whichever the customer shall choose. This does not affect your statutory rights.

Comment

While this term is not compulsory, the *CRA* 2015 does require a supplier to state if he provides any guarantee.

Again, this is essentially a voluntary undertaking. The last sentence is, however, required by the CRA *2015* in precisely those circumstances where such a voluntary undertaking is given. It has the effect of reminding the customer that he always has his rights against the supplier under *CRA* 2015

It should also be realised that the rights which a consumer, as opposed to a business customer, has that the goods are of satisfactory quality and reasonably fit for their purpose cannot be excluded or limited, and that any term in the contract to such effect is illegal by virtue of the *Consumer Protection from Unfair Trading Regulations* 2008 (SI 2008/1277).

8. While we use only reputable carriers and ensure that the goods are packed securely, we cannot accept any liability for any damage or deterioration in the goods which occurs, for whatever reason, while the goods are in transit to you.

Comment

We include this clause because suppliers might be tempted to use some such clause, based perhaps on previous experience, but only to advise that such clauses no longer have any effect and should not be used. While such clauses remain valid in business to business contracts, they were rendered ineffective in the case of consumer contracts by *CRA 2015*. In the case of a consumer contract, risk now passes only on delivery to the consumer unless when handed to a carrier selected by the consumer other than from a list provided by the suppler. In such a case, risk passes to the consumer when in possession of the carrier so selected.

---

9. The property in the goods remains with the supplier until payment has been received in full.

Comment

This takes advantage of the provision in *SGA 1979* relating to the passing of property. If this provision is not used, property, and hence the full rights of ownership, will pass once a contract is made and agreed for specific goods. (see A2.26). If property is retained by the supplier as recommended, then the goods remain his and can be repossessed. These provisions continue to apply to consumer contracts.

---

10. The price of this product is £120.00 inc VAT at the standard rate.

Comment

The Consumer Contracts (Information, Cancellation and Additional Charges) Regulations 2013 (SI 2013/3134) require the price to be stated 'inclusive of taxes'. This appears to rule out saying '£100 plus £20.00' even though the calculation of the total price is straightforward. In fact, it is not even necessary to say that the price given does include VAT. It is enough for the purposes of the Regulations that it does include VAT.

---

11. Please add £3.50 postage charges to the value of the goods ordered when calculating the overall amount you have to pay.

Comment

The 2013 Regulations require the contract to indicate any delivery costs which may be payable. If no delivery costs are payable, this does not have to be stated, but of course the supplier can indicate this if he wishes. The supplier can also indicate that delivery costs will be imposed on certain levels of order by value.

---

12. To place your order with us, please fax, phone or email on or at the following freephone numbers or address.

13. The cost of your calling us on the number given will be [state cost] and the call will last for approximately [state period].

Comment

The 2013 Regulations provide that the cost of contacting the supplier must be stated if this is other than the 'basic rate'. Accordingly, if it is necessary to make the call by a premium rate number, the costs of doing so must be stated. The costs of communication need only be stated if they exceed the basic rate, though there is nothing to stop a supplier from giving the costs of communication not exceeding the basic rate.

The Regulations also provide that, if a consumer makes contact about an existing contract, any call costs must be at no more than the basic rate.

---

14. Should the goods you have ordered for any reason become unavailable, we reserve the right to offer you goods of an equivalent or better value. You may return any such replacement goods at our cost by use of a reply-paid label.

Comment

There is no requirement in law to offer replacement goods when the intended goods become unavailable, but this clause can be regarded as good customer policy.

---

15. By entering this contract, you agree to make monthly payments of £310.

Comment

The 2013 Regulations require, in the case of contacts of indefinite duration, or a contract containing a subscription, a statement of the costs

---

per billing period or, where such contracts are charged at a fixed rate, the total monthly costs.

16. Please Note: We cannot accept orders from those under [specify an age here appropriate to the product in hand] without the countersignature of a responsible adult.

Comment

There is no legal requirement for any such statement but is still sound policy to include it.

17. We may contact you in the future with further offers, or supply your details to carefully selected third parties. Please tick the boxes alongside if you do not wish to hear from us [ ] or from third parties [ ].

Please tick this box [ ] if you are happy for us or third parties to contact you by email or SMS.

Comment

Under the *Privacy and Electronic Communications (EC Directive) Regulations 2003 (SI 2003/2426)*, consumers must be given separate choices in relation to further communication by, on the one hand, email, SMS or fax; and, on the other, any other form of communication. The former requires an opt in, the latter an opt out. A box is not necessary, so long as the consumer's options are clearly indicated, but it is the easiest method of complying with the law. If there is no intention to make further communication, no action is required and nothing need be stated.

Prior consent to contact by email or SMS is, however, not required in the following circumstances:

(a)   the sender has obtained the contact details of the recipient of that electronic mail in the course of the sale or negotiations for the sale of a product or service to that recipient;

(b)   the direct marketing is in respect of that person's similar products and services only; and

(c)   the recipient has been given a simple means of refusing (free of charge except for the costs of the transmission of the refusal) the use of his contact details for the purposes of such direct marketing, at the time that the details were initially collected, and, where he did not initially refuse the use of the details, at the time of each subsequent communication.

This final requirement means that, on the occasion of the subsequent communication, a further opt in box, or its equivalent, is to be provided.

Where contact is made with a consumer by email or SMS, the identity of the person on whose behalf the communication has been sent must be given along with a valid address to which the recipient of the communication may send a request that such communications cease.

Where a consumer has registered his fax or phone number with the register maintained by the Office of Communications, the Regulations state that no unsolicited fax or phone communication can be made with such person for direct marketing purposes.

Under the provisions of the *Data Protection Act 2018*, direct marketers who have details of customers on file can continue to market them but must provide an opt out. See too the General Data Protection Regulations (GDPR).

18. {Name of supplier and address} together with contact details.

Comment

The 2013 Regulations require the trader to provide its trading name and the geographical address where it is established and, where available, phone, fax and email contact details. If the trader is acting on behalf of another trader, the geographical address of that other trader must also be given. The Regulations further require that, if different from the address where a trader is established, then the trader must give the geographical address of the place or business and, where the trader acts on behalf of another, the geographical address of that other where the consumer can address any complaints.

19. As part of our continuing service to you, the customer, we have established a helpline whose address is {Insert address}. It can be contacted between 8am and 5.30pm on the following numbers {Insert number}.

Comment

The 2013 Regulations do not require any kind of complaint procedure. What they say is that, where applicable, the contract must provide details of the existence and the conditions of after-sale customer assistance, after sales service, and commercial guarantees. They also require, where applicable, details of any complaints handling policy.

Alternatively, the following can be used:

> 'Should you require our help or advice in making the best use of your purchase, please contact our helpline on… '

20. We subscribe to the following code of conduct []. Please ask us if you would like to see a copy.

Comment

The 2013 Regulations require details of adherence to a code of conduct to be indicated, if applicable.

---

21. We belong to an out of court complaint and redress mechanism which we can use to avoid court procedures in the event of a dispute arising between us. Should you wish to use it, we will provide all appropriate details.

Comment

The 2013 Regulations require this only where applicable.

Under the provisions of the *Alternative Dispute Resolution for Consumer Disputes (Competent Authorities and Information) Regulations 2015 (SI 2015/542)*, where a trader is obliged to use alternative dispute resolution services provided by an ADR entity under:

(a)   an enactment, or

(b)   the rules of a trade association to which the trader belongs,

the trader must provide the name and website address of the ADR entity:

(c)   on the trader's website, if the trader has a website, and

(d)   in the general terms and conditions of sales or service contracts between the trader and a consumer: see Part 4 of the 2015 Regulations.

Where a trader has exhausted its internal complaint handling procedure when considering a complaint from a consumer relating to a sales contract

---

or a service contract, the trader must inform the consumer, on a durable medium:

(a)   that the trader cannot settle the complaint with the consumer;

(b)   of the name and website address of an ADR entity which would be competent to deal with the complaint, should the consumer wish to use alternative dispute resolution, and

(c)   whether the trader is obliged, or prepared, to submit to an alternative dispute resolution procedure operated by that ADR entity.

An organisation offering ADR must be approved by the Chartered Trading Standards Institute.

These regulatory bodies can also approve schemes: Ofgem, Civil Aviation Authority, Gambling Commission, Ofcom, Financial Conduct Authority, Legal Services Board, lead enforcement authority for purposes of Estate Agents Act 1979.

A 'consumer' is defined as an individual acting for purposes which are wholly or mainly outside that individual's trade, business, craft or profession. Reference to a 'trader' is a person acting for purposes relating to that person's trade, business, craft or profession, whether acting personally or through another person acting in the trader's name or on the trader's behalf.

Presentation of contract terms   C1.4

As required by the 2013 Regulations, you must give consumers the information listed below in a way that is clear, comprehensible and appropriate to the means of distance communication before they enter into a contract with you. In addition, if you provide this information on a durable medium you must make sure that it is legible.

A durable medium is defined as paper, email or other medium that:

•   allows the information to be addressed personally to the recipient;

•   enables the recipient to store the information and access it for future reference (this includes you placing the information in your customer's personal account area of your website, which they can access by logging in);

•   allows unchanged reproduction of this information.

The information that you are required to give is as follows:

(a)   The main characteristics of the goods, services or digital content. You must give as much information as the means of communication allows.

(b)   Your identity, such as your trading name.

(c)   The geographical address where you are established and, where applicable, a telephone number, fax number and email address to allow consumers to be able to contact you quickly and efficiently. Online sellers must provide an email address; an online contact form is not sufficient (see below).

(d)   If you are acting on behalf of another trader, their identity and geographical address.

(e)   If you, or the trader that you are acting for, have a different address for consumer complaints this must also be given.

(f)   The total price of the goods, services or digital content inclusive of tax (such as VAT). If this cannot be calculated in advance you must say how this will be calculated.

(g)   All delivery charges or any other costs. If these cannot be calculated in advance you must state that they are payable

(h)   The monthly, or billing period, costs of open-ended contracts or subscriptions.

(i)   Any additional costs for using a specific means of distance communication to make the contract – for example, if you make an extra charge for buying by phone as opposed to online.

(j)   The arrangements for payment, delivery or performance and the time that you will take to deliver the goods, perform the services or supply the digital content.

(k)   If you have one, your complaint-handling policy. Providers of services (this includes online sellers of goods, according to European Union guidance) should have a complaint-handling policy in place as required by the Provision of Services Regulations 2009. In addition, CTSI approved codes of practice and some trade associations and professional bodies will also require a policy to be in place, which must be made available to consumers.

(l)   The conditions, time limits and procedure for exercising a right to cancel, if there is one (the next section covers cancellation in detail). This information may be provided by correctly filling in and providing the 'Model instructions for cancellation' provided by the Regulations

(m)   If you are expecting consumers to pay the costs of returning the goods after cancellation you must tell them, or if the goods cannot normally be returned by post (they are too large, for example) you must advise consumers of the cost of returning them. This information may be provided by correctly filling in and providing the 'Model instructions for cancellation' (see above).

(n)   If you are offering a service contract that a consumer can expressly ask you to start within the cancellation period, you must tell them that they will be required to pay you the reasonable costs of the service that you have delivered up to the time of their cancellation within the cancellation period. This information may be provided by correctly filling in and providing the 'Model instructions for cancellation' (see above).

(o)   If there are no cancellation rights for specific goods, services or digital content that you offer, or there are circumstances in which consumers will lose their right to cancel, you must inform them of this.

(p)   If you are selling goods you should remind consumers that the goods you sell must be in conformity with the contract – for example, you might say: 'It is our responsibility to supply you with goods that meet your consumer rights. If you have any concerns that we have not met our legal obligations please contact us'.

(q)   If you offer any after-sales consumer assistance, services or guarantees you must make consumers aware of this and any applicable conditions.

(r)   If you are a member of a code of conduct you must inform consumers how they can obtain a copy of the code – for example, by providing a link to the code sponsor's website.

(s)   If the consumer will be entering into a contract of a fixed duration, they must be informed what this is. If the contract has no fixed length, or can be extended automatically, the consumer must be informed of the conditions under which they can terminate it.

(t)   You must inform consumers if there is a minimum duration under a contract – for example, a minimum period for a mobile phone contract.

(u)   If consumers are required to give deposits or other financial guarantees you must inform them of this obligation and any applicable conditions.

(v)   Digital content functionality. This includes information about its language, duration, file type, access, updates, tracking, internet connection, geographical restrictions and any additional purchases required.

(w)   Digital content compatibility (information regarding both hardware and other software).

(x)   The existence of any 'alternative dispute resolution' schemes that you are subject to and how to access them (see 'Additional information required for online sellers' below for further information that online sellers must provide regarding alternative dispute resolution schemes) [If the means of distance communication that you are using limits the space or the time that is available to provide the information, these items may be provided in a different but appropriate way]. For example, a TV shopping channel may decide to give the detailed information on its website, during the sales call, or through a combination of the two.

Cancellation form   C1.5

If a right of cancellation exists the consumer must be given, or have access to, a cancellation form, which must be in the following form (please note that this has been placed in a box for illustrative purposes):

Model cancellation form

To [here the trader's name, geographical address and, where available, fax number and email address are to be inserted by the trader]:

I/We [★] hereby give notice that I/We [★] cancel my/our contract of sale of the following goods [★] / for the supply of the following service [★],

Ordered on [★] / received on [★],

Name of consumer(s),

Address of consumer(s),

Signature of consumer(s) (only if this form is notified on paper),

Date

[★] Delete as appropriate

Contracts outside the Regulations C1.6

The Regulations do not cover contracts for:

- gambling, including participating in the National Lottery (covered by gambling legislation);

- financial services, such as banking, credit, insurance or personal pensions – however, credit and insurance facilities will be affected if supplied with contracts for goods or services or when offered as an optional extra that the consumer must opt out of;

- the construction of new buildings (or substantially new buildings by the conversion of existing buildings, such as a barn conversion) and the sale of immovable property – however, the construction of extensions to existing buildings will be covered;

- residential letting contracts, but estate agency contracts for their work in connection with the sale or letting of properties are covered;

- the supply of consumables by regular rounds people, such as the delivery of milk – these visits must be frequent and regular to a consumer's home, residence or workplace;

- package travel contracts;

- timeshare and long-term holiday products, including resale and exchange contracts;

- purchases from vending machines;

- single telecom connections, such as payphones and internet café connections.

Acknowledgment of order   **C1.7**

The supplier's system should be so set up that, where an order is sent by email, an acknowledgement of order is immediately sent back to the consumer by email. This reply should:

- clearly spell out the goods or services which have been ordered;
- the price and the method of payment;
- a reference number for the contract;
- delivery date;
- place of delivery (that is, if the goods are to be sent to the consumer's home or are to be collected by him);
- an email address for queries and also a phone number;
- the geographical address of the supplier's place of business;
- any registration numbers appropriate to the supplier's business;
- the supplier's website address; and
- arrangements for cancellation and refunds.

The reply should also indicate that it should be printed off and retained by the consumer.

Privacy statement   **C1.8**

The reply should further contain a privacy statement on these lines: 'This email and any attachment are confidential and intended solely for the use of the individual to whom it is addressed. If you are not that individual, please pass it to that individual and notify us at the above email address.' See too compliance with the *Data Protection Act 2018* and the GDPR.

The reply should also state that, if it is in fact the case, the e-mail reply has been swept for the presence of all known computer viruses.

Internet-related terms

Failure in transmission   **C1.9**

The contract should state: 'We cannot be held responsible, and accept no liability for, any failure in transmission by you and where, for whatever reason, your transmission is corrupted, fails to arrive, or arrives after an undue delay, or is received in an unintelligible form'. This provision should not only appear in the terms and conditions, but it should appear on the order page, so that it is clearly conveyed to the consumer before any contract is made with them. Since, furthermore, this is a term which precedes the formation of any contract, it will not be subject to the provisions of the *Unfair Contract Terms Act 1977* or the *Consumer Rights Act* 2015

Avoiding a premature offer C1.10

It should be clearly stated on the order page, that any display of goods or services is not an offer, but nothing more than an invitation to treat. If the website amounts to an offer, then the consumer can accept that offer, at the price stated, and thus give rise to a binding contract. If the website is, however, just an invitation to treat, then the consumer makes the offer which the supplier can then accept or reject in his absolute discretion.

> **Case Example**
>
> The Kodak website offered digital cameras at £100 instead of £330. More than 5000 customers emailed an acceptance, and received an automated email reply confirming the offer and accepting it. This created a binding contract.

The website should specifically state: 'Nothing contained in this website amounts to an offer to supply the goods or services, and any order from a customer can be refused at our absolute discretion.'

Electronic commerce requirements C1.11

Where your contract is concluded by an electronic means, and places the consumer under an obligation to pay, you must ensure that information items 'a', 'f', 'g', 'h', 's' and 't' above are clearly, and prominently, brought to the consumer's attention immediately before they place their order.

You must also ensure that consumers expressly acknowledge that they are under an obligation to pay when they place their order. If you are using a button or similar function to enable the consumer to place their order this must be labelled in an easily legible manner with the words 'order with obligation to pay'; you may use different phrases, such as 'buy now', 'pay now' or 'confirm purchase', as long as they have a similar effect. If you do not meet this requirement the consumer will not be bound by the contract.

If you are concluding a contract through a website you must indicate in a clear and legible manner, at the very latest at the beginning of the ordering process, whether any delivery restrictions apply and the payment means that you will accept.

Using telephone calls to conclude a distance contract   C1.12

You must start the conversation with the following information if you are calling consumers with the aim of concluding distance contracts:

- your identity;
- the identity of the person on whose behalf you are making the call, if you are calling on behalf of another business;
- the commercial purpose of the call.

Confirming distance contracts   C1.13

Once you have entered into a distance contract you must give the consumer confirmation of the contract on a durable medium. Your confirmation must include information items 'a' to 'x' above. You will not need to do this if you have already given this information on a durable medium prior to the conclusion of the contract.

You must give this information to the consumer no later than when the goods are delivered (so you could include it in the package with the goods), before performance of the service begins or, for digital content that is not on a tangible medium, within a reasonable time (which may mean that it has been sent, but not received, before the digital download begins).

Unsolicited commercial communications   C1.14

The 2013 Regulations state that if you send unsolicited goods to consumers they are not obliged to pay for them and can keep them as an unconditional gift. Consumers do not have to take any action, such as informing you, if they receive unsolicited goods, they can just keep them. Under *the Electronic Commerce (EC Directive) Regulations 2002 (SI 2002/2013)*, a service provider shall ensure that any unsolicited communication sent by him by electronic mail is clearly and unambiguously identifiable as soon as it is received.

Conclusion of contracts   C1.15

Unless parties who are not consumers have agreed otherwise, the 2002 Regulations state that where a contract is to be concluded by electronic means a service provider shall, prior to an order being placed by the recipient of a service, provide to that recipient in a clear, comprehensible and unambiguous manner:

- the different technical steps to follow to conclude the contract;

- whether or not the concluded contract will be filed by the service provider and whether it will be accessible;

- the technical means for identifying and correcting input errors prior to the placing of the order, and

- the languages offered for the conclusion of the contract.

Unless parties who are not consumers have agreed otherwise, a service provider shall indicate which relevant codes of conduct he subscribes to and give information on how those codes can be consulted electronically.

The above requirements shall not apply to contracts concluded exclusively by exchange of electronic mail or by equivalent individual communications.

Where the service provider provides terms and conditions applicable to the contract to the recipient, the service provider shall make them available to him in a way that allows him to store and reproduce them.

Placing of the order **C1.16**

Unless parties who are not consumers have agreed otherwise, the 2002 Regulations where the recipient of the service places his order through technological means, a service provider shall:

- acknowledge receipt of the order to the recipient of the service without undue delay and by electronic means; and

- make available to the recipient of the service appropriate, effective and accessible technical means allowing him to identify and correct input errors prior to the placing of the order.

For the purposes of the first bullet point above:

- the order and the acknowledgement of receipt will be deemed to be received when the parties to whom they are addressed are able to access them; and

- the acknowledgement of receipt may take the form of the provision of the service paid for where that service is an information society service.

The foregoing requirements shall not apply to contracts concluded exclusively by exchange of electronic mail or by equivalent individual communications.

Right to rescind contract C1.17

Where a person:

- has entered into a contract to which the 2002 Regulations apply; and
- the service provider has not made available means of allowing him to identify and correct input errors as required above,

he shall be entitled to rescind the contract unless any court having jurisdiction in relation to the contract in question orders otherwise on the application of the service provider.

Checklist C1.18

- Are you aware of the distinction between 'off-premises' contracts and distance selling contracts and the requirements for each?
- Are you fully aware of the applicability of the *Consumer Contracts (Information, Cancellation and Additional Charges) Regulations 2013 (SI 2013/3134)* and the *Electronic Commerce (EC Directive) Regulations 2002 (SI 2002/2013)* and what they require?
- Have you considered the application of the *Data Protection Act 2018* and the GDPR in distance selling consumer contracts and the need to include details in the privacy statement?
- Are you aware of the timeline within which the supplier must perform the contract under the 2013 Regulations?
- Have you considered the provisions of the *Consumer Protection from Unfair Trading Regulations 2008* and their application to distance selling?
- Are you aware of the rights to 'cooling off' period which must be given to the consumer?
- Have you made the consumer aware of cancellation rights and provided a cancellation form?
- Are you aware of the provisions for acknowledgement of an order?
- Are you aware of the requirements for using telephone calls for concluding a distance contract?
- Have you considered the details to be provided to the consumer when confirming distance contracts?
- Are you aware of the restrictions concerning unsolicited commercial communications?
- Have you considered the applicability of the *Alternative Dispute Resolution for Consumer Disputes (Competent Authorities and Information) Regulations 2015* where ADR services are provided by an ADR provider?

C2:
Hire Purchase Contracts

At a glance C2.1

- A hire purchase agreement is concerned with leasing of goods to the hirer with an option to purchase them.

- A hire purchase contract is distinguishable from a conditional sale agreement.

- Hire purchase agreements are regulated by the Consumer Credit Act 1974 (as amended).

- Certain pre-contract information and explanation must be provided to the debtor before the hire purchase contract is concluded.

- Certain agreements are outside the ambit of the CCA 1974 and therefore exempt from its requirements.

- Certain formalities are mandatory and must be complied with under the Consumer Credit (Agreements) Regulations 1983 to ensure that the hire purchase agreement is regulated.

- Specific formalities must be complied with before termination of the hire purchase contract.

Definition C2.2

In law, a hire purchase agreement is a bailment, or leasing of goods, with an option to purchase them.

Case Example: *Helby v Matthews* **[1895] AC 471**

In this case, the court recognised the basic structure of the modern hire purchase agreement – a contract of bailment or lease whereby ownership is retained by the supplier of goods (the bailor), and the hirer (or bailee) obtains mere possession coupled with an option to buy the goods on payment of the agreed sum, usually nominal, on exercising that option.

Hire purchase v conditional sale   C2.3

A contract of hire purchase is to be distinguished from a conditional sale.

> **Case Example:** *Lee v Butler* **[1893] 2 QB 318**
>
> It was held that where the buyer commits himself at the outset to buying the goods, and agrees to pay the purchase price in instalments, that is a conditional sale agreement. The difference between this and a hire purchase agreement is that, as pointed out above, the latter is an agreement to hire goods with an option to purchase. In a conditional sale agreement, in contrast, the buyer commits himself at the outset to make the purchase of the goods. In practice, of course, there is no real difference in the agreements.

> **Case Example:** *Forthright Finance Ltd v Carlyle Finance Ltd* **(unreported, 28 January 1997)**
>
> It was held that a contract is a contract of conditional sale if the buyer is obliged to pay all the instalments, even though the contract provides an option not to take the title.

> **Case Example:** *Close Asset Finance v Care Graphics Machinery Ltd* **[2000] CCLR 43**
>
> By contrast, in a contract of hire purchase, a party has an option to buy, and is not legally obliged to acquire title, even if the option price is nominal and one that a person would almost certainly pay, given the amount of the previous instalments.

Regulated hire purchase agreements   C2.4

The *Consumer Credit Act 1974* (*CCA 1974*) (as amended by the *Enterprise Act 2002* and the *Consumer Credit Act 2006*) regulates hire purchase agreements regardless of the amount of credit extended.

Before the contract is made   C2.5

Pre-Contract Information

Pre-contract credit information is to be provided in a standard form as set out in The Standard European Consumer Credit Information Form ('SECCI') (covering such matters as the type of credit, costs of the credit, early repayment): see Schedule 1 to the *Consumer Credit (Disclosure of Information) Regulations*

2010 (SI 2010/1013). There is an exemption for agreements entered into for business purposes or where the credit provided is in excess of £60,260: see *Consumer Credit (Exempt Agreements) Order 2007 (SI 2007/1168).* For further exemptions see: *Consumer Credit (Exempt Agreements) Order 1989 (SI 1989/869* as further amended in 1999 and 2006).

Pre-Contract Explanation

Before the contract is made, the creditor must provide the debtor with an adequate explanation of certain matters in order to place him in a position enabling him to assess whether the agreement is adapted to his needs and his financial situation. These matters are:

(a) the features of the agreement which may make the credit to be provided under the agreement unsuitable for particular types of use;

(b) how much the debtor will have to pay periodically and, where the amount can be determined, in total under the agreement;

(c) the features of the agreement which may operate in a manner which would have a significant adverse effect on the debtor in a way which the debtor is unlikely to foresee;

(d) the principal consequences for the debtor arising from a failure to make payments under the agreement at the times required by the agreement including legal proceedings and, where this is a possibility, repossession of the debtor's home; and

(e) the effect of the exercise of any right to withdraw from the agreement and how and when this right may be exercised.

The above provisions do not apply if the credit provided exceeds £60,260.

Pre-Contract Advice

The debtor must be advised to:

(i) consider the pre-contract credit information; and

(ii) where this information is disclosed in person to the debtor, that the debtor is able to take it away.

The creditor must provide the debtor with an opportunity to ask questions about the agreement, and must advise the debtor how to ask the creditor for further information and explanation. This does not apply if the credit exceeds £60,260.

Creditworthiness

The creditor must also determine the creditworthiness of the debtor.

Copy requirements C2.6

The most common situation is where the customer selects the goods to be obtained on hire purchase, and signs a form setting out the details of the agreement. It is then up to the dealer, or a third-party finance house, to accept the offer contained in the form signed by the customer.

First and second copies C2.7

Before the agreement is made, the creditor must, if requested, give to the debtor without delay a copy of the prospective agreement (or such of its terms as have at that time been reduced to writing). This will not apply if the agreement is entered into for business purposes or if the credit provided exceeds £60,260. Nor do these provisions apply if at the time the request is made, the creditor is unwilling to proceed with the agreement. If this requirement is not complied with, the debtor has the right to sue for damages.

On signing the offer document, the customer becomes entitled to a copy of it.

A second copy must be delivered to the customer within seven days of the agreement being made. This will occur when the other side signs the agreement and posts it to the customer. If a finance company is involved, what happens is that the finance company itself buys the goods from the dealer, and itself enters into the hire purchase agreement with the customer.

It is less common for all the relevant parties to sign the agreement at the same time. If this is the case, though, the document signed by the customer is the complete contract, and he is entitled to just one copy.

Consequences of failure to comply C2.8

If the copy requirements are not complied with, under *CCA 1974* the agreement cannot be enforced against the consumer unless the court grants an enforcement order. An enforcement order may be made conditional on such terms as the court thinks fit. This also applies where there is a failure to provide the pre-contract credit information (see C2.4.1).

Exempt agreements C2.9

A number of agreements are outside the remit of the *CCA 1974*. Under the *Consumer Credit (Exempt Agreements) Order 1989 (SI 1989/869)*, an agreement will be exempt if the number of repayments is not more than four, and are to be made within 12 months. Many agreements secured on land are exempt; as are agreements made with high net-worth individuals; and agreements where the credit provided exceeds £25,000 and the agreement is entered into for business purposes: see the *Consumer Credit (Exempt Agreements) Order 2007 (SI 2007/1168)*. There is also an agreement for low-cost credit where the rate of interest does not exceed the lower of 13% or 1% above base rate. This typically applies to debtor–creditor agreements, such as a bank loan.

Status of customer C2.10

For an agreement to be within the jurisdiction of *CCA 1974*, and hence regulated by it, the customer must be an 'individual'. This is defined by *s 189(1)* of the *CCA 1974* (as substituted by the *Consumer Credit Act 2006*) to include a partnership consisting of two or three persons not all of whom are bodies corporate; and an unincorporated body of persons which does not consist entirely of bodies corporate and is not a partnership.

Form of regulated agreement C2.11

Since the form and content of a regulated hire purchase agreement is subject to the provisions of the *Consumer Credit (Agreements) Regulations 1983 (SI 1983/1553)*, there is little room for variation. The Regulations state that, apart from any signature, the mandatory contents set out below must be easily legible and, where applicable, be of a colour which is readily distinguishable from the background medium upon which the information is displayed; and apart from that inserted in handwriting, be of equal prominence, except that headings, trade names and names of parties to the agreement may be afforded more prominence whether by capital letters, underlining, larger or bold print or otherwise. Note, too, that the order set out below is mandatory. Note also that the mandatory information is to be shown together as a whole and shall not be preceded by any information apart from trade names, logos or the reference number of the agreement or interspersed with any other information or wording apart from subtotals of total amounts and cross references to the terms of the agreement.

The Regulations apply only to:

(a) agreements secured on land;

(b) agreements under which the creditor provides the debtor with credit exceeding £60,260; and

(c) agreements entered into by the debtor wholly or predominantly for the purposes of a business carried on, or intended to be carried on, by him.

Online agreements and signature C2.12

> **Case example:** *Bassano v Toft* **[2014] EWHC 377**
>
> It was held that a regulated agreement within the meaning of the *Consumer Credit Act 1974* could be concluded electronically. There was nothing in

the Act to suggest that regulated agreements should not be capable of electronic signature, and there were no policy reasons why a signature could not be affixed and communicated electronically.

Precedent – Specimen Hire Purchase Contract (when within the 1983 Regulations)

C2.13

1. HIRE PURCHASE AGREEMENT REGULATED BY THE CONSUMER CREDIT ACT 1974

This is an agreement under which we [as owners] agree to hire out to you [as customer] the goods described below.

2. KEY FINANCIAL INFORMATION

Comment

Under this heading, the agreement will specify:

- the amount of credit;
- the total charge for credit;
- the duration of the credit;
- the timing and amount of repayments;
- the APR (accompanied, if relevant, by a statement that no account has been taken in the calculation of the APR of any variation which might occur in any amount forming part of the total charge for credit). The APR must, if appropriate, also be accompanied by 'variable'.

3. OTHER FINANCIAL INFORMATION

Comment
- A description of the relevant goods.
- Their cash price.

- The amount of any advance payment.

- The total charge for credit (with or without a list of its constituent parts).

[If the amount or rate of any item in the total charge for credit can vary, then the item immediately above is to be replaced by a statement of the rate of interest, and the total amount of other charges (which can be expressed by reference to a percentage or formula if the charge cannot be stated as an amount).]

- The total amount payable (except in the case of variable agreements as referred to immediately above).

- A statement (if relevant) that the APR has been calculated with no account of any change or variation which enters into its calculation.

- Where the provision immediately above applies, a statement indicating the circumstances in which a variation may occur, and when (if this is known, when the customer gets the document for signature).

4. KEY INFORMATION

Comment

- If relevant, a description of any security given by the customer.

- If relevant, an indication on charges applicable on default.

- If relevant, an indication of any term which provides for default charges not included in the charge for credit.

- If relevant, a statement that the agreement cannot be cancelled.

- If the agreement is for more than one month, examples must be given based on the amount of credit to be provided under the agreement or the nominal amount of either £1,000 or £100, showing the amount that would be payable if the debtor exercised the right under s 94 of the *Act* to discharge his indebtedness on the date when:

  (a) a quarter of the term of the agreement elapses;

  (b) half of the term elapses; and

  (c) three quarters of the term elapses,

  or on the first repayment date after each of those dates.

There must also be a statement explaining that, in calculating the amounts shown, no account has been taken of any variation which might occur under the agreement, and that the amounts are accordingly only illustrative.

(*Section 94* of the *CCA 1974* gives an individual, at any time, the right to pay off the hire-purchase agreement ahead of time.)

MISSING PAYMENTS

Missing payments could have severe consequences and make obtaining credit more difficult.

YOUR RIGHT TO CANCEL

Once you have signed this agreement, you will have a short time in which you can cancel it. The creditor will send you exact details of how and when you can do this.

Comment

This applies only if the agreement is cancellable (this will be when the negotiations leading up to the agreement included oral representations made in the presence of the customer made by the other party to the contract or someone acting on his behalf).

The cancellation period is five days from the day after the customer has received his second copy of the agreement.

The copy requirements in the case of cancellable agreements are set out in *ss 62–64* of the *CCA 1974* as follows:

- If the agreement is personally presented to the customer, and it becomes executed on signature by him, a copy of the agreement must be given to him at the same time.

- The position is the same in the more likely case when the agreement is presented personally to him and the agreement does not become executed on his signature (meaning that the other side has yet to sign).

- If an unexecuted agreement is sent to the customer for signature, a copy must be sent at the same time.

- When both signatures have been applied, so that the agreement becomes executed, a copy must be sent or delivered to the customer

---

by post within the seven days following the application of the second signature.

Where the agreement is cancellable, the required copies must contain a cancellation notice (see below) and must be sent by post within the seven days following the day when the last signature was applied.

If the requirements as to copies are not complied with, the agreement can be enforced only on a court order.

IMPORTANT – YOU SHOULD READ THIS CAREFULLY

STATUTORY NOTICE RELATING TO A REGULATED HIRE PURCHASE AGREEMENT

YOUR RIGHT TO CANCEL

You recently made a hire purchase agreement [1] with [2]. You have a right to cancel if you wish by sending or taking a WRITTEN notice of cancellation to [3]. You have FIVE DAYS starting with the day after you received this notice. You can use the form provided. If you cancel the agreement, any money you have paid, [goods given in part-exchange (or their value) and property given as security] [4] must be returned to you. You will not have to make any further payment.

If you already have any goods under the agreement, you should not use them and should keep them safe. (Legal action may be taken against you if you do not take proper care of them.) You can wait for them to be collected from you and you need not hand them over unless you receive a written request. [If you wish, however, you may return the goods yourself] [5]. [You are warned that it would be dangerous and could be in contravention of Health and Safety legislation for you to attempt to disconnect and return the goods yourself] [6].

[You will not, however, be required to hand back any goods supplied to meet an emergency or which have already been incorporated, for example in your home. But you will still be liable to pay for emergency goods or services or for any goods which have been incorporated by you or one of your relatives] [7].

[Note: Your notice of cancellation will not affect [your contract for life assurance] [your contract for insurance] [your contract of guarantee] [your contract to open a current account] [your contract to open a deposit account] [8]. [The place where your financial obligations consequent upon cancellation of this agreement are shown is [9] [10] [11]].

439

Comment

1   Owner to insert reference number, code or other identification details.

2   Owner to enter its name.

3   Creditor to insert name and address of person to whom notice may be given.

4   Words in square brackets to be omitted if inapplicable.

5   Owner to include the words in the first set of square brackets unless the words in the second set are applicable; eg in a case where the subject matter of the agreement is liquefied petroleum gas of greater than 150 litres water capacity.

6   Creditor to omit words in square brackets if not applicable.

7   Creditor may omit words in square brackets where inapplicable.

8   Creditor to omit words in square brackets if not applicable.

9   Creditor to insert clear reference to the place where these obligations appear.

10   Creditor may include words in square brackets were applicable.

11   Creditor to omit words in square brackets where inapplicable.

The above wording is prescribed by the *Consumer Credit (Cancellation Notices and Copies of Documents) Regulations 1983 (SI 1983/1557)*. Capital letters can be replaced by other forms of prominence.

In those cases where the notice of cancellation rights is included in the copies of agreements, the first paragraph under YOUR RIGHT TO CANCEL should read: 'Once you have signed, you will have for a short time a right to cancel this agreement. You can do this by sending or taking a WRITTEN notice of cancellation to [1].

1   Creditor to insert name and address of person to whom notice may be given, or an indication of the person to whom notice may be given, together with a clear reference to the place in the document where his name and address appear.

Again, the capital letters can be replaced by any other form of prominent lettering.

CANCELLATION FORM

(Complete and return this form ONLY IF YOU WISH TO CANCEL THE AGREEMENT.)

To: _____ [1]

I/we hereby give notice that I/We wish to cancel the agreement [2].

Signed: _____

Date: _____

Name: _____

Address: _____

Comment

1   Owner to insert name and address of person to whom notice of cancellation can be given.

2   Owner to insert reference number, code or other identification details.

Again, the capital letters can be replaced by any other form of prominent lettering.

This cancellation form is applicable whichever of the forms set out above is used. It is important to remember, however, that the customer does not have to use the cancellation form provided. *Section 69(1)* of the *CCA 1974* states that any written notice of cancellation which, however expressed, and whether or not use is made of the cancellation form provided, is effective to cancel the contract if it indicates an intention to withdraw from the contract. The notice has the effect of cancelling the agreement.

TERMINATION: YOUR RIGHTS

You have a right to end this agreement. To do so, you should write to the person you make your payments to. They will then be entitled to the return of the goods and to [the cost of installing the goods plus half the rest of the total amount payable under this agreement, that is] [half the total amount payable under this agreement, that is]* £x**. If you have already paid at least this amount plus any overdue instalments and have taken reasonable care of the goods, you will not have to pay any more.

Comment

*   Creditor to insert the appropriate passage in square brackets where the amount calculated in accordance with the provisions of *s 100* of

the *CCA 1974* applies. If the agreement provides for a sum below the minimum prescribed in *CCA 1974*, both passages in square brackets are to be omitted.

★★ Creditor to insert the amount calculated in accordance with the provisions of *s 100* of the *CCA 1974* or such lesser sum as the agreement may provide.

Under *s 100* of the *CCA 1974*, a customer can terminate at any time and if he pays all of any installation charges specified in the agreement and 50% of the total price. The agreement can always provide for a smaller sum.

The courts are unwilling to hold that a customer has voluntarily terminated an agreement unless the full consequences of doing so are considered to have been fully appreciated by that consumer.

Case Example: *Bridge v Campbell Discount Co Ltd* **[1961] 2 All ER 97**

The House of Lords held that a party had not terminated the contract but was writing to advise the other side that he was compelled to break the contract when he wrote: 'Owing to unforeseen personal circumstances I am sorry but I will not be able to pay any more payments on the Bedford Dormobile. Will you please let me know when and where I will have to return the car? I am very sorry regarding this but I have no alternative.'

REPOSSESSION: YOUR RIGHTS

If you do not keep your side of this agreement but you have paid at least [the cost of installing the goods plus one third of the rest of the total amount payable under this agreement, that is] [one third of the total amount payable under this agreement, that is]★ £x★★ the creditor may not take back the goods against your wishes unless he gets a court order. (In Scotland he may need to get a court order at any time.) If he does take the goods without your consent or a court order, you have the right to get back any money that you have paid under this agreement.

Comment

★ Creditor to insert the appropriate passage in square brackets.

★★ Creditor to insert the amount calculated in accordance with the provisions of *s 90* of the *Act*.

Section 90 of the *CCA 1974* provides for what are called 'protected goods'. If one-third of the total price has been paid, the creditor requires a court order to repossess. *Section 91* provides that a creditor who repossesses protected goods without a court order releases the consumer from all liability under the contract and must repay all sums paid.

IMPORTANT – READ THIS CAREFULLY TO FIND OUT ABOUT YOUR RIGHTS

The Consumer Credit Act 1974 lays down certain requirements for your protection which should have been complied with when this agreement was made. If they were not, the creditor cannot enforce this agreement without getting a court order.

The Act also gives you a number of rights:

(1)   You can settle this agreement at any time by giving notice in writing and paying off the amount you owe under the agreement [which may be reduced by a rebate]★ [Examples indicating the amount you have to pay appear in the agreement.]★★

(2)   If you received unsatisfactory goods or services paid for under this agreement [, apart from any bought with a cash loan,]★★★ you may have a right to sue the supplier, the creditor or both.

(3)   If the contract is not fulfilled, perhaps because the supplier has gone out of business, you may still be able to sue the creditor.

If you would like to know more about your rights under the Act, contact either your local Trading Standards Department or your nearest Citizens' Advice Bureau.

Comment

★   Creditor to insert phrase in square brackets in any agreement where rebate would be payable on early settlement under the agreement or the *Consumer Credit (Early Settlement) Regulations 2004 (SI 2004/1483)*.

★★   Creditor to insert phrase in second pair of square brackets in any agreement for fixed-sum credit for a term of more than one month.

★★★   Creditor to insert phrase in square brackets in any multiple agreement, of which, at least one part is a debtor-creditor-supplier agreement falling within *s 12(b)* or *(c)* of the *Act* and at least one part is a debtor-creditor agreement falling within *s 13(c)* of the *Act*.

It should be realised that the above applies only in the case of the traditional three-party hire purchase agreement, where the supplier in fact sells to a finance company which then enters the agreement with the consumer. If only two parties are involved, the owner/creditor and the customer, the following is the mandatory requirement.

IMPORTANT – READ THIS CAREFULLY TO FIND OUT ABOUT YOUR RIGHTS

The *Consumer Credit Act 1974* lays down certain requirements for your protection which should have been complied with when this agreement was made. If they were not, the creditor cannot enforce this agreement without getting a court order.

The Act also gives you a number of rights. You can settle this agreement at any time by giving notice in writing and paying off the amount you owe under the agreement [which may be reduced by a rebate]★. [Examples indicating the amount you might have to pay appear in the agreement.]★★

If you would like to know more about your rights under the Act, contact either your local Trading Standards Department or your nearest Citizens' Advice Bureau'.

Comment

★ Creditor to insert phrase in square brackets in any agreement where rebate would be payable on early settlement under the agreement or the *Consumer Credit (Early Settlement) Regulations 2004 (SI 2004/1483)*.

★★ Creditor to insert phrase in second pair of square brackets in any agreement for fixed-sum credit for a term of more than one month.

This is a Hire-Purchase Agreement regulated by the Consumer Credit Act 1974. Sign it only if you want to be legally bound by its terms.

Signature(s)

Of Debtor

Date(s) of signature(s).

The goods will not become your property until you have made all the payments. You must not sell them before then.

Comment

Note. The creditor may omit 'Dates(s) of signature(s)' where that date is not required. This relates to an agreement which is not cancellable and the date is given in the document on which the unexecuted agreement became an executed agreement. Note too that the above mandatory requirements must appear in a box.

It is stated that the goods must not be sold prior to property in them passing. This does not necessarily mean, however, that a sale or disposition before then will not pass property to a third party. The *Hire Purchase Act 1964* provides that a third party, other than a dealer, taking a motor vehicle in good faith when that vehicle is still subject to a hire purchase agreement or conditional sale agreement will receive a good title.

Case Example: *G E Capital Bank Ltd v (1) Stephen Rushton (2) Richard Jenking* **[2005] EWCA Civ 1556**

G had lent money to a motor dealer (T) under a master trading agreement to enable T to purchase motor vehicles for the purposes of its business. The agreement provided that title to a purchased vehicle remained vested in the bank until the whole sum advanced in relation to that vehicle had been repaid. T ran short of money and approached R for a loan. The loan had been provided by R's friend, the second respondent (J), through J's company, which took a debenture from T to secure the loan. Some weeks later J demanded repayment of that loan and in order to repay it T sold its remaining stock of vehicles to R. R with the assistance of J took possession of the cars and stored them pending disposal. T went into liquidation. The bank took proceedings against R and J seeking the return of the cars or their value, damages for conversion and interest. G submitted that R (1) had not been a private purchaser; (2) had not acted in good faith.

It was held that *HPA 1964* drew a clear distinction between a private purchaser who obtained the protection of *HPA 1964* and a trade purchaser who did not. The trade purchaser carried on a business that consisted of purchasing motor vehicles for sale and the private purchaser did not. The expression 'carries on a business' could in an appropriate context refer to a single transaction in the way of business. The purpose of the legislation was to provide protection to those who did not buy in the course of trade. In context, the reference in *HPA 1964* to a person carrying on a business that consisted wholly or partly of purchasing motor vehicles for the purpose of offering or exposing them for sale was intended to direct attention not only to the business of the purchaser immediately before and at the time of the disposition but also to the purpose for which the vehicle was bought. This meant that a person was not necessarily to be regarded as a private purchaser simply because he had not previously bought motor vehicles with a view to selling them in the way of business. When R bought the vehicles from T he had not taken any steps to set himself up as a motor dealer but he clearly decided to purchase them as a business venture with a view to selling them at a profit. At the time he bought the vehicles, R was a trade purchaser and not a private purchaser within the meaning of the Act. As a result, R did not obtain a good title to the vehicles when he bought them from T.

It was also held that, in order to assess R's good faith, it was necessary to know what he thought the cars were worth when he purchased them, as to which the evidence was far from clear. R clearly believed that he was buying at a discount to the trade price. The discount appeared to be about 20% and that was not strong evidence of dishonesty. There were insufficient grounds for overturning the lower court's decision that R had acted in good faith.

Case Example: *Welcome Financial Services Ltd v Nine Regions Ltd (t/a Log Book Loans)* **(unreported; 22 April 2010)**

The appellant company (W) appealed against a decision that the respondent company (N), and not W, was beneficially entitled to the proceeds of sale of a motor vehicle. W provided credit, including personal loans and car finance through hire purchase agreements. N provided 'no credit check' loans to individuals with a bad credit history secured against the debtor's vehicle, title to which was assigned to N by means of a bill of sale. W had entered into a hire purchase agreement with an individual (S) who wished to buy a car. It was an express term of the agreement that title to the vehicle remained with W and that S must not sell the car. Three days later S, in breach of the terms of her agreement with W, assigned the vehicle to N pursuant to a bill of sale as security for a loan. S defaulted on the loan with N. N repossessed the car and sold it. The judge held that N was a 'private purchaser' within the meaning of the *Hire-Purchase Act 1964* so that S could transfer a good title and N was entitled to retain the proceeds. The term 'private purchaser' was used in contradistinction to a 'trade or finance purchaser' so that a private purchaser meant a purchaser who, at the time of the disposition made to him, did not carry on any such business as was described in *s 29(2)*. W submitted that the judge had erred in her interpretation of the definition contained in *HPA 1964, s 29(2)*.

It was held that the judge was wrong to hold that the purpose of the purchase of the car in the instant case by N was not for the purpose of offering or exposing it for sale within the Act. The fact that S's borrowing was for unrelated purposes was irrelevant. N had the undoubted ulterior purpose of purchasing the vehicle as a security, partly 'for the purpose of offering or exposing [it] for sale' in the event of the borrower's default, as acknowledged by N's own terms and conditions in the bill of sale. The evidence on the number of such vehicles having to be sold was not important if it was part of N's business plan to do so as a last resort in the event of default. A significant number were sold at auction albeit a small percentage of those secured. N was a long way from being the 'private purchaser' envisaged by the Act. A purpose of N in purchasing the vehicles, although not the purpose, was to sell them in the event of default by the borrower under the loan agreement.

The court said that the judge was also wrong to hold that N did not fall within the Act because the finance provided was not for the purpose of, or in any way linked to, the acquisition by the user of the car. The Act did not say that the undoubted bailment needed to be linked to the acquisition of the vehicle under hire purchase. Parliament intended the Act to cover all business situations where motor cars acted as security for finance, not just hire purchase and conditional sale agreements. That would cover the situation where the main purpose was to provide finance to a high risk sub-prime customer for potential substantial reward at an exorbitant rate of interest necessarily secured with the vehicle in their ownership bailed back to the borrower. In context, N was not within the ambit of a consumer such as a private purchaser. Finance companies were not designed to fall within the protection of the definition of a private purchaser. It would go against the purpose of the legislation if N were to be able to claim protection because it used a bill of sale rather than a hire purchase agreement or a conditional sale agreement. W was entitled to the proceeds of sale of the vehicle.

Importantly, as pointed out above, the customer might be a business, and hence would be capable of passing a good title to goods subject to a hire purchase agreement under other provisions recognised by the *Factors Act 1889* and the *Sale of Goods Act 1979*. A factor, or mercantile agent, can also pass a title to a bona fide third party.

In addition, title can pass by operation of the doctrine of estoppel. It will always be a question of fact as to whether the circumstances show that there has been an estoppel, that is to say that a person – by his conduct – should be estopped or prevented from denying what he has led another person to believe is the case.

Case Example: *Central Newbury Car Auctions Ltd v Unity Finance Ltd* **[1957] 1 QB 371**

A car was obtained on hire purchase from the claimant and driven away with the registration book. The defendant then declined the proposal for a hire purchase agreement, the car being sold to a third party. It was held that the car still belonged to the auction house. Its allowing the customer to have possession did not amount to a representation that he had the right to sell. The registration book was not a document of title and indeed contained a warning that the person in whose name the vehicle was registered might not necessarily be the owner.

Case Example: *Moorgate Mercantile Leasing Ltd v Twitchings* **[1976] 3 WLR 66**

Moorgate was a finance company, which owned a car which was let on hire purchase to a customer. Before completing the payments, the customer sold it to a car dealer. Both Moorgate and the dealer were members of Hire Purchase Information (HPI) Ltd which operates a register of hire purchase agreements available for inspection by members. Moorgate had carelessly failed to register the agreement, the result being that HPI told the dealer that no such agreement was outstanding. The dealer accordingly claimed that Moorgate were estopped from denying that the customer was the owner of the car. The claim failed; Moorgate had made no representations to the dealer.

The only statement to the dealer was that made by HPI, namely that there was no hire purchase agreement relating to the car in question. That statement was true and had, in any case, not been made by Moorgate since HPI was not its agent. It was true that Moorgate had been careless, but this was not the same as 'negligence' unless Moorgate were in breach of a duty to take care. Moorgate were not obliged to join HPI, nor under a duty of care to register agreements. No estoppel could therefore be made out, and Moorgate were entitled to succeed in their claim against the dealer. Since this case, however, HPI have written into its terms of membership an absolute duty to register, so that if the facts of this case were to recur, the result might well be different.

5. NAMES AND ADDRESSES OF TWO WITNESSES TO CUSTOMER'S SIGNATURE:

Signature: _____

Address: _____

_____

Signature: _____

Address: _____

_____

Comment

This provision is optional, since there is no legal requirement for witnesses.

6. DECLARATION BY CUSTOMER

By signing this agreement you are declaring that:

(a)   your name and address as contained in this agreement are correct;

(b)   all the information you have given us whether in this contract or in the course of negotiation are correct;

(c)   you accept that we rely on that information when deciding whether or not to make this agreement.

Comment

This provision is not a statutory requirement. Effectively, it gives the owner a right to sue for breach or for misrepresentation in the event of any inaccuracies.

Further terms   **C2.14**

There will, of course, be other terms which the owner will wish to incorporate and these are considered below.

Incorporating these further terms   **C2.15**

Section 61(1)(b) of the *CCA 1974,* however, does say that the contractual document must embody all the terms of an agreement other than implied terms (though these can be included if the owner wishes). In this context, *s 189(4) CCA 1974* provides that an agreement embodies a contract term if it refers to it, thus allowing incorporation by reference. Breach of this provision renders an agreement improperly executed and hence enforceable only on a court order.

PAYMENT

All payments must be made not later than the date stipulated in this agreement. If this provision is not complied with, we reserve the right to charge interest at the rate charged for credit under this agreement. Interest will be calculated on a daily basis from the date the amount falls due until such time as it is received and will run both before and after any judgment (such obligation to be independent of and not to merge with any judgment). If you are making payments by post, we advise the use of recorded or registered delivery. Should you not make use of such services, the onus is on yourself to prove despatch and receipt of the payment by ourselves.

Comment

The passage in brackets above avoids the fact that the law does allow for interest to be payable up to judgment date, but not after it, unless there is a provision in the agreement allowing for post-judgment interest.

Case Example: *Director General of Fair Trading v First National Bank plc* **[2002] 1 All ER 97**

The Director General sought a declaration that this provision was unfair, and hence unenforceable, under the provisions of the *Unfair Terms in Consumer Contracts Regulations 1994 (SI 1994/3159)* (these have been replaced, without any relevant difference, by the *Unfair Terms in Consumer Contracts Regulations 1999 (SI 1999/2083)*). *Regulation 3(2)(b)* excludes from the scope of the Regulations a term which defines the main subject matter of the contract or which concerns the adequacy of the price or remuneration, as against the goods or services sold or supplied. The House of Lords accepted that the disputed clause was not within this provision, and hence subject to the fairness test imposed by the Regulations.

It then ruled that the clause was not unfair. It said that the provision could not be said to cause a significant imbalance in the parties' rights and obligations to the detriment of the consumer to an extent which was contrary to the requirement of good faith, this being the test laid down by the Regulations. The essential bargain was that the bank would make funds available to be repaid, over a period, with interest. Neither party could suppose that the bank would willingly forgo any part of its principal or interest.

The House of Lords pointed out that the customer did have certain remedies open to him under *CCA 1974*, but that there was no requirement for the agreement to indicate their presence.

It should be noted that *s 92* of the *CCA 1974* states that a customer cannot be obliged to pay interest on sums outstanding at a rate exceeding the contractual rate of interest.

OWNERSHIP OF THE GOODS HIRED

The goods hired to you under this agreement remain our absolute property until such time as you have fulfilled all conditions, relating to payment or otherwise, necessary for property to vest in yourself.

Comment

For the ability of a customer to pass title regardless of any such clause, see the above 'Specimen of a Hire Purchase Contract' at C2.12.

CUSTODY OF GOODS

You must maintain the goods in good condition and repair at your own expense. Should you have been provided with the goods by a third party, you must not allow that third party to retain the goods or to have any lien over them. You will at all times be responsible for any loss or damage incurred by the goods, fair wear and tear excepted, even if such loss or damage arises because of events beyond your reasonable control.

Comment

This clause cannot in fact prevent the customer from giving a lien over the goods, since a third party is not bound by the agreement, but the giving of a lien would amount to a breach of contract, thus allowing the owner to terminate under further provisions of the contract (see below).

This clause can also be used in conjunction with *s 80* of the *CCA 1974*. This allows the owner, where the agreement requires the customer to keep the goods under his control, to require the customer, following notice in writing, to advise the owner within seven working days of the whereabouts of the goods.

YOUR DETAILS

You must notify us in writing of any change in your address within seven days of such change taking effect.

Comment

It is of obvious importance for the owner to know the whereabouts of the customer, and hence of the goods. Failure to inform the owner of a change of address would be a breach of contract and hence allow the owner to terminate the agreement (see below).

INSPECTION OF THE GOODS

You must allow us or a representative of ours to inspect the goods on due notice and at all reasonable times.

Comment

It is likely that, in the vast majority of cases, the owner would never want to exercise this right, but it could be useful in the case of high-value goods, such as cars.

INSURANCE

You must keep the goods insured under a fully comprehensive policy of insurance at your own expense. You must notify us of any loss or damage to the goods and hold any moneys payable under the policy in trust for us. You irrevocably authorise us to collect the moneys from the insurers. If a claim is made against the insurers we may at our absolute discretion conduct any negotiations and effect any settlement with the insurers and you agree to abide by such settlement.

Comment

The customer, as hirer of the goods, has an insurable interest in the goods although he is not the actual owner. By using this clause, the customer is committed to taking out the widest possible level of cover. Although he may be the person to receive the insurance payment, he holds it in trust for the owner.

YOUR RIGHT TO END THE AGREEMENT

You have the right to terminate this agreement as set out in the TERMINATION: YOUR RIGHTS notice set out in this agreement. You must then at your own expense return to us the goods together with, in the case of a motor vehicle, the registration document, the road fund licence and any current test certificate.

Comment

This builds on the statutory right of termination referred to above. *CCA 1974* does not prevent the imposition of expenses where the customer does exercise his right to terminate.

OUR RIGHT TO TERMINATE THE AGREEMENT

In the event of the happening of the following, we will have the right, after serving notice on you at your last known address, to terminate this agreement if:

- you fail to keep to any of the terms of this agreement, express or implied;

- you commit any act or bankruptcy or have a receiving or bankruptcy order made against you or you petition for bankruptcy, or are served with a creditor's demand under the *Insolvency Act 1986* (or any re-enactment thereof), or go into administrative receivership, or make a formal composition or scheme of arrangement with your creditors, or call a meeting of them, or, other than for normal purposes of amalgamation and reconstruction, wind up your business;

- execution is levied or sought against any of your assets or income;

- the landlord of the premises where the goods are situated threatens or takes any steps to distrain on the goods;

- where you are a partnership, the partnership is dissolved;

- you have given false or misleading information in connection with your entry into this agreement;

- the goods are destroyed or the insurers treat a claim under the policy referred to above; or

- you fail to notify us of any change of address or you move to live permanently outside the United Kingdom.

If we do terminate this agreement, then subject to the provisions covered by REPOSSESSION: YOUR RIGHTS contained in this agreement, we may resume possession of the goods. You will also have to pay all outstanding payments and such further amount, as appropriate, as will make up one half of the total purchase price payable under this agreement. If you have failed to take reasonable care of the goods, you may be liable to compensate us for this.

Comment

The foregoing clause gives the right to terminate and is not concerned with whether any terms infringed are conditions or warranties.

It recognises, particularly in relation to partnerships and winding up, that *CCA 1974* covers not just individuals, but also partnerships and any legal entity not consisting entirely of bodies corporate and which is itself not a partnership.

The reference to 'implied terms' ensures that the owner's right to terminate exists not just in relation to the terms expressly written in the agreement. The right will apply also in relation to any duties implied on

---

the customer by law. The customer is, for example, under a common law duty to accept delivery of the goods (*National Cash Register Co v Stanley* [1921] 3 KB 292) and hence any breach of this implied duty would entitle the owner to terminate the agreement.

It limits the customer's liability to 50% of the purchase price. This limit is not mandatory, but is aimed at avoiding the rule against penalty clauses.

Case Example: *Bridge v Campbell Discount Co Ltd* **[1962] AC 600**

The House of Lords ruled that a provision requiring the customer to pay two-thirds of the hire purchase price was not a liquidated damages clause, but an unenforceable penalty clause instead.

Owner's obligations before termination   **C2.16**

It is important to realise that restraints are imposed by *CCA 1974* on the owner when he seeks to invoke such a termination clause. *Sections 76, 87* and *98* require the issue of notices on the customer to be in the form specified by the *Consumer Credit (Enforcement, Default and Termination Notices) Regulations 1983 (SI 1983/1561)*. Where the customer is actually in breach of the agreement, he must be given at least 14 days after service of the notice to make good the breach (*CCA 1974, s 88(2)*).

Reference should also be made here to the discussion of Protected Goods under the REPOSSESSION:YOUR RIGHTS clause above.

EXPENSES

You will be required to pay on demand any expenses and legal costs which we incur for:

(a)   finding your address if you change your address without notifying us, or of us finding the goods if they are not at your address; or

(b)   taking such steps as, in our discretion, are considered necessary, including but without limitation any court action, to recover the goods or to obtain payment for them.

YOUR RIGHT TO A REBATE

You have a statutory right at any time to pay all amounts payable under this agreement, and any such early settlement may entitle you to a statutory rebate. Any notice you give to make use of this right must be in writing.

Comment

This reflects the provisions of s *94* of the *CCA 1974* and of the *Consumer Credit (Rebate on Early Settlement) Regulations 2004 (SI 2004/1483)*. If the agreement provides for a higher level of rebate than that provided for in the Regulations, the customer is entitled to the higher rebate (*Home Insulation Ltd v Wadsley* [1988] CCLR 25).

LIMITATION OF LIABILITY

Except where you are dealing as a consumer as that term is defined in the *Consumer Rights Act 2015*, your rights under that Act, or under any other provision, whether statutory or existing by virtue of implication of law, are hereby excluded.

Comment

The exclusion of consumers from this clause (broadly speaking those who are not taking the goods in the course of a business) recognises the fact that, under *CRA*, terms implied as to description, quality and fitness for purpose cannot be excluded vis-à-vis such customers.

Case Example: *R&B Custom Brokers Co Ltd v United Dominions Trust* **[1988] 1 WLR 321**

The claimant company obtained a car from the defendant finance company. A term in the agreement excluded the implied terms as to the condition or quality of the car or its fitness for purpose. The car was the second or third which the claimant had acquired on credit terms. They were in business as shipping brokers and freight forwarding agents. This particular car had been obtained for business and personal use. The Court of Appeal ruled that the purchase was only incidental to the claimant's business activity and that a degree of regularity was required before that transaction could be said to be an integral part of the claimant's business. Since the car was, at the most, the third acquired on business terms, that degree of regularity was lacking. The company had, therefore, dealt as a consumer. See too *Feldaroll Foundry plc v Hermes Leasing (London) Ltd* [2004] EWCA Civ 747.

If the customer does not deal as a consumer, then the clause is valid if it can be shown by the owner to be reasonable. While it cannot be said with certainty that a total exclusion clause such as this one would fail the reasonableness test, it is always possible. Accordingly, the owner might like to replace the total exclusion with a limitation of its maximum liability to a specified sum, or a sum worked out by a given formula, such as limiting liability to the value of the contract.

It is also possible to attempt to have the best of both worlds by using a clause which provides for a total exclusion, but which adds that 'in the event of the foregoing being deemed by any court or arbitrator to be unreasonable, liability shall be accepted up to the value of the contract' or such other limitation as is deemed appropriate.

MISCELLANEOUS

This agreement is personal to you and may under no circumstances be assigned by you to any third party.

We may in our absolute discretion assign the agreement to any third party we think fit.

Comment

The owner is allowed by virtue of the above to assign the agreement to a third party. This can take place when the business is sold or taken over, or when the owner factors his debts (ie sells them to another in return for payment of the right to collect debts which would otherwise be due to the owner).

When within the 2010 Regulations   C2.17

Agreements regulated by the *Consumer Credit Act* (as to which see C2.3 and C2.8) are covered by these Regulations except:

(a)   an agreement secured on land;

(b)   an agreement under which the creditor provides the debtor with credit which exceeds £60,260; and

(c)   an agreement entered into by the debtor wholly or predominantly for the purposes of a business carried on, or intended to be carried on, by him.

Note, though, that the Regulations will apply in such cases too if the pre-contract credit information has been supplied (see C2.4.1).

The form and content of contracts within the 2010 Regulations is as below.

Hire Purchase Agreement regulated by the Consumer Credit Act 1974

Agreement Number:

Between us, the Owner, and you, the Customer, for the supply of the goods referred to below on the terms listed hereunder.

Owner:

Address:

Tel, fax, email:

Customer (name, address, phone, fax, email):

Credit intermediary (if applicable) address, phone, fax, email:

Goods (description of goods)   Cash Price Inc VAT

This agreement finances the supply of the specific goods/services described above. Except where the cash price of the goods is greater than £30,000 or less (but more than £100) or the amount of credit exceeds £60,260, or you enter this agreement wholly or predominantly for the purposes of your business, if the goods or services are not supplied to you or are supplied only in part or do not conform to the supply contract, you have the right under the Consumer Credit Act 1974 to seek redress from us if you are unable to obtain redress from the supplier. In other circumstances, you can seek redress from us or the supplier in your absolute discretion.

Insurance

Address:

Policy No; Date insurance commenced; Expiry date

Financial particulars: Net; VAT @20%

Total cash price of goods:

Total cash price (inc VAT):

Advance payment part exchange; Cash

Amount of credit:

Balance payable by:

A first instalment (including document fee if charged) of ... followed by ... instalments each in the sum of ... followed by a final instalment (including option to purchase fee if charged) in the sum of ...

Each instalment is due and payable on the same day of each month commencing one month after the date of this agreement or, if (a) is inserted here [ ] this date.

We will provide the amount of credit to you on the making of this agreement by paying such amount to the dealer or other supplier of the goods.

Interest:

Term of agreement: [ ] months.

Document fee; rate of interest: [ ]% pa fixed.

Total charge for credit including any default charges (as below): £[ ];APR: [ ]%.

Total amount payable: £ ... ; calculated at the time of making the agreement, on the assumption that the agreement remains in force for the term of the agreement and that you promptly perform your obligations under this agreement.

Balance payable: £ ....

Security (insert details of security if required).

Terms and conditions

Default interest and charges

We may charge you default interest in accordance with clause 10 of the Terms and Conditions of the agreement, at the rate stated on the agreement per annum calculated daily for each day you still owe the payment. We can charge this interest even after we have obtained a court judgment against you.

We may also require payment of our reasonable charges arising from late payment for (a) each payment reminder letter or document to which you are not otherwise entitled; (b) each cheque, card payment, standing order or direct debit which is rejected, dishonoured, stopped or otherwise not paid by you.

Where known at the date of the agreement, our costs for the above are, for (a) £30, and for (b) £30 and otherwise as we will notify you. See also clause 10(b) for our costs for enforcing the agreement, which includes recovery of our costs or charges payable by us to third parties acting on our behalf.

Other charges not relating to default

A charge of 2% of the value of the transaction will be payable on payments made by credit card.

Missing payments

Missing payments make obtaining credit more difficult and could have severe consequences such as the possibility of our taking possession of the Goods/Vehicle, legal proceedings, bankruptcy proceedings, or your home being repossessed.

Statement of account

You have a right under the Act (unless you enter into the agreement for business purposes) to receive, on request and free of charge, at any time during the period of the agreement, a statement in the form of a table showing:

(a)   the details of each instalment owing under the agreement;

(b)   the date on which each instalment is due, the amount and any conditions relating to the payment of the instalment; and

(c)   a breakdown of each instalment showing how much comprises:

(i)   capital repayment,

(ii)   interest payment, and

(iii)   if applicable, any other charges.

Right of withdrawal

You have the right under the Act to withdraw from the agreement, without a reason, in accordance with the provisions below. You must then make the payment set below on:

(a)   the day on which the agreement is made, or

(b)   the day on which you receive a copy of the executed agreement, or

(c)   where you have previously been provided with a copy of the unexecuted agreement, the day on which we inform you in writing that:

(i)   the agreement has been executed,

(ii)   the executed agreement is in identical terms to the unexecuted agreement, a copy of which has already been given to you, and

(iii)   that you have the right to receive a copy of the executed agreement, if you request it before the end of the period for withdrawal.

Notice of your intention to withdraw from the agreement may be given orally by telephoning us on: 08448 463463; by a personal visit to our business address shown on the agreement or by writing to us; or by leaving written notice at, our business address shown on the agreement, or by facsimile transmission to us on: 08448 469024, or by email to us at: info@billingfinance.co.uk

Once you have given us notice of your intention to withdraw from the agreement, you must pay to us at our address shown in the agreement, without delay and no later than 30 calendar days beginning with the day after the day you gave us notice of withdrawal, the amount of credit provided under the agreement together with interest from the date the credit was provided to the day we receive full payment in cleared funds. Interest will accrue at the interest rate provided for in this agreement. You may pay us by cash, cheque, bankers draft, or by whatever other method of payment is agreed by you and us. You may contact us by any of the means shown above.

Early repayment

You have the right, under the Act, at any time to repay in full or in part the outstanding balance under the agreement, less any rebate to which you may be entitled under s 95 of the Act. To do this you must give us notice, by any of the methods shown above, of your intention:

(a) to fully discharge your indebtedness under the agreement, or

(b) to partially discharge your indebtedness under the agreement and pay to us the amount as notified to you by us before the end of the period of 28 days beginning with the day following our receipt of your notice, or on or before any later date specified in that notice.

Partially discharging your indebtedness will have the effect of reducing your monthly instalments for the remainder of the term of the agreement. The term of the agreement will not reduce.

Supervisory authority

The supervisory authority under the Consumer Credit Act 1974 is the Financial Conduct Authority, 25 The North Colonnade, Canary Wharf, London E14 5HS.

If you have a complaint you should write to us and we will endeavour to resolve it as soon as possible. If you enter into the agreement for non-business purposes you have the right to refer any unresolved complaint to the Financial Ombudsman Service, South Quay Plaza, 183 Marsh Wall, London, E14 9SR. Web: www.financial-ombudsman.org.uk. Telephone: 020 7964 1001. Email: complaint.info@financial-ombudsman.org.uk

If you enter into the agreement for business purposes you may still have this right.

Termination and repossession

You may terminate the agreement at any time before the final payment is due, by giving us written notice at the address shown under Right of Withdrawal above. You must then immediately pay us the amount by which one half of the Total Amount Payable exceeds the sums paid and the sums due in respect of the Total Amount Payable immediately before termination. We will notify you of the amount due.

1 Hire purchase

We enter into the hire purchase agreement with you for the hire to you of the Goods/Vehicle, on the hire purchase terms set out in the pages of your agreement and the terms below.

2 Payment to you

(a)   You must pay the Advance Payment, if any shown, on or before signing the agreement.

(b)   You agree to pay us the Total Amount Payable (less any Advance Payment paid) by the instalments and at the times shown in the agreement. Any Option to Purchase Fee, included in the final instalment, is only payable if you want to become the owner of the Goods/Vehicle, as set out in clause 8.

(c)   It is essential that you make all payments in full and on time (see clauses 10 and 11). If you pay by cheque you will be responsible for any payment lost in the post.

3 Safekeeping if the Goods/Vehicle

You must keep the Goods/Vehicle safely at your address. You may not sell or part with possession of the Goods/Vehicle or transfer your rights under the agreement. You may only part with the Goods/Vehicle to have it repaired. You may not use the Goods/Vehicle as security for your outstanding debts or liabilities. You may not take the Goods/Vehicle outside the United Kingdom or use it for hire or reward without our consent.

4 Caring for the Goods/Vehicle

(a)   You must keep the Goods/Vehicle in good working order and condition at your expense. You are responsible for all loss of or damage to, the Goods/Vehicle even if caused by events beyond your control, except for loss or damage due fair wear and tear.

(b)   You must not let a repairer, or any other person to whom you owe money, keep the Goods/Vehicle as a result of your not paying the money you owe.

(c)   You must make sure that any test or inspections required by law or by the insurer are carried out.

(d) Unless we have consented in writing, you may not make any alterations or additions to the Goods/Vehicle (including fixing a personalised or non-original number plate). Any alterations or additions made without our consent will become our property.

(e) You must allow our representative to inspect and test the Goods/Vehicle at all reasonable times.

5 Change of address or name

You must let us know, in writing, within seven days of any change of your address or name.

6 Insuring the Goods/Vehicle

You must insure the Goods/Vehicle and keep it insured at all times at your expense with a reputable insurer, to its full replacement value under a fully comprehensive policy against such risks as are ordinarily insured against. You must tell us and your insurer about any loss or damage to the Goods/Vehicle within 48 hours of the loss or damage happening, and whether you or anybody else will be making a claim against the insurer.

(a) You agree to hold in trust for us any insurance monies you may receive.

(b) You authorise us to negotiate and settle any claim with your insurer; and to receive any monies from the insurer under the policy. You may not withdraw this authority and you agree to accept any settlement we may reach with the insurer. You will still need to pay us any outstanding balance under the agreement. Unless we end the agreement, pursuant clause 11, the agreement will continue even if the Goods/Vehicle is lost or damaged.

(c) If you enter into the agreement for your business purposes, you must also obtain adequate insurance cover for employer's liability to third parties and liability for negligence and loss, damage or injury arising out of your use and possession of the Goods/Vehicle.

7 Operator's Licence

If the vehicle is a goods vehicle:

(a) you must be licensed under the Goods Vehicle (Licensing of Operators) Regulations 1995, and

(b) you must:

(i) confirm that you hold a valid operator's licence and agree to furnish us with a copy within seven days of the date of the agreement and at least annually following our request; and

(ii)   agree not to do anything which might result in the loss of that licence or which might result in the Vehicle being taken away under the Goods Vehicles (Enforcement Powers) Regulations 2001, SI 2001/3981.

8 Ownership of the Goods/Vehicle

We remain the owner of the Goods/Vehicle until you have, (a) paid to us all the instalments shown in the agreement and all other amounts which may become payable by you to us under the agreement and (b) you exercise the option to purchase by paying the Option to Purchase Fee shown in the agreement or, if none is shown, by notifying us in writing of your decision to retain the Goods/Vehicle. Until then your rights are only those of a hirer of the Goods/Vehicle.

9 Your right to end the agreement

You may end the agreement by taking the steps set out in the notice 'Termination: Your Rights' shown in the agreement. You must then (at your own expense) return the Goods/Vehicle to us together with the registration document, tax disc and MOT test certificate. You must also pay to us any further amount mentioned in the notice.

10 Default interest and charges

(a)   If you fail to pay us any amount you owe us under this agreement by the due date we may, in addition to our other rights, charge you default interest on that amount from the due date of payment until its receipt by us at the interest rate shown in the agreement, both before and after any judgment.

(b)   You agree to pay us any costs and charges shown in the agreement, which may become payable by you, and our reasonable legal and other costs for enforcing the agreement, including any payable to third parties.

11 Rights of other people

Nothing in the agreement will give any person, other than us or you (or anyone who takes over from us or any person to whom we have transferred our rights under the agreement), any rights under the agreement.

12 Our right to end the agreement

12.1 We will be entitled to assume that you refuse to comply with the terms of the agreement and to end the agreement, after giving you a default notice if:

(a)   you break any of the provisions of clauses 2, 3, 4 or 6 of the agreement;

(b) you provide false information when entering into the agreement;

(c) the Goods/Vehicle is destroyed or treated as a total loss under any insurance claim;

(d) you entered into the agreement for the purpose of your business and you stop trading or, if you are a partnership, the partnership is ended or court action has commenced to end it;

(e) you have done anything which would allow any of your belongings, property, income, or savings to be legally removed to pay off any of your debits; or

(f) any of the following happens:

(i) a statutory demand (that is, a written demand for payment of debt of at least £750, which, if not paid in full, may result in bankruptcy proceedings being brought against you) is not paid in 21 days, or any steps are taken by you or anyone else to declare you bankrupt;

(ii) you take steps to enter into an arrangement or debt management plan with you creditors;

(iii) a bailiff or other office controls or seizes the Goods/Vehicle or any of your assets following a court order; or

(iv) landlord of premises where the Goods/Vehicle is situated threatens, or takes steps, to seize or in any other way control the Goods/Vehicle or any of your assets.

12.2 If we end the agreement, subject to your rights as set out in the notice, 'Repossession: Your Rights', we may take back the Goods/Vehicle from you and you must pay to us:

(a) all instalments and other sums which have become payable by you to us under this agreement, and

(b) the outstanding balance of the Total Amount Payable, less:

(i) any Option to Purchase Fee and any rebate of charges to which you may be entitled; and

(ii) any money we receive from selling the Goods/Vehicle after we have deducted the cost of recovery, insurance and storage.

13 Exclusion

(a) If you are dealing as a consumer, as described in the *Consumer Rights Act 2015*, nothing in this agreement will take away your rights under that Act. (These relate to our holding title in the Goods/Vehicle, the Goods/Vehicle's correspondence with description and the quality or fitness of the Goods/Vehicle.)

(b) In all other cases:

(i)   you must inspect the Goods/Vehicle and use your own skill and judgement to decide whether it is of satisfactory quality and fit for your intended purpose; and

(ii)   we will not be responsible for the quality of the Goods/Vehicle or whether it is fit for its intended purpose, or whether it matches any particular description or specification.

14 General

(a)   In the agreement 'Act' means the Consumer Credit Act 1974; 'Terms' include, without limitation, the Terms and Conditions; 'Goods/Vehicle' means the Goods/Vehicle described in the agreement and includes any replacements, renewals and additions, to which we or any insurer may agree. Words and expressions to which meanings have been given on page 1 of the agreement shall have those meanings in these terms. Headings to clauses shall not affect the interpretation of any terms.

(b)   References to any act or regulation include any amendments to that act or regulation.

(c)   If at any time we allow you to do something which is against any of the terms of the agreement, this will not prevent us from insisting that you strictly follow the terms at any later time.

(d)   If two or more of you have signed the agreement as the Customer, you are liable jointly and severally, that is together as well as separately under the agreement. This means that either of you can be held fully liable for the obligations of the Customer under the agreement.

(e)   If you discharge part of your indebtedness under the agreement early we may, by written notice to you, vary the amount of remaining instalments or the remaining duration of the agreement, which may also automatically result in increasing the APR.

(f)   You may at any time request us to communicate with you by email. You must then provide us with an email address and provided we are practicably able to do so, we will send you statements, documents, notices and letters (other than default notices) by email. It shall be deemed effective service if we write to you or email you at your address or email address last known to us.

(g)   We may transfer our rights and responsibilities under the agreement to another person. This will not take away any of your rights or responsibilities under the agreement. You may not transfer any of your rights or responsibilities under the agreement to another person.

(h)   English law will apply to the agreement. If you entered into the agreement in Scotland, words that are not in current use in Scotland will have their nearest equivalent meanings.

15 When the agreement comes into force

The agreement will only come into force if and when you and we, or our authorised representative, have signed it.

Disclosing your data

We may use personal information about you which we acquire in connection with any application you make to us, or any agreement you enter into with us, to manage your agreement and for statistical or market research purposes. If we transfer, change or assign your agreement to a third party or if we employ a third party to manage any aspect of your account, we may pass relevant information about you to them. Your personal data may also be used for other purposes with your specific consent or, in limited circumstances, where required by law or permitted under the *Data Protection Act 2018* and the UK GDPR.

Data Protection Act

Under the *Data Protection Act 2018* and the UK GDPR, you have a right to access certain personal records we, credit reference agencies and fraud prevention agencies hold about you. This is called a 'subject access request', which you can make by writing to legaldepartment@billingfinance.co.uk A fee may be payable, but we will not charge you until we have told you how much the fee is and what it is for, and you have told us you still want to proceed.

This is a Hire Purchase Agreement regulated by the Consumer Credit Act 1974. Sign it only if you want to be legally bound by its terms.

Signature of Customer:

......

Owner's Signature:

Signed for and on behalf of the Owner:

Date ... which is the date of this agreement.

Unregulated hire purchase agreements   C2.18

An agreement will fall outside *CCA 1974* if the agreement is exempt (see C2.8) or the customer is not an individual, defined in *s 189(1)* of the *CCA 1974* (see C2.9).

Where an agreement is outside *CCA 1974*, none of the requirements as to form will apply. There are no common law requirements as to the form and content, as to copies, or as to cancellation or termination. Nor is there any requirement that the contract must be in writing and signed, though, as a practical matter, both are usual and to be recommended.

Applicability of enactments   C2.19

The contract will be subject to the provisions of the *Supply of Goods (Implied Terms) Act 1973*, if made with a business, or the *Consumer Rights Act 2015* if made with a consumer. Each implies into such contracts terms as to conformity with description, satisfactory quality and reasonable fitness for purpose. Similarly, the *Unfair Contract Terms Act 1977* and the 2015 Act will apply in relation to exclusion clauses.

Unauthorised dispositions   C2.20

The provisions relating to sales by a customer of goods subject to a hire purchase agreement will also apply (see the discussion above in relation to the 1983 Regulations specimen contract).

Termination   C2.21

The termination by breach of an unregulated hire purchase agreement will be governed by the terms of the agreement alone. It would be common, therefore, to find in such an agreement a clause similar to that given above. Such a clause will, of course, be subject to the rules against penalties, and hence will be valid only if it represents a genuine pre-estimate of likely loss. If a clause is rejected as being a penalty, the owner will remain able to sue for damages representing his actual loss.

Where the agreement provides for termination by death, bankruptcy, liquidation, moving abroad and such like, the agreement may specify for the payment of minimum sums in the event of such events happening.

> **Case Example:** *Re Apex Supply Co Ltd* **[1942] Ch 108**
>
> It was held that the occurrence of any such event could not be regarded as a breach of contract, and hence the rules as to penalty clauses were inapplicable.

In the event of voluntary termination by the customer, where the agreement provides for a minimum payment, and the customer gives notice of termination, returning the goods, the position at common law is that the minimum payment is to be made since there is no breach and the rules as to penalties cannot apply. The effect is that the customer may be better off if he breaks the agreement since he can then argue that the sum is payable on breach and is potentially a penalty.

The owner's right to repossess $\qquad$ C2.22

Where the agreement is not regulated, an owner's right to repossess in the event of a breach is wider than that allowed under *CCA 1974* where the agreement is regulated. If the goods remain in the customer's possession, the owner may repossess at any time.

If there has been a wrongful disposition of the goods, the owner can claim the goods from the person in possession. No court order is needed but if, as a matter of practicality, one has to be obtained (eg because access to the goods is physically impossible without trespassing), the owner can bring an action for wrongful interference under the provisions of the *Torts (Interference with Goods) Act 1977*. The Act gives the court the discretion not to order repossession. Where the goods have been bought by an innocent third party, and the provisions discussed above as to an innocent third party obtaining title apply, obviously no order can be made. In that case, there are two alternatives, which are:

- an order for the return of the goods, but giving the third party the option of paying damages; or
- damages.

The damages would be the unpaid balance of the total price payable under the agreement, the result effectively being that the obligations under the agreement have been transferred from the customer to the third party. The third party would be able to sue the customer for the amount paid.

If the owner does attempt to repossess the goods where the customer has paid a substantial amount under the agreement, a court may take the view that, in the interests of fairness, some relief should be granted to the customer. The point has never been decided but in *Snook v West Riding Investments Ltd* [1967] 1 All ER 518, 527, Lord Denning spoke of the customer's 'valuable equity' in goods subject to a hire purchase agreement.

Unfair relationships $\qquad$ C2.23

The provisions of *CCA 1974*, as amended by the *Consumer Credit Act 2006*, allowing the court to reopen an agreement where there is an unfair relationship are not restricted to regulated agreements. In this context, *CCA 1974* covers any agreement between an individual (see C2.9) where the relationship between the parties is unfair.

If the relationship is unfair, the court can reopen it and make such order as is just in all the circumstances of the case.

The fairness of a relationship is to be judged by reference to:

- its terms, or the terms of any related agreement (ie any previous agreement with the lender consolidated by the new agreement and any linked transaction, such as payment protection insurance);

- the way in which the creditor has exercised or enforced his rights under the agreement or any related agreement; and

- anything else done, or not done, by or on behalf of the creditor (before or after the agreement, or any related agreement, is made).

> **Case Example:** *MBNA Europe Bank Ltd v Thorius* **(unreported Newcastle County Court, 21 September 2009)**
>
> An unfair relationship had arisen within the meaning of the Act in the light of the standard advice to the defendant to take out Payment Protection Insurance when combined with the receipt by MBNA of undisclosed commission.
>
> See too *Yates and another v Nemo Finance and another* (Unreported, Manchester County Court; 14 May 2010).

> **Case Example:** *Link Financial Ltd v Wilson* **[2014] EWHC 252**
>
> A loan obtained to pay for the capital purchase of a holiday timeshare gave rise to an unfair relationship between the creditor and the debtor because the related timeshare purchase agreement provided that the debtor would forfeit the whole capital asset for non-payment of management charges.

> **Case Example:** *Scotland v British Credit Trust Ltd* **[2014] EWCA Civ 790**
>
> A misrepresentation by double-glazing salesmen about the need to purchase payment protection insurance when taking out a loan was properly taken into account by the court as something 'done by, or on behalf of, the creditor' when determining whether the relationship between the creditor and the debtor was unfair.

Conditional sale agreements C2.24

For the nature of a conditional sale, see C2.3.

Unauthorised dispositions C2.25

The position of the customer who takes goods under a conditional sale agreement as regards any further disposition by him during the currency of the agreement is generally identical to that of the customer under a hire purchase agreement. The customer under a conditional sale agreement is, however, also a person who has agreed to buy, and hence, potentially, can also pass title to an innocent third party under *s 25* of the *Sale of Goods Act 1979*. The right to pass title under this provision is, however, restricted by *SGA 1979* to those cases where the agreement is not a consumer credit agreement (see C2.8 for exempt agreements).

Requirements as to regulated conditional sale agreements C2.26

The provisions discussed in relation to regulated hire purchase agreements apply almost in their entirety to regulated conditional sale agreements. Any references in the agreement to a hire purchase agreement will, of course, have to read conditional sale agreement.

The discussion as to unregulated hire purchase agreements above is equally apposite to unregulated conditional sale agreements.

C3:
Online Terms and Conditions of Sale

At a glance C3.1

- Such contracts fall under the *Consumer Contracts (Information, Cancellation and Additional Charges) Regulations 2013 (SI 2013/3134)* ('Regulations') as well as the ordinary law of contract. Note that the Regulations only apply to contracts with consumers (ie to individuals not acting in the course of a business). A 'consumer' is defined as 'an individual acting for purposes which are wholly or mainly outside that individual's trade, business, craft or profession'.

- Specific detail must be presented in the online contract.

- There are special requirements to note as to mode of delivery and time for performance.

- There is a general right to cancel a contract, but this is somewhat limited in the case of a contract for the provision of a service.

- There are obligations as to when the mandatory information is to be supplied.

- There are also obligations as to how this information is to be provided.

- There is room for choosing just where the information is located.

- Some of the information is to be presented in a written or 'durable medium' which is available to and accessible by the consumer.

- The mandatory information is not exhaustive, however, and other contract terms can always be included.

- There are tight controls on the use of exclusion clauses.

Excepted contracts C3.2

The 2013 Regulations do not cover any contract. Regulation 6 of the Regulations states:

'These Regulations do not apply to a contract, to the extent that it is –

(a)   for –

(i)   gambling within the meaning of the Gambling Act 2005 (which includes gaming, betting and participating in a lottery); or

(ii) in relation to Northern Ireland, for betting, gaming or participating lawfully in a lottery within the meaning of the Betting, Gaming, Lotteries and Amusements (Northern Ireland) Order 1985;

(b)   for services of a banking, credit, insurance, personal pension, investment or payment nature;

(c)   for the creation of immovable property or of rights in immovable property;

(d)   for rental of accommodation for residential purposes;

(e)   for the construction of new buildings, or the construction of substantially new buildings by the conversion of existing buildings;

(f)   for the supply of foodstuffs, beverages or other goods intended for current consumption in the household and which are supplied by a trader on frequent and regular rounds to the consumer's home, residence or workplace;

(g)   within the scope of Council Directive 90/314/EEC of 13 June 1990 on package travel, package holidays and package tours;

(h)   within the scope of Directive 2008/122/EC of the European Parliament and of the Council on the protection of consumers in respect of certain aspects of timeshare, long-term holiday product, resale and exchange contracts.

The Regulations do not apply to contracts –

(a)   concluded by means of automatic vending machines or automated commercial premises;

(b)   concluded with a telecommunications operator through a public telephone for the use of the telephone;

(c)   concluded for the use of one single connection, by telephone, internet or fax, established by a consumer; and

(d)   under which goods are sold by way of execution or otherwise by authority of law.'

Distance selling   C3.3

Online sales are a form of distance selling and, as such, are subject to the provisions of the 2013 Regulations when made with a consumer and if the contract is not an excepted contract: see C3.2. It should be borne in mind, though, that the law of contract also applies, in particular, the rules relating to offer and acceptance. The material provided over the internet would amount to an invitation to treat, not an offer, meaning that it is the consumer who makes the offer, which the supplier is entitled to reject in his absolute discretion. This could be important if, as has happened, the internet advertisement states a much lower price for the goods than was intended. It should also be realised that, if the wording is to such effect, then the on-screen copy could immediately amount to an offer which a consumer could immediately accept. Under the 2013 Regulations, making information available to a consumer applies only if the consumer can reasonably be expected to know how to access it: Regulation 8 to the 2013 Regulations.

Contract terms required by the Regulations   C3.4

There is no need for the on-screen contract to be presented as a formal document, but it must contain at least the following detail as set out in Schedule 2 to the Regulations:

- the main characteristics of the goods or services, to the extent appropriate to the medium of communication and to the goods or services;

- the identity of the supplier (such as the supplier's trading name);

- the geographical address at which the trader is established and, where available, the trader's telephone number, fax number and email address, to enable the consumer to contact the trader quickly and communicate efficiently;

- a description of the main characteristics of the goods or services;

- the total price of the goods or services including all taxes or where the nature of the goods or services is such that the price cannot reasonably be calculated in advance, the manner in which the price is to be calculated. It does not appear permissible to give the total price for the goods or services in the form: '£100 plus £20 VAT'. It seems that the only permitted statement is 'Price £120'. In this case, it seems permissible to add 'inclusive of £20 VAT';

- there must be a statement of the relevant delivery costs and any other costs; and

- the arrangements for payment, delivery, performance, and the time by which the trader undertakes to deliver the goods or to perform the services.

The arrangements for payment could embrace online means for paying, usually by entering credit card details, or by allowing for sums to be deducted directly from a bank account.

Requirements as to statement of performance C3.5

The stated arrangements as to performance will show how delivery is to be made, for example, by despatch to the consumer's home address or to a central collection point such as the nearest post office. It does not seem necessary to indicate just how the goods will be delivered (eg by mail, parcel post, courier), though these can be stated and often are. These provisions in the contract as to performance can be linked to further provisions in the 2013 Regulations as to the time of performance (see immediately below).

Time of performance C3.6

Unless the contract says otherwise, the supplier must perform the contract without undue delay and, in any event, within 30 days from the day after the contract was made: Regulation 42 of the 2013 Regulations. If, therefore, the supplier expects to provide the goods six weeks from the order, the arrangements for performance should state this. If, though, he expects no problem with performing within 30 days, then nothing further need be said. Unless the contract states otherwise, the contract is to be treated as including a term that the supplier must deliver the goods to the consumer.

Cancellation C3.7

Notice must be given of the consumer's right to cancel. This should state that the consumer can cancel the contract at any time up to 14 calendar days from the day after receipt of the goods without giving any reason: Regulations 29 and 30 to the 2013 Regulations. In addition, there must be an indication as to how the consumer can exercise his right to cancel. If cancellation is effected under clause 29, the cancellation ends the obligations of the parties to perform the contract. The supplier need only collect the goods if it has offered to do so: Regulation 35 to the 2013 Regulations. Otherwise, the burden of return falls on the consumer who must send them back to the supplier or hand them over to the trader or a person authorised by the trader to receive them. The address to which goods must be sent is: (a) any address specified by the trader for sending the goods back; (b) if no address is specified for that purpose, any address specified by the trader for the consumer to contact the trader; (c) if no address is specified for either of those purposes, any place of business of the trader.

The consumer has a maximum of 14 calendar days in which to return the goods or hand them over. The consumer must bear the direct cost of returning goods unless the supplier has agreed to bear those costs; or the supplier has failed to provide the consumer with the information about the consumer bearing those costs as required under Schedule 2 to the 2013 Regulations. Under the 2013 Regulations, the notice of cancellation must be in writing or in another 'durable medium' available to and accessible by the supplier, which would thus include fax or email and, arguably, a message left by answer-phone. The term 'durable medium' means paper or email or any other medium that: (a) allows information to be addressed personally to the recipient, (b) enables the recipient to store the information in a way accessible for future reference for a period that is long enough for the purposes of the information, and (c) allows the unchanged reproduction of the information stored. The contract must indicate the ways in which the consumer must provide the notice of cancellation. The contract must also indicate if there is no right to cancel or that the right to cancel might be lost.

Miscellaneous requirements **C3.8**

The contract must indicate the cost of using the means of distance communication for the conclusion of the contract where that cost is calculated other than at the basic rate. Note that no phone call must cost more than the basic rate where a consumer is seeking information on an existing contract: Regulation 41 to the 2013 Regulations. If in those circumstances a consumer who contacts a supplier in relation to a contract is bound to pay more than the basic rate, the contract is to be treated as providing for the supplier to pay to the consumer any amount by which the charge paid by the consumer for the call is more than the basic rate.

In the case of a contract of indeterminate duration or a contract containing a subscription, the contract must indicate the total costs per billing period or (where such contracts are charged at a fixed rate) the total monthly cost. There must also be an indication of the duration of the contract, where applicable, or, if the contract is of indeterminate duration or is to be extended automatically, the conditions for terminating the contract. Where applicable, there must be an indication of the minimum duration of the consumer's obligations under the contract.

The contract must show the geographical address at which the trader is established and, where available, the trader's telephone number, fax number and email address, to enable the consumer to contact the trader quickly and communicate efficiently. Where applicable, the trader's complaints-handling procedure should be shown.

It does not seem necessary for there to be a specific reference for 'complaints' in the contract. It would be enough if, for example, the address was given as one to which queries can be directed. Where applicable, there must also be a statement concerning the existence and the conditions of after-sales customer assistance, after-sales service and commercial guarantees. If the supplier claims to be bound by a code of practice, there must be an indication as to how copies of the code can be obtained. Where applicable, there must be a statement as to the possibility of having recourse to an out-of-court complaint and redress mechanism, to which the trader is subject, and the methods for having access to it. Under Regulation 44 of the 2013 Regulations, it is the duty of an enforcement authority to consider any complaint made to it about a contravention of the Regulations unless the complaint appears to be frivolous or vexatious.

In the case of a sales contract, there must be a reminder that the supplier is under a legal duty to supply goods that are in conformity with the contract.

With regard to the passing of risk, under a sales contract the goods remain at the supplier's risk until they come into the physical possession of the consumer, or a person identified by the consumer to take possession of the goods: Regulation 43 of the 2013 Regulations. Regulation 43 does not apply if the goods are delivered to a carrier who is commissioned by the consumer to deliver the goods and is not a carrier the supplier named as an option for the consumer. In this case, the goods will then be at the consumer's risk on or after delivery to the carrier.

Where the contract concerns the supply of digital content, it must indicate the functionality, including applicable technical protection measures, of the digital content. Where applicable, any relevant compatibility of the digital content with hardware and software that the trader is aware of or can reasonably be expected to have been aware of should be mentioned.

If the trader makes a telephone call to the consumer with a view to concluding a distance contract, the trader must, at the beginning of the conversation with the consumer, disclose: (a) the trader's identity, (b) where applicable, the identity of the person on whose behalf the trader makes the call, and (c) the commercial purpose of the call: Regulation 15.

Contracts concluded by electronic means   **C3.9**

Regulation 14 to the 2013 Regulations require the following in the case of a contract concluded by electronic means.

If the contract places the consumer under an obligation to pay, the trader must make the consumer aware of the following in a clear and prominent manner and directly before the consumer places the order:

- the main characteristics of the goods or services, to the extent appropriate to the medium of communication and to the goods or services;

- the total price of the goods or services inclusive of taxes, or where the nature of the goods or services is such that the price cannot reasonably be calculated in advance, the manner in which the price is to be calculated;

- where applicable, all additional delivery charges and any other costs or, where those charges cannot reasonably be calculated in advance, the fact that such additional charges may be payable;

- in the case of a contract of indeterminate duration or a contract containing a subscription, the total costs per billing period or (where such contracts are charged at a fixed rate) the total monthly costs;

- the duration of the contract, where applicable, or, if the contract is of indeterminate duration or is to be extended automatically, the conditions for terminating the contract; and

- where applicable, the minimum duration of the consumer's obligations under the contract.

The trader must ensure that the consumer, when placing the order, explicitly acknowledges that the order implies an obligation to pay.

If placing an order entails activating a button or a similar function, the trader must ensure that the button or similar function is labelled in an easily legible manner only with the words 'order with obligation to pay' or a corresponding unambiguous formulation indicating that placing the order entails an obligation to pay the trader.

The trader must ensure that any trading website through which the contract is concluded indicates clearly and legibly, at the latest by the beginning of the ordering process, whether any delivery restrictions apply and which means of payment are accepted.

Comment

If a guarantee is offered, this must comply with the provisions of the *Consumer Rights Act 2015*.

The requirements are:

- The guarantee must set out in 'plain and intelligible language' the contents of the guarantee, and the 'essential particulars' needed for making use of the guarantee, such as its duration, territorial scope and name and address of guarantor (which can be non-geographical).

- If asked by the consumer, the guarantor must provide him with the guarantee within a reasonable time.

- The guarantee must be in English when the goods are offered within the United Kingdom.

It should also be remembered that, if a guarantee offers to remedy any defects in the goods, it must also indicate that this will not affect the consumer's statutory rights: *Sale and Supply of Goods to Consumers Regulations 2002 (SI 2002/3045)*. It refers to the fact that, quite apart from the guarantee, the consumer might also be able to sue under the *Sale of Goods Act 1979*.

Implications of the Data Protection Act 2018 and GDPR   C3.10

The *Data Protection Act 2018* ('*DPA 2018*') regulates the processing of personal data of data subjects and should be read together with the EU General Data Protection Regulations ('GDPR') (*Regulation (EU) SI 2016/679*), which is incorporated into UK law. They have significant implications for online services and supply of goods. For a broader context, see too the *Digital Economy Act 2017* and the data protection aspects under the 2017 Act; and the *Network and Information Systems Regulations 2018, SI 2018/506*.

The *DPA 2018* and the GDPR protects individuals with regard to the processing of data, in particular by:

(a)   requiring personal data to be processed lawfully and fairly on the basis of the data subject's consent or another specified basis; and

(b)   conferring rights on the data subject to obtain information about the processing of personal data and to require inaccurate personal data to be rectified: *s 2, DPA 2018*.

Everyone responsible for using personal data must comply with the strict 'data protection principles'. They must ensure that the information is:

- used fairly, lawfully and transparently;
- used for specified, explicit purposes;
- used in a way that is adequate, relevant and limited to only what is necessary;
- accurate and, where necessary, kept up to date;
- kept for no longer than is necessary;
- handled in a way that ensures appropriate security, including protection against unlawful or unauthorised processing, access, loss, destruction or damage.

Under the *DPA 2018* and the GDPR, the data subject has the right to find out what information is being stored about the person. These include the following rights:

- The right to be informed about how the person's data is being used.
- The right to access personal data.
- The right to have incorrect data updated.
- The right to have data erased.
- The right to stop or restrict the processing of a person's data.

- The right to data portability (allowing the person to get and reuse that person's personal data for different services).

- The right to object to how the person's data is processed in certain circumstances.

The GDPR has the objective of harmonising a majority of data protection in the EU, but it should be noted that in certain circumstances the GDPR leaves it to Member States as to how certain provisions will be implemented as laws will vary in certain areas between the Member States.

The GDPR applies to the 'processing' of personal data. Article 4(1) of the GDPR defines personal data as information that can be used 'directly or indirectly' to identify a person. The definition is broad and can include email addresses, Cookie data and IP addresses. The term 'processing' is defined broadly as

> 'any operation or set of operations which is performed on personal data or on sets of personal data, whether or not by automated means, such as collection, recording, organisation, structuring, storage, adaptation or alteration, retrieval, consultation, use, disclosure by transmission, dissemination or otherwise making available, alignment or combination, restriction, erasure or destruction'.

This can include sharing a list of customers' telephone numbers, sending direct marketing mails, or asking people to complete a contact form on a website.

The GDPR applies to any person or organisation that offers goods and services in the EU; or which monitors the behaviour of people in the EU: Article 3. In practice, compliance with the GDPR may take the form of providing details in an organisation's privacy policy, which must be written in clear and simple language that users can understand; comprehensive by covering all aspects of the personal data processing activities; and easily accessible.

Article 13(1)(a) of the GDPR requires an organisation to provide its users with 'the identity and contact details of the controller and, where applicable, of the controller's representative'. The term 'controller' refers to the data controller who will decide how and why personal data is processed.

Article 13(1)(b) of the GDPR requires an organisation to provide 'the contact details of the data protection officer, where applicable'. Depending upon the size of the organisation and whether it routinely processes sensitive personal data, a Data Protection Officer (DPO) may need to be appointed, who can be an individual or an organisation.

Article 13(1)(c) of the GDPR requires the organisation to provide information about 'the purposes of the processing for which the personal data are intended including the legal basis for the processing.' Personal data cannot be processed unless there is a specific purpose and a legal basis for doing so. In this regard,

Article 6 of the GDPR sets out six legal basis for processing a person's personal data as follows:

(1)   The organisation has the person's consent to do it.

(2)   The organisation needs to process the personal data in order to fulfil or enter into a contract with them.

(3)   The organisation is legally required to process the personal data.

(4)   Failing to process their personal data would put their life or someone else's life at risk.

(5)   The organisation is carrying out a task in the public interest or with legal authority.

(6)   The organisation has a legitimate interest in processing the personal data, in which case the organisation must set out the legitimate interest and undertake a legitimate interest assessment.

Based on the above, a standard internet contract could be as follows.

A model contract   **C3.11**

ABC Co Ltd, 123 Any Street, Any Town AA1 1AA

To supply 1 garden shredder at a total cost of £299 (add £6.50 delivery charges for all orders under £300).

[Complete here details of your credit card and billing address. If the address to which the goods are to be delivered differs, please also provide this address.] A surcharge of x% will be added to all payments by credit and/or debit card. (*This provision to be added when appropriate.*)

The above equipment will be delivered to your address within 30 days.

While we are confident that your use of these goods will be trouble free, we are anxious to deal with any problems which might arise. Please address any queries to us at the above address or contact us on _____.

All goods and prices displayed here are subject to availability and are liable to be withdrawn at any time without notice.

You should be aware that we are obliged to supply you with goods which conform to the contract.

IMPORTANT: Please note that you have a right to cancel this contract. You can do this at any time up to fourteen (14) calendar days starting with the day after the goods are delivered to you. If you do wish to cancel, you must notify us in writing or its equivalent. You may also use the model cancellation form. Any cancellations by phone must be confirmed in writing within the permitted cancellation period. You will then be required to return the goods to us at your expense.

[Note: The supplier can always say here instead that he is prepared to accept the cost of return delivery and will, for instance, send a reply paid label or arrange for the collection of the goods himself.]

If you are under 18, we cannot accept your order.

[To comply with the *Data Protection Act 2018*, there should also be some such notice as the following]:

Please click here if you wish to opt out and do not want us to send you further information or supply your details to third parties. It is important that the personal data we hold on you is accurate and current. Please keep us informed if your personal data changes during your working relationship with us. Should you wish to amend the personal data that we hold for you, please contact us at [email address].

We will not be responsible for any losses arising directly or indirectly from any inaccurate and/or incomplete information provided to us by you.

[To comply with the *Privacy and Electronic Communications (EC Directive) Regulations 2003 (SI 2003/2426)* there should be some such notice as the following where any follow up might be by email or SMS]:

Please click here if you do not wish us to contact you in the future by email or SMS.

Consent is not required for any further email marketing as long as it relates to goods similar to those which were the subject of the first order. Such marketing must itself be accompanied by an indication of how the consumer can, in future, opt out of emails or SMS. Apart from the costs of opting out, this must incur no charge.

When the mandatory information is to be provided   C3.12

The details must all be provided 'prior to the conclusion of the contract'. It should be realised that it is the consumer who makes the offer, which is then accepted (or rejected) by the trader. Presumably, 'in good time' means in such time as will allow the consumer to consider the terms before proceeding with the order.

For information regarding additional important requirements set out by the *Electronic Commerce (EC Directive) Regulations 2002 (SI 2002/2013)* see C1.13.

Form of presentation of required information   C3.13

All of the provisions above under the 2013 Regulations must be provided in a 'clear and comprehensible manner appropriate to the means of distance communication': Regulation 9. This would require them to be easily legible, and not, for example, such that flash on and off the screen so that reading them is difficult. 'Comprehensible' does not appear to mean that the terms and conditions must be in English, since any language is comprehensible to those who speak it, and because a consumer faced with a language he does not speak is always free to ignore the offer. It presumably does require that, given the language can be understood, the above provisions are expressed with due clarity. Certain exceptions from the display of information apply when the means of distance communication allow limited space or time to display the information.

Location of information   C3.14

It also seems possible for the provisions to be elsewhere than on the page containing details of the offer. If there is a link to the provisions, so long as this is clearly indicated, that would suffice. In principle, it is possible for the on-screen page to indicate that the provisions are available from an address, perhaps itself postal, which will be sent to the customer by post. All information is thought to be provided before the customer's offer is accepted.

Optional terms   C3.15

The provisions referred to above are mandatory. The supplier is always free to add to them. To ensure that they are binding, they should either be presented in exactly the same way as the mandatory provisions are, or presented in a way which satisfies the contractual requirements as to incorporation. Thus, the on-screen order form can, to incorporate any optional terms, simply:

- say that full terms and conditions are available on request (stating where they can be obtained);
- provide a link to a page where they can be read; or
- state them in full with the other provisions on the order form.

Possible optional terms   C3.16

Such further terms could include:

> 'Property in the goods does not pass to you before payment is made in full.'

Comment

It is no longer possible to say that risk passes on despatch. Under the provisions of both the 2013 Regulations and the *Consumer Rights Act 2015*, risk cannot pass before delivery where the buyer is a consumer. Where the buyer is acting in the course of a business, however, such a term as to risk can be employed.

The supplier may also wish to provide a guarantee, though this is optional. Should he wish to do so, it could be phrased as follows:

> 'Should these goods fail in normal use within 12 months of purchase, we will repair or replace them at our expense.'

Further requirements as to guarantees are imposed by the *Consumer Rights Act 2015*. The guarantee must set out, in plain, intelligible language, the contents of the guarantee and the 'essential particulars' which are necessary for claims to be made under it. In particular, the guarantee must state its duration, its territorial scope, and the name and address of the guarantor. In addition, if the goods circulate in any part of the United Kingdom, the guarantee must be in English.

Thus, the guarantee could go on to state:

> 'This guarantee applies only in relation to goods purchased in the United Kingdom. Should you require to make use of the guarantee, send the goods securely packaged, postage paid, to [address]. We will then examine the goods and, if appropriate, replace them or repair them, all at our own expense. For any queries, please contact [email/phone/fax details].'

Comment

The contract should not make any attempt to exclude or limit the rights of a consumer to goods which are of the contract description, which are of satisfactory quality and which are reasonably fit for their purpose. This is because such provisions, when used in a consumer contract, are not only void under the *Consumer Rights Act 2015*, but could possibly also give rise to a criminal offence under the *Consumer Protection from Unfair Trading Regulations 2008 (SI 2008/1277)* referred to above.

Special provisions as to the supply of services C3.17

For the most part, the foregoing provisions apply as much to internet contracts for the supply of a service as they do to the supply of goods. There are, however, some points unique to service contracts, as set out below.

Cancellation C3.18

In the case of a service contract, the service must not be provided unless the consumer has expressly requested its provision. The right to cancel is lost if the service is fully performed and the consumer has acknowledged that he would lose his right to cancel. Where the contract is not fully performed and the consumer exercises the rate to cancel, the consumer must pay an appropriate sum.

Special provision is made for the supply of digital content during the cancellation period. Digital content is defined as 'data which are produced and supplied in digital form'.

The 'warning notice' C3.19

The additional information must, in the case of a service, indicate that the right to cancel might be affected by any start of performance of the contract. There is no mandatory wording for this notice, but it could read: 'You have a right to cancel this contract at any time before 14 days has passed from the day after this contract was made. You can cancel by notice in writing or any other durable means (such as by fax). If, however, we start to perform our side of the contract with your agreement before you exercise this right to cancel, your right to cancel could be lost.'

Exclusion and limitation clauses C3.20

There is restricted scope for the use of exclusion or limitation clauses. The *Consumer Rights Act 2015* imposes on those providing a service an obligation to use reasonable care and skill and further provides that such a term cannot be excluded. To attempt to exclude this term could even give rise to a criminal offence under the *Consumer Protection from Unfair Trading Regulations 2008 (SI 2008/1277)*.

Checklist C3.21

- Are you fully aware of the application to the contract of the *Consumer Contracts (Information, Cancellation and Additional Charges) Regulations 2013 (SI 2013/3134)* and of the *Electronic Commerce (EC Directive) Regulations 2002 (SI 2002/2013)*?

- Have you made sure that all the information required by those Regulations has been supplied?

- Are you sure that the relevant information will be supplied at the time and in the manner required by those Regulations?

- Have you made sure that your on-screen copy is couched in terms of an invitation to treat and not an offer?

- Have you set out how you intend to perform the contract?

- Are you fully aware of the rights of the consumer to cancel and how long the cooling off period lasts?

- Has thought been given to providing alternative goods should the original ones become unavailable?

- Are you sure that you have considered any problems which might arise from applications from those under age?

- Is all the contractual information located or placed where it can be accessed in accordance with the Regulations?

- Have you made use of the fact that the Regulations allow you to add terms and conditions of your own choosing?

- In the drafting of any exclusion clauses, have you been fully aware of the restrictions imposed on their use?

- Have you complied with data protection rules?

C4:
Online Terms and Conditions for the Supply of Software

At a glance

- *The Consumer Contracts (Information, Cancellation and Additional Charges) Regulations 2013 (SI 2013/3134)* and the *Electronic Commerce (EC Directive) Regulations 2002 (SI 2002/2013)* apply to such contracts.

- The normal law of contract also applies, in particular the rules as to offer and acceptance.

- Such contracts can only be contracts for the supply of services.

- There are specific requirements and which are mandatory as to what must go into the particular contract under the 2013 Regulations.

- Careful consideration must be given to calculating the delivery charges.

- Cancellation rights can easily be lost in this particular context. The provisions as to payment and countermanding payment are of particular importance here.

- Substitute software can be offered.

- Where applicable, there must be details of the trader's complaints handling policy.

- Details of any after-sales service or guarantee are to be given if provided, though there is no compulsion to provide either of these.

- There are requirements as to the time and manner in which the mandatory information is presented.

- There is scope for deciding where the information is to be provided.

- Certain information is to be in writing or some other durable medium.

- Apart from the terms made mandatory by the *2013 Regulations* the supplier is free to add his own terms and conditions to the contract. These could cover various matters such as systems support, copying restrictions, virus warnings and the like.

- There is scope for the use of exclusion or limitation clauses in contracts.

Issues   C4.2

In this context, where there is no question of a disk being supplied, the supply of software online can only be the provision of a service (see Chapter A4). It will therefore be a service contract.

Such sales are a form of distance selling and, as such, are subject to the provisions of the 2013 Regulations. It should be borne in mind, though, that the law of contract also applies, in particular the rules relating to offer and acceptance.

Offers and invitations to treat   C4.3

The internet copy would amount to an invitation to treat, not an offer, meaning that it is the consumer who makes the offer, which the supplier is entitled to reject in his absolute discretion. This could be important if, as has happened, the internet advertisement states a much lower price for the item than was intended. The copy should be carefully drafted since, in certain circumstances, it could in fact amount to an offer rather than an invitation to treat.

Contract terms required by the Regulations   C4.4

There is no need for the on-screen contract to be presented as a formal document, but it must contain at least the following detail under Schedule 2 to the 2013 Regulations.

(1) The identity of the supplier, such as a trading name.

(2) A description of the main characteristics of the software, to the extent appropriate to the medium of communication.

(3) The total price of the software including all taxes, or where the nature of the services is such that the price cannot reasonably be calculated in advance, the manner in which the price is to be calculated. The price shown must be the price inclusive of VAT, and it does not appear permissible to say, for example, £100 plus £20 VAT. There is no need to say that the price includes VAT.

(4) The geographical address at which the trader is established and, where available, the trader's telephone number, fax number and email address, to enable the consumer to contact the trader quickly and communicate efficiently.

(5) Where applicable, all additional delivery charges and any other costs or, where those charges cannot reasonably be calculated in advance, the fact that such additional charges may be payable.

Determining delivery costs

It is far from clear how this requirement will operate in this context if it is assumed, as it seems proper to do, that the costs of downloading are delivery charges. Internet connections are invariably either freephone, via broadband (so the consumer is only paying for his broadband subscription and nothing extra to communicate with the supplier) or at local rates. The supplier will not know this, nor will he necessarily know how long it will take the consumer to download the software. This problem is compounded if the supplier is outside the United Kingdom. It seems that the best the supplier can do is to give an approximate time for downloading and to say that the costs will depend on applicable connection rates. As a solution to this issue, it may be permissible to define 'delivery' as being limited to the transfer of possession of goods, thus meaning that there can be no delivery costs in the context of downloading software.

(6) There must be a statement of the arrangements for payment, delivery or performance and the time by which the trader undertakes to perform the services. The arrangements for payment could embrace online means for paying, usually by entering credit or debit card details, or by allowing for sums to be deducted straight from a bank account. It should be indicated that there is a supplement for payment by debit or credit card. Remember that under the *Consumer Rights (Payment Surcharges) Regulations 2012 (SI 2012/3110)*, the surcharge applied for a payment must be no more than allows the trader to recoup its costs.

The stated arrangements as to performance will be easily and automatically covered by the instructions for downloading.

Given the nature of this particular transaction, it is obviously unnecessary to give any dates for performance.

(7) Notice must be given of the consumer's right to cancel the contract. This should state that the consumer can cancel the contract at any time up to 14 calendar days from the day after conclusion of the contract (see further (12) below): Regulations 29 and 30 to the 2013 Regulations.

(8) There must be a statement of the cost of using the means of distance communication, if the cost is more than the basic rate. In practical terms, this provision has no application to Internet dealing since calls will either be free or at local rates.

(9) In the case of a contract of indeterminate duration or a contract containing a subscription, the total costs per billing period must be given or (where such contracts are charged at a fixed rate) the total monthly costs. For instance, the supply of software might be for downloading anti-virus software every time an update to cover new viruses is made necessary.

(10) The duration of the contract must be stated where applicable, or, if the contract is of indeterminate duration or is to be extended automatically, the conditions for terminating the contract.

(11) If the intended software is unavailable, the supplier may wish to offer the consumer an alternative of equivalent quality and price. If he wishes to do so, and the option is his, this information must be provided.

(12) The supplier shall inform the consumer that, unless the parties agree otherwise, he will not be able to cancel the contract once the performance of the services has begun with his agreement.

(13) Where a right to cancel exists, there must be a statement as to the conditions, time limit and procedures for exercising that right. A consumer is always to be provided with a model cancellation form, but does not have to use it. Any clear statement as to cancellation suffices. If the consumer does use the online form, the trader must communicate to the consumer an acknowledgement of receipt of the cancellation on a durable medium without delay. It is difficult to see that an on-screen communication by the trader is in itself on a durable medium.

(14) Where applicable, there must be a statement of the functionality, including applicable technical protection measures, of digital content.

(15) Where applicable, there must be a statement of any relevant compatibility of digital content with hardware and software that the trader is aware of or can reasonably be expected to have been aware of.

(16) Where applicable, there must be a statement of the possibility of having recourse to an out-of-court complaint and redress mechanism, to which the trader is subject, and the methods for having access to it.

(17) If the trader claims to be bound by a code of practice, there must be a statement as to where copies can be obtained.

When this information is to be given   C4.5

The details must all be provided prior to the conclusion of the contract.

Manner of presentation   C4.6

The 2013 Regulations state that if the required information is presented on a durable medium, then it must be legible. The term 'durable medium' is defined as any paper or email, or any other medium that: (a) allows information to be addressed personally to the recipient, (b) enables the recipient to store the information in a way accessible for future reference for a period that is long enough for the purposes of the information, and (c) allows the unchanged reproduction of the information stored.

It seems unlikely that something shown on screen can be regarded as presented on a durable medium, though this may suffice since the information can be printed or saved to file. Accordingly, such a requirement seems limited to postal communications. The Regulations do say that, if there are limitations as to time and display, as there may well be with internet advertising, then not all the required information need be shown, and there can instead be an indication where the other information is to be found. The following is the information which must appear even where there are limitations as to time and space:

- the identity of the trader (such as the trader's trading name);

- the total price of the goods or services inclusive of taxes, or where the nature of the goods or services is such that the price cannot reasonably be calculated in advance, the manner in which the price is to be calculated;

- where applicable, all additional delivery charges and any other costs or, where those charges cannot reasonably be calculated in advance, the fact that such additional charges may be payable;

- in the case of a contract of indeterminate duration or a contract containing a subscription, the total costs per billing period or (where such contracts are charged at a fixed rate) the total monthly costs;

- where a right to cancel exists, the conditions, time limit and procedures for exercising that right in accordance with regulations;

- the duration of the contract, where applicable, or, if the contract is of indeterminate duration or is to be extended automatically, the conditions for terminating the contract.

Location of terms C4.7

It also seems possible for the provisions to be elsewhere than on the page containing details of the offer. If there is a link to the provisions, so long as this is clearly indicated, that would suffice. In principle, it is possible for the on-screen page to indicate that the provisions are available from an address which will send them to the consumer by post. Since, however, the supplier must provide the relevant terms in good time before the contract is made, this would impose severe practical limitations, and this is an option which should not be considered.

Additional payments C4.8

Under a contract between a trader and a consumer, no payment is payable in addition to the remuneration agreed for the trader's main obligation unless, before the consumer became bound by the contract, the trader obtained the consumer's express consent. There is no express consent (if there would otherwise be) for the purposes of this paragraph if consent is inferred from the consumer not changing a default option (such as a pre-ticked box on a website).

Confirmation of the contract C4.9

The trader must give the consumer confirmation of the contract on a durable medium. It is difficult to see that an on-screen display is on a durable medium, unless one assumes that the ability to print out or save to file fulfils this requirement.

The confirmation must include all the information referred to in C4.4 unless the trader has already provided that information to the consumer on a durable medium prior to the conclusion of the distance contract.

Where the contract is for the supply of digital content not on a tangible medium, such as an online download, and the consumer has given the consent and acknowledgment to download during the cancellation period, the confirmation must include confirmation of the consent and acknowledgement.

The confirmation must be provided within a reasonable time after the conclusion of the contract, but in any event before performance begins of any service supplied under the contract.

The confirmation is treated as provided as soon as the trader has sent it or done what is necessary to make it available to the consumer.

Losing the right to cancel   **C4.10**

The 2013 Regulations provide for the loss of the right to cancel in the case of digital downloads as follows:

Under a contract for the supply of digital content not on a tangible medium, the trader must not begin supply of the digital content before the end of the cancellation period unless –

(a)   the consumer has given express consent, and

(b)   the consumer has acknowledged that the right to cancel will be lost.

The consumer ceases to have the right to cancel such a contract under regulation if, before the end of the cancellation period, supply of the digital content has begun after the consumer has given the consent and acknowledgement as above.

Where a contract is cancelled and digital content has been supplied, not on a tangible medium, in the cancellation period, the consumer bears no cost for supply of the digital content, in full or in part, in the cancellation period, if –

(a)   the consumer has not given prior express consent to the beginning of the performance of the digital content before the end of the cancellation period;

(b)   the consumer gave that consent but did not acknowledge when giving it that the right to cancel would be lost, or

(c)   the trader failed to provide the required confirmation (see C4.9).

Rights and remedies under the Consumer Rights Act 2015

The *Consumer Rights Act 2015* states that digital content must conform to its description, be of satisfactory quality and be reasonably fit for its purpose: See Part 1, Chapter 3 to the *CRA 2015*. The trader must also have the right to supply that content. If the digital content damages a device or digital content, and the damage is of a kind that would not have occurred if the trader had exercised reasonable care and skill, the consumer is entitled to compensation. The payment the consumer is entitled to is the cost of replacing the device or digital content that is damaged.

None of the foregoing provisions can be excluded from the *CRA 2015*.

Where digital content is supplied which does not conform to the contract, the consumer has rights as to repair, replacement, a price reduction and a refund.

Precedent – Standard Internet Contract for Software
C4.11

ABC Co Ltd

123 Any Street

Any Town

AA1 1AA

DETAILS

Agreement for the provision of anti-virus software at a total cost of £29.99. Please note: we cannot advise specifically on how much your connection charges will be for downloading. We would advise that downloading time depends on the quality of the line and the modem strength, but, under normal circumstances, downloading should not take more than 60 minutes.

[To comply with the *Data Protection Act 2018 and the UK GDPR*, there should also be some such notice as the following]:

> 'Please click here if you wish to opt out and do not want us to send you further information or supply your details to third parties.'

[To comply with the *Privacy and Electronic Communications (EC Directive) Regulations 2003 (SI 2003/2426)* there should be some such notice as the following where any follow up might be by email or SMS]:

'Please click here if you do not wish us to contact you in the future by email or SMS.'

Consent is not required for any further email marketing so long as it relates to goods or services similar to those which were the subject of the first order, but such marketing must itself be accompanied by an indication of how the consumer can in future opt out of emails or SMS. Apart from the costs of opting out, the opt-out must incur no charge to ensure compliance with the Data Protection Act 2018 and the UK GDPR.

CREDIT CARD DETAILS

Complete in the on-screen box details of your credit card and billing address. If the address to which the software is downloaded is different from the billing address, please also provide this address. Please note that there is a surcharge of x% for the use of a credit or debit card.

HELPLINE

While we are confident that your use of the software will be trouble free, we are anxious to deal with any problems which might arise. Please address any queries to us at the above address or contact us on: _____.

All services and prices displayed here are subject to availability and are liable to be withdrawn at any time without notice.

IMPORTANT: Please note that you have a right to cancel this contract. You can do this at any time up to fourteen days starting with the day after the contract between us is concluded. You can cancel this contract at any time within the permitted period by clicking on the 'not confirmed' button placed beneath the payment box or using the model cancellation form we have made available. You do not have to use this form. Please note: If you commence downloading, then your right to cancel is lost.

If you are under 18, we cannot accept your order. Please click here to confirm that you are aged 18 or over.

Model Cancellation Form

'To [ABC Co Ltd

123 Any Street

Any Town

AA1 1AA (fax number/email address where applicable)

I hereby give notice that I cancel my contract for the supply of the following service ordered on [date)

Name of consumer

Address of consumer

Signature of consumer

Date'

Other terms and conditions C4.12

The foregoing represent the terms and conditions made mandatory by the *2013 Regulations*. Other terms can be added by the supplier to provide the appropriate safeguards.

Restrictions on copying C4.13

This software is supplied solely for your use. It must not in any circumstances be copied, other than by way of providing a back-up copy, nor may copies be supplied, whether free of charge or for a payment, to any third party.

Comment

The obvious intent of this provision is to safeguard the supplier's intellectual property rights, in particular his copyright in the software.

Virus warning C4.14

Although we make every effort to ensure that no form of virus is transmitted to you in the course of your downloading this software, YOU ARE STRONGLY ADVISED TO ENSURE THAT YOU HAVE UP TO DATE ANTI-VIRUS SOFTWARE INSTALLED.

Comment

The supplier of the software cannot be liable for the effects of any virus which might already be present on the consumer's system. It may be, however, that there is a virus in the software being downloaded.

It should be noted that, under the *Consumer Rights Act 2015*, digital content must be of satisfactory quality and reasonably fit for its purpose, and these obligations cannot be excluded. The Act also gives consumers the right to damages for any loss caused by a virus present in the software.

Note: the 2013 Regulations, where applicable, require there to be a statement in the contract as to, the functionality, including applicable technical protection measures, of digital content.

Technical support   C4.15

The following can be used to provide technical support:

> The following technical support services are available to you. You can visit our website at www _____ or you can visit our support services website at www _____.
>
> You can also email us at advice@ _____ and enter [supplier to insert heading] as the subject of your email to obtain the index of our documents. You can also call us on [012345678] on our fax back service and request document number [123456] for our index of documents. Technical support is also available during normal working hours from [012345678].
>
> You can also visit the online forums by typing [XXXX] into your search engine. Online volunteers and forum managers offer advice on our products when issues are posted on bulletin boards. If any issues or problems are uncovered, they will be posted on our website.

System requirements   C4.16

The following can be used as an example:

> It is your sole responsibility to ensure that you are operating a system which can support the software downloaded by you.

Note: the 2013 Regulations require there to be a statement, where applicable, of any relevant compatibility of digital content with hardware and software that the trader is aware of or can reasonably be expected to have been aware of.

Installation issues   C4.17

In terms of installation issues, the following can be used as an example:

> If there is a failure at any point in the installation of the software, a complete uninstall will then be performed. It is therefore important not to close the installation prematurely by clicking on the 'close' button. No liability can be accepted if there is any such premature closing, whether by deliberate action or by some extraneous event beyond our control, such as a failure in the public electricity supply system.

Exclusion of liability   C4.18

The *Consumer Rights Act 2015* provides that no contract term can exclude the duty of a supplier of digital content to provide content which conforms to its description, is of satisfactory quality or which is reasonably fit for its purpose. Nor can the trader exclude his duty to have the right to supply such content. It could be that any clause seeking any such exclusion will give rise to an offence under the *Consumer Protection from Unfair Trading Regulations 2008 (SI 2008/1277)*.

Checklist   C4.19

- Are you fully aware of the applicability of the *Consumer Contracts (Information, Cancellation and Additional Charges) Regulations 2013 (SI 2013/3134)* and the *Electronic Commerce (EC Directive) Regulations 2002 (SI 2002/2013)* and what they require?

- Are you also aware of the fact that normal contract law also applies, in particular the rules as to offer and acceptance?

- Are you aware of what information is made mandatory by the 2013 Regulations?

- Have you given proper thought to how the delivery charges will be calculated?

- Has there been a clear indication as to the right to cancel and how this right can be lost?

- Has there been a clear statement as to the duration of the offer?

- Has a proper geographical address been given for complaints?

- Have any requirements as to data protection been observed?

- Are you sure you have complied with the requirements as to the time by which and the manner in which the mandatory information is to be provided?

- Have you given proper regard as to where this information is located?

- Have you complied with the requirements as to material being in written or other durable form?

- Have you considered the use of terms and conditions beyond those required by the 2013 Regulations?

- In particular, have you thought of adding such terms as clearly prevent unauthorised copying, virus warnings or setting up helplines?

- Have you realised the severe limitation imposed on the use of exclusion clauses?

- Have you complied with the *Data Protection Act 2018* and the UK GDPR?

Index